FARM PLANNING AND CONTROL

Farm Planning and Control

SECOND EDITION

C. S. BARNARD
Lecturer in Land Economy
University of Cambridge

J. S. NIX
Senior Lecturer in Farm Management
Wye College, University of London

CAMBRIDGE UNIVERSITY PRESS
CAMBRIDGE
LONDON · NEW YORK · MELBOURNE

Published by the Syndics of the Cambridge University Press
The Pitt Building, Trumpington Street, Cambridge CB2 1RP
Bentley House, 200 Euston Road, London NW1 2DB
32 East 57th Street, New York, NY 10022, USA
296 Beaconsfield Parade, Middle Park, Melbourne 3206, Australia

First published 1973
Reprinted 1976, 1978
Second edition 1979

Printed in Malta by Interprint Ltd

Library of Congress Cataloguing in Publication Data

Barnard, Christopher Stephen,
Farm planning and control.

Bibliography: p.
Includes index.
1. Farm management. 2. Farm management – Great Britain. I. Nix, John, joint author. II. Title. S561.B277 1979 658′.93 79–10572

ISBN 0 521 22658 9 hard covers
ISBN 0 521 29604 8 paperback

(first edition

ISBN 0 521 08738 4 hard covers
ISBN 0 521 29079 1 paperback)

Contents

Notice to readers

Although the rate of inflation in Britain has fallen substantially compared with a few years ago, the trend in prices of farm inputs and outputs is still steadily upwards, with considerable unpredictable fluctuations around this trend. The prices used in the second edition relate for the most part to levels during 1977–78. It is to be remembered, however, that the examples are concerned simply to demonstrate principles, concepts and methods, and these are in no way invalidated by price changes.

October 1978

Preface to the first edition

It is a common aphorism today that farming is no longer simply a way of life but is just as much a business requiring careful planning, organisation and control. This is supported by the rapid strides that have been made recently in the theory and practice of the business organisation of farms.

The growing importance of the subject is demonstrated in many ways. Farm planning and management now receive far more rigorous treatment in university curricula than was formerly the case, including the setting up of specialist postgraduate degrees and diplomas in farm management. In recent years also, an increasing number of farm management courses have been mounted in agricultural colleges and farm institutes. At the same time, a new category of farm adviser has come into being – the farm management specialist working in such bodies as the Agricultural Development and Advisory Service and the Milk Marketing Board, and in private commercial firms. In addition, accountants and land agents have spread their activities into the farm management field and many bank managers take an active interest in the subject. Last, but not least, there is a growing awareness amongst farmers of the need for business methods in farming. More and more of them accept that the profitability of their farming is as much dependent on the hours they spend in their farm offices as in their fields and barns – as is endorsed by the rapid growth of the Farm Management Association over the past five years.

Although this book is presented primarily as an intermediate text for students in universities and colleges, it is hoped that it will prove of value to many others requiring a sound and practical knowledge of modern farm planning and control, including farmers, farm managers and their advisers. In order to facilitate comprehension by the non-specialist, the mathematical treatment of topics has been kept to a minimum. In addition, use is made of appendices to individual chapters, either to elaborate particular points or to add detail to them.

The book is divided into four parts:

I The organisation of resources
II The organisation of enterprises
III The combination of enterprises
IV The control of resources and enterprises

These parts follow one another in logical sequence, the general theme being that, in order to make the most economic use of the resources at his disposal, the farmer has to decide what resources to use, how to organise their use within individual enterprises and how to combine the enterprises into an integrated farming system. Lastly, if these efforts are not to be largely wasted, he must initiate the keeping of suitable records to provide both planning data and a system of checks and controls when his plans are put into practice. Throughout, detail is subordinated to principle so that the reader may gain a clear insight into the processes involved in farm planning and control. Examples are given to demonstrate these principles, not to suggest what farmers necessarily ought to do in any particular situation.

The authors are indebted to Mr Stuart Wragg, Director of the Agricultural Economics Research Unit at the University of Bristol, for his many useful comments on the final draft of the manuscript. They would also like to thank Miss Joan Maskell and Mrs Daphne O'Flaherty for their patient and painstaking handling of the typescript.

C.S.B.
J.S.N.

November 1972

Preface to the second edition

Although the second edition retains the same broad structure as the first, the text has been enlarged and expanded in several ways. First, the important topic of uncertainty, whose ramifications run throughout the book, is now treated in a new Chapter 16, which also includes an appendix on decision analysis. Secondly, long-term planning and development are dealt with more explicitly, both in terms of general planning principles (Chapter 13) and in relation to budgetary analysis (Chapter 14). Thirdly, sections have been added on focus-loss and MOTAD (Chapter 17), on allowing for seasonal variability in matrix construction (Chapter 18) and on systems simulation models (Chapter 21), as well as appendices on growth theory (Chapter 13), on the hand calculations and basic equations used in linear programming (Chapter 15) and on inflation accounting (Chapter 19). Fourthly, the list of selected reading at the end of the book has been divided by chapters. Lastly, the opportunity has been taken to metricate and update the figures and, in some instances, to substitute new examples.

The authors would like to thank all those who have made useful suggestions on how the book might be improved, and hope that, in following on from the first edition, it will continue to provide a basic text in many universities at home and overseas, and to serve the needs of many others whose interest lies within the field of farm planning.

C.S.B.
J.S.N.

October, 1978

SELECTED METRIC CONVERSION FACTORS

(approx. figures, with accurate figures in brackets)

Metric to British		*British to Metric*	
1 hectare = 2½ acres	(2.471)	1 acre = 2/5 hectare	(0.405)
1 kilogram = 2¼ lb.	(2.20)	1 lb. = ½ kilogram	(0.45)
50 kilograms = 1 cwt.	(0.984)	1 cwt. = 50 kilograms	(50.8)
1000 kilograms = 1 ton	(0.984)	1 ton = 1000 kilograms	(1016)
1 tonne = 1 ton	(0.984) (2 204.6 lb.)	1 ton = 1 tonne	(1.016)
1 kg/ha = 0.9 lb./acre	(0.89)	1 lb./acre = 1.1 kg/ha	(1.121)
100 kg/ha = 4/5 cwt./acre	(89 lb.)	1 cwt./acre = 125 kg/ha	(125.5)
1000 kg/ha = 8 cwt./acre	(7.95)	1 ton/acre = 2500 kg/ha	(2511)
1 tonne/ha = 2/5 ton/acre	(0.398)	1 ton/acre = 2½ tonnes/ha	(2.511)

(kg/ha = kilograms per hectare)

1 litre = 0.220 gal.		1 gal. = 4½ litres	(4.55)
		= 4½ cu. decimetres	(4.55)
1 sq. metre = 1¼ sq. yds.	(1.20)	1 sq. yd. = 0.85 sq. metres	(0.836)
1 cu. metre = 1¼ cu. yds.	(1.31)	1 cu. yd. = 0.75 cu. metres	(0.76)
100 cu. decimetres = 3½ cu. ft.	(3.75)	1 cu. ft. = 28 cu. decimetres	(28.32)
1 centimetre = 2/5 inch	(0.39)	1 inch = 2½ centimetres	(2.45)
1 metre = 3¼ feet	(3.2)	1 foot = ⅓ metre	(0.305)
1 metre = 1.1 yard	(1.09)	1 yard = 0.9 metre	(0.914)
1 kilometre = ⅝ mile	(0.62)	1 mile = 1.6 kilometres	(1.609)
1 kw = 1⅓ h.p.	(1.34)	1 h.p. = ¾ kw	(0.75)

PART I

THE ORGANISATION OF RESOURCES

1: The planning environment and the managerial function

The purpose of planning

The first question which arises is why farm planning should be regarded as necessary. The answer may be sought by turning to the tenets of production economics embodied in what is known as the 'theory of the firm'. The firm represents the business or decision-making unit in an industry and involves the producer (or 'entrepreneur') in the manipulation of resources in order to obtain output. In farming, the farm is the firm and the farmer or manager the entrepreneur. The need to plan production arises from three basic factors:

1. Individuals have various wants which they seek to satisfy.
2. The means available to satisfy these wants are in scarce supply.
3. The means available can be put to many different uses.

The planning problem is thus one of allocating scarce resources amongst various uses in a way that best satisfies the wants of the individual.

Thus far, we have simply a general statement as much applicable to a consumer allocating his income amongst his many competing needs as to a producer deciding what to produce. It may now be considered in greater detail in the context of farming.

Objectives

The wants of individuals are expressed as objectives which they aim to fulfil. Clearly producers must have an objective (or objectives), otherwise there would be nothing to guide their choice between alternative courses of action. Moreover, it is evident that for a rational body of planning principles and procedures to be propounded, there must be the basis of a common or standardised objective. The theory of the firm assumes that, in the short term, where planning is only for a year or so ahead, producers aim to maximise the profit from the resources at their command. In other words, they are assumed to be aiming for that particular output which gives a greater profit than any other form of output and seeking to obtain it in the most profitable possible way.

However, even if profit maximisation may be regarded as an important short-term objective, it is by no means the only one, nor is it necessarily the most pressing. This is particularly the case in farming, where there are many other objectives, both financial and non-financial, arising largely from the intimate relationship that exists between the farmer, his family, his workers, his farm and his farming. It is illustrated in a general way by the unwillingness of farmers to give up farming, even when they are aware that their capital and labour could bring in higher and more certain rewards in other occupations. In short, they are strongly motivated to survive as farmers. This may be expressed more directly as a desire for stable rather than maximum profits or for the assurance that they are unlikely to fall below some specified level. Among non-financial motives there are the preference for familiar enterprises, even if these do not have the financial potential of others less well known; the satisfaction gained from high, even if uneconomic, crop and livestock yields; and the retention of long-employed workers on sentimental rather than economic grounds. While such objectives which obscure the profit motive must obviously not be ignored in farm planning, they do not take the place of profit maximisation as the primary objective (in most forms of planning, at least). Instead, they may exert their influence in two main ways. In the first, they are not included directly as part of the planning process but provide additional criteria by which to assess alternative plans. For example, a maximum profit plan with a high degree of variation from season to season may be rejected in favour of one with a lower but more stable profit. The second and more common case, is where objectives other than profit-maximising ones are included directly in the planning process, thus limiting the freedom with which the profit motive can be pursued. For example, suppose the inclusion of potatoes on an arable farm would lead to maximum profits, but the farmer is not prepared to go to the effort of obtaining and organising the casual labourers required to assist at harvest. The objective of planning is still to maximise profit, but within the more limited framework resulting from the exclusion of potatoes. Or again, suppose because of fear of 'buying-in' disease, a farmer on a small dairy holding insists on rearing his own heifer replacements although greater profit could be expected to accrue if all of the land were to be devoted to milking cows. Planning still aims at maximising profit, but within the limits imposed by having to devote some resources to rearing. All profit-maximising plans are bounded by the resources available, and non-profit-maximising objectives, which may be inherent in personal preferences and attitudes, simply draw the boundaries more closely together. Thus the qualification 'within limits' is always implied when considering profit maximisation in practical planning.

Use of the profit motive in planning enables non-financial objectives to be evaluated in financial terms, in that money acts as a common denominator in making decisions. For example, if a farmer insists on carrying on an enterprise that is not justified on purely financial grounds, the difference between the profits of the plans with and without the enterprise represents the cost of his particular choice and allows him to come to a more balanced judgement on it. Similarly, the cost of a worker employed in excess of the number required to achieve maximum profit is the fall in profit consequent upon employing him. In both cases, potential profit forgone is used to place a value on the farmer's preferences.

When the planning horizon extends to longer periods of time, short-term profits may be deliberately reduced in order to promote long-term objectives. This does not mean that the profit-maximising principle has been abandoned, but that the emphasis is now more on the growth of farm resources, leading to both increased earning power and increased asset value in the future. For example, a farmer may acquire more land in the hope that it will eventually both appreciate in value and increase his profits, but in doing so he may leave himself with insufficient ready money to finance his current operations, so that his short-term profits are reduced. Even when no new assets are acquired, the maintenance and perhaps enhancement of the value of existing resources demonstrates how short-term opportunities may be outweighed by longer-term considerations. Rotations designed to conserve the fertility and condition of the soil offer a classic example. Although larger short-term profits might be realised by 'overcropping' with the more paying crops, this could lead to declining land values and earning power in the future. (The farmer would be 'living off capital'.) Thus, while short-term tactics are to maximise profits from year to year, limits are imposed by the longer-term strategy of conserving or expanding resources on the farm.

Scarce resources

A shortage of the means of production confronts farmers in two ways. First is the scarcity in the industry as a whole of resources suited to the needs of farming, which throws farmers into competition with one another for the available supplies. Not surprisingly land is foremost in this respect, as is indicated by the difficulty that new entrants to farming have in obtaining a holding, or that an established farmer, wishing to enlarge his property, has in getting land contiguous to his farm. Similarly with labour, for even when a surplus is available in rural areas, it may not have the specialised skills called for by modern farming methods. Secondly the farmer or intending farmer is restricted, as an individual, by the amount of capital he is able to acquire. In consequence, even if farming resources were abundantly available, he would be limited in the amount of land he could rent or mortgage, in the number of workers he could hire and in the quantity of goods and services he could employ. Such scarcities render it necessary for him to plan the use of those resources that he is able to acquire.

An added problem is that some resources are likely to be relatively more scarce than others. In part, this arises from the reasons considered above. For example, one farmer with a sufficiency of workers may be unable to obtain enough land to keep them fully employed, while another with a sufficiency of land may lack the labour and capital needed to farm it intensively. Another major cause stems from the indivisible or 'lumpy' nature of many farm resources, which can only be acquired in discrete amounts. Regular labour, for example, is hired by the man and not by the hour. Machines come in specific sizes capable of servicing a given amount of land. Land too, which at first sight would appear to be the most highly divisible of resources, is nevertheless normally gained not by the hectare but by the farm – namely, a parcel of hectares. The result is that resources are seldom likely to be in that ratio to one another where they are all fully employed and earning maximum profits. For example, the equivalent of two and a half men may be required to manage a given area for maximum profit. If the farmer employs two men, labour is scarce relative to land, while if he employs three, land is scarce relative to labour. Similarly, a farmer may have a cowshed sufficient for sixty cows, a herd size too large for one man but not sufficiently large to keep two men fully employed. Where such imbalance occurs, the major concern is with those resources that are relatively the scarcest, for it is they that limit the amount of production and profit that can be obtained. Consequently, of the many resources on the farm, they must be husbanded the most carefully, both by being used in a technically effective manner and by being devoted to those lines of production that bring in a high return to them.

Alternative use of resources

If farm resources could only be devoted to single lines of production, a large part of the planning process would be rendered unnecessary.

However, the fact that resources can usually be used in alternative enterprises constitutes the nub of planning, for the farmer's main problem is to find those uses for his resources that best achieve his objectives. Not unexpectedly, the range of choice is wider for some farmers than for others, particularly as so much depends on the character of natural resources, such as soil type, climate and topography. For example, lowland farmers on relatively flat, fertile land have many more opportunities available to them than upland farmers on thin, impoverished, rain-leached soils. Nevertheless, on most farms land can be used for more than one purpose, labour can be employed on various tasks and non-specialised fixed capital, such as dutch barns and tractors, can perform a variety of functions.

The task of planning is rendered still more complex because there are usually many ways of organising production within individual enterprises, so that the balance between different resource inputs can be varied. For example, in obtaining a specific output in milk production – assuming resources and cows of a given quality – hectares required per cow vary with the balance between purchased and home-grown foods, the types of food produced and the intensity with which they are grown and stocked; labour and capital requirements vary with whether a cowshed or parlour system is adopted, the degree and sophistication of capital equipment and the type and layout of buildings. All vary according to the level of yield of the cows. Similarly, in crop production, labour and capital requirements for a given output vary with the degree of mechanisation, the types of machine, the way field operations are organised and the level of inputs, such as seeds, fertilisers and sprays. It follows that achievement of the planning objective is as much dependent on the way resources are used within individual enterprises (enterprise organisation) as on the way they are allocated between enterprises (enterprise combination). The principle to guide the producer is that he should select the cheapest methods of operation within each enterprise (that is, those methods that minimise the input of scarce and expensive resources) consistent with obtaining that level of output beyond which no further profit is possible.

Committed and uncommitted resources

The breadth of the planning problem also depends on the extent to which resources have already been committed to farming. Take the situation facing an intending farmer. Until he has obtained a farm, his capital – made up of the money he is able to raise from his own resources and by borrowing – is fluid, in the sense that it is uncommitted to farming. He is thus faced not only with problems of allocating resources such as have already been considered, but also with the much bigger problem – in that decisions taken will have more far-reaching and long-lasting effects – of what resources to select in the first place. Should he, for example, seek a farm in a mainly arable or a mainly livestock area? Should he attempt to rent a larger farm or to buy a smaller one? Should he look for a farm in good condition or one which, because it is in poorer heart, may cost less? Should he seek an isolated farm or one nearer a town?

Once he has obtained a farm, however, and manned and equipped it, his planning problem becomes more restricted. Much of his previously fluid resources are now committed in the guise of land, labour, buildings and machinery, which comprise a short-term framework within which he must formulate his plan. In the longer term, it may be modified considerably by the acquisition or disposal of resources. For example, the labour force may be reduced, new buildings erected and, possibly, the holding extended. In such cases the established farmer is in a position analogous to that of the intending farmer, in that he has to make decisions on investment in resources.

To summarise thus far, the basic tenets behind most forms of planning are that:

1. The farmer is limited in the resources that he can acquire.
2. Within the framework imposed both by his limited resources and by his preferences and motivations, he selects enterprises and determines the amount of output to be obtained from each and the methods to be used in obtaining it.
3. His aim is to maximise profit (given the above conditions).
4. Furthermore, because of resource indivisibilities, it is the resource (or resources) that is (or are) the most limiting, relative to his other resources, from which profitability must be maximised.

Dynamic nature of production

It might appear that once the farmer had formulated a sound plan and put it into practice, further planning would be unnecessary and he would only have to concern himself with the day-to-day running of the farm. That this is not so stems from the dynamic nature of the environment in which production is undertaken. Several factors contribute to this.

Changing resource patterns

As has already been acknowledged, the farmer may deliberately decide to change the balance between his resources so that replanning becomes necessary. Even where this is not the case, it may be forced on him as labourers reach retiring age and capital items come to the end of their useful lives. Such cases frequently involve far more than just straightforward replacement by a new worker, building or piece of equipment. For example, there may be no housing available for a new worker unless the farmer erects it himself. Livestock production, which may have been maintained simply because an existing building was available, may be incapable of covering the capital cost of a new one. There may be no directly comparable new machine to replace an old one. In all such instances, a course of action has to be decided upon, so that some form of planning is necessary.

Changing technical relationships

The farmer is faced with a constant stream of advances in technology which, whether they concern resources or products, imply changing relationships between inputs and outputs. Such innovations take many forms. For example, new machinery or improved versions of existing types, new materials, such as herbicides and pesticides, new techniques in crop and livestock husbandry, new varieties of crops and strains of livestock. The farmer has to keep abreast of such advances if he is to maximise his long-term gains and remain competitive with other farmers. This is to imply not that he necessarily takes up more than a small proportion of innovations, but that he should at least assess the financial effects of adoption or non-adoption of those that are pertinent to his farming system and which might have important implications for it.

Changing prices

Price changes concern both the goods and services that the farmer purchases and the produce that he sells. Profit, as the relatively small balance between costs and receipts, is very sensitive to changes in either. For example, on a farm where costs amount to some 75 per cent of receipts (which is typical of many farms in the United Kingdom) a 5 per cent fall in receipts accompanied by a 5 per cent rise in costs reduces profit by 35 per cent. The points of concern to the farmer are, first, whether a change in prices is likely to be fairly permanent, as opposed to being simply a short-term phenomenon (such as fluctuations in product prices due to seasonal gluts and shortfalls in supplies), and, secondly, whether it is sufficient to warrant alterations in his farming system. If the answer to the first question is in the affirmative, some form of evaluation is called for in order to reach a decision on the second.

Uncertainty

Closely allied to the dynamic environment of farming is the uncertainty that accompanies farming operations and which affects inputs and outputs in both the short and long term. Uncertainty as to the future complicates decision making, because it results in imperfect knowledge of many of the planning data, which not only vary over time but do so in an unpredictable manner.

Although it is usual to distinguish between risk, where sufficient information is available to allow expectations based on statistical probabilities to be formulated, and uncertainty, where information is not sufficient, most situations facing farmers may be regarded as uncertain. For example, although an experienced pig producer may, over the years, gain a good idea of the extent of the mortality to be anticipated in his herd and thus be able to evaluate it as a risk to which a cost can be assigned, with many other more important variables, such as the levels of feed and pigmeat prices, no such calculation is possible. In short, even given that the boundary between risk and uncertainty is largely a matter of degree, few farmers are in a position to predict levels of risk on any valid statistical basis.

This is not to imply that producers are absolved from forming expectations, for without them planning would be impossible, but that the latter must be based largely on subjective judgement, which will vary from farmer to farmer for any particular situation. In this way, a 'quasi-risk' situation is established so that planning data can be quantified. At the same time, it implies that there cannot be an optimal solution for any individual year (except fortuitously), but that in a run of years the solution may approximate to the optimum.

Uncertainty can be recognised as short-term or long-term in nature and to affect products, factors and prices.

Product uncertainty

The yields of crops and livestock vary from season to season, due largely to natural factors over which the farmer often has little control. Such variation is particularly marked with crops and also with those forms of livestock production that are subject to the vagaries of the climate. Figure 1.1 shows how the yields of some of the more important arable crops, in two areas of contrasting soil type in East Anglia, varied from year to year. It is noticeable, if account is taken of both the direction and the degree of variation, that different crops in any one area did not respond in the same manner to seasonal stimuli, and that this was also largely true of the response of the same crop in the

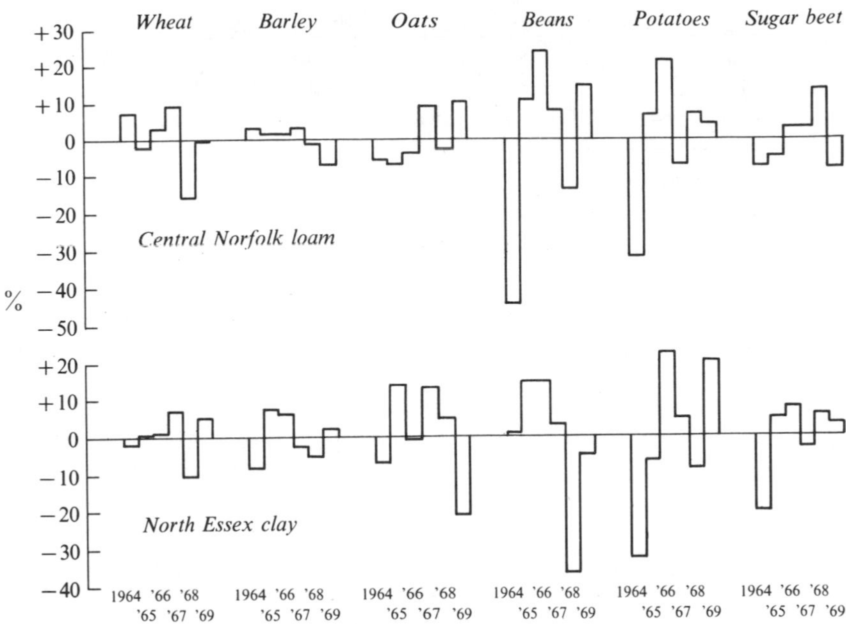

Fig. 1.1. Seasonal variation in crop yields (per cent annual variation around six-year mean [= 0])

two different areas. For example, in Norfolk in 1964, wheat and barley yields were above average while for the remaining crops they were below average (although to different degrees), as was also the case with wheat and barley in Essex. Livestock yields may vary in a similar way. For example, the mortality rate of both ewes and lambs in flocks lambed outdoors is directly affected by the relative severity of the weather, while the yields of all grazing livestock may be indirectly affected by the season's influence on fodder supplies. In the case of those livestock that are largely buffered against the effects of climate by being kept indoors under controlled environmental conditions the incidence of disease nevertheless causes output to vary, as indeed it does with all crops and livestock.

The standard of management is important in this respect, for it is frequently possible to reduce, if not to prevent, variation in output. For example, the quick recognition of the early signs of trouble combined with the prophylactic spraying of crops or inoculation of livestock may do much to reduce the incidence of disease and its consequent effects on output. Again, a generally high standard of husbandry with crops, such as the use of sound seed stock, timeliness in carrying out operations and the correct adjustment of harvesting machinery; and with livestock, such as ensuring that animals breed regularly and are fed correctly on good quality food, can all help to reduce variation in output.

In the longer term, output uncertainty is largely a product of technical change and innovation. For this reason, a farmer may be uncertain whether to replace a known and tried variety of cereal with a new and potentially higher-yielding one; whether the likely gains in crop yields will make the installation of an irrigation system worthwhile; whether a change in policy on breeding or feeding or the supply of replacements will be justified in the light of their bearing on livestock output. Such uncertainties in essential planning data may make him shy of seizing new opportunities or of adopting untried techniques that might bring increased profits.

Factor uncertainty

Natural forces also cause variation in inputs from season to season. This is perhaps most pronounced with labour and machinery use on arable farms. In a bad season such as, for instance, one of above-average rainfall on a heavy-land farm, not only may labour and machine availability for tasks like ploughing be reduced, because there are fewer days on which work is possible, but requirements per ha may also be increased, because of slower work rates on those days when it is feasible to get onto the land. In consequence, the farmer is unable to tell with any certainty how long different tasks will take to complete or how well they will dovetail into one another, and his farm plans should make allowance for such variation. Other inputs such as fertilisers, sprays and supplementary foods for grazing livestock also vary with the season, although they do not on the whole present undue problems of a planning nature.

In the longer term, factor uncertainty may arise for several reasons. One is the uncertainty of technical change that may quickly render obsolescent recently purchased plant and machinery. Another is institutional uncertainty concerning the supply of inputs, such as: whether hired labour will be readily available in a district in the future; whether it will be possible to obtain or expand contracts or quotas; whether contract services are likely to be available in difficult seasons and whether land will be lost to non-agricultural uses. There is also the personal uncertainty, particularly on the one-man farm, that illness may disrupt the farming system or that the farmer may not be able to cope as he becomes older.

Price uncertainty

Although the future levels of both factor and product prices are subject to uncertainty, it is the latter that on the whole display more variation, particularly in the short term. The basic cause stems from seasonal variations in output, such as have already been considered. As the demand for the more staple products is inelastic, a large decrease in prices is needed to dispose of a surplus, while prices may rise considerably if there is a shortfall. In addition, uncertainty as to the action being taken by other farmers adds to fluctuations in supply and thus in prices. For example, an arable farmer who, because of an unfavourable autumn, has been unable to plant his full area of winter wheat, may be uncertain whether it would be better to make up the unsown area next year with spring barley or spring wheat. If he knew how other farmers in the district were reacting, he would be in a better position to avoid the aggravation of what might be an unbalanced supply situation. In a similar way, a time-lag between the initiation of production and the sale of the ensuing output may change the balance of supplies in the two periods and cause wide price fluctuations, as demonstrated by the pig cycle.

The main variation in short-term factor prices is likely to occur with those items that are purchased from other farms, such as piglets, calves, store animals, hay and straw. Being primary products they are subject to variation in market supply, and thus price, for the reasons already considered.

Longer-term uncertainties as to prices arise largely from institutional causes. Shifts in demand, such as a move from grass-fed to grain-fed meats, or to a greater use of convenience foods; changes in government support policies, such as increases in the prices of some products relative to others, or shifts in the level of production grants; and changes in the buoyancy of the economy as a whole, all lead to long term variation, and therefore uncertainty, in both factor and product prices.

The result of product, factor and price variation is that farm profits are also very changeable and uncertain. In consequence, the farmer may put considerable weight on objectives such as income stabilisation, which influence his plans in terms both of the type and the number of enterprises that he carries. It may also make him cautious of making longer-term investments, because of the uncertainty of their outcomes.

The managerial function and the decision-making process

Stages in farm planning and control

So far attention has been directed towards the reasons why farm planning is a necessary and continuing process and something has been seen of the environment of change and uncertainty in which it takes place. Planning the use of resources, however, is simply one of a chain of operations that itself constitutes one of the managerial functions concerned with the making and execution of decisions. This chain is shown schematically in flow-chart form in Figure 1.2.

Compilation. Once it has been recognised that there is a problem to be solved, for instance, that profits are falling or that a building is in need of replacement, the first step is to seek out and assemble the information necessary for its solution. For example, in the case of a decision whether or not to replace an outdated piggery, the data required includes the costs of alternative structures, the financial performance of the pig enterprise and the alternative uses to which the capital might be devoted. Or, if falling profits are the problem, data are needed concerning available resources and the inputs and outputs of current and potential enterprises. Analysis of the data is usually a fundamental part of this stage in order to check that current standards are reasonable, and perhaps also to search for weaknesses in organisation that might point to the direction that planning should take.

Planning. The next stage is to formulate answers to the problem in hand, making use of the data that have been compiled. In many cases, more than one solution is required. For example, with building replacement, a plan assuming that the building is replaced and another assuming it is not will probably be the minimum number to be calculated. Commonly, the need for additional information is revealed during the planning process, either because there prove to be insufficient data to enable solutions to be obtained or because the process of planning throws up fresh ideas. For this reason step 3 shows a return to the first stage if more data are required.

Several years may be required to carry through some plans, as for example when a dairy herd is enlarged by relying solely on retaining a greater than normal number of home-reared heifers. In such cases, the solution obtained initially usually assumes that the new system is fully operational, so that its merit can first be assessed. Thereafter, it may be necessary to produce 'development' plans that cover the change-over period between the present and the proposed systems.

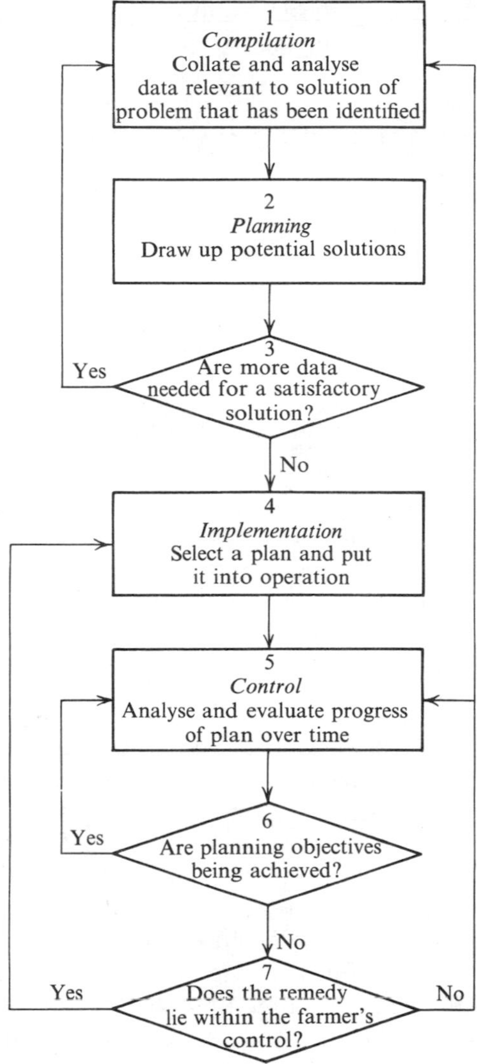

Fig. 1.2. Stages in farm planning and control

Implementation. Once planning is complete, implementation follows as the next stage. This may imply doing nothing (negative action), for planning may have revealed that the best course is simply to accept things as they stand. An example is where the current organisation of a farm remains optimal, although changing prices have lowered profits.

It may also imply selecting from a number of solutions the plan which most nearly satisfies the planning objectives.

Control. Assuming that positive action has been taken and that a plan has been or is being implemented, the next stage is to check on progress. This is essential for several reasons.

1. Planning takes place in an environment of imperfect knowledge. Some of the assumptions made in 'paper' plans may, in the event, turn out to be incorrect, so that modifications and adaptations are required.
2. Even if the planning data prove to be broadly correct, some of the targets set or assumptions made may not be fully achieved in practice. The sooner this is made clear the better, particularly in the case of those plans that may take several years to complete.
3. Although an established farming system may have been running according to plan, the dynamic environment in which it is operated may begin to render it out of date. For example, changing price relationships may call for a change in the balance of enterprises, or new techniques may make available new opportunities.
4. In the short term, natural factors such as bad weather and disease may upset the running of a plan. It is important to distinguish these seasonal effects from more permanent changes.

Control thus implies not just scrutiny of the progress of some change in the farming pattern but regular checks on the whole system, even if it has been operated successfully for many years. It is for this reason that, in the flow chart, the question is posed whether planning objectives are being achieved. If the answer is in the affirmative, a return is made to the control stage, implying that checks will continue to be maintained in the future. If the answer is that planning objectives are not being achieved, the cause may be any of the factors considered above. These may also be divided into factors which the farmer should be able to remedy, such as building-up to a given herd or flock size, and those that are beyond his power to control, such as the effects of institutional price fixing. If the answer to the question posed in step 7 is that the farmer should be able to remedy the situation, a return is made to stage 4. In short, he should take action to implement the plan in the manner originally proposed. For example, if anticipated livestock yields are not being achieved because of an outbreak of disease, implementation would imply attempting to stamp it out, as the plan would be based on the assumption of healthy, not diseased, animals. If, on the other hand, it results from factors beyond the farmer's power to rectify, the action to be taken depends on the cause. Where it is simply due to short-term seasonal factors, such as lowered crop yields due to bad weather, while in other respects objectives are being achieved, no action has to be taken and a return is made to the control stage. Where, however, it originates from longer-term trends, such as changing price relationships, a return to the first stage is indicated, in other words, planning should be initiated in order to find what changes, if any, should be made to the farming system.

Control of plans is thus a vital management function. Without it, time spent on gathering and analysing data and on formulating plans may be largely wasted. It also acts as some insurance against the farmer being overtaken by longer-term adverse trends or failing to take advantage of favourable ones. For this reason, it receives detailed attention in the final part of the book.

Decision making

The essential role of management is to take decisions, for it is clear that if there were no decisions to be made, there would be no need for managers. Decisions are called for in all the stages of planning and control shown in Figure 1.2. First, with the dawning realisation that there is a problem in need of solution, the decision has to be taken to find out more about it. Next, when data are being compiled, it has to be decided whether there is sufficient information to enable the problem to be solved. Once a solution (or solutions) has been obtained the decision must be taken whether to leave things as they are or to take positive steps to implement a plan. In the latter case, it has to be decided which plan to select (when there is more than one), and how and when to start putting it into practice. Finally, in the control stage, a judgement has to be made on whether objectives are being achieved and, if not, what action should be taken.

These are by no means the only types of decision that management is called on to make. For example, there are decisions concerning the day-to-day operation of the farm, such as whether the corn is fit to cut, or what should be done if an essential piece of machinery breaks down. Largely these are short-term, technical matters outside the scope of this book. Then there are decisions to be made concerning the organisation and control of capital and labour, including the determination of when to invest, where to obtain capital, when to replace machinery and how to get the best from the labour force. Such aspects are treated in Chapters 3, 4 and 5. Marketing decisions also have to be made; for example, whether to store a crop or at what season to sell livestock or their output. Such problems receive attention in Chapters 10 and 12.

Management thus has to take decisions in many spheres of activity, which are embraced in the main theme of this book. This may be summarised as a study of problems involved in the pursuit of bounded profit maximisation on farms, and of methods by which they can be solved. As such, it is concerned with the organisation of resources, with planning their use, both within and between enterprises, and with the control of plans both during their implementation and afterwards.

2: Basic principles and concepts of planning

Farmers often have little patience with economic principles and tend to dismiss them as theoretical ideas of little or no relevance to practical people. It is perfectly true that the considerable variations and uncertainty that occur in farming make it difficult to obtain precise data in order to provide neat answers for each individual farm situation. Nevertheless, knowledge of these principles is important to orderly thinking and thus to good decision-making. It helps the farmer or farm manager to realise what information he needs in order to make the decisions with which he is faced. It also helps narrow down the large number of alternatives between which a choice often lies. The principles are subconsciously used by successful farmers to a greater extent than they often realise.

The sequence of decisions in farm planning

The decisions that have to be taken in farm planning are no different fundamentally from those that need to be taken in manufacturing industry. They are covered by what is known in production economics as the 'theory of the firm'. Three basic questions have to be answered, the logical sequence of which would appear to be:

1. *What* to produce? That is, what enterprise, or combination of enterprises, should be chosen? To answer this question, 'product–product' relationships are studied.
2. *How* to produce? That is, what combination of resources (alternatively called factors, or inputs) should be used to produce the enterprises selected? The total supply of some resources is limited, thus restricting the choice. Here 'factor – factor' relationships are relevant.
3. *How much* to produce? That is, what level of output should be aimed at in each enterprise? To this end 'factor–product' relationships are examined.

The answers to all three of these questions on any one farm are in practice very largely interrelated. Furthermore it is not always as easy as might be thought to distinguish between what constitutes a difference in enterprise (considered in 'what' to produce) and what comprises a difference in method of production (considered in 'how' to produce). Certainly the choice made between different methods, for example, alternative ways of supplying bulk feed for cows in the winter, may have far more widespread effects on a farm's economy than the choice between two different crops, such as wheat or barley.

The first step in deciding on a farm policy is obviously to narrow down the possible choice of enterprises, using in particular the comparative advantage of the farm and the farmer's skills and personal preferences. After that, however, on any farm with more than one enterprise, all three types of decision have to be taken together, since all are affected by limitations on the resources available. The choice between different products and their level (i.e. number of hectares, number of head) is inevitably affected by how they are to be produced, and how they are to be produced is influenced largely by factor–product relationships, which are used in deciding how much of a product to produce (and, implicitly, how much of any given variable resource should be used). Thus decisions have to be taken about the use of resources in individual enterprises before the optimal, or a near-optimal, size (in hectares or numbers) of the different enterprises can be decided. This is why the 'organization of enterprises' (Part II) precedes the 'combination of enterprises' (Part III) in this book.

Consequently the three questions are considered below in the order: how much, how and what to produce. Before looking further at these, however, certain basic concepts common to all of them are defined and explained.

Some basic concepts

The marginal principle

The margin refers to an added unit, or the last unit, either of output or input. In both cases it can be measured either in physical or financial terms. Thus, as regards output, in referring to the return obtained from one more unit of input, or one more unit of output, this can be either the *marginal physical product* or the *marginal revenue* (or *marginal return*), that is, the addition to total physical product or total revenue made by one more (or the last) unit of input, or output. As regards inputs, reference can be made to the additional physical quantity of resources needed to produce one more (or the last) unit of output, or to the *marginal cost* of producing one more unit of output, or of supplying one more unit of input.

A marginal change is normally symbolized either by Δ or by δ, as used in calculus. In mathematical terms this need not necessarily refer to an additional unit, but possibly to any point on a continuous function, that is, to the *rate of change* at any particular point. Marginal product, for example, can therefore be depicted as Δ product/Δ input and marginal cost as Δ cost/Δ output.

If the level of output has no effect on the price per unit received, as is usually the case in farming, where the individual producer is usually supplying only an insignificant part of the total production of a commodity, the marginal revenue (or return) of additional (equal units of) *output* is constant. This is in contrast to the marginal return to additional (equal) units of *input*, which usually declines after a point, when added to one or more fixed factors of production, as will be described and illustrated below.

Similarly, the marginal cost of additional units of *input* is constant if the amount required does not affect the price per unit of input. The marginal cost of additional (equal units of) *output*, by contrast, usually rises.

Average relationships are quite different. The average (physical) product, revenue or return is simply the total production or revenue divided by the number of units of either output or input. In the former case, the average return on the individual farm is normally constant, being equal to the price per unit of output.

Average input, or cost, is the total input, or cost, divided by the total number of units of either input or output. In the former case, the average cost on the individual farm is normally constant, being equal to the price per unit of input.

The law of diminishing returns

This is probably the best known law in economics. It states that when one or more variable inputs are added to one or more fixed inputs the extra production obtained will, after a point, decline. The fact that one or more of the resources involved in production are fixed in quantity is essential to this principle. It is thus alternatively called the 'law of variable proportions'. It describes a factor – product, or input – output, relationship. It is most often used with regard to a single variable factor, but, as is implied by the words 'one or more' above, it can also be considered with respect to combinations of different types of input, for example, fertiliser plus labour and machinery.

The law is illustrated by Figure 2.1, which shows a *production function*, *OX*: that is, the response of production to the addition of one or

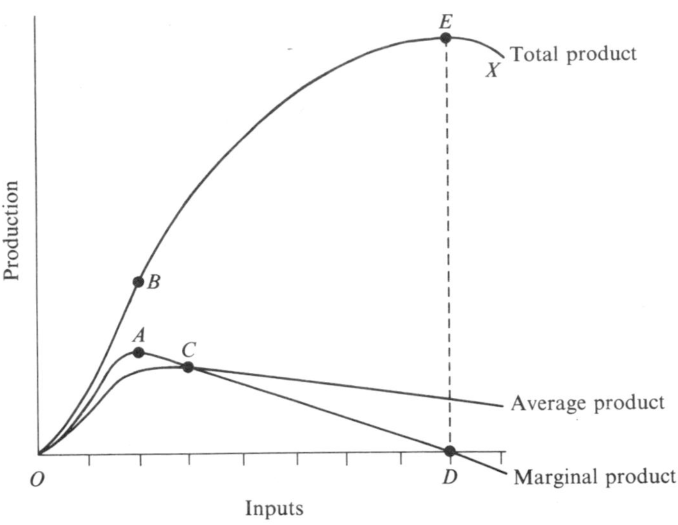

Fig. 2.1. Diminishing returns: total, average and marginal product

more variable inputs to one or more fixed factors of production. Because, as has already been said, in agriculture the individual producer usually provides such a small part of total output that the level of his supply does not affect the market price, the revenue curves are the same shape as the curves of physical production: at all levels of input the amount of physical production is simply multiplied by the same price per unit of output. Similarly, total costs at any level comprise the number of units of input times the same price per unit of input. (A monopoly situation would be different, in that extra production would mean a lower sale price and an extra demand for inputs could raise their prices.)

There are a number of relationships to note between the curves in Figure 2.1. Marginal product begins to decline (*A*) at the point of inflexion of the total product curve, that is, where the slope of the latter begins to decline (*B*). Average product is at a maximum where it is intersected by the marginal product curve (*C*). Marginal product is zero (*D*) at the level of input where total product is at a maximum (*E*). These relationships are further illustrated by the figures in Table 2.1.

Although the law of diminishing returns could refer to all three curves it should normally be related to marginal returns. Marginal returns may not necessarily increase to begin with, as shown in Figure

TABLE 2.1. *Illustration of the law of diminishing returns* (kg of nitrogen applied to barley – hypothetical data)

Kg of N applied per ha	Total product[a] (tonnes)	Marginal product[b] (kg)	Average product[b] (kg)	
10	0.40	400	400	
20	0.91	510	455	Maximum MP
30	1.35	440	450	MP ≃ AP
40	1.71	360	428	
50	1.96	250	392	
60	2.11	150	352	
70	2.19	80	313	
80	2.23	40	279	
90	2.25	20	250	Maximum TP
100	2.25	0	225	MP = Zero
110	2.23	−20	203	Negative MP
120	2.20	−30	183	

[a] Total product excludes the production obtained with no nitrogen applied.
[b] Marginal and average product relate to successive additions of 10 kg.

2.1. They may decline from the outset, in which case both marginal product (MP) and average product (AP) decrease from the same initial point, marginal product falling faster, as shown in Figure 2.2.

The significance of this law in determining how much of a variable factor should be used in order to maximise profit is described on pp. 26–30.

The marginal rate of substitution

This measures the rate at which one factor, or one product, substitutes for another. In the case of factor–factor substitution, the level of production is assumed to remain the same. Thus, the rate at which factor X substitutes for factor Y is the amount of Y which is replaced by one additional unit of X without affecting production. Similarly, in the case of product – product substitution, the same amounts of inputs are assumed. Hence, the rate at which product X substitutes for product Y is the amount of Y which has to be sacrificed in order to produce an additional unit of X, with the same level of resource use.

The 'additional unit' implies a marginal relationship. Hence the term, 'marginal' rate of substitution. This rate of substitution might possibly be constant, meaning that it is the same whatever the relative amounts of factors X and Y being used, or of products X and Y being

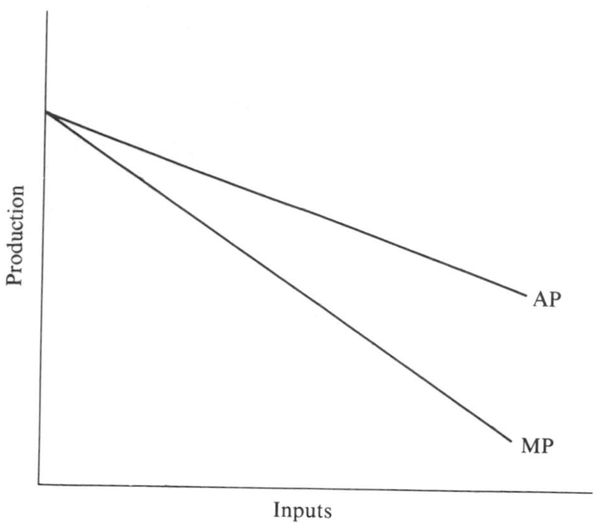

Fig. 2.2. Average and marginal products (no initial increasing returns)

supplied. In this case any line joining all possible combinations of factors *X* and *Y* that may be used to produce a given amount of a particular product (called an iso-product curve, or product contour), or all possible combinations of products *X* and *Y* that can be produced with a given amount of resources (called a production possibilities curve), must be straight. This is shown in Figure 2.3*A*.

It is far more likely, however, owing largely to the operation of the law of diminishing returns, that the marginal rate of substitution will alter according to the combinations of factors, or products, being used at any one point. In the factor – factor case the curves are then as shown in Figure 2.3*B*. This implies a diminishing rate of substitution. That is to say, the more factor *X* is substituted for factor *Y*, the less of factor *Y*

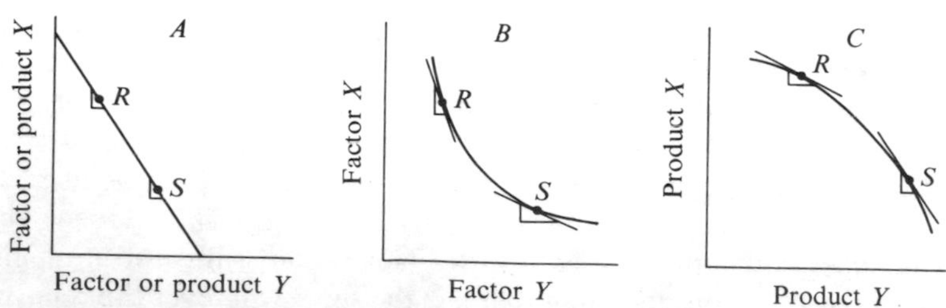

Fig. 2.3. Marginal rate of substitution

that is replaced by each additional unit of factor *X*. In the product–product case the curves would be as shown in Figure 2.3*C*, which denotes an *increasing* rate of substitution. That is, the more product *X* is substituted for product *Y*, the more of product *Y* that has to be sacrificed in order to allow each additional unit of *X* to be produced.

The slope of the curve at any point measures the marginal rate of substitution at that point, which can be written as $\Delta Y/\Delta X$. This can be measured by drawing a tangent at that point, as shown in Figure 2.3. Considering the tangents to points *R* and *S* on the curves, the vertical line on each of the right-angled triangles measures ΔX and the horizontal line ΔY. In Figure 2.3*A*, $\Delta Y/\Delta X$ is the same at *R* as at *S* (or anywhere else on the line), indicating a constant rate of substitution. In Figure 2.3*B*, $\Delta Y/\Delta X$ is smaller at *R* (where more of *X* and less of *Y* is used) than at *S*, implying a diminishing marginal rate of substitution (similarly, $\Delta X/\Delta Y$ is greater at *R* than at *S*). In Figure 2.3*C*, $\Delta Y/\Delta X$ is greater at *R* (where more of *X* and less of *Y* is produced) than at *S*, which means an increasing marginal rate of substitution (similarly, $\Delta X/\Delta Y$ is smaller at *R* than at *S*).

These relationships are further illustrated and their significance demonstrated in discussing 'how to produce' and 'what to produce' in later sections of this chapter.

The law of equi-marginal returns

This law states that limited resources should be allocated in such a way that the marginal return to those resources is the same in all the alternative uses to which they might be put. If the marginal returns in different uses were in fact unequal, it would clearly pay to transfer some of the resource from the use where its marginal return is lowest to the use where its marginal return is highest. This process should continue until marginal returns are equal in all alternative uses.

As will be seen below, this law has significance for all three questions: how much to produce, how to produce and what to produce. Difficulties that arise in trying to implement this principle in practice are discussed later (pp. 42–3). It is illustrated in Table 2.2. Given the knowledge of marginal returns to additional units of capital as shown in that table, the profit-maximising distribution of £12,000 worth of capital is as shown. The same example can be used to illustrate the next concept.

Opportunity cost

This concept is a corollary of the law of equi-marginal returns and has considerable practical significance. The opportunity cost of

TABLE 2.2. *Illustration of the law of equi-marginal returns*

Capital invested	Additional profit (£) per £1000 invested in: Fertiliser	Machinery	Drainage	Buildings	Livestock
1st £1,000	**3,500**	**2,000**	**3,000**	**1,800**	**2,500**
2nd £1,000	**2,750**	1,600	**2,000**	1,400	**2,300**
3rd £1,000	**2,000**	1,200	1,000	1,000	**2,100**
4th £1,000	1,500	800	500	700	**1,900**
5th £1,000	750	400	400	400	**1,700**

Assuming £12,000 to be the maximum amount of capital available, the figures in bold print represent the returns to the investments that should be made in order to maximise profits. The principle of opportunity cost is satisfied, in that the added profit from the marginal £1,000 is £1,700 (invested in livestock), and this exceeds the best alternative return, which is £1,600 (in machinery).

The profits are discounted to present values (see Chapter 3, pp. 61–2).

using a resource in a given way is the value forgone by not using it in the most profitable alternative way. For example, in Table 2.2, the opportunity cost of using another (i.e. a 13th) £1000-worth of capital for drainage would be £1600, which is its value in the next most profitable use (machinery).

Where other costs associated with the alternative use are the same, the opportunity cost is measured by the gross value of the output forfeited. If they are different a net value has to be used. For example, the most appropriate measure in determining the allocation of fixed quantities of land and labour is not the outputs of the different enterprises but the gross margins (see p. 45). When allocation is optimal, resources have been used in the most profitable way, which means the returns to those resources must be at least as high as their opportunity cost, that is, their return in the next most profitable use. If this were not so the opportunity cost would exceed the value obtained in the chosen use and some potential extra profit would have been forfeited.

This concept is fundamental to the optimal allocation of scarce resources, which is the essence of farm planning. It affects all three of the decisions listed above: what to produce, how to produce, and how much. Consequently, the term is used repeatedly throughout this book, and especially in Part III.

How much to produce

The question of determining the level of a variable input, and therefore the level of output, which gives the maximum profit is closely linked to the law of diminishing returns. The optimal point can be found by valuing the total product at different levels of input and plotting the total revenue (TR) and total cost (TC) on the same graph (Figure 2.4). Because the cost of each additional unit of input (MC) is assumed to be constant, total cost is represented by a straight line. Since profit equals TR–TC, maximum profit is obtained at the point where the vertical distance between the TR curve and the TC line is at its greatest. This is further illustrated, by figures, in Table 2.3, which expresses the physical data of Table 2.1 in financial terms.

The point of maximum profit can also be found by considering marginal revenue and marginal cost. These are illustrated by the data in Table 2.3 and Figure 2.5, which includes the marginal revenue (MR) and average revenue (AR) curves and the marginal cost (MC) and average cost (AC) curves. The last two are both represented by a single horizontal line, since, with the input scale along the horizontal axis, MC = AC = the price per unit of the input. The only rational area in which to produce is between *A′*, that is, where AR is at a maximum (*A*), and *B*, where MR reaches zero. Up to input level *A′*, average profit per unit of input (which is AR–AC) is still increasing; therefore total profit must obviously still be rising. Beyond point *B* extra costs are being borne for a lower total output, the MR becoming negative beyond

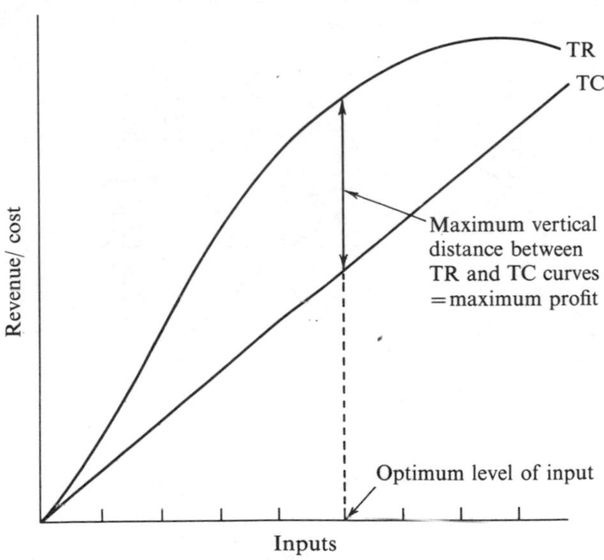

Fig. 2.4. Maximum profit point, I: total curves

TABLE 2.3. *Level of variable input at which profit is maximised*

Kg of N applied per ha	Total revenue (£)	Marginal revenue (£)	Average revenue (£)	Total cost (£)	Marginal cost = Average cost (£)	Total revenue less total cost (£)
10	32.00	32.00	32.00	2.40	2.40	29.60
20	72.80	40.80	36.40	4.80	2.40	68.00
30	108.00	35.20	36.00	7.20	2.40	100.80
40	136.80	28.80	34.20	9.60	2.40	127.20
50	156.80	20.00	31.36	12.00	2.40	144.80
60	168.80	12.00	28.13	14.40	2.40	154.40
70	175.20	6.40	25.03	16.80	2.40	158.40
80	178.40	**3.20**	22.30	19.20	**2.40**	**159.20**[a]
90	180.00	1.60	20.00	21.60	2.40	158.40
100	180.00	0	18.00	24.00	2.40	156.00
110	178.40	−1.60	16.22	26.40	2.40	152.00
120	176.00	−2.40	14.67	28.80	2.40	147.20

The figures above are based on the physical data in Table 2.1 (successive additions of 10 kg of N to 1 hectare of barley).

Assumed price of barley: £80 per tonne.

Assumed price of nitrogenous fertiliser: 24p per kg.

[a] 80 kg represents the optimal application, total revenue less total cost being maximised. Marginal revenue approximately equals marginal cost, and is lower than marginal cost at the next application shown (90 kg).

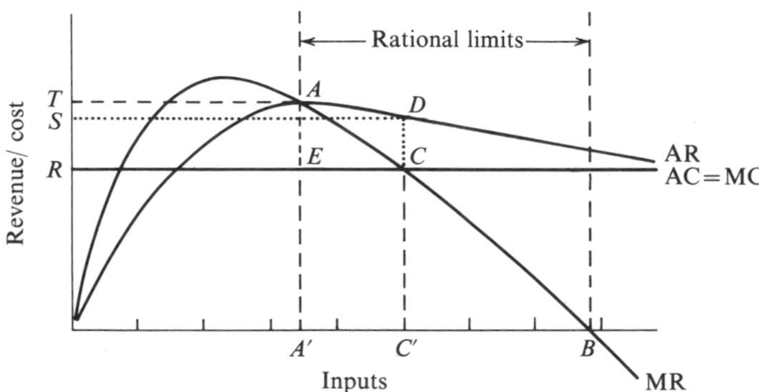

Fig. 2.5. Maximum profit point, II: marginal (and average) curves

this point, which is obviously uneconomic. The optimum level of input is at C', where MR equals MC (point C), since up to this point the extra revenue obtained from the last unit of input exceeds the extra cost of that input, and beyond that point the extra revenue produced is less than the extra cost incurred to obtain it. Referring back to Figure 2.4, the maximum vertical distance between the TR curve and TC line is where the slope of the former (which measures MR at any point) equals (i.e. is parallel to) the slope of the latter (which measures MC). The maximum profit point on the TR curve is thus where a line drawn parallel to the TC line is tangential to the TR curve.

With fertiliser representing the variable input and barley the product, marginal cost can be expressed as (extra) kg of fertiliser × price per kg of fertiliser, and marginal revenue as extra kg of barley (i.e. the resulting increase in production) × price per kg of barley. At the most profitable point, as we have seen, these two are equal. Alternatively, the equation can be written as follows:

$$\frac{\Delta \text{ Barley}}{\Delta \text{ Fertiliser}} = \frac{\text{Price per kg of Fertiliser}}{\text{Price per kg of Barley}}.$$

Using the figures in Tables 2.1 and 2.3, at an application of between 80 and 90 kg of N per hectare, this is

$$\frac{30}{10} = \frac{24\text{p}}{8\text{p}}.$$

Cross-multiplying, this gives:

30 kg (Δ Barley) × 8p (Price per kg of Barley)
= 10 kg (Δ Fertiliser) × 24p (Price per kg of Fertiliser) = £2.40.

It should be noted that at point *C* the average profit per unit of input (which is *DC′–CC′*) is less than at point *A* (where the average profit per unit of input is *AA′–EA′*), since the average return is lower and the average cost is the same. However, this lower profit per unit of input is being obtained on a larger number of inputs. The area *DCRS* represents the profit being made and this exceeds area *AERT* by the area *AEC*.

Figures 2.4 and 2.5 present the situation from the point of view of what happens to production and revenue when extra (equal) units of input are added. The same relationships can be indicated from the opposite point of view, namely, the effect on costs when a producer endeavours to obtain extra (equal) units of additional output with certain resources, or inputs, fixed in quantity; for example, when successive additions of 100 litres per annum per dairy cow, or successive additions of 1 tonne per ha of potatoes, are sought. The corollary of diminishing returns to added (equal) units of input is increasing costs

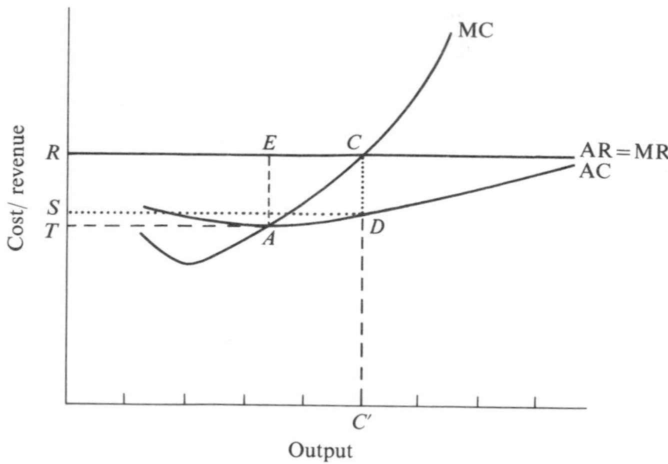

Fig. 2.6. Maximum profit point, III: increasing costs

of added (equal) units of output. This is illustrated in Figure 2.6. The horizontal axis now represents units of output, instead of input as in Figures 2.4 and 2.5. The cost curves fall at first and then rise. The marginal cost curve cuts the average cost curve where the latter is at a minimum. This time it is the marginal revenue (MR) and average revenue (AR) curves which are represented by a single straight line, since with constant additional units of output MR = AR = the price per unit of output. The optimum level of production is at *C′*, where MR = MC (point *C*). The profit is represented by the area *DCRS*, which exceeds area *AERT*, even though the profit per unit of output is lower, *AC* being higher at *D* than at *A* and *AR* being constant. Eventually *AR* would become equal to *AC* (where *TR* = TC), when profit would clearly have fallen to zero.

It must be stressed that the point where MR = MC is only optimal if as many of the variable inputs are available as may be wanted. If a resource is limited then the law of equi-marginal returns (see p. 25) applies and the principle of opportunity cost has to be considered. Then a point to the left of *C* in Figures 2.5 and 2.6 would be optimal. If in fact the resource is available in any quantity that may be demanded, the law of equi-marginal returns is automatically satisfied if the point where MR = MC is obtained in all alternative uses.

How to produce: the principle of substitution

In deciding how to produce a particular product the principle of substitution is applied. This is concerned with factor–factor relationships, and is used to help determine the optimum combination of variable resources to produce a given output. The concept of the marginal rate of substitution (p. 23 above) is used in applying this principle.

Curves on a graph which show different possible combinations of factors to produce a given output are called product contours (or iso-product curves). As was seen on pp. 23–4, if these are drawn as straight, parallel lines, as for example line *CD* in Figure 2.7, a constant marginal rate of substitution is implied. The further the lines are from the origin the higher the output level. With a constant marginal rate of substitution, provided both resources are available in unlimited quantities, using only the resource with the lower cost will obviously give the higher profit. To illustrate this in Figure 2.7, the broken line *XD* and those parallel to it are iso-cost lines, that is, they join all combinations of the two factors with the same total cost. Hence, if *CD* is the level of output sought, it is cheapest to produce it by using quantity *D* of factor *B* and none of factor *A*. Any other choice would lie on a higher iso-cost line. If the slopes of the two lines happened to coincide then it would be immaterial which factor, or combination of factors, were chosen.

The more likely relationship, however, is one of diminishing

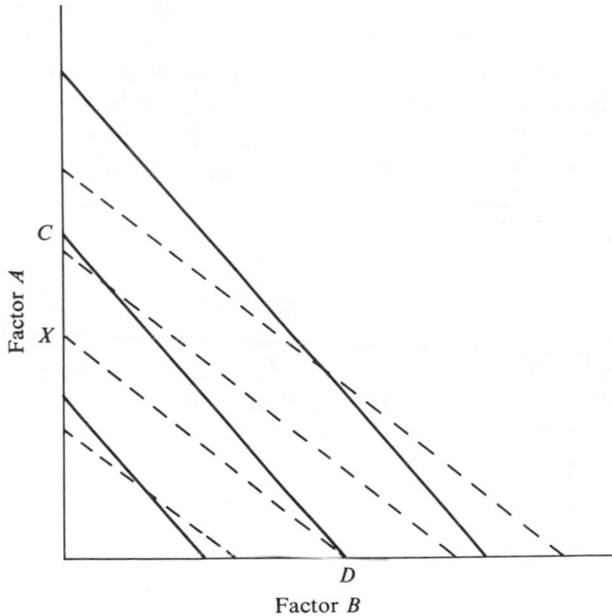

Fig. 2.7. Product contours and iso-cost lines: constant marginal rate of substitution

TABLE 2.4. *Combinations of land and fertiliser to grow barley*

Kg of N applied per ha	Yield of barley per ha (tonnes)	Combinations to produce 1 tonne of barley		
		Land (ha)	Nitrogen (kg)	
0	2.50	0.400	0	
10	2.90	0.345	3.45	
20	3.41	0.293	5.87	*A*
30	3.85	0.260	7.79	*B*
40	4.21	0.238	9.50	
50	4.46	0.224	11.21	*C*
60	4.61	0.217	13.02	*D*
70	4.69	0.213	14.93	
80	4.73	0.211	16.91	
90	4.75	0.210	18.95	

The data are derived from Table 2.1.

It is assumed that 2.5 tonnes of barley per ha can be produced without any nitrogen being applied.

marginal rates of substitution. This is a corollary of the law of diminishing returns, and is illustrated by the data in Table 2.4. This is derived from the figures in Table 2.1 (excluding the 3 highest levels of application), and shows different combinations of land and fertiliser (which requires working capital) that could be used to produce a tonne of barley. Taking points *A* and *B*, between which fertiliser application is increased from 20 to 30 kg per ha, the same production as at *A* can be achieved at *B* by applying 1.92 more kg of N to 0.033 ha less land. This means that the marginal rate of substitution of (1 kg of) N for land is 0.017, that is,

$$\frac{\Delta \text{ Land}}{\Delta \text{ Fertiliser}} = \frac{0.033}{1.92} = 0.017.$$

Increasing fertiliser from level *C* (50 kg/hectare) to *D* (60 kg/hectare), however, gives a marginal rate of substitution of only 0.004 (0.007/1.81) demonstrating that increasing (equal) additions of fertiliser replace less and less land for a given output.

These relationships would be very important to farm planning decisions if both factors were variable or, indeed, if both were limiting. A more likely example of two variable resources is represented by different combinations of hay (representing bulk fodders in general) and concentrates, to produce different levels of, say, milk yield from a

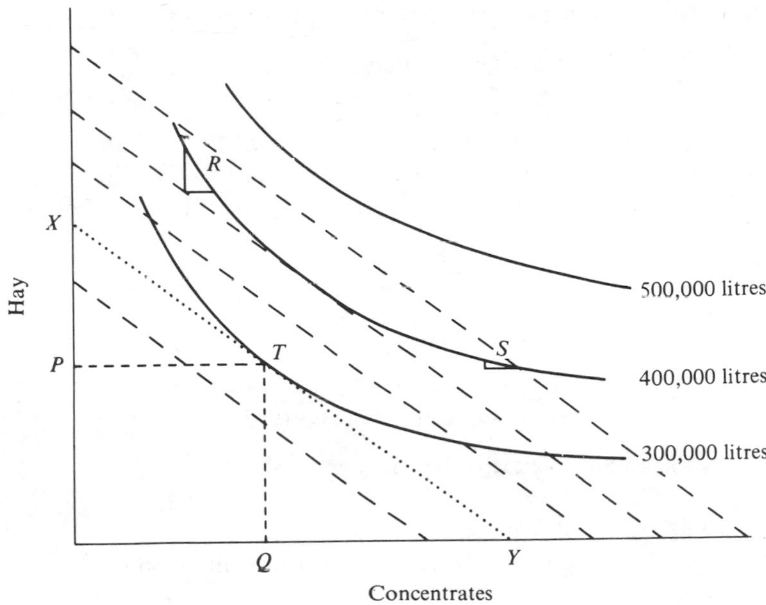

Fig. 2.8. Product contours and iso-cost lines: diminishing marginal rate of substitution

given number of cows during the winter. The greater the input of one variable with the other variable (and all other factors) fixed in quantity, the lower the marginal return – as is to be expected from the law of diminishing returns. Typical product contours are shown in Figure 2.8. Their shape represents diminishing marginal rates of substitution, as illustrated above and in Figure 2.3*B*. The (broken) iso-cost lines are straight, as in Figure 2.7.

The optimal point at any given level of output, which is called the *least cost outlay*, or the *least cost combination*, is where an iso-cost line is tangential to the relevant product contour. This is obviously the lowest iso-cost line touched by the product contour. To illustrate, point *T* in Figure 2.8 shows the optimum combination of hay (amount *P*) and concentrates (amount *Q*) needed to produce 400,000 litres of milk from a given number of cows, *XY* being the tangential iso-cost line. At this point the slopes of the two lines are equal: hence, the marginal rate of substitution equals the price ratio of the two factors, that is,

$$\frac{\Delta \text{ Hay}}{\Delta \text{ Concentrates}} = \frac{\text{Price per unit of Concentrates}}{\text{Price per unit of Hay}}.$$

This is the same as saying that at this point (by cross-multiplying):

$$\Delta \text{ Hay} \times \text{Price per unit of Hay} = \Delta \text{ Concentrates} \times \text{Price per unit of Concentrates.}$$

Suppose the price of concentrates to be £105 per tonne and the price of hay £35 per tonne; that is, the ratio is 3:1. The optimal point is where 1 kg of concentrates just replaces 3 kg of hay. At that point,

$$\frac{\Delta \text{ Hay}}{\Delta \text{ Concentrates}} = \frac{3}{1},$$

which equals the price ratio of the two:

$$\frac{\text{Price per unit of Concentrates (£105)}}{\text{Price per unit of Hay (£35)}}.$$

To put this in an alternative form:

$$3 \text{ kg of hay at 3.5p per kg} = 1 \text{ kg of concentrate at 10.5p per kg.}$$

If, at any point,

$$\frac{\Delta \text{ Hay}}{\Delta \text{ Concentrates}} > \frac{\text{Price per unit of Concentrates}}{\text{Price per unit of Hay}}$$

then some hay should be replaced by concentrates until the two are equal, since it means that Δ Hay × 3.5p is exceeding 10.5p (where Δ Concentrates = 1 kg). If the marginal rate of substitution of concentrates for hay were *less than* the price ratio, then some concentrates should be replaced by hay, until the two are equal.

If two factors have to be combined in fixed proportions then each level of output will be simply depicted by a dot on the graph, showing the required amount of each resource.

The principle with three or more resources remains the same. Solutions cannot then be found graphically, but linear programming (see Chapter 15) can be used to find, for example, the cheapest combination of feedingstuffs to make a ration of a given nutritional standard.

The above analysis has assumed both (or all) factors to be freely available in whatever amounts are required. If, however, one of the resources is in limited supply, the law of equi-marginal returns and the principle of opportunity cost have to be applied (see pp. 25–6 above). In other words, the marginal return of the resource in all its alternative uses has to be taken into account. There might for example be an optimal combination of labour and machinery for the production of potatoes, assuming both to be available in any quantities required. But if capital is scarce and labour is plentiful it will probably pay to use more labour and less capital than this, because the combination is only optimal if the resources are correctly valued, which necessitates using opportunity costs where resources are limited. Similarly, if capital is readily available but labour is in short supply – either overall or at certain times of the year – then it will probably pay to use more capital than would otherwise appear to be optimal, owing to the high opportunity cost of labour. As will be seen in Part III, certain planning techniques take opportunity cost fully into account in allocating resources between competing uses.

The present section, 'How to produce', can be further linked to the previous section, 'How much to produce', through Figure 2.9, which again illustrates a factor–factor relationship. Let us suppose that the two variable factors are fertiliser and labour, which are being applied to a fixed quantity of land, and that these are associated with a fixed amount of other inputs. The inputs along the horizontal axes in Figures 2.4 and 2.5 could be simply fertiliser, with all other factors, including labour, given: this would be indicated by line *AB* in Figure

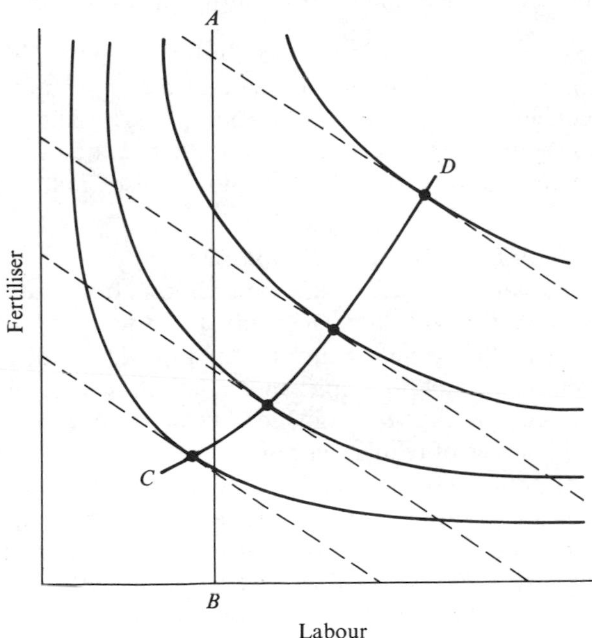

Fig. 2.9. The expansion path

2.9, which illustrates diminishing returns, more and more fertiliser being needed to achieve successive equal increments in production. Or the inputs could represent constant additional input costs of the optimal combination of fertiliser and labour at each level of production. In practice the latter situation would normally be presented in the form of Figure 2.6, showing rising marginal costs. The optimal combination of factors, or inputs, at different levels of output can be traced along line *CD* in Figure 2.9, known as the *expansion path* (or scale line). The increasing distance between successive product contours (which represent equal additions to production levels) with increasing distance from the origin represents diminishing returns to the fixed factors of production.

What to produce

The following principles and concepts are all relevant to the optimal choice of enterprises on a farm:

The principle of product substitution;
Complementary and supplementary relationships;
The law of equi-marginal returns – principle of opportunity cost.

The last two concepts, which are closely linked, have already been defined (pp. 25–6) and it has been seen that they are also relevant to decisions concerning how and how much to produce. They will not be referred to again in this section, therefore, but their fundamental importance to allocative planning decisions must again be stressed.

The principle of product substitution

This principle states that a farmer should choose, from each group of competing enterprises revelant to his circumstances, that which will provide him with the best net return for the farm as a whole. This can be illustrated by a simple example, shown in Figure 2.10, which illustrates a product–product relationship. Let us assume that a farmer with given resources of regular labour and capital can produce either sugar beet or potatoes on 40 hectares of his land. Sugar beet yields 35 tonnes per ha and potatoes 25 tonnes per ha. He can thus produce either 1400 tonnes of sugar beet or 1000 tonnes of potatoes or any combination of the two (e.g. 700 tonnes of sugar beet and 500 tonnes of potatoes at point *X*). The relative prices or, more specifically, gross margins (see page 45) will determine the most profitable choice. Suppose the gross margin for sugar beet is £15 per tonne and for potatoes £27 per tonne.

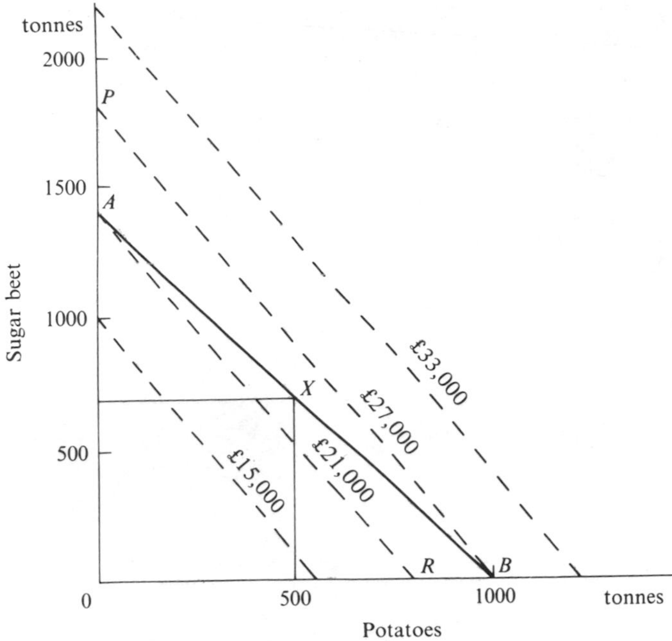

Fig. 2.10. Production possibilities 'curve' and iso-gross margin lines: constant marginal rate of substitution

An all-sugar-beet policy would give a total gross margin of £21,000 and all-potatoes £27,000. The farmer would thus choose the latter.

Line *AB* in Figure 2.10 is known as the production possibilities line (or curve). It links all combinations of the two crops that can be produced with the given basic farm resources. Line *PB* and others parallel to it are iso-gross margin lines, often called iso-revenue lines (or curves), since they link all combinations of the two crops giving the same total gross margin (e.g. $PB =$ £27,000, $AR =$ £21,000). Maximum profit is obtained at the point where the production possibilities line touches the highest iso-gross margin line. In Figure 2.10 this is point *B*. If the slope of the two lines were identical, then all points on the production possibilities line would give the same total gross margin and all possible cropping combinations would be equally profitable.

The relationship indicated by the line *AB* is one of a constant rate of substitution (see p. 23 above). At any point on the line 1 tonne of potatoes substitutes for 1.4 tonnes of sugar beet, that is,

$$\frac{\Delta \text{ Sugar Beet}}{\Delta \text{ Potatoes}} = 1.4.$$

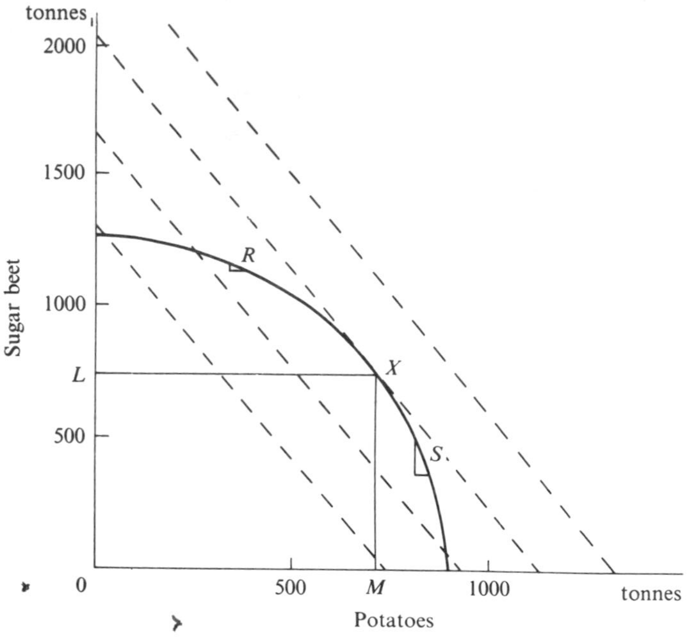

Fig 2.11. Production possibilities curve and iso-gross margin lines: increasing marginal rate of substitution.

It is far more likely, however, that the marginal rate of substitution will be not constant but increasing (see pp.24–5, Figure 2.3*C*). That is to say – returning to our example – as potatoes are increased the marginal sacrifice, or loss, of sugar beet becomes greater and greater. This is illustrated in Figure 2.11. At *R*, where few potatoes are grown, only a relatively small amount of sugar beet is lost if more potatoes are produced:

$$\frac{\Delta \text{ Sugar Beet}}{\Delta \text{ Potatoes}} \text{ is about } 0.5\,;$$

at *S*, a relatively large amount is sacrificed:

$$\frac{\Delta \text{ Sugar Beet}}{\Delta \text{ Potatoes}} \text{ is about } 2.5.$$

This relationship occurs mainly for rotational reasons (especially control of disease in this case) and because of timeliness of operations (given the amount of labour and machinery available at any one time during the year).

The iso-gross margin lines in Figure 2.11 have the same slope as in Figure 2.10, the optimal point being the point where one of these lines is tangential to the production possibilities curve. This is at point X, where L tonnes of sugar beet and M tonnes of potatoes are produced. This is obviously the highest total gross margin obtainable from any combination of the two crops.

Since the point of tangency is where the slopes of the two lines are equal, the optimal point is located where the marginal rate of substitution equals the gross margin ratio between the two crops, which is 15:27, or 1:1.8; that is, where the loss of sugar beet for the addition of 1 tonne of potatoes is 1.8 tonnes. In equation form, this is where

$$\frac{\Delta \text{ Sugar Beet}}{\Delta \text{ Potatoes}} = \frac{\text{GM of Potatoes}}{\text{GM of Sugar Beet}} \left(\text{in this example, } \frac{1.8}{1} = \frac{27}{15}\right).$$

To put this in yet another way, by cross-multiplying, the optimal point is where Δ Sugar Beet $\times$ GM of Sugar Beet $=$ Δ of Potatoes $\times$ GM of Potatoes. At point X, $1.8 \times £15 = 1.0 \times £27 = £27$.

If, at any point,

$$\frac{\Delta \text{ Sugar Beet}}{\Delta \text{ Potatoes}} < \frac{\text{GM of Potatoes}}{\text{GM of Sugar Beet}}$$

potatoes should be substituted for sugar beet (since Δ Sugar Beet $\times$ GM of Sugar Beet would then be less than Δ Potatoes $\times$ GM of Potatoes). If

$$\frac{\Delta \text{ Sugar Beet}}{\Delta \text{ Potatoes}} > \frac{\text{GM of Potatoes}}{\text{GM of Sugar Beet}}$$

then sugar beet should be substituted for potatoes. This last equation could be re-written: if

$$\frac{\Delta \text{ Potatoes}}{\Delta \text{ Sugar Beet}} < \frac{\text{GM of Sugar Beet}}{\text{GM of Potatoes}}.$$

Competitive, complementary and supplementary relationships

In Figure 2.11, the marginal rate of substitution is always negative, that is, if one product is increased, some of the other product has to be sacrificed. This is the most common relationship between enterprises, and means that the two products are competing with one another for resources. Sometimes, however, an increase in one product may actually *increase* the total production of the other, through some beneficial effects – over a limited range. This is known as *complementarity*

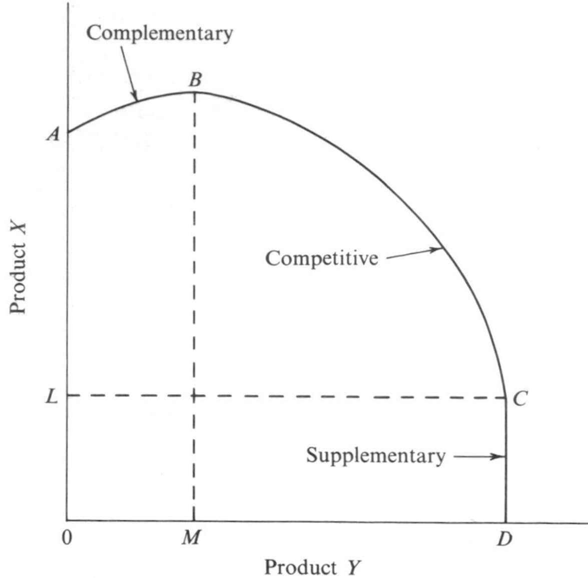

Fig. 2.12. Complementary, competitive and supplementary relationships

and is illustrated by sector *AB* on the production possibilities curve shown in Figure 2.12; the introduction of Product *Y*, up to point *B* (= amount *OM* of *Y*) actually increases the total output of product *X*. Sometimes one product can be introduced without any effect on the output of the other product, over a certain range; this is known as *supplementarity* and is shown by *CD* on Figure 2.12: the introduction of product *X*, up to point *C* (= amount *OL* of *X*), has no effect on the output of product *Y*. Between *B* and *C* the products are *competitive*, since one product can be increased only at the expense of some reduction in the output of the other.

An example of complementarity is the introduction of some beef animals on grassland previously stocked only with sheep. The output of sheep may actually rise, up to a point, because the different grazing habits of the two types of animal may improve the sward and because the rest from sheep provided by grazing beef is likely to reduce the incidence of sheep diseases. Another example might be the introduction of a break crop on a farm previously growing continuous cereals (see also Chapter 12, pp.270–1). Again, the introduction of a sheep flock on an all-arable farm should, by utilising arable by-products, increase the value of those by-products, besides providing additional fertility. On some soil types at least, straw-yarded cattle might be held to have a complementary relationship with a crop such as potatoes, because of the extra yield resulting from the application of farmyard manure.

Supplementarity involves the use of spare or surplus resources, i.e. resources that would otherwise be wasted. Thus their use does not affect the output of enterprises already on the farm (unless they compete for *other* resources – see below). For instance, a catch-crop utilises land during months when the main crops do not require it. As another example, the vining pea crop requires its harvesting labour mainly in July, which is a relatively slack time on many farms, coming between hay-making and the cereal harvest. The classic case is a yarded beef enterprise on an arable farm (also referred to above with regard to complementarity), which often utilises a winter labour surplus and sometimes old buildings and yards with perhaps no other use. Although by-products are included above under complementarity, they might equally be regarded as illustrating supplementarity, in so far as they relate to intermediate products (or feed resources) that might largely be wasted if there were no livestock enterprise to consume them.

It is important to appreciate that these complementary and supplementary relationships between enterprises only operate up to a point and do not necessarily hold for all resources on the farm. Thus a grazing livestock enterprise, after a certain point, will no longer increase the total output of cereals, although it will still probably increase the cereal output *per hectare*. After a point (*B* on Figure 2.12 for example) it becomes competitive, even though it is still having a beneficial effect on the other product. Again, one product may be supplementary to others in the use of *some* resources and yet be competitive for others. Thus vining peas have a supplementary effect as regards seasonal labour requirements, but are competitive for land. The beneficial and dovetailing effects can be extremely complex.

Diversification versus specialisation

Finally, in deciding what to produce, a farmer has to decide to what extent he should specialise or, alternatively, diversify his production. There is an increasing trend towards specialisation on farms. Increasing dependence on large, expensive machines adds to the importance of economies of size (see p.47). Increasing technical complexity and the economic necessity for a high level of proficiency in production, and sometimes marketing, puts an additional premium on the concentration of both management and manual labour on fewer enterprises. By specialisation, the particular comparative advantages of the farm and the farmer or manager can be fully exploited and it should be possible to gain benefits through buying and selling greater quantities of particular inputs and products.

On the other hand there have always been powerful arguments in favour of diversification. The best-known is the desire to combat risk and uncertainty: if the yield or price of a product falls drastically for any reason, it is obviously less likely to be calamitous if there are several enterprises on the farm rather than just that one. Some years are bad for some products but good for others. The other major reasons for diversification are embodied in the complementary and supplementary aspects just described. In fact the whole concept of rotations, particularly as embodied in the Norfolk four-course, is bound up with these mutually beneficial interrelationships between the individual farm enterprises.

There are other worthwhile reasons for diversification. Some farms, especially those with a large area, have a diversity of soils and topography, suitable for a variety of enterprises. Large differences in the distance between the farmstead and buildings add to the likelihood of having more than one enterprise. Some farmers would find too little interest or too little to occupy them with only one enterprise. Furthermore, the integration of enterprises with differing cash flow patterns may reduce the overall capital requirement.

Practical difficulties

There is no denying that many problems exist in trying to apply the principles outlined above to practical situations. The analysis is static, whereas we live in a dynamic world: techniques and prices change continually, there is a time-lag between starting production and ultimately selling the product, the future is uncertain, production is largely subject to the weather and to attacks by pests and diseases, considerable variations can exist between, for example, the soil in one part of a field and that in another, and between different cows in the herd, and knowledge about the relationships that exist is far from perfect. Further complications arise because of the existence of joint costs and joint products,[1] and the complementary and supplementary aspects

[1]Joint costs are costs which are shared between two or more products: their allocation between products can therefore only be arbitrary, e.g. a baler may be used for both hay and straw; tractors and much of the labour on farms with more than one enterprise are further examples. Joint products relate to items of output produced together, e.g. lamb and wool, grain and straw; sometimes the proportions of the two can be altered, within limits.

referred to above. The fact that many inputs can be applied only in large, indivisible, units rather than in small amounts at a time also creates difficulties. Nevertheless, an understanding of these principles, even though they can be applied only imperfectly, does assist producers to approach problems logically. As will be seen in subsequent chapters, these principles are incorporated in planning techniques in such a way as to help practical people to arrive at practical decisions.

Fixed and variable costs

One of the most important concepts, and one of the most frequently misunderstood, is that of fixed and variable costs. It is fundamental to a considerable number of planning decisions and techniques. In economic theory, a fixed cost is defined as one which does not change when the level of output alters (i.e. it applies to a resource that is fixed in quantity); by contrast, a variable cost is one which *does* change when the level of output alters (i.e. it applies to a variable resource). The terms refer to the *total* of each category of cost, not to costs *per unit* of production. It is important to remember that the 'level of output' may be interpreted in different ways. It may refer to increases in production per hectare of crop or per head of livestock, in which case, as we have seen, variable costs tend to rise at an increasing rate as output is increased, owing to the effect of the law of diminishing returns. On the other hand, the optimum level of variable costs per hectare or per head may have been decided, using the equation of marginal revenue and marginal cost, and changes in output may then only be referring to changes in the number of hectares grown or the number of livestock kept[1]. In this case, which costs are fixed and which are variable depends very much both on the extent of the change and the time period being considered.

In management decision-making, the costs which can be taken as fixed and those which can be regarded as being variable in any particular situation depend on the type of problem being studied and, as has already been said, on the time period involved. Probably the best word to indicate where the line should be drawn between the two is 'escapable', or 'avoidable'. In the long run all costs in farming are variable, in the sense that the farm and all the associated assets can be sold and the business wound up.

Fixed costs are those which are given, in any situation, and cannot be altered. In the short run, therefore, they should not influence the

[1]As will be seen below, the distinction made between fixed and variable costs in defining a 'gross margin' is based on this interpretation.

decision being taken. The only costs which are relevant are those that can be avoided, i.e. those that are affected by the decision taken; these are the variable costs. Let us consider some examples.

Suppose an all-arable farmer is trying to decide whether or not to introduce a dairy herd. All the costs which he could avoid by not doing so are variable at this point in time; these will include the depreciation and interest on the extra buildings needed and the livestock. Suppose he decides to introduce the dairy unit and then wishes to consider what level of yield to aim for. His fixed costs, as far as this decision is concerned, now include not only the annual costs of the land, buildings and the cows themselves, but also the cost of the maintenance ration and most at least of the labour and machinery expenditure. These will be the same whether he aims for 3000 litres a cow or 6000. The only variable costs will be the concentrate ration and perhaps some relatively small addition to labour costs, veterinary expenses and cow depreciation – because of stricter culling. With higher yields the fixed costs per litre fall but the variable costs rise: it is the marginal cost (the addition to variable costs) that determines the optimum level (where MR = MC). This is illustrated in Figure 2.13, which represents an extension of Figure 2.6.

To take another example, an early potato producer finds himself faced with a price slump. Prices are so low he wonders whether the crop is worth harvesting. He knows he cannot hope to recoup his total

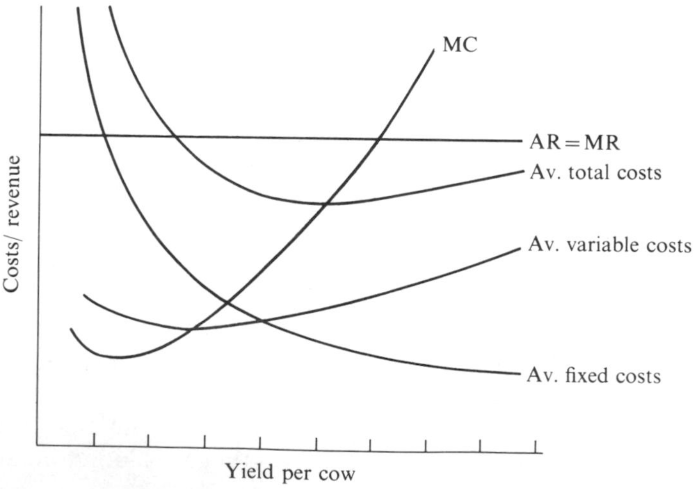

Fig. 2.13. Cost curve relationships

costs of production. However, the costs which he has already incurred – including all the costs of growing and materials – are irrelevant to the decision whether or not to harvest the crop. So are depreciation on harvesting and storage equipment, and the day wages of regular labour, since these costs will remain the same regardless of the decision. The only relevant costs, i.e. the variable costs in this context, are those which he can avoid by not harvesting the crop: these are the cost of casual labour for harvesting, overtime, fuel and repair costs for tractors and harvesting machinery, and any transport and marketing expenses. As long as the price received covers these costs the crop is worth harvesting, since there will then be something left over to help cover the fixed costs (i.e. the costs already incurred), whereas otherwise the fixed costs would represent a total loss. In other words, he will thereby minimise his loss. Clearly he could not stay in early potato production if this happened every season. Over a period of years, obviously, total costs must be covered if a farmer is to stay in business – assuming the farm is his sole means of livelihood.

Gross margins

Some confusion has arisen over the terms 'fixed' and 'variable' costs with the widespread use of the gross margin concept in farm management since about 1960. This is because the same terms are applied in defining gross margins, but the interpretation of fixed and variable costs used assumes a specific planning situation, whereas, as has been seen in the previous section, there are in fact many different possible situations that can occur in farm management, where the interpretation of the terms (i.e. those resources which can be assumed to be fixed and those that can be assumed to be variable) is quite different.

For the purpose of defining gross margins, a farm is assumed to have a given set of resources – land, labour and capital – and the decision being made is how to utilise these 'fixed' resources (or costs) over the next production period (usually taken to be one year). In this context, the costs which are 'variable' are those that differ according to which enterprises are selected, and the size of those enterprises, i.e. the number of hectares grown or the number of head of livestock. To be regarded as variable costs in the gross margin sense, therefore, costs have to satisfy two criteria, which are also satisfied by the enterprise outputs: they must (*a*) be specific to a single enterprise and (*b*) vary approximately in proportion to the size of the enterprise.

The gross margin of an enterprise is its enterprise output less the variable costs attributable to it. For arable crops the variable costs consist primarily of seed, fertiliser, sprays, and contract work and casual labour hired specifically for that enterprise. For non-grazing livestock, concentrate feed is easily the main variable cost,[1] others being veterinary and medicine expenses, and some mainly minor miscellaneous expenses. For grazing livestock, the variable costs are as for non-grazing livestock plus those of the forage crops – mainly seed and fertiliser for grass.

The enterprise output is the total value of the production of the enterprise. It is not necessarily the same as gross output, which is defined as sales plus subsidies plus (or minus) any increase (or decrease) in valuation, less purchases of livestock. It also includes the value of any produce consumed on the farm, e.g. by the household or hired workers, or transferred to another enterprise, e.g. home-produced barley fed to pigs, or dairy heifers transferred from the rearing enterprise to the milk production enterprise. The value of transfers to another enterprise must be deducted from the output of that enterprise, in the same way as livestock purchases. Such calculations are avoided if only the combined output is required, e.g. of a rearing and a fattening pig enterprise.

The total gross margin of all the enterprises on the farm has to cover the total fixed costs and provide a profit. In other words, total farm gross margin less total fixed costs = farm profit (or loss). The fixed costs include rent or mortgage repayments and interest, depreciation on buildings, regular labour, power and machinery expenses (depreciation, repairs, fuel, etc.) and general overhead expenses. Part at least of the fuel and repair costs could in fact be correctly described as variable costs in the gross margin context, but their importance is not usually considered sufficient to make it worthwhile to do the large amount of recording needed for these costs to be allocated; hence they are normally included in the fixed costs. Further practical problems that arise when calculating and using gross margins are discussed in Chapter 20.

Some costs are specific to a single enterprise and yet are not allocated in calculating gross margins per unit of production. This is because they do not satisfy the second criterion stated above, i.e. they do not

[1] This statement assumes that the value of livestock at the start of a fattening period, or livestock depreciation in the case of breeding (or 'productive') livestock, is deducted in arriving at their 'output' (see next paragraph). Sometimes these items (especially livestock depreciation in e.g. egg, lamb or milk production) are included instead as variable costs.

vary in proportion to the size of the enterprise. They form a given total sum, at least over a certain range of enterprise size. Examples are a full-time cowman and depreciation on a potato harvester. A cowman is usually paid extra for looking after more cows, but a major part of his wage is usually at a given level whether he is looking after 40 cows or 100. A potato harvester of given capacity might be applicable to any area from, say, 15 to 30 ha, beyond which a larger harvester would be needed. Because of the fixed cost element, the costs per cow or per hectare in these cases would fall as the enterprise size increased; this contravenes the proportionality criterion for variable costs in the gross margin model.

Fixed costs, as defined in gross margin analysis, are thus of two types: those virtually absolutely fixed, e.g. rent or mortgage expenses (excluding buildings) and general overhead expenses, which will remain the same whatever enterprises are selected and whatever their size, and those which will vary but only in 'steps': these are the 'indivisible' or 'integer' costs, e.g. buildings and machinery depreciation, regular labour. The three types are illustrated graphically in Figure 2.14.: *A* shows total costs in each case and *B* shows costs per hectare or per head. When considering major changes in enterprise size possible changes in these integer costs are clearly as important – sometimes far more so – than the variable costs as defined in gross margin terminology.

Some find it useful to conceive of fixed and variable costs as used in the gross margin context as 'flow' and 'stock' resources respectively. The 'fixed' resources, such as land and regular labour, generate a continuous flow of services; this flow continues whether they are used or not. The variable inputs, such as fertiliser and seed, are obtained from a stock: their cost is incurred only as and when required. The latter costs can be turned on and off, as if by a tap, while costs such as rent, the wages of regular labour and machinery depreciation 'flow on' continuously: if unused they are wasted – they cannot be stored, nor can their cost be stopped – at least not in the short run.

Economies of size and scale

Economies of size are obtained by spreading fixed (or integer) cost items over a larger output, as depicted in Figure 2.14 *B*. The effect is also illustrated by the declining average fixed cost curve in Figure 2.13 (and is illustrated again in Chapter 4, p. 85). As the growing scarcity and cost of farm labour increases the necessity for larger and more expensive items of mechanisation, so the importance of this cost-spreading effect increases.

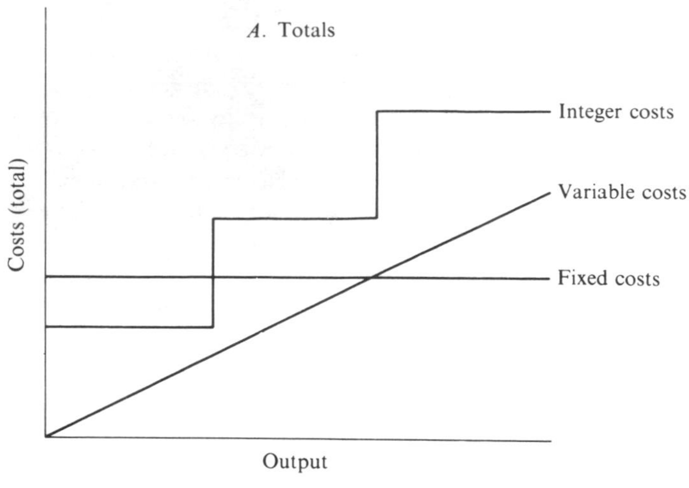

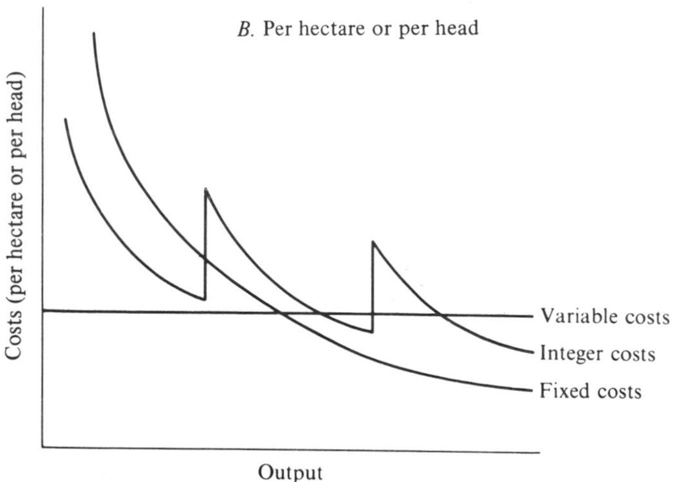

Fig. 2.14. Fixed, variable and integer costs

Such economies are often described as economies of scale, but strictly speaking the latter is a different concept. Economies of *size* relate, as illustrated above, to the spreading of one or more items of fixed cost over a greater production (e.g. more hectares of a crop, more head of livestock, more milk from a given number of cows). Increases in *scale* relate to proportional increases in *all* the factors of production taken together; that is, the ratios of the various factors of production remain the same while the overall size of the business is increased. Let us suppose that a certain farm with a given area and given numbers of men and machines, producing a given set of enterprises, could be exactly duplicated. On the face of it there is no reason why the second unit should not have exactly the same costs and returns as the first, and thus give an identical profit. This would be called constant returns to scale. It is difficult to conceive of such an example occurring in most types of farming; but it could happen in pig or poultry production.

In fact there *would* be both economies and diseconomies in such situations, largely through external factors. Diseconomies arise from increasing scale largely because one of the factors of production *cannot* be increased in the same proportion as other factors, namely management. Assistant managers can be employed, but the chain of command lengthens, co-ordination becomes more difficult, decision-taking is likely to become slower and less effective. Economies and diseconomies of size are further discussed in Chapter 4 (p. 114).

3: The organisation of capital – general

Types of farming capital

'Capital' in farming refers to the total finance required in order to operate a farm business. In the case of an owner-occupier this includes the purchase of land with its associated facilities: roads, drains, ditches, hedges and at least most of the buildings. This may be variously referred to as landlord's capital, fixed capital, or long-term capital, and is discussed further in Chapter 4.

The present chapter relates mainly to the remaining capital – that needed to equip, stock and run the farm. This is normally called 'tenant's' capital, even though fewer than half of British farms are now rented. Tenant's capital may be divided into medium-term and short-term capital. The former consists of plant and machinery and breeding (or 'production') livestock – such as dairy cows, beef cows, ewes and sows. Some include breeding livestock in fixed capital on the grounds that the farm would lose a major source of revenue if such stock were sold; however, several points can be made against this argument and such livestock are better considered as being medium-term capital. Pig and poultry houses expected to last no longer than ten years are also often supplied by the tenant on rented farms and are better regarded as medium-term capital than long-term capital. Both medium and long-term capital supply a 'flow' of services, as it were, over time; most medium-term capital items provide this flow for a period of up to ten years, whereas many long-term capital assets do so for considerably longer.

Short-term capital is alternatively called circulating, or working, capital. It is that capital required to finance the production cycle, from the beginning of production (e.g. preparing the ground for a crop, or buying weaners to fatten) until the ultimate sale of the product. It includes 'trading', or 'temporary', livestock (e.g. livestock being fattened), seed, fertiliser, feedingstuffs, labour, machinery running expenses, various sundry items, rent on a tenanted farm and living expenses. The production period may be long, e.g. over 18 months for winter wheat stored until early summer, or traditional beef

TABLE 3.1. *Types of farming capital*

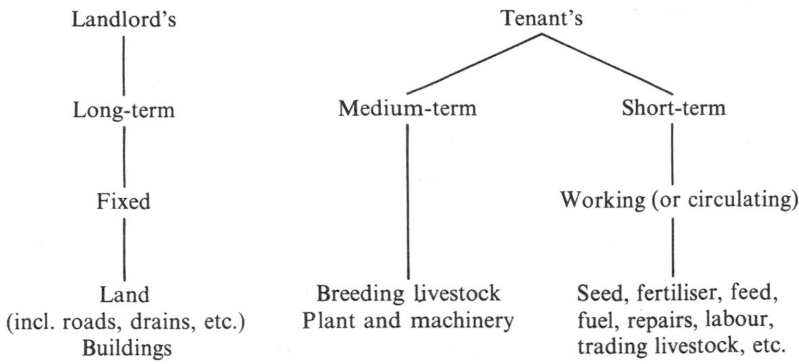

fattening from the calf stage, or short, e.g. 3 or 4 months for fattening purchased beef stores, or fattening weaner pigs for pork production. Also, a farmer buying down-calving heifers or point-of-lay pullets will find his cash receipts from them soon exceeding his subsequent cash outlay. For many farms it is impossible to define a single production period, since different enterprises overlap and receipts from one product finance the costs of another. The different types of capital are summarised in Table 3.1.

Capital requirements

Table 3.2 indicates the level of tenant's capital requirements for various types of farm in England and Wales. These are national average figures obtained by averaging the opening and closing valuations. The 'livestock, mostly sheep' figures are low because most of the holdings are hill farms. Disregarding these and specialist pig and poultry farms, the average total figure is about £500 per ha. Clearly the breakdown of this total varies very much with the type of farming, but the usual range for most lowland farms is £100 to £150 per ha for machinery, £100 to £400 for livestock (both breeding and trading), and £100 to £150 for the remaining short-term capital.

Several points need to be made concerning these figures. To begin with, they do not relate to the amount of capital needed to begin farming, which is substantially higher. The machinery figures are average written-down values. A full complement of machinery, mainly bought new, would cost £450 to £650 per ha on 100 hectares or more, depending on the size and type of farming (see further Chapter 4, p. 80). Breeding livestock too would almost certainly cost more initially than

TABLE 3.2. *Tenant's capital for different types of farming, 1976–7* (£ per hectare)

	Medium-term capital		Short-term capital			
Type of farming	Machinery	Breeding livestock	Trading livestock	Crops	Other	Total
Specialist dairy	126	238	67	25	35	491
Mainly dairy	100	139	72	38	35	384
Livestock, mostly sheep	15	45	10	4	3	77
Livestock, cattle and sheep	55	77	87	23	17	259
Cropping, mostly cereals	103	17	34	65	55	274
General-cropping	161	20	47	112	74	414
Mixed	122	67	112	72	56	429
Pigs and poultry	174	112	247	65	67	665

Note: The above figures are averages from farms of between 275 and 4,199 standard man days in size. They are the averages of opening and closing valuations.

Source: *Farm Incomes in England and Wales, 1976–77*. Ministry of Agriculture, Fisheries and Food (data derived from the Farm Management Survey).

the average value over their whole life. How much total tenant's capital is needed to start farming obviously depends on the system and intensity of farming to be practised. For example, an all-arable 200-hectare farm would require about £750 per ha, comprising £550 for machinery and £200 for working capital. An all-grass 40-hectare dairy farm starting with 80 down-calving heifers and cows would require about £1500 per ha, consisting of £400 for machinery, £1000 for livestock and £100 for working capital.

Even as an estimate of the *average* value of tenant's capital on an established farm, survey data such as those presented in Table 3.2 tend to understate the true position. The machinery figures should be a fair assessment, since realistic depreciation rates are used in the data calculations, as far as possible. However, livestock figures are usually undervalued in farmers' accounts, partly through inertia but mainly for tax reasons. Although these valuations are not necessarily accepted by survey personnel and indeed positive steps are usually taken to ensure that the figures are realistic, livestock still tend to be valued conservatively, and an addition of 20 per cent would give a more accurate assessment of the true value of livestock. Furthermore, 'historic' data, however recent, obviously understate the current figures during periods of inflation.

Assessing working capital requirements from annual accounts is notoriously difficult. It is usual to take either the closing valuation or the average of the opening and closing valuations of trading livestock, cultivations, seed and fertiliser used for unharvested crops, crops in store including hay, silage and straw, and materials in store such as fertiliser, seed and feedingstuffs. As a measure of working capital requirements for an individual farm this may be totally misleading; it is only necessary to compare the April closing valuation on a cereal-growing farm with its grain still in store with that of a virtually identical farm which sold its grain at the end of March. The same point can arise with fattening beef cattle. For this reason different calculations are sometimes used. For example, one method of estimating total tenant's capital is to add together the closing valuation of machinery, the opening valuation of livestock and total current expenses, including the value of the occupier's time (for living expenses) and home-grown foods brought forward from the previous year, and deduct from this receipts from livestock and livestock products. But however elaborate the calculation, the result can still only be an estimate, since it is the pattern of receipts and expenses during the year that determines the amount of working capital required (see pp. 54–6 below) and there is no simple and quick way of estimating this from the annual accounts. There is also the question of whether it is the average requirement throughout the year or the peak requirement that is being sought. Calculations have shown that the apparently crude method of averaging opening and closing valuations does give an acceptable approximation to average requirements for a group of farms, even if it is suspect for individual farms within the group. Compared with cash flow calculations the method underestimates the average tenant's capital requirements by between 1½ and 6 per cent, according to the type of farm. The understatement is most serious in the case of cropping farms.

Assessing capital requirements

Detailed calculations are necessary for the individual farmer requiring to estimate how much capital he needs to pursue his proposed system of farming. He may have a limited amount of capital available and wish to check whether it is sufficient to enable him to carry out the desired system. If it is not, he will have to amend his system, adjust his proposed pattern of payments and sales, or try to obtain more capital. The calculations needed take the form of what is variously known as a capital diary, capital budget, capital profile, or cash flow statement, in which the ebb and flow of capital over given periods of time are assessed.

Other reasons for making these calculations are to help obtain credit from a bank manager, who can see how the applicant proposes to spend the money and the likely seasonal requirements, and for use in budgetary control (see Chapter 20). Annual cash flow statements are also used for calculating returns on capital by the discounted cash flow method (see pp. 61–8).

The length of the time periods required has first to be decided. The shortest period normally considered is monthly. The longest is usually quarterly, unless only a broad idea is wanted over, say, a five-year period, in which case a four-monthly or even half-yearly period may be acceptable – provided capital restrictions are unlikely to be too critical. If the calculation is made for longer than 2 years, however, it is almost certain to need revision after 1 or 2 years. A quarterly assessment can clearly be prepared more quickly than a monthly one. Not only is less arithmetic involved (in that there are fewer columns to add and subtract) but less exact information is needed as to when a receipt is to be expected or a bill is likely to be paid, and there are fewer allocation decisions to make. On the other hand, even a quarterly period may disguise a particular peak: a lot of money may have to be paid out at the beginning of the quarter and perhaps the bulk of the quarter's receipts may not materialise until near the end of the period. A two-monthly period is an acceptable compromise, although comparatively rarely used.

There are two alternative ways in which the statement can be set out. One is in the form of a diary. An example is shown in Table 3.3. In the *pro forma* only the columns and column headings are given. For each period, say a month, both a monthly and a cumulative balance are calculated. Where the latter is being measured against the amount of capital available, the money already spent at the beginning of the diary period (e.g. for machinery or livestock) can be either subtracted from the capital available or added to the cumulative balance and the total compared with the amount of capital originally available. Thus if, say, the borrowed money spent at the start is £10,500 and the overdraft limit is £15,000, the cumulative balance at the end of each period can be compared with the £4500 remaining, or the £10,500 can be added to the cumulative balance at the end of each month (as shown in Tables 3.3 and 3.4) and the total compared with the £15,000 limit.

TABLE 3.3. *Cash flow diary*

Month	Receipts Item	(£)	Payments Item	(£)	Monthly balance (£)	Cumulative balance (£)
						– 10,500[a]
April	Milk	2,760	Feedingstuffs	660		
	Cull cow	300	Seed	360		
	Calves	180	Fertiliser	1,350		
			Wages	540		
			Fuel and repairs	225		
			Rent	1,860		
			Living expenses	240		
			Sundries	120		
		3,240		5,355	–2,115	–12,615
May	Milk	2,550	Feedingstuffs	300		
	Cull cow	290	Wages	570		
	Calves	260	Fuel and repairs	270		
			New trailer	820		
			Living expenses	240		
			Sundries	110		
		3,100		2,310	+790	–11,825

[a]Brought forward.

The alternative layout is illustrated in Table 3.4. Here the periods are given along the top and the receipts and expenses down the left-hand side. Some organisations provide printed forms with the required layout. The headings for receipts are usually inserted by the person using the form, since the items can vary so widely from farm to farm, but many of the cost items are common to all farms and are therefore often printed on the forms. In general this layout is to be preferred to that shown in Table 3.3, because items are less likely to be forgotten when entering receipts and expenses, and the periodic balances are made within the columns instead of across them.

Some important differences compared with budgets used for estimating profitability (see Chapter 14) must be remembered. Only actual cash payments and receipts are included. Thus depreciation charges and valuations are ignored. On the other hand, all capital payments and receipts, including the cost of machinery and buildings

TABLE 3.4. *Cash flow statement*

Item	April (£)	May (£)	June (£)
Receipts			
Milk	2,760	2,550	2,460
Cull cows	300	290	
Calves	180	260	70
Grants			
Other capital receipts			
Other receipts			
Sub-total	3,240	3,100	2,530
Payments			
Feedingstuffs	660	300	210
Livestock			
Seed	360		
Fertiliser	1,350		620
Wages	540	570	610
Fuel and repairs	225	270	290
Contract hire			
Rent	1,860		
Living expenses	240	240	280
Tax			
Capital payments		820	1,050
Sundries	120	110	135
Sub-total	5,355	2,310	3,195
Monthly balance	−2,115	+790	−665
Cumulative balance[a]	−12,615	−11,825	−12,490

[a] −£5,500 brought forward.

and grants received thereon, are entered. Private drawings, for living expenses, are also normally included. Interest payments, loan repayments, and estimated tax payments should also be included when the calculation is made in order to assess total cash needs.

Sometimes the cash flow statement is used only to estimate the extra capital required (or possibly the capital saved) by a change in farm policy or by a new investment project. In this case the same rules apply as for a partial budget (see pp. 315–17; only the *changes* in receipts and expenditure should be included.

Return on tenant's capital

Figures described as 'return on tenant's capital' are often given in reports from university departments of agricultural economics, as

TABLE 3.5. *Return on tenant's capital for different types of farming in south-east England* (based on results for two years: 1975–6 to 1976–7)

Type and size of farm		Average return (%)	'Premium'[a] return (%)
Mainly milk	under 60 ha	15	26
	60–120 ha	22	30
	over 120 ha	19	29
Mainly arable	under 100 ha	23	38
	100–200 ha	18	28
	over 200 ha	36	55
Milk and arable	under 200 ha	31	46
	over 200 ha	26	36
Mainly sheep/cattle	under 100 ha	12	23
	over 100 ha	24	23
Sheep/cattle and arable	under 100 ha	22	39
	over 100 ha	15	24
Milk, sheep/cattle and arable		18	26
Mainly pigs/poultry		30	38
'Mixed', with pigs/poultry		26	44
Intensive arable – fruit		34	58
Intensive arable – hops and fruit		15	30
Intensive arable – field vegetables		48	67

[a]'Premium' figures are averages of the fifty per cent showing the highest return.
Source: *Farm Business Statistics for South-East England.* Wye College, University of London (data derived from the Farm Management Survey).

illustrated in Table 3.5. The calculation is derived from the formula:

$$\frac{\text{Management and Investment Income}}{\text{Total Tenant's Capital}} \times 100.$$

Several observations need to be made concerning these estimates. First, they are obviously dependent upon the accuracy of the estimate of tenant's capital – a problem discussed above (pp. 52–3). Insofar as these estimates are likely to be on the low side, the figures for return on capital are to that extent exaggerated. Secondly, the 'return' part of the calculation is the management and investment income; in the derivation of this figure a sum is included in costs for the value of the unpaid labour of the farmer and his family and an estimated rent is charged on owner-occupied farms, ownership expenses being excluded (see further Chapter 20, pp. 524–5). On the other hand, any interest payments are excluded from costs and, furthermore, no charge is allowed for management; thus this return has not only to provide interest on the capital invested and a reward for risk-taking, but also payment for management, which is normal practice in agriculture. In industry, management is far less likely to be supplied by the owner of the capital, and directors' fees and managers' salaries are included in costs when calculating the profit figure used in estimating return on capital. Finally, it is more realistic to base depreciation on replacement costs rather than historic costs.

Bearing these reservations in mind, the university figures usually average about 15 per cent over a period of years. The 'premium farms', defined as the most profitable half of the sample, usually return about 25 per cent, sometimes more – especially in the case of arable farms on fertile soils. If a charge for management were included in costs, the average figure would be approximately halved and the 'premium' figure would be reduced by about one third.

While estimates can be made of the return on total tenant's capital on different types of farm, figures for individual enterprises tend to be rather meaningless. This is partly because of the wide variation between farms, not only in enterprise profitability but especially in the capital employed in production. Thus one might contrast the capital tied up in a modern 'cow palace', complete with tower silos and automatic feeding, and that in a farm with nothing more than an old milking bail or cowshed, relying in the winter on silage stored in an open clamp. Similarly in cereal production: one farmer may have all the latest equipment, including an expensive fully automated corn store, while another may have all the work done by a contractor and sell the grain off the field. In such circumstances a single average figure for an enterprise has little meaning.

More important still is the allocation problem on the mixed farm. First there is the difficulty of allocating costs shared by more than one enterprise in calculating individual enterprise profit. Secondly there is the task of allocating capital items shared by more than one enterprise in estimating the capital requirements of individual enterprises. In estimating working capital requirements there is the added problem of the seasonality and interaction of payments and receipts for different enterprises. Only for a specialist pig or poultry unit does the calculation have any meaning on a mixed farm. The task is virtually impossible for crops, except where monoculture is practised. There are also the complementary and supplementary relationships between enterprises to take into account (see Chapter 2, pp. 39–41).

The only calculations of capital return that are relevant to decision-making in farming are those involving the total capital in the farm and returns on marginal capital expenditure. We shall return to these points later in this chapter.

Investment appraisal

A farmer may contemplate expanding his cow numbers, growing more potatoes instead of sugar beet, investing in irrigation equipment, introducing a pig unit, or making some other change in farm policy involving either a small or large amount of extra capital. There are various ways of evaluating such projects. All the methods described in the present section require initially at least a partial budget (see pp. 315–17), in order to estimate the extra profit arising from the investment. Most projects also require a calculation of the change in cash flow if the additional working capital needed (or possibly the amount saved) is to be estimated at all accurately. Frequently, however, the extra profit is simply related to the initial capital cost of the project.

Rate of return

The most common method is to assess the rate of return from the investment by the simple calculation:

$$\frac{\text{(Additional) Profit}}{\text{(Additional) Capital Required}} \times 100.$$

Profit is calculated after charging depreciation, but no interest payments are deducted; interest on borrowed capital has to be paid out of the return on capital that is being calculated. With regard to depreciating assets, the capital required is sometimes taken to be the initial sum required (plus any additional working capital) and sometimes the average capital investment during the life of the project (Table 3.6). For the former it is argued that this is the total sum that has to be found. For the latter it is said that the allowance for deprecia-

TABLE 3.6. *Rate of return on capital*

£2000 invested.

Extra profit after deducting depreciation: £200 a year.

Return on Initial Capital $= \frac{200}{2{,}000} \times 100 = 10$ per cent.

Return on Average Capital $= \frac{200}{1{,}000} \times 100 = 20$ per cent.

tion which is deducted is available for reinvestment – possibly in a sinking fund to replace the asset – and that, at any one time, the average written-down value (or amount of capital outstanding) is approximately half this sum (assuming an asset is kept until it is virtually valueless; otherwise the average value is higher). Certainly in calculating the overall return on total tenant's capital it is the current sale value of the assets that is normally used. Discounted cash flow calculations (see below, pp. 61–8) indicate that return on initial capital is below the true return and is therefore too harsh an estimate of the profitability of the investment; this concept is therefore useful if it is considered desirable to subject the project to a severe test. On the other hand, the average return calculation gives too high a return and is not to be recommended (see further, pp. 68–70).

Another problem is that of deciding whether to use the peak working capital requirement or the average amount needed during a production period in the assessment of the capital employed in the project. Although it is obviously true that the peak amount is needed at some stage, interest on a bank overdraft is paid only on the actual sum owing. It is therefore usual to take the average figure.

Pay-back period

The pay-back period is a simple 'rule-of-thumb' concept. It is the time taken to repay the capital cost of the project. It is calculated by dividing the total capital cost by the additional profit created, before charging depreciation. Thus, if a project costs £5000 and generates £1000 a year additional 'profit' (ignoring depreciation in calculating costs), the pay-back period is 5 years, that is, the capital is recovered in that time. Interest payments should be deducted from profit in making the calculation. The period may be calculated before or after allowing for tax; the former is more usual but the latter is more realistic.

Such a crude measure is easy to criticise. In particular, it ignores the value of the project after the pay-back period is completed. Thus one investment may pay back in three years and then cease to be of any further value, while another may take twice the time but continue to generate further profits for many more years. Nevertheless this simple yardstick is widely used, since it is both easy to understand and takes the important aspect of risk into account, even if only in a rough and ready way. This is because the sooner a loan can be written off the smaller is the risk of economic circumstances changing adversely before the capital sum is repaid.

Discounted cash flow: principles

The pay-back period deals only inadequately with the possible variability of the rates of cash flow over time, and the rate of return calculation fails altogether to take this important aspect into account.

Supposing there were three investment projects, each requiring £1000 capital, which would result in the annual cash flows (cash returns less cash expenses) shown in Table 3.7. All three investments give a total net cash flow of £1750. Deducting depreciation (assuming a complete write-off after five years) gives a total profit of £750, or £150 a year, representing a rate of return on the initial investment of 15 per cent in each case.

However, Project *C* is preferable to *B*, and *B* preferable to *A*, because the net cash flow is generated more quickly in *C* than *B*, and in *B* than *A*. The quicker the return, the more can be earned by re-investment. Furthermore, the quicker the money is returned the less risky the investment – other things being equal. The further into the future a forecast is made, the more uncertainty there is about possible future changes in demand, supply, prices, costs and technology. For these two reasons, therefore – reinvestment and risk – money earned sooner is worth more than the same amount of money earned later. This is true even apart from the effect of inflation on the value of money over time.

This 'time value of money' factor is incorporated into the principle of compounding and discounting. In applying these concepts, it is usual to discount future cash flows to a present value, making use of 'discount factors'. These give the present value of a sum of money (the unit taken is normally £1) to be received at a date *n* years in the future at various rates of interest. A complete table of discount factors is given in Appendix 3.1, Table 3.14. To select a few examples for illustrative purposes, Table 3.8 shows how the further one goes into the future and the higher the rate of interest, the lower the discount factor. The present value of £100 received in 5 years' time is £71.3

TABLE 3.7. *Comparison of three investments: annual net cash flows (£)*

	Year 1	Year 2	Year 3	Year 4	Year 5
Project *A*	250	300	350	400	450
Project *B*	350	350	350	350	350
Project *C*	450	400	350	300	250

TABLE 3.8. *Examples of discount factors* (present value of £1)

Year	Rate of Interest 7%	10%
1	0.935	0.909
5	0.713	0.621
10	0.508	0.386

(100 × 0.713) at a 7 per cent rate of interest and £62.1 at 10 per cent; the present value if received in 10 years' time is £50.8 at 7 per cent and £38.6 at 10 per cent. To put this another way, if £50.8 were invested today at 7 per cent compound interest it would be worth £100 in 10 years' time, whereas at 10 per cent only £38.6 would need to be invested for this to amount to £100 in 10 years' time. These sums do not take account of inflationary trends and consequent changes in the value of money. The general formulae for compounding and discounting are given in Appendix 3.1.

Table 3.9 illustrates the large differences that can occur in the present values of equal net cash flows (£1500) occurring at quite different times and rates in the future. The present value of the net cash flows from Project I, which start at a high level in the first year and then decrease until they finish in year 5, is £1209 (81 per cent of the total net cash flow), while that of the net cash flows from Project II,

TABLE 3.9. *Present value of future net cash flows*

Year	Net cash flow (£) Project I	Net cash flow (£) Project II	Discount factor (10%)	Present value (£) Project I	Present value (£) Project II
1	500	—	0.909	455	
2	400	—	0.826	330	
3	300	—	0.751	225	
4	200	—	0.683	137	
5	100	—	0.621	62	
6	—	100	0.564	—	56
7	—	200	0.513	—	103
8	—	300	0.467	—	140
9	—	400	0.424	—	170
10	—	500	0.386	—	193
	1,500	1,500		1,209	662

which do not start until year 6 and then increase until they terminate in year 10, is £662 (only 44 per cent of the total net cash flow). At a lower rate of interest the present values would be higher and the difference less, and at a higher rate of interest they would be lower and the difference greater.

When the annual net cash flows are a virtually constant sum per annum the calculation of present values is far easier, because annuity tables can be used. These give 'annuity factors', that is, the present value of a constant annual amount over a period of *n* years, at varying rates of interest. Each is the sum of the discount factors for the individual years in the period. Examples are shown in Table 3.10. Thus, £100 a year for five years (i.e. £500 in total) has a present value at 7 per cent interest of £410 (100 × 4.10), and at 10 per cent interest of £379. Over ten years the present values are £702 at 7 per cent and £614 at 10 per cent. Again looking at this in the reverse way, £614 invested to-day at 10 per cent would provide an annual income of £100 a year for 10 years (capital plus interest). Appendix 3.1, Table 3.15, gives a full table of annuity factors.

TABLE 3.10. *Present value of a constant annual sum*

Number of years	Rate of interest 7% (annuity factors)	Rate of interest 10% (annuity factors)
5	4.10	3.79
10	7.02	6.14

Discounted cash flow: application

Calculating the annual net cash flows and their present value are essential parts of investment appraisal by the 'discounted cash flow' (DCF) technique. It is normally assumed that the net cash flows occur as lump sums at the end of each year. The sum invested in a project must include an allowance for working capital – usually taken as the average amount required during the production period. If the assets employed in the project still retain some value at the end of the investment period being considered, this value (called the 'terminal value') is added to the cash flow of the final year together with any recoverable working capital. The investment period taken is the estimated economic life of the project; in order to cover risk aspects – especially the obsolescence factor in the case of buildings and machinery – it is usual to err on the conservative side. Printed forms are available for the necessary calculations, given that the annual net cash flows have already been estimated (see pp. 53–6 above). A relatively simple example is shown in Table 3.11. A more complete form, including tax calculations, is shown in Table 3.12. The latter incorporates another vital feature of investment: namely, feasibility, in terms of how quickly borrowed capital can be repaid, or whether the annual net cash flow is sufficient to allow payment of interest and repayments of capital as required by the lender.

There are two alternative DCF methods: the 'net present value' and the 'discounted yield' (or 'internal rate of return').

Net present value is obtained by subtracting the amount of the initial investment from the present value of the net cash flows – allowing for subsequent additional capital inputs where these apply. The example shown in Table 3.11 illustrates how this is done. To take an even simpler example, if the initial sum invested in both Projects I and II in Table 3.9 were £600, the former would give a net present value (at 10 per cent rate of interest) of £609 (£1209 – £600) and the latter one of £62 (£662 – £600). An interest rate has to be selected in order to calculate the present value: this could be the rate of borrowing plus, possibly, an allowance for risk and trouble (see further below). If the net present value is positive the project is estimated to be worthwhile, in the sense of being able to return that rate of interest and more. If it is negative then clearly the opposite applies.

The discounted yield is that rate of interest which makes the present value equal to the initial cost of the investment, that is, which makes the net present value zero. This is the rate of interest which the project can just afford to pay. It is found by trial and error. Thus, to return again to Project II in Table 3.9, it has already been calculated that at 10 per cent the present value is £662, compared with the initial investment of £600. A rate of 11 per cent gives a present value of £611 and 12 per cent gives £566. Thus the discounted yield is 11 + ($\frac{11}{45} \times 1$), that is, $11\frac{1}{4}$ per cent (11 being 611 – 600, and 45 being 611 – 566).

The fact that the present value had already been estimated at a rate of interest leaving only a small net present value made this calculation a simple one, but in general the procedure is the same. It is first necessary to estimate a range between which the discounted yield is likely to fall, then to calculate and interpolate as shown. To take another

TABLE 3.11. *Discounted cash flow: simple example*

Year	Capital (less grants)	Budgeted cash margin	Net cash flow	Present value of annual net cash flows: 15% Factor	15% Product	20% Factor	20% Product
	(£)	(£)	(£)		(£)		(£)
0	(–)52,500	—	–52,500	1.000	–52,500	1.000	–52,500
1	(–)13,500	4,500	–9,000	0.870	–7,830	0.833	–7,497
2	(+) 2,700	12,000	14,700	0.756	11,113	0.694	10,202
3		13,500	13,500	0.658	8,883	0.579	7,816
4		15,000	15,000	0.572	8,580	0.482	7,230
5		15,000	15,000	0.497	7,455	0.402	6,030
6		15,000	15,000	0.432	6,480	0.335	5,025
7		15,000	15,000	0.376	5,640	0.279	4,185
8		15,000	15,000	0.327	4,905	0.233	3,495
9		15,000	15,000	0.284	4,260	0.194	2,910
10	(+)36,000[a]	15,000	51,000	0.247	12,597	0.162	8,262
		Net present value			+9,583		–4,842

The example is based on doubling the size of a dairy herd, from 80 to 160 cows; 50 down-calvers are purchased in year 1 (when a new parlour is erected and much of the other building expenditure is incurred), and 30 in year 2. Nearly a third of their forage requirement is obtained by improving the stocking rate on existing grassland (by additional use of fertiliser) from 0.69 to 1.53 forage hectares per cow, the remainder by reducing the barley area. Replacement heifers are contract reared. A capital grant of 30 per cent on buildings is assumed, paid a year in arrears.

[a]Terminal value (cows only).

Discounted yield calculation $= 15 + \dfrac{9{,}583}{14{,}425^{*}} \times 5 = 18.3$ per cent approx.

* 14,425 = 9,583 + 4,842.

Notes:

1. Where most or all the capital is spent in year 0 (i.e. before production begins in year 1), year 0 may alternatively be omitted from the table, and the amount of capital invested is then subtracted from the sum of the discounted cash flows from years 1 to (10) to give the net present value.

2. Where both the net present value (at x%) and discounted yield are required, and the net present value shows x% to be very different from the discounted yield, three discounting columns will be needed, one for x% (to give net present value), the others at y% and z%, to allow the calculation of the discounted yield.

TABLE 3.12. *Form for complete appraisal of investment project: discounted cash flow and feasibility*

Year	Annual net cash flow before tax[a]	Income before tax[b]	Allowances against tax: Depreciation	Allowances against tax: Interest	Allowances against tax: Total	Taxable income[cd]	Tax (at t%)[e]	Annual net cash flow after tax[d]	Present value of annual net cash flows: x% Factor	x% Product	y% Factor	y% Product	Feasibility: Capital repayments	Interest payments	Annual deficit or surplus[f]	Cumulative deficit or surplus[f]
	(£)	(£)	(£)	(£)	(£)	(£)	(£)	(£)		(£)		(£)	(£)	(£)	(£)	(£)
0																
1																
2																
3																
4																
5																
.																
.																
n																
							Totals:		—		—				—	—

[a] Including all capital expenditure (including working capital) less capital grants and terminal value; interest payments are (normally) omitted.
[b] Calculation of (extra) profit, before charging depreciation (or interest).
[c] Income before tax less total allowances.
[d] Note that there may be a net *reduction* in tax in some (usually earlier) years.
[e] The time-lag in tax payments must be allowed for.
[f] If the project is clearly feasible, in the sense that annual net cash flows after tax exceed capital repayments and interest payments, the final two columns may be replaced by one headed 'outstanding balance', which is calculated by subtracting, each year, the capital repayment from the capital outstanding.

example, Project *A* in Table 3.7 might be assumed to give a rate between 15 and 25 per cent. The present value at 15 per cent is £1124 and at 25 per cent £892, compared with the initial investment of £1000. The required rate is therefore $15 + (\frac{124}{232} \times 10)$, where 124 is 1124 − 1000, 232 is 1124 − 892, and 10 is 25 − 15. The result is approximately $20\frac{1}{4}$ per cent. This is slightly inaccurate, because the relationship is not linear; the nearer the point is to midway between the limits selected the greater the error. The difference is barely significant, however, particularly considering that the cash flows are only estimates. In this example the point is midway and the true rate is in fact just under 20 per cent. It is possible to get closer by further calculations but this is rarely worthwhile. Table 3.11 further illustrates the calculation of the discounted yield, using net present values instead of present values; as can be seen, the calculation is virtually identical.[1]

Where the net cash flow is constant the calculation is much easier. It is necessary only to find that annuity factor which makes the present value of the constant annual sum equal to the initial amount invested. This is done by dividing the annual net cash flow into the original investment. To take as an example Project *B* in Table 3.7, the calculation is: (1000)/(350) = 2.86. The rate of interest is then read off from the annuity table (Table 3.15), looking along the line giving the duration of the project in years (here 5) until 2.86 is reached. It may be necessary to interpolate a fraction between adjacent rates; in this example the result is almost exactly 22 per cent.

Much has been written about the relative advantages of the two alternative DCF assessments. The debate largely concerns anomalies that can occur – especially with the discounted yield method. Many of the potential difficulties are unlikely to arise in practical farming examples and so will not be pursued in detail here.

The net present value is simpler to calculate and avoids many of the complications that may arise with the discounted yield. On the other hand it gives the answer as a lump sum. This may prove difficult to evaluate and complicates the problem of comparing different projects costing different amounts. A second difficulty is that of deciding on the discount rate to be used, especially as the ranking of alternative projects may differ according to the discount rate chosen. The decision

[1] Applications of the discounted cash flow technique to farming examples are given in: Kerr, H. T. W. (1966) *Methods of Appraising New Capital Investment in Agriculture*. Farmers' Report No. 161, Dept. of Agricultural Economics, University of Nottingham. Helme, W. H. and James, P. J. (1969) 'Evaluating Capital Investment Projects by D. C. F. Techniques'. *Farm Management*, **1**, No. 5.

is largely subjective. In particular, the rate of interest to be paid if the capital is borrowed and the amount to be allowed for risk should be taken into account. The latter will depend not only on the nature of the project but also on the personal financial situation and temperament of the individual concerned. It is possible also to think in terms of the returns that can be earned in alternative investments, especially when using one's own capital, but this point will be taken care of when DCF is in fact being used to compare different projects.

The discounted yield calculation avoids these two problems, although the need for personal judgement cannot be altogether escaped. It provides a specific rate which can be assessed with regard to the cost of borrowing, possible alternative investments, the degree of risk, personal considerations and so on. The decision is still therefore largely subjective. Where alternative projects are being considered, comparable earning rates are given for investments of different magnitudes. On the other hand complications can arise. The yield is in fact affected by the amount of capital invested – very small investments can give very high yields. Again, if large negative cash flows occur in the later years of a project's life – because of further capital investment – the answer can be made virtually meaningless. Small negative flows are unlikely to have much effect and where doubt exists the 'extended yield' method may be used. This consists of discounting the negative flow back one year at the normal cost of capital and subtracting it from the cash flow in that year, thus 'absorbing' the negative amount. If a negative sum results, it is necessary to discount a further year back, until a positive sum is obtained. This is illustrated in Appendix 3.2. The normal discounting procedure is then pursued using the positive sums in order to obtain the discounted yield. Negative cash flows in the middle of a project's life do not usually cause any problems.

Despite the difficulties, the discounted yield method is normally to be preferred as giving a more meaningful answer. It has been argued that the wrong order of ranking can be given when different investments are being compared, but in practice this is only likely to happen when the differences in discounted yield are small, in which case other factors will determine the final choice. Once the net cash flows have been calculated relatively little extra work is needed to calculate *both* net present values and discounted yields.

Discounted cash flow and the rate of return: an assessment

On pp. 59–60 there was some discussion about whether the simple rate of return method of assessing return on capital in the case of depreciating assets should use the initial capital cost or the average capital investment in the calculation. The discounted yield falls between the rates of return obtained by these alternatives. In fact, for investments lasting 5 to 15 years, when the rate of return on initial capital is 10 per cent and on average capital 20 per cent, the discounted yield is almost exactly halfway between, i.e. about 15 per cent. However, this is only the case when the anticipated annual net cash flows are fairly constant, or are expected to fluctuate – but unpredictably – around a fairly constant level (because, for example, of weather effects).

The discounted yield falls closer to the rate of return on initial capital (that is, the lower per cent return) and further from the rate of return on average capital:

(*a*) the longer the life of the investment,
(*b*) the higher the rate of return,
(*c*) the higher the net cash flow in the later years of the investment compared with the earlier years.

When the opposite circumstances obtain, the discounted yield is closer to the rate of return on average capital (that is, the higher per cent return).

It must always be remembered that all these calculations of return, whether simple or complex, are dependent on the accuracy with which the net cash flows are forecast. Many factors may cause departures from the assumptions made: the level of expertise of management and staff, weather, future price and cost levels, and so on. Given that these variations can and will occur, there seems little point in worrying too much about the niceties of the calculations. Thus, where the annual net cash flow earnings are expected to be fairly constant or to fluctuate unpredictably about a constant level, the following short-cut estimates of the discounted yield are suggested for depreciating assets. (WO period = write-off period; RRIC = rate of return on initial capital.)

1. Where (i) the WO period is 5 years or less,
   (ii) the WO period is 6 to 10 years and the RRIC is 15 per cent or less,
   (iii) the WO period is 11 to 20 years and the RRIC is 10 per cent or less,

   calculate the return on capital as being approximately midway between the rates of return on initial capital and average capital, that is, by calculating the rate of return on $\frac{2}{3}$ of the original investment.

For example, if £5000 is invested and £500 is the annual net return (after deducting depreciation, but ignoring interest charges), the calculation is:

$$\frac{500}{3333} \times 100 = 15\%.$$

2. Where (i) the WO period is 6 to 10 years and the RRIC exceeds 15 per cent,
   (ii) the WO period is 11 to 20 years and the RRIC is between 10 and 25 per cent,
   (iii) the WO period exceeds 20 years and the RRIC is 10 per cent or less,

   calculate the rate of return on 80 per cent of the original investment. That is, using the same example as above:

$$\frac{500}{4000} \times 100 = 12\tfrac{1}{2}\%.$$

3. Where (i) the WO period is 11 to 20 years and the RRIC exceeds 25 per cent,
   (ii) the WO period exceeds 20 years and the RRIC exceeds 10 per cent,

   take the return on capital to be the RRIC ($= \frac{500}{5000} \times 100 = 10\%$).

In borderline cases, use method 1 rather than 2, or 2 rather than 3 if there is a tendency for the cash flow to be higher in the earlier years, for example, because of tax allowances on machinery. Take 2 rather than 1, or 3 rather than 2 if the cash flow is likely to be lower in earlier years and increase in later years.

It must however be stressed that the full DCF calculation should be used wherever the annual cash flow is expected to vary substantially (apart from unpredictable fluctuations). This is especially so where the variation is both up and down (rather than increasing or decreasing steadily over the period) and where further periodic investments are to be made during the life of the project. Taxation aspects can become quite complex, and if these are to be properly evaluated the full procedure is necessary. The tax effect is not normally included in the short-cut methods referred to and the estimated return is therefore before tax, whereas DCF calculations normally include tax allowances and payments and thus give the results after tax.

Maximum return on total capital

It is often said that the main objective of a profit-conscious farmer should be to obtain the highest possible return on capital. In fact this is not necessarily a worthwhile or even sensible aim in itself, because obtaining a higher return on capital may be at the expense of a lower income. For example, consider a farmer producing only cereals. His capital investment might be kept as low as £100 per ha by having all the work done on contract and selling the grain off the field at harvest time; on the other hand, he might erect drying and storage facilities and store the grain until the following late spring or early summer, raising his capital costs to £250 per ha (the cost of the land being ignored in both cases). In the first case, the farmer may obtain a profit (before deducting interest payments) of £25 per ha, giving him a return on capital of $(25/100) \times 100 = 25$ per cent, while in the latter he may get a profit of £50 per ha, with a return on capital of $(50/250) \times 100 = 20$ per cent. Even allowing for the difference in interest payments, the farmer's net income is some 50 per cent higher by taking the second course even though his return on capital is lower.

The relevant economic concepts here are diminishing returns and marginal cost versus marginal revenue. By investing £150 of additional capital the farmer obtains an extra income of £25 per ha (before charging interest), or nearly 17 per cent on initial capital, which is well worthwhile. It is not the *average* return, but the *marginal* return that is the more important. As long as marginal revenue exceeds marginal cost (the cost of borrowing plus an allowance for risk) the investment is worthwhile and income will be increased, even if this decreases the *average* return on capital.

If capital is the most limiting factor on the farm, and more than a certain sum cannot possibly be obtained, then it *is* economically logical to say that the profit-oriented farmer should strive to maximise his return to that amount of capital. That is the same as saying he should aim to maximise his income. Even where capital is less limited it does make economic sense to argue that he should aim to maximise the return to the amount of capital he is investing. This is different from arguing that that amount of capital should be invested which will give the highest possible return on capital. On the contrary, he should not be worried if investing more reduces his average return, providing the extra investment is justified in its own right.

While the 'marginal cost' of a person's own capital is often stated as being the return available on gilt-edged securities plus an allowance for risk, the level is largely subjective. The more capital a farmer has, the lower the returns available from additional investments on the farm are likely to be. He may on the one hand be prepared to chance more and more risky investments, thus raising his 'marginal cost' in terms of the return expected to justify the risk. On the other hand, he may be prepared to settle for his existing farming programme, but invest in the farm purely for reasons of personal pleasure or prestige, with little consideration for the rate of return.

Where capital is limited, or where someone is endeavouring to maximise the return to a *given* level of capital investment, the principle of equi-marginal returns is applied. This means that capital should be allocated between alternative investments in such a way as to give the same marginal return in all of them. In practice this level of perfection is impossible to attain, for many reasons. Apart from the problem of uncertainty, there is the major difficulty of factor indivisibility, or 'lumpy' inputs. However, it is possible to seek to satisfy the opportunity cost principle, which is the corollary of equi-marginal returns. This means that any additional capital put into the business should not only give a worthwhile return, but should be allocated in such a way as to give the highest possible return; in short, the farmer should make as certain as possible that the capital cannot be invested in another way which would yield a still greater return.

This question of *allocation* of capital is an important one, even where there is no intention of investing *additional* capital. It may be possible to re-allocate the amount of capital already in the business so as to give a higher return. With this aim in mind farmers often ask what the return on capital is to different enterprises. This point has already been discussed, on p. 58. Even if such figures could be calculated, the results would only be averages and could be completely misleading as guides to the marginal return to extra investment in each enterprise. The only sensible approach is to consider the *marginal* capital requirements of different enterprises and methods of production in a given farm situation. This entails estimating how much extra or how much less working capital would be required if enterprises were expanded or started, reduced or given up altogether, as well as how much extra investment in livestock, machinery and buildings would be needed, or how much capital could be released by the sale of livestock, machinery or buildings (known as 'salvage value'). The effect of possible reallocations can be measured by means of capital partial budgets together with ordinary partial budgets (see Chapter 14). Alternatively, more complex procedures like DCF or more comprehensive approaches such as linear programming may be used (see Chapter 15).

The marginal return on capital used to expand existing enterprises where no extra fixed capital is required is often very high. On the other hand the level is frequently exaggerated. For example, it is sometimes claimed that an extra cow can add, say, £100 (its gross margin) for an extra £150 capital, i.e. a 67 per cent return. However, unless the land is currently understocked, this figure would seem to ignore the cost of the extra grazing and winter bulk fodder required, whether obtained by additional fertiliser, greater dependence on bought feed, or a reduced area of other crops.

Return on equity and the principle of increasing risk

Finally, it is necessary to distinguish between the return on the total capital in the farm business and the return to the farmer's *own* share of that capital, which is known as his *equity*. The latter return is calculated from profit less interest payments on borrowed money. The point here is that loan capital in farming is normally lent at given rates of interest, whatever the net earnings on that capital prove to be. Consequently, if the return on total capital is above this rate, the return on the farmer's equity is inflated, the more so the smaller is his equity. Conversely, if the return on total capital is less than the borrowing rate, the return to the equity is deflated, and in fact some loss of equity will ensue if a large proportion is borrowed at fixed interest rates. This is the basis of the 'principle of increasing risk', which states that the higher the proportion of borrowed capital the greater the risk of bankruptcy if bad results are obtained.

TABLE 3.13. *The principle of increasing risk*

	Proportion of total capital borrowed				
	(0%)	(25%)	(50%)	(75%)	(85%)
Borrowed capital	0	5,000	10,000	15,000	17,000
Own	20,000	15,000	10,000	5,000	3,000
Total	20,000	20,000	20,000	20,000	20,000
15% profit	3,000	3,000	3,000	3,000	3,000
Less interest on loan at 8%	—	400	800	1,200	1,360
Return on equity	3,000	2,600	2,200	1,800	1,640
%return on equity	15	17½	22	36	55
4%profit	800	800	800	800	800
Less interest on loan at 8%	—	400	800	1,200	1,360
Return on equity	800	400	0	−400	−560
% return on equity	4	2⅔	0	—	—
10% loss	2,000	2,000	2,000	2,000	2,000
Plus interest on loan at 8%	—	400	800	1,200	1,360
Loss on equity	2,000	2,400	2,800	3,200	3,360
% loss of equity	10	16	28	64	100

Note: 'Profit' refers to the net margin obtained before deducting interest payments.

The principle is illustrated in Table 3.13, where 'profit' refers to the net margin obtained before deducting interest payments. When good profits are made, for example, 15 per cent on total capital compared with a borrowing rate of 8 per cent, a very high return on equity can be obtained when a large proportion of the total capital is borrowed: thus it is 55 per cent where 85 per cent is borrowed (22 per cent on total capital would give a 100 per cent return on equity). Where only 4 per cent is made, however, not only is no return on equity obtained where more than 50 per cent is borrowed, but part of that equity is lost also. With a 10 per cent loss and 75 per cent borrowing, nearly two-thirds of the equity is lost, and with 85 per cent borrowing bankruptcy ensues. Hence the bank manager's interest in the potential borrower's net capital as a percentage of the total assets of the business. The ratio of own capital to loan capital is referred to as 'gearing'. Thus a person borrowing only 20 per cent of total capital employed is said to be 'low geared' (4:1), whereas a person borrowing 75 per cent is very highly geared (1:3). Other important aspects of the balance sheet are examined in Chapter 19.

Rules for capital use on farms

Many of the following points relating to capital expenditure in farming are well known and often repeated. They will therefore be dealt with only briefly. Nevertheless, their importance cannot be overstressed.

(i) It can be fatal for the business to run short of capital for fertilisers, livestock and feed by investing too large a proportion of available capital in longer-term assets such as machinery and buildings. The return on the former is usually by far the higher. This point is particularly important for those starting farming with limited capital. Fertiliser, feedingstuffs and livestock directly *generate* the income which is the source of profits that can be ploughed back into the business. Other types of capital investment, e.g. machinery and, especially, buildings, *assist*, or *maintain*, production, but are of little use by themselves. It is certainly true that investment in machinery and buildings can often increase profits by reducing costs, given that there is enough capital available for them to be fully utilised. Nevertheless, the first priority where capital is short should be to invest in those items which are best able to generate a surplus that can be used subsequently to expand, buy machinery and erect better buildings. To follow the reverse procedure, and to lack the capital to utilise fully the money invested in plant and equipment, can be financially disastrous. In some cases production is impossible without at least some investment in equipment and buildings, but this should be kept to a minimum where capital is scarce. Of course a farmer and his staff cannot live in perpetual squalor. If the investment priorities have been right and the farmer is nevertheless unable to afford either to expand or improve his working or living amenities in, say, five years, his only sensible course is to give up farming.

(ii) Some investments do not depreciate and may even appreciate, e.g. a herd or flock of breeding livestock, while others lose their value, sometimes rapidly, e.g. machinery and buildings. The first type of capital can be withdrawn and reinvested and is therefore to be preferred to the second, which, by and large, cannot. It is true that, after a certain age, an individual animal will depreciate in value, but a breeding unit is normally being constantly replenished by young stock.

(iii) When borrowing to invest in a depreciating asset, full repayment should be planned within the expected life of the asset.

(iv) Capital should be conserved wherever possible, by seeking all ways of improving income without any major capital expenditure, for example, by improving crop yields or margin over concentrates per cow.

(v) If expansion is required and additional investment in plant or buildings is called for, the enterprises to expand are those proving to be the most profitable.

(vi) Trying to revive an enterprise giving a poor return by investing more capital in it is usually futile.

(vii) In general, those areas for investment should be selected where it is possible to evaluate the return, rather than those where the benefits promised are vague and may well prove to be illusory.

(viii) If a new type of production is being tried, whenever possible the technical and economic problems likely to be encountered should be assessed by beginning on a small scale and costing the enterprise carefully, avoiding heavy expenditure on specialist machinery and buildings until the enterprise has proved itself.

(ix) Unless a high level of income allows the farmer to be indulgent, buildings should be erected as cheaply as the technical requirements and personal and amenity considerations will permit, particularly specialised buildings. They are likely to be quickly obsolescent, however elaborate and however much is spent (see further Chapter 4, pp. 105–8).

(x) Farmers should not seek the will-o'-the-wisp of technical perfection. In these days of continual technical progress such an aim is unattainable and the attempt to achieve it can lead to considerable capital losses.

(xi) When new innovations occur, particularly those requiring a lot of capital, it pays to 'wait and see'. A farmer is then able to learn from the experience of others, and discover whether there are any real benefits or likely snags. There are always some who are unable to resist a new idea and can afford to be pioneers. In the case of machinery, if an innovation proves to be successful its cost is likely to fall as demand increases and mass production is introduced.

(xii) Once a major investment is made, it should not be subjected to every possible chop and change as new ideas arise (see also points (x) and (xi)). Relatively few machinery or building innovations are so clearly economically advantageous, in terms of either reducing running costs or increasing output, to justify writing off a previous heavy investment in a very short time.

(xiii) As far as possible, the investment should be flexible in the sense of allowing for alternative uses. Many machines and buildings today are specialised, but where there is a choice between specialist and general-purpose-type buildings and equipment, with similar technical merits and costs, the general-purpose alternative should be selected (see further, Chapter 4, pp. 107–8). For example, flexibility is an important factor in favour of floor storage of grain compared with moist grain storage in sealed silos.

(xiv) Farmers should try to avoid being unduly tempted by considerations of taxation allowances, unless they have exceptionally high incomes. It has to be remembered that any additional profit that results is subject to the same rate of tax as is allowed on the capital investment. Of course, if the investment has an object other than that of raising profits, then that is another matter (see further Chapter 4, pp. 104 and 109).

(xv) Finally, and especially important: a farm business may be producing a good net return, well above the interest rate on borrowed capital, and yet it may still get into serious financial difficulties. There could be insufficient liquidity of funds, and the business could even become insolvent. (These aspects are further discussed in detail in Chapter 20, pp. 545–7). Such problems may arise because out of the net margin the farmer has to pay not only the interest on his loans, but also living expenses, tax and loan repayments. It is not simply the level of profit and the interest rate that are relevant, but also the proportion of total capital borrowed and the period over which repayments have to be made. Similar points arise when examining the feasibility of a farmer borrowing to *expand* his business, except that in this case living expenses can be ignored unless they are expected to rise; on the other hand, a higher proportion of the extra net margin will have to be paid in tax.

Appendix 3.1: Compounding, discounting, tables of discount and annuity factors

The following notation is used below:

r = rate of interest (note, 1 per cent is expressed as 0.01)
n = number of years.

Compounding

At a 7 per cent rate of compound interest:

The value of £1 at the end of 1 year is £1.07.
The value of £1 at the end of 2 years is $£1.07^2 = £1.145$.
The value of £1 at the end of 3 years is $£1.07^3 = £1.225$, etc.

The general formula is:

$$(1 + r)^n$$

Discounting

At a 7 per cent rate of compound interest (or discount rate):

The present value of £1 after 1 year is $£\frac{1}{1.07} = £0.935$.

The present value of £1 after 2 years is $£\frac{1}{1.07^2} = £\frac{1}{1.145} = £0.873$.

The present value of £1 after 3 years is $£\frac{1}{1.07^3} = £\frac{1}{1.225} = £0.816$.

The general formula is:

$$\frac{1}{(1 + r)^n}.$$

The general formula for the present value of an annuity is:

$$\frac{1 - [1/(1+r)^n]}{r}.$$

TABLE 3.14. *Discount factors for calculating the present value of a future cash sum receivable in year n* (per £1).

	(Percentage)											
Year	5	6	7	8	9	10	12	15	20	25	30	40
1	0.952	0.943	0.935	0.926	0.917	0.909	0.893	0.870	0.833	0.800	0.769	0.714
2	0.907	0.890	0.873	0.857	0.842	0.826	0.797	0.756	0.694	0.640	0.592	0.510
3	0.864	0.840	0.816	0.794	0.772	0.751	0.712	0.658	0.579	0.512	0.455	0.364
4	0.823	0.792	0.763	0.735	0.708	0.683	0.636	0.572	0.482	0.410	0.350	0.260
5	0.784	0.747	0.713	0.681	0.650	0.621	0.567	0.497	0.402	0.328	0.269	0.186
6	0.746	0.705	0.666	0.630	0.596	0.564	0.507	0.432	0.335	0.262	0.207	0.133
7	0.711	0.665	0.623	0.583	0.547	0.513	0.452	0.376	0.279	0.210	0.159	0.095
8	0.677	0.627	0.582	0.540	0.502	0.467	0.404	0.327	0.233	0.168	0.123	0.068
9	0.645	0.592	0.544	0.500	0.460	0.424	0.361	0.284	0.194	0.134	0.094	0.048
10	0.614	0.558	0.508	0.463	0.422	0.386	0.322	0.247	0.162	0.107	0.073	0.035
11	0.585	0.527	0.475	0.429	0.388	0.350	0.287	0.215	0.135	0.086	0.056	0.025
12	0.557	0.497	0.444	0.397	0.356	0.319	0.257	0.187	0.112	0.069	0.043	0.018
13	0.530	0.469	0.415	0.368	0.326	0.290	0.229	0.163	0.093	0.055	0.033	0.013
14	0.505	0.442	0.388	0.340	0.299	0.263	0.205	0.141	0.078	0.044	0.025	0.009
15	0.481	0.417	0.362	0.315	0.275	0.239	0.183	0.123	0.065	0.035	0.020	0.006
20	0.377	0.312	0.258	0.215	0.178	0.149	0.104	0.061	0.026	0.012	0.005	0.001
25	0.295	0.233	0.184	0.146	0.116	0.092	0.059	0.030	0.010	0.004	0.001	—
30	0.231	0.174	0.131	0.099	0.075	0.057	0.033	0.015	0.004	0.001	—	—
40	0.142	0.097	0.067	0.046	0.032	0.022	0.011	0.004	0.001	—	—	—

TABLE 3.15. *Annuity factors, i.e. discount factors for calculating the present value of a future constant annual cash sum receivable in years 1 to n inclusive* (per £1 per annum)

	(Percentage)											
Year	5	6	7	8	9	10	12	15	20	25	30	40
1	0.95	0.94	0.93	0.93	0.92	0.91	0.89	0.87	0.83	0.80	0.77	0.71
2	1.86	1.83	1.81	1.78	1.76	1.74	1.69	1.63	1.53	1.44	1.36	1.22
3	2.72	2.67	2.62	2.58	2.53	2.49	2.40	2.28	2.11	1.95	1.82	1.59
4	3.55	3.47	3.39	3.31	3.24	3.17	3.04	2.85	2.59	2.36	2.17	1.85
5	4.33	4.21	4.10	3.99	3.89	3.79	3.60	3.35	2.99	2.69	2.44	2.04
6	5.08	4.92	4.77	4.62	4.49	4.36	4.11	3.78	3.33	2.95	2.64	2.17
7	5.79	5.58	5.39	5.21	5.03	4.87	4.56	4.16	3.60	3.16	2.80	2.26
8	6.46	6.21	5.97	5.75	5.53	5.33	4.97	4.49	3.84	3.33	2.92	2.33
9	7.11	6.80	6.52	6.25	6.00	5.76	5.33	4.77	4.03	3.46	3.02	2.38
10	7.72	7.36	7.02	6.71	6.42	6.14	5.65	5.02	4.19	3.57	3.09	2.41
11	8.31	7.89	7.50	7.14	6.81	6.50	5.94	5.23	4.33	3.66	3.15	2.44
12	8.86	8.38	7.94	7.54	7.16	6.81	6.19	5.42	4.44	3.73	3.19	2.46
13	9.39	8.85	8.36	7.90	7.49	7.10	6.42	5.58	4.53	3.78	3.22	2.47
14	9.90	9.29	8.75	8.24	7.79	7.37	6.63	5.72	4.61	3.82	3.25	2.48
15	10.38	9.71	9.11	8.56	8.06	7.61	6.81	5.85	4.68	3.86	3.27	2.48
20	12.46	11.47	10.59	9.82	9.13	8.51	7.47	6.26	4.87	3.95	3.32	2.50
25	14.09	12.78	11.65	10.67	9.82	9.08	7.84	6.46	4.95	3.98	3.33	2.50
30	15.37	13.76	12.41	11.26	10.27	9.43	8.06	6.57	4.98	4.00	3.33	2.50
40	17.16	15.05	13.33	11.92	10.76	9.78	8.24	6.64	5.00	4.00	3.33	2.50

Appendix 3.2: DCF: illustration of the 'extended yield' method

Two examples are considered, with the following net cash flows in three successive years:

Example *A*:	1500	1500	– 1000
Example *B*:	750	750	– 1000

The normal rate of interest is assumed to be 8 per cent.

In Example *A*, the negative cash flow is 'taken back' one year, as follows:

$$1500 - \frac{1000}{1.08} = 1500 - 926 = 574.$$

The revised net cash flows thus become:

$$1500 \qquad 574 \qquad 0.$$

In Example *B*, a negative amount still occurs when the negative cash flow is discounted one year back:

$$750 - \frac{1000}{1.08} = 750 - 926 = -176.$$

It is thus necessary to go back a year further, as follows:

$$750 - \frac{176}{1.08} = 750 - 163 = 587.$$

The revised net cash flows thus become:

$$587 \qquad 0 \qquad 0.$$

4: The organisation of capital – machinery, buildings and land

MACHINERY

Annual machinery costs average between 15 and 20 per cent of total costs on most types of farm in the U.K., except for non-intensive arable holdings, where the figure is 20 to 25 per cent. Over £300 millions are spent each year by British farmers on tractors and other machinery. The average written-down value of machinery and equipment is currently about £125 per ha – excluding highly intensive small farms and extensive upland farms. To equip a farm exceeding 100 hectares entirely with new machinery at 1978 prices would cost £450 to £650 per ha, according to the choice of enterprises and the degree of specialisation, even without any undue elaboration. The cost on the smaller farm would be considerably greater and could only be kept down by a combination of specialisation, buying second-hand and hiring contractors.

Every extra £10 per ha spent on machinery adds between £2.50 and £4.50 per ha to annual machinery expenses, if interest on capital is included. The question is whether this extra cost is worthwhile.

Justification for mechanisation

Reduced drudgery

Expenditure which eliminates or at least reduces sheer hard and dirty work may have little or no immediate economic justification. Examples are expensive equipment for fully automated grain handling or slurry and farmyard manure disposal, sack hoists, pallett handling. In some circumstances there may be little or no cost savings to compensate for the equipment costs. However, such investments may have an indirect benefit in helping to attract and retain good quality staff.

Increased returns

Five alternative ways of increasing returns may be listed:

(i) *Directly increased yields.* An example is irrigation. Average annual costs if no sourceworks (reservoir or borehole) are needed will be approximately £100 per ha and with sourceworks £150 or more. On most soils in the south-eastern half of Britain the consequent increased returns over a period of years from early or maincrop potatoes should well cover these costs, but many other crops would fail to do so.

(ii) *Increased yields through more efficient cultivations.* For example, use of a subsoiler, or having available a wide range of implements to allow for large variations in soil conditions.

(iii) *Increased yields through improved timeliness.* This has played a large part in increasing crop yields in the past 25 years, especially perhaps for preparing the ground, drilling and planting in late springs. However, this must not be overdone, and panic buying of additional machinery in particularly difficult seasons should be avoided. There comes a point where the extra benefit to be obtained, say, one year in five is insufficient to cover the extra depreciation and interest charges borne every year. On the other hand, if the extra cost is small compared with the potential benefits it is false economy to be too frugal. For example, paying an extra £1000 for a larger, faster drill may seem extravagant, but with, say, 150 hectares of cereals, it only needs an increased yield of 0.015 tonnes per ha to cover the £1.25 per ha extra annual costs.

(iv) *Increased price through improved quality.* Examples are high quality grain cleaners and equipment which reduces damage to potatoes during harvesting and subsequent handling.

(v) *Increased price through storage.* This is illustrated and discussed in Chapter 12, p. 266.

Reduced costs

The main reason for mechanisation is to reduce costs, especially labour. A separate section is therefore devoted to this subject below (pp. 94–5).

Replacing labour

This is given a separate heading from the one above because mechanisation is often forced on a farmer through his inability to obtain suitable labour, even though he would prefer it to machine work if it were available. On the other hand some farmers prefer to mechanise, even where labour is available and possibly slightly cheaper, because it reduces their personnel problems.

Reductions in labour requirements through mechanisation can be enormous. For example, the average number of labour-hours per hectare needed to produce a cereal crop in 1930 was 135; for a well-mechanised farm the figure is now 10 or even less, despite much higher yields. The single-row sugar beet harvester reduced labour-hours per hectare for knocking and topping to a tenth of their former level (from 100 to 10).

In all cases the basic approach needed to help decide whether further expenditure on machinery is worthwhile is partial budgeting (see Chapter 14, pp. 315–17), that is, measuring the added receipts or costs saved against the added costs of mechanisation, always bearing in mind capital availability and the return from possible alternative investments where capital is scarce. Frequently, however (referring to the second justification above), there is considerable doubt about the likely addition to receipts. In this case break-even budgeting should be used (see Chapter 14, pp. 393–4).

Total farm machinery costs

Annual machinery costs per hectare for six different types of farm are shown in Appendix 4.4, Table 4.6. The approximate breakdown of the total between depreciation, repairs, fuel, contract work and vehicle tax and insurance over all types and sizes is 25 per cent, 30 per cent, 22½ per cent, 17½ per cent and 5 per cent respectively. Interest is not included in these costings, the farm surplus having to cover interest payments as well as provide the profit.

Obviously these costs vary according to the intensity of the farming system. An alternative, therefore, is to relate the costs to the number of tractor units.[1] Tractor units are akin to standard man-days (see Chapter 5, pp. 132–3), i.e. they are not the *actual* tractor hours worked on the farm, but average tractor hours per hectare of crop or per head of livestock for all types of tractors, farm size and conditions. They are used as a means of obtaining an objective measure of the amount of machinery work on a farm, according to the crops and livestock on that farm. In the UK, the tractor units for each enterprise are given in

[1] Both costs per hectare and costs per tractor unit can be used, with reservations, to measure the efficiency of machinery use (see further Chapter 20, pp. 535–7).

TABLE 4.1. *Calculation of total tractor units and cost per unit*

Enterprise	Hectares or number of head	Tractor units per ha or per head	Total tractor units
Potatoes	20	55	1,100
Wheat	30	12	360
Barley	60	12	720
Ewes	400	1.5	600
	Total tractor units		2,780

Total annual machinery costs: £8,062.
Annual machinery costs per tractor unit: £2.90.

management handbooks. An example of the calculations is shown in Table 4.1, with costs per tractor unit for six farm types shown in Appendix 4.4, Table 4.7. It is important to remember that the costs represent not only the tractor expenses but the total annual machinery costs, including a share of the farm car(s) and any other farm vehicles, such as a van or landrover.

Depreciation, the highest single machinery cost item, is related to the machinery valuation. Valuations for different farm types and sizes are shown in Appendix 4.4, Table 4.8 (some more general figures are included in Table 3.2).

Estimating machinery costs for budgeting

When preparing a budget for a new farm, there are three methods that can be employed to estimate machinery costs. The easiest and quickest is to take a per ha figure from published 'standards', or average data for various types and size of farm, where available. This could be inaccurate, especially if the farm differs considerably in intensity from the average. The second alternative takes more time: it is to calculate the total number of tractor units (see above) for the farming system employed and multiply by the average cost per tractor unit for that farm type, again where published data from farm surveys are available. This allows for intensity, but still ignores specific farm circumstances, including soil type and size of labour force. The third is the most time-consuming but the most accurate: namely, to calculate individual machinery requirements for that farm and cost them separately for depreciation, repairs, fuel, etc., as described in the next section, using published tables where no better individual estimate can be made.

Any contract work is calculated separately and added to the total. Such a calculation may possibly be cross-checked against one of the first two methods. The farm vehicles, including the farm car, must not be forgotten. More will be said on choice of machine size and numbers in a later section of this chapter (pp. 95–100).

When budgeting for changes to an existing farm, past accounts for the farm may be utilised. To begin with, the level of machinery costs to be expected if the farming system remained unchanged should be calculated. In doing this, allowance must be made for inflation and the figures should be 'normalised', that is, adjusted for any abnormalities in previous years, such as extra high depreciation through exceptionally heavy capital expenditure in a particular year. Following this, changes can be estimated on the basis of the third alternative outlined above. Thus, it must be decided whether more or larger machines are necessary, and, if so, the depreciation and repairs for these can be estimated and added, together with the estimated extra fuel costs (for tractors, combine, grain drier, etc.), to the 'normalised' figure for the existing system.

Machinery costs: further details

This section gives further details of each main item of machinery expense, in the context of costing the operation of individual machines. All but the interest and labour items are also used in estimating machinery costs for the whole farm. Individual machine costings, including labour and often interest, are made for several reasons: to compare the costs of operating different types and sizes of machine, to compare the cost of owning a machine with the cost of hiring, leasing or engaging a contractor, and, sometimes, in the costing of an individual enterprise, for purposes of negotiating prices. This involves the use of 'unit costs': for example, labour is costed by multiplying the number of hours it is used on a particular job by the labour cost per hour, calculated from the actual wages paid plus other costs such as insurance. Reservations about such procedures are expressed in several places in this book. Enterprise costings in general are criticised in Chapter 12 (pp. 260–2), and especially in Chapter 20 (pp. 537–9). Later in this chapter the shortcomings of unit cost comparisons are stressed, mainly on the grounds that they normally ignore interrelationships between different activities on the farm and the opportunity costs of the resources involved.

For convenience, annual operating costs of machinery may be divided into fixed and running costs. Fixed costs (not used here in the

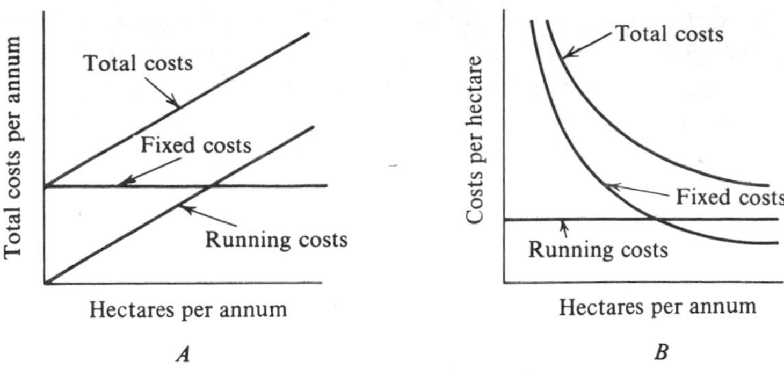

Fig. 4.1. Annual fixed and running costs

gross margin sense) comprise those costs which remain the same per annum regardless of the amount the machine is used, namely, depreciation (to a large extent), housing, interest and tax. Running costs are those which vary according to the use made of the machine, namely, labour, tractor use where required, fuel and repairs. Fixed costs are fixed *in total*, but decline *per ha* (or per tonne) as the annual use of the machine is increased. Running costs vary *in total* in proportion to annual use, but are approximately constant *per ha* (or per tonne). These relationships are illustrated in Figure 4.1.

A. *Fixed costs*

(i) *Depreciation*. This is not a cash payment: it is an estimate of the amount by which the value of a capital item falls in a given period, and thus represents the cost of ownership of that item. The capital asset is supplying, as it were, a flow of services over time. Annual depreciation is a charge against the year's profits, that is available to build up a reserve fund out of which the asset can be replaced when required. Inflation – plus possibly machine improvement – may well mean that the fund will be insufficient fully to pay for the machine's replacement, because the purchase price of a replacement machine may be higher than that paid for the current machine. This can be allowed for by adding a percentage to the annual allowance for depreciation, sufficient to allow funds to be accumulated equal to the anticipated cost of replacement. (See further, Appendix 19.4, pp. 522–3.)

Depreciation may occur for three reasons: (*a*) obsolescence, (*b*) gradual deterioration with age, (*c*) wear and tear with use. The first two factors limit the economic life of the machine in years. The third limits the life in hours of use, if it is intensively employed. If the third factor predominates over the first two, which is not uncommon on large farms, depreciation is no longer fixed per annum (regardless of use) and can be taken instead as a constant sum per ha (or per tonne), like running costs.

There are three main ways of calculating depreciation, all of which are illustrated in Table 4.2 and Figure 4.2:

(*a*) the straight-line method, in which the estimated total depreciation during the time the machine is expected to remain on the farm (i.e. purchase price minus sale, trade-in or scrap value) is divided by the number of years the machine is on the farm; it is thus a constant sum per annum.

(*b*) The diminishing balances method, in which a constant percentage is taken of the written-down value, which is the value of the machine remaining after deducting total depreciation to date; with this method, annual depreciation obviously decreases as the machine gets older.

(*c*) The sum-of-the-years'-digits method, in which a declining fraction of the estimated total depreciation (as calculated for the straight-line method) is taken each year. The denominator is the sum of the individual years the machine is expected to be retained on the farm;

TABLE 4.2. *Alternative methods of calculating depreciation*

	Annual depreciation			Written-down value		
Year	*A*	*B*	*C*	*A*	*B*	*C*
1	225	500	400	1,775	1,500	1,600
2	225	375	350	1,550	1,125	1,250
3	225	281	300	1,325	844	950
4	225	211	250	1,100	633	700
5	225	158	200	875	475	500
6	225	119	150	650	356	350
7	225	89	100	425	267	250
8	225	67	50	200	200	200

Example: machine costing £2,000; estimated scrap value after 8 years, £200.

A = Straight-line method.
B = Diminishing Balances method (25%).
C = Sum-of-the-Digits method.

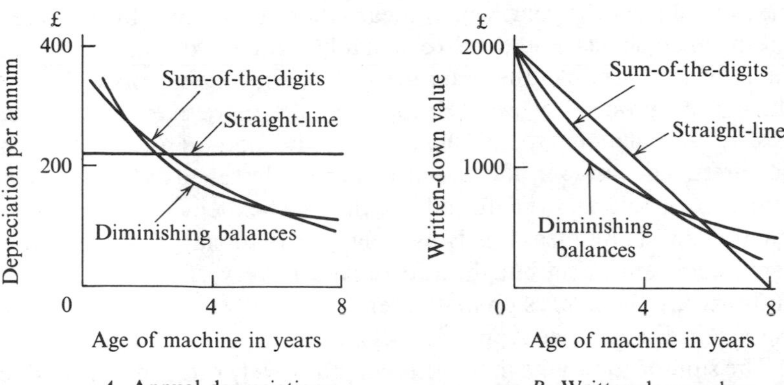

A. Annual depreciation *B.* Written-down values

Note: the curves in this figure are not intended to coincide exactly with the figures in Table 4.2.

Fig. 4.2. Methods of calculating depreciation

for example, if the period were 8 years, the denominator would be 36 (i.e. 8 + 7 + 6 + 5 + 4 + 3 + 2 + 1); the numerator is the years of life remaining at the start of the year. The fraction is, therefore, for an 8 year period, $\frac{8}{36}$ in year 1, $\frac{7}{36}$ in year 2, and so on, until it is $\frac{1}{36}$ in year 8.

The effect of intensive use shortening the machine's years of useful life can be allowed for in the diminishing balances method by increasing the annual percentage used to write down the value of the machine. In the other two methods a similar increase in cost per annum will be effected by a combination of decreasing the number of years the machine is expected to be on the farm and reducing the trade-in value of the machine; if the machine is in any case kept until it is of scrap value only, the effect will be entirely through the reduced period on the farm.

The straight-line method is the simplest and the one normally used in budgeting, since then the concern is usually only with the average annual cost of the machine; similarly, repair costs are estimated as an average annual sum.

For calculating depreciation and hence written-down values for individual machines in the annual accounts it is usual to use the diminishing balances method. This reflects more accurately than the straight-line method the way in which the sale value of a machine drops after purchase, that is, quickly at first, more slowly as it gets older. In the profit and loss account, therefore, the annual depreciation calculated in this way approximates to the reduction in the value of the machine during the year, which means that the written-down value in the balance sheet should be reasonably close to the actual current value of the asset. As the machine gets older, repair costs will rise as the depreciation falls, thus helping to give a more even total annual cost for the machine than if the straight-line method were used in the accounts. The number of calculations can be lessened by using a single diminishing balances rate for all but the more expensive items, such as tractors and combines; this is especially true for larger farms, where some items are being bought and replaced every year. Annual wear-and-tear tax allowances on machinery are usually made on a diminishing balances basis (see Appendix 4.1).

The sum-of-the-digits method is comparatively rarely used, but does have some advantage over the other two. It gives similar results to the diminishing balances method, but the annual depreciation is lower in the first year or two (unless the machine is kept only a short time) and towards the end of its life, and a little higher in the middle years, which may more accurately describe the fall in value over time of some machines.

The estimated useful life of different types of machine with varying intensities of use, and the annual fall in value with different frequencies of renewal, are shown in Appendix 4.4, Tables 4.9 and 4.10.

(ii) *Interest on capital.* This item is included in accounts for tax assessment purposes if interest is actually being paid, but not otherwise. In partial budgeting, however (and sometimes in complete budgeting also), it is usually allowed for even where the farmer is not borrowing the money. The rate charged is normally the minimum opportunity cost, that is, what he could obtain by investing the money in safe securities instead.[1] A higher rate may be charged if preferred, e.g. because capital is very short, or to allow for risk. However, it is not charged, whether borrowed or not, if the intention is to calculate the return on the investment. Interest has to be paid out of this return. Tax relief on interest payments can be – and usually is – allowed for in discounted cash flow calculations (see further Chapter 3).

[1] It is of course true that if a farmer, assuming he does not buy the machine, leaves the money unused in his current account, inclusion of interest overstates the cost of his owning the machine. There is also the point that in partial budgeting to evaluate the worthwhileness of buying a machine, interest on extra or reduced working capital requirements should also be included to be accurate, especially where the farmer is operating on a bank overdraft.

In budgeting it is the average annual interest charge over the life of the machine that is included. A common convention is to allow the rate of interest on half the initial cost (or half the rate of interest on the whole of the initial cost) on the grounds that the machine is gradually being written off over its life, the depreciation charges being re-invested until needed to replace the machine. This underestimates the cost, especially when the machine is replaced early. A more accurate calculation is to charge the expected average rate of interest over the time the machine is on the farm on the following sum: (initial cost + trade-in value) ÷ 2, which represents the average value of the machine while it is on the farm. It would obviously come to the same thing to charge half the rate of interest on the whole sum (initial cost plus trade-in-value). This still assumes simple rather than compound interest, however. To allow for this an amount exceeding half the interest rate must be charged, e.g. approximately 5 per cent, not 4 per cent, when 8 per cent is the expected average rate (see Table 4.3 and the footnote to that table).

(iii) *Insurance, road tax and housing.* Insurance on machinery is typically about 0.4 per cent of the insured value. Housing may vary from between nothing, where a machine is kept outside, and a substantial sum, where

TABLE 4.3. *Repayments of capital and interest per £1,000 borrowed.*

Rate of interest	No. of years					
	5	10	15	20	30	40
5	231	130	96	80	65	58
6	238	136	103	87	73	66
8	251	149	117	102	89	84
10	264	163	132	117	106	102
12	278	177	147	134	124	121
15	299	200	171	160	153	150
20	334	239	214	205	202	200

The average annual capital repayment can be calculated simply by dividing £1,000 by the number of years over which repayment is made. Deducting the resulting figures from the annual repayments shown in the table gives the average annual interest payment.

special accommodation has been recently erected; often, however, barn space will be used for another purpose for part of the year. Although savings in maintenance costs and possibly depreciation are to be expected from housing, no studies have been made in Britain comparing such savings with the depreciation, interest and maintenance of the buildings required. Such accommodation tends rather to be regarded as part of the basic fixed equipment of a farm, along with the land, roads and a house (see p. 109 below). But a new owner-occupier farmer short of capital with no machinery accommodation would find it difficult to justify more than a tractor-shed, at least in the short run. If he felt housing of machinery to be essential this would be an additional point in favour of his using contractors.

B. Running costs

(i) *Labour*. In cost accounting terms labour for operating a machine should be charged according to the number of hours employed. However, in partial budgeting, used for purposes of deciding whether or not to purchase a machine, the cost is often rightly omitted. This is done where it is considered that regular labour is available to do the work, so that no extra labour cost will be incurred, and no other enterprise will suffer as a result of taking on the extra task. However, where other enterprises *are* competitive for labour at such times, its opportunity cost must be allowed for. Without time-consuming calculations, only an arbitrary assessment can be made and the simplest practice is to charge on the basis of the actual cost per hour, as in cost accounting. This could however be a considerable underestimate of its real cost if the work is needed at critical times, to such an extent as to make the calculation potentially highly misleading. The full implications may only be understood and evaluated by making a completely new farm plan.

(ii) *Tractor use*. Where a tractor is used and no tractor costings are available on the farm it may be possible to obtain an appropriate charge from a published management handbook, and calculate the cost according to the number of hours the tractor is employed. As with labour, however, it is misleading to include depreciation (or interest) when partial budgeting, if the job does not make it necessary to buy more or larger tractors and no other work is delayed to the detriment of farm profits.

(iii) *Fuel.* This cost obviously varies in proportion to the number of hours the machine is employed. For many machines, however, all fuel costs are included in the tractor charge.

(iv) *Repairs.* Although total repair costs for a machine rise with increased use they are unlikely to do so proportionately. This is because repairs are partly a function of age as well as use, e.g. the cost of batteries and defects through rusting (Figure 4.3). Table 4.11 in Appendix 4.4 shows annual repair costs for different machines as percentages of their initial costs, at varying levels of annual use.

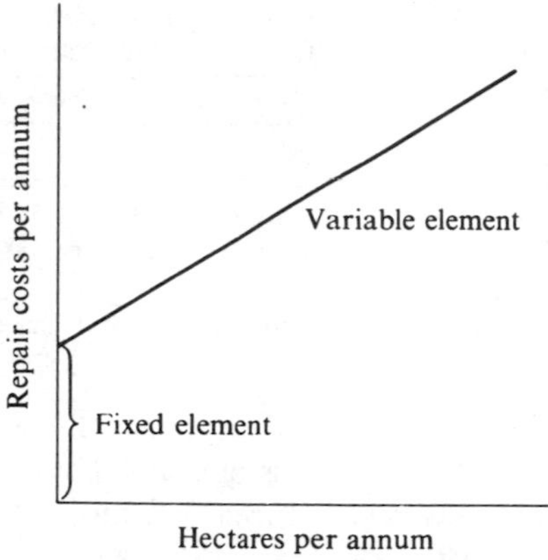

Fig. 4.3. Machinery repair costs per annum

The relevant items of cost are added to give the total costs of operating an individual machine. The calculations can be per hour, per ha or per tonne. Costs per hour can be translated into costs per ha or per tonne by relating them to the rate of work, i.e. dividing by ha or tonnes per hour. The approximate rate of work of a machine or implement in hectares per hour can be calculated by the formula: 0.083 × km per hour × working width in metres. This allows for turning, stoppages and rests (the absolute theoretical maximum being 0.1 × kmph × width in metres). However, when allowance is made for preparation and starting in the morning and travelling to and from the field, the actual rates of work achieved per hour over the whole working day are unlikely to be quite so high.

An illustration of an individual machine costing is given in Table 4.4 at four different levels of use.

TABLE 4.4. *Example of individual machine costing: sugar beet harvester*

	Annual use							
	5 ha		10 ha		25 ha		50 ha	
	total (£)	per ha (£)	total (£)	per ha (£)	total (£)	per ha (£)	total (£)	per ha (£)
Depreciation	350	70	350	35	350	14	560	11
Interest	180	36	180	18	180	7	180	4
Other	50	10	50	5	50	2	50	1
Fixed costs	580	116	580	58	580	23	790	16
Labour	80	16	160	16	400	16	800	16
Tractor	100	20	200	20	500	20	1,000	20
Repairs	90	18	140	14	250	10	400	8
Running costs	270	54	500	50	1,150	46	2,200	44
Total costs	850	170	1,080	108	1,730	69	2,990	60

Cost of machine: £3,000. Maximum economic life: 8 years or 250 ha harvested.
Scrap value: £200. Interest: 10 per cent (on diminishing value).
Insurance and Housing: £50.
Running Costs per ha: labour, £16; tractor, £20; repairs, vary with use.

Own machine versus contractor

From Figure 4.1*B* and Table 4.4 it is obvious that it cannot pay to buy a machine for work on a very small area. The more work the machine is given, the lower the cost per hectare, because of the spreading of the fixed costs. At some area the costs must become less than the alternatives, which may be hiring a contractor or using hand labour. The area at which the costs are equal is the 'break-even' point.

Take, for example, a small farmer who at present employs a contractor to combine-harvest his cereal crops. He has enough capital to buy a reliable four-year old second-hand combine-harvester for £3200. He decides he should write this off over six years, allowing £200 value at the end of this time. Depreciation is thus £500 a year and interest and other fixed costs are approximately £200. Labour, repairs and fuel are estimated to total £11.50 per ha. The contractor charges £30 per hectare.

Figure 4.4 represents the situation graphically. The break-even area (X) can be calculated by dividing the annual fixed costs by the saving in contractor's charges less the running costs per ha, i.e. $700 \div (30 - 11.50)$ = approximately 38 ha. That is, if his average annual area is less than 38 ha it will pay him to continue hiring the contractor; if greater, it will be cheaper for him to buy the machine.

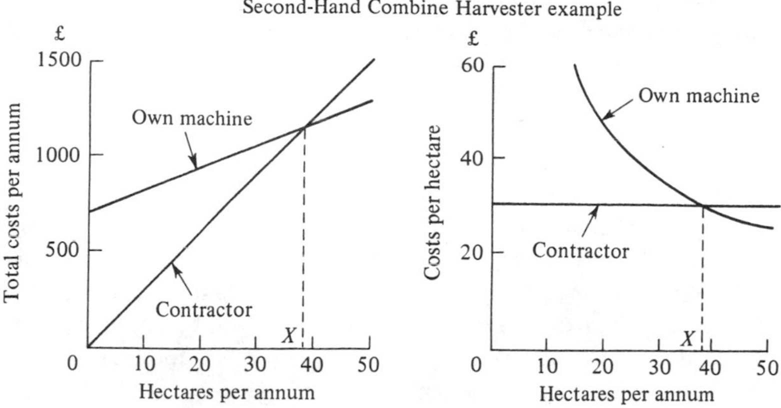

Fig. 4.4. Contractor versus own machine

Several points must be made regarding this calculation. These relate not only to this example, but to any decision involving machine purchase versus hiring a contractor. First, the farmer may feel he can manage this job without extra staff and without other work getting behind, in which case he can exclude the labour cost (£1.50 per hour and £3.50 per ha) from the calculation, i.e. 700 ÷ (30 − 8) = 32 ha break-even point. On the other hand, the cereal harvest may be his peak labour period, in which case labour may be worth more than £1.50 an hour at such times – especially if casual labour is difficult to obtain in the district.

He may be able to spread the fixed costs by doing contract work for other farmers, or by sharing the machine with others. The latter will be referred to again below.

Of major importance is the timeliness factor. If the contractor is unreliable, or has a large area of his own or other farmers to harvest, then the yield may suffer considerably (e.g. through grain shedding), or extra costs may be incurred (e.g. more grain drying – especially if this also has to be done by a contractor). With his own machine he can choose his own time to operate. This is of considerable importance with some jobs, such as grain harvesting or spraying, but less important with others, e.g. sugar beet harvesting (up to a point), or hedging and ditching.

On the other hand, the farmer with his own machine is in a less flexible capital position than when he employs a contractor. Technical developments may make his machine suddenly obsolete; he then has the choice of disposing of it at a very low price or of incurring higher running costs or greater crop losses than a new machine would provide. Even if there are no such technical advances, he may decide to give up the crop – or farming altogether, and he may obtain only a poor price for his machine, particularly if other farmers are abandoning the enterprise at the same time. The contractor's charge, by contrast, can be switched off like a tap at any time.

Finally, if capital is scarce and profitable alternative opportunities for investment exist on the farm, it may still be better to employ the contractor even though buying a machine appears to be cheaper. The return on capital from buying the machine should be compared with the return from the alternative investments (see Chapter 3), and the principle of opportunity cost applied.

Machine versus hand

An alternative decision may be whether to buy a machine to replace hand labour. Let us take potato harvesting as an example. A machine costing £6000 is being considered; the soil is suitable for machine-harvesting, with on average four pickers on the machine, costing £50 per ha. Carting costs are assumed to be the same for both machine and hand harvesting.

Fixed costs on the harvester are estimated at £1300 a year and running costs at £100 per ha (including £50 labour for picking off). At present harvesting costs £100 a year plus £35 per ha running costs for the spinner and £140 per ha for hand picking. A break-even area can be calculated, by dividing the difference in annual fixed costs by the difference in running costs per ha, i.e. (1300–100) ÷ (175–100) = 1200 ÷ 75 = 16 hectares.

As with the contracting alternative, however, there are other factors to be considered. Both the point about flexibility made above and the possibility of more profitable alternative uses for limited capital have to be remembered. Any differences in work quality must be considered – in this case total yield per hectare and percentage of tubers damaged. But of even greater relevance is the labour-saving aspect.

If the picking is at present being done by casual labour and the same type of labour will also be employed on the back of the harvester, then the above calculations will be acceptable, since virtually all the cost difference will be represented by a change in direct cash outgoings. If, however, the labour is provided by regular staff in both cases, the calculation represents an over-simplification. Only if the £90 per ha difference in picking labour results in an actual cash saving will the calculation stand. The difference in labour-hours required may be turned into cash either by reducing the number of regular staff employed – which is certainly possible if the potato harvesting time represents the main labour peak during the year – or by finding other productive work for the labour to do in the time saved. The latter can be achieved either by introducing new enterprises or by replacing relatively low gross margin enterprises by higher gross margin enterprises, e.g. more potatoes or wheat in place of barley. Whichever course is taken it will be very much a coincidence if the saving in labour costs or additional gross margin amounts to exactly £90 per hectare.

In deciding the worthwhileness of buying a machine to replace hand labour, therefore, a partial budget is usually needed (see further Chapter 14, pp. 315–17 and the example in Table 14.1).

The following items should be considered:

Debits (Added costs and reduced returns)	*Credits* (Costs saved and added returns)
Fixed costs of new machine	Fixed costs of any machinery replaced
Net increases in fuel and repair costs	Net decreases in fuel and repair costs
	Regular labour costs saved
	Casual labour costs saved
Valuc of any reduction in saleable yield or quality	Value of any increase in saleable yield or quality
Gross margin of enterprises deleted or reduced in size	Gross margin of new enterprises or additions to existing enterprises

It will be apparent from the foregoing analysis that the substitution of machinery for hand labour may have many repercussions on the farm economy, through the ensuing effect on seasonal labour requirements and hence cropping possibilities. These interactions may be so great that they can be fully appreciated only by re-planning the whole farm, as has already been suggested above (p. 90). If mechanisation makes possible an expanded area of the crop being mechanised, the fixed costs of the machine will be spread over a larger area, although it must also be remembered that other machines already on the farm would then be less fully utilised.

Number and size of machines

Given that the farmer has decided to mechanise an operation, he must decide how many machines, and of what size, to purchase. A host of factors enters into such a decision. First he must calculate the *rate of work* needed, by dividing the area (or tonnage) to be handled by the *hours or days available* to do the work. Next he must select the number/size of machine(s) with sufficient *capacity* to accomplish this. For example, he may have 200 hectares of cereals, estimate that he must complete harvest in 15 working days, or 150 combining hours, and thus require a combine (or combines) that will average 1.33 ha per hour. He may consider a number of alternative machines, calculate their capacities (i.e. average rate of work in hours × available hours to do the work) and select from those with sufficient capacity to do the job. The choice will clearly be affected by the prices of the different machines. The urgency of subsequent operations must also be considered.

A major problem, however, is that 'available hours' cannot be known exactly, nor in fact can the rate of work. Both vary according to seasonal weather and related factors. Even if the range is known there is still a difficult choice to be made, since a higher capacity machine will give greater timeliness and thus a higher yield (e.g. through less shedding losses in grain) and/or lower ancillary costs (e.g. for grain drying, or having to hire a contractor to complete the harvest in difficult seasons). However, the benefit gradually becomes less as capacity increases for a given work requirement, both because the gain in any one season declines and because in an increasing proportion of seasons there is no benefit at all. At the same time the larger capacity machines result in an increasing annual cost. The situation is depicted in Figure 4.5. Thus, while it is easy to condemn excess capacity and over-

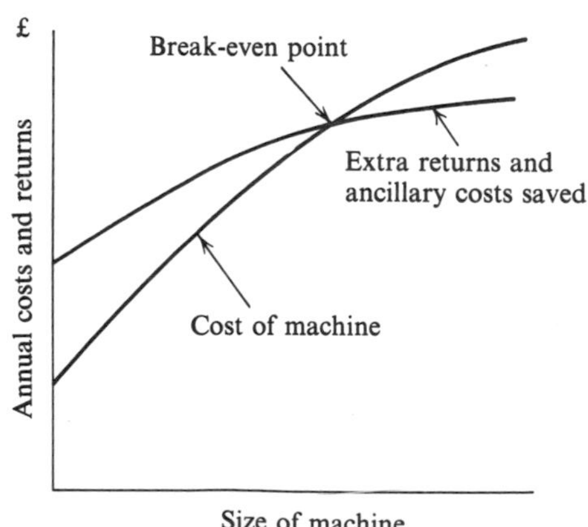

(N.B. some economies of size,
e.g. in labour use, assumed)

Fig. 4.5. Annual costs and benefits with increased machine size

mechanisation, making optimum decisions in the choice of machinery is in fact extremely complex, and would still be so even if full and certain information were available about the way in which yields decline and costs increase over time in different seasons. A way of tackling this problem using simulation is outlined in Appendix 4.2.

Sometimes there is a straight choice between different machines, one having higher initial costs but lower running costs than the other. The break-even point can be calculated by dividing the difference in fixed costs by the difference in running costs. For example, an oil drying unit for a grain drying plant may cost £2000 as against £1300 for electricity, with the former costing £1 per tonne in fuel and repairs and the latter £1.80. The annual fixed costs are £320 and £208 respectively. The break-even throughput is (320–208) ÷ (1.80–1.00) = 112 ÷ 0.80 = approximately 140 tonnes dried a year, with electricity the cheaper below this level and oil above it. This is shown graphically in Figure 4.6.

In most cases, however, the main running cost saved is labour. Thus there might be a choice, as in Figure 4.7, between machines *A*, *B* and *C*. *A* is relatively cheap but requires substantial amounts of labour; *C* is expensive but is extremely labour-saving; *B* falls between the other two. In the simplest situation the same rate of work per day may be assumed. The machines could be costed over varying areas and the results could be as shown in Figure 4.8I. This indicates a lowest cost alternative for each area. It sometimes happens that the lower labour costs of the more expensive machines never compensate for

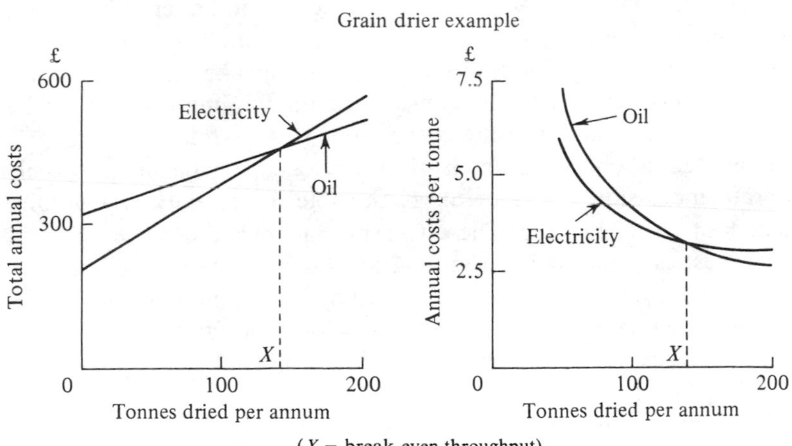

Fig. 4.6. Choice of machine type

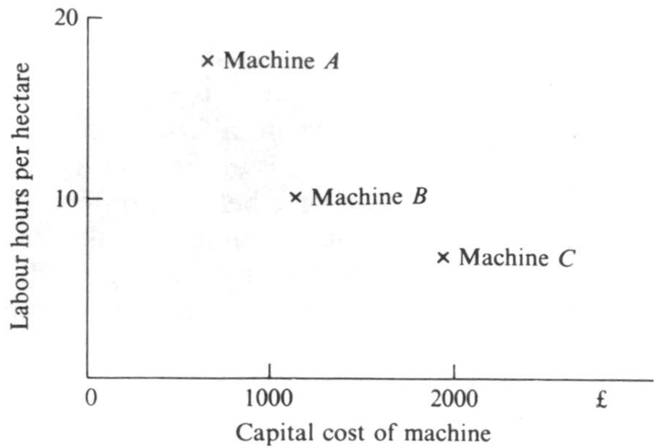

Fig. 4.7. Labour versus capital in machinery choice

their higher initial costs, at any area; the cheapest machine thus appears to be the 'best buy' over the whole range.

In practice, however, two complications arise. First, both capital and labour have varying opportunity costs according to their availability relative to alternative uses. This is a case of factor–factor substitution (see Chapter 2, pp. 30–5) and the optimum choice depends on the relative *real* costs of the two factors. If labour is scarce at the time when the job has to be done, it may well pay to have a more expensive machine, even though unit cost comparisons as described above (pp. 84–92) imply that costs per hectare are higher than for a cheaper machine. Similarly, if capital is scarce and alternative profitable investments exist, it may pay to make do with the cheaper machine, even though labour savings appear to make a more expensive machine worthwhile. Only by considering the full implications for the whole farming system can the correct decision be reached.

The second complication is that the cheaper machines usually operate more slowly; often this is the sole reason why they require more labour per hectare. The different machines thus have different capacities, as illustrated in Figure 4.8II (where only two machines are shown, in order to simplify the diagram). The timeliness aspect discussed earlier therefore affects the decision. The farmer also has the choice between two (or more) smaller machines and one large capacity machine.

Decisions regarding choice of machine, therefore, cannot be separated from those relating to whole farm planning. In particular, seasonal labour availability, timeliness and capital availability affect the

I

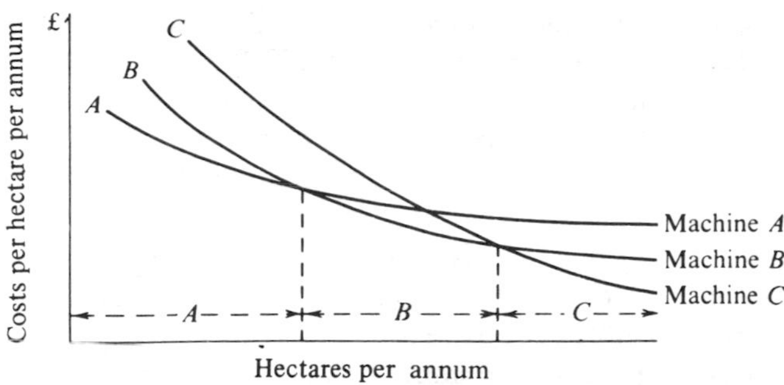

(The lowest cost machine over the relevant area is indicated above the horizontal axis)

II

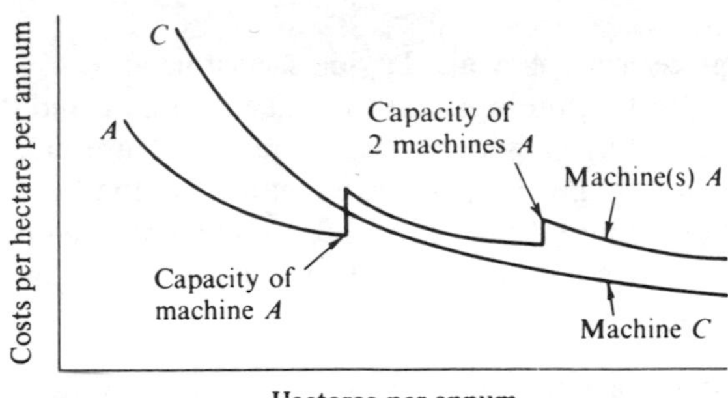

(Machine *A* gives the lowest cost up to its capacity, but at greater areas machine *C* gives a lower cost than having 2 or 3 machines *A*)

Fig. 4.8. Machine size and cost per ha: (I) same capacities; (ii) different capacities

optimum choice. At the very least, decisions regarding machinery choice should only be taken in the light of the information shown by a gang-work day chart (see Chapter 5, p. 140), which shows the number of men available and the way they are deployed at different times of the year. More information can be obtained by means of linear programming (see Chapter 15), re-running the matrix with different assumptions concerning the quantity of labour available and the level of mechanisation.

In choosing the number and size of tractors required for a farm the same factors apply, namely, the labour supply, capital availability and timeliness – all related, of course, to the cropping and stocking of the farm. At the simplest level all but the last can be ignored and the number of medium-sized tractors calculated by summing total tractor units (see p. 82 above), deducting 800 for the first tractor and assuming that one extra is needed for each subsequent 1200 units. At a higher level the gang work-day chart would be used. Beyond that, linear programming could be employed. Simulation (Appendix 4.2) may also be used but is unlikely to be practicable at the individual farm level. The especially high-powered tractors (over 80 kW) are costly per unit of power and are also expensive in ancillary equipment. They are unlikely to be economic except on large areas being run by an exceptionally small labour staff and where they can help to solve problems caused by periods of excessive labour demand; even then alternatives such as contracting should be considered, particularly where soil compaction could be a problem.

Replacement policy and buying second-hand

The factors affecting the optimum replacement date and the wisdom or otherwise of buying second-hand equipment are closely linked. The main points are given below; the first five are the most important, the others being more difficult, perhaps impossible, to measure. The term 'early replacement' means replacing a machine within 3 years of buying it new.

1. Rate of depreciation, i.e. actual annual loss in value. The slower this is, the more likely is early replacement to be worthwhile, since it will involve a smaller loss in value.
2. Rate of increase in repair costs. The faster these increase, the more beneficial early replacement is likely to be, because the saving in repair costs will be greater.
3. Interest rates. The lower the rate, the more early replacement is to be recommended, since the higher interest charges involved in this policy will then be less onerous.
4. Availability of capital. The more plentiful this is, the stronger the case for early replacement, because there are less likely to be more profitable ways of using the extra capital tied up.
5. Annual use. The more intensively the machine is used the more is early replacement favoured, for two reasons: the depreciation cost per hour is lower (trade-in value depending more on age than condition, and more on condition than actual use) and breakdowns are more costly in terms of loss of timeliness.
6. Reliability. The less reliable the machine becomes with increased age the more will early replacement pay; the more intensive the use the more important is reliability (see 5 above).

7. Improvements in the machine. The greater these are, the more early replacement is to be encouraged. They must, however, be real, not imaginary or superficial improvements, and result either in higher yields, better quality of work, or reduced running costs.

8. Morale/psychological factors. If having new machinery is an important factor in retaining good staff and the farmer's own self-esteem depends to any extent on new machines, he may need to replace his equipment earlier. Peace of mind (because of freedom from breakdowns) could also be included here, although too often this is far from being provided by a new machine, particularly in its first season.

The principle of holding cost and operations analysis techniques can be invoked to aid the replacement decision and are briefly described in Appendix 4.3. Such studies as have been done, however, reveal that there is little to choose between fairly early (i.e. at 3 or 4 years old) and later replacement, provided the machine is used reasonably close to capacity. In such cases the imminence of a large overhaul or repair bill, a good trade-in price offer, or a good harvest (i.e. high profit and therefore a high tax year) is enough to encourage replacement, and often the balance is so fine that these are totally valid reasons.

It is not possible to give a list of different machines with their optimum replacement periods. This is mainly because of variations between farms in two of the factors listed above: availability of capital and the annual use made of the machine. The trade-in, or second-hand, price is in fact a reflection of all the points made above blended together. If one replacement period were optimal for everyone there would be no second-hand market and second-hand price. It is because the second-hand price provides a delicate balance that time of replacement is a difficult decision. The same applies to buying new or second-hand: where capital is plentiful and the machine is intensively used buying new is economically justified; where the opposite conditions apply second-hand machinery should be preferred, the lower annual fixed costs compensating for the probability of higher running costs and more breakdowns – which are less critical with less work to be accomplished. In between there is inevitably a fairly balanced case for one or the other.

Alternatives to owning and contracting

Leasing and *hiring* of machinery achieve one of the main advantages obtained by engaging contractors, namely, the conservation of capital – or its release for other uses. They miss the other advantages, such as the provision of extra labour during peak labour periods, but also avoid the drawbacks, especially possible loss of timeliness. It is difficult to generalise about relative costs because agreements tend to vary in detail. By and large, however, leasing and hiring are likely to be slightly more costly than owning a machine. The business firms concerned have to cover their overhead expenses and naturally expect to make a profit. Tax allowances (see Appendix 4.1) complicate the comparison: a farmer loses the potential tax saving through high initial allowances that can be obtained by replacing a machine in a high-profit year, but all lease and hire payments are tax allowable. Either way, the after-tax cost difference is usually small and leasing and hiring are certainly worth considering where capital is short and profitable alternative investments exist. Like engaging contractors, they (particularly hiring) have the advantages of certainty and flexibility: the cost is known in advance (unlike depreciation on a machine that is owned) and – at least in the case of hiring – can more or less be stopped at any time. The fixed payments for hiring normally include maintenance and repairs; the main benefits then go to the intensive user, since he is most likely to have high depreciation (through frequent replacement) and high annual repair costs. However, the large user is less likely to be short of capital than the smaller farmer, and forfeits more tax savings.

Despite much publicity, machinery *sharing* – or, more formally, syndicate ownership – is not popular in Britain. The advantages are that less capital is required per user, and fixed costs per hectare (or per tonne) are reduced by spreading depreciation and interest charges over a larger throughput. The smaller farmer, however, can achieve the same advantages by buying either a smaller machine, if one is available, or a second-hand one; he can then use it when he wants to and obtain the full benefit of timeliness. If the machine is smaller, however, the job takes more time; if it is second-hand its quality of performance may be inferior and breakdowns are more likely to occur, although these are less vital to a small farmer than to a large user.

Because sharing may cause a farmer to lose yield or endure extra ancillary expenses, and much frustration, in a bad season, a better case can be made for sharing the use of fixed or portable barn equipment or machines used for jobs where timeliness is less critical, e.g. hedgers and ditchers. Otherwise, if trouble is to be avoided, the total planned use should be kept safely within the capacity of the machine in an average season and the method of allocation and responsibility for costs, together with the order of use, must be carefully detailed and understood. There are other benefits from sharing, which are likely to increase in importance in the future: it is a means of obtaining the use of a high output machine using relatively little labour; it encourages labour-sharing on gang-work, e.g. silage-making; and it is likely to lead to the shared ownership of the full range of ancillary equipment, e.g. labour-saving drying and storage facilities with a combine-harvester.

Reasons for excessive machinery costs: a summary

The following factors may all contribute to an excessive level of machinery costs, as indicated, possibly, by one of the efficiency measures described in Chapter 20 (pp. 535–7).

1. Over-mechanisation of non-peak period jobs, with no compensating cost savings.
2. Mechanisation of peak-period work but with no saving in the labour bill, because the work was previously done by regular labour staff which cannot be reduced for various reasons – possibly the existence of other, unmechanised, peak periods – and no cropping changes have been made.
3. Mechanisation without the necessary ancillary equipment, e.g. high-output combine-harvesters with inadequate or non-existent grain handling and drying facilities; or high-powered tractors without the equipment to make full use of the power.
4. Excess capacity: too many or too large (and too new) machines; increased yields are obtained in difficult seasons, but at too high a price; this is often caused by panic buying in bad seasons.
5. Insufficient specialisation, that is, too many, too small enterprises, each with a full complement of machinery.
6. Small farmers buying new instead of reliable second-hand machines: on the small farm the risk of loss through breakdowns is less, the savings in repairs through buying new are lower, and the opportunity cost of capital is usually higher.
7. Too early replacement – on farms where the intensity of use is insufficient to justify such a policy; up-to-dateness and reliability are bought at too high a price; because the trade-in price tends to depend more on age than condition, depreciation costs per hour of use are high and the savings made in repair bills are insufficient to compensate.
8. Too much machinery purchased for tax-reducing reasons; most tax allowances are made only on the actual depreciation that occurs – like any other cost (see Appendix 4.1). There may be some benefit from replacing machines in a high-profit year, especially with high first-year allowances; (for this reason it is useful to try to estimate the annual profit before the end of the year; whole farm budgetary control (see Chapter 21) helps considerably; some accountants will prepare

11-month accounts for the purpose). However, any consequent increase in profits, for example, because of higher yields or a lower labour bill, is taxed, thus offsetting the tax saved by allowances on expenditure. If no such benefit is expected, it is true that the net cost of the machinery or plant is reduced by taxation allowances, but only by reducing profits. This may be justifiable where a farmer deliberately chooses to spend part of his income in this way for personal satisfaction instead of on non-farm items, such as a boat or colour television.

9. Contracting – the wrong balance, i.e. too little use made of contractors on small farms or too much on big farms, where it would be cheaper to purchase the equipment to do the work. However, shortage of capital, management time or expertise may justify contract services on larger farms in some circumstances.

10. Excessive repair costs, through too little maintenance, ill-usage, inadequate skill or equipment for the farmer or his staff to do the simpler jobs on the farm, or use of a high-cost repairs firm. There might, on the other hand, be excessive maintenance: too-frequent overhauls and renewals, or a large workshop and full-time mechanic not justified by the size of the business.

11. Excessive fuel costs. The main cause is likely to be electricity instead of oil for heating, where a large amount is used.

12. Wasteful livestock mechanisation, e.g. mechanised feeding in piggeries or for dairy herds, the equipment needed for tower silos, organic irrigation. There are circumstances where these may be justified, but often the savings are minute and the benefits illusory, especially in relation to the high level of costs involved. Careful scrutiny is thus required before such investments are made and certain relevant questions must be asked. Is labour (or some other) cost *really* being saved? Is a yield benefit *certainly* going to occur? Is a labour bottleneck being overcome – and, if so, will this enable a man to look after *more* livestock without any loss of efficiency, and would this be the right policy for the whole farm in terms of the use of total resources, especially capital and land? Is there a cheaper way of obtaining the same result?

BUILDINGS

Justification and costs

Many of the points made above with regard to investment in machinery apply equally to buildings. Buildings may be erected (*a*) in order to be able to introduce or expand the size of an enterprise; (*b*) to increase output per head or per ha from an existing enterprise, e.g. by erecting a specialised farrowing house to reduce piglet losses, or a grain or apple store to achieve higher prices; (*c*) to save feed costs, e.g. in bacon production; or (*d*) to save labour. From the economic standpoint returns must be increased or costs be saved (or a combination of both) sufficiently to cover the additional annual building costs. A partial budget (see Chapter 14) can be drawn up, with interest on capital included in costs. Alternatively, interest may be omitted and the return on capital estimated as shown in Chapter 3, perhaps for comparison with other possible investments. When government grants are paid, the calculations of worthwhileness to the farmer should be related to the net cost after the grant has been deducted.

The main items of building costs are depreciation and interest, which have both been fully discussed above (pp. 85–9). Straight-line depreciation is used for buildings, based on their economic life. If the building is durable, of a type unlikely to become obsolescent and used for an enterprise unlikely to be abandoned, 15 years may be taken, or even 20 years for a multi-purpose building, such as a large free-standing barn. For specialist buildings, however, it is unwise to take a period longer than 10 years. Experience during the last 20 years has shown how rapidly and unexpectedly buildings can become obsolete. Even if obsolescence is unlikely the farmer should expect to 'see his money back' within a reasonable time and be suspicious of any investment that needs more than ten years to pay for itself. However, taking a period longer than ten years only reduces annual costs slightly, and the rate of reduction decreases as the period taken lengthens. This point is illustrated by the figures in Table 4.3 (p. 89) and Figure 4.9. Because of the high risk of obsolescence, potential investors occasionally go to the other extreme and insist on depreciating over less than 10 years, even possibly 5. While this may occasionally be justified, especially with a high risk enterprise such as broilers, many reasonable investments could not withstand such high fixed charges, and might therefore be wrongly rejected.

To complete the fixed costs an allowance needs to be made for maintenance and repairs (or 'upkeep') and insurance. Clearly the figure will vary according to the quality and expected life of the building and the use to which it is put: the normal range is between 1 and 3 per cent of the original cost per annum, the figure for insurance usually being approximately 0.125 per cent of the value.

It is sometimes useful to think in terms of the maximum sum that it is economic to invest in buildings and plant. This depends on the extra

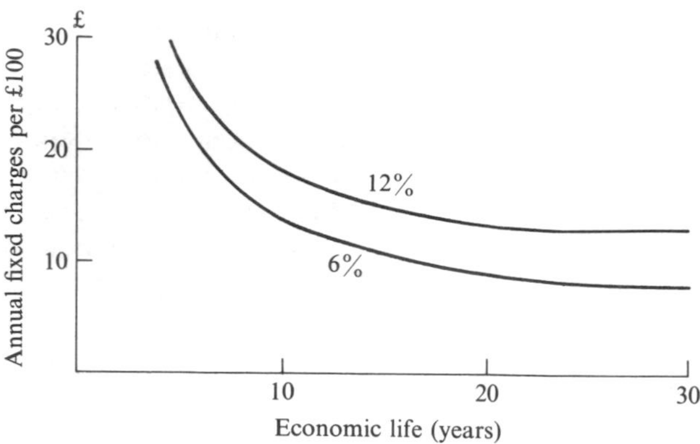

Fig. 4.9. Annual fixed charges (depreciation and interest) at two rates of interest and economic life in years

income expected, the economic life assumed for the building and the interest rate charged. Allowance must also be made for a return on the extra capital apart from buildings, say at 15 per cent. The maximum investment formula is then as follows:

$$\frac{100}{\text{Annual fixed charges (\%)}} \times \text{Extra Margin (less 15\% on other capital).}$$

For example, suppose a farmer selling weaner pigs expects an extra margin from an enlarged sow herd of £75 per sow, after allowing for all extra costs apart from building charges and interest on the livestock and working capital. He wants a return of at least 8 per cent on his capital invested in buildings and equipment and wants to write the buildings off in 10 years; his annual amortisation charge is thus 14.9 per cent (see Table 4.3); 2 per cent added for upkeep makes a total annual fixed charge of approximately 17 per cent. Livestock values and extra working capital average £100 per sow, on which he wants 15 per cent return. The maximum economic investment in buildings per sow is:

$$\frac{100}{17} \times 75 - (0.15 \times 100) = \frac{100}{17} \times (75 - 15) = 5.88 \times 60 = \text{£}353.$$

It must be stressed that this is the *maximum*, not the *recommended* level of investment, which should obviously be kept below the maximum if possible, provided the income is unaffected, or declines by less than the saving in fixed charges.

Type of building

Given that a farmer has decided to erect a certain type of building e.g. a covered yard, capital availability should clearly affect his decision whether to erect a cheap structure likely to last 10 years at most, or whether to erect something more substantial, certain to endure at least 20 years. Supposing he has the choice between two buildings which would satisfy a particular purpose equally well, one costing £3000 and likely to last only 10 years, and another, costing £4250, certain to last for 20. At first the latter would appear to be the obvious choice, since the former would cost £6000 over 20 years (being replaced after 10) and the latter only £4250. However, the farmer could invest a sum now to obtain the £3000 needed in 10 years' time to replace the cheaper building. At 7 per cent he would need to invest £1525 ($=3000/(1.07)^{10}$), making a total investment of £4525, compared with £4250 for the more durable building. But if he can earn 20 per cent on his capital on the farm he has only to invest £485 ($=3000/(1.20)^{10}$) now to get £3000 in 10 years' time, making a total investment of £3485, which is £765 less than the £4250 for the better building. It is true that inflation would affect the issue. If building costs rose by 5 per cent per annum the replacement would cost £4890 ($= 3000 \times (1.05)^{10}$) in 10 years' time and the farmer would need to invest £2485 now at 7 per cent, making a total of £5485, which is much more expensive than the better building. But at 20 per cent only £775 need be invested now to be worth £4890 in 10 years' time and the total cost for the two cheaper buildings would be only £3775. Furthermore, the building with the shorter life gives him greater flexibility: he may wish to change his methods, give up the enterprise or even give up farming after 10 years, or certainly before 20 years are up; or building techniques may improve.

Farmers are tempted, often quite rightly, to invest in multi-purpose rather than specialist buildings, for reasons of flexibility, particularly as their less specialised nature may also mean that they are cheaper. However, for some enterprises a specialist building may make a bigger profit for a farmer in 10 years than a cheaper flexible one in 20 or more. An example can be taken from pig fattening. Suppose a farmer wishes to fatten 240 baconers at a time. A specialised house costing £70 a pig with an economic life of 10 years gives an annual building cost, at 8 per cent interest, of £10.45 per pig space; the equivalent figure for a general-purpose type building costing £40 a pig with an economic life of 20 years is £4.10. But if the food conversion rate (kg of food per kg liveweight gain) in the former were 0.5 better than in the latter, the annual saving in feed costs would be approximately £10 per pig space, which well exceeds the extra building costs. The 'break-even' difference in conversion rate would be 0.3. Of course, if specialised fittings for general-purpose buildings were available which would give results as good as specialised buildings, the best of both worlds could be obtained. It also seems certain that the skill of the labour and management is a more important determinant of livestock profitability than the quality of the buildings; this is probably even truer of cattle than of pigs and poultry.

Labour saving

If expenditure on buildings is incurred mainly to save labour, it must be remembered that labour costs are low compared with feed costs, averaging, for example, approximately 6 per cent of output in pig fattening and egg production, compared with 75 to 85 per cent for feed (the cost of weaners or flock depreciation having been deducted in the calculation of output). It could therefore be very shortsighted to reduce labour if this resulted in a worsened feed conversion rate (unless, possibly, it enabled the herd to be expanded – see Chapter 5, p. 129). On the other hand, this is no excuse for wasted labour in livestock production. It may be easier to cut labour costs considerably than to make even a small reduction in feed costs, if opportunities for the latter have already been fully exploited. Any cost savings are significant where margins between receipts and total costs are narrow. Thus a 25 per cent saving in labour costs would increase average profits in pig production by some 15 per cent. Although there must come a point where labour is too fully 'stretched' and costly mistakes can occur, there is no clear correlation between labour hours per head of livestock and livestock performance. A farmer who is an indifferent labour manager is also very likely to be an indifferent feed manager. Many piggeries have a high labour usage, not because the pigs are particularly well looked after, but because either the building layout or work methods employed are poor.

The point needs to be made once more that labour-saving, to be economically worthwhile, must result either in a smaller staff or in more productive work done. The most effective way usually is to expand the enterprise on which building expenditure has been made, provided, of course, that the enterprise is profitable and its expansion represents the best use of available capital and other farm resources. This last point must be watched carefully in the case of grazing livestock. It is easy to underestimate the additional bulk fodder requirements of an enlarged herd of beef cattle or dairy cows and followers and thus overestimate the potential return.

Taxation

From the point of view of annual profits, the same basic point relating to tax arises with buildings as with machinery: tax relief is made through depreciation allowances, but any addition to profits made by the investment is subject to tax at the same marginal rate. For the landlord or owner-occupier, however, the possible effect on the value of the entire property has to be considered. The amount which a new building adds to the sale value of a farm is probably well below its written-down value, especially in the first few years. Nevertheless, if a high marginal rate of tax is being paid this increased value may be worthwhile; in the UK, furthermore, building expenditure can be deducted from the increased value of a property when calculating capital gains tax.

Other investment aspects

It happens to some extent with machinery, but even more so with buildings, that it is often very difficult, sometimes impossible, to quantify the benefits obtained. Implement sheds, for example, might be assumed to give a longer life and lower repair bills for the equipment housed, but it is rather pointless to attempt complicated calculations of return on capital. With improvements to the farmhouse, to take an extreme example, no economic measure of benefit is possible.

In such cases it has to be accepted that certain structures are part-and-parcel of the land, as are the farm roads and a certain amount of concrete or tarmac in the farmstead: these fixtures are part of the basic capital structure of the entire farm or estate and can only be regarded as such. A certain amount is necessary before the property can be farmed at all, and this also includes some of the directly productive buildings, such as cow accommodation on a heavy land farm in a high rainfall, all-grass, essentially dairying part of the country. These investments can only be considered as part of the land, and their annual cost can only be looked at, even by an owner-occupier, as part of the 'rent' for the farm as a whole. The question then is whether the farmer is capable of making a living from the land, paying that level of 'rent'. For someone buying bare land and trying to make a farm of it, the 'rent' will be the total annual charge he has to pay on the land and the minimum buildings required to farm it.

On an existing farm, where the buildings are almost derelict and the surface of the farmstead and roads are in a similarly poor condition, a farmer has three choices. He must either (*a*) be prepared to live with it and be able to make a sufficient living to keep him on the farm as it is, or (*b*) be both willing and able to improve the property and still be capable of making a living from it, or (*c*) give it up, either to someone more desperate to farm or someone with sufficient capital available to be able to afford the necessary expenditure. Such essential investments may or may not be replacements for almost worthless buildings, but they must be regarded in the same light. It may be difficult to make even an approximate calculation of the benefits of a new building compared with the one it is replacing, and the fact that it is likely to incorporate improvements as well as being a replacement (e.g. a new type of dairy parlour) complicates the comparison in any case. But sooner or later the building *has* to be replaced and the question then is whether the additional annual building costs can be covered by the profits from the enterprise, or possibly the whole farm.

Parts of the above discussion also relate to a final point, namely, that investments may not necessarily be made for economic reasons, whether related to a specific project or to the whole farm. Farmers who can afford it may choose to spend part of their income or capital to reduce anxiety, e.g. by having an exceptionally high capacity grain drier, or to make life easier, e.g. by having a fully automatic grain handling unit. Or, further, wealthy farmers and landowners or new entrants into agriculture may choose to spend part of their income or wealth on improving the amenity of a property or in possessing the latest idea in buildings and equipment, regardless of any potential economic benefit. There is little point in subjecting such investments to economic scrutiny: they are simply alternative ways of spending capital or income, like yachts or Caribbean holidays.

LAND

Renting versus buying

The main 'traditional' arguments in favour of owner-occupation are that it provides absolute security of tenure and freedom of action for the farmer: because he knows he will stay on the farm as long as he wishes he will 'farm for posterity'; furthermore, he is not subject to exploitation by excessive rents. In favour of the landlord–tenant system is the fact that much less capital is needed to farm – thus a person with farming skills but little capital is enabled to apply those skills; further points are that owner-occupiers may misallocate their financial resources between ownership and farming, and that the separation of functions of farm and estate management allows specialised skills to be used for each. Other arguments in favour of the landlord–tenant system, especially in relation to large estates, are that rent levels are more flexible than mortgages, which might help carry farmers more easily through periods of economic depression, and that enlightened landlords can help less well-educated tenants with ideas for farm improvement. From the national viewpoint, too, it could be argued that fear of eviction may provide a stronger motivation to farming the land well than security of tenure.

Some of these points have even greater validity in present-day conditions, others have far less. In the UK, legislation has given tenants and, to a large extent, their sons, almost complete security of tenure, freedom of cropping and fair rents. From the landlords' viewpoint, the reduction in their control, together with taxation and worsening economics of land ownership, have caused many to sell part or all of their land, or to farm more of their land themselves when their tenants leave the farm or die. Consequently the person with little capital has far less chance now of obtaining a farm. Very often land has been bought by sitting tenants. This is partly because they are able to buy the land relatively cheaply, since the non-vacant possession price is considerably below the price with vacant possession, partly because ownership ensures that their families can stay on the farm in perpetuity, and partly for other ownership advantages discussed later.

The difference in capital requirements and return on capital for owning land and farming are now considerable. The following figures are typical of UK farms exceeding 20 hectares in 1978:

	Capital Value per ha (£)	*Average Return per ha* (£)	*Return on capital* (%)
Land (including buildings, etc.)	3,000	30[a]	1
'Tenant's capital' (Livestock, machinery, etc.)	600	90[b]	15
Total (owner-occupier)	3,600	120	3.3

[a] Assuming a rent of £50 and ownership expenses of £20 per hectare.
[b] Management and investment income (see Chapter 20, p. 525).

Economics of buying land

Despite these figures, land is still being bought for farming. The reason is partly negative: it is difficult to obtain a farm to rent, especially without personal connections. Even if obtainable, the rents that have to be tendered are often at least double the average rent levels for sitting tenants; a high level of farming is required if such rents are to be afforded.

Yet to buy land at £3000 per ha, at a 12 per cent mortgage rate over 30 years, costs over £370 per ha per annum. This is more than treble the average return given above (£120 per ha). Of course it is not normally possible to borrow 100 per cent of the purchase price. But even if only one third is borrowed and the rest supplied from the purchaser's own funds, ignoring the interest forgone on that capital, a high level of farming would be needed to make the venture pay. It would probably mean farming at above average intensity, which would require far more tenant's capital than the average of £600 per ha stated above, particularly at the outset. Furthermore, money borrowed for tenant's capital also bears interest and has to be repaid.

Why then do people continue to invest in farmland? There are a number of reasons:

(i) Prestige (social standing),
(ii) Amenity and sporting value,
(iii) Capital transfer tax relief (in the UK),
(iv) Other (annual) tax benefits,
(v) Long-term stability of the real value of land (hedge against inflation),
(vi) Capital gains – including the speculative element (for example, the possibility of part of the land being sold for development – although development taxes could largely reduce the gains from the latter).

The last two are closely allied but not quite the same thing. Land prices in the UK increased eight-fold between 1960 and 1977 and twelve-fold between 1950 and 1977. This rise in value obviously adds substantially to the economic benefits of land ownership, even despite capital gains tax. However, this is of limited relevance to the person who has to earn his living from farming. He has to pay interest and mortgage repayments out of current income; growth in capital value will be of benefit only if he gives up farming or at least sells part of his land.

Farm enlargement

There is another very important factor, however. The discussion above relates to someone wishing to enter farming. Many farmers, of course, buy land for expansion. While some of the points listed above are still relevant, a number of new arguments apply:

(i) *Spreading fixed costs.* Often the extra land can be farmed with little extra in the way of regular labour and machinery, and possibly buildings. Certainly any increase is likely to be less than proportionate. This represents economies of size. (On the other hand it can also happen that a well integrated unit can become just a little too large and incur uneconomic 'jumps' in regular labour and equipment requirements.)

(ii) *Adjoining land infrequently available.* The knowledge that the chance to obtain adjoining land may occur only once or twice in a lifetime is often the deciding factor.

(iii) *Spreading the additional fixed charges.* A farmer who already owns his present farm outright often thinks of the extra mortgage as a 'rent' over the whole of his land. Economically this is false thinking – extra costs borne should be set against extra revenue earned. Nevertheless it is common practice, the extra rent calculation operating as a crude measure of feasibility.

(iv) *Tax relief on interest payments.* This could be a major factor for an existing farmer paying high marginal rates of tax, especially if his standard of living is satisfied at a lower income level.

(v) *Expanding future land base.* The farmer may well be looking to the future. Extra land will give him greater flexibility. He may anticipate that future technical developments could require a larger farm to derive full benefit from them. He may have sons who will wish to farm in the future.

(vi) *Expectation of further increase in land prices in future.* Bearing the points in (v) in mind, the farmer may feel the longer he delays expansion the higher will be the land price. Even if he thinks he may later decide that he does not want the extra land, he will feel fairly certain that the value of his capital will rise rather than fall as a result of acquiring it.

Economics of farm size

It is meaningless to generalise about an optimum farm size. This varies according to the type of farming, location, objectives and the managerial ability available. There are both advantages and disadvantages of large farms, which are described briefly below. Clearly the points for and against small farms are the same, but in reverse.

To take the advantages first. Economies of size are obtained (see Chapter 2, pp. 47–8): equipment can be used to its full capacity, thus reducing fixed costs per unit of production to the minimum. Large-scale, expensive, labour-saving specialist equipment can therefore be justified as well as afforded; this point increases in importance as labour becomes scarcer and more expensive. Specialist employees can concentrate their acquired skills and experience on a single enterprise instead of having to be Jacks-of-all-trades, with less time wasted moving from one job to another; furthermore, up to a point, the larger the enterprise, the lower the labour cost per unit of output. These technical benefits are accompanied by commercial-financial-marketing advantages. The larger producer has greater bargaining power and transport costs per unit are lower with large quantities: thus he is in a better position to obtain premiums in selling and discounts in buying. He can also more easily obtain credit. Another major advantage is that the large-scale producer has greater flexibility: he has a wider choice of enterprises, can more readily alter his policy with changing economic and personal circumstances, and can – if circumstances allow – opt for a low cost–low output policy more easily than his small-scale neighbour, assuming the latter has only his farm to provide him with a living. Finally, the farmer can become a specialist manager, or afford to employ a specialist manager, instead of having to combine manual and managerial duties.

On the other hand, less individual care and attention is possible on the larger farm; this is especially important in agriculture because of its high dependence on nature and the consequently ever-changing circumstances, which require frequent and quick decisions. Control is more difficult, with men employed over a wider area, and perhaps several jobs going on at once. A system of assistant or joint managers and, or, foremen can provide the necessary control, but only at a greater cost per unit of production than the smaller-scale farmer working alongside his men much of the time. Thus managerial and office overheads will almost certainly be higher on the large farm. There is also more risk of wasted resources and yield losses because of the diminished control. Finally, farmers can often expand only by adding land scattered over a wide area, because of the infrequency with which opportunities for obtaining adjoining land occur; this again adds to transport costs and the difficulties of supervision and control. Obviously these potential disadvantages can be minimised by first-class top-level management.

Appendix 4.1: Taxation allowances on machinery and buildings

Taxation allowances vary widely from country to country and from year to year. No attempt will, therefore, be made here to explain what the current allowances are; instead we shall simply illustrate the main types. In the UK these are normally referred to as wear-and-tear (or annual), initial and investment allowances. Where capital (investment) grants are paid, which are straight cash rebates to offset the initial cost of a machine, the allowances are made on the net cost after grant.

In the UK, wear-and-tear allowances on machinery are calculated by the diminishing balances method (see p. 86): a constant percentage of the written-down value is allowed against tax each year. (However, for some time 100 per cent has been allowed in the first year.) On buildings, allowances are made on a straight-line basis (see p. 86).

An initial allowance is an additional percentage given in the year of purchase. It may be optional. The allowance is deducted in arriving at the value of the machine on which wear-and-tear allowances are made after the first year.

An investment allowance, also, is normally made in the year of purchase. It differs from an initial allowance in that it is not used to

TABLE 4.5. *Tax allowances on machinery*

	Wear-and-tear allowance only		Initial allowance		Investment allowance		Initial and investment allowance	
Year 1	ATA	WDV	ATA	WDV	ATA	WDV	ATA	WDV
	500	1,500	600[a]		200[b]		600[a]	
			500		500		200[b]	
			1,100	900	700	1,500	500	
							1,300	900
Year 2	375	1,125	225	675	375	1,125	225	675
Year 3	281	844	169	506	281	844	169	506

Example: machine costing £2,000 (after any capital grant): investment allowance (where made) 10 per cent; initial allowance (where made) 30 per cent; annual wear-and-tear allowance 25 per cent.

ATA = annual tax allowances. WDV = written-down value.
[a] = initial allowance;
[b] = investment allowance; all others are wear-and-tear allowances.
After year 3, the annual tax allowance simply continues at 25 per cent (the assumed wear-and-tear allowance) of the written-down value.

reduce the written-down value on which the annual wear-and-tear allowances are subsequently made. Thus, when applied to buildings, for example, if the rate were 10 per cent, allowances would be obtained on 110 per cent of the initial cost, over 10 years.

All three types of allowance are illustrated for machinery in Table 4.5.

Tax adjustments are usually made when the machine is sold, to allow for the difference between sale price and written-down value. Thus, if in the example in Table 4.5 the machine were sold towards the end of the 3rd year for £1000, a sum, called a *balancing charge* in the UK, would be deducted from total machinery tax allowances. In the example, the sum would be either £156 (£1000 – 844) or £494 (£1000 – £506). If, on the other hand, the sale price were *below* the written-down value (say £400), an extra tax allowance would be made to make up the difference. This is called a *balancing allowance*, which in the example would amount to either £444 (£844 – £400) or £106 (£506 – £400).

Appendix 4.2: Systems simulation as an aid to machinery selection

Much interest has been shown in recent years in *systems research*, or the *systems approach* to problem-solving. By a *system* is meant a combination of interrelated factors which can be considered separately from other systems. It is argued that studying parts of a system in isolation, without considering what happens to the whole complex, is bound to be inadequate. Furthermore, most systems have dynamic, or 'time-dependent', elements, that is, the state of the system will change over time; they are also frequently affected by uncontrollable elements, so that future outcomes cannot be predicted with certainty.

Simulation methods can be used to examine the working of a system. First a model is developed or synthesised to represent the 'real world' system being studied. This is necessary because it is usually impossible or impractical to experiment on the actual system itself. Secondly, the model is used, normally with the aid of a computer, to predict the behaviour of the system, that is, to study the effects of changes in its structure or of different management policies. Such study, known as *systems simulation*, may be used to determine improved managerial policies, or to detect particularly sensitive points in the system (variations in which have a very important effect on its operation and which therefore warrant especially firm control), or to design entirely new systems. The term *systems analysis* is given to the observation and experimental part of the approach, that is, the attempt to explain the detailed structure of the system, while the term *systems synthesis* is used for the constructive part – the design and control of modified or wholly new systems, using the knowledge gained from the analysis.

It could reasonably be argued that techniques described in Part III of this book, such as linear programming, must then be considered to be simulation methods, since they, too, use a model to represent a system (e.g. a farm) on which 'experiments' can be carried out to try to devise an improved system. However, the term 'simulation' is usually reserved for situations where the models involved differ from those used in recognised mathematical programming techniques. Furthermore, the time-dependent and uncertainty aspects are likely to be incorporated, which is in contrast to the static and deterministic approach of at least some of the techniques described in Part III (see Chapter 17, p. 413).

Systems simulation has been used to a limited extent for decisions regarding the choice of machinery, either in a given farm situation or for general guidance in a specific region. A model is constructed which combines the relevant variables and their interaction to represent reality. To take an example, the operation for which the approach has been mainly used is grain harvesting.[1] The variables included are: biological tolerances – crop yield, shedding losses; weather constraints – harvest time limits, rain-free days, moisture content; and machine performance – rate of work, operating hours per day. For some of these variables a range of values, instead of a single value, is included, e.g. the number of rain-free days, the rate of work[2].

A large number of 'trials' are then run on the computer, possibly 1000 or more, over a range of areas and seasons. In each run values are selected at random from the range of each distribution and the effect on total harvesting costs is calculated using the interactions between the variables. A range of results over *n* simulated harvest years

[1] See, for example; Donaldson, G. F. (1970) *Optimum Harvesting Systems for Cereals*. School of Rural Economics and Related Studies, Wye College, University of London. van Kampen, J. H. (1971) 'Farm Machinery Selection and Weather Uncertainty' Chapter 14 in Dent, J. B. and Anderson, J. R. (eds.) *Systems Analysis in Agriculture*. John Wiley and Sons Australasia Pty. See also Chapters 1 and 2 on systems analysis and simulation in general.

[2] These are known as 'stochastic' variables, and when a frequency distribution (i.e. the number of times each value is likely to occur) can be defined the situation is described as being 'probabilistic'. This is in contrast to the 'deterministic' approach, when a single value only is given, with assumed certainty.

is thus obtained, from which the mean value, range and frequency distribution can be measured. This procedure can be repeated for a number of different harvesting systems, varying the size of combine-harvester and associated grain drying unit. The results are then used as an aid in deciding which harvesting system to select in any given situation.

Whatever the merits of this method, however, it takes a long time to construct the model. Variables have to be quantified, often including frequency distributions, and the interactions between them have to be accurately established. The research involved certainly helps in understanding how the system works and in determining the most important variables, but it is too expensive to be used for the individual farm – unless most of the relationships have already been specified in the construction of previous models. Where general guidelines are provided, the final choice has still to be made by the manager using his judgement – although the result of his choice and the alternatives will have been made clear to him, assuming the model has been fully and accurately defined.

Appendix 4.3: Machinery replacement – the principle of 'holding cost'[1]

Apart from fuel and servicing, which in this analysis are taken to be constant per hour of use regardless of age, the main costs of owning and operating a machine, excluding interest on capital, are depreciation and repairs. The combination of capital cost (i.e. initial cost) plus total repair costs to date gives the 'holding cost' of a machine. Given that repair costs per hour increase with age, the holding cost curve will be as shown (*AB*) in Figure 4.10*A*, *OA* being the initial cost. The horizontal axis can represent either hours of work or age in years (with constant hours of use per annum the same scale could represent both). Assuming no trade-in value (scrap value would simply lower the curve *AB* slightly and not affect the argument) the minimum cost per-hour (or year) is obtained by replacing the machine after *Y* hours (or years), *X* being the point where the line *OC* is tangential to the curve *AB*. Here the holding

[1] The term was first used by Fox, A. H., 'The Theory of Second-Hand Markets'. *Economica*, **XXIV**, No. 94, May 1957. It was illustrated and developed for farm machinery by Dunford, W. J. and Rickard, R. C., 'The Timing of Machinery Replacement'. *Journal of Agric. Econ.*, **XIV**, No.3, May 1961. See also Mathieson, M. C., 'A Comment' and 'A Rejoinder' by Dunford and Rickard in *Journal of Agric. Econ.*, **XIV**, No. 4, Dec. 1961.

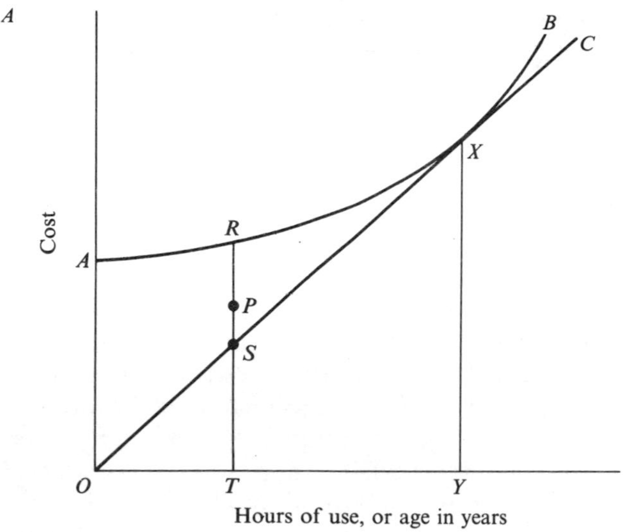

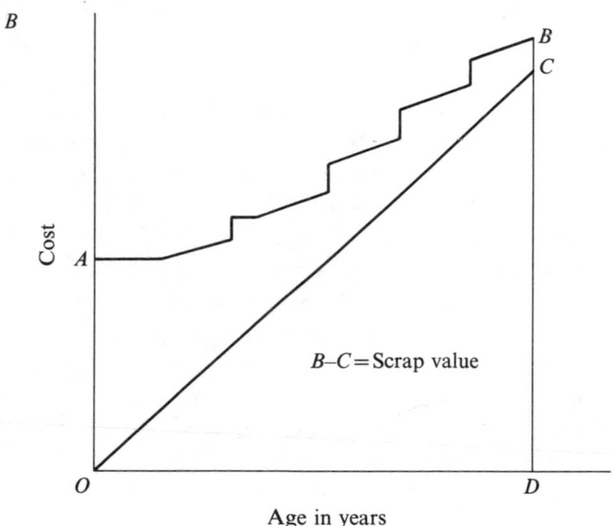

Fig. 4.10 The principle of holding cost

cost per hour (or year) is £XY/OY hours (or years). In order for the combined cost of depreciation and repairs to be lowered by trading the machine in earlier, the trade-in value would have to exceed the difference in vertical height between the holding cost curve AB and the line OX at any given age or number of hours worked. Thus, at OT the trade-in value must equal at least RS, if the cost is to be lowered.

Other factors, however, may affect the decision, as outlined in the main text of this chapter (pp. 100–1). These include some types of tax allowance, improvements in the machine's performance, the risk of breakdowns, or simply personal preference for a new machine. To return to the above example, if a trade-in value of less than RS is accepted (e.g. RP), the value of the estimated benefits should exceed the difference (PS) for the replacement to be worthwhile.

Two difficulties arise over this analysis. First, repair costs per hour of use may not rise continually, but may be low at first and then become constant, so that no point of tangency; as shown in Figure 4.10*A*; can be obtained. Secondly, repair costs tend in practice to rise in 'jumps' (e.g. when new tyres or a major overhaul are needed) but, again, possibly with no tendency to rise (when 'smoothed') over time. However, the same basic analysis can still be used, the lowest cost still being achieved by replacing where initial cost plus cumulative repair costs less trade-in value is at its lowest. The relevant diagram, which incorporates a scrap value for the machine ($= DB - DC$), is shown in Figure 4.10*B*. If the trade-in value at any age is never as high as the difference in vertical height between the lines OC and AB, the lowest cost is achieved by keeping the machine until it is beyond repair, say after D years. Since repair costs are a function partly of hours of use per year and partly of age in years, the exact shape of the line AB will vary with different intensities of use (i.e. hours of work per annum).

Operations analysis techniques have been developed to tackle the replacement problem. At their most straightforward they use only simple arithmetic. Total depreciation at any given date (which is the original cost less the declining trade-in value) is added to the cumulative total of repairs and the age is found at which this total cost per year is at its lowest; this procedure has close affinities to the holding-cost principle just described. More complex procedures exist, incorporating discounting, but these are too long and complicated to describe in the context of this book. In any case their usefulness is limited by the number of unquantifiable factors involved and the difficulty in predicting even those factors that *are* quantifiable, such as future costs.

Appendix 4.4: Further tables on machinery costs.

TABLE 4.6. *Annual machinery costs per hectare, 1976–7.*

Farm type	Deprecia-tion (£)	Repairs, VTI (£)	Fuel and Elec. (£)	Contract (£)	Total (£)
Mainly dairying					
under 60 ha	13.2	39.3	26.4	13.4	92.3
60–120 ha	12.4	25.6	15.8	13.4	67.2
over 120 ha	10.8	21.8	15.7	10.5	58.8
Mainly arable					
under 100 ha	13.4	20.6	14.6	19.8	68.4
100–200 ha	13.8	20.6	11.3	6.6	52.3
over 200 ha	13.5	18.7	10.0	7.7	49.9
Dairy and arable					
under 200 ha	21.2	31.5	20.0	11.1	83.8
over 200 ha	12.9	19.9	13.9	10.3	57.0
Mainly sheep/cattle					
under 100 ha	5.6	12.8	7.8	9.8	36.0
over 100 ha	10.5	15.4	10.0	4.8	40.7
Sheep/cattle and arable					
under 100 ha	9.0	17.6	9.4	11.4	47.4
over 100 ha	11.2	17.7	11.4	6.0	46.3
Intensive arable					
(field vegetables)	23.5	40.4	23.1	15.4	102.4

VTI = vehicle tax and insurance.

Source: *Farm Business Statistics for South-East England* (Supplement for 1978). Wye College, University of London.

TABLE 4.7. *Annual machinery costs per tractor unit, 1976–7*

Farm type	Deprecia-tion (p)	Repairs, VTI (p)	Fuel and Elec. (p)	Contract (p)	Total (£)
Mainly dairying					
under 60 ha	40	115	80	43	2.78
60–120 ha	50	97	62	51	2.60
over 120 ha	45	90	65	39	2.39
Mainly arable					
under 100 ha	58	87	66	84	2.95
100–200 ha	62	91	49	30	2.32
over 200 ha	57	77	42	31	2.07
Dairy and arable					
under 200 ha	69	114	73	42	2.98
over 200 ha	56	88	61	48	2.53
Mainly sheep/cattle					
under 100 ha	28	66	42	49	1.85
over 100 ha	42	65	41	22	1.70
Sheep/cattle and arable					
under 100 ha	41	81	43	52	2.17
over 100 ha	47	74	47	25	1.93
Intensive arable					
(field vegetables)	65	101	58	46	2.70

VTI = vehicle tax and insurance.

Source: *Farm Business Statistics for South-East England* (Supplement for 1978). Wye College, University of London.

TABLE 4.8. *Machinery valuations per hectare, 1976–7.*

	(£)		(£)
Mainly dairying		Dairy and arable	
under 60 ha	152	under 200 ha	173
60–120 ha	113	over 200 ha	111
over 120 ha	104	Mainly sheep/cattle	
Mainly arable		under 100 ha	60
under 100 ha	124	over 100 ha	94
100–200 ha	123	Sheep/cattle and arable	
over 200 ha	116	under 100 ha	88
Intensive arable (field vegetables)	209	over 100 ha	102

Source: *Farm Business Statistics for South-East England* (Supplement for 1978). Wye College, University of London.

TABLE 4.9. *Estimated useful life of machinery* (years)

Equipment	Annual use (hours)				
	25	50	100	200	300
Group 1					
Ploughs, cultivators, toothed harrows, hoes, rolls, ridgers, simple potato planting attachments, grain cleaners	12+	12+	12+	12	10
Group 2					
Disc harrows, corn drills, binders, grain drying machines, food grinders and mixers	12+	12+	12	10	8
Group 3					
Combine harvesters, pick-up balers, rotary cultivators, hydraulic loaders	12+	12+	12	9	7
Group 4					
Mowers, forage harvesters, swath turners, side-delivery rakes, tedders, hedge cutting machines, semi-automatic potato planters and transplanters, unit root drills, mechanical root thinners	12+	12	11	8	6
Group 5					
Fertiliser distributors, combine drills, farmyard manure spreaders, elevator potato diggers, spraying machines, pea cutter-windrowers	10	10	9	8	7
Miscellaneous					
Beet harvesters	11	10	9	6	5
Potato harvesters	—	8	7	5	—
Milking machinery	—	—	—	12	10

	Annual use (hours)					
	500	750	1,000	1,500	2,000	2,500
Tractors	12+	12	10	7	6	5
Electric motors	12+	12+	12+	12+	12	12

Source: Culpin, C. (1968) *Profitable Farm Mechanisation.* Crosby Lockwood & Son.

TABLE 4.10. *Depreciation: average annual fall in value* (per cent of new price)

Frequency of renewal (years)	Complex. High depreciation rate e.g. potato harvesters, mobile pea viners, etc.	Established machines with many moving parts, e.g. tractors, combines, balers, forage harvesters	Simple equipment with few moving parts, e.g. ploughs, trailers
	(%)	(%)	(%)
1	34	26	19
2	24½	19½	14½
3	20[a]	16½[a]	12½
4	17½[b]	14½	11½
5	15[c]	13[b]	10½[a]
6	13½	12	9½
7	12	11	9
8	11	10[c]	8½[b]
9	(10)	9½	8
10	(9½)	8½	7½[c]

[a]Typical frequency of renewal with heavy use.
[b]Typical frequency of renewal with average use.
[c]Typical frequency of renewal with light use.
Source: Baker V., University of Bristol.

TABLE 4.11. *Estimated annual cost of spares and repairs as a percentage of purchase price*[a] *at various levels of use*

	Approximate annual use (hours)				Additional use per 100 hours ADD
	500	750	1,000	1,500	
	(%)	(%)	(%)	(%)	(%)
Tractors	5	6.7	8.0	10.5	0.5

	Approximate annual use (hours)				Additional use per 100 hours ADD
	50	100	150	200	
	(%)	(%)	(%)	(%)	(%)
Harvesting machinery					
Combine harvesters, self-propelled and engine driven	1.5	2.5	3.5	4.5	2.0
Combine harvesters, pto. driven, metered-chop forage harvesters, pick-up balers, potato harvesters, sugar beet harvesters	3.0	5.0	6.0	7.0	2.0
Other implements and machines					
Group 1					
Ploughs, cultivators, toothed harrows, hoes, elevator potato diggers } Normal soils	4.5	8.0	11.0	14.0	6.0
Group 2					
Rotary cultivators, mowers, binders, pea cutter-windrowers	4.0	7.0	9.5	12.0	5.0
Group 3					
Disc harrows, fertiliser distributors, farmyard manure spreaders, combine drills, potato planters with fertiliser attachment, sprayers, hedge-cutting machines	3.0	5.5	7.5	9.5	4.0
Group 4					
Swath turners, tedders, side-delivery rakes, unit drills, flail forage harvesters, semi-automatic potato planters and trans-planters, down-the-row thinners	2.5	4.5	6.5	8.5	4.0
Group 5					
Corn drills, milking machines, hydraulic loaders, simple potato planting attachments	2.0	4.0	5.5	7.0	3.0
Group 6					
Grain driers, grain cleaners, rolls, hammer mills, feed mixers, threshers	1.5	2.0	2.5	3.0	0.5

[a]When it is known that a high purchase price is due to high quality and durability, or a low price corresponds to a high rate of wear and tear, adjustments to the figures should be made.

Source: Culpin, C. (1968). *Profitable Farm Mechanisation*. Crosby Lockwood & Son.

5: The organisation of labour

Labour costs – including the value of the farmer's own manual labour – average 20 to 30 per cent of total costs on a high proportion of farm types, including those where dairying, cereal production and beef and sheep are major enterprises. The proportion is highest on intensive arable and fruit farms, where it can be as much as 40 per cent.

Special features of farm labour as a resource

As one of the basic farm resources, labour has certain special features, although the first two mentioned below are not unique to this particular factor of production.

First, the service of regular labour is supplied as a continuous flow. It cannot be stored until wanted, like seed or fertiliser. If labour is unused at any time it is wasted for good.

Secondly, regular labour comes in 'indivisible' units. It is not possible to hire half a man. This point is of special relevance in agriculture because of the small numbers employed on the majority of farms. Most farmers who employ any workers at all have only one or two men. 'Saving a man' is thus a very different proposition compared with a factory employing thousands of workers. Some flexibility is provided, however, by the use of overtime and the employment of casual or contract labour. From the cost standpoint too, the employment of a proportion of youths or women adds flexibility.

Thirdly, on a high proportion of farms some of the manual labour, often all, is supplied by the farmer himself.

Fourthly, and most important of all, is the human factor, about which more will be said at the end of this chapter. Apart from questions of man management, social or sentimental reasons often limit a farmer's scope for achieving greater economic efficiency. In particular, older workers are often retained because they (and possibly their forefathers) have been on the farm for a long time, even if it could be run better and more profitably without them. The importance attached to these aspects, and the constraints thereby imposed, clearly vary from farmer to farmer.

Various ways of *measuring the efficiency of labour use* are described and discussed in Chapter 20 (pp. 535–7). To summarise here, labour cost per ha, even when compared with farms of a similar type and size, is at best a crude measure, because differences in system intensity are not taken into account. Net output per £100 labour is affected by many factors which have little or nothing to do with labour efficiency. Labour efficiency indices based wholly on physical measures – thus eliminating the financial aspects – are weakened by the inadequacy of the enterprise standards employed. Other indices combine physical measures of labour requirements and the level of wages paid.

Farm output, enterprise efficiency and labour use

Output comprises yield and price. In general, labour requirements are increased relatively little when higher yields result from factors other than increased inputs of labour itself, such as soil fertility. There is some impact on harvesting: heavier crops of potatoes, for example, need more loading and carting, but hand picking time is determined by the number of tubers rather than their size.

It is the *marginal* return to labour that is important in decisions concerning the size of labour force to employ, not the possible effect on net output per £100 labour, which, as is pointed out in Chapter 20 (p. 528), depicts an *average* relationship only. Suppose, for example, a farmer at present has a net output of £22,500 and a labour cost of £7500. He estimates that by employing another man, at a cost of £3250, net output can be increased by £5500, from which £4250 extra costs must be deducted (including labour, but excluding the additional bought feed and seed already deducted in the calculation of net output). Thus he will be £1250 better off. That this has happened despite the net output per £100 labour having fallen from £300 to just over £260 emphasises the fact that comparative efficiency ratios based on *average* relationships may be misleading as guides to future action to increase profitability. The example illustrated above can occur especially on arable farms, when high output arable crops such as potatoes or vegetables are introduced or expanded, these being particularly labour-consuming enterprises.

It may be false economy to attempt to manage with less labour if, as a consequence, yield levels fall or feed efficiency suffers. For example, increasing dairy cows from 70 to 100 per man could reduce labour costs per cow from £72 to £65, but this would be offset by a loss in yield of as little as 65 litres (less than $1\frac{1}{2}$ per cent). With bacon pigs, a reduction of 0.1 in the feed conversion rate means a fall of some £1500 in the profit made on 2000 bacon pigs a year – a typical output for one pigman in labour-saving buildings. Thus it may be worthwhile to pay higher wages for extra skill or to employ some casual or part-time labour to enable the stockman to devote more time to the stock, instead of spending his time on drudge work such as slurry clearing.

The 'indivisible' nature of the regular labour resource does however complicate the problem. Thus if a farmer expanded from 70 to 100 cows and took on another cowman, costing £4000 a year, the additional cost compared with paying more to the one cowman could be £25 or more per head, which is equal in value to some 240 litres a cow. The 'jumps' in labour cost per head that occur as the number of men is increased are illustrated in Figure 5.1. The one-man-labour-cost-per-cow curve illustrates economies of size; these are large at first but gradually level out until the cost reduction for extra cows becomes small. However, even if a yield loss of 200 litres a cow is anticipated, it is still cheaper to have one man rather than two with 100 cows, if the one man can cope. Obviously the type of parlour and other buildings and the impact of the expansion on the rest of the farm economy are other vital aspects to be taken into account. This problem does not arise, however, when expansion is in terms of extra 'man units' (say of 70 or 80 cows each) at a time.

Similar issues may arise with an expansion in the size of a pig herd.

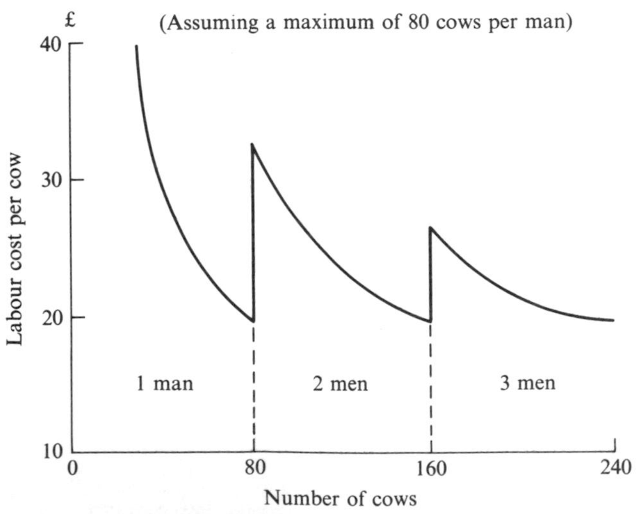

Fig. 5.1. Labour cost per cow and herd size

A fall in feed conversion efficiency as a result of expansion with only one pigman employed is not necessarily uneconomic, even if the increase in food cost per pig exceeds the saving in labour cost per pig. Two comparisons need to be made: one with the expansion assuming a second man is employed, the other with the existing situation, i.e. with no expansion. To illustrate from Table 5.1, *A* is the existing situation. In *B*, the food conversion rate and profit per pig are worsened, but the total profit is better than for *A* or *E* (two men). In *C*, however, the food conversion ratio is further worsened, so that, even though the profit is still increased above the present figure (*A*), it would be better to employ a second man (*E*). In *D*, the worsening in feed conversion rate is so great that total profit is reduced.

With crops the problem incorporates the seasonal aspects of production. For example, in the case of sugar beet, suppose chemical weed control plus mechanisation of spring hoeing, with virtually no hand work, reduces yields by five tonnes per ha, causing a loss of output of £100 per ha after allowing for transport costs saved. With 20 hectares of sugar beet there is thus a £2000 loss of crop. The factors determining whether or not this would pay were discussed in the previous chapter (pp. 94–5). Savings in casual labour costs may offset this loss. Or, if the farm could be run with one regular man less, the change would be worthwhile. Possibly the labour saving would enable more high gross margin crops to be grown, including additional sugar beet if an extra quota is obtainable.

Output can also be increased by achieving higher prices. The amount

TABLE 5.1. *Illustration of labour performance in pig production*

	A	*B*	*C*	*D*	*E*
Number of men	1	1	1	1	2
Number of pigs per year	1,400	2,100	2,100	2,100	2,100
Assumed food conversion rate					
(kg food per kg liveweight gain)	3.40	3.50	3.55	3.60	3.35
	(£)	(£)	(£)	(£)	(£)
Output per pig	35.00	35.00	35.00	35.00	35.00
Labour cost per pig	2.50	1.90	1.90	1.90	3.20
Food costs per pig	26.52	27.30	27.69	28.08	26.13
Other costs per pig	4.00	4.00	4.00	4.00	4.00
Total costs per pig	33.02	33.20	33.59	33.98	33.33
Profit per pig	1.98	1.80	1.41	1.02	1.67
Total profit	2.772	3,780	2,961	2.142	3.507

of labour used for an enterprise is likely to have a minor influence on price compared with other factors, such as variety or breed, and skill or date of selling. Often there is no labour effect at all. Two examples may be quoted however: rogueing may affect grain price, and extra time and care in handling and riddling could affect potato prices. These examples preclude raising prices through fulfilling part of the marketing function, e.g. pre-packing potatoes, grading apples, or selling eggs direct to the consumer. In some cases such work may be undertaken without raising total farm labour costs, by making use of labour not fully employed.

Other factors affecting labour productivity

Many factors determine the output per £100 labour costs on a farm, apart from yields and prices. These factors are: capital expenditure on machinery and buildings; enterprise size; field size and shape; soil type; seasonality of labour requirements; employment of casual labour; work organisation; wage levels; man management. They mainly affect the cost side, but the last two in particular also affect output.

Capital expenditure

Labour substitution by capital expenditure in the form of machinery or buildings has already been fully discussed in Chapter 4. The point particularly to be stressed is that for this to be economic labour costs must actually be reduced – by saving casual labour or decreasing the size of the regular labour force – or the labour saved must be used to increase output. Simple comparisons between the annual extra costs of buildings and machinery and the saving in labour-hours multiplied by wage costs per hour are virtually meaningless for the purpose of aiding decisions on the individual farm.

The efficiency measure net output per £100 labour makes no allowance for such capital expenditure, and other labour efficiency measures make very little. Obviously a farmer who has spent considerable sums on high output machinery or labour-saving buildings should have a much better labour efficiency figure than one who has spent very little. Net output per £100 labour and machinery does at least allow also for machinery expenditure.

Enterprise size

Up to a point, the larger an enterprise the lower are labour costs per ha or per head (see also above, p. 128). One reason is that most farm jobs require a fixed element of time regardless of the number of hectares or livestock. This is the time needed to get to the place where the job has to be done, size up the task, prepare the machinery or materials required, and perhaps make adjustments once the work begins. A similar set time is needed at the end of the task, to clean the parlour and units after milking, for example. The actual work itself, while in operation, varies more or less in direct proportion to the number of hectares or livestock – given the conditions and equipment available. This is illustrated in Figure 5.2.

However, the above point is not always sufficient in itself to explain the very high labour inputs per head that can arise in small livestock units, especially when run by the farmer, possibly with the help of his family. Often the building layout and ancillary equipment are extremely poor from the point of view of saving labour, but in addition the unit is frequently a full-time occupation only because there is no other work to do and either no means or no desire to increase the size of the unit.

Larger enterprises also allow more specialisation and the opportunity to acquire additional skills, compared with the Jack-of-all-trades moving from one enterprise to another throughout the day. Thus labour costs per unit of output as measured by weight of crop or litre of milk may fall even faster than when production is measured by hectares or cows. On the other hand, as has been discussed already in this chapter, results may deteriorate if the labour becomes over-

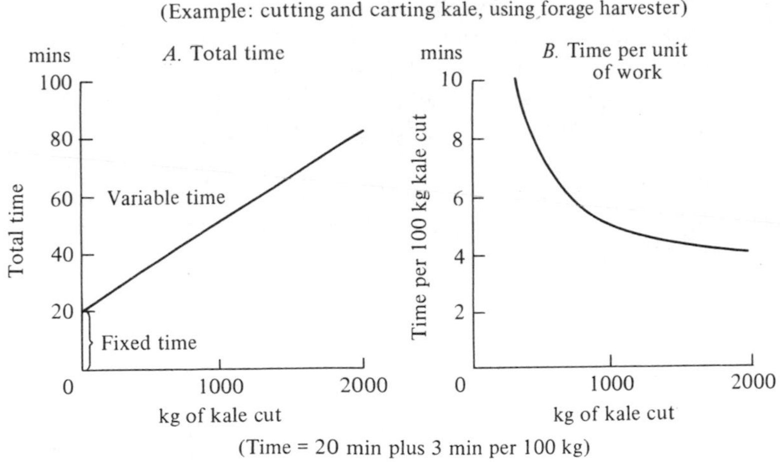

Fig. 5.2. Effect of fixed time on work-rates

extended, in which case labour costs per unit of output could begin to rise after a point. Livestock studies have demonstrated the former effect but not the latter. Smaller units are often shown to have poorer outputs per head of livestock than larger units. It is not however known how much of this is due to differences in labour skill and how much to other factors, especially managerial ability. As regards the possibility of worsening results with very large size, common sense would suggest that this must happen after a point, but there is little if any factual evidence to support the view.

Field shape and size

There are four benefits from combining small fields into larger fields: saving time on field operations; reducing the time and money spent on hedging or fencing; reducing the percentage of unproductive land in hedgerows and headlands; and reducing infestation from hedgerow weeds and the number of birds and animals feeding on the crops. On the other hand larger fields may make the control of stocking rate and pasture management more difficult and expensive and reduce the protection from the elements accorded by hedgerows to livestock and sometimes to crops and soils. There are also the ecological and aesthetic aspects to be considered.

The advantages decline as field size increases. The main benefits are derived from removing really small fields, of less than 2 hectares. Above 8 hectares the proportionate benefits become small, in terms of both loss of productive land and work time. However, the shape of the field is very important, and in fact row length is more significant than area with regrad to work time. There is little saving with a length exceeding 500 metres (N.B. 500 metres × 200 metres = 10 hectares). Beyond this, such problems as re-filling drills in the middle of fields instead of on the headlands begin to proliferate.

Other factors

The other factors affecting labour productivity listed at the beginning of this section are discussed in detail in the remaining sections of this chapter.

Planning farm labour requirements

The standard man-days calculation

In some cases the number of regular workers required to run a farm is obvious – particularly with smallish areas. Where this needs to be calculated, however, the simplest method is by using 'standard man-

TABLE 5.2. *Standard man-day calculation of labour requirements*

250 ha farm:		SMD
140 ha of cereals (straw burnt)	× 2 =	280
40 ha of cereals (straw baled)	× 3 =	120
20 ha of potatoes	× 28 =	560
50 ha of grazing	× 1 =	50
500 ewes	× 0.5 =	250
	Total	1,260
Less: casual labour for potato picking, 20 × 12 =		240
		1,020
Plus: 15 per cent (of regular labour requirement) for maintenance		153
Total SMD (regular workers)		1,173
1,173 ÷ 300 (per man) = 3.9		

The number of regular workers required is therefore 4, or 3 if the farmer works manually most of the time.

days' (once called 'man-work units'). A standard man-day is eight hours of work supplied by an average worker. In the UK the numbers of standard man-days required (per annum) per hectare for the different crops, and per head, for various categories of livestock, are listed in university and Ministry farm data publications. The total number of standard man-days needed for the farm is calculated by multiplying the hectares of crops and numbers of livestock by their respective standard man-day requirements. The number of days supplied by casual labour is deducted and 15 per cent is added for general maintenance work. It is assumed that a man provides 300 standard man-days annually. Allowance is made for any manual labour supplied by the farmer himself. An example is given in Table 5.2. Alternatively, no addition is made for maintenance work and stockmen are assumed to provide 300 standard man-days a year and other workers 250, the difference being explained by the limitations on fieldwork imposed by natural factors.

This method has the advantage of simplicity and it can be used to give at least a quick and general idea of labour requirements. It does however suffer from a number of major inadequacies.

Criticisms of the standard man-day calculation

First, as regards livestock enterprises, the number of stockmen required for housed animals depends largely on the type, condition and layout of the buildings, together with the equipment and work methods employed. Some small units may be dealt with by field workers or the farmer part-time; others require one or more full-time stockmen. In other words it is necessary to think in terms either of units employing one man or more, with or without assistance from other staff or the farmer, or supplementary enterprises run by the farmer, field-workers or general farm workers part-time.

Secondly – and particularly important – labour requirements vary considerably during the year, from season to season. This is especially true of crops. The exception is livestock housed all the year round, when labour needs are fairly evenly spread; but even these often have occasional peaks that have to be considered, e.g. manure disposal.

Thirdly, the requirements depend on the type and size of machines being used. To give an extreme example, operating a small bagger combine may require over 7 man-hours per hectare, whereas a large capacity tanker combine may need less than one man-hour per hectare.

Fourthly, labour requirements vary according to the type of soil. There are two effects here: one is the time taken for an operation, the other is the time available. Regarding the former, there is little or no difference for many jobs, e.g. drilling or rolling, but others, such as ploughing and cultivating, are affected. It is the difference in time available that is the more important. The heavy land farmer requires more men and machines – or at least higher capacity machines – to do a given amount of work, because he has a shorter period when soil conditions are suitable.

There are also variations between men themselves, their rate of work and their willingness to work overtime, and lesser points such as field size.

Seasonality

In order to allow for seasonality, requirements can be estimated for different periods of the year; these can be illustrated graphically on a labour profile. Usually calendar months are taken, but four-weekly, half-monthly or two-weekly periods are acceptable alternatives. The shorter the period the more accurate is the profile, but there is also a danger of suggesting over-rigidity, whereas for many jobs there is some flexibility as to timing. It is not essential to cover the whole year; it is the peak periods that are important from most aspects. Not only current peaks but those that may occur with a change in system are relevant. Examples of data requirements are given in Table 5.3, for the

TABLE 5.3. *Examples of labour-hours per month* (premium levels)

	Winter wheat (excl. straw) (per ha)	Spring barley (excl. straw) (per ha)	Straw baling and carting (per ha)	Maincrop potatoes[a] (per ha)	Grass[b] (for grazing only) (per ha)	Sheep (per ewe)
January	—	—	—	—	—	0.25
February	—	—	—	—	—	0.25
March	0.4	3.8	—	3.1	0.7	0.75
April	0.9	0.4	—	4.4	0.7	0.3
May	—	0.4	—	0.9	0.4	0.25
June	—	—	—	—	0.4	0.3
July	—	—	—	1.1	0.4	0.15
August	2.0	2.7	2.8	0.7	0.2	0.15
September	2.0	—	2.1	9.1	0.2	0.15
October	4.5	0.7	—	36.5	—	0.15
November	0.9	1.3	—	6.5	—	0.15
December	—	0.7	—	0.7	—	0.15

[a]Excluding casual labour on harvester and riddling, bagging and loading.
[b]Assuming undersown three-year leys.
Source: Nix J. (1977) *Farm Management Pocketbook* (eighth edition). Wye College, University of London.

enterprises in the earlier 250-hectare farm example (Table 5.2). The results are illustrated in Figure 5.3. The labour available varies seasonally according to the effect of bad weather and the amount of overtime that can be worked in daylight.

On an existing farm with labour records (see Chapter 19, pp. 503–4) the farm's own data can be used. Where standard data are used all but the second of the criticisms made of the standard man-day calculation can be levelled also at the labour profile.[1] The breakdown of work requirements according to the time of year does however facilitate adjustments for special conditions.

Reducing labour peaks

The following are ways in which a labour peak may be reduced:

[1] If standard data were available in more detail than is generally the case, showing variations for different soils and machines, for example, instead of a single set of figures per enterprise, their use would be more acceptable.

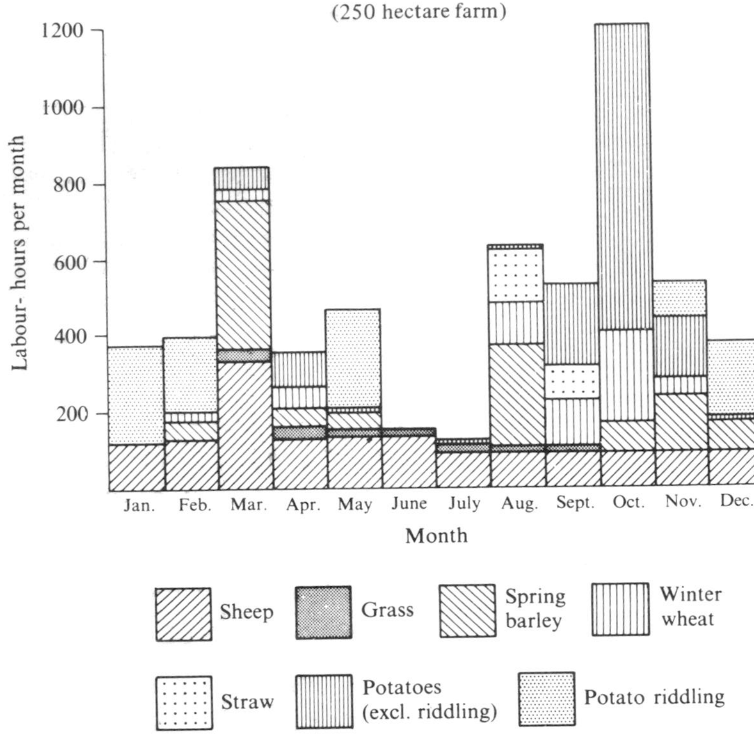

N.B. Casual labour on the potato harvester is excluded

Fig. 5.3. Labour profile

(i) *Working more overtime*. Unless fatigue is likely to be critical this is probably the cheapest way of overcoming peaks, and includes continuing fieldwork after dark with the aid of headlamps. It also helps retain the keenest and fittest men by giving them the opportunity for extra earnings. This is not true of all men of course: some have less need or ambition for extra money than others and some care more for their leisure time. The last point is particularly relevant as regards weekend work.

(ii) *Greater use of casual labour*. Three types of casual labour employment may be distinguished. First there is employment of gangs of workers for specific major tasks, such as potato picking or sugar beet hoeing. If mechanisation of these jobs is either impossible or considered unsatisfactory because of possible yield loss or soil damage, casual labour is the ideal solution because the cost has to be borne only while that specific job is being done, in contrast to regular labour, which must be 'carried' through the year.

Secondly, there is more general help at busy times of the year. Examples are the springtime on farms where both sheep and barley are important enterprises and where lambing and sowing time may clash, or silage-making time on a mainly dairy farm, or in August–September on cereal-growing farms, particularly where a lot of straw has to be carted before potatoes or sugar beet are lifted. One or more students can often be employed to help with jobs such as lambing or bale-carting.

In some areas, especially where intensive vegetable growing and/or fruit production is practised, 'regular casual' labour can form an important part of the staff. Such labour comprises women employed continually for several months, possibly for as much as half of the year. They move from one job to another and are retained even if there is a gap in productive jobs in order to keep their services, particularly where demand for such labour is high relative to supply. Where housewives are supplying such labour they often do not want to work in the winter – at least not outside – and so are quite content to be released from employment once the peak summer–autumn period has passed, and re-engaged in the spring.

(iii) *Use of contractors*. It is sometimes forgotten when considering the hiring of contractors that the farmer is getting the use not only of a machine but also, usually, of skilled labour. This can be important in such tasks as silage-making on a farm where dairying or beef are major enterprises, combining or baling straw where cereals are important, or autumn ploughing where a large area of winter wheat is grown as well as substantial quantities of potatoes and sugar beet. A well-known difficulty is that peak jobs are often ones for which timeliness is very important, e.g. combining, haymaking; the contractor must therefore be reliable. On the other hand timeliness is rather less critical for jobs such as sugar beet harvesting and autumn ploughing, although it obviously cannot be ignored.

(iv) *Mechanisation to reduce labour requirements*. Here there are two possible levels of decision. One is whether to mechanise a job at present being performed manually. This was a major problem in the past, e.g. introduction of a combine-harvester to reduce the labour needed from 70–100 man-hours per ha to 7–10 (excluding straw collection). Many jobs are now so universally mechanised that this decision does not arise, but it can still occur, potato harvesting being an example. The decision is often complicated by uncertainty as to the workability of the machine under adverse conditions and fears of yield reduction or crop damage.

The other level of decision is size of machine, given that the job is to be mechanised, or has already been mechanised. For example, combine-harvesters of widely varying capacities are available at prices ranging from £10,000 to £40,000. A partial analysis can be undertaken, comparing the labour cost saved with the extra costs of a larger machine, but the main problem is the opportunity cost of the labour saved and the capital invested in machinery. The integration of the whole farming system with different possible levels of labour force and machinery complements needs to be considered (see also Chapter 4, pp. 94–100, and Part III).

(v) *Improving gang organisation*. Another possibility is the more effective synchronisation of work by studying work methods, travelling time, size of loads and so on. In this way, more work may be achieved by the same labour force in the same time. This is an aspect of work study considered below.

(vi) *Changing the cropping*. This alternative is quite different from the other five possibilities discussed, since they have all assumed the cropping to be given – although it is true they may all be combined with cropping changes.

The first possibility here is only a partial solution. Thus, different varieties of a crop may be grown with different growing or ripening characteristics to help spread a peak. For example, a variety of winter barley may be grown in the certain knowledge that it will enable part of the cereal crop to be harvested before the spring barley and winter wheat are ready, probably in July in southern England. However, after a while it becomes difficult to draw a line between what constitutes a different variety and what constitutes a different crop. For example, early, second early and maincrop potatoes or different varieties of grass seed may be regarded as either.

Obviously a peak can be lowered by growing less of the crop, or one of the crops, responsible for that peak. This can be replaced by crops whose main labour demand comes at a relatively slack time. A classic example is reducing an autumn peak by growing less winter wheat, maincrop potatoes or sugar beet, and growing more (or introducing) peas to fill a trough in July. Alternatively, early and second early potatoes may replace part of the maincrop potato area.

It should always be remembered that this is essentially a whole-farm planning problem. The relative gross margins of the different crops have to be built into the planning process, as described in Part III.

(vii) *Extension of time period.* A further possibility – although not one that commends itself to many farmers – is to extend the time period during which a task is to be performed, even if this means accepting some loss in yield. It is certainly possible that the subsequent spreading of a labour peak may cause savings in the combined labour and machinery costs greater than the resulting loss in receipts, and it may be more profitable than reducing the area of the crop. This point is complicated by the variations that occur between weather and soil conditions in different seasons, a matter of considerable importance that is referred to further elsewhere in this chapter and in Chapter 4.

A few further points are worthy of mention. One is that on many farms, especially smaller holdings, there are reserves of family labour that can be called upon to help at peak times. Another is that with the continual reduction in the size of the labour force it can be argued that there is no longer any slack time on farms, because there is always enough maintenance work to be done when workers are less busy on crop field work. Although there is some truth in this it is to some extent counteracted by the fact that modern machinery enables the essential field work to be done much more rapidly than even a few years ago. Finally, it is a mistake to try to level out the labour requirements *too* much over the year; apart from the obvious need to allow time for holidays, trouble is likely to arise if labour is expected to be kept at full stretch for the whole year: most people can work very hard for long hours in bursts of activity which last several weeks at a time, but it is too much to expect them to keep this up continually. In any case, some flexibility must be allowed in order to be able to cope with bad seasons.

Gang-work day charts

Two criticisms may be levelled at the labour profile described and illustrated above. First, it is rarely sufficiently specific about the actual jobs being done – although more of such detail could in fact be included than is usual practice. Secondly, it ignores the concept of gang size:

20 labour-hours could mean 1 man for 20 hours or 4 men for 5 hours. Total labour-hours per month may indicate that four men are required to run a farm, but perhaps at some periods of the year two jobs may need to be going on concurrently, the gangs for the two tasks together requiring six men. A gang-work day chart shows, for specific jobs, the number of men needed and the number of days required. This is the type of detail needed if the farmer is to be able to see precisely how he may be able to improve a labour situation by re-planning.

The information required to plot the chart is as follows:

The size of each enterprise;
A list of the jobs to be done for each enterprise;
The number of workers required for each job;
The rate of work for each job, in hectares per day;
The limits to the time period in which each job must be done;
The number of days available when work is possible within each time period.

The rate of work and size of enterprise give the number of days needed for each job, e.g. at 0.8 ha a day for potato harvesting, 20 hectares will require 25 days. The rates of work and days available should

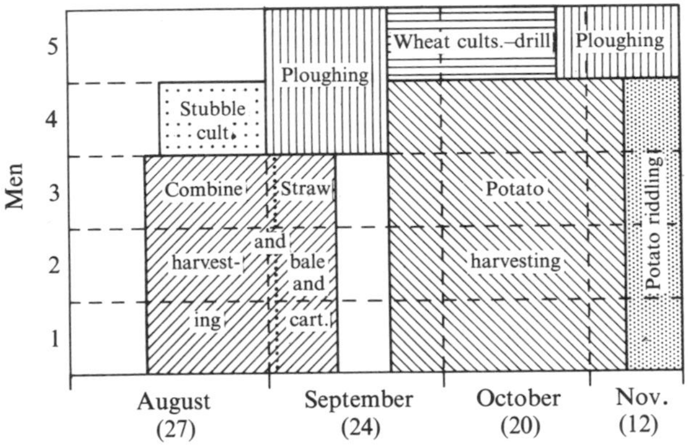

N.B. 1. Figures in brackets are the number of '8-hour days' when fieldwork is possible.
2. If two men were required simultaneously on wheat preparation and drilling, either the potato harvesting gang would have to be reduced to three or additional help would be needed from the farmer, a stockman or a casual worker

Fig. 5.4. Gang-work day chart

both be in terms of '8-hour days' (e.g. 4 of 10 hours would count as 5 'days'). The number of work days available in each period allows for the effect of bad weather on soils and the possibility of overtime work. As with the labour profile, it is not always necessary to prepare the chart for the whole year; it may well be sufficient to concentrate on the peak period or periods. An example is shown in Figure 5.4.

All the relevant data about the farm and its workers are incorporated in the work rates specified and times available, e.g. size of machines, type of soil, willingness to work overtime. In the UK, several planning data booklets give labour days available per month, sometimes for different soils – but not, as yet, for different regions. Because the relevant information is given in more detail than in a labour profile, the precise ways in which peaks may be removed or at least reduced in size can be more easily discerned, e.g. by buying a larger machine which either needs fewer men to operate it or completes the work in fewer days, possibly both.

Allowing for bad weather

A major difficulty with any method of labour planning is allowing for bad weather – the problem of variations between seasons. The usual method is to reduce the time available for fieldwork in terms of hours per man along the vertical axis of a labour profile, or in days per month along the horizontal axis of a gang-work day chart. The effect of a given amount of rainfall on the time that fieldwork is ruled out depends on the duration of that rainfall, climatic factors at the time, including wind and sunshine, the time of year, and the type of soil. The latter affects some tasks more than others and some hardly at all.

The allowances are made, on the best evidence available (limited though this may be), usually on the basis of the average season. Assuming the estimates have been reasonably accurate, this means that – for a 'full' section of the profile or chart – there will be more than enough time available in some years but not enough in others. Worse than average seasons can be allowed for either by assuming slower rates of work (that is, increasing the labour requirements) or by reducing the time available (as indicated in the previous paragraph), or even both. This is largely a matter of judgement; the farmer's attitude to risk and his aptitude for coping with difficult seasons need to be considered. Certainly the labour-time assumed to be available can be reduced, given the required information, to ensure that the labour force can cope seven or eight years in ten. It is a mistake to take this too far however. A farm cannot be planned with a guarantee that all jobs can be fitted in at the right time ten years out of ten. If this were necessary no one would ever start farming. There is always emergency action available, e.g. calling in contractors, extra casual or family help, or working more overtime. Few people would want to plan their farm on the basis of having to work at full pressure every year, but it is in the nature of farming that occasional years call for exceptional measures. In extreme seasons there may be partial or even complete crop losses; these should be allowed for in calculating the enterprise gross margins.

Furthermore, it is possible to build in 'floaters'; for example, limited amounts of manual work that are sometimes provided by the farmer or manager on the larger farm, or by family labour not regularly employed on the farm, can be omitted from the labour plans in the knowledge that these are additional sources of labour that can be called upon in a bad season. Again, it is a mistake to include all possible hours of overtime in the time available. Most field workers are not prepared, in any case, to work regularly every evening and every weekend. They will normally do so, however, in limited spells, particularly to catch up in a difficult season – especially as bad weather probably means they have been working less overtime than usual in previous weeks. A reasonable compromise is to include half the maximum available overtime, leaving the other half to cover emergencies. These 'floaters' also help cope with problems arising through men going sick.

Work study

Work study is a subject in its own right and only the briefest of outlines of the techniques employed will be given here.[1] It must be stressed that the object of work study is not to make men work *harder* but to enable them to work *more effectively*. The aim, therefore, is to try to *ease* the tasks, to eliminate sheer drudgery and thus allow the worker more time to use his specialist skills. Hence the USA term 'work simplification'. Using a hosepipe instead of buckets to convey water is a simple example, but it effectively illustrates this salient point.

Two other aspects of work study are worth stressing. One is the importance of the outside observer trained to be critical of everything he sees. Wasteful practices are not always obvious – above all to those

[1] For a more detailed description see, for example, Harvey, N. (1958) *Farm Work Study*. Farmer and Stockbreeder Publications.

who have been doing a job in a particular way all their working lives. The other is that the workers involved should always be consulted and understanding reached before the study begins.

Work study consists of two parts: method study and work measurement.

Method study

As the name implies, this involves the detailed investigation of the method of doing a particular job. The procedure has five parts:

1. Record – how is the job done *now*?
2. Examine – critically; to improve or simplify.
3. Devise – a new method; check whether economically sound where capital investment is required.
4. Install – put the new method into operation.
5. Check – that the performance is as expected.

There are three main methods of recording:

1. *The flow process chart.* This records the activities of workers, movement of materials (including crops and livestock) and the use of tools and machines. It can be a 'man-type' or 'materials-type' chart, according to which is the more important aspect of the recording. Each part of a task is classified as either operation (an actual job is performed), inspection (checking or weighing), transport (movement), storage (materials only) and delay (waiting, idle). Times and distances travelled can be added alongside each where appropriate. The object is to reduce the number of these parts of a job as far as possible, but especially those classified as transport and delay. Only operation and inspection are taken to be productive.

There is also the *outline process chart*, which is more general, covering operation and inspection items only. At the other extreme there is the *two-hand process chart*, which examines the detailed movement of each hand in performing a task, e.g. picking apples.

2. *String diagram.* A plan is made of the area in which work is being done. Pins are placed at the various work points e.g. at the position of machines, stores, doors, etc. Movements are recorded and represented on the plan by thread. The total length of thread shows the distance travelled in doing the work, and the relative thickness of combined lengths of thread between any two points shows the amount of back-tracking involved. Obstacles are clarified. The investigator then attempts

to devise new routes, re-position machines, stores, doors, etc. to eliminate backtracking as far as possible and reduce the total distance walked in doing the job.

3. *Multiple activity chart.* This is used to study the balance of jobs where gangs, or teams, are working together on a task. There are a series of columns alongside one another, each of which represents one of the workers in the team, and a vertical time-scale. Each chart represents a 'cycle' of work, e.g. cutting, loading, transporting, unloading, and spreading two loads of silage into a clamp, and each part of the task is indicated by a different type of marking in the columns. The chart thus shows how much time each worker is spending on the different parts of the job. Wasted time, e.g. waiting in the field for the previous trailer to finish filling, is marked in black. The object is to try to eliminate as much wasted time (called 'enforced idle time') as possible – possibly by changing the size of the machine (a forage harvester in the example above) or the number and size of trailers. This enables either the same gang to do more work in the same time or a smaller gang to do the same work in the same time. Unfortunately, in field work, the varying distances of the different fields from the farmstead can make it difficult to devise a combination of men and machines that comprises an 'exact fit' in all cases. Time spent travelling is dictated as much – possibly more – by the quality of the road or track surface as by the distance or type and size of vehicle.

Because of the problem of synchronising the work of different members of a gang doing different jobs, and time lost for the whole team when breakdowns occur, it is usually found that the smaller the gang the smaller the number of labour hours per hectare used to do a particular task. However, this often involves wasting machine time (as with one-man combine- or forage-harvesting). Furthermore, less work is done in a day, which means reduced timeliness; loss of crop or reduced quality could occur because the job takes longer. These factors have to be weighed one against the other.

Critical examination. This is the essence of work study. In the first place 'key' operations are selected for critical examination, which involves asking a series of questions about each of these operations, as given below. If an apparently key operation in fact proves to be unnecessary the examination of lesser tasks associated with it, e.g. 'getting ready' and 'putting away' tasks, is automatically eliminated. The questions are:

(*a*) *What* is achieved? Is it necessary? Can it be eliminated?
(*b*) *Where* is it done? Why there? Where else could it be done? Where *should* it be done?
(*c*) *When* is it done? Why then? When else could it be done? When *should* it be done?
(*d*) *Who* does it? Why that person? Who else could do it? Who *should* do it?
(*e*) *How* is it done? Why that way? How else could it be done? How *should* it be done?

Question (*a*) is of primary importance, followed by question (*e*). Technical considerations must be taken into account, including *how well* the job is done. If question (*e*) suggests the use of new equipment or machines, the worthwhileness of the capital expenditure will need to be evaluated.

Work measurement

This involves timing workers, with the aid of a stop watch. A task is broken down into 'elements', with clear 'break points' between them. The lengths of the elements depend on the amount of detail required. 'Rating' has to be used; this is a measure of how quickly the person being timed is working compared with the average person (average = 100). The 'observed time' is converted to 'standard time' by adjusting according to the rating. In order to calculate 'work unit time' a 'relaxation allowance' and a 'contingency allowance' are added. The relaxation allowance depends on the energy expended in the job, the posture, ease of movement, etc.: an addition of 15 per cent is average, with a range from about 10 per cent minimum up to 30 per cent or so for heavy work.

Thus, as an example, one might have:

(*a*) Observed time: 2.10 minutes

(*b*) Standard time (after rating): $\frac{110}{100} \times 2.10 = 2.31$ minutes

(*c*) Work unit time (after adding allowances): $\frac{120}{100} \times 2.31 = 2.77$ minutes

This technique is used for setting piece-work rates, or incentive schemes based on work rates. Basically a rate would be fixed at which the 'average worker' would earn an average day-wage rate if he took 2.77 minutes to do the above task. On piece-work rates it is estimated that output in a given time is increased by an average of 30 per cent.

Application of work study to agriculture

Work study has been described as 'organised common sense'. This is an apt description, but it is *essential* for the job to be examined critically from 'outside'. Certainly work study is no substitute for good management and technical knowledge. It should not be employed until the worthwhileness of having the enterprise on the farm at all has first been checked, or if it is felt that mechanisation or new techniques will eliminate or substantially alter the task in the near future.

Work study should be concentrated on seasonal peaks and repetitive chores. The time saved is then more likely to be translated into a cash saving by reducing the size of staff, or into higher output by enabling the same labour force to cope with more livestock. There is less scope for work study in agriculture than in industry, however, because of the high proportion of non-peak and non-repetitive tasks. Furthermore, the variation in conditions makes standardisation difficult. There is more scope in horticulture, especially in glasshouse production.

The family farmer, as well as the farmer employing a large staff, can benefit from the application of work study principles. He often works very hard for a poor living. The results of work study can provide him with more time either to use for leisure, of which he often has far too little, or to stop and think, or to add to the size of his business by expanding an existing enterprise or introducing a new one.

The point has already been made that labour accounts for a relatively small proportion of total costs in livestock production, especially pigs and poultry. Nevertheless, savings can still be worthwhile, especially if they allow the expansion of a profitable enterprise. Certainly, however, any deleterious effect on yields or feed costs must be carefully watched for, since a small worsening in these can soon wipe out the benefit of any labour saving.

Few farm businesses are large enough to justify the employment of a team of private work study consultants. The technique will be used in the future mainly as a research tool to study important labour-using tasks or to determine the best operation of new machines or methods, in order to establish basic principles that can be applied on farms in general.

Labour saving in and around buildings

Most work study carried out on farms has inevitably been associated with work in and around the buildings, especially in regard to the tending of livestock. Except for milking and egg collection, much of the work on livestock relates to feeding, littering and clearance of manure.

These work study exercises on individual farms have together revealed a number of general points with regard to the main ways of saving work, which are listed below. It needs to be stressed that work performance in buildings depends as much, or even more, on the work methods employed as on the layout of the buildings.

(*a*) Minimise transport and daily movement of fodder and litter, e.g. by self-feeding silage, or 'easy-feeding'. i.e. placing silage in portable mangers alongside the clamp.
(*b*) Store materials near where they are required, e.g. store straw on the clamp silo alongside the bedded area. This is closely related to point (*a*).
(*c*) Handle in bulk wherever possible.
(*d*) Make use of gravity wherever possible.
(*e*) Provide smooth paths and containers with rubber tyres where transport is unavoidable.
(*f*) Provide easy access for food and litter where this *has* to be brought from another point; try to avoid having to open and shut gates, if possible by putting the feed in the mangers, etc. from outside the building or yard itself. If large quantities *have* to be brought into a building, ensure that doors are wide enough for a tractor and trailer to enter.
(*g*) Lay on water wherever possible.
(*h*) Have separate sets of tools wherever required and make sure they are always returned to a recognised place after use, e.g. brooms and shovels. Make sure, too, that the tools are suitable, e.g. a 2 kg, 400 mm aluminium shovel is estimated to enable three times the amount of work to be done in the same time as a 5 kg, 300 mm steel shovel.

These may seem to be trifling and obvious points. But it is surprising how much time is wasted because they are often ignored. Especially to be avoided is carrying forkfuls and bucketfuls of food, water and litter, or pushing wheelbarrows, long distances and into almost inaccessible places.

Incentive payments

Most work in agriculture is paid at time-rates, with overtime. The majority of workers are regular staff on a weekly wage which, in the UK, may be at the statutory minimum rate for a given number of hours' work, but often includes a premium, either to reward special skill or long service, or because it is necessary in order to attract workers of adequate calibre in competition with other farmers or local industries. Incentive payments are often made, however, and in a sense even the premiums just referred to may contain an incentive element.

The main features of a good incentive scheme are as follows:

(*a*) It should be fair to both sides.
(*b*) It should be easily calculated and understood.
(*c*) The payment should be received shortly after the work is completed.
(*d*) It should depend solely, or at least mainly, on the efforts of the individual worker.
(*e*) It should not encourage bad quality work or waste of other resources.
(*f*) It should be effective. Payments made at a high rate over an expected 'norm' are more effective than 'flat rates'.

Incentive schemes in agriculture may be used either to increase physical output or to encourage and reward extra care, skill or responsibility. They can be divided into direct and indirect schemes.

1. *Direct payments*. These relate to (*a*) piece-work rates, when the entire earnings at the time are based on the rate of work, or (*b*) bonuses added to 'day-work' earnings, based on output, numbers of stock tended, quality achieved or the rate of work. There is limited scope for paying piece-work rates in agriculture because of the difficulty of obtaining standardised conditions – variations occur in the weather, soils, the state of a crop. It is thus difficult to establish a 'fair rate' over a period and a man's earnings do not relate solely to his own efforts (see point (*d*) above). As was pointed out earlier in this chapter in discussing the application of work study, there is more scope in horticulture.

An indirect benefit of piece-work is improved timeliness, e.g. in beet hoeing, or ploughing heavy land in the autumn. The faster a man does the job the more his total earnings are increased. With field-work it is more valuable to pay, for example, £2 bonus for every hectare ploughed over 2 hectares a day, rather than a flat rate of 50p per ha. The marginal incentive is then very much greater. The size of the bonus can be varied according to the pressure of work at the time, or the urgency of getting the task done quickly for timeliness reasons. The larger the farm the more there is to be said for such payments. This is partly because it is more worthwhile to work out the appropriate rates and partly because supervision is more difficult and management more remote. Furthermore, with smaller farms, calculations are complicated because the men change tasks more frequently. The quality of work must be checked and reductions made, or the scheme abandoned, if it deteriorates.

Bonuses based on output are fairly common in livestock production. Examples are those linked to milk yield per cow, weaners reared per sow, and lambing percentage. In all cases, as with field-work, the incentive is greater if it is fixed at a high rate per unit of output above an expected average level, rather than at a low rate on all output, e.g. 1.5p per litre above 4000 litres a year rather than 0.3p per litre on all milk produced. There are three snags to this, however. Firstly, it is not easy to translate an annual yield per cow norm into a monthly figure, particularly where there is seasonal calving; therefore payments may have to be made less frequently. Secondly, such a bonus is more dependent than the flat rate on factors outside the stockman's control which influence yield, e.g. silage quality. Thirdly, it encourages uneconomic levels of inputs even more than a flat rate: it pays the worker to aim for maximum physical production rather than optimum economic production (where marginal cost equals marginal revenue), especially by the feeding of excessive quantities of concentrates. Either there has to be complete trust that the man will not do this, or the total amount of concentrates fed has to be controlled by the farmer, or the scheme should be based on a margin over concentrates (or feed conversion rate with pigs). The latter requires more recording and calculations, but these may be done in any case for an enterprise costing scheme, probably run by an 'independent' outside agency.

2. *Indirect payments*. These relate to profit-sharing schemes. Such schemes are not widespread; where tried in farming they have often proved unsuccessful and been abandoned. There are two main snags. First, they are *too* indirect: they depend more on the efforts of other workers, the farmer's decisions, and chance elements such as prices and weather than on the individual's own contribution. Secondly, profits are bound to fluctuate; after a while the bonus tends to be taken for granted and considered to be a regular part of annual income; when profits fall and the bonus drops or even ceases, the worker is apt to become disgruntled, perhaps even to feel he is being cheated. Profit-sharing schemes are only really successful with a small, knowledgeable staff who get on well together and work as a team, possibly participating in managerial decisions. Such a bonus is far more applicable to the farm manager, who is responsible for the operation of the whole business unit. But he, too, has to be philosophic if profits – and his bonus – fall through no fault of his own.

Because of the above difficulties, many farmers prefer – once they are sure about a worker's capabilities and character – to pay him the flat weekly bonus above the minimum statutory wage referred to at the beginning of this section, the level depending on his experience and degree of responsibility. Such bonuses engender mutual trust and confidence between worker and employer, and the regularity of the bonus is usually preferred to uncertain, irregular payments.

Man management

Man management is probably the most important aspect of running a successful business. It has been defined as 'the skill of controlling and energising an employee in the execution of his tasks, so that the employee's effort, sense of responsibility, and attention to detail, are the best possible in the circumstances'.[1] It is an enormous subject, incorporating as it does all the behavioural sciences, such as psychology, sociology, social psychology and applied anthropology, and it is only possible, in the context of this book, to skim over the surface. This section, therefore, briefly outlines some of the more important aspects.

It can justifiably be argued that good managers of men are born, not made; that is, that they have inherent qualities in their characters that make men respect and want to please them – qualities which cannot be taught. Nevertheless, it is also true that an awareness and understanding of the importance of motivation and good communications, for example, adds substantially to the effectiveness of a manager.

A leader's responsibility is 'to get work done through people'. Good leadership means good teamwork – a contented staff who are working because they know what needs to be done and care that it is done well, in contrast to men who are doing a task only because they have been told to.

A manager can improve his qualities of leadership by an understanding of human *motivation*, which is derived from man's basic needs. These are usually stated in the following order:

1. Physical. Food and shelter are obviously primary requirements for survival.

2. Safety, or security. Protection is needed from forces that threaten continued existence. Economic forces that could undermine a person's standard of living may be included here.

3. Social. People need love and friendship. They want to feel that

[1] Griffith, D. J. (1968) 'What Is Personnel Management?' *Farm Management*, **1**, No. 3.

they 'belong', are accepted by society, that somebody cares what happens to them.

4. Ego, or esteem. People like to feel self-confident, to feel they are respected and that their work is appreciated.

5. Self-fulfilment, or self-development. People like to feel a sense of achievement.

The first two of these are referred to as the physiological, or 'primitive', needs, and the last two as the sociological–psychological, or 'higher', needs, the third being part physiological and part sociological. They are placed in order of their 'basic' importance; obviously, if the first is not provided the rest become irrelevant. Nevertheless, the last two are extremely important and become more so, relatively, as the standard of living of a population rises. People have to devote less of their time to achieving the first two and begin to concern themselves more and more with the last two. After a point – which varies from individual to individual, depending on their needs or desires for material objects and services – the level of income becomes less important than the satisfaction derived from work. Financial incentives therefore begin to lose their effectiveness as motivators.

The 'ego' needs include status, a feeling of importance. Staff at any level like their efforts, their part in the overall plan, to be recognised, and they will respond to such recognition. It is not easy to separate the ego needs entirely from the need for self-fulfilment. Thus the term 'pride in his work' covers both. It is this pride, or sense of achievement, that so often distinguishes a contented, good employee from an apathetic, indolent one. The former has his self-respect. People like to feel they have a contribution to make, that their lives possess some significance, that it matters whether they exist or not. They also like to feel that they are being fairly treated. In a low-status job, with no recognition, employees are often on the defensive, anxious to prove they are as good as anyone else; feeling aggressive, they are easily led by the demagogue. The need for self-fulfilment relates to a person's innate desire to realise his potential; hence the demand on the part of many for more responsibility, for chances of further advancement. An important aspect of management is the art of delegation: delegating tasks to others both releases management time and effort and adds to other people's satisfaction. It is true that some men are contented with a fairly simple task well done, but others are never happy unless they are 'fully stretched'. Where these aspects of motivation and the different needs of different men are fully recognised, there is a happy staff with high morale.

Another vital aspect of man management is *communications*. These may be either 'horizontal' that is, between staff at a similar level in the hierarchy, 'downwards' or 'upwards'. A manager's wishes must be conveyed 'downwards' accurately and fully and in a clear way that can be fully understood by the employees. Less frequently appreciated is the need for good 'upwards' communications. This partly relates to 'feedback' type of information, such as the results of recording, or messages concerning the veterinary needs of animals, but also covers receiving suggestions and complaints from personnel. Employees closest to a particular job work more enthusiastically if their suggestions are listened to and considered. Frequently, too, there are feelings of stress, frustration, unfairness and often these can be prevented from 'boiling over' by talking things over, informally, with the men concerned. Sometimes what is lacking, individually, is a clear appreciation of exactly what they are responsible for and who they are directly responsible to: a clear job description for each worker and sub-manager has much to commend it. Talking with individuals about their problems, both personal and occupational, often makes them happier and builds up their self-confidence; this inevitably improves their work. To show sympathy and understanding is not a sign of weakness.

The point made in the last paragraph with regard to taking the staff's suggestions into account in making decisions ties in closely with the conclusion arrived at in discussing motivation: namely, that esteem and self-fulfilment are becoming increasingly important motivators and monetary rewards alone are losing their effectiveness. Furthermore, this links in with one of the essential requirements of 'management by objectives' (see Chapter 21, pp. 571–3)–namely, involving the staff in decision-making. 'Participative management' encourages staff to understand the importance of their work, makes them care more about the result, and stimulates a feeling of community interest – that 'they are all in it together'. A sense of group loyalty and membership of a team is engendered.

The tendency in modern management is therefore to move away from the 'Theory *X*' to the 'Theory *Y*' type of organisation, as propounded by McGregor.[1] The distinction between these summarises the change needed in attitudes towards labour management. Theory *X* organisations are based on the assumptions that people hate work,

[1] McGregor, D. (1960) *The Human Side of Enterprise*. McGraw-Hill.

that they have to be driven, threatened or bribed to work hard, and that they are unambitious, shun responsibility, and want only security and to be told what to do. Theory *Y* organisations, on the other hand, assume that people want to work, that they work better if they know and help formulate their own objectives than if they are driven, and that the more satisfaction they get from their job the more effort they put into it.

PART II

THE ORGANISATION OF ENTERPRISES

6: An introduction to enterprise organisation

It was seen in Chapter 1 that the planning of the use of farm resources breaks down into the twin problems of discovering the best way of organising individual enterprises and the best way of fitting them together into an overall farming system. The first requires the farmer to look inwards at his enterprises in order to decide the methods and techniques to adopt in running them. The second requires him to look outward from them, to see how they compete against or complement one another in their use of scarce resources. Although this part of the book concentrates on enterprise organisation, it does not imply that the two sides of planning can be divorced from one another, for both are closely linked aspects of the same general problem and must, in practice, be considered together.

Enterprise organisation and fixed resources

Before proceeding further, it is pertinent to consider what is meant by an 'enterprise'. In the commonly accepted sense, enterprises are distinguished from one another by virtue of their different end-products: for example, barley as opposed to sugar beet, or table poultry as opposed to eggs. This may not, however, always suffice in the context of economic planning, where the distinction between enterprises rests on their giving different returns to fixed resources. The first part of Table 6.1 demonstrates that in this sense barley and sugar beet are, indeed, distinct enterprises, as they give different returns to land and autumn labour. But by the same count, so are sugar beet I and sugar beet II, where the differences arise because of the contrasting techniques employed. Thus from the planning point of view each way of handling sugar beet constitutes a separate enterprise.

The importance of the organisation within enterprises is illustrated in the second part of Table 6.1, where the first two plans maximise gross margin for different combinations of land and autumn labour, given the opportunities specified in the first part of the table. In plan (*A*) autumn labour is plentiful relative to land so that sugar beet I, giving higher returns to land but lower returns to labour than sugar beet II,

TABLE 6.1. *Enterprise organisation and fixed resources*

1. *Returns to resources*			
	1 hectare Barley	*1 hectare Sugar Beet I*[a]	*1 hectare Sugar Beet II*[b]
Gross margin (£)	250	530	510
Autumn labour required (hrs)	5	31	18
Gross margin per hour autumn labour (£)	50	17	28

2. *Resource patterns and enterprise organisation*

	Gross margin (£)	(£)
A. Resources available		
Land 100 hectares		
Autumn labour 1,020 hours		
Sugar beet maximum 20 hectares		
Optimal plan		
20 ha sugar beet I	10,600	
80 ha barley	20,000	30,600
B. Resources available		
Land 100 hectares		
Autumn labour 760 hours		
Sugar beet maximum 20 hectares		
Optimal plan		
20 ha sugar beet II	10,200	
80 ha barley	20,000	30,200
C. Resources available		
As in *B* above		
Sub-optimal plan		
10 ha sugar beet I	5,300	
90 ha barley	22,500	27,800

[a] Sugar beet I: not hand-hoed; harvested by a single-row, side-delivery machine with a team of three men.

[b] Sugar beet II: hand-hoed; harvested by a one-man dumper machine.

is included. In plan (*B*), labour is scarcer, and sugar beet II displaces sugar beet I. Thus the methods of production to be adopted in enterprises are just as much influenced by the pattern of fixed resources as is the combination of enterprises, and choosing the most suitable organisation in the light of fixed resources is a vital part of the planning process. Plan (*C*) shows the effect of a choice of enterprise organisation which is incorrect in view of the available fixed resources. Although there are the same amounts of land and labour as in plan (*B*), sugar beet I, which makes comparatively extravagant use of labour, is included in the place of sugar beet II and, in consequence, the gross margin is £2400 lower.

This example also makes it clear that decisions concerning the most appropriate enterprise organisation must precede those concerned with combining the enterprises into an overall farm plan, a point of considerable importance in practical farm planning. If the planner makes use of a computer, he can readily allow for different methods of production within enterprises, by including them as separate activities in the model. With non-computer planning techniques, however, this is usually impracticable, because the arithmetic becomes too burdensome; it is common practice, therefore, to assume only one way of organising each enterprise. It is thus important that the organisation selected should be the one that would fit in best, not only with the pattern of available resources, but also with the other enterprises likely to be included in the plan. The planner, therefore, has to prejudge which particular enterprise organisation is likely to be the most suitable in a given farm situation. As long as those resources that are relatively the scarcest can be clearly defined in advance, this may not pose too difficult a problem. Often, however, this is not possible and a 'standard' enterprise organisation may be assumed that is not fully appropriate to the fixed resource pattern of the farm. In such cases, the organisation chosen should be reviewed once a plan has been formulated and it has become clear where the main resource scarcities lie. In addition, the example illustrates the danger of holding rigid and preconceived notions of the best way of running an enterprise, as is not uncommon with the protagonists of this or that system of production. Their claims are usually based on experience gained under a specific set of farm conditions and may be of little relevance to farms differently situated.

Enterprise organisation and efficiency

The preceding discussion also shows that sound enterprise organisation implies more than simply running an enterprise in a technically efficient manner. The prime task in enterprise organisation is to select the most suitable way of operating an enterprise in the context of the fixed resource pattern on the farm and here economic considerations – the maximisation of farm profit – are of paramount importance. Having selected the method of production within the enterprise, the task is then to operate it so that more output cannot be obtained from the same resources nor, conversely, the same output be obtained from less. While this is largely a matter of technical efficiency, it naturally has economic consequences. In short, the ultimate goal is neither a suitable system run with indifferent technical efficiency nor an unsuitable system run with a high standard of efficiency, but a combination of the desirable features of both.

Closely linked with these two aspects of enterprise organisation is the need for caution when interpreting enterprise efficiency standards, whether physical or financial. These are concerned simply with technical or economic efficiency *within* the enterprise. But, as has been seen, the purely internal economy of an enterprise must always be viewed against the background of total farm resources (and other enterprises), with a view to economising on those resources that are relatively the scarcest. For example, it is not necessarily inefficient for one farmer to feed twice the quantity of concentrates as another to cows with similar yields, for it may be a deliberate policy of heavy feeding in order to conserve scarce farm land. Again, an above average use of labour may be due not to any inefficiency, but to labour being relatively plentiful, while capital for labour-saving innovations is scarce or can be more profitably employed in other alternatives.

A similar need for caution arises when viewing the cost economies that may arise when an enterprise is enlarged. From the point of view of the individual enterprise, the optimal size of unit is reached when the maximum output is obtained from the fixed resources devoted to it, so that resource input per unit of output is at its lowest. However, the size that is optimal for the enterprise may not be so from the farm point of view. For example, suppose a full-time shepherd (paid £3365 a year) looks after a lowland flock of 300 ewes on 36 hectares, with labour cost (assuming a lambing percentage of 140) of £8 per lamb. He could readily manage another 100 ewes, which would lower the labour cost to £6 per lamb. But if the gross margin from the present use of the 12 extra hectares required is £250 per hectare, whereas the sheep bring in only £120 per hectare, lowering labour cost per lamb by 25 per cent reduces farm gross margin by £1560. In short, the overriding need is to view enterprises from the standpoint of the whole farm economy.

In addition, problems involved in the internal organisation of enterprises are frequently regarded as though they were unique to those enterprises. In terms of detail this may be true, but in regard to general principles it is not so. For instance, the general principles to be taken into account in deciding the best seasonal pattern of production are the same whether the product involved is milk, eggs or fat lamb. Throughout this part of the book, therefore, detail is subordinated to principle, with the aim of showing the processes involved in working towards sound enterprise organisation. The examples that follow are presented, not as solutions to specific problems, but to demonstrate the way in which they may be solved. The main weight is given to livestock enterprises, both because they present more complex problems than cropping enterprises and because they commonly incorporate a cropping element.

Structure and classification of livestock enterprises

All livestock production may be looked on as an amalgam of three separate but interlocking enterprises. The first is the basic or 'parent' enterprise, from which stems a specific sale product. The second and third are concerned with supplying the parent enterprise with food and replacement stock respectively. Although these are themselves a form of output – sometimes being sold off the farm – they are only a half-way stage, as they become inputs to further production. (Technically they are known as 'intermediate commodities'.) This concept of 'enterprises within enterprises' is perhaps at its most obvious in milk production, for all three activities are usually carried out on the same farm. The parent enterprise produces milk, the replacement enterprise supplies it with heifers to replace discarded cows, and the forage enterprise supplies the other two with grazing and conserved grass. The relationship is less obvious in, say, a herd of fattening pigs in which weaners and all food requirements are purchased. But, although in such cases the farmer has relegated the production of the intermediate commodities to other farmers and carries on the parent enterprise alone, he has nevertheless at some stage had to make the decision to buy weaners rather than to rear them himself, and to use only purchased food, rather than growing at least a proportion on the farm. Furthermore, decisions taken in the past are not irrevocable, and as prices and other factors change the farmer still has to assess whether his policy is the correct one.

When allowance is made for the many different ways in which each of these enterprises can be organised, the magnitude of the decision-making task in livestock production may be better appreciated. The farmer has to decide not just whether to produce meat or eggs or milk, but what techniques to employ in producing them; not just whether to purchase food or grow it on the farm, but what foods to purchase or grow and, in the latter case, how to grow and utilise them; not just whether to buy or to rear replacements, but how many and, if home-reared, by what system.

In addition, since livestock production is a dynamic process, many decisions concerning organisation are continuing ones. One outstanding example is the changing relationship between feed input and product output, which calls for frequent adjustments to the ration. The livestock producer thus has a host of decisions to make, some of the more important of which are considered in subsequent chapters. Starting with the parent enterprise, a major problem is the level of yield at which to aim, particularly in view of the high level of fixed costs in livestock production. There follows a consideration of the relationship between feed input and product output and of how optimal rates of feeding should be determined. In turn, this leads to the problem of what foods to feed from among the bewildering choice that is usually available. Next, seasonal aspects are considered, with the aim of providing criteria for deciding the time of year to lay the emphasis on production. Finally problems concerned with the last of the 'enterprises within enterprises' – the supply of replacements – are studied, especially the pros and cons of purchasing versus home-rearing replacements, and at what stage to replace animals.

Although, as mentioned previously, the broad principles behind these many problems are the same whatever type of livestock is being considered, differences of emphasis arise when putting them into practice. In consequence, it is helpful to classify livestock enterprises into four groups, within each of which the emphasis remains much the same, as in Table 6.2.

TABLE 6.2. *Classification of livestock enterprises*

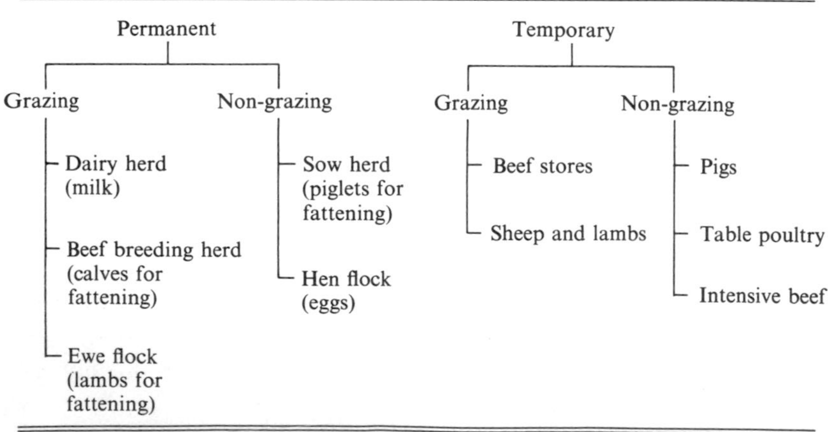

Permanent v temporary. The primary division is based on the fact that temporary livestock are *themselves* the end-product and are thus animals destined to be sold fat (or as stores), while it is the *output* from permanent livestock that is sold and not the animals themselves – at least, not until they are culled at the end of their productive life. (Their particular forms of output are shown in brackets in Table 6.2.) As will be seen later, this distinction is important when considering yield, feed conversion and seasonal aspects of production.

Grazing v non-grazing. The secondary division relates to land use on the farm. With grazing livestock, it is nearly always necessary to devote at least some farm land to the provision of grazing and bulky fodder, and the stocking rate achieved becomes an important factor affecting profit per hectare. With non-grazing livestock fed only concentrated foods, it is possible for the farmer to purchase all his feed from outside the farm, so that none of his own land is involved, and production is reduced to a 'manufacturing' process taking place entirely in buildings.[1]

Continuous v intermittent production. Finally a distinction (not shown in Table 6.2) may be made between continuous and intermittent production. The former implies an unbroken process or series of processes, so that there are always livestock on the farm, while in the latter case there are intervals when there are no animals. This distinction arises from the time element in production and is particularly relevant to temporary livestock. With continuous production, if the length of the process for each batch of animals is increased, the throughput of animals in any fixed time period falls. With intermittent production, batches are independent of one another, so that lengthening the process does not affect throughput. Most forms of permanent livestock fall into the continuous category, although there are the occasional

[1] An apparent anomaly may be noted, in that intensive or 'barley' beef is included in the temporary *non-grazing* group. Although the animals are inherently grazing stock, they are, for all intents and purposes treated as non-grazing stock on the farm, and are thus placed in this category.

In a similar manner, under some systems, non-grazing stock may make demands on farm hectares, as with free-range poultry or sows housed out of doors. However, such land may be regarded mainly as exercise ground and as a site for production, rather than as a provider of food.

'flying' herds or flocks. Temporary livestock may fall into either category. For example, a single batch of pigs for fattening may be purchased each summer in order to utilise empty cattle accommodation. On the other hand, a specialist pig keeper will have batches of animals continuously throughout the year.

With this classification in mind, we turn in the next chapter to examine the first of the principles of livestock organisation, that of the relationship between fixed costs and yield.

7: Livestock yield and fixed costs

Fixed costs in livestock production

'Fixed' and 'variable' costs have different connotations, according to the context in which they are used. In this chapter we shall be discussing them in relation to changes in livestock output. However, output may vary both because of alterations in the numbers of animals in a herd or flock and because of changes in their individual yields. For example, a milk producer, with an annual herd yield of 160,000 litres from 40 cows averaging 4000 litres, might obtain an extra 20,000 litres by raising herd numbers to 45 with no change in cow yields, or by keeping herd size constant and raising yields to 4500 litres. In the first case, with the extra cows and assuming resources are not initially under-utilised, many extra inputs will be required, so falling in the variable category. These will include more land to provide additional maintenance rations, extra purchased feed for production, extra AI fees and the like, and possibly additional accommodation and labour. In the second case, with raised output from the cows – given that they already have the capacity for the higher yields – the only major variable item will usually be the additional food needed to stimulate the extra milk; that is, the production ration.[1]

Changes in size of unit are largely a matter of enterprise combination on the farm (the subject of the next part of the book) whereas, by contrast, variations in yield levels are mainly a question of organisation within the individual enterprise. The latter aspect is our concern here, so we shall assume that, in a herd or flock of given size and in a short-term situation, virtually all costs except the production ration are

[1] If the cows are near the limit of their yield capacity, and extra feed will not stimulate any worthwhile amount of extra output, other items may become variable if an attempt is made to raise the yield potential. For example, there may be higher replacement costs, arising from stricter culling and more costly breeding, or higher miscellaneous costs because of more detailed veterinary attention. In addition, in those types of production where output consists of young animals, of which weaner production is one example, the need for extra food is in part the consequence rather than the cause of extra output.

fixed in relation to yield. In this chapter, fixed costs may thus be defined as: the maintenance ration; livestock labour; maintenance of buildings and equipment; provision of replacement stock; miscellaneous items, such as veterinary and power bills.[1]

The consequent high ratio of fixed to variable costs is illustrated in Table 7.1, which gives examples from all the major groups in our previous classification. Fixed costs range from roughly sixty per cent of total costs in milk and intensive beef production to near enough eighty per cent in fat pig, piglet, egg and winter beef production and up to eighty-five per cent in fat lamb production.

TABLE 7.1. *Fixed and variable costs in livestock production*

	Intensive beef	Dairy cow	Bacon pig	Breeding sow	Laying hen	Winter beef store	Lowland ewe
Class[a]	T/NG (%)	P/G (%)	T/NG (%)	P/NG (%)	P/NG (%)	T/G (%)	P/G (%)
Fixed costs							
Maintenance ration	28	19	24	43	49	12	40
Other	29	39	51	35	30	67	45
Total	57	58	75	78	79	79	85
Variable costs							
Production ration	43	42	25	22	21	21	15
Total costs	100	100	100	100	100	100	100

[a] P = Permanent, T = Temporary, G = Grazing, NG = Non-Grazing.

Fixed costs, yield and profits

The implications of such high levels of fixed costs are considered in Figure 7.1*A*. Two levels of fixed costs are shown – one low, the other high – the latter representing the position in livestock production. In addition, there are the variable costs, which are taken to be the same in each case and which display diminishing returns, so that as output per animal rises, proportionately greater amounts of input are required for successive increments of output. The 'break-even' points where total costs (the sum of fixed and variable costs) are just covered by receipts occur at *L′* and *H′*, the intersections of the total receipts and

[1] In some cases, costs such as replacement and veterinary attention are, in fact, variable, as in the example of bacon production (p. 175 below).

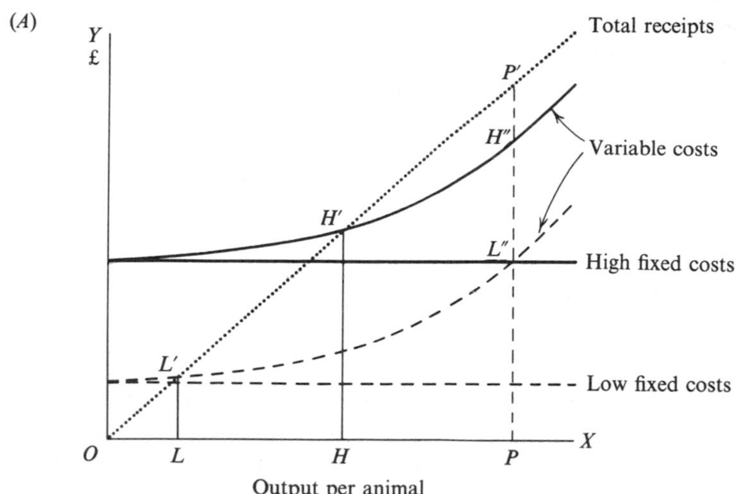

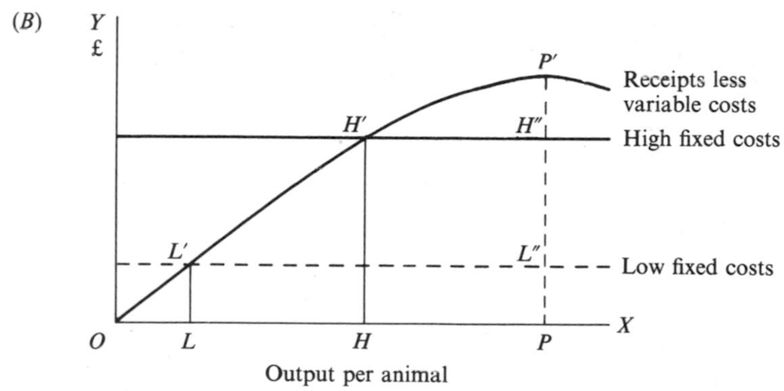

Fig. 7.1. Fixed costs and 'break-even' output

total costs curves. Thereafter a profit starts to be made. *OL* and *OH* are the amounts of output required to attain the respective break-even points (the break-even outputs) in conditions of low and high fixed costs respectively, while *OP* is the output that achieves the maximum profit in each case (*P′L″* and *P′H″*).

It is clear that a far greater output is required to cover high fixed costs than low. The practical implication for the producer is that he must achieve good yields from his livestock if he is to have any chance of making a worthwhile profit.

Figure 7.1*B* is derived from Figure 7.1*A*, but variable costs are deducted from receipts instead of being shown separately, thus demonstrating more clearly that only receipts less variable costs (and not total receipts) are available to defray the fixed costs. The points L' and H', where this curve cuts the two fixed cost curves, give the same break-even outputs *OL* and *OH* as before. This treatment suggests a formula that may be used to calculate break-even output:

$$\text{Break-even Output} = \frac{\text{Fixed Costs}}{\text{Receipts less Variable Costs}}$$
per unit of output

Fixed costs may be calculated for the herd or flock or for the individual animal. The formula is simplified by using average variable costs instead of marginal costs and consequently break-even output is exaggerated in those cases where diminishing returns are operating.[1] However, this is of small consequence, for we are seeking, not a precise measure, but simply a rough guide to the level of output that must be achieved before a profit can be made, and it is preferable for this to be over rather than under-stated. In any case, it has to be recognised that, in practice, precise input–output functions are seldom, if ever, available on farms, so that averages have to be used.

We now turn to examples of the practical application of the break-even output formula, with two aims in mind: first, to give some indication of how much output is taken up in simply covering fixed costs in different types of livestock production, and secondly, to demonstrate how the producer can calculate the position in his own herd or flock. In doing so, it is helpful to return to our previous classification of livestock with its division into 'permanent' and 'temporary' livestock.

Break-even output – permanent livestock

In the case of permanent livestock where the animal itself is not traded, output takes the form of litres of milk, dozens of eggs or numbers of calves, lambs or piglets.

[1] Average variable costs are obtained by dividing total variable costs incurred for a given output by that output, thus assuming constant returns to each unit of input. In Figure 7.1*B*, assuming an output of *OP*, the receipts-less-variable-costs curve becomes a straight line joining *O* and P', and this pushes the break-even outputs to the right of *OL* and *OH*.

TABLE 7.2. *Financial results for 80-sow breeding herd*

1. *Trading account*			
Expenses	(£)	*Receipts*	(£)
Food	16,439	1,472 × 25 kg piglets	27,968
Labour	3,839		
Miscellaneous and overheads	4,292		
Replacement[a]	480		
	25,050		
Profit	2,918		
	27,968		27,968
2. *Data re-arranged*			
Fixed costs			(£)
Food for sow and boar maintenance			10,845
Labour			3,839
Miscellaneous and overheads			4,292
Replacement			480
			19,456
Variable costs Piglet feed and extra feed to lactating sows			5,594
Receipts			27,968
Variable costs per piglet	(£5,594/1,472)	£3.8	
Receipts per piglet	(£27,968/1,472)	£19.0	

[a] Replacement is the cost of gilts introduced into the herd less the value of cull sows, adjusted for valuation changes.

Source: Based on Ridgeon, R. F., *Results for 1977. Pig Management Scheme*. Agric. Econ. Unit, Dept. of Land Economy, Cambridge University.

Sow breeding herd. The first example is of a sow breeding herd, as it offers a straightforward case in calculating break-even output. The costs and returns of producing piglets for sale at an average weight of 25 kg are shown in trading account form for an eighty-sow herd in the first part of Table 7.2. To put these data into a form suitable for calculating break-even output it is first necessary to divide the costs into their fixed and variable elements, as is done in the second part of the table. Variable costs, in this case, are those that vary with the number of piglets produced and are taken to be simply the food fed directly to the piglets (creep feed and starter ration) together with that part of the food for lactating sows which is varied according to their litter size. The remaining costs are taken as fixed.[1] Secondly, receipts and variable

[1] Certain other small items that vary with the number of piglets produced, for example, the piglets' share of the cost of vet and medicines, are not included in variable costs but remain as part of fixed costs. This simplification, however, has a negligible effect on the break-even calculation.

costs for the herd are divided by the number of piglets produced, so that they are expressed 'per piglet'. The break-even output can now be calculated.

$$\text{Break-even output: (per 80 sows)} \quad \frac{\pounds 19{,}456}{\pounds 19.0 - \pounds 3.8} = 1{,}280 \text{ piglets.}$$

In this example, 1280 piglets (16 per sow), amounting to 87 per cent of the total output of 1472 piglets, have to be produced before fixed costs are covered and a profit starts to be made. Looked at in another way, 1280 piglets make no profit while the remaining 192 each make £15.2 (the difference between receipts and variable costs per piglet).

Table 7.3 demonstrates the need for a good output in a more conventional manner, *viz*., the spreading of fixed costs. As output rises from 14 to 19 piglets, fixed costs are spread more thinly, falling from £17.4 to £12.8 per piglet, while variable costs are assumed unchanged over this range of output. (If output continued to rise, extra variable costs would be incurred per unit output at some point. For example, earlier weaning would raise the amount of piglet feed needed.) Thus total costs fall as output increases. Below 16 piglets per sow (the break-even output) receipts do not cover costs and a loss is made. Thereafter, a profit accrues which increases with increasing output.

Dairy herd. Milk production, where litres of milk constitute output, is taken as our second example of break-even output in permanent

TABLE 7.3. *Sow breeding herd – output and profits*

	No. of piglets per sow per year					
	14	15	16	17	18	19
	(£)	(£)	(£)	(£)	(£)	(£)
Fixed costs per sow	243	243	243	243	243	243
Per piglet						
Fixed costs	17.4	16.2	15.2	14.3	13.5	12.8
Variable costs	3.8	3.8	3.8	3.8	3.8	3.8
Total costs	21.2	20.0	19.0	18.1	17.3	16.6
Receipts	19.0	19.0	19.0	19.0	19.0	19.0
Profit/Loss	−2.2	−1.0	—	0.9	1.7	2.4
Profit/Loss per sow	−31	−15	—	15	31	46

TABLE 7.4. *Costs and returns in milk production*

			Per cow (£)	(£)
Receipts	4,500 litres milk			450
Fixed costs	Bulky fodder and grazing		85	
	Labour		72	
	Miscellaneous		74	
	Replacement		20	
			251	
	Deduct value of calf		40	
Net fixed costs				211
Variable costs (1.44 tonnes concentrates)				180
Total costs				391
Profit				59
Receipts per litre (45,000p/4,500)		10p		
Variable costs per litre (18,000p/4,500)		4p		

Source: Based on National Milk Costings. Compiled by the Economics Division, Milk Marketing Board.

livestock. If, as in Table 7.4, purchased and home-grown concentrates are taken as the only variable costs, fixed costs total £251 a cow, from which it is convenient to deduct the value of a calf, giving 'net' fixed costs of £211.[1] With receipts and variable costs of 10p and 4p respectively, break-even output is:

$$\text{Break-even output: (per cow)} \quad \frac{21{,}100\text{p}}{10\text{p} - 4\text{p}} = 3{,}517 \text{ litres}$$

In this case 78 per cent of total production per cow (3517 litres out of 4500) are required to break even, while the remaining 983 litres give rise to the profit of £59 per cow.

Lowland ewe flock. Our final example is of fat lamb production from a lowland ewe flock lambing in March (Table 7.5). Variable costs consist simply of the concentrates fed to the ewes before and after lambing, on

[1] Although bulky foods and grazing in fact supply some production, they are, in the present context, treated entirely as fixed costs – which for all practical purposes they are. Nonetheless, a proportion could be allocated to variable costs (as in Table 7.1) if desired.

TABLE 7.5. *Costs and returns in fat lamb production* (Lowland flock – late lambing)

			Per 100 ewes (£)	(£)
Receipts	142 fat lambs			3,053
Fixed costs				
	Fodder and grazing (10 ha)		1,116	
	Labour		546	
	Miscellaneous		289	
	Replacement		407	
			2,358	
	Deduct value of wool clip		270	
Net fixed costs				2,088
Variable costs (concentrates)				423
Total costs				2,511
Profit				542
Receipts per lamb (£3,053/142)		£21.50		
Variable costs per lamb (£423/142)		£ 2.98		

Source: Based on Thomas, W. J. K., *Lowland Sheep – Economics of Lamb Production in England 1976* (flock size 150–299 ewes).

the basis that the lambing percentage (as measured by the number of lambs tailed) is heavily dependent on the ewes receiving adequate nutrition at that time.[1] The value of the wool clip may conveniently be deducted from fixed costs, giving a net value of £2088. With receipts and variable costs per lamb of £21.5 and £2.98 respectively, break-even output is:

$$\text{Break-even output: (per 100 ewes)} \quad \frac{£2{,}088}{£21.50 - £2.98} = 113 \text{ lambs.}$$

As a lambing percentage of 113 is thus required to break even and the actual percentage is 142, this represents 80 per cent of output, the profit of £542 arising from 29 out of the 142 lambs.

Break-even output – temporary livestock

There may appear to be scant opportunity to vary output with temporary livestock – where the animal itself is traded – when the maximum numbers dictated by such factors as the accommodation available

[1] The lambs receive no concentrates but 'grow with the grass'.

have already been reached. However, temporary livestock are kept for the purpose of putting on flesh, so that their output consists of gains in liveweight. Variation in output thus depends on finishing animals at different weights. Nevertheless, this is not the complete picture, for some types of stock – bacon pigs, for example – are fattened to within fairly closely defined limits, so that there is little opportunity to vary output by manipulating finishing weights. In such cases, *time* may be saved by attaining the required finishing weight more rapidly. With intermittent production this leads to a saving in fixed costs, such as the maintenance ration, while with continuous production there is a greater throughput of animals, and therefore a greater output of liveweight from the unit during the year.

As both the time and weight dimensions of production from temporary livestock may be, in varying degrees, either fixed or flexible, there are several possible combinations, of which the more pertinent are:

(*a*) A flexible finishing weight in a given time span (output variable and time fixed).
(*b*) A given finishing weight in a flexible time span (output fixed and time variable).
(*c*) A flexible finishing weight in a flexible time span (output variable and time variable).

This classification may conveniently be called upon in applying the break-even output formula to different types of temporary production.

Flexible finishing weight in a given time span

This combination implies a more or less fixed period available for the process, but a market weight that can vary within quite wide limits. In consequence, for a given weight of animal at the start of the process, final sale weight is a direct function of the daily rate of liveweight gain achieved. The fattening of forward beef stores in yards in winter on arable farms is one example. The need to fit production into the period between the end of the late-autumn rush of work and the commencement of the spring load dictates a process of about five months, within which the weight added to the beasts may vary. Similarly, the fattening of beef stores in summer is mainly confined to the period when the grass is actively growing.

Since the time span is fixed, the situation is analogous to that in permanent production and the break-even output necessary to cover the 'block' of fixed costs incurred in the period can be calculated. Furthermore, this may be usefully related to the time available, by calculating the rate of daily liveweight gain needed to break even, which is the minimum rate that must be achieved if a loss is not to be incurred.

Fattening beef stores in winter. Fattening beef stores in winter on a diet of bulky fodder and concentrates may be taken as an example, using the data in Table 7.6. Twenty weeks are available for the process, stores being purchased at 380 kg and sold at the end of the period at 500 kg. The fixed costs, which remain the same whatever the weight added to the animals, amount to £265.6 per beast, and the cost of meal for production £72.6, or 60.5p per kg of flesh added. The sale price is 68p per live kg, a gain of 15p on the purchase price of 53p per kg.

TABLE 7.6. *Costs and returns in fattening yarded beef* (20 week period)

			Per beast	
			(£)	(£)
Receipts	1 fat beast (500 kg at 68p)			340.0
Fixed costs				
	Purchased store (380 kg at 53p)		201.4	
	Maintenance ration		40.0	
	Labour		14.0	
	Miscellaneous		10.2	
				265.6
Variable costs	Meal for production			72.6
Total costs				338.2
Profit				1.8
Variable costs per kg liveweight added (7,260p/120 kg)		60.5p		

Source: Based on unpublished data from beef production surveys. Farm Economics Branch, Cambridge University.

In order to calculate break-even output, the break-even formula has to be adjusted to allow for the fact that the receipts for the finished beast include the sale value of weight put on the animal before it arrives on the farm. This is accomplished by deducting the weight at purchase multiplied by the sale price per unit weight from fixed costs, so that the break-even formula becomes:

$$\frac{\text{Fixed costs} - (\text{Purchase weight} \times \text{Sale price per unit output})}{\text{Receipts} - \text{Variable costs per unit output}}$$

Entering the data from our example:

$$\text{Break-even output: (per beast)} \quad \frac{26{,}560\text{p} - (380\text{ kg} \times 68\text{p})}{68\text{p} - 60.5\text{p}}$$

$$= \frac{26{,}560\text{p} - 25{,}840\text{p}}{68\text{p} - 60.5\text{p}} = \frac{720}{7.5} = 96\text{ kg}.$$

There is no profit until animals have gained 96 kg, which in 20 weeks (140 days) means an average daily liveweight gain of 0.69 kg (96 kg ÷ 140). In fact, a gain in liveweight of 0.86 kg daily is achieved, amounting to 120 kg over the whole period. Thus 80 per cent of output (0.69/0.86 × 100) bears no profit.

Given finishing weight in a flexible time span

This combination implies that animals must be fattened to within fairly narrow weight ranges, but that more or less time may be taken in doing so. Bacon production has already been quoted as one example where, in order to attain top grades, deadweight must lie within a few per cent of a given weight (which varies with different market outlets). Another example is that of beef production, where there is a contract between the farmer and the butcher to produce carcasses close to a specific weight. In this type of production (as seen on page 173), increased rates of daily liveweight gain enable the process to be completed in less time, thus reducing those costs per animal, such as the maintenance ration and labour, that vary with time, and raising the throughput of animals in continuous production.

Bacon pig production. Our example in Table 7.7 is of bacon production in a one-man unit operated continuously the year round, with accommodation for 500 pigs at a time. Weaners are bought on average at 26 kg, and sold at 92 kg 130 days later so that annual throughput is 1400 fat pigs (2.8 batches of 500 pigs each). Fixed costs consist of the food to supply maintenance requirements for 500 pig places for a year, together with labour and overhead costs. The variable costs cover, in addition to the production ration, the purchase of weaners and miscellaneous costs such as medicines. This is because the total weight of flesh added in the unit during the year depends on the numbers of animals passing through. Thus if the production process is speeded up, so that throughput rises, not only do more production rations have to be fed, but more weaners also have to be provided.

TABLE 7.7. *Costs and returns in bacon production* (per annum) (continuous production)

			per 500 pig places (£)	(£)
Receipts	1,400 baconers (at 92 kg liveweight)			76,440
Fixed costs				
	Maintenance ration		15,375	
	Labour		2,495	
	Overheads		1,437	
				19.307
Variable costs				
	Purchased weaners (at 26 kg)		27,860	
	Production ration		16,657	
	Miscellaneous		1,906	
				46,423
Total costs				65,730
Profit				10,710
Receipts per pig (£76,440/1,400)		£54.60		
Variable costs per pig (£46,423/1,400)		£33.16		

Source: Based on Ridgeon, R. F., *Pig Management Scheme Results for 1977*. Agricultural Economics Unit, Dept. of Land Economy, Cambridge University.

With fixed costs of £19,307 and with receipts and variable costs of £54.60 and £33.16 respectively, break-even output is as follows:

$$\text{Break-even output: (per 500 pig places)} \quad \frac{£19{,}307}{£54.60 - £33.16} = 901 \text{ pigs.}$$

Thus 901, or 64 per cent, of the total output of 1400 pigs are required to cover fixed costs. This is equivalent to 1.8 batches (of 500 pigs each), so the break-even period for adding 66 kg a pig (the difference between weaner and sale weights) is 203 days (365/1.8), with a daily liveweight gain of only 0.33 kg (66/203). In practice, with a fattening period of 130 days, the daily liveweight gain is 0.51 kg.

Flexible finishing weight in a flexible time span

This combination allows the possibility of attaining higher weights by prolonging the production period. In so doing, more is disbursed on those costs which vary with the length of the production period, so that the output necessary to cover them also rises.

We may illustrate this with our former example of yarded beef production (Table 7.6). Previously, the animals were fattened from 380 kg to 500 kg in 20 weeks. Suppose it is practicable to take them to 530 kg – a total gain of 150 kg – in 24 weeks, assuming, for the sake of simplicity, that costs (excepting that of the store) rise in proportion to the extra weight added and the additional time taken. The break-even formula becomes:

$$\frac{28{,}165\text{p} - (380\text{ kg} \times 68\text{p})}{68\text{p} - 60.5\text{p}} = \frac{28{,}165\text{p} - 25{,}840\text{p}}{68\text{p} - 60.5\text{p}} = \frac{2{,}325}{7.5} = 310\text{ kg}.$$

This compares with the 96 kg necessary to break even with the shorter period and the lighter weight. Furthermore, it shows that it is not worthwhile to prolong production, as the weight added – 150 kg – is *less* than the break-even output of 310 kg.
[*Proof*: selling 530 kg at 68p brings in £360, whereas costs amount to £372 (fixed costs £281 and variable costs £91).]

Practical implications

At the start of this chapter it was contended that because of the heavy burden of fixed costs in livestock production, good yields are essential if they are to be covered and a worthwhile profit made. The particular examples quoted in this chapter – taken from surveys of production on farms – confirm that in general this is likely to be the case, for they all show that by far the greater proportion of output carries no profit but simply goes to pay off fixed costs. The first part of Table 7.8, which

TABLE 7.8. *Profit and non-profit bearing output*

Type of product:	Bacon	Milk	Fat lamb	Winter beef	Piglets
Productive unit:	(pig place)	(cow)	(ewe)	(store beast)	(sow)
1. *Output*	pigs	litres	lambs	kg flesh	piglets
Non-profit bearing	1.80	3,517	1.13	96	16.0
Profit bearing	1.00	983	0.29	24	2.4
Total	2.80	4,500	1.42	120	18.4
Non-profit bearing output as percent of total (%)	64	78	80	80	87
2. *Profit*					
Current	£21	£59	£5.42	£1.80	£36.5
With 5% more output[a]	£24	£72	£6.73	£2.25	£50.5
Increase (%)	14	22	24	25	38

[a] Receipts less variable costs (pro rata) on 5 per cent more output added to current profit.

summarises the previous examples, shows this proportion to range from 64 per cent of total output in bacon pig production up to 87 per cent in pig breeding. It is not surprising, therefore, that yields which are inadequate in relation to the fixed costs incurred are one of the commonest causes of unsatisfactory profits in livestock production.

In addition, the fact that the proportion of profit-bearing output is relatively low implies that quite modest increases in yield will add markedly to profit-bearing output and to profit, because, with fixed costs already covered, the extra receipts have only to defray the extra variable costs. This is demonstrated in the second part of Table 7.8, where it is assumed that total output rises by 5 per cent – with variable costs rising in proportion. As a result, profits rise by between 14 and 38 per cent.

While this example makes the general point, it is over-simplified, in that it ignores the potential effects of diminishing returns. As has been seen in Chapter 2, margins begin to fall once the point is reached where the value of extra output does not cover the extra costs of obtaining it. In some cases livestock may be close to this point, although, if average costs are less than receipts, the fact may be disguised. [For example, average costs might be 8p per unit of output and receipts 10p. Yet the last (marginal) unit of input might have cost 12p, so that a loss was incurred on it.]

However, it is unlikely that diminishing returns are a serious problem at the levels of output being achieved in many livestock units. In such cases, relatively modest increases in output may well give rise to benefits of the order of those shown in Table 7.8.

The profit advantage accruing to good yields and a high proportion of profit-bearing output is demonstrated in Table 7.9, which compares the results of low and high-yielding groups of dairy herds. Although the high-yield herds incur higher costs – amounting to a total of £13 per cow – combined with lower receipts per litre, this is more than offset by their excellent yield. Consequently 54 per cent of their output is profit-bearing, compared with only 17 per cent in the low-yield group, and profit per cow is five times as great.

An alternative route to worthwhile profits might appear to be that of keeping fixed costs low, rather than obtaining high yields. Indeed, some producers set out to do this as a matter of deliberate policy. Such 'low cost' systems, however, have their snags.

The first is that, as there is a certain inevitability about fixed costs, it may be difficult to reduce them significantly, particularly in the established unit where there may be very little room for manoeuvre. For

TABLE 7.9. *Yield and profit in milk production*

	Low-yield group		High-yield group	
No. of herds	49		108	
	Per cow			
Yield (litres)	2,964		4,882	
	(£)	(£)	(£)	(£)
Receipts		140		221
Fixed costs				
Maintenance ration	27		28	
Labour	48		32	
Miscellaneous	34		40	
Replacement	5		7	
	114		107	
Deduct calf value	28		37	
Net fixed costs		86		70
Variable costs		37		66
Total costs		123		136
Profit		17		85
Receipts per litre (p)	4.7		4.5	
Variable costs per litre (p)	1.2		1.35	
Break-even output per cow	$\frac{8{,}600p}{4.7p - 1.2p}$ = 2,457 litres		$\frac{7{,}000p}{4.5p - 1.35p}$ = 2,222 litres	
Output as per cent of total				
Non-profit bearing (%)	83		46	
Profit bearing (%)	17		54	

Source: Based on National Milk Costs, 1972–3 compiled by the Economics Division, Milk Marketing Board.

example, in specialised pig or poultry production a large part of the fixed costs consists of food for maintenance, often fed on an '*ad lib.*' basis. Providing rations are properly balanced and there is no undue waste, there is only limited opportunity to reduce its cost. Again, if labour and buildings are both being used to capacity (the assumption made in this chapter), the only way to use them more efficiently is to raise yield and so increase annual throughput. Looked at from another angle, even if fixed costs are kept low, they are still likely to amount to the greater part of total costs and therefore reasonable yields are required to cover them adequately.

The second drawback arises from the close link between fixed costs and livestock performance. It is the fixed costs that set the limits on output and, within these limits, the producer largely determines the actual level of yield by manipulating the variable costs. Cutting fixed costs may thus imply an undue restriction on the potential output from the livestock unit. To take some examples, attempting to keep replacement costs down by buying or rearing second-rate stock or by replacing animals less frequently almost inevitably implies having to accept lower levels of output. Similarly, housing animals in inadequate buildings or reducing the labour input to the point where stockmen have insufficient time to carry out essential tasks, including keeping on the alert to detect potential outbreaks of disease, are not likely to pay in the long run.

Lastly, a policy of keeping costs low does not usually distinguish between fixed and variable costs. In consequence, with variable costs cut too, the very output that is capable of bringing in a profit may be lost.

In short, although it is possible to run successful 'low cost' systems, there is always the danger that undue constraints may be placed on livestock performance and that the value of output lost will more than offset the costs saved. The two groups of herds in Table 7.9 may be used to illustrate this point (although it is not claimed that they demonstrate a causal relationship between fixed costs and yield). Although total costs in the low-yield group are £13 per cow lower than in the high-yield group (£123 compared to £136), this is more than offset by the fact that yield per cow is also 1918 litres less; this difference, valued at the margin over variable costs of the high-yield herds (3.15p), amounts to a reduction in margin of some £60. It seems hardly likely that cutting costs still further would offer a very practical means of recouping the profit forgone.

Thus far, yield has been examined in relation to fixed costs, the concern being with minimum rather than with optimal levels of output. At the same time, the simplifying assumption has been made that the level of variable costs remains the same per unit of output, regardless of the level of yield. It is now time to drop this simplification and to think in terms of optimum economic yields, the subject of the next chapter.

8: Yield, variable costs and optimal feed conversion

The most profitable level of output from an animal is determined by the interplay of variable costs and yield (see Chapter 2, pages 26–30, for the principles determining how much to produce). Adherence to the simplifying assumption of the last chapter, that variable costs per unit output remain the same whatever the yield, would imply that, once fixed costs were covered, profit would rise at a constant rate proportional to additional output, until the yield capacity of the animal was reached. In short, the maximum yield of which the animal was capable would always be the most profitable. That this is not necessarily so acknowledges that at some stage diminishing returns are encountered, so that the most paying yield becomes that where the value of a unit of output is just matched by the cost of the variable input required to obtain it. To proceed beyond this point results in extra variable costs exceeding the value of extra output, so that profit begins to fall.

If the short-term view is still taken, that the production ration is the only significant variable cost, the problem facing the producer is one of increasing food input step by step until the cost of the last unit is just recouped by the output it stimulates. At this point the margin between the total cost of the production ration and total returns is greatest and, if fixed costs are deducted, the profit per animal is also highest. (Refer back to Figure 7.1, p. 167, where feeding for output *OP* gives the greatest profits, *P'H"* and *P'L"*, in conditions of high and low fixed costs respectively.) From the economic viewpoint, this can be regarded as the optimal level of feed input or, conversely, as the optimal level of product output, or by combining them both, the optimal ratio between food cost and product sales.

Time and output combinations

It was seen in the previous chapter that the time factor plays an important part in livestock production. It is necessary, therefore, to review the principle of optimal economic rates of feeding in the light of the different types of production outlined on page 173, namely:

permanent production:	output variable and time fixed;
temporary production:	output variable and time fixed,
	output fixed and time variable,
	output and time variable.

Permanent production – output variable and time fixed

Permanent livestock are normally on the farm all the year round, so that a year may be conveniently regarded as the fixed time period. During the year, costs are incurred for items such as the wages of the stockmen and the provision of maintenance rations, which, as we have seen, do not vary with changes in the level of output. It follows that achieving the optimal ratio between feed costs and the value of output results in the highest margin with which to meet the fixed costs, and consequently leaves the greatest profit.

Of the various categories of permanent livestock, this concept of optimal feeding is really applicable only to dairy cows. It should, in theory at least, apply also to egg production, but here there is conflicting evidence as to the extent to which diminishing returns obtain. It also has little application to lamb and weaner production, where obtaining extra output is far more dependent on other factors, such as raising fecundity or reducing mortality.

Temporary production – output variable and time fixed

As the length of the process is fixed, this combination is directly comparable with permanent production. A 'block' of fixed costs is incurred over the period and achieving the greatest daily margin between receipts and the cost of the production ration results in the highest profit. This is illustrated in Table 8.1, which takes as an example the fattening of pigs over 120 days (which could be assumed to be the period that cattle yards are available in summer for the fattening of one batch of pigs). The second part of the table shows the response, in terms of liveweight gain per day, to three different levels of feeding (based on experimental results of restricted, *ad lib.*/restricted and *ad lib.* feeding – here designated 'low', 'moderate' and 'high' respectively – and assuming, for the sake of simplicity, an average response over the period and similar quality carcasses). The high level of feeding gives the greatest daily margin over the production ration (24.23p) and thus, as the last part of the table shows, the greatest margin in the period as well (£29.08). To this must be added the sale value of the weight of the pig at the start of the process; the resultant margin of £37.31 best covers the fixed costs of £34.89, leaving a profit of £2.42.

TABLE 8.1. *Optimal feed rates. Temporary production – output variable and time-fixed* (pig fattening example)

1. *Data*

Fattening period 120 days	
Fixed costs in period (per pig)	(£)
Purchase 13½ kg weaner	12.00
Maintenance ration, average 1.27 kg daily at 12.5p	19.05
Non-feed costs	3.84
Total	34.89
Variable costs Meal at 12.5p per kg	
Sale price 61p per kg liveweight	

2. *Daily response per pig*

	Feed rate for production[a] (1) (kg)	Live-weight gain (2) (kg)	Meal cost (1) × 12.5p (3) (p)	Receipts (2) × 61p (4) (p)	Margin over production ration (4) – (3) (5) (p)
Low	0.87	0.56	10.88	34.16	23.28
Moderate	1.19	0.64	14.88	39.04	24.16
High	1.38	0.68	17.25	41.48	24.23

[a]Average daily input of meal less 1.27 kg for maintenance.

3. *Covering fixed costs per pig in period*

	Margin in period (5 above) × 120 (1) (£)	Sale value of initial weight 13½ kg × 61p (2) (£)	Total margin (1) + (2) (3) (£)	Fixed costs (4) (£)	Profit (3) – (4) (5) (£)
Low	27.94	8.23	36.17	34.89	1.28
Moderate	28.99	8.23	37.22	34.89	2.33
High	29.08	8.23	37.31	34.89	2.42

Source: Response rates based on Braude, R., Townsend, M. J., Harrington, G. and Rowell, J . G. (1958) *J. Agric. Sci.* **51**, 208.

Temporary production – output fixed and time variable

When animals are being fattened to a given weight but the time available can vary, matters are quite different, and it becomes necessary to distinguish between intermittent production, with only the odd batch of animals fattened, and continuous production, where batches follow one another in succession.

Intermittent production. As the amount of weight to be added is fixed, the aim must be to produce it for the lowest cost. This involves balancing the cost of the production ration, which varies with the rate of daily liveweight gain, against those costs, such as the maintenance ration, which vary with the length of the process. In short, costs must be divided into weight-variable and time-variable categories with the object of discovering their least-cost combination.[1] In addition, there are other non-recurrent costs that vary neither with the weight added nor with the length of the process and which, therefore, have no direct part to play in determining optimal feed rates.

The first part of Table 8.2–based on exactly the same data as Table 8.1, but with the difference that the pigs must be fattened to a given weight (91 kg) – divides costs into these three categories. The non-recurrent costs consist of the purchase price of the weaner and certain other items, such as the cost of transport and veterinary attention. Of the costs that vary with the length of process, by far the biggest item is the maintenance ration, but, as in this example, there may be other items, such as the cost of labour. The weight-variable costs consist simply of the meal fed to add weight to the pigs. The second part of the table shows that the different levels of feeding result in three possible combinations of meal input and length of process, ranging from an extended production period and low meal input to a shorter period and higher meal input (cols. 3 and 4). In the circumstances assumed, the combination resulting from the low rate of feeding pays best.

Given a specific physical relationship between feed input and product output, the most profitable rate of feeding is determined by the relative cost of time-variable and weight-variable inputs. Figure 8.1 – still using the pig example – maps the areas where each rate of feeding is optimal for different cost levels (see Appendix 8.1 for the method of calculation). If the unit cost of time-variable inputs is less than 1.41 times

[1] It will be appreciated, from the principles discussed in Chapter 2, that we are concerned with a factor – factor relationship in which time-variable and weight-variable costs are the respective inputs and a given weight added is the output.

TABLE 8.2. *Optimal feed rates. Temporary production – intermittent process, output fixed and time variable* (pig fattening example)

1. *Data*

Fatten from 13½ kg to 91 kg liveweight

Time-variable costs (per pig daily)	(p)
Maintenance ration, 1.27 kg meal daily	15.88
Other costs (labour, water rate, etc.)	1.62
Total daily	17.50
Weight-variable costs Meal at 12.5 per kg	
Fixed costs (non-recurrent) per pig	(£)
Purchase 13½ kg weaner	12.00
Other costs (vet., transport, etc.)	1.90
Total	13.90

Sale price 61p per kg liveweight = £55.5 per pig

2. *Balancing time-variable and weight-variable costs*

	Feed rate for production (meal daily) (1) (kg)	Liveweight gain (daily) (2) (kg)	Days to add 77½ kg 77½/(2) (3)	Meal consumed for production (1) × (3) (4) (kg)
Low	0.87	0.56	138	120
Moderate	1.19	0.64	121	144
High	1.38	0.68	114	157

	Time-variable costs (3) × 17.5p (5) (£)	Weight-variable costs (4) × 12.5p (6) (£)	Total (5) + (6) (7) (£)	Sale price less non-rec. costs £55.5 – £13.9 (8) (£)	Profit (8) – (7) (9) (£)
Low	24.15	15.00	39.15	41.6	2.45
Moderate	21.18	18.00	39.18	41.6	2.42
High	19.95	19.62	39.57	41.6	2.03

Source: See Table 8.1.

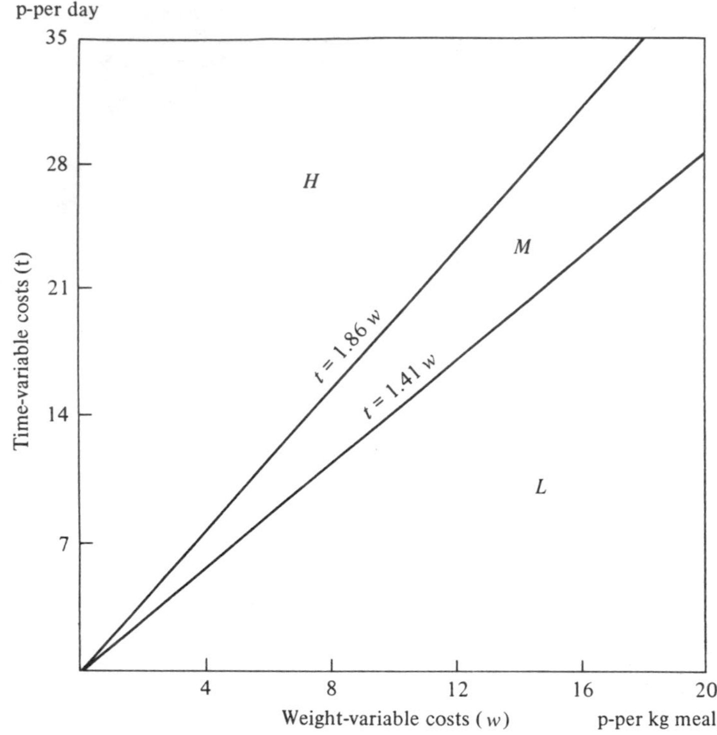

Fig. 8.1. Costs and optimal feed rates

that of weight-variable inputs (as in Table 8.2, where the unit cost of time-variable inputs is a little below that level at 1.4 (17.5/12.5)) the low rate of feeding is optimal, while if it is more than 1.86 times as high, the high rate of feeding is best. Between these ratios the moderate rate is applicable. In short, where the cost of time-variable inputs is low compared with the cost of weight-variable inputs, it is better to feed for a lower daily weight gain over a longer period of time, thus conserving food fed for production at the expense of extra maintenance rations (and any other time-variable costs). Conversely, if time-variable inputs are relatively costly, it is preferable to feed more intensively so as to speed up the production process (always allowing for any qualitative differences in the carcasses).

In many instances, three factors may make time-variable costs relatively high, so that the latter course of action is more relevant than the former. First, while weight-variable costs consist simply of food fed for production, time-variable costs may include items such as labour in addition to the food fed for maintenance. Secondly, the maintenance ration makes up a significant proportion of the total food consumed by livestock – the more so if animals are fed for relatively low rates of gain. For example, in the intensive production of beef ('barley' beef) or of pigmeat, the maintenance ration averages around 40 per cent of the total feed input. Lastly, with non-grazing livestock, where one type of ration is fed for both maintenance and production, the food cost per kg is as high for the former as for the latter. This contrasts with grazing livestock, where the maintenance ration may come from relatively cheap bulky fodder (although, as we shall see in the next chapter, this cheapness may be more illusory than real if its production is evaluated in terms of alternative opportunities forgone).

Where one type of ration is fed for both maintenance and production, and provided the maintenance ration is the only time-variable cost, the optimal rate of feeding is simply that which results in the minimum total consumption of food. This is achieved by balancing the extra food fed to intensify the daily rate of liveweight gain against that saved by a reduction in the length of the process. For instance, in adding 77½ kg liveweight in the pig example in Table 8.2, 138 days are required at the low level of feeding, which averages 2.14 kg meal daily (for maintenance and production), compared with 114 days and 2.65 kg meal daily at the high level of feeding. The latter thus saves 511 kg meal (138 – 114 days × 2.14 kg) because of the shorter period, but requires an extra 58 kg (114 days × 2.65 kg – 2.14 kg) because of the more intensive feeding. On balance, 7 kg less meal is fed on the more restricted diet (295 kg overall compared with 302 kg).

The correct pricing of inputs may present problems. Those concerned with valuing feedstuffs are considered in the next chapter, but there are also other time-variable inputs, such as labour. It may appear uncertain whether the latter should be charged and, if so, what rate is pertinent. In such instances, it is necessary to call on the principle of 'opportunity cost' (as expounded in Chapter 2) and to determine what is the most profitable alternative use for labour at the time. In many cases, intermittent production is a 'sideline' activity, designed to absorb surplus labour for which there is no alternative use and which is therefore not chargeable. This may, for example, be the situation on an arable farm where a batch of pigs is fattened in winter. As there is surplus labour at that time which is not chargeable, time-variable costs are reduced, so that an extended period of fattening may be best. If, however, the same production is undertaken in summer in order to utilise empty cattle yards, labour may incur quite a high charge in alternative uses, so that with higher time-variable costs an intensive feed policy to cut down the length of the process may be more appropriate.

Continuous production. Where batches of animals follow one another in succession, it is not the return on individual batches that is of concern, but the return to the unit over a given time period, usually a year. It follows, therefore, that in seeking optimal rates of feeding, the position is the same as with either permanent production, or with temporary production where the time period is fixed (pp. 182–83), and that achieving the highest daily margin between output and the production ration gives the best cover of the fixed costs incurred during the year. If we revert to the pig example, it would be anticipated that the high rate of feeding is optimal, for Table 8.1 shows it to give the greatest daily margin. In the event, the first part of Table 8.3 shows that this is not the case, for it is the moderate rate that gives the greatest annual profit. This apparent anomaly does not imply that our first premise is

TABLE 8.3. *Optimal feed rates. Temporary production – continuous process, output fixed and time variable* (pig fattening example)

1. *Annual profit*

	Fattening period[a] (1) (days)	Batches per annum 365/(1) (2)	Profit per batch (pig)[a] (3) (£)	Annual profit (2) × (3) (4) (£)
Low	138	2.64	2.45	6.47
Moderate	121	3.02	2.42	7.31
High	114	3.20	2.03	6.50

[a]See Table 8.2.

2. *Feeder's and market margins*

	Feeder's margin		Market margin (loss)		Profit	
	per pig (£)	per year (£)	per pig (£)	per year (£)	per pig (£)	per year (£)
Low	8.12	21.44	−5.67	−14.97	2.45	6.47
Moderate	8.09	24.43	−5.67	−17.12	2.42	7.31
High	7.70	24.64	−5.67	−18.14	2.03	6.50

Source: See Table 8.1.

incorrect, but that other factors are affecting the outcome – firstly, the 'market' margin, i.e. the gain or loss between buying and selling prices on the initial weight and, secondly, the level of the other 'fixed' costs. Part 2 of the table splits profit into the market margin (including, for convenience, the fixed cost element) and the 'feeder's' margin, i.e. the gain or loss on the weight actually added on the farm (consisting of the value of the latter less the weight- and time-variable costs).

If the buying and selling prices were such that the market margin was zero, the high rate of feeding would indeed be optimal, bringing in a profit (feeder's margin) per pig place of £24.64 per year. However, the 13½ kg weaner costs £12 to buy, but the same weight is sold for only £8.23 (13½ kg × 61p), so that with the fixed costs of £1.9, a loss of £5.67 results. In consequence, the highest annual profit is made by moving from the high to the moderate rate of feeding, so reducing the loss on the market margin by £1.02 (£18.14 – £17.12) while accepting that the feeder's margin also falls, but by a lesser amount – £0.21 (£24.64 – £24.43).

As buying and selling prices of livestock are seldom the same, feeding for the greatest margin over the production ration is thus not necessarily the way to achieve the highest annual profit in *continuous production*. If market margin is negative it may be worth feeding less intensively, in order to reduce the throughput of animals and so cut the market loss. Conversely, if it is positive, it may be worth feeding more intensively, so that by producing more batches advantage is taken of the market gain. In addition, the degree to which annual profit in continuous production is affected by the market margin depends in part on the proportion of weight at purchase to final sale weight. In the example in Table 8.3 it is only 15 per cent (13½ kg out of 91 kg), but in other types of production it may rise far higher. For example, in intensive beef production it amounts to 25 per cent if weaned calves are purchased around 100 kg and sold fat at 400 kg. Or in porker production, if weaners are purchased at 25 kg and sold fat at 66 kg, it rises to 38 per cent. To put the latter example in another way, 38 per cent of the final weight is purchased from outside the farm and is thus affected by differences between purchase and sale prices, while the remaining 62 per cent is added on the farm and is unaffected by such price differences.

Temporary production – output and time variable

The widest choice of possible outcomes confronts the producer when animals can be finished at different weights and the time span can also vary. This implies freedom to achieve different levels of output, either by varying the rate of feeding in a given time period, or by varying the time period for a particular level of feeding. In consequence, this situation gives rise to many combinations of time-variable and weight-variable inputs. For example, if in pig fattening the farmer is free to produce either porkers or cutters, with a choice of three different levels of feeding, he has six potential processes from which to select. The principles involved, however, are precisely those that have already been considered and it is only the wider range of choice that complicates matters, particularly when account is also taken of seasonal and qualitative aspects.

In determining whether to carry animals on to heavier weights by prolonging the period of feeding, a commonly advocated guide is one based on the probability of receipts for the extra flesh added covering the additional costs of producing it. If they are likely to do so, the heavier weight and longer period are to be preferred and vice versa. If production is intermittent this is indeed the case, as is shown by the example of porker and cutter production in Table 8.4. Compared with pork production, fattening to cutter weight involves adding another 16 kg liveweight by prolonging the feeding period by four weeks. Doing so adds £2.2 to receipts per pig, whereas costs increase by only £1.8. Cutter production thus had an advantage of £0.4 per pig over pork production. However, if production is continuous account must also

TABLE 8.4. *A comparison of pork and cutter production in 1968*

Per pig	Pork	Cutter
Liveweight gain[a] (kg)	49	65
Fattening period[b] (weeks)	14	18
	£	£
Receipts	13.2	15.4
Costs	11.4	13.2
Profit	1.8	2.2
Annual throughput per pig place	3.47	2.74
Annual profit per pig place (£)	6.2	6.0

[a] From 8 weeks of age and 18 kg liveweight.
[b] Allowing one week clear between batches.
Source: Ridgeon, R. F. and Sturrock, F. G. (1969), *Economics of Pig Production.* Agric. Econ. Report No. 65. University of Cambridge, Dept. of Land Economy.

be taken of throughput, since annual profit is a combination of the numbers of animals processed and their profit per head. It is thus necessary to ensure that any gain in profit per head resulting from prolonged production is not more than offset by a reduction in throughput, as is the case in this example, where pork production gives a slightly higher annual profit per pig place.[1]

Summary

In seeking optimal rates of feeding, it is clear that matters are more complex than might at first seem the case, for, although use has deliberately been made of the same basic example of pig production, the most paying level of feeding has varied according to circumstances. The high rate of feeding was best when output could be varied but time was fixed, whereas with output fixed and time varying the best level was the low rate with single batches, or the moderate rate if production was continuous.

Differences in the optimal rate of feeding mainly depend on whether the time period for the process can be regarded as fixed. Apart from those cases where its length is predetermined by circumstances on the farm, all types of continuous production can be regarded as though time were fixed. This is because even if the length of the individual process is capable of variation, it is the annual profit rather than the profit per batch that is important, and thus a year becomes the fixed time period. In those types of production where time is fixed, the aim should be to obtain the greatest daily margin between output and the production ration, as this gives the best cover of the fixed costs incurred in the period. An exception to this rule may occur when the time taken for the individual process can be varied and differences between buying and selling prices dictate a different rate of fattening than that at which the return over the production ration is at a maximum.

This leaves only those cases of intermittent production where the time span is able to vary. Here it is a question of finding the least-cost balance between time-variable and weight-variable inputs in producing a given level of output.

The position may be summarised as follows:

[1] It must be acknowledged that it is more usual for the higher profit per pig of cutter production to be sufficient to offset the lower throughput, so that it results in the higher annual profit.

Production	*Output*	*Time*	*To maximise profit feed for:*
Continuous	Variable	Fixed	Maximum daily margin over the production ration. If the time for individual process can vary, take account also of any market margin.
	Fixed	Variable	
	Variable	Variable	
Intermittent	Variable	Fixed	
	Fixed	Variable	Least cost combination of time and weight-variable inputs to produce a given output.
	Variable	Variable	

Diminishing returns

So far, we have simplified the discussion by assuming an average relationship between food input and product output over the time span of the process. In practice, as an animal becomes heavier more food is required to add a given amount of output. The producer thus faces two types of diminishing returns: first, 'short-run' diminishing returns if daily feeding is intensified and secondly, 'long-run' diminishing returns over the whole of the production cycle, as the animal increases in weight and food conversion efficiency declines. While the former affects the choice of the rate of feeding to adopt from day to day, the latter is important in determining when production should be terminated in those cases where there is a choice of finishing weights. Table 8.5 illustrates these two factors, with an example from the closing stages of intensive beef production, and at the same time exemplifies the data ideally required to help decision making. The animals are assumed to be nine months old and to weigh 327 kg when put on to the different rates of feeding, while the costs incurred up to that stage amount to £240. Not only are there decreasing increments in weight to extra feed in each month – for example, in the tenth month each additional 27 kg fed above the lowest rate adds 9 kg and 6 kg liveweight respectively – but with any particular rate of feeding, food conversion efficiency declines over the three-month period. For instance, feeding at the high rate requires 5.3 kg meal per kg liveweight gain in the tenth month (218/41), 5.7 kg in the eleventh (245/43) and 6.5 kg in the twelfth (272/42). Time-variable costs are incurred for labour and a little hay (the bulk of the maintenance ration being included in the cost of meal).

The calculation of cumulative profit at the end of the month enables decisions to be reached about both the optimal rate of feeding and, where there is freedom of choice, the optimal weight to which to fatten. This may be illustrated for our various categories of production (assuming that there is no move from one rate of feeding to another during the process).

TABLE 8.5. *Diminishing returns and production decisions in intensive beef production* (hypothetical data)

1. *Intermittent* (per beast)

Length of process	Feed rate	Meal fed[a]	Closing weight[b]	Opening cost[b]	Meal cost (10p per kg)	Time vc	Cumulative values at close: Costs (5) + (6) + (7)	Receipts (4) × 74p	Profit (9) − (8)
(1) (months)	(2)	(3) (kg)	(4) (kg)	(5) (£)	(6) (£)	(7) (£)	(8) (£)	(9) (£)	(10) (£)
	L	164	353	240	16.4	1.5	257.9	261.2	3.3
10	M	191	362	240	19.1	1.5	260.6	267.9	7.3
	H	218	368	240	21.8	1.5	263.3	272.3	9.0
	L	191	379	257.9	19.1	1.5	278.5	280.5	2.0
11	M	218	403	260.6	21.8	1.5	283.9	298.2	14.3
	H	245	411	263.3	24.5	1.5	289.3	304.1	14.8
	L	218	409	278.5	21.8	1.5	301.8	302.7	0.9
12	M	245	445	283.9	24.5	1.5	309.9	329.3	19.4
	H	272	453	289.3	27.2	1.5	318.0	335.2	17.2

TABLE 8.5. (cont.)
2. *Continuous*

Length of process[c] (months)	Batches per annum	Feed rate	Profit per beast (£)	Annual profit (£)
		L	3.3	3.8
10.3	1.16	M	7.3	8.5
		H	9.0	10.4
		L	2.0	2.1
11.3	1.06	M	14.3	15.2
		H	14.8	15.7
		L	0.9	0.9
12.3	0.97	M	19.4	18.8
		H	17.2	16.7

[a]For maintenance and production.
[b]Values are cumulative.
[c]Allowing 10 days clear period between batches.

Intermittent production – output variable and time fixed. If the time available for the process is limited by farm circumstances but the finishing weight can vary, it is a matter of seeking the highest profit in the given time period. For example, if the latter is ten months, the highest profit (£9.0) results from the high rate of feeding, and if the period is twelve months, the moderate rate (£19.4) is the most profitable.

Intermittent production – output fixed and time variable. As the finishing weight is fixed but the period of fattening can vary, the highest profit for the fixed weight must be sought. For example, assuming a beast of about 407 kg is required, the selection lies between eleven months' production with the moderate and high rates, selling at 403 kg and 411 kg respectively, or twelve months' production at the low rate, selling at 409 kg. The resultant profits are £14.3, £14.8 and £0.9, so the high rate of feeding with sale at eleven months is the best.

Intermittent production – output and time variable. With complete flexibility of time and output it is simply a question of selecting that length of process and rate of fattening that gives the highest profit. In our example, this is the twelve-month process with the moderate rate of feeding, resulting in a profit of £19.4.

When production is continuous, the annual throughput must be calculated, as in the second part of the table.

Continuous production – output fixed and time variable. If it is again assumed that a beast of about 407 kg is needed, there is the same range of choice between rates of feeding and length of process as was considered above for intermittent production. The one difference is that the choice must be based not on profit per batch, as before, but on annual profit. The latter runs at £15.2, £15.7 and £0.9 for the relevant processes, with the high rate of feeding and sale at eleven months optimal by a small margin.

Continuous production – output and time variable. The highest annual profit (£18.8) is obtained by the twelve-month process in conjunction with the moderate rate of feeding.

It should be stressed once more that Table 8.5, based as it is on hypothetical data, simply demonstrates the effect of diminishing returns in temporary livestock production and underlines the types of information required to enable sound economic decisions to be made. That it represents an idealised situation will become clear from the section that follows.

Practical problems

Thus far we have been concerned simply with the economic principles of feed conversion. It is now time to relate them to some of the practical difficulties that arise in obtaining and applying the necessary data, which may lead to considerable modifications to the theoretical ideal. Problems arise both from the nature of livestock production itself and from the way that production is organised on farms.

The outstanding feature of any livestock process is its dynamic nature. Not only is it spread over time, so that many and continuing inputs are required (unlike crop production where there are often only single applications of items such as seed, fertilisers and sprays), but the physical relationship between input and output changes with the stage of production. We have already seen that with fattening stock more food is required to put on a given output as animals grow in size and weight. Similarly with permanent stock, such as dairy cows and laying hens, daily food requirements vary because output rises to a peak and then declines as the process advances. Furthermore, animals are individuals, and even if they are at the same stage of production they will not all respond in the same way to given inputs.

The implications of this are that animals must be rationed individually and that constant adjustments must be made to their rations. With only a few animals this might not create undue difficulties, but the trend is increasingly towards large units. It is, for example, becoming fairly commonplace for one man to tend 100 dairy cows or 1500 fattening pigs or 12,000 laying hens, while still larger man-units are not unknown. In such circumstances the opportunity to ration animals individually is remote, if not impossible. At the same time, the difficulty is further aggravated by the growing trend towards *ad-lib.* feeding, as with the intensive production of eggs, poultry, beef and pigmeat. Whether the feed to the whole unit is in free or restricted supply, any control on the amount eaten by the individual animal – through, for example, competition with other animals – bears no relationship (other than the purely fortuitous) to economic rationing. The same conditions apply when ruminants are grazing.

Further difficulties may arise because of unavoidable variations in the pattern of feeding due either to seasonal changes, as with a shift from a winter to a summer regime in a dairy herd, or to variations in the quality of feedstuffs, such as hay or silage. Even where these changes mainly concern the maintenance ration, they may still be expected to influence the relationship between the production ration and output.

Finally, seasonal price variations in many livestock products mean that the economically justifiable rate of feeding may change. For example, in milk production, the rate at which concentrates are fed to obtain the last litre of output can vary by as much as twenty per cent between the low summer and the high winter prices. Matters are made more complex with fattening stock, because the relevant price for determining the intensity of fattening is an anticipated selling price, and not necessarily the prices ruling during the period when the output is actually being obtained.

Quite apart from problems arising from the dynamic nature of production, there is the question of whether the data required should be sought from outside the farm or from the farm itself. It has already been suggested that individual farm animals are in a sense unique, and this applies also to other factors which influence the relationship between feed input and product output on particular farms. These include, amongst other things, the ability and stockmanship of those tending livestock, the type and quality of housing, the standard of hygiene adopted, the types and composition of foods and food supplements, the frequency of feeding and the degree of competition among free-housed animals. The list is almost endless and its implication is clear. Even if data are available from outside the farm, they can usually be no more than a guide to the type of relationship that the farmer can anticipate with his own animals. This in itself serves a useful purpose, but it is unlikely to be adequate for making individual production decisions. Thus, with established enterprises, the farmer must rely largely on generating his own data, which, while being the generally accepted procedure in milk production, happens far less often in other lines of production.

Assembling the necessary information is a formidable task, for the reasons that have been considered, although the degree of difficulty varies with the type of production. Problems are less acute if animals are housed so that there is some control over their environment, if the production process is fairly rapid, if feeds are both concentrated and purchased – thus reducing variations in quality and the problem of valuing them – and if there is no marked seasonal pricing. Most of these conditions, for example, apply to the production of pigmeat, but are absent from the less intensive systems of beef production. Nonetheless, a degree of simplification is obviously needed, and this may come about in two main ways.

The first is to treat animals as groups instead of as individuals, so that the group, and not the animal, becomes the technical unit of production in which feed input is related to product output. The degree to which this necessitates a departure from individual treatment depends on the resource situation on the individual farm. At one end of the scale, labour shortage and 'open-plan' buildings may dictate that the whole herd or flock constitutes the group. At the other end of the scale, it may be practicable to split animals into small batches of roughly similar potential, as occurs when pens of fattening cattle are 'levelled-up'. In between these extremes there may be a few relatively large groupings, as when dairy herds are divided into high-yielding, low-yielding and dry cows. Clearly, the more closely the animals in a group match up to one another, the more nearly does group response provide a reasonable basis of rationing.

The second way of simplifying the problem is to extend the time period over which the response to feed is measured. For example, dairy cows are commonly rationed on the basis of their weekly production, while with fattening animals the period may be a month or longer. If the feed–product relationship is changing only slowly, an extended period may be an acceptable basis for determining optimal levels of feeding; but if it is changing fairly rapidly, then the shorter the period the better.

Feed conversion ratios and feeding efficiency

Before leaving the problem of determining optimal feed rates it is pertinent to consider the part that feed conversion ratios can play, for they have the advantage of being relatively easy to calculate.

At their simplest they relate food input to product output in purely physical terms, such as kg meal per kg liveweight gain or per dozen eggs or per litre of milk. With non-grazing stock, food input includes both the maintenance and the production requirements. In this form the ratios are commonly referred to as measuring 'feed conversion efficiency' (FCE), with the implication that the lower the input of food per unit of output, the greater the efficiency of feeding. As the prices of feedstuffs vary widely, matters may be taken a stage further by calculating a partly financial standard, such as the cost of meal per kg liveweight gain. Where the price of output may vary also, for example, due to different gradings, a wholly financial standard, such as the cost of meal per £100 livestock output, may be calculated. The implication of such standards, however, remains the same as for the purely physical ratios, namely that the lowest food cost is optimal.

It is apparent, if we cast our minds back to the previous beef example (Table 8.5), that such ratios cannot necessarily locate the most economic rate of feeding, because this varies with the degree of flexibility in time and output and depends on whether production is continuous or intermittent. More explicitly, Table 8.6, based on our previous pig example, shows that both physical and financial conversion ratios

TABLE 8.6. *Optimal rates of feeding and conversion ratios* (pig-fattening example)

Rate of feeding:	Low	Moderate	High
Production data (per pig)			
Liveweight gain daily (kg)	0.56	0.64	0.68
Days to add 77½ kg liveweight	138	121	114
Meal consumed (kg)	295	298	302
Conversion ratios			
kg meal per kg liveweight gain	3.81	3.85	3.90
Meal cost per £100 output (£)	78.0	78.8	79.9
Financial results[a]			
Profit per pig (£)	2.45	2.42	2.03
Batches per pig place per annum	2.64	3.02	3.20
Profit per pig place per annum (£)	6.47	7.31	6.50

[a] See Table 8.3.
Source: See Table 8.1.

indicate that the low rate of feeding is the most efficient. If production is intermittent this is indeed the case, under the circumstances assumed. With continuous production, however, the highest annual profit results from the moderate, not the low, rate of feeding.

It is clear that feed conversion ratios used in this way are unreliable guides to optimal economic feed rates. This is in accord with the theoretical principles discussed in Chapter 2, which show that economic optima are based on marginal criteria whereas, in contrast, conversion ratios are based on average criteria (and assume the lowest point on the average factor input or cost curve to be optimal). Nonetheless, this does not mean that they are to be dismissed as being of no value, for improved conversion ratios are commonly accompanied by higher profits. There are two main reasons why this should be so.

The first concerns technical efficiency. Up to now, it has tacitly been assumed that producers are operating on the most technically efficient function between input and output, and are simply concerned with locating the optimal position on it. This implies that they can neither obtain more output from a given input, nor, conversely, the same output from a smaller input. Clearly, this is often not the case, so that moving closer to the correct feed–product relationship leads to improved conversion rates and profits (see Appendix 8.2.).

The second reason is that most conversion ratios include the maintenance part of the ration, so that as output increases they reflect not just the response to additional feeding but also the spread of the fixed

TABLE 8.7. *Yield, conversion ratios and margins in egg production* (per bird per annum)

Egg output	216	264	264
Meal requirement	(kg)	(kg)	(kg)
For maintenance	30	30	30
For production	10	12	18
Total	40	42	48
Meal input per dozen eggs	2.2	1.9	2.2
Financial results	(p)	(p)	(p)
Egg receipts (33p per doz.)	594	726	726
Meal cost (12p per kg)	480	504	576
Margin	114	222	150

part of the ration over greater output. Since poor conversion ratios are often the result of indifferent yields, with the maintenance ration spread over too few units of output (rather than from the onset of markedly diminishing returns), raising yields achieves a better spread and results in higher profits and more satisfactory conversion ratios.

Table 8.7 illustrates this with an example from egg production. The first column shows that with only 216 eggs per bird, the maintenance requirement comes to 75 per cent of total feed input and the conversion ratio is poor, at 2.2 kg meal per dozen eggs, with the margin over meal cost per bird correspondingly low, at 114p. If, as in the second column, production is 264 eggs (with the production ration rising in proportion), the conversion ratio falls to 1.9 kg meal per dozen eggs and the margin nearly doubles to a level of 222p per bird. The third column shows that even if markedly diminishing returns were encountered in obtaining the additional eggs, the production ration could nevertheless rise nearly two times (from 10 kg to 18 kg) before the conversion ratio reached the same level as that of the lower-yielding bird (assuming that a bird would consume this quantity of meal).

Table 8.7 also brings out another important point about the use of conversion ratios, namely, that it is vital to know the level of output associated with a particular ratio. Under the circumstances assumed, 2.2 kg meal per dozen eggs, although a poor standard, brings in a larger margin when associated with a yield of 264 eggs than with 216 eggs. It is doubly important to know the yield level when dealing with conversion ratios which include only the production ration. For example, with milk production, 0.2 kg of concentrates per litre appears to be a far better standard than 0.4 kg per litre. However, if the former is associated with a yield of 3000 litres per cow and the latter with 5000 litres, and if milk is priced at 10p per litre and concentrates at 12p per kg, the resultant margins over concentrate cost are as follows:

3000 l @ 10p = £300. 3000 l × 0.2 kg concs. @ 12p = £ 72. Margin £228.
5000 l @ 10p = £500. 5000 l × 0.4 kg concs. @ 12p = £240. Margin £260.

The higher yielding cow with the poorer conversion rate nets an additional £32 margin.

To summarise, while conversion ratios cannot be relied on to indicate the position of optimal economic feed conversion, they do provide producers with a guide to their relative technical efficiency, without which economic efficiency can never be fully attained, and they thus have a useful service to perform.

Appendix 8.1: Mapping optimal feed rate boundaries with variations in the cost of time-variable and weight-variable inputs

The optimal balance between time-variable and weight-variable inputs for producing a given output can be determined by marginal analysis, namely,

$$\Delta T \times P_t = \Delta W \times P_w \qquad (1)$$

where ΔT is the amount of change in time-variable inputs consequent upon a given amount of change in weight-variable inputs ΔW, and P_t and P_w are their respective unit costs.

This formulation is used in Figure 8.1 to determine the equal cost boundaries – where it is a matter of indifference from the economic viewpoint which of the two feed rates on either side of the boundary is adopted – using the data in Table 8.2.

Between low and moderate feed rates

$$\Delta T = 17(138 - 121) \quad \text{and} \quad \Delta W = 24(144 - 120)$$

substituting in equation (1): $17P_t = 24P_w$

$$P_t = 1.412P_w$$

Between moderate and high feed rates

$$\Delta T = 7(121 - 114) \quad \text{and} \quad \Delta W = 13(157 - 144)$$

substituting in equation (1): $7P_t = 13P_w$

$$P_t = 1.857P_w$$

Appendix 8.2: Feed conversion ratios and technical and economic efficiency

Figure 8.2 demonstrates, for a given resource situation, two levels of input that obtain a given level of output together with their associated conversion ratios (units of input per unit of output, measured on the right-hand scale). One is technically efficient and the other technically inefficient (in that it is possible to obtain more output for each level of input). C and F are points of maximum technical efficiency on each of the total food cost curves and occur where there is the lowest input per unit of output, as shown by points C' and F' on the conversion ratio

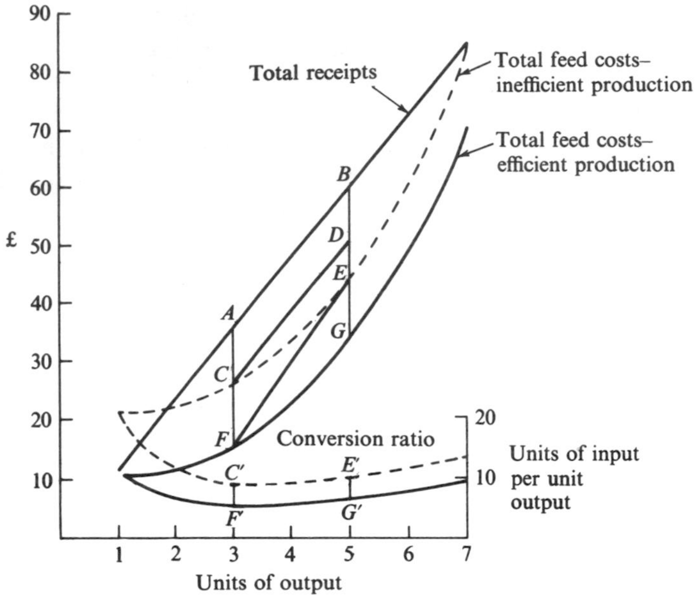

Fig. 8.2. Technical and economic efficiency

curves, and *AC* and *AF* are the associated margins over feed cost. *E* and *G* are points of maximum economic efficiency, giving the maximum margins *BE* and *BG* respectively (where the total receipts curve is at a maximum distance from the two feed cost curves).

If a producer at point *C* on the inefficient function moves along that same curve to the point of maximum economic efficiency *E*, he makes *DE* extra margin, and the conversion ratio deteriorates slightly from *C′* to *E′*. If, however, he moves from *C* to *F*, the point of maximum technical efficiency on the efficient function, he makes *CF* extra margin, which is nearly twice as great as *DE*, and at the same time the conversion ratio improves markedly from *C′* to *F′*.

It can be hypothesised that in practice when producers become more efficient they move both towards more effective functions and towards the economic optimal positions on them. Thus, in our example they move in the area *CEFG* (and *C′E′F′G′* in respect of conversion ratios), so that both margins and conversion ratios are likely to improve.

9: The selection of feedstuffs

If only one type of feedstuff were available to the livestock producer, he would (as we saw in the previous chapter) simply be concerned with how much of it to feed. As he is, in practice, confronted with a wide range of alternative feeds, he has also to decide which of them to use and this may include choosing between buying foods such as barley, beans and hay, as opposed to growing them on the farm. The selection is widest with grazing livestock, for there are both concentrated and bulky foods from which to choose. As the latter are commonly grown on the farm and there are alternative methods of producing them – for example, grass conserved as hay or as silage, or kale unthinned and grazed direct or thinned and cut and carted to the cattle – selecting the most appropriate method of production adds to the size of the problem.

Economic principles

The basic problem facing the producer is to select that food or combination of foods which provides a given livestock output at least cost. Two examples, each involving only two foods at a time, are given in Table 9.1. The first shows different combinations of soya-bean meal and corn producing 0.45 kg gain on broilers initially weighing 0.68 kg. The first ration is relatively high in corn but low in soya-bean meal. As the latter is increased in the ration, the amount of corn is reduced, but by smaller and smaller quantities for each successive addition of soya-bean meal. If corn is valued at 10p and soya-bean meal at 16p per kg, the saving in corn outweighs the cost of extra soya-bean meal (col. 4) up to the third feed combination (*C*). As column (5) shows, mix *C* thus produces 0.45 kg gain at least cost (990p). The last two columns illustrate the effect of price changes on the least-cost mix. When soya-bean meal is relatively costly compared with corn (col. 6) the least-cost ration – mix *B* – consists more of corn and less of soya-bean meal, whereas when it is relatively cheap (col. 7) the balance tips the other way and mix *D* costs the least.

The second part of the table shows different combinations of bulky

TABLE 9.1. *Least-cost feed combinations*

1. *Broiler production* (Combinations of soya-bean meal and corn (maize) to produce 0.45 kg gain on broilers weighing 0.68 kg – per 100 broilers.)

Mix	Soya-bean meal (1) (kg)	Corn (2) (kg)	Corn saved for each 4.5 kg soya-bean added (3) (kg)	Value of corn saved for each 72p soya-bean added[a] (4) (p)	Total cost[a] (5) (p)	Total cost when: soya-bean: 20p corn: 8p (6) (p)	Total cost when: soya-bean: 15p corn: 12p per kg (7) (p)
A	15.0	85.8	—	—	1,098	986	1,255
B	19.5	70.8	15.0	150	1,020	956	1,142
C	24.0	60.6	10.2	102	990	965	1,087
D	28.5	53.8	6.8	68	994	1,000	1,073
E	33.0	48.6	5.2	52	1,014	1,049	1,078
F	37.5	44.7	3.9	39	1,047	1,108	1,099

[a] Corn 10p per kg, soya-bean meal 16p per kg.

Source: Based on Heady, E. O., Balloun, S. and Townsley, R. J. (1966) *O.E.C.D. Documentation in Food and Agriculture* **81**, 35.

2. *Beef production* (Combinations of silage and cereal in winter fattening of steers adding 68 kg and 91 kg liveweight respectively.)

68 kg					91 kg				
Mix	Silage (1) (kg)	Cereal (2) (kg)	kg cereal saved for each 227 kg silage added (3) (kg)	Total cost[b] (4) (£)	Mix	Silage (1) (kg)	Cereal (2) (kg)	kg cereal saved for each 227 kg silage added (3) (kg)	Total cost[b] (4) (£)
A	1,475	186	—	36.08	*E*	1,475	271	—	42.45
B	1,702	138	48	35.88	*F*	1,702	231	40	42.85
C	1,929	95	43	36.06	*G*	1,929	200	31	43.94
D	2,156	66	29	37.29	*H*	2,156	183	17	46.06

[b] Cereal 7.5p per kg, silage 1.5p per kg.

Source: Based on Wragg, S. R., Godsell, T. E. and Williams, G. (1966) *O.E.C.D. Documentation in Food and Agriculture* **82**, 70.

food and concentrate that add two different amounts of gain to steers in winter. Precisely the same type of relationship is revealed as in the broiler example, namely, that as more of one food (silage) is added savings are made in the other (cereal), but at a decreasing rate. If cereal is valued at 7.5p and silage at 1.5p per kg, mix *B* is cheapest when adding 68 kg liveweight and mix *E* when adding 91 kg.

Although these examples have been concerned with only two foods at a time – while in practice a far wider choice is usually available – they make it clear that to determine least-cost rations the farmer needs, first, to be aware of the different combinations of feeds that will result in a given output. To put it another way, he needs to know the rates at which feeds substitute for one another in a ration, as illustrated by column (3) in each part of the table (see also Appendix 9.1). Secondly, he must know what values to place on the different foods.

Rates of substitution between feeds

It was seen in the last chapter that many practical difficulties arise in determining optimal feed rates, largely because of the dynamic nature of production and the trend towards larger units. It was also seen that there are reservations about the validity of attempting to apply such experimental data as exist to individual farm situations. These difficulties apply with equal force to the determination of rates of substitution between feedstuffs so that it is hardly surprising that producers tend to fall back on simple rules of thumb, such as that 4 kg concentrates are equivalent to 7 kg hay, or 1 kg silage is equivalent to 2.5 kg kale. The assumption underlying their use is that foods substitute for one another in constant proportions regardless of whether they constitute a small or a large proportion of the total ration. Indeed, the same assumption is inherent to the metabolisable and net energy systems of rationing used in the UK (see Appendix 9.2) and in systems used in other countries, such as those based on starch equivalents or total digestible nutrients.

The consequences of assuming constant rates of substitution are two-fold. First, except for the rare occasions when prices are such that the cost of one feed added is exactly offset by the value of another feed saved so that it is a matter of indifference which of them is fed (see Chapter 2, p. 31), the ration will consist of only one food (or as much of it as it is technically feasible to feed). Secondly, this will not necessarily be the least-cost ration. Reference to beef production (68 kg gain) in Table 9.1 makes this clear. If the net energy of corn is 8MJ and silage 1 MJ per kg *crude* weight, the implication is that 1 kg of the former always replaces 8 kg of the latter. Given their respective prices of 7.5p and 1.5p per kg, adding 1 kg of grass silage to the ration costs 1.5p but saves only 0.94p worth of corn ($\frac{1}{8}$ × 7.5p). Conversely adding 1 kg of corn costing 7.5p saves 8 kg of grass silage worth 12p. It is thus implied that ration *A* – with the maximum corn and the minimum silage – should be fed at a cost of £36.08. This is slightly more costly than ration *B* (which at £35.88 costs the least), and on a batch of 100 animals would add £20 to the feed bill.

How far the assumption of constant rates of substitution will be wide of the mark, and will therefore lead to false evaluation of the least-cost ration, is likely to vary according both to the make-up of the ration and to the types of food that are being fed. With regard to the former, there is some evidence that, for any particular level of output, near constant substitution rates may apply over quite a wide range of combinations of two feeds. At the same time, this is least likely to be so at the 'extremes' of the ration, where one food or the other is dominant and wider than 'normal' ratios may be expected to obtain.

As to the types of food, those that are reasonably alike in their composition – for example, cereals such as oats and barley, or pulse crops such as peas and beans, or oil feeds such as groundnut cake and soyabean meal – may be expected to substitute approximately in proportion to their energy contents (assuming that they have similar proportions of dry matter). On the other hand, this is unlikely to be the case where feeds are dissimilar, as when concentrates are substituted for bulky foods. The inclusion of the latter also intensifies the problem, because they may vary widely in their composition even in a single season, due largely to climatic factors and to the stage of growth at harvest, hay and silage being particularly notorious in this respect.

Appetite limits

Another relevant factor, when bulky foods (particularly coarse fodders such as hay and straw) are being substituted for concentrates, is the effect on the appetite of the animal. In obtaining a unit of energy from a bulky fodder, an animal has to consume more dry matter than if it were obtained from a concentrate. For example, to obtain 100 MJ of metabolisable energy, a dairy cow would eat about 7 kg dry matter if the feed were barley, 12 kg if it were seeds hay and 14 kg if it were barley straw. In consequence, if feeding is to the limit of appetite, adding more bulk in order to save concentrates entails a reduction in the amount of nutrient intake, which may in turn place an undue restriction on output. Table 9.2 demonstrates this for dairy cows fed to appetite limits

TABLE 9.2. *Feed substitution and appetite limits in milk production* (per cow daily)

1. *All hay ration*			
Food costs	(p)	Receipts	(p)
Hay 18 kg at 3.5p	63	Milk 11.4 litres at 12p	137
Margin	74		
	137		137
2. *Hay and concentrate ration*			
Food costs	(p)	Receipts	(p)
Hay 9½ kg at 3.5p	33	Milk 18.2 litres at 12p	218
Concentrates 9 kg at 12p	108		
	141		
Margin	77		
	218		218

Source: Based on Langley, J. A. (1965) *O.E.C.D. Documentation in Food and Agriculture* **71**, 121.

in mid-lactation. Those fed only hay yielded 11.4 litres daily, but those for which concentrates replaced half the hay (so stepping up nutrient intake but leaving dry matter intake virtually unchanged) yielded 6.8 litres more. The resultant gain in receipts of 81p more than offsets the extra cost of 78p for the more concentrated ration, leaving on balance 3p more margin daily with which to defray non-feed costs.

Practical action

While having to rely mainly on the assumption of constant rates of substitution between foods, the livestock producer may be able to bring a greater degree of precision into his rationing in several ways (see also Appendix 9.2). First, foods can be tested for their feeding value. This is particularly necessary with foods such as hay and silage that vary widely in composition, and helps to eliminate one of the uncertainties in feeding. It is also important where feeding is to the limit of appetite and there is a danger that animals may not receive sufficient nutrients when food quality is poor. Any cost of laboratory analysis may well be more than recouped, in that the knowledge of feeding values so gained, permits more accurate rationing and the avoidance of both lost production through under-feeding when values are low, or wasted food through over-feeding when values are high. Furthermore, the producer must be prepared to limit the amount of bulky fodder fed to high-yielding animals, even if its quality is good, which admittedly is no easy task if 'self-feed' or 'easy-feed' systems are in operation. Secondly, it should be borne in mind that rates of substitution between foods are likely to widen as the ration consists more and more of one particular type of food. Finally, it may be possible for the farmer to build up a personal store of knowledge concerning substitution rates between the types of food fed on his farm, which allows both for the conditions under which they are fed and the type of stock that receive them.

The valuation of feedstuffs

The second problem in seeking least-cost feeding is to place correct values on alternative foodstuffs. As the first part of Table 9.1 shows (cols. 5, 6 and 7), changes in the costs of feeds in a mix may alter the make-up of the least-cost ration. Conversely, incorrect valuations of foods may mean that the mix selected (or it may be a single feed) is not the least-cost one.

Foods may be placed in the following categories for the purpose of valuing them:

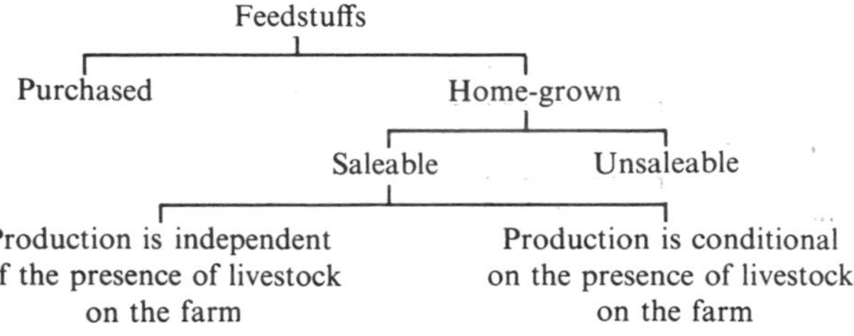

The prime distinction is between purchased and home-grown foods. The latter break down into three further groups: crops that are unsaleable (or, at least, are normally so) and are thus grown only because there are livestock on the farm to consume them; crops which, although saleable, are grown for the same reason; and finally, saleable crops which, although fed to livestock, are not basically grown for that purpose.

Purchased foods

This is the most straightforward group of foods to deal with, for they should be valued at the prices that must be paid for them. As, however, the latter need to be known before decisions can be taken on the composition of least-cost rations, difficulties may sometimes arise in determining them in advance of any actual purchase, and in relating them to quality, particularly in the case of bulky foods such as hay and straw.

Home-grown, saleable foods not specifically grown for livestock

If a crop that is saleable is grown on the farm independently of the livestock – because it would continue to be grown even if there were no livestock, being sold instead of fed – the anticipated sale price is its appropriate value. This is often the case with barley, part of which may be sold and part fed to pigs. Although the feed barley never leaves the farm, it is nevertheless really a cash crop that has been diverted to the pigs. If barley prices are high, use of sale value may indeed reveal that it is better to sell all the barley and buy an alternative feed for the livestock.

Home-grown, saleable foods specifically grown for livestock

Although, like the previous group, foods in this group are marketable, they are grown only because they are required for feeding to livestock. Thus, if the livestock unit were to be eliminated, they would be replaced by other more profitable crops, and this gives a clue to the way in which they should be valued. The real cost to the farmer of growing the feed crop is the value (gross margins) of the alternative activities that would replace it, together with those costs that would be saved if it were no longer grown (variable costs in a planning sense).

A single example serves to illustrate the valuation of home-grown foods for both this and the previous category. An 80-ha arable farm is run on a rotation of four 20-ha shifts – break crops, wheat, barley, barley – with the barley all fed to a 30-sow breeding and fattening herd. It is feasible for wheat to replace up to half the barley in the third shift (but no more because of disease risk), so the present and potential organisations are:

Present Organisation		*Potential Organisation*	
Break crops	20 hectares	Break crops	20 hectares
Wheat	20 hectares	Wheat	20 hectares
Barley	20 hectares	Wheat	10 hectares
		Barley	10 hectares
Barley	20 hectares	Barley	20 hectares

Each hectare of barley incurs £76 variable costs and yields 4 tonnes grain which could be sold for £80 per tonne. Wheat yields 4.5 tonnes per hectare, selling at £85 per tonne, which with variable costs of £90 gives a gross margin of £292 per hectare.

To determine the real costs of growing barley for pig feed, it is necessary to distinguish between the 30 ha that are an essential part of the arable rotation and would continue to be grown even if there were no pig unit, and the 10 ha that could be switched to wheat and are only grown because there are pigs on the farm. The appropriate value for the former is the potential sale price of barley of £80 per tonne. The other 10 ha, however, must be valued in terms of the wheat that they displace. The gross margin forgone from wheat is £292 per ha, which, together with the £76 per ha variable costs of growing barley that would be saved if wheat were to be grown, amounts to £368 in all. This is the real cost of a hectare of barley which, with a yield of 4t per hectare, amounts to £92 per tonne, £12 higher than the price at which barley could be sold. If the farmer could buy barley for less than £92 per tonne he should turn 10 ha of the barley in the third shift over to wheat and instead purchase the 40 tonnes of production forgone. Conversely, if barley cost more than £92 per tonne to buy, he should carry on as at present, growing his full feed requirements on the farm.

Home-grown, unsaleable foods

The final group of foods comprises those crops such as grazing, kale and silage that are not normally traded and in consequence have no recognised sale value. Since they are grown only because there are livestock to feed, their value must be determined precisely as for the previous group, namely, in terms of forgone alternatives. An additional complication is that they often require a very different pattern of fixed resources, such as labour and capital, than do the crops that could replace them, so far more may be involved than a straightforward substitution between two crops only.

The valuation of unsaleable fodders may be illustrated by an arable farm of 60 ha run by the farmer and his son, on which there is a herd of 36 dairy cows, the maximum number that the cowshed permits. With all replacement heifers purchased, the cows require 15 ha of leys for grazing and another 5 ha for making into some 100 tonnes of silage (variable costs £100 per ha). In addition, 38 tonnes of hay are purchased for about £33 per tonne. The rest of the land is under 36 ha of barley (gross margin £250 per hectare) and 4 ha of sugar beet (gross margin £600 per hectare).

As work on silage making and sugar beet (still hand-singled) clash, the farmer is wondering whether he should stop growing the 5 ha of leys for silage and instead purchase another 38 tonnes of hay. To determine whether this is worthwhile, it is necessary to calculate the real costs of the silage. The farmer reckons that, if silage were to be eliminated, sufficient labour would be released to enable him to grow another hectare of sugar beet (for which he should be able to obtain the necessary contract), while the remaining 4 ha would be put into barley. His present and potential cropping are thus:

Present cropping	(hectares)	*Potential cropping*	(hectares)
Barley	36	Barley	40
Sugar beet	4	Sugar beet	5
Grazing leys	15	Grazing leys	15
Silage	5		
	60		60

The real cost of the 5 ha of silage is thus the value that would be gained from 1 ha of sugar beet and 4 ha of barley if silage making were to cease, together with the variable costs that would be saved on the latter:

	£
Value of fixed resources in alternative uses	
4 ha barley at £250 gross margin per hectare	1,000
1 ha sugar beet at £600 gross margin per hectare	600
Saving in variable costs	
5 ha of leys for silage at £100 per hectare	500
Real cost of 5 ha silage	2,100

As the 38 tonnes of hay that would replace the silage would cost on average £1254, compared with the real silage cost of £2100, the farmer decides to rely in future entirely on purchased hay. He is also encouraged to do so because the price of hay could rise to £55 per tonne (£2100/38t) before it would be a matter of indifference whether he made the silage or purchased the hay (see also Appendix 9.3).

If the comparison is between two home-grown fodder crops, the principles of valuing them remain exactly the same. Suppose, for instance, that the farmer in the previous example is contemplating using the 5 ha of leys for hay (40 tonnes from 2 cuts) instead of for silage. As haymaking does not clash with sugar beet singling, the introduction of 5 ha of hayed leys into the *potential* cropping organisation shown previously would simply require the sacrifice of 5 ha of barley at a cost of £1250. If the variable cost of hay is £105 per ha, total real cost amounts to £1775. Thus, other things being equal, haymaking is preferable on financial grounds to silage-making, while purchasing hay is better than either (in this example).

Instances may occur where a fodder crop is regarded as an essential part of a rotation, for which at the same time there is no feasible alternative. Livestock may thus sometimes be kept simply because the crop is available, rather than the crop being grown because there are animals to be fed, so that the planning problem is to determine the most suitable type of livestock to use the crop. The fattening of beef on grass, grown as a break between cereals, may sometimes be undertaken for this reason. Although it is possible to calculate the real cost of such break crops – and this involves crediting them with the extra output that their inclusion stimulates from cash crops – it is in practice simpler to regard them as being without cost, so that they always have priority over alternative feeds. Care, however, must be taken that such break crops do not expand beyond that area where they can be economically justified on rotational grounds. Permanent pasture may fall into a similar category, if some or all of it can be ploughed and brought into rotation. That part which is unploughable can be regarded as being without cost, but that which is ploughable must be assessed in real terms.

By-products, such as sugar beet tops, straw and pea haulm, may appear to fall into much the same category, but here it is necessary to assess whether any of the resources required for their harvest have alternative uses. For example, sugar beet tops may seem to offer a 'free' fodder, but their utilisation may be costly in real terms, both through the diversion from other productive tasks of the labour required to collect them during what is usually a busy period, and through the planting of a smaller acreage of winter wheat, because ploughing and seed-bed cultivations have to be delayed until the tops are cleared from the land.

Feed substitution and the time factor

Our concern up to now has been simply with problems of determining least-cost rations for a given quantity (and quality) of livestock output. It may, in addition, be necessary to take account of the time factor in relation to least-cost feeding for, with temporary stock, different feeds or mixes may result in different rates of daily gain and thus varying time spans for the completion of the process. The situation is thus analogous to that of allowing for time when seeking optimal levels of feeding, and the summary in the previous chapter (pp. 191–2) is pertinent to least-cost rationing also. If the time span of the process can be regarded as fixed, the aim must be to obtain a given output at least cost. If time can vary, however, throughput must also be considered.

To illustrate this, Table 9.3 presents experimental results of feeding two rations, containing different levels of protein, to fattening pigs.

TABLE 9.3. *Least-cost rations and rates of fattening in pig production*

1. *Margin per pig*

	Meal fed to add 68 kg flesh (kg)	Meal price per kg (p)	Meal cost per pig (£)	Receipts less weaner cost per pig[a] (£)	Margin per pig (£)
High protein	226	14.00	31.6	37	5.4
Low protein	262	11.85	31.0	37	6.0

2. *Margin per annum* (per 100 pig places)

	Daily livewt. gain (kg)	Time to add 68 kg (days)	Annual throughput[b]	Margin per pig (£)	Annual Margin (£)
High Protein	0.61	111	302	5.4	1,631
Low Protein	0.53	128	264	6.0	1,584

[a] Receipts per pig £55 less £18 weaner cost..
[b] Allowing 10 days clear between batches.
Source: Based on Morgan, J. T., Green, F. R., Costain, R. A. and Williams, E. F. (1959) *J. Agric. Sci.* **52**, 170.

Section 1 shows that those on the high-protein diet consumed 226 kg of meal in gaining 68 kg liveweight (23 to 91 kg), which was 36 kg less than the 262 kg consumed by those receiving the low-protein meal. Nevertheless, if it is assumed that the high and low-protein meals cost 14p and 11.85p per kg respectively, the latter, in spite of the higher meal input, results in a slightly lower cost of meal per pig. If, for purposes of illustration, it is further assumed that carcass quality is the same in each case (although in fact, the pigs on the low-protein diet carried significantly more fat and less lean), the low-protein diet gives a greater margin per pig.

However, this is to disregard the time factor for, as the second part of the table shows, pigs on the low protein diet required an extra 17 days (128 compared with 111) to gain 68 kg. With intermittent production, the low-protein meal is optimal, as long as time-variable costs, if any, for the extra 17 days do not exceed £0.6 per pig – the difference in margin per pig between the two rations. With continuous production, account must be taken of the number of batches per pig place per annum, which amounts to 3.02 and 2.64 for the high and low-protein rations respectively (allowing 10 days clear between batches). Section 2 of the table translates this into terms of a 100-pig fattening house and shows that high-protein feeding leaves the higher annual margin because greater throughput more than offsets a lower margin per pig. (This example is naturally not meant to imply that a more expensive meal combined with a shorter production cycle is always to be preferred in continuous production for, quality considerations apart, low protein meal has only to fall in price from 11.85p to 11.76p per kg for it to become optimal.)

Summary

In considering the principles of least-cost feeding, it has been seen that ideally different rations should be related to livestock performance, in terms of both a given quantity and quality of product. In practice, however, both may vary with changes in the pattern of feeding. For example, in milk production different rations may impose varying limits on total yield (as was seen in Table 9.2), while in pig fattening one meal may lead to different proportions of fat to lean and differing killing-out percentages from another. Nonetheless, given the necessary data (as in Table 9.3, for example), allowances can be made for such quantitative and qualitative variations in output.

However, more often than not the producer has no relevant data to guide him, and is forced back on the assumption that foods substitute for one another in direct ratio to their nutrient content. Where this is the case, substitutions between the individual foods to be included in a ration are best assessed in terms of the cost of the whole mix and not simply of the individual ingredients. For example, a producer seeking the cheapest protein feed with which to balance the carbohydrate in a pig-fattening ration should compare the cost of the different rations, rather than the cost of protein in the individual foods. This is because the quantities of other constituents in the ration are likely to alter with changes in the source of protein.

Fortunately, problems in least-cost rationing are not equally serious in all cases. At one end of the scale, substitutions between similar purchased concentrates are relatively easy to calculate, because their values are readily determined and the assumption of constant rates of substitution may not be too wide of the mark. At the other end of the scale, the greatest difficulties are likely to be encountered in comparisons that include home-grown bulky foods. The reason is that, on the one hand, variations in type and quality of food may make physical rates of substitution hard to determine and, on the other, the values to be attached to them are not immediately obvious. As has been seen, in order to determine meaningful values the producer has to involve himself in farm planning, so that foods are priced in terms of the relative availability of resources and the alternative uses to which they can be put on the individual farm.

The maximisation of margin over feed cost

Two distinct but closely related aspects of feeding have now been considered. One has been concerned with the level of feeding that results in the greatest margin between its own cost and the value of the output that it induces, the other with the pattern of feeding that costs the least for a given level of output. It is now time to draw these two sides of feeding together for neither of them, taken in isolation, necessarily

TABLE 9.4. *Intensity of feeding and feed substitution in pig production*[a] (fattening from 23 kg to 73 kg liveweight)

Ration[b] Milk (%)	Ration[b] Grain (%)	Total feed Milk (l)	Total feed Grain (kg)	Time (weeks)	Carcass Lean (%)	Carcass Price (cents/kg)	Margin[c] per pig ($)	Margin[c] per week ($)
1. *Intensity*								
1.0	1.0	850	77.6	27.5	58.6	46.0	15.17	0.55
1.5	1.5	682	68.1	15.4	54.4	44.9	16.21	1.05
2.0	2.0	627	62.6	10.8	50.5	41.8	14.60	1.36
2.5	2.5	686	66.7	9.4	47.0	37.7	10.92	1.16
2. *Substitution*								
1.5	1.5	682	68.1	15.4	54.4	44.9	16.21	1.05
2.0	1.0	818	41.8	14.4	54.1	44.9	16.76	1.17
2.5	0.5	1,041	17.3	13.6	53.3	44.3	16.89	1.24
3.0	0.0	1,227	0.	13.1	52.0	43.4	16.08	1.22
3. *Optimal rations*								
per pig:								
2.0	0.0	1,241	0.	21.8	58.8	46.0	17.97	0.82
per week:								
1.5	3.5	418	88.5	9.1	48.7	39.6	12.73	1.40

[a] Based on computed averages for experimental diets fed in trials conducted at Wollongbar Agricultural Research Station, N.S.W., Australia.

[b] Dry matter of the two feeds in terms of proportions of the pig's bodyweight. For example, a pig weighing 27 kg on a diet of 2% milk and 3% grain would receive a ration of 0.54 kg milk dry matter and 0.81 kg grain until next weighing day.

[c] When separated milk costs 0.684 cents a litre and wheat 7.067 cents per kg.

Source: Based on Battese, G. E., Duloy, J. H., Holder, J. M. and Wilson, B. R. (1968) *J. Agric. Econ.* **XIX**, 3.

leads to the maximum margin over feed cost. For this to be achieved it is necessary to determine the pattern and intensity of feeding that provides the optimal level of output at least cost. These two aspects are considered in Table 9.4, which is based on the results of an Australian pig feeding trial. Fattening was to a fixed weight of 73 kg on a ration based on skim milk and wheat, fed in various combinations and at various levels of intensity, ranging from two to five per cent of bodyweight. In arriving at the margin per pig and per week, fixed costs, such as those involved in producing weaners, are deducted, but not labour cost, interest or building maintenance. Allowance is made for the effect of different rations on carcass quality. Of the two criteria of optimality, margin per pig is applicable to intermittent production and margin per week to continuous production.

In the first part of the table the proportion of milk to grain in the diet is kept constant (at fifty per cent), while the weight of the ration (in terms of dry matter) rises from two to five per cent of bodyweight. The concern is therefore with the particular intensity of feeding that should be selected. If production is intermittent, so that selection is based on margin per pig, ration $M = 1.5$, $G = 1.5$ gives the highest margin of \$16.21.[1] If production is continuous, however, more intensive feeding, $M = 2$, $G = 2$, is best, for, although it leads to a fall of \$1.61 (\$16.21 – \$14.60) in the margin per pig, the reduction of nearly five weeks in the fattening period raises the margin per week by \$0.31 (\$1.36 – \$1.05).

In the second part of the table the level of the ration remains the same in each case at three per cent of bodyweight, but the proportion of skim milk varies between fifty and one-hundred per cent of the total. The concern is thus with the particular make-up of the ration that gives the best results. With both intermittent and continuous production this is ration $M = 2.5$, $G = 0.5$, with a margin per pig of \$16.89 and per week of \$1.24. A comparison of these results with those in the first part of the table shows that the optimal 'substitution' ration gives a higher margin

[1] As noted above, this is when no time-variable costs, such as labour, are charged. If they amounted to \$0.35 per week, it would be a matter of indifference whether ration $M = 1.5$, $G = 1.5$ or ration $M = 2$, $G = 2$ was selected, as shown below:

Ration (M)	(G)	*Margin per pig* (\$)	*Period* (weeks)	*Time-vc per week* (\$)	*Total time-vc* (\$)	*Margin less time-vc* (\$)
1.5	1.5	16.21	15.4	0.35	5.39	10.82
2.0	2.0	14.60	10.8	0.35	3.78	10.82

If they were to rise higher than this, ration $M = 2$, $G = 2$ would become optimal.

per pig than the optimal 'intensity' ration – \$16.89 compared with \$16.21 – but a lower weekly margin – \$1.24 compared with \$1.36.

Thus, taken in isolation, neither the intensity with which a given mix is fed, nor the variation in composition of a fixed weight of ration, necessarily leads to maximum profits, as is further demonstrated in the last part of the table, which shows the optimal rations when allowance is made for the full range in both these factors. With intermittent production, ration $M = 2$, $G = 0$ gives the highest margin per pig – \$17.97 – and with continuous production, ration $M = 1.5$, $G = 3.5$ gives the highest margin per week – \$1.40. It is only by taking into account both the *level* and the *composition* of the ration that optimal results can be derived.

Table 9.5, based on the previous example of the final stages of intensive beef fattening in Table 8.5 (p. 193), takes matters a stage further,

TABLE 9.5. *Feed conversion and substitution in intensive beef production* (hypothetical data)

1. Intermittent

Month	Feed rate	Cumulative profit per beast Meal *A* (£)	Meal *B* (£)	Meal *C* (£)
10	Low	3.3	3.7	3.6
	Moderate	7.3	8.1	7.9
	High	9.0	9.9	9.8
11	Low	2.0	2.2	2.3
	Moderate	14.3	13.9	14.7
	High	14.8	14.6	18.2
12	Low	0.9	1.0	1.1
	Moderate	19.4	17.6	18.9
	High	17.2	17.0	18.3

2. Continuous

Length of process[a] (months)	Batches per annum	Highest profit in month: Meal	Feed rate	Profit per beast (£)	Annual profit (£)
10.3	1.16	*B*	High	9.9	11.5
11.3	1.06	*C*	High	18.2	19.3
12.3	0.97	*A*	Moderate	19.4	18.8

[a] Allowing 10 days clear between batches.

in that alternative meals are assumed to be available. In addition to the meal fed at different levels in Table 8.5 (which becomes meal *A* in Table 9.5), there are now two alternative meals – *B* and *C* – that cost respectively less and more than meal *A* and result in different rates of growth.[1] Given such data, the farmer can determine which ration to use, at what rate to feed it and when to terminate production. For instance, if production consists simply of an occasional batch of animals, meal *A* fed at the moderate rate for a twelve-month period gives the highest profit per beast (£19.4). On the other hand, if production is continuous, meal *C* fed at the high rate for eleven months is optimal (£19.3 per annum).

In the final analysis, it has to be acknowledged that data as comprehensive as in Tables 9.4 and 9.5 are rarely available to the individual farmer. By contrast, Table 9.6, although based on experimental data, shows the type of information that the farmer might collate for himself. It is based on the assumption, which is common practice in milk production, that concentrates are rationed, and that bulky fodder is then fed to the limit of appetite. Additional concentrates in the ration not only result in hay being saved, but at the same time stimulate extra milk output (because more nutrients can be consumed before appetite becomes limiting, see Table 9.2). Consequently, instead of simply balanc-

TABLE 9.6. *Feed conversion and substitution in milk production* (per cow for a 28-day period at mean stage of lactation)

Ration	Feed combinations Concs: (kg)	Hay (kg)	Milk yield (l)	Feed cost[a] Concs: (£)	Hay (£)	Total (£)	Receipts[b] (£)	Margin (£)
A	0	508	320	0	17.8	17.8	38.4	20.6
B	63.6	470	394	8	16.5	24.5	47.3	22.8
C	127.2	407	448	16	14.2	30.2	53.8	23.6
D	190.8	343	486	24	12.0	36.0	58.3	22.3
E	254.4	267	513	32	9.3	41.3	61.6	20.3
F	318.0	165	523	40	5.8	45.8	62.8	17.0

[a] Concentrates 12.5p and hay 3.5p per kg.

[b] Receipts 12p per litre.

Source: Based on Langley, J. A. (1965) (from estimates by Heady, E. O. et al. 1956) *O.E.C.D. Documentation in Food and Agriculture*, **71**, 121.

[1] For simplicity, only cumulative profits are shown. They are, however, derived in the same way as those illustrated in Table 8.5.

ing the cost of extra concentrates against the value of hay saved, as would be the case if only a single level of output were being considered, account has also to be taken of the value of the extra milk. For example, in moving from ration *A* to ration *B*, an extra £8 is incurred for 63.6 kg concentrates. This not only saves 38 kg hay worth £1.3, but at the same time allows the production of 74 litres more milk worth £8.9; so the substitution is worth making. By contrast, moving from ration *E* to ration *F* results in a saving of hay worth £3.5 and an increase in milk output of £1.2, which is insufficient to offset the extra £8 spent on concentrates. In fact, in the circumstances assumed, it is ration *C* that brings in the greatest margin.

Patterns of feeding and land use

The pattern of feeding adopted with grazing livestock, for which a large proportion of the foods are normally home-grown, may have important repercussions on land use. The choice of foods directly affects the animals' hectare requirements which, in turn, tend to be inversely correlated with margins per ha. Feeding patterns that result in high stocking densities thus raise the ability of livestock activities to compete with other enterprises for land, usually a scarce resource on farms.

There are three types of feed substitution that may lead to an increased stocking density. The first is to replace existing fodder crops by others of higher potential output per ha. For example, if sufficient labour is available for thinning and harvesting them, kale and mangolds are capable of giving twice the nutrient output (metabolisable energy) per ha compared with grass treated with moderate intensity and conserved as hay or silage. In a similar manner, a higher output per ha from grassland may be obtained by the substitution of existing species of grass by more productive types and by species that extend the grazing season.[1]

The second way is to substitute purchased foods for home-grown ones. This is commonly done with concentrated foods, although often in a negative sense, in that there was never any intention of growing them (or a substitute) on the farm in the first place, so that they are a supplement to home-grown foods rather than a substitute. Neverthe-

[1] Methods of raising productivity that are more concerned with better production and utilisation – rather than substitution – of existing crops also link in closely here. They result either from better cultural practices, such as the more intensive use of fertilisers, or from reducing waste on existing levels of output, as when pastures are stocked more intensively or when barn-dried hay replaces naturally cured hay.

less, the implication remains that if the crop or a similar one could be grown on the farm, land is saved by not doing so. It is less common with marketable bulky fodders, such as hay and straw, although where scarcity of land is a major problem their purchase does offer one solution to the pressure on it.

The last method is to substitute by-products for fodder crops specifically grown for livestock. On the whole, this is mainly applicable to farms where there is at least some arable land. Examples are the substitution of sugar beet tops for kale, of pea haulm silage for grass silage and of straw for hay.

Table 9.7 shows the potential of these types of substitution for raising gross margin per ha in semi-intensive beef production, where calves are purchased in the autumn and sold fat in the spring eighteen months later, when they weigh about 460 kg. The calves receive concentrates and hay in the first winter after they have been early weaned. They are turned out to grass in May when about seven months old and subsequently yarded again by the end of October. In their second winter they receive concentrates, hay and silage. Bulky fodder requirements (as column 1 shows) amount to 0.44 ha per head – 0.2 ha grazed and 0.24 ha conserved, the latter providing 1 tonne hay and 1.5 tonnes silage. Gross margin amounts to £51 per beast and £116 per hectare.

The first substitution (column 2) is to replace the 1 tonne of home-grown hay per cow with purchased hay at £30 per tonne. Although the gross margin per beast falls by £15, gross margin per hectare rises by a similar amount because of the saving of hay land. Furthermore, the price per tonne of hay could rise to £33.5 before gross margin per ha would fall to its former level. (With hay at £33.5 per tonne, the gross margin per beast falls by a further £3.5 to £32.5, which divided by the reduced land requirement of 0.28 ha gives £116 per hectare.)

In the second substitution (column 3), the grassland requirement is reduced by 0.12 ha per beast, by a combination of a better choice of species and by improved cultural practices, including heavier use of fertiliser and paddock grazing. Gross margin per head falls by £5 because of the extra expenditure on the grassland (variable costs on grass rise by £45 per ha), but gross margin per ha rises to £144 – 24 per cent above its original level.

The third substitution (column 4) depends on the use of by-products. In the second winter, sugar beet tops and pea haulm silage replace the grass silage and straw replaces part of the hay. As a consequence, 0.12 ha are saved and fodder variable costs also fall by £9. Gross margin per ha rises by 62 per cent to £188 per hectare.

TABLE 9.7. *Feed substitution, stocking density and gross margin per hectare* (Per beast) (semi-intensive beef example).

	(1) Basic method		(2) Bought hay		(3) Intensive grassland		(4) By-products		(5) Measures (2) and (3)		(6) Measures (2) (3) and (4)	
		(£)		(£)		(£)		(£)		(£)		(£)
Receipts		290		290		290		290		290		290
Variable costs												
Calf		64		64		64		64		64		64
Concentrates		129		129		129		129		129		129
Miscellaneous		10		10		10		10		10		10
Bought hay		—		30		—		—		30		22
Home grown fodder	(ha)		(ha)		(ha)		(ha)		(ha)		(ha)	
Grazing	0.20		0.20		0.14		0.20		0.14		0.14	
Hay	0.16		—		0.12		0.12		—		—	
Silage	0.08		0.08		0.06		—		0.06		—	
	0.44		0.28		0.32		0.32		0.20		0.14	
		36		21		41		27		24		17
Total variable costs		239		254		244		230		257		242
Gross margin		51		36		46		60		33		48
Gross margin per hectare		116		129		144		188		165		343
Index		100		111		124		162		142		296

Finally, the last two columns show the effect of combining the previous measures. In column 5, the intensification of grassland and the purchase of hay are brought together, as would be feasible on a purely grassland farm. Hectare requirements fall by over a half and gross margin rises to £165 per ha, over 40 per cent above the original level. Column 6 adds to this the use of by-products, which might be possible on an arable farm. Gross margin per ha rises nearly three times to £343.

It will be clear from our earlier discussion of the valuation of home-grown foods that substitutions such as these must not be considered in isolation from the rest of the farm, for they may compete with other enterprises for the use of fixed resources additional to land. For example although, as mentioned earlier, kale and mangolds when thinned are capable of giving a higher nutrient output per ha than hay or silage, their considerable requirements of labour may clash with the needs of other crops, such as sugar beet and potatoes. Indeed, this is a prime cause of their relative unpopularity to-day. In addition, even if the existing cropping pattern is not directly influenced by such substitutions, the area that is saved must earn at least as much margin as in its existing production. For example, if 100 beasts were being fattened on the original system (column 1, Table 9.7) they take up 44 ha and give a total gross margin of £5100. If hay is purchased (column 2) the area required falls to 28 hectares and gross margin to £3600. Thus the 16 hectares saved must at least bring the gross margin on the total area back to £5100 if the substitution is to be worthwhile. In short, unless they can earn £1500, or £94 per ha, the original system remains the better one. Similarly, when the purchase of hay is combined with the intensification of grassland use (column 5), so that the area for 100 beasts falls from 44 to 20 ha and gross margin falls by £1800, the 24 ha saved must earn at least £75 per hectare for the substitution to be worthwhile.

These substitutions have been considered in the light of the scarcity of land and the consequent need to raise the intensity of its use in livestock production. If other resources, such as labour and capital, are relatively more scarce, accepting a lower return per ha in order to give a higher return to these resources may be the more appropriate course of action. This is particularly likely to be true if the livestock activities themselves are expanded becasue of improved stocking rates – rather than the land saved being used for other purposes – for there may be considerable capital requirements for more purchased feed, stock and buildings.

Appendix 9.1: Marginal rates of substitution of feedstuffs and least-cost rations

It will be appreciated, from the principles expounded in Chapter 2, that the least cost ration for a given level of livestock output is specified by the following equations:

$$\Delta B/\Delta A = P_a/P_b \qquad (1)$$

or

$$\Delta A \times P_a = \Delta B \times P_b \qquad (2)$$

where ΔB is the decrease in the quantity of feedstuff B consequent upon ΔA, an increase in the quantity of feedstuff A, and P_b and P_a are their respective prices per unit weight. Equation (1) establishes that the least cost ration (under conditions of diminishing returns) obtains when the marginal rate of substitution of the two feedstuffs ($\Delta B/\Delta A$) is inversely equal to their price ratio, and equation (2) – which is obtained from equation (1) by cross-multiplication – when the value of the feed added equals the value of the feed saved. The latter formulation is represented by column (4) of the broiler example in Table 9.1, which is based on *average* marginal rates of substitution between discrete mixes of soya-bean meal and corn. The precise least-cost ration is not specified by any of the rations shown, but falls between mix *C* and mix *D* (at the point where 72p of soya-bean meal added equals 72p of corn saved). It could be solved exactly by the use of calculus, given the underlying production function expressing the relationship between the two feeds and broiler output.

Although the use of simple arithmetic to derive marginal rates of substitution is thus less precise than algebraic formulation, it may be justified for practical use on two counts. First, as farmers must rely to a large extent on their own data, to which the application of sophisticated forms of analysis is inappropriate, their approach to least-cost rationing must be based on an understanding of the principles involved, coupled with the application of simple arithmetic. Secondly, there are often occasions when inputs must, for technical reasons, be in discrete amounts and cannot be varied continuously, as for example when a feed hopper in a milking parlour delivers concentrates in set 'doses'. (We may also note that these same comments apply to obtaining the optimal level of output, as considered in Chapter 8.)

Those wishing to pursue further the use of production functions in livestock feeding are recommended to refer to any of the OECD publications mentioned in Tables 9.1 and 9.2.

Appendix 9.2: Metabolisable energy

A system of rationing based on metabolisable energy (ME) replaced the former starch equivalent (SE) system in 1976, and is detailed in *Energy Allowances and Feeding Systems for Ruminants*, Ministry of Agriculture, Fisheries and Food Technical Bulletin 33 (1975). In essence it is based on principles put forward by Blaxter in 1965, in the Agricultural Research Council's *The Nutrient Requirements of Farm Livestock. No. 2. Ruminants*, but includes, in addition, a variable net energy (NE) system for cattle and sheep. The relationships underlying the systems are expressed as simple, linear equations, and have to be applied within the context of the problems discussed in Ch. 8.

Appendix 9.3: Real cost of home-grown fodder crops

The real cost of growing a fodder crop has been seen to be made up of:

(*a*) The variable costs of the fodder crop;

(*b*) The value (gross margin) of the alternative activities that would replace it if it were not to be grown.

More precisely, the latter is made up of the value – or 'net' opportunity cost – of the resources required by the fodder crop that are 'scarce', in the sense that they are currently fully utilised.

The valuation of scarce resources may be illustrated by the arable/dairy farm example (pp. 210–11) where land and labour in May/June (sugar beet singling and silage making period) are the fully utilised resources.

Net opportunity cost of one hectare of land

If one ha of land is released (independently of labour) from the silage crop, it will be replaced by one ha of barley (it cannot be put into sugar beet because more labour is required, nor into cows as numbers are already at their maximum). The gross margin of a hectare of barley is £250 and this is therefore the net opportunity cost of one ha of land.

Net opportunity cost of one hour of May/June labour

If one hour of labour is released from silage making (independently of land) it will be replaced by 0.013 (1/75th) ha of sugar beet (which requires 75 hours per ha of May/June labour). Land for the extra beet grown will be taken from barley. Balancing the gains and losses:

Selection of feedstuffs

	(£)
Gain 0.013 ha of sugar beet at £600	8.00
Sacrifice 0.013 ha of barley at £250	−3.33
Net opportunity cost of 1 hour labour	4.67

These values may be applied to one acre of silage production in order to obtain the real cost of the latter.

Real cost of one hectare of silage

	(£)	(£)
Use of scarce fixed resources		
Land: 1 ha at £250	250	
Labour: 15 hours at £4.67	70	
		320
Use of variable resources		
Seed, fertiliser etc.		100
Real cost per hectare		420

10: The influence of season on livestock production

There is commonly some degree of flexibility in the time of year when the livestock producer initiates production and sells the ensuing output. It is most apparent with temporary livestock, of which the semi-intensive production of beef is one example. Calves may be purchased in the autumn and sold fat eighteen months later in spring or, conversely, they may be purchased in spring and sold eighteen months later in autumn. Or, in either case, the process may be prolonged and the animals sold, for instance, at twenty-one rather than eighteen months. Another example is the traditional fattening of beef stores, which may commence in spring with the animals sold fat off grass in autumn, or commence in autumn with the animals yarded and sold fat in spring.

The position is much the same for those permanent livestock whose output consists of young animals, such as the ewe flock or the beef or pig breeding herds. For example, the ewe flock may be lambed down early in January with lambs sold fat from April onwards, or lambing may be later in March with sales commencing towards the end of June. Again, with lowland single-suckled beef herds, calving may range from late autumn to spring, with the sale of store beasts falling mainly in autumn in each case.

There remain those permanent livestock where there is more or less continuous output the year round – as exemplified by milk and egg production – and where, in consequence, seasonal factors may appear to be of little relevance. However, in such cases, the producer may bring seasonal forces to bear by varying the volume of output at different times of the year. For example, a milk producer has the three broad possibilities of calving his cows mainly in autumn, so that some two-thirds of the milk output falls in the winter months, of calving them in spring and so putting the emphasis on summer milk, or of spreading his calvings so that there is near enough level production the year round.

As livestock processes are capable of seasonal variation, the producer is faced with a choice as to their timing. He needs, in consequence, to be aware of the way in which seasonal shifts in production affect the economic outcome through their bearing on yields, on costs and on prices. Although we now consider them one at a time, these factors are, in practice, closely interwoven.

Seasonal production and yield

In many cases the timing of production influences the physical yields of livestock. This is most evident when animals are kept under 'natural' conditions, rather than being buffered against them by a closely controlled environment, such as with intensive egg production in a battery unit.

In milk production, for example, one study revealed that cows calving in October to December averaged a yield some twelve per cent higher than those calving from May to June.[1] Furthermore, this was so, not just between herds where calvings were concentrated in spring as opposed to autumn, but also between cows in the same herds calved at those different times. The 'flushing' effect of spring grass played a part in this, in that the output of autumn calvers declined less rapidly than that of spring calvers after the peak of lactation had been reached. Somewhat similarly, a study of egg production found that birds kept under natural conditions and coming into lay in September gave over one-third more eggs than those coming into lay in February, due largely to different patterns of light intensity in relation to stage of lay.[2] Another example is given by lowland, out-wintered, ewe flocks, where the lambing percentage may be ten to fifteen per cent higher for the flock lambed under relatively equable conditions in March and April, compared with that lambing under harsher conditions in December and January. Yet again, the yield of beef stores (namely, their rate of liveweight gain in a given period) may differ materially for animals fattened on grass in summer, compared with those fattened in yards in winter.

These examples make it clear that the producer is often able to influence the level of yield of his animals by his choice of the time of the year when he starts production.

[1] *Report of the Breeding and Production Organisation.* Milk Marketing Board, No. 19 (1968–9) 109.

[2] Maw, A. J. G. and Maw, W. A. (1928) *Scientific Agriculture* (Ottawa) **IX**, No. 4, 201.

Seasonal production and prices

The prices of many livestock products – as Figure 10.1 shows – vary with the time of year. Often this is the consequence of institutional price fixing, but it may also result from interaction between supply and demand or some combination of the two.

Milk, for example, is higher priced in winter than in summer, largely to ensure an adequate supply of the higher-cost winter milk. Prices are lowest in early summer when milk can be produced largely from grass. For similar reasons, beef prices show the same general pattern as milk prices, although to a less marked extent and with the trough falling later. Egg prices are highest in mid-winter, because the supply is then at its lowest, whereas sheep prices reach their peak in spring, when the first of the output from early-lambed flocks is reaching the market.

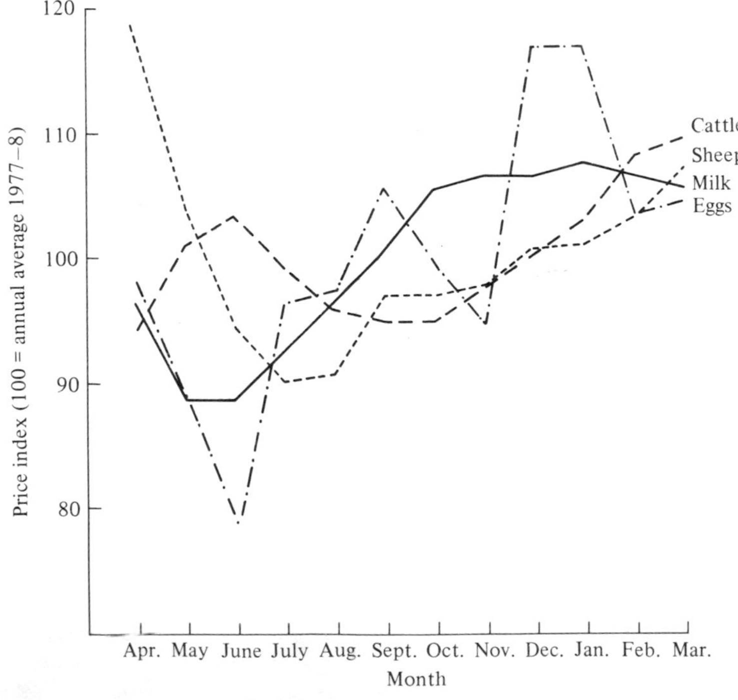

Fig. 10.1. Seasonal pricing

It follows that the producer can raise his returns from livestock either by selling fat or store stock when prices are high or by manipulating production from permanent livestock so that peak output coincides with peak prices.

Seasonal pricing and length of process with temporary livestock – intermittent production

Previously it was suggested that where it is feasible to carry animals to heavier weights by prolonging the length of the process (p. 190 and Table 8.5), production should continue for as long as extra receipts cover extra costs. This, however, was under conditions of constant prices over time. Seasonal pricing, by contrast, may result in the apparent anomaly that it pays to continue production when receipts for the extra weight added do not cover the costs of obtaining it or, conversely, to terminate production although receipts still cover extra costs.

In examining why this should be so, use is made of a previous example of intensive beef production. Section 1*a* of Table 10.1 repeats the data for the *low* rate of feeding from Table 8.5, but in addition distinguishes between feeder's and market margins in each month. (Refer back to p. 189 for definitions of these terms.) With sale price constant from month to month at 74p per kg, it is clear that production should be terminated at the end of the tenth month, because in the ensuing months extra receipts (column 4) do not cover extra costs (column 5). Consequently, the feeder's margin is negative (column 6). At the same time, as prices do not change, the market margin is zero.

Section 1*b* of the table assumes that there is seasonal pricing, the price per kg liveweight rising slightly from 74p to 76p and 77p in months eleven and twelve respectively. In these two months, the costs of the extra output are still not covered by the extra receipts, so that the feeder's margin is again negative. However, as the price rise, of 2p and 3p per kg respectively, also applies to the weight added before the start of the month, there is a positive market margin which is more than sufficient to offset the loss on feeding (in spite of the small changes in prices deliberately assumed). On balance, the overall margin (column 8) rises throughout, so that it is worthwhile feeding to the end of the twelfth month. For example, the effect in the eleventh month of constant prices may be compared with that of rising prices:

TABLE 10.1. *Seasonal pricing and feeder's and market margins* (intensive beef production)

Month	Sale price per kg	Weight: At start	Weight: Added	Value added (3) × (1)	Extra Costs[a]	Margin: Feeder's (4) − (5)	Margin: Market (2) × p^b	Margin: Both	Cumulative values at end of month: Costs	Cumulative values at end of month: Receipts	Cumulative values at end of month: Profit (10) − (9)
	(1)	(2)	(3)	(4)	(5)	(6)	(7)	(8)	(9)	(10)	(11)
	(p)	(kg)	(kg)	(£)	(£)	(£)	(£)	(£)	(£)	(£)	(£)
1*a*. *Low feed rate (prices constant)*											
10	74	327	26	19.2	17.9	1.3	—	1.3	257.9	261.2	3.3
11	74	353	26	19.3	20.6	−1.3	—	−1.3	278.5	280.5	2.0
12	74	379	30	22.2	23.3	−1.1	—	−1.1	301.8	302.7	0.9
1*b*. *Low feed rate (prices rising)*											
10	74	327	26	19.2	17.9	1.3	—	1.3	257.9	261.2	3.3
11	76	353	26	19.8	20.6	−0.8	7.1	6.3	278.5	288.1	9.6
12	77	379	30	23.1	23.3	−0.2	3.8	3.6	301.8	315.0	13.2
2*a*. *High feed rate (prices constant)*											
10	74	327	41	30.3	23.3	7.0	—	7.0	263.3	272.3	9.0
11	74	368	43	31.8	26.0	5.8	—	5.8	289.3	304.1	14.8
12	74	411	42	31.1	28.7	2.4	—	2.4	318.0	335.2	17.2
2*b*. *High feed rate (prices falling)*											
10	74	327	41	30.3	23.3	7.0	—	7.0	263.3	272.3	9.0
11	72	368	43	31.0	26.0	5.0	−7.4	−2.4	289.3	295.9	6.6
12	71	411	42	29.8	28.7	1.1	−4.1	−3.0	318.0	321.6	3.6

[a] Meal cost and time-variable costs as in Table 8.5.
[b] p = Difference in price per kg between the start and end of the month.

	Constant prices	*(74p)* (£)	*Rising prices*	*(74p to 76p)* (£)
Value of output added in 11th month	26 kg at 74p	19.3	26 kg at 76p	19.8
Costs incurred in month		20.6		20.6
Loss on feeding (feeder's margin)		−1.3		−0.8
Gain on initial weight (market margin)		—	353 kg at 2p	7.1
	Net loss	−1.3	Net gain	6.3

In the same way, declining prices affect the weight previously added and, in consequence, production may need to be terminated even though the value of flesh added is sufficient to cover the costs of obtaining it. Sections 2*a* and 2*b* of the table illustrate this for the high rate of feeding. Under constant prices it is worth extending the process to twelve months, but with the price falls assumed in section 2*b* the negative market margin more than offsets the gain on feeding, so that production should cease at the end of the tenth month.

In addition, any other age-linked price differentials, such as the influence of age on grading, have a precisely similar effect to that of seasonal pricing and, like the latter, can be allowed for by calculating cumulative values as in columns 9 to 11 of Table 10.1.

Seasonal pricing and length of process with temporary livestock – continuous production

Where production is continuous with one batch following on after another, a complicating factor is that unless the process lasts exactly a year (or multiples thereof) each successive batch of animals is sold in a different month. For example, if the process lasts nine months with the first batch sold in September, the second batch is sold in June of the following year, the third in March of the year after and so on. In consequence, if there is marked seasonal pricing, each batch sells at a different price and the optimal timing of production must be based not on a single batch but on a number of batches that may extend over several years.

The main issue is the effect that the length of the individual process has on the degree of choice between different patterns of selling dates and how, in turn, the latter are affected by seasonal pricing. A subsidiary issue concerns the length of the cycle before price patterns start to repeat themselves. If the nine-month process is again taken, and it is assumed that production of the first batch starts on 1 January, the whole cycle is as follows:

Batch no.	*Starting date*	*Year*	*Selling date*	*Year*	*Months elapsing*
1	1 Jan.	1	30 Sept.	1	9
2	1 Oct.	1	30 June	2	9
3	1 July	2	31 Mar.	3	9
4	1 Apr.	3	31 Dec.	3	9
5	1 Jan.	4	......		36

The length of the cycle before the price pattern starts to repeat is three years and by that time four batches have been sold, giving a combination of four selling dates (March, June, September and December). It follows from this that the choice of selling patterns is limited to three (still assuming monthly starting and selling dates) namely:

Selling pattern (*a*) January, April, July, October;
(*b*) February, May, August, November;
(*c*) March, June, September, December (illustrated above).

If the length of the individual process is six months instead of nine, the complete cycle lasts only one year, during which two batches of animals are sold. There is thus a choice of six selling patterns, each consisting of two selling dates as follows:[1]

Selling pattern (*d*) January, July;
(*e*) February, August;
(*f*) March, September;
(*g*) April, October;
(*h*) May, November;
(*i*) June, December.

Given an expected monthly price distribution (which for long cycles has to be estimated for several years ahead), the total returns accruing to different selling patterns can be compared. Suppose, for example, that prices are distributed so that there is relatively little price movement the year round except for a short-lived and marked seasonal peak. This situation is represented in the form of an index in which January's price is 100.

Jan.	*Feb.*	*Mar.*	*Apr.*	*May*	*June*
100	101	103	105	130	105

[1] See Table 10.3, Appendix 10.1, for further examples.

July	Aug.	Sept.	Oct.	Nov.	Dec.
103	101	100	99	98	99

If, for simplicity, these values are taken as absolute values per animal (in £'s), receipts may be calculated for the selling patterns for the nine- and six-month processes. With the former, selling patterns (*a*) and (*c*) return £407 over the three-year cycle, while (*b*) returns £430. With the latter, pattern (*h*) returns £228 over the one-year cycle while the other five selling patterns bring in between £202 and £204. Thus, not unexpectedly, in both cases selling patterns that include the peak selling price (in May) give the highest return, while there is little to choose between the other patterns.

In contrast, another price distribution may be taken, where, although there is a greater difference between peak and trough prices, there is a more gradual build-up to, and fall-away from, the peak.

Jan.	Feb.	Mar.	Apr.	May	June
100	110	120	130	140	130
July	*Aug.*	*Sept.*	*Oct.*	*Nov.*	*Dec.*
120	110	100	90	80	90

Because of the more even price distribution, the three selling patterns of the nine-month process each bring in £440, and the six of the six-month process £220. It is thus a matter of indifference which seasonal pattern is chosen from the viewpoint of simple undiscounted returns.

The problem of selecting an optimal price pattern is thus to some extent mitigated in that the more marked and abrupt the peak in seasonal prices, the more is it necessary for it to be included, while with smoother changes through the year there is less to choose between different selling patterns. The number of selling dates included in the complete cycle is also a relevant factor in this respect, for the fewer there are, the more likely it is that different selling patterns will give different returns. The extreme example is the twelve- or twenty-four-month process which includes only one selling date and thus gives a choice of twelve selling patterns.[1]

[1] In addition, prices may change more or less frequently than monthly, as assumed here. Given all the data uncertainties, however, there would probably be little to be gained by distinguishing price changes for periods shorter than a month.

This analysis of the influence of seasonal pricing on the continuous production of temporary livestock is not meant to imply that once the producer has embarked on particular cycles of production he is inflexibly committed to them. A change may be made from one selling pattern to another by the introduction of an idle period (or, in other words, by switching for a time to intermittent production) or, perhaps, by varying the length of the individual process. Indeed, if the length of the process is not rigidly fixed, the selection of the optimal length should be based on the effect it has on selling patterns and throughput. Greater confidence will naturally be placed in the likely outcomes of short as opposed to long cycles and on the early stages of a long cycle rather than on its later stages. Furthermore, allowance must be made for the fact that the selection of optimal selling patterns depends on the evaluation of cash flows over time. In some cases, resort to formal discounting techniques may be necessary in order to clarify the situation (see Chapter 3), but frequently accumulating the undiscounted sale values as the cycle proceeds is sufficient (see Appendix 10.2 for examples).

Seasonal production and costs

Lastly, costs are influenced by the season of production. In this respect, the producer who is attempting to assess the cost changes consequent upon a proposed shift in seasonal output needs to distinguish between seasonally avoidable and seasonally unavoidable costs. The latter are those costs that, even if they should differ from one time of the year to another, are nevertheless an essential and unavoidable part of the overall system. As such, they have no part to play in decisions concerning seasonal production, whatever the selling pattern selected. Account thus needs to be taken only of the seasonally avoidable costs, that is, those costs that could actually be saved by switching production from one season to another. (There is thus a close parallel to the concept of 'conventional' fixed and variable costs in planning, with the difference that here costs are fixed or variable purely in the context of whether or not they change with seasonal shifts in production.)

The relative balance between seasonally avoidable and unavoidable costs varies with the type of livestock production. For example, many of the costs of milk production in an established herd fall into the seasonally unavoidable category. Maintenance rations in winter, which consist largely of conserved feeds, are more expensive than those supplied by grazing in summer. However, as they have to be fed the year round in order to keep the cows alive, their cost is unavoidable and does not change with shifts in seasonal production. Similarly with labour, where requirements are higher in winter because of extra cleaning and littering and handling of feedstuffs, and whose cost, therefore, is largely independent of whether more or less milk is produced at that time. On the other hand, the production ration is the only seasonally avoidable cost of any practical significance.

Failure to distinguish between seasonally avoidable and unavoidable costs may lead to incorrect evaluation of the likely effect of a change in the balance of seasonal production. Suppose, for example, that a dairy farmer with fairly level output all the year round is wondering whether it would be worthwhile putting a greater emphasis on seasonal production. In comparing the margin per litre of winter and summer milk, he mistakenly includes the cost of labour and the cost of providing bulky fodder and grazing for maintenance:

Margin per litre	*Winter*		*Summer*	
	(p)	(p)	(p)	(p)
Receipts		11.0		9.0
Costs – production ration	5.0		3.2	
– maintenance ration	2.5		2.0	
– labour	2.6	10.1	1.7	6.9
Margin		0.9		2.1

The much higher estimated margin per litre in summer suggests that more emphasis ought to be placed on production at that time. However, as the costs of the maintenance ration and labour would remain unaffected by a shift in the balance between winter and summer milk, they should be excluded from the calculation. The true margin is therefore simply that of receipts over the costs of the production ration, with a slight advantage of 0.2p per litre in favour of winter milk (6p compared with 5.8p). Thus in any comparison of seasonal production, only those items that will actually change should be included.[1]

In contrast to milk production, where most costs are seasonally unavoidable, are those types of production where they are largely avoidable. The seasonal calving pattern in single-suckled beef herds is one example. With spring calving outwintering may be possible, whereas with autumn calving extra costs may be incurred for labour and build-

[1] An alternative, which however involves more calculations, is to compare the *annual* profits from production where the emphasis is on output in winter and summer respectively.

ings necessary for inwintering. Similarly with the finishing of forward beef stores, where the choice may lie between fattening on grass in summer or in yards in winter. As these represent two distinct processes which do not overlap, most costs can be regarded as seasonally avoidable, although the fixed resources, such as labour and buildings, are only chargeable if they are at the same time in short supply. For example, the winter fattening of beef often relies for its labour supply on men who are surplus to other requirements at that time. Such surplus labour still has to be paid whether or not winter fattening is carried on and should not, therefore, be charged when comparing it with summer production. Conversely, if labour is in short supply, its cost to the cattle is either its value in alternative activities from which it has to be withdrawn or else the cost of hiring extra labour specifically for the livestock.

In summary, when evaluating seasonal costs, account should be taken only of those items that definitely change as a consequence of seasonal shifts in production. Furthermore, where this involves fixed resources, they must be valued in 'real' terms.

Seasonal production and the interaction of yield, price and cost

In deciding on the optimal timing of production, account must be taken of the combined effect that season has on yields, prices and costs. Often these work in opposition to one another. For example, the pattern of calvings in a dairy herd which results in the highest milk yield per cow does not necessarily give the highest average price per litre. Also, the relatively low cost of finishing beef on grass in summer is usually offset by a lower sale price per beast. However, in spite of these complications, the aim is to discover the seasonal pattern of production that gives the greatest margin between seasonal output (yield × price) and seasonal costs – as previously defined.

The production of fat lamb from an early and a late-lambed lowland ewe flock may be taken as an example. The former is lambed down in January with the bulk of the lambs sold fat in April, while the latter is lambed down in March with sales concentrated in July. Table 10.2 assesses the effect of these different seasonal patterns of production on physical output, prices and costs. The output of fat lamb per 100 ewes is 820 kg lower in the early-lambed flock, as a consequence of two factors. First, as climatic conditions are harsher with early lambing, the proportion of lambs that survive is lower than with late lambing. Secondly, the growth rates of the early lambs are also slower,

TABLE 10.2. *Seasonal production – early v. late lambing* (lowland flock) (per 100 ewes)

	Early lambing (January)	Late lambing (March)	Difference (late–early)
Physical output			
Lambs sold	130	145	+15
Weight at sale[a] (kg)	16	20	+4
Total weight sold (kg)	2,080	2,900	+820
Cull ewes	20	17	−3
Price per kg (p)	123.5 (April)	112.5 (July)	−11
Value output	(£)	(£)	(£)
Lambs	2,569	3,262	+693
Cull ewes (at £18)	360	306	−54
Total value output	2,929	3,568	+639
Seasonally avoidable costs			
Purchase replacements	875 (25)	770 (22)	−105
Concentrates	550 (5t)	462 (4.2t)	−88
Fodder vc	600 (10 ha)	725 (14.5 ha)	+125
Total	2,025	1,957	−68
Margin	904	1,611	+707
Margin per hectare	90.4	111.1	+20.7

[a]Estimated dressed carcass weight.

Source: Davidson, J. G. (1969) *Farm Planning Data.* Agric. Econ. Unit, Department of Land Economy, Cambridge University.

which, coupled with the need to market the lambs as early as possible, means that they are sold at lighter weights.

Offsetting this lower physical output is the higher price received per kg for the early lambs, as they come onto the market at a time of relative scarcity of fresh lamb. In consequence, although the late-lambed flock still has an advantage of over £600 output over the early-lambed flock, this is proportionately much less than the relative difference between physical outputs.

Finally, the pattern of seasonally avoidable costs differs in the two flocks. The early-lambed flock incurs higher costs for replacement (as flock life is shorter) and also for concentrates to supplement the diet of both ewes and lambs. On the other hand, the late-lambed flock incurs extra costs for the additional land required to provide grazing for the lambs. All these differences taken together result in a margin to the late-lambed flock that is nearly eighty per cent higher than that in the early-lambed flock.

This, however, is not the whole picture, for there are also differences to be considered in the use of fixed resources in the two flocks. Land use is the most obvious, for the late-lambed flock requires an additional $4\frac{1}{2}$ hectares per 100 ewes and, if this can earn over £157 margin per ha, early lambing is preferable, as the following break-even budget shows:

Margin per 100 ewes			
Late lambing	(£)	*Early lambing*	(£)
14.5 ha at £111.1	1,611	10 ha at £90.4	904
		Alternative production	
		4.5 ha at £157.1	707
14.5	1,611	14.5	1,611

There is also the question of labour. If there is labour to spare all the year round, it should not be included in the calculation of seasonal costs. If not, the peak labour requirements for late lambing, falling in March to April and coinciding with the rush of spring cultivations on arable farms, are more likely to lead to the withdrawal of labour from alternative tasks than in the early-lambed flock, where peak requirements fall in January. In consequence a labour shortage in spring would tend to favour early lambing.

Appendix 10.1: Length of process and selling patterns

Table 10.3 shows, for processes of varying duration, the length of the overall cycle before price patterns start to repeat, the number of selling dates (or batches sold) in each cycle, and the number of selling patterns from which the producer must choose. The latter range from one to twelve. Where it is one, sales will have been made in every month by the time the cycle is completed, so that there is only one selling pattern and no choice exists. Where it is twelve, sales occur in only one month in the cycle, so that there is the greatest degree of choice between twelve selling patterns. In between these two extremes there are a varying number of alternatives as with the nine-month process where, as has already been seen, there are three alternative selling patterns.

Appendix 10.2: The evaluation of alternative selling patterns

Although alternative selling patterns, in cycles that take only one or two years to complete, may be compared in terms of the total returns

TABLE 10.3. *Length of process and choice of selling patterns*

Length of individual process months (1)	Length of cycle[a] months (2)	Selling dates per cycle (2)/(1) (3)	No. of selling patterns 12/(3) (4)
1	12	12	1
2	12	6	2
3	12	4	3
4	12	3	4
5	60	12	1
6	12	2	6
7	84	12	1
8	24	3	4
9	36	4	3
10	60	6	2
11	132	12	1
12	12	1	12
15	60	4	3
18	36	2	6
21	84	4	3
24	24	1	12

[a] Before the selling pattern starts to repeat. The length of the cycle is given by the LCM of col. (1) and 12.

accruing to the whole cycle, this may not suffice with those that take several years. In the latter case, one possibility is to discount the cash flows to their present values, as described in Chapter 3. Often, however, it is sufficient simply to accumulate the undiscounted cash flows in the order that they occur and then to compare them.

For example, taking the second price distribution on page 233, it was noted that the three selling patterns–(*a*), (*b*) and (*c*)–of the nine-month process all returned £440 over the three-year cycle. Assuming that the cycle is started near the beginning of the year, part 1*a* of Table 10.4 shows the order in which selling dates fall for the three selling patterns, while part 1*b* shows the selling prices that obtain. In part 1*c*, the latter are accumulated as the cycle advances. It is clear that in the circumstances assumed, selling pattern (*c*) is optimal, for it brings in a greater return over the first three batches. (It also has the advantage of starting earlier than the other two selling patterns, assuming the producer is in all cases in a position to commence production at the beginning of the year.)

The time of the year when the first process is initiated is also important, for it affects the order of selling dates within each selling pattern. For example, the last part of the table shows cumulative sale values

TABLE 10.4. *Evaluation of selling patterns*

1*a*. *Selling patterns for nine-month process*

Selling pattern[a]	Start first batch	Sell batch: No. 1	No. 2	No. 3	No. 4
(*a*)	Feb.	Oct. Yr 1	July Yr 2	Apr. Yr 3	Jan. Yr 4
(*b*)	Mar.	Nov. Yr 1	Aug. Yr 2	May Yr 3	Feb. Yr 4
(*c*)	Jan.	Sept. Yr 1	June Yr 2	Mar. Yr 3	Dec. Yr 3

1*b*. *Sale values per batch*

Selling pattern[a]	Start first batch	Sale values:[b] Batch No. 1 (£)	No. 2 (£)	No. 3 (£)	No. 4 (£)	Total (£)
(*a*)	Feb.	90	120	130	100	440
(*b*)	Mar.	80	110	140	110	440
(*c*)	Jan.	100	130	120	90	440

1*c*. *Cumulative sale values*

Selling pattern[a]	Start first batch	Cumulative sale values:[b] Batch No. 1 (£)	Nos 1, 2 (£)	Nos 1, 2, 3 (£)	Nos 1, 2, 3, 4 (£)
(*a*)	Feb.	90	210	340	440
(*b*)	Mar.	80	190	330	440
(*c*)	Jan.	100	230	350	440

2. *Cumulative sale values*

Selling pattern[a]	Start first batch	Cumulative sale values:[b] Batch No. 1 (£)	Nos 1, 2 (£)	Nos 1, 2, 3 (£)	Nos 1, 2, 3, 4 (£)
(*a*)	Aug.	130	230	320	440
(*b*)	Sept.	140	250	330	440
(*c*)	July	120	210	310	440

[a] As defined on pp. 231–2.
[b] See p. 233.

when production is started six months later than assumed previously. Selling pattern (*b*), and not selling pattern (*c*), is now optimal.

Finally, if the cost of producing different batches varies with season, the analysis can take the same form as that propounded, except that costs are deducted from receipts to give net cash flows.

Appendix 10.3: Overlapping versus single batches in continuous production

The analysis of selling patterns in continuous production (pp. 231–4) has assumed that only single batches of animals are carried at any one time. In many cases, however, overlapping batches of animals at different stages of production are kept. The consequences are threefold. First, the more production is broken down into overlapping batches, the more evenly are sales spread over the year, so that seasonal price differences are of less importance. Secondly, the choice between alternative selling patterns is reduced. Thirdly, each complete cycle is lengthened because of the effect of 'starting-up' and 'closing-down', so that assuming a given throughput of animals per cycle, there is a reduction in throughput over a given time period.

The eight-month process may be taken as an example. With only a single batch of animals at a time the complete cycle lasts two years and there are four selling patterns – each of three dates – from which to choose, namely,

(i) Jan., May, Sept. (iii) Mar., July, Nov.
(ii) Feb., June, Oct. (iv) Apr., Aug., Dec.

If the same number of animals as in the single batch are carried in two batches at four-monthly intervals, there is still a choice of four selling patterns, but the complete cycle lasts an extra four months. If four batches are carried at two-monthly intervals the choice of selling patterns falls to two:

(i) Jan., Mar., May, July, Sept., Nov.
(ii) Feb., Apr., June, Aug., Oct., Dec.,

and the cycle lasts two and a half years.

Finally, if batches are started every month, there is only one selling pattern and it takes two years and seven months to process a given number of animals.

The lengthening of cycles in this manner looms large when only single cycles at a time are considered. It becomes proportionately of less importance the larger the number of cycles over which production is continued, because the time taken in 'starting-up' and 'closing-down' is spread more thinly. In any event, the disadvantage of the extra cycle time resulting from overlapping batches may be more than offset by a more effective use of buildings and a reduction in the risk of unforeseen changes in the balance of seasonal prices invalidating the selected selling pattern.

11: The provision of replacements

Once any livestock process has been initiated, replacement stock must be provided if it is to continue. With most permanent livestock, only a proportion of the animals are normally replaced each year, either because they die or because they fall below an acceptable standard due to disease, other disorders, old age or poor genetic capacity. With temporary livestock, however, the provision of replacements is a more fundamental part of the process, for when one batch has been sold they must all be replaced, if production is to continue on the same scale.

It was seen earlier (Chapter 6) that replacement stock are end-products in their own right and yet are also inputs to further production. This is most obvious when different stages of production are carried out on separate farms. For example, one farmer may produce weaned piglets and sell them to another, who fattens them for sale as baconers. Or again, dairy heifers may be reared by one farmer who undertakes no milk production and sold to another who keeps a milking herd but rears no replacements.

In consequence, economic decisions relating to replacements fall into two categories. The first concerns the replacement unit as an independent activity with its own output and involves problems of organisation similar to those already considered; for example, what feeds to select and what amounts to feed. The second concerns the replacement unit in its role of providing the parent activity with replacements, and involves such problems as whether to purchase replacement stock or to rear them on the farm and, if the latter, how many to rear and to what age. It is this second aspect that is our main concern here, although in practice these two sides of planning are closely linked. For example, the method of rearing adopted within the replacement unit may determine the desirability of rearing on the farm.

Purchased v. home-reared replacements

Perhaps the most fundamental question facing the livestock producer is whether to rear his own replacements or instead to rely on purchasing them. In some cases the answer is largely determined for him, in that there is no readily available supply of sound replacement stock, so that they must be reared on his own farm (unless contract rearing is feasible). In others, the production of replacements is a highly specialised process usually carried on by firms ancillary to farming, as with the production of day-old chicks for broiler or egg-laying flocks. Between these two extremes there are enterprises, such as the fattening of cattle and pigs, where it is common to find some farmers rearing their own replacements and others purchasing them from outside the farm.

The decision whether to rear or buy – where the choice exists – is not immediately obvious and clear-cut, for two main reasons. The first is that home-rearing takes up farm resources, many of which could be profitably employed in alternative activities. This is most marked with grazing livestock, because land is involved. Secondly, there are many reasons for farmers rearing their own replacements which are not readily measured in purely financial terms. The avoidance of risk ranks high amongst these: the risk of bringing disease onto the farm; the risk of being unable to obtain supplies of the right kind of animal at the time they are needed; the risk of having to pay too high a purchase price to permit a fair profit. Another is that home-rearing enables the capital which would be required as a lump sum if replacements were purchased, to be accumulated in relatively easy stages. In addition, many farmers have an interest in rearing their own animals that goes beyond purely financial gain.

In the circumstances, it is perhaps not surprising that replacements are often reared as a matter of course as part of the parent enterprise, with no clear thought given as to whether it is economically justified. The least the producer can do, however, is to attempt to put a value on those factors that are not readily quantifiable, by comparing the cost of purchasing with that of home-rearing. If the latter should prove to be more expensive, he is then in a position to assess whether the extra cost is a reasonable premium to pay for a reduction in risk, for the accumulation of capital or for the satisfaction of a preference.

The cost of purchasing replacements is simply the market price that the producer anticipates he must pay for the type and quality of animals that he requires. (Although, if capital to purchase them were so scarce that it had to be withdrawn from other uses, its real cost would have to be assessed in the light of the consequent effect on farm income.) With home-rearing, the real costs must be calculated (in a manner similar to that demonstrated for home-grown foods in Chapter 9) by adding together the variable costs of rearing and the gross margin forgone by the withdrawal of scarce fixed resources from other opportunities.

Dairy herd example

An example may be taken from milk production. A farmer on a mixed-arable farm rears his own replacements for his one-man yard and parlour unit of 48 Friesian cows. With herd life averaging four years, 12 down-calving heifers are required annually, although 15 are in fact reared to give a greater margin of choice, the 3 surplus being sold. Allowing for calf mortality, 17 heifer calves are retained annually, while the remainder, together with all bull calves, are sold at four days old.

The farmer wonders whether he is justified in rearing his own heifers, and decides to calculate their real cost. He reckons that if heifers are no longer reared the cowman could manage another 7 cows (making 55 in all, for which present accommodation is sufficient), which would require 5 hectares more forage. As 15 ha would be released from the heifers, there would be a balance of 10 ha which would be put into arable rotation, divided equally between beans, wheat and barley.

The variable costs of rearing the 15 heifers which would no longer be incurred if replacements were purchased, together with the value of the 17 heifer calves that would be available for sale, are calculated to be:

Variable costs no longer incurred:	(£)
Concentrates	1,575
Miscellaneous	150
Forage variable costs (15 hectares)	795
Heifer calves now available for sale (17)	680
	3,200

From this total may be deducted the value (£930) of the 3 down-calving heifers no longer available for sale, leaving a net saving of £2,270.

Next the gain from allocating land and labour to extra cows and arable crops instead of to rearing is calculated.

Gross margin from 7 extra cows	(£)	(£)	(£)
Receipts			
Milk	3,150		
Calves	280		
Cull cows	394	3,824	
Variable costs			
Concentrates	1,260		
Miscellaneous	140		
Purchase replacements (at £325)	650		
Forage variable costs (5 hectares)	225	2,275	
Gross margin			1,549

Gross margin from 10 hectares arable land	(£)	(£)
Beans (3.3 hectares)	766	
Wheat (3.3 hectares)	1,050	
Barley (3.3 hectares)	850	
		2,666
Total gain in gross margin		4,215

The real cost of bringing the 12 heifers into the herd is the sum of the net variable costs saved and the gross margin gained if rearing ceases, namely, £6485 (£2270 + £4215), giving a real cost per head of £540.

In addition, the break-even price between rearing and buying may be calculated. With a herd of 55 cows, 14 replacements must be purchased annually. If the £650 replacement cost for the extra cows is excluded, the gain from not rearing rises to £7135 (£6485 + £650). This represents the maximum price – £510 per head – that could be paid before (financially at least) it is better to keep to the present system of a smaller milking herd combined with home-rearing. As the farmer reckons that heifers of similar quality to his own could be purchased for £325 each (£4550 in all), the annual premium that he is paying for the greater peace of mind of home-rearing amounts to £2585 (£7135 – £4550), a sum he regards as excessive. However, as an alternative to a larger herd with replacements purchased, he considers the possibility of retaining his existing herd size and of continuing to rear replacements but with less resources – particularly land – devoted to the latter. He reckons that if he were to rear only the minimum requirement of 12 heifers annually (keeping back 14 calves and buying in the occasional replacement if necessary), and if the age of first calving were lowered, it should be possible to reduce the area taken up by young stock by one-third – from 15 to 10 ha – so that the break-even price falls to £6002, as below:

Variable costs of rearing 12 heifers	(£)	(£)
Concentrates	1,260	
Miscellaneous	120	
Forage variable costs (10 hectares)	530	1,910
Sale of 14 heifer calves		560
Margin from 7 extra cows on 5 hectares (no replacement charged)		2,199
Gross margin from 5 hectares of arable rotation		1,333
		6,002

The premium paid for home-rearing now amounts to £1452 (£6002 – £4550) a level deemed acceptable by the farmer.

Pig fattening example

Another example may be taken from pig production. In this particular case, with no land directly involved, the real cost of producing weaned piglets hinges mainly on the availability of labour. A farmer at present has a one-man pig unit in which some 1250 purchased weaners are fattened to bacon weight each year. Because of uncertainties about the regular supply of weaners, he is thinking of rearing his own, in which case the one-man unit would consist of 40 breeding sows with an output of 665 baconers annually. Modifications would also be necessary to buildings in order to provide farrowing accommodation. In order to calculate the real costs of home-rearing, the variable costs (including the amortisation of building costs) of the 40-sow unit must be added to the gross margin forgone from the 585 (1250–665) baconers no longer produced. An alternative procedure – adopted in Table 11.1 – is to compare the margins of the present and proposed organisations. Home-rearing results in £2873 less margin than when weaners are pur-

TABLE 11.1. *Purchasing v. home-rearing in pig production*

1. *Fattening only. Production of 1,250 baconers annually*				
	per baconer		*annual total*	
	(£)	(£)	(£)	(£)
Output Bacon pig		55		68,750
Variable costs				
Food	28		35,000	
Miscellaneous	1		1,250	
Purchased weaner	19	48	23,750	60,000
Gross margin		7		8,750
2. *Breeding and fattening. 40 sows producing 665 baconers annually*				
			annual total	
			(£)	(£)
Output 665[a] bacon pigs at £55			36,575	
13 cull sows at £60			780	37,355
Variable costs				
Sows				
Food and miscellaneous	40 at £265		10,600	
Farrowing accommodation	£9,000 amortised at 12% over 10 years		1,593	
Baconers				
Food and miscellaneous	665 at £29		19,285	31,478
Margin				5,877

[a] 17 baconers per sow less 15 gilts for breeding.

chased. From these data, the real costs of home-rearing may be derived:

	(£)	(£)
Variable costs of 40-sow breeding unit		
Food and misc. less £780 for cull sows	9,820	
Amortisation of buildings	1,593	11,413
Gross margin forgone on 585 baconers		
585 baconers at £7		4,095
		15,508

The real cost of providing home-reared piglets thus averages £23.3 each (£15,508/665). This compares with purchasing at £19 per head when the total cost for 665 replacements is £12,635. The farmer, however, considers it is worth incurring the extra cost of home-rearing, as over half of it arises from adaptations to buildings, which should still be in sound condition when the ten-year amortisation period is completed.

Temporary livestock – maximum purchase price

The profitability of fattening livestock, where replacements are purchased, depends as much on the ability of the producer as a buyer (and seller) of livestock as on his technical competence in carrying out the fattening process. As was seen in Chapter 8, these two sides of fattening may be measured by the market and feeder's margins respectively. For example, suppose a farmer purchases 400 kg stores in spring at 54p per kg – £216 each – and incurs variable costs of £16 each, mainly for grazing. If the animals are sold fat in the autumn for £285 per head – 500 kg at 57p per kg – the gross margin amounts to £53 per head (£285 – £232), which may be broken down into the feeder's and market margins.

	(£)	(£)
Feeder's margin		
Sell 100 kg weight gain at 57p	57	
Less variable costs	16	41
Market margin		
Sell 400 kg at 57p	228	
Buy 400 kg at 54p	216	12
Gross margin		53

In this instance, as the selling price is 3p per kg higher than the purchase price, market margin is positive. However, as in practice prices are usually higher in spring than in autumn, it may often be negative. Taking the same example, but assuming the purchase price in spring is 63p per kg:

	(£)	(£)
Feeder's margin		
Sell 100 kg weight gain at 57p	57	
Less variable costs	16	41
Market margin		
Sell 400 kg at 57p	228	
Buy 400 kg at 63p	252	−24
Gross margin		17

The rise of 9p per kg (from 54p to 63p) in the purchase price of store animals thus gives a negative market margin of £24 and lowers gross margin to one-third of its former level.

In cases where gross margin is extremely sensitive to the level of market prices, the producer can do something to protect himself against low or even negative margins by calculating the maximum purchase price that he can afford to pay for an animal in order to break even. The latter is simply the anticipated sale value of the animal less the variable costs of fattening it. Stated as an equation:

$$p = c(a + b) - d \tag{1}$$

where p = maximum purchase price
a = weight at purchase
b = weight gain on farm
c = selling price per unit weight
d = variable costs.

Substituting the data from the previous example in equation (1):

$$\begin{aligned} p &= 57\text{p}\ (400\ \text{kg} + 100\ \text{kg}) - £16 \\ &= £285 - £16 \\ &= £269 \end{aligned}$$

If the farmer pays more than £269 for replacements – or about 67p per kg – the gross margin becomes negative, implying that it would be better to leave idle the land required for fattening, rather than to stock it with beef animals.

However, this is simply the short-term position that ignores both the need in the longer term for a positive contribution to fixed costs and also the likelihood that the land has a positive value in other uses, such as for making and selling hay or for agistment. To be justified, the beef animals must earn as least as much per ha as such alternative uses. The maximum purchase price may be adjusted to allow for this, by incorporating the required margin per beast e in equation (1) as below:

$$p = c(a + b) - (d + e). \tag{2}$$

If, for example, the land can earn £130 per ha in alternative uses and a beef animal requires 0.3 ha, each beast must earn at least £39. Allowing for this margin in equation (2):

$$\begin{aligned} p &= 57\text{p}\ (400\ \text{kg} + 100\ \text{kg}) - (\pounds 16 + \pounds 39) \\ &= \pounds 285 - \pounds 55 \\ &= \pounds 230 \end{aligned}$$

Compared with the break-even price, the effect is thus to lower the purchase price per beast by the £39 of required margin, so that buying price must now not rise above 57.5p per kg (23,000p/400kg).

Admittedly, all the data in the calculation are uncertain. If, however, the calculation of the maximum purchase price of replacements does no more than prevent the farmer's competitive instincts getting the upper hand and leading him to bid away any prospect of a profit at his local market, a useful purpose will have been served.

Frequency of replacement

The producer may be able to choose how often he replaces his animals. With temporary livestock, decisions about the frequency of replacement are bound up with the optimal length of process, which is influenced by the level of market margin and by seasonal factors (aspects already considered in Chapters 8 and 10). Where there is continuous production, shortening the length of the individual process leads to the need for a greater number of replacement stock and thus to a rise in the annual cost of replacement. The latter, and any associated cost changes, must at least be covered by a commensurate gain in receipts, due to greater throughput or to a more paying seasonal distribution of production, if it is to be worthwhile.

With permanent livestock, the decision when to replace is partly taken out of the hands of the producer because deaths, accidents, diseases and other disorders dictate the introduction of replacement stock in order to maintain herd or flock numbers. Nonetheless, there remain those animals that are 'normal' and healthy, so that it is not immediately obvious whether or not they should be replaced. Often they are culled simply because replacements happen to be available. However, even if the latter are potentially more productive than the animals they are displacing, a high pricc may be paid for unnecessarily frequent replacement, particularly when home-rearing involves a large slice of scarce farm resources, as with dairy heifers.

The problem of when to replace permanent stock resolves itself into the interplay of two factors. On the one hand, output is likely to rise with more frequent replacement. This is due mainly to the more rigorous culling of the less productive animals that it permits and, to a lesser extent, to animals being culled at a younger age before their yields have started to diminish significantly. On the other hand, replacement costs per unit of output also rise, because with a shorter life there is less total output over which to spread them. In consequence, the optimal age of replacement is reached when the average margin between output and replacement cost is at its greatest.

Pig breeding herd example

An example may be taken from pig breeding, assuming the following average pattern of output per sow according to age from first service.[1]

Year from first service	*Annual weaner output per sow*
1	16
2	19
3	17
4	14
5	9

As gilts usually have smaller litters than sows, annual output rises from the first to the second year, when the peak is reached. Thereafter it declines as sows become older, because of lower conception rates and a falling-off in litter size.

These data are used in Table 11.2 to illustrate the optimal average replacement age for healthy sows in a hypothetical herd producing weaners for sale. (For the sake of simplicity this is shown in years, assuming two litters per annum.) It is assumed that maiden gilts are purchased as replacements some two months before being served and by the time of first service have cost £78 in purchase price and food. Cull sows fetch £53 on average, so that net replacement cost is £25. Weaners sell for £19 each.

The first part of the table shows the cumulative value of weaner sales over a period of five years, from which replacement cost is deducted. (The latter is assumed to remain constant regardless of age, because the cull sows are normally sold for slaughter rather than for further breeding, so that increased age has a negligible effect on their value.) The consequent cumulative margin over replacement cost is divided by the relevant number of years, to bring it to an annual average margin,

[1] Based partly on evidence from Dutch experience. *Varkens* (1965), Bedrijfseconomische Beschrijvingen, Landbouw-Economisch Instituut.

TABLE 11.2. *Optimal age of replacement. Pig breeding example*

1. *Annual margin over replacement cost*

			(per sow)		
Sows retained for (years)	1	2	3	4	5
Annual weaner output	16	19	17	14	9
Cumulative weaner output	16	35	52	66	75
	(£)	(£)	(£)	(£)	(£)
Cumulative value output	304	665	988	1,254	1,425
Net replacement cost	25	25	25	25	25
Cumulative margin over replacement cost	279	640	963	1,229	1,400
Average margin over replacement cost	279	320	321	307	280

2. *Herd margin over replacement cost* (100 sows over 6 years)

Sows replaced every: (1) (year)	Cumulative margin per sow (2) (£)	Multiplier[a] [6/(1)] 100 (3)	Herd margin (2) × (3) (4) (£)	Fall in margin compared with replacement every 3 years (5) (£)
1	279	600	167,400	25,200
2	640	300	192,000	600
3	963	200	192,600	—
4	1,229	150	184,350	8,250
5	1,400	120	168,000	24,600

[a] The number of times the herd is replaced in a six-year period multiplied by the number of sows in the herd.

which in this example rises to its peak in the third year. Ignoring for the moment the actual performance of individual sows, the implication is that herd margin will be reduced if healthy sows are replaced on average either more or less frequently than the optimum of every three years, as is demonstrated in the second part of Table 11.2, for a 100-sow herd over six years.

Dairy herd example

A calculation similar to that made for the pig herd is shown in Table 11.3 for the first seven lactations in a dairy herd, where the peak yield

TABLE 11.3. *Optimal age of replacement. Dairy herd example*

	(per cow)						
Lactation number:	1	2	3	4	5	6	7
Yield per cow (l)	3,319	3,660	4,050	4,246	4,387	4,060	3,610
Cumulative yield (l)	3,319	6,979	11,029	15,275	19,662	23,722	27,332
	(£)	(£)	(£)	(£)	(£)	(£)	(£)
Cumulative milk value (at 10p per l)	332	698	1,103	1,528	1,966	2,372	2,733
Net replacement cost							
Heifer cost	325	325	325	325	325	325	325
less cull cow	250	225	200	175	150	145	140
and calves	35	70	105	140	175	210	245
	40	30	20	10	0	−30	−60
Cumulative margin over replacement cost	292	668	1,083	1,518	1,966	2,402	2,793
Average margin over replacement cost	282	334	361	380	393	400	399

per cow is reached in the fifth lactation.[1] As it is assumed that the value of cull cows decreases with age, net replacement cost is not constant from year to year as it was in the pig example. The average margin over replacement cost is at its greatest after six lactations and thereafter begins to decline.

Practical implications

Both these examples are intended simply to demonstrate the principles involved and not to suggest the desirable age of replacement in practice. However, providing the producer is prepared to collect sufficient data to enable the optimal replacement age (the age when average margin over replacement cost is at its highest) to be calculated in his herd or flock, it can serve as a rough guide as to when animals should be replaced. How it is used depends on whether or not animals continue to be individually recorded once the optimal replacement age has been established. In either case the concern is not with those obvious 'poor-doers' which would continue to be culled as the occasion arose (and which would be excluded from the calculation of standard replacement age), but with those that are not clearly sub-standard. The latter, in those cases where livestock are treated as a unit and are not individually recorded, would remain in the unit at least until they attained the

[1] See Wood, P. D. P. (1970), *Animal Production* **12**, 253.

optimal replacement age. They would then be culled, unless, even though unrecorded, they were obviously of outstanding productivity. Although the application of a standard replacement policy to the whole unit has the advantage that the number of replacements required each year is known fairly precisely, it has the disadvantage that indifferent performers may be carried past the stage when they should have been replaced and, conversely, that above-average performers may be replaced too soon.

Where animals are individually recorded, their retention or rejection depends on how their performance relates to the standard performance of the unit. On the one hand, there is the animal that may need to be replaced early because of relatively poor performance to date. On the other hand, there is the animal whose performance has been above average, but which has reached the standard optimal replacement age. In both cases, retention or rejection depend on whether past performance suggests that the animal's output in an additional period of production will be sufficient to attain at least the optimal margin over replacement cost. If this is considered likely, the animal is retained; if not, it is culled. For example, using the pig data in Table 11.2, a sow, in order to attain the optimal margin over replacement cost in a fourth year, would need to have a potential output of 17 weaners which, at £19 each, near enough equals the optimal margin of £321 per sow. (For further discussion, see Appendix 11.1.)

This is assuming that a replacement is immediately available. Where this is not so (or if there is spare accommodation or grazing available, even if another animal does enter the livestock unit), the animal should be retained, providing – and for as long as – the value of its output is sufficient to cover the expenditure that could genuinely be saved if it were to be culled. The latter usually applies simply to the provision of food and, in the case of grazing livestock, to the production ration only; few, if any, other costs can be saved in the very short term.

Frequency of replacement and opportunity cost of home-rearing

So far it has been assumed that replacements are purchased so that their cost per head is independent of the frequency of replacement. If they are home-reared, however, this may no longer hold true, for the more young stock are reared, the greater the amount of farm resources that must be devoted to them, and this may entail the sacrifice of alternative opportunities of increasing value, so that their real cost per head rises. This is particularly likely to be the case with grazing livestock, because land is involved.

Take, for example, a 120-cow dairy herd where, with five-year herd life, 30 down-calving heifers are produced annually (the extra 6 are to permit a wider choice), requiring 30 ha of land. If heifers were not reared, 25 ha of the land would remain in grassland (needed for rotational purposes) supporting beef production with a gross margin of £65 per ha, and the remaining 5 ha would be devoted to barley with a gross margin of £255 per ha. The total gross margin forgone by the use of the land for heifer rearing is thus:

	(£)
25 ha in beef at £65 gross margin per hectare	1,625
5 ha in barley at £255 gross margin per hectare	1,275
	2,900

This amounts to £97 (£2900/30) per replacement reared.

Suppose now that the cows were replaced every three years, so that 50 replacements occupying 50 ha would be required, the additional 20 ha coming from barley:

	(£)
25 ha in beef at £65 gross margin per hectare	1,625
25 ha in barley at £255 gross margin per hectare	6,375
	8,000

Although the land requirement per heifer reared remains the same (at 1 hectare), the value forgone per head rises by two-thirds to £160 (8000/50), because of the higher earning rate of the extra land sacrificed in order to accommodate more frequent replacement.

Appendix 11.1: Permanent livestock – optimal age of replacement

Output necessary to justify retention

It might appear that the decision whether or not to carry an animal for an extra period of production should be based simply on whether it could better the output that could be obtained from a replacement, less the net cost of that replacement. If this criterion is applied to the pig data in Table 11.2, the output that a sow would have to achieve in order to justify retention is as follows:

		(£)	(£)
Output anticipated in 1st year of production from replacement gilt			304
deduct	cost of replacement less	78	
	value of cull sow	−53	25
			279

An output of £279 is equivalent to approximately 15 weaners (at £19), yet if a sow (Table 11.2) has 15 (and not 14) weaners in a 4th year, margin over replacement cost is £312, so it still should not be kept. The calculation above falls into error, because account is taken only of the first year of production from the replacement, and not the potential flow, assuming it is kept for the optimal period of three years. In addition, replacement cost is allocated entirely to one season. Rectifying these faults:

	(£)
£988 output anticipated from replacement gilt to optimal replacement age (3 years) gives annual average of:	329.3
£25 net replacement cost gives annual average over 3 years of:	8.3
	321.0

A sow must thus be capable of producing 17 weaners if it is to cover this sum and so justify retention.

As Table 11.2 shows, £321 is the optimal margin over replacement cost. The formula that establishes the minimum physical output necessary to attain the optimal margin (where net replacement cost does not vary with age) is given in equation (1) below:

$$O = m/p \tag{1}$$

where O = physical output required
m = highest average margin over replacement cost
p = price per unit output.

Substituting the data in Table 11.2 into equation (1):

$$O = 321/19$$
$$= 16.9 \text{ weaners}$$

Once calculated, this standard becomes the yardstick against which to compare the potential output of sows in the example herd, in order to decide whether or not to retain them for another production period.[1]

If net replacement cost does vary with age (as is assumed in the dairy herd example in Table 11.3), equation (1) is modified as follows:

$$O = (m + r' - r)/p \qquad (2)$$

where r is the current net replacement cost

r' is the net replacement cost if the animal is replaced after a further period of production

and the other coefficients are as in equation (1). For instance, suppose that in our pig example net replacement cost were to rise from £25 to £35 per sow between the third and fourth years. The output necessary to justify keeping a sow for a fourth year would amount to:

$$\begin{aligned} O &= (321 + 35 - 25)/19 \\ &= 331/19 \\ &= 17.4 \text{ weaners.} \end{aligned}$$

Or, to take another example, suppose that in the dairy herd in Table 11.3 a cow has been kept for six years. The yield she must give in a further lactation if her retention is to be justified is:

$$\begin{aligned} O &= \{400 + (-)\,60 - (-)\,30\}/0.10 \\ &= \{400 - 60 + 30\}/0.10 \\ &= 370/0.10 \\ &= 3{,}700 \text{ litres} \end{aligned}$$

Discounting to present value

As the optimal margin over replacement cost is based on cash flows over a number of years, it may be desirable to allow for the 'time-value' of money by discounting to present values (see Chapter 3).

In exemplification we revert to the pig example in Table 11.2 and discount the annual cash flows and the net replacement cost at 10 per cent.

[1] It must be stressed that it is not suggested that such standards should be inflexibly applied without reference to other factors such as: the availability of replacements; the state of the market in respect of the price of purchased replacement and cull stock; the effect of the number of animals culled at any particular time on total herd or flock numbers.

Year	Output (£)		Discount factor	Present value (£)	Net replacement cost (£)	Present value (£)
1	304	×	0.909	276.3	25	22.7
2	361	×	0.826	298.2	25	20.6
3	323	×	0.751	242.6	25	18.8
4	266	×	0.683	181.7	25	17.1

From these data, the discounted average annual margin over replacement cost can be calculated.

Year	*1*	*2*	*3*	*4*
Present value of:	(£)	(£)	(£)	(£)
Cumulative output to date	—	276.3	574.5	817.1
Output in current year	276.3	298.2	242.6	181.7
Total cumulative output	276.3	574.5	817.1	998.8
Net replacement cost	22.7	20.6	18.8	17.1
Cumulative margin over replacement cost	253.6	553.9	798.3	981.7
Average annual margin over replacement cost	253.6	277.0	266.1	245.4

Taking account of the time-value of money results in the optimum margin over replacement cost occurring in the second year, instead of the third as before. Equation (3) below allows the calculation of the level of physical output required to enable the optimal margin to be maintained:

$$O = m_d - (r - r_d)/p_d \qquad (3)$$

where O, m, p and r are as previously and the subscript d indicates that they are discounted to present values. The expression $(r - r_d)$ acknowledges that by keeping an animal for an extra production period (assumed here to be one year) the cost of replacement is put back in time, so saving the difference between the cost of replacing it now and of replacing it in the future.

Substituting the discounted data above in equation (3):

$$O = 277 - (25.0 - 22.7)/17.3^1$$
$$= 15.9 \text{ weaners.}$$

Discounting has thus reduced the required output that a sow must attain if it is to be retained, from 16.9 to 15.9 piglets.

[1] £19 discounted for 1 year at 10 per cent.

Establishing standardised data

Problems arise in the establishment of standardised data in a livestock unit, because as animals become older, the numbers on which to draw become smaller, due to increasingly heavy culling. For example, one study (Pettit, G. H. N. (1940) *J. Agric. Sci.* **XXX**, iii, 485) of the age distribution of nearly 4000 dairy cows revealed that first, second and third calvers accounted for two-thirds of total numbers; fourth, fifth and sixth calvers for one quarter; and seventh, eighth and ninth calvers for only onc-twelfth. In consequence it may be necessary, in the period when standards are being determined, to retain animals for longer than has been the practice in the past, to ensure an adequate sample in the higher age groups. If it should happen, however, that average margin over replacement cost starts to fall at a fairly early stage, there would be no need to retain the older animals, and the problem would be avoided.

12: Crops and cropping

Crop costing

To many people the economics of crop production is associated almost entirely with crop enterprise costing. The latter is illustrated in Table 12.1, the example being an above-average crop of maincrop potatoes. The costs are classified first by operations and materials and secondly by factors of production. Such costings are normally required as a necessary basis for price negotiations where government guarantees are operating or where contract prices are being fixed. Furthermore, if trends over time are considered, they do give some broad idea, together with normalised returns, of how the general profitability of the crop is changing. However, for reasons explained in detail in Chapter 20 (pp. 537–9), such costings have little relevance for the purposes of individual farm planning. Many of the costs can only be allocated arbitrarily, especially the general farm overheads, and cropping changes are unlikely to result in profit changes in the way suggested by these figures. Of special importance would be the effect of such changes on the total labour bill, as determined by seasonal requirements and the proportion of hired and family labour.

To illustrate from Table 12.2, suppose Farmer *A* has a 40-hectare arable farm with 5 hectares of sugar beet. He gets a rather poor yield and his costs are high. Consequently complete costings show the crop making a loss of £30 per ha. On the other hand his barley yield is above average and the crop shows a profit of £80 per ha. But if the farmer gave up growing sugar beet and substituted 5 more hectares of barley he would not be £550 (£110 per ha) better off, but poorer by about £350, quite apart from any rotational considerations and consequent effect on yields. This is because he would in fact save nothing in labour charges. He would be worse off by 5 times the difference in gross margin per ha (£350 for sugar beet minus £250 for barley), less some saving in power and machinery expenses.

On the other hand Farmer *B*, growing 25 hectares of sugar beet on a 200 hectare farm, has an above-average beet yield and the same barley yield as Farmer *A*. His crop costs may suggest that he would be £3750

TABLE 12.1. *Example of enterprise costing: maincrop potatoes* (all figures are £ per hectare)

I. COSTS	
A. Operations/materials	
Cost item	(£)
Ploughing	18
Seedbed cultivations and fertiliser distribution	25
Fertiliser	140
Seed	280
Chitting seed	40
Planting	52
Post-planting cultivations and spraying	60
Spray materials	60
Bags	75
Total growing costs	750
Harvesting/picking	150
Carting and clamping	70
Storage	60
Riddling and bagging	80
Total harvesting, storage, riddling costs	360
Rent	50
Share of general overhead expenses and sundries	110
Total costs[a]	1,270
B. 'Factor costs'	
Fertiliser	140
Seed	280
Spray materials	60
Bags	75
Labour	255
Tractor costs	90
Machinery depreciation and repairs	120
Buildings	90
Rent	50
General overheads, etc.	110
Total costs[a]	1,270
II. OUTPUT	
30 tonnes of ware at £50	1,500
2 tonnes of chats at £12.50	25
Total output	1,525
III. PROFIT	255

[a]Excluding farmyard manure, management and interest on capital.

TABLE 12.2. *Enterprise profit or loss and gross margins*

	Farmer *A*	Farmer *B*
1. *Sugar beet* (per hectare)		
Yield (tonnes)	28	40
Receipts (£)	600	850
Enterprise costs (£)	630	600
Profit (or loss) (£)	–30	250
Gross margin (£)	350	500
2. *Barley* (per hectare)		
Yield (tonnes)	4.5	4.5
Receipts (£)	340	340
Enterprise costs (£)	260	240
Profit (£)	80	100
Gross margin (£)	250	250

worse off by giving up sugar beet (£150 per ha difference in profit × 25) – again ignoring rotational and general yield implications. It is however unlikely that the change in profits would be of this magnitude. If substituting cereals for sugar beet enabled him to reduce his regular labour staff by two men he might even be *better* off, assuming he has the type of soil or enough other break crops to stand such a change without a reduction in cereal yields.

It is the combined effect of the change in total gross margin and total fixed costs that will determine whether or not a change in cropping is economically worthwhile, and complete enterprise costing and comparisons of net profit per hectare may be entirely misleading in this respect.

Profit factors

The determinants of crop profitability can be classified as follows:

(*a*) Yield per hectare
(*b*) Price per unit of output } = Output per hectare
(*c*) Variable costs per hectare } = Gross margin per hectare $(a \times b) - c$
(*d*) Labour and machinery costs per hectare

These will now be considered in turn.

Yield

There can be no doubt that increasing yield is the most likely and most rewarding way to increase the profitability of crop production. This is not to imply that such improvements are easy, particularly where the possibilities have been exhaustively examined over a period of years.

Three ways may be distinguished, excluding at this stage rotational considerations:

(i) *by increasing the input of a variable factor*, for example, by applying more fertiliser, or spending more on better quality seed.

This involves the application of the law of diminishing returns and the principle of increasing the input of the variable factor until marginal revenue equals marginal cost. This has already been illustrated in Chapter 2 (pp. 27–30) and therefore will not be repeated here. Because no two seasons and no two soils are exactly alike in terms of response, it is impossible to establish exactly optimal levels of all variable factors for every field on the farm. Furthermore other husbandry factors, such as time of drilling, may affect the optimal application. Nevertheless, experimental data and past experience have to be sifted with this principle in mind, thinking in terms of the most likely type of season and response for each soil type.

Having established the optimal, or near-optimal, levels for fertiliser, seed and sprays, their cost can be estimated and deducted from the estimated output to give the 'margin over materials', which is the gross margin if no casual labour or contract work is hired for the crop. This assumes that the materials are freely available and the farmer has sufficient funds or credit to purchase these amounts. If this is not so (for example, if fertiliser were rationed or the farmer could not afford the optimal amounts), the law of equi-marginal returns would have to be applied to give the optimal allocation of the limited quantity between crops (Chapter 2, pp. 25–6).

Rothamsted surveys have indicated that many potato and sugar beet growers in the Eastern Counties apply *more* than the likely optimum amounts. On the other hand some cereal growers deliberately choose to apply less than the likely optimum, in order to reduce the risk of a laid crop and the resulting difficult and slow combining and crop losses in a bad harvest season.

(ii) *by introducing a new factor or technique*, e.g. a new seed variety, a different type of chemical control, irrigation.

The relevant principle here is much the same as in (i) above, that is, comparison between the marginal return and the marginal cost, to see whether the former appears adequately to cover the latter, taking into account any element of uncertainty involved and any extra capital required. This time, however, it is not the optimum position along a

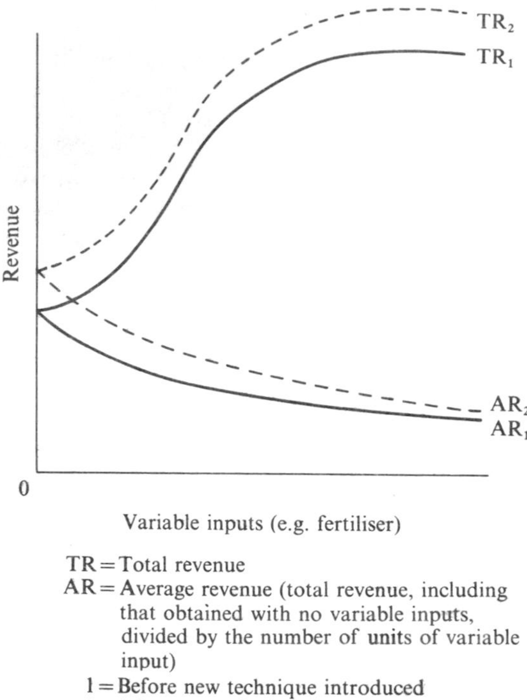

Fig. 12.1. Introduction of new technique: shift in revenue curves

single response curve that is being considered, but a 'jump' onto a new curve. This is illustrated in Figure 12.1. The marginal response to, and therefore optimum level of, the variable inputs such as fertiliser may also be affected.

The method normally applied to test the worthwhileness of introducing a new technique is partial budgeting (see further Chapter 14, pp. 315–17). This is illustrated in Table 12.3 for the introduction of irrigation for maincrop potatoes.

(iii) *by improved cultivating and harvesting practice*. This is a question of husbandry skill, which lies outside the scope of this book. Nevertheless, its crucial importance must be stressed. In particular it is a question of the *timeliness* of operations, including time of sowing and fertiliser application, and covers such vital considerations as keeping off the land, especially heavy soils, until conditions are right, and avoiding moisture loss in the spring and early summer, especially on the

TABLE 12.3. *Irrigation of potatoes*
Assumptions: 20 hectares of potatoes grown; initial cost of equipment: £7,500

Added costs (per annum)	(£)	Added returns (per annum)	(£)
Depreciation on equipment	725	4 tonnes per hectare	4,450
Interest on capital	475		
Repairs	200		
Overtime labour	200		
Harvesting, storage, riddling the heavier crop	900		
	2,500		
Added profit[a]	1,950		
	4,450		4,450

[a] Before deducting water charges.

lighter, drought-prone soils. *Methods* of sowing, fertiliser application and weed control are also highly relevant.

Some further points in relation to yields and costs are discussed in Appendix 12.1.

Price

The second way to try to increase returns is by obtaining a higher price. Price can be increased in two ways, apart from sheer bargaining power and marketing knowledge and skill: (*a*) by improving *quality*, or (*b*) by improving the *time of marketing*.

In both cases extra costs are usually incurred and the problem again is to decide, with the aid of partial budgeting, whether the extra returns make the extra costs worthwhile. However, higher quality sometimes means lower yield. Since costs may be the same in this instance, the question is whether the extra price is enough to compensate for the lower yield, which is a simple multiplication sum once the relevant facts are known. In the early 1950s this point was well illustrated with feeding versus malting barley, the varieties favouring the former giving a higher yield but achieving a lower price: 3 tonnes per ha of Kenia barley at £25 a tonne was better than 2.25 tonnes of Spratt Archer at £30. With the arrival of the dual-purpose Proctor variety the issue became less clear-cut: quality tended to be dependent on soils and seasons rather than variety and the price differential became less well-defined. A similar issue in some areas was to decide between Majestic and King Edward maincrop potatoes. The question was whether, on a particular soil type over a number of seasons, the extra yield usually obtained from Majestics was enough to compensate for the lower price. The difference averaged £3.50 per tonne; nearly 28 tonnes of ware Majestics at £16.50 per tonne were needed to equal in value 23 tonnes of Edwards at £20.

Improvement of price by timely marketing frequently entails storage and all the associated costs. Grain storage is an important example to many farmers. The costs include depreciation and interest on the plant and equipment, interest on the grain stored, loss of weight through additional drying, and extra handling and drying costs. The total for wheat could be as shown in Table 12.4, assuming the plant and equipment costs £50 per tonne after deducting any available grants.

In order to cover the costs listed, therefore, with interest on capital charged at 10 per cent, at least an extra £16 per tonne must be obtained for the crop – assuming a storage period of 8 months. It should however be added that unless grain can be sold immediately from the field, some at least of the barn plant and equipment costs would probably be necessary simply to handle the grain during harvest prior to sale.

Instead of charging interest on capital as shown, an alternative approach is to estimate the extra net returns likely to be obtained, excluding interest charges, and calculate the return on the capital in-

TABLE 12.4. *Annual costs of grain storage*

	Cost per tonne (£)
Depreciation (10 years)	5.00
Interest (10% on written-down value)[a]	3.15
Interest on wheat stored 8 months (10%)[b]	5.00
Loss of weight[c]	1.90
Extra handling and drying costs	0.95
Total	16.00

[a] For the reasoning behind this item and its calculation, see Chapter 4, pp. 88–9.

[b] Interest on the value of the stored crop is charged because if it were sold at harvest time, the receipts could be used to reduce outstanding loans – and thus interest payments upon them – or alternatively they could be invested and so be earning a return. In the latter case, if valuable possible investments on the farm are being forgone because of shortage of working capital, the opportunity cost of capital tied up in crop storage could well exceed the 10 per cent allowed.

[c] The allowance for loss of weight assumes that ¾ of the crop needs an extra 2 per cent of moisture extracted for storage, compared with the moisture content at which the crop could be sold without price penalty at harvest time. It assumes that, on average, ¼ of the crop could be combined at this lower safe moisture content without need for drying. A 2 per cent moisture extraction causes a reduction in weight of approximately 25 kg per tonne of grain. Clearly this loss will not occur if the moisture is added back before sale or if the grain is stored in moist grain silos or preserved by means of chilling or the use of propionic acid.

vested. Discounting techniques can be employed, as demonstrated in Chapter 3.

Variable costs

Another way in which the gross margin may be increased is by making savings in the variable costs (as defined in gross margin analysis). Such costs usually constitute between a third (as for cereals) and a half (as for potatoes) of total crop enterprise costs, but they are not easy to reduce. This is in contrast to pig and poultry production, where variable costs – primarily feed – are some 80 per cent of total costs (assuming livestock purchases and depreciation are deducted from output and not, therefore, included in costs) and one of the main ways to try to increase profitability is to reduce these costs.

Some opportunities do exist, however. These include the following:

(i) Mixing straight fertilisers instead of buying compound fertilisers. Savings of several pounds per tonne may be possible, but few farmers are prepared to accept the work and trouble involved, and imperfect mixing would lead to deleterious results.
(ii) Economising in fertiliser by placement, e.g. in potato growing.
(iii) Soil analysis in order to avoid wasting fertiliser; for example, surveys frequently show excessive use of phosphatic fertilisers.
(iv) Timely cultivations to avoid the cost of weedkillers. The main savings are likely to be through stubble cultivations to control such weeds as couch grass, for which the chemical cost of control is high. But even for the more straightforward weed problems the extra costs of harrowing are very minor compared with the cost of spraying, including materials. Furthermore, there appears to be increasing evidence that 'routine' spraying may often be doing more harm than good.
(v) Retaining home-grown seed. Examples here are sowing a small amount of pedigree cereal seed each year for use the subsequent year, and frequent insecticide spraying of part of the potato crop from which the seed is retained.
(vi) Reducing or eliminating contractors' charges, by buying a machine and doing a job with farm labour. Capital costs per hectare can be kept down by buying second-hand equipment, or by sharing with neighbours. Obviously this will not *necessarily* be economic, but it may be worth investigating (see further Chapter 4, pp. 92–4).

(vii) A special example of this would be buying a lorry to reduce or eliminate contractors' charges for transport, e.g. of sugar beet, which can be very high. The likelihood of this being worthwhile is clearly increased if the lorry can be used for other purposes at other times of the year.

(viii) Reducing casual labour costs by mechanising the job where feasible, e.g. potato harvesting.

From the contents of this list it is clear that no substantial economies in variable costs are likely, except for the last three, which simply involve replacing variable cost items by additional fixed costs – although the intention is clearly that there will be on balance a reduction in *total* costs. Apart from the examples quoted, any attempt to reduce variable costs by means of reducing the input level of fertiliser or expenditure on seed will usually decrease output more than costs, thus reducing profits instead of increasing them. This is assuming that the producer's input level is either close to or below the optimum point, where marginal cost equals marginal revenue.

Labour and machinery

On arable farms, labour and machinery costs together amount to about 50 per cent of total costs – more on intensive arable holdings. Thus any cost saving is most likely to come from this sphere. Combined labour costs and annual machinery expenses can be as little as £75 per hectare on a highly mechanised, mainly cereal-growing farm on light land, and as much as £350 or more on a highly intensive arable farm specialising in field vegetables – even excluding casual labour costs.

The basic problem with crops is not the total annual labour requirement, as it is with some types of livestock, but the seasonal needs. Ways of tabulating this material have been described in Chapter 5. Supposing a peak to exist in the seasonal labour demand for regular labour, seven ways of overcoming the problem were outlined in that chapter, namely: working more overtime, greater use of casual labour, use of contractors, mechanisation, improving gang organisation, extension of the time period (especially for sowing and harvesting), and changing the cropping. In order to avoid needless repetition these points will not be discussed again in this chapter, but it must be stressed that the consequent brevity of the present section very much understates the importance of the subject on mainly arable farms. The efficient organisation and integration of men and machines are major factors affecting the profitability of any farm, but they have a particularly large relative importance on the arable unit, and much of the content of Chapters 4 and 5 is therefore very closely linked to this chapter.

Choice of cropping

On an arable farm the first priority for investigating ways of increasing profitability is to examine the level of yields, prices and variable costs of the existing crops – as described in previous sections of this chapter – to see whether the total gross margin of the farm can be increased by improving the individual gross margins of the crops already being grown, with no (or at least a less than commensurate) increase in fixed costs. Once this has been done the further alternatives open for increasing profitability are as described in some detail for farming systems in general in Chapter 14 (pp. 329–30). They can be briefly summarised as follows:

(i) Retain the same cropping policy, but reduce combined labour and machinery costs, possibly by substituting machinery for labour.
(ii) Substitute some high for low gross margin crops, with the same complement of regular labour and machinery.
(iii) Substitute high for low gross margin crops with added labour and/or machinery costs; obviously the object is to raise total gross margin more than fixed costs are increased.
(iv) Substitute low for high gross margin crops with reduced labour and/or machinery costs; clearly the aim must be to save more in fixed costs than the reduction in total gross margin. This may involve more mechanisation but a large reduction of labour, which is the essence of the case for farm simplification: namely, cutting out small areas of roots, for example, and expanding the cereal enterprise.
(v) Substitute high for low gross margin crops *and* make savings in the combined labour and machinery costs. This is difficult to achieve.

The best choice depends on many factors, including the farmer's objectives, his capital position, and his relative crop margins. The same planning concepts and techniques are needed as for a livestock farm or a mixed crops and livestock farm. These are described in detail in Part III.

On any farm specialising in cash crop production there are several special economic features that have an important bearing on the choice of crops. One is the integration of different crops and varieties in order to avoid excessive and prolonged peaks and troughs in the seasonal labour demand; this has already been referred to above and discussed fully in Chapter 5 (pp. 135–9). Another is the large yield variations that can occur through the impact of weather, pests and diseases. Since costs are relatively little affected this can lead to wide variations in annual profits – more so than with many forms of livestock production. A further feature is the unevenness of the cash flow often found on cash cropping farms. Working capital requirements tend to be high, because of the long time that may occur between preparing the ground and selling the crop – especially if it is stored for a long period. There is no continuous inflow of cash as in dairying, egg production and, often, in pig production (see further Chapter 3). A combination of crops, which are affected differently by changing weather conditions and which have different cash flow patterns, will help alleviate both the problem of profit variability and that of uneven cash flow. Finally, there are the complementary, supplementary and competitive interrelationships, to which the rotational effect is closely linked. These are now discussed.

Crop interrelationships

In the choice of crops, the three types of enterprise interrelationship described and illustrated in Chapter 2 (pp. 39–41) have to be borne in mind: namely, complementarity, competitiveness and supplementarity. A complementary relationship is often taken simply to imply that one enterprise assists another, in the sense of increasing its profitability. The whole rationale of the Norfolk 4-course or any other rotation is based on this concept. The 'break' crops 'rest' the land, improve the structure and fertility of the soil, enable the land to be cleaned, break the disease cycle, and so on, thus improving the yield of subsequent cereal crops, and they may also supply by-products for livestock, which in turn provide added fertility for cash crop production. In its stricter interpretation, however – as explained in Chapter 2 – the 'rest' crop not only improves the yield *per hectare* (and/or reduces the costs) of subsequent crops, but actually improves the *total* yield of the other crop.

To take an example, if this were to occur by giving an almost-continuous barley field a rest one year in six, the five barley crops would have together to produce a higher yield than the six would produce under continuous barley. For example:

6 crops of barley at 3.7 tonnes = 22.2 tonnes; 6 × £200 GM = £1,200
5 crops of barley at 4.5 tonnes = 22.5 tonnes; 5 × £265 GM = £1,325

The gross margin from the break crop would be additional benefit. Such a very large yield increase (averaged over *all* the five years) is unlikely to occur. What is more likely from the break is:

5 crops of barley at 4.0 tonnes[1] = 20 tonnes, 5 × £225	GM =	£1,125
Plus 1 year ley (or other break crop) at, say, £175	GM =	£ 175
	Total	£1,300

[1] 4.25 tonnes falling to 3.75 tonnes over the 5 years.

In other words, the *combination* gives a better total gross margin than monoculture. This does not necessarily mean that it is more profitable, since fixed costs and interest charges might possibly rise by more than the increase in total gross margin. These points are discussed in more detail later in this chapter.

The second relationship is competitiveness. If the crops are perfectly competitive it implies that they substitute for each other at a constant rate; (see Chapter 2, pp. 23–4). For example, suppose 40 hectares of cash root crops (potatoes and sugar beet) are being grown on a farm. A constant rate of substitution would mean that increasing the potato area by 2 hectares would cause a loss in sugar beet gross margin of, say, £400, whether the farmer was initially growing 32 hectares of potatoes and 8 of beet, 20 of each, or 8 of potatoes and 32 of beet.

Such a relationship might be considered reasonably realistic in an example such as this – although in fact there is likely to be *some* changing effect as the proportions of the two crops vary, at least because of the timeliness of operation factor. Once different *types* of crops are considered, however – for example, beans and wheat – it is clear that the marginal rate of substitution (see Chapter 2, p. 23) will vary. This is in fact the type of relationship described earlier as complementarity in the more general sense – namely, that one crop 'helps' another. In practice most crop relationships are of this type – they are neither *perfectly* competitive nor *strictly* complementary.

Given the physical rates of substitution between two types of crop and their relative gross margins it is possible to say which of the two should be grown, or which combination. In the case of perfect substitutes, all one or all the other should be grown, according to the price relationships (Chapter 2, p. 37). With imperfect substitutes it is still possible that only one crop should be grown for maximum profitability.

It is more likely, however, that the most profitable plan would involve growing some of each crop, unless they are of the same type.

Finally there is the supplementary relationship – where increased production of one crop has no effect at all on the production of another. This implies the use of spare resources which can be utilised by another crop without any detriment to other crops being grown. For example, pea harvesting may utilise 'spare' labour in July, grain maize can utilise 'spare' combine capacity in November, a catch crop may utilise 'spare' land in certain months.

As discussed in Chapter 2, in practice none of these relationships is clear-cut. Two crops may be supplementary in terms of one resource (e.g. seasonal labour), but competitive for another (e.g. land). Two crops may be complementary in the sense of being of mutual benefit as regards yield and yet competitive for certain resources – especially land. Furthermore, the optimum point as depicted in Figure 2.11 (p. 38) is obviously a great deal more complicated to obtain when many different crops are involved. Apart from the question of the increased complexity of the calculations there is the problem of defining these relationships over a considerable number of different cropping combinations and varying seasons. Finally, the calculations above have assumed labour and machinery costs and capital requirements to be given; obviously this is unlikely to be true.

This is not to imply that these relationships can therefore be forgotten. On the contrary, they are an essential part of the thinking involved in arriving at an optimum cropping combination and all have to be built into the planning process, as far as the data available will allow.

The economics of rotations

The economics of crop rotations are very largely tied up with the three types of interrelationship between different crops discussed in the previous section. These concern not only the effect on yields but also the use of resources. Obviously, both aspects – production and the levels of resource use required – need to be considered in determining a crop rotation for a particular farm. The farmer's attitude to work and worry and capital expenditure will also have a major influence, as well as the quality of the soil and the necessity to maintain, or possibly improve, its future productivity.

Many of these points can be illustrated by looking specifically at the effect of introducing a break crop on a farm that is at present growing continuous cereals. The possible financial effects on the whole farm are five-fold:

(i) The gross margin of the break crop itself.

(ii) The effect on the variable costs of the cereal crops. Fertiliser and spray costs (especially expensive chemicals to control grass weeds) should be reduced for subsequent cereal crops.

(iii) The beneficial effect on the yields of the following cereal crops. This is a complicated question and one on which opinions and experimental evidence vary widely. Much depends on the soil type.

(iv) The effect on the cereal cropping. The main point here is that most farmers will only grow wheat after a break crop, and winter wheat tends to have a substantially higher gross margin than barley.

(v) The effect on the fixed cost structure of the farm, which will relate primarily to the requirements of the break crop for labour, machinery and buildings. Of particular importance will be the extent to which its labour demands occur at already busy times of the year rather than non-peak periods, and whether or not additional, specialist equipment or buildings are needed. Thus field beans, for example, fit in fairly well as regards seasonal labour needs and require no extra specialist equipment. Grain maize integrates even better from the point of view of labour, but needs additional harvesting (and sometimes drilling) equipment; this can be hired instead of bought, but the contract charges will then reduce the gross margin. The introduction of leys for livestock can raise fixed costs substantially – additional buildings may be needed, conservation equipment, and possibly extra labour. There is also the extra capital required for livestock and the interest on that capital to be considered. Working capital requirements may also rise. Sheep are likely to add less to fixed costs than beef, which in turn will normally have a smaller effect than dairying.

The first four effects can be combined to measure the likely difference in total gross margin of different rotations. Despite the conflicting evidence and hence the uncertainty concerning the assumptions that have to be made, particularly as regards the yield effect (iii above), it is worthwhile endeavouring to quantify the relationships involved. Thus the possible yield effect, assuming average quality soils, may be estimated to be as shown in Table 12.5*A*, which also includes the resulting gross margins, allowing for the effect on variable costs as well as output. Combining these into a number of alternative rotations, the

TABLE 12.5. *Rotational effects on yields, gross margins and profits*

A.	Yield (tonnes)	GM (£ per hectare)
Winter wheat:		
first crop after 1-year break	4.8	332
second crop after 1-year break	4.4	296
first crop after 2-year break	5.0	350
second crop after 2-year break	4.7	323
Spring barley:		
second crop after 1-year break or third crop after 2-year break	4.3	254
third/fourth crop after 1/2-year break	4.0	230
fourth/fifth crop after 1/2-year break	3.9	222
continuous	3.7	206
Oats: after 3 to 5 years of cereals	4.1	220
Break crops, e.g. field beans	—	190
B.	Average GM (£ per hectare)	Profit (£ per hectare)
1. Continuous barley	206	16
2. 1-year break, 1 wheat, 3 barleys	246	56
3. 1-year break, 2 wheats, 2 barleys	254	64
4. 2-year break, 2 wheats, 3 barleys	256	66
5. Oats, 1 year break, 2 wheats, 3 barleys	249	59

total gross margins and profits per hectare are shown in Table 12.5*B*, assuming fixed costs of £190 per hectare in all cases.

There are obviously many alternative rotations that could be tried, the results depending mainly on the assumptions made regarding yields. The problem is to establish, often on variable soils on any one farm, comparative figures for the different cereals in different parts of the rotation that are reasonably accurate taken over a longish period. However, granted this difficulty, it is clear that the beneficial effect of break crops on the subsequent cereal crops may well raise farm profits substantially, despite their possibly modest gross margin figures when looked at in isolation. Even if the gross margin from the break crop were only £150 per hectare the overall gross margins from rotations 2 to 4 in Table 12.5*B* would only be lowered by between £8 and £12 per hectare – still substantially better than continuous barley on the assumptions made.

It is not only the total gross margin that matters, however. There is still the fifth effect listed above to be taken into account, namely, the effect on fixed costs. It is conceivable that on a large farm some break crops, by helping spread labour and machinery peaks, could actually reduce overall fixed costs per hectare. However they are more likely to be raised, in ways already illustrated above. The introduction of other possible break crops, not yet mentioned in this section, would almost certainly raise fixed costs – unless contractors or casual labour were used on a major scale, thus reducing their gross margins. Examples are potatoes, sugar beet and field vegetables, for either processing or direct sale. In all cases there would be difficulty in obtaining quotas, contracts and marketing outlets. If they can be introduced, however, they lift the overall gross margin considerably. Thus if potatoes were the one-year break (or one of the two-year breaks) in the above rotations, the total farm gross margins would rise by between £50 and £70 per ha with an average crop, that is, to over £300 per ha. Farms with rotations such as three-year leys (utilised by a dairy herd) followed by three years of cereals, or one-third cash roots and two-third cereals, have overall gross margins in the order of £350 to £400. Although fixed costs are obviously substantially higher, the profit potential is also certain to be greater.

Appendix 12.1: Further points in relation to yields and costs

1. It should be noted that attempts to increase yield usually entail increased inputs – at least as far as (i) and (ii) on pp. 263–4 are concerned. Total and per hectare costs will therefore rise, both because of higher growing costs (cause) and higher harvesting costs (effect). However, total costs *per unit* of output (i.e. per kg or per tonne) will often fall – at least up to a point. This is mainly because a large proportion of the crop costs are given once the decision to grow the crop has been taken, whatever the yield obtained (cf. livestock, Chapter 7). Such costs include rent, a minimum seed cost, and labour and machinery costs for cultivating, sowing and harvesting. These are the *fixed* costs in this context.[1] Such costs obviously fall continually, per unit of production, as yield increases. The extra costs incurred in order to raise yields and harvest the heavier crop are the *variable* costs in this context.

[1] In contrast to the gross margin context, when the decision to grow the crop (and the area, if grown) has not yet been taken.

TABLE 12.6. *Effect of increasing yield on costs: potatoes*

Yield (tonnes per ha)	Fixed costs per ha (£)	Variable costs per ha (£)	Total costs per ha (£)	Fixed costs per tonne (£)	Variable costs per tonne (£)	Total costs per tonne (£)	Marginal costs per tonne* (£)
17	1,000	0	1,000	58.8	—	58.8	—
20	1,000	30	1,030	50.0	1.5	51.5	10
23	1,000	70	1,070	43.5	3.0	46.5	13
26	1,000	120	1,120	38.5	4.6	43.1	17
29	1,000	185	1,185	34.5	6.4	40.9	22*X*
32	1,000	320	1,320	31.3	10.0	41.3	45*Y*
35	1,000	530	1,530	28.6	15.1	43.7	70
38	1,000	830	1,830	26.3	21.8	48.2	100

* Approx. mean for the 3-tonne increment.

Note: The terms 'fixed' and 'variable' costs are not used here in the gross margin sense – see text.

The effect is illustrated for potatoes in Table 12.6. There are various features to note:

(*a*) Up to point *X* (29 tonnes per ha), variable costs per tonne are rising, but less fast than fixed costs per tonne are falling, so that total costs per tonne are falling.

(*b*) Beyond point *X*, variable costs per tonne are rising faster than fixed costs per tonne are falling; hence total costs per tonne are rising.

(*c*) If potatoes are worth £45 a tonne at point *Y* (32 tonnes per ha) marginal cost equals marginal revenue. Thus it is economic to increase production from *X* to *Y*, even though total costs are rising not only *per hectare* but also *per tonne.* However, it is uneconomic to continue beyond point *Y*, since marginal costs then exceed marginal revenue.

2. Another point to appreciate is that while extra yield normally increases harvesting costs, the amount of the increase is usually small compared with the value of the increased output. Thus, with potatoes, the extra harvesting cost is unlikely to exceed £5 per tonne compared with a value of at least £30 per tonne, or, with cereals, £5 per tonne compared with a value of at least £65 per tonne (these figures exclude extra storage, however). In fact a heavy, clean crop of cereals is easier and quicker to harvest than a lighter crop infested with weeds and grasses. One crop where the proportion is higher is sugar beet, especially where grown a long way from the factory; the extra harvesting

and transport costs can then be some £4 or £5 per tonne, out of a total value ranging from £20 to £25.

3. The point has already been made in Chapter 2 (pp. 43–5) that the division of costs into fixed and variable items depends upon the decision being considered and the relevant time span. An example was given (p. 45), pointing out that just prior to harvesting a crop most of its costs are 'fixed', in the sense that they have already been incurred and are therefore inescapable. In fact, even more of the total costs are fixed, in this context, than when considering point (1) above. If market price has fallen very low, the relevant question is whether the return for the crop will be sufficient to cover the harvesting and marketing variable costs yet to be borne if the crop is harvested, that is, those that will be avoided if the crop is left in the ground. If these are exceeded then there will be something left to help offset the costs already borne. If the season is a late one, of course, and if conditions are wet, the farmer will have other factors to take into account: the effect of deteriorating conditions on the yields of other crops waiting to be harvested, the possible soil damage, the effect on his subsequent cropping plans. Nevertheless, the only relevant *cost* items are those mentioned. Whether or not the *total* costs of the crop will be covered is irrelevant so far as this particular decision is concerned – although it will obviously affect his decision whether or not to grow the crop another year.

PART III

THE COMBINATION OF ENTERPRISES

13: Principles and procedures in planning enterprise combination

Background to planning enterprise combination

The previous part of the book was concerned with planning the organisation within individual enterprises. The present part considers ways of planning their combination into an overall farming system. Although, as has already been stressed, these two sides of planning must not in practice be divorced from one another, it is assumed for the moment that the enterprises to be combined into a farming system are organised in an optimal manner.

All systems of planning are based on models, which are abstractions from the real world in that they contain only part of the detail that exists in practice. An efficient farm planning model should ideally contain just sufficient information to enable the planning situation to be encompassed realistically. On the one hand, nothing is gained if a solution is obtained using a superfluity of data when the same result could have been achieved with less. Indeed, the reverse is rather the case, because more time is required to handle the extra data and there is a greater chance of errors occurring. In addition, a large amount of data may make it more difficult to discern the really significant relationships. On the other hand, there is no virtue in pruning the amount of information in a model to such an extent that solutions are likely to be either unfeasible or else inferior, in terms of stated objectives, to those that could have been obtained. Admittedly, unless the planner is well versed in handling similar planning situations, it may not be easy for him to distinguish in advance between the information which is likely to influence solutions and that which is not. In this event, there would seem to be some merit in the suggestion that models should, in the first instance, consist of the minimum of data and if, in consequence, solutions are inadequate or unrealistic, adjustments can then be made to put matters right.

Most planning models are based on a distinction between fixed and variable resources – a concept already introduced in Chapter 2. Any plan is bounded by a specific set of fixed resources – whose constraints cannot be exceeded in the plan – and requires variable inputs if it is to be operated (as well as liquid assets to purchase them and to service the fixed resources). A suitable starting point for planning a farm would seem logically to be that of the purely short-term situation presented by the existing pattern of fixed resources, enterprises and techniques. The solution obtained in this way will be prevented from unlimited development by one or more of the fixed resources running short (although, conversely, many resources will be only partly used). Further development may then be sought by adding new resources or by cutting down on existing ones, by incorporating new techniques or by considering fresh lines of production. The plans generated in this way may suggest the most suitable path of development for the farm in the future, so that short-term planning merges into longer-term planning. Thus, in the latter case, not only is enterprise combination being planned, but resource combination as well.

As was seen in Chapter 1, economic planning involves the manipulation of limited resources among alternative opportunities in order to satisfy the bounded objective of maximising profit. It follows that any planning procedure must contain three essential elements:

1. An objective,
2. Scarce resources,
3. Alternative ways – the enterprises – of using the resources to attain the objective.

An objective

The tenets of production economics hinge on the assumption that the aim in planning the allocation of resources is to maximise profit. As already seen, however, farmers commonly have other objectives as well, of which account must be taken in practical planning if solutions are to be acceptable. In most forms of planning this is achieved, not by abandoning the profit-maximising principle, but by including 'personal' or 'managerial' constraints that limit the freedom with which it can be pursued. In an analogous manner, constraints are also included to ensure that the long-term productivity of resources is not harmed in the pursuit of maximum short-term profits.

Furthermore, it is often gross margin that is maximised in farm planning and not profit, which is derived by the deduction of fixed costs. In many cases this gives the same result as if profit itself had been maximised. In some cases, however, an enterprise may come into the solution at a level that does not cover the cost of some fixed resource that is specific to it, such as specialised labour or machinery. In consequence, the maximum gross margin plan is lower than the maximum profit plan, which would exclude both the resource and the enterprise.

Resources and constraints

The resources available to the farmer act as a framework within which he must plan his system of farming. On the one hand there are the visible, material resources, such as land, labour, buildings and machinery. Obviously, the farmer cannot grow a greater area of crops than he has suitable land available, keep more housed livestock than his accommodation allows or exceed the capacities of his labour and machinery. On the other hand, and perhaps less obviously, there are also non-material factors that may just as effectively limit his freedom of action. Examples are: the need to obtain contracts in order to produce crops like sugar beet or vining peas and the subsequent limitations on their area when obtained; the necessity, even in this prophylactic age, of keeping within certain rotational limits if disease and weed-free crops are to be maintained; the need to take account of restrictions arising out of personal preferences and attitudes to risk. To disregard such non-material constraints in planning could result in solutions just as absurd as those that might be obtained if material resources were ignored.

A distinction may also be made between those resources required by more than one enterprise – the 'shared' or 'common' resources – and those that are specific to individual enterprises. Examples of the former are: arable or grassland that may be cropped or stocked in alternative ways, non-specialist labour, such as general arable workers, and non-specific machinery and buildings, such as tractors and dutch barns. Examples of the latter include specialist labour, such as cowmen or pigmen, specific-purpose machinery, such as potato or sugar beet harvesters, and single-product buildings, such as piggeries, milking parlours and broiler houses. Although both categories have a part to play, it is competition between the enterprises for the shared resources that constitutes the nub of the planning process.

In addition, the concern is with those resources that are relatively the scarcest, for selecting the enterprises that give the maximum returns to them also maximises the return to the whole complex of resources that comprises the farming unit. For example, if labour is scarce relative to land, enterprises such as cereals and pulses and the 'ranching' of cattle are likely to be selected because they give a good return to labour. Conversely, if land is scarce relative to labour, enterprises that give a high return to land, such as potatoes, sugar beet, vegetables and intensive livestock, are more appropriate. Although it is frequently impossible to decide in advance which resources will prove to be limiting – so that it becomes part of the planning process to detect them – it is at least possible to distinguish some of those that can never be so, and which can therefore be excluded.

For example, planning labour use on the arable farm hinges on the peak periods of work, so nothing is gained if the slack periods, which they dominate, are included too. Or again, in some cases labour may be obviously more limiting on production than machine capacity or livestock accommodation, so the latter can be excluded from planning.

Resource–enterprise relationships

Before turning to the types of fixed resource incorporated in farm planning, it is relevant briefly to consider what bearing they have on the enterprises.

First, the resources available to the farmer distinguish the feasible from the unfeasible enterprises. The latter need to be further divided into those enterprises that are never likely to be a practical possibility on the farm – mainly because of unfavourable natural factors – and those that, although not feasible at the actual time of planning, may become so in the future. This may be because the fixed resources required, such as contracts or specialised buildings or machinery, are not available on the farm at the moment or because some technological innovation awaits fruition. Thus the longer the time horizon of the plan, the more enterprises are likely to be feasible, a point that should not be overlooked in moving from short-term to long-term planning. The feasible enterprises constitute a 'short list' from which those for actual inclusion in a plan are selected. As seen earlier, the relative balance between different resources plays a part in this.

Secondly, the fixed resources place a limit on the maximum level of production from individual enterprises. This results both from the quantities of resources available, which determine the maximum area of crops and numbers of livestock, and from their quality, which limits yields per hectare and per animal.

Thirdly, fixed resources influence the level of input both of other fixed resources and of variable resources. Again, both quantitative and qualitative aspects play a part. With the former, economies of size may obtain if sufficient resources are available to permit large-scale units. For example, a farmer with an extensive area of arable can use big, high-capacity machines, so attaining lower inputs of labour and machinery per unit output than a neighbour with a small area. Similar gains are possible with large as opposed to small livestock units. The quality of a fixed resource may affect inputs both directly and indirectly. For example, a lower input of fertiliser per unit of crop output on a fertile, peat soil, compared with a light, 'hungry' soil, may be the direct effect of a lower fertiliser dressing per ha and the indirect effect of a higher crop yield per ha. Labour and machinery use may be similarly affected. Again, in intensive livestock production, the quality of buildings may affect both labour requirements and the amount of feed consumed by animals.

Lastly, the fixed resources determine the most suitable organisation to be adopted within individual enterprises, as was considered in the previous section. Thus, for example, if labour is the outstandingly scarce resource on a farm, not only should those enterprises be selected that make relatively low demands on it, but they should also be organised in a way that uses it most sparingly.

It is thus clear that account must be taken of both the quantitative and qualitative influence of fixed resources on the enterprises. While the former may be fairly readily assessed when data for planning are being assembled, this may not always hold true for the latter. Data should preferably be collected on the individual farm so that they reflect resource quality, although this is not possible if the farmer is establishing a new enterprise or if he has only recently occupied the farm. In such cases recourse to standardised data is necessary. It must be kept in mind, however, that the assumption of a standard enterprise performance that does not accord with the nature of the fixed resources on an individual farm can be a major source of error in farm planning. Standards should therefore be obtained from sources where conditions compare as closely as possible with those on the farm being studied. In addition, the opportunity should be taken to check the results actually achieved as soon as is practicable.

Resource categories

Resources can be divided into six major categories, in terms of the ways in which they constrain farming systems, namely: land, labour, capital, personal, institutional and husbandry constraints. The first three represent material resources and the last three non-material resources. (They are considered only briefly here, but further details of the type of information required for planning are given in Appendix 13.1.)

Land. Land is a complex resource, in that it influences enterprises through its location; through natural factors associated with it, such as soil type and fertility, slope, altitude and climate; and through other man-made attributes, such as drainage, field size, roads, fences and piped water. These factors do not work in isolation from one another.

For example, a heavy soil that is suitable for cropping in a low rainfall area may only be suitable for grassland in an area of high rainfall. Or again, land under grass near the farmstead may be suitable for dairy cows, while similar grassland sited some distance away or cut off by a busy road is not. Because of the number of factors involved, it is not uncommon to find more than one category of land on the same farm, and some degree of simplification may be needed to deal with it in planning. One way is to divide the land into separate 'blocks' according to the enterprises that each can support, or according to differences in enterprise performance that result from variations in land quality. These can then be planned as separate units that share a common pool of other resources such as labour and machinery.

Labour. With labour the main distinctions are between family and hired labour – the latter both regular and casual – and, for all categories, between general and specialist labour. In the case of family labour, the amount of time that the farmer is prepared to devote to manual as opposed to managerial tasks varies considerably. Providing, however, he is willing to help out in rush periods, he may have virtually the same effect on a plan as the employment of an extra man. Although hired labour consists mainly of regular workers, casual labour may still have an important part to play for, by supplementing the regular labour force at peak periods, it may enable reductions in the level of the latter.[1] The distinction between general and specialist labour is necessary because, while the former is a shared resource that is competed for by more than one enterprise, the latter is specific to single enterprises.

Since, in the case of arable cropping, labour constraints operate through the peak periods, the latter must be analysed in respect of the number of productive days likely to be available and also those tasks that require men to work in gangs (see Chapter 5). Matters are simpler where specialist labour is involved on livestock, because it is often sufficient simply to express the labour constraint as the maximum number of animals that can be handled.

Capital. Capital can be divided into fixed capital that is already committed in a material form, such as buildings, machines, fences and

[1] In a similar way, the use of contract services, although involving the hire of machinery, also includes a labour element. For example, the use of contract ploughing in autumn may be an essential factor in releasing regular labour for team-work operations, such as potato harvesting.

roads, and liquid capital (also variously called fluid, circulating and working capital) that is not yet committed, such as cash in the bank or in hand. Both categories may act as constraints on the farming system. Those arising from fixed capital – which, as has been seen, may be specialised or general purpose – are expressed mainly as capacities of machines or buildings.

Liquid capital is required to pay for variable inputs, such as fertilisers and feedstuffs; to service the fixed resources, such as rent or mortgage payments, wages bills, the costs of repairing and replacing equipment and machinery and of maintaining buildings; to defray personal expenditure, including living expenses and tax liabilities; and to generate a surplus for new investment. Shortage of liquid capital may thus be just as effective as a constraint on both long-term growth and short-term operations as a deficiency of fixed capital. In the short term, the timing of operations may be important in its effect on the ebb and flow of liquid capital, which is generated by sales on the one hand and consumed by expenditure on the other.

Personal. Included under this heading are constraints that arise through the farmer as an individual, as an operator and as a manager. His qualities in these respects may be vital to the success of the farm, but may be hard to assess unless previous evidence is available concerning his capabilities.

Attitudes to the uncertainty of farming operations and the willingness or otherwise to accept risks (which may be contingent on the relative availability of capital) are important in this context. The farmer who is prepared to take risks may adopt a system that would be quite unacceptable to another who is more cautious and whose main aim is a stable and reasonably assured income from year to year. Attitudes to output uncertainty may be included in those models not specifically designed to cater for risk aversion – which includes the majority (known as 'deterministic' models) – as constraints excluding or limiting the size of enterprises which the farmer regards as 'risky'. This is a relatively blunt instrument to use, however, because it prejudges the issue and may exclude enterprises that, although risky on their own, are reasonably stable when operated in combination with others, due to their reacting differently to varying seasonal conditions. Input uncertainty may be handled by carrying sufficient fixed resources, such as men and machines, to enable operations to be completed in unfavourable seasons. Again, this is not a wholly satisfactory way of meeting the situation, because it may be better to accept some losses in unfavourable seasons in order to avoid having to pay for an excess of resources in more favourable ones. (Such measures are considered in greater detail in Chapter 16, pp. 383–9, 391.)

Closely allied with attitudes to uncertainty are the farmer's subjective preferences for this or that enterprise. These may be expressed negatively, so that he is not prepared to countenance certain enterprises on his farm or positively, so that he insists on including an enterprise that might not otherwise enter the plan.

Institutional. Institutional constraints arise from factors operating outside the farm gate and are largely concerned with whether it is possible to market certain products, even if they can be produced successfully on the farm. This often involves the location of the farm, which needs to be situated reasonably close to a processing plant if products such as sugar beet, vining peas and broilers are to be sold. In addition, even if location is favourable, contracts still have to be obtained. In a similar way, quotas may be imposed by authorities such as the Potato and Hop Marketing Boards. The relatively narrow breadth of the market for certain products, such as herbage seeds and vegetables, may also act as a constraint on their production on the individual farm.

Husbandry. Husbandry constraints are largely concerned with preserving the long-term fertility and condition of the land and with controlling disease, so that satisfactory levels of output can be maintained. They are at their most obvious as rotational constraints, which may apply either to individual crops, such as sugar beet or potatoes, or to groups of crops, such as cereals or pulses. They usually take the form of maximum permissible crop areas – in absolute or proportionate terms – although for crops such as leys, minimum limits may be imposed. (In a similar way, maximum constraints on crops like cereals may imply a minimum limit on other crops such as leys.) Closely connected with rotation are certain crop 'ties' or 'links', where the production of one crop is bound up with that of another. Examples are the need to include a suitable cereal as a nurse crop if seeds are to be undersown, or to follow a proportion of the land in sugar beet with a spring-sown crop, as all the land is not cleared in time for the planting of autumn-sown crops.

Enterprises

The enterprises are the third element in any planning procedure, representing alternative ways of using the fixed resources in seeking to attain the objective. We have already seen how they are linked to the resources, and it now remains to consider the information that is required about them before planning is possible. This falls under three heads:

1. Financial returns;
2. Requirements of variable inputs;
3. Requirements of fixed resources.

Financial returns. Without information on the financial returns to be expected in the enterprises, it would be impossible to attain the bounded objective of maximising net income, because there would be no criterion on which to base their selection.

Returns are made up of an expected yield multiplied by an expected price. Both are subject to considerable year-to-year variation, yet in deterministic models, such as we are dealing with here, data are single-valued and are assumed to be known with certainty. It is clear that when planning there is little value in using data based on single years, as they may be atypical, particularly in the case of crops. Instead, a run of at least three years is required to give an adequate picture. Although it might seem preferable to go back for a considerably longer period, if possible, the difficulty is then encountered that factors such as varieties and techniques may have been different in the past. To use such data for planning in the future could be positively misleading. One ameliorating feature is that a plan will often accommodate quite considerable changes in enterprise returns before a new plan is rendered necessary. In addition, providing the relative balance in the returns *between* different enterprises is fairly accurately assessed, failure to obtain a high degree of precision within individual enterprises may not be very important.

Variable input requirements. Variable inputs are those items, such as fertilisers and feedstuffs, the use of which alters in direct proportion to changes in the balance of individual enterprises, within a given framework of fixed resources (see Chapter 2, pp. 45–7). For example, if a pig fattening unit is expanded (within the present capacities of labour and buildings) additional weaners and food have to be supplied. Or if land in barley is expanded at the expense of beans, extra seed and fertiliser are required for the barley, while less are needed for the beans. Many factors affect the level of variable inputs. They include the quality of the fixed resources, the intensity of production, the methods adopted and the efficiency with which they are applied. One feature that helps in their estimation is that they tend to stay more or less unchanged from year to year.

The financial returns and the variable costs have one feature in common, namely, they both vary together with changes in the size of enterprises. Deducting the variable costs from the output of an enterprise leaves the gross margin and it is the latter that becomes the guide as to which enterprises to select in seeking to maximise net income.

Fixed resource requirements – 1. Maximum size of enterprise. Although the fixed resources available at any particular point in time constitute a planning framework, they do not by themselves determine the maximum size (output) of an enterprise, for the latter depends also on the amount of fixed resources required per unit of the enterprise. Stated as a formula:

$$\text{Maximum size of enterprise} = \frac{\text{Fixed resource available}}{\text{Fixed resource requirement per unit of enterprise}}.$$

Table 13.1 gives an example from milk production. The various resources available (column 1) when divided by the requirements per cow (column 2) give the maximum number of cows that can be carried (column 3). As a result of imbalance between resources, the limits imposed on herd size differ for each resource, with winter labour the most restrictive at 60 cows.

As with the variable inputs, the unit requirements of fixed resources vary with the production methods adopted and the relative efficiency with which they are applied. It follows that it is possible to raise the

TABLE 13.1. *Fixed resources in milk production*

Fixed resource	(1) Availability	(2) Requirement per cow	(3) Max. no. of cows (1)/(2)	(4) Gross margin[a] per unit resource £300/(2) (£)
Land	48 hectares	0.6 hectares	80	500
Livestock labour:				
winter 6 months	1,800 hours	30 hours	60	10
summer 6 months	1,800 hours	24 hours	75	$12\frac{1}{2}$
Accommodation	68 cows	1	68	300

[a] Gross margin per cow = £300.

limits imposed on an enterprise, both by lowering fixed resource requirements and by acquiring more fixed resources.

2. *Returns to Fixed Resources*. Knowledge of fixed resource requirements is also needed to enable the return (gross margin) to the resources used in different enterprises to be calculated as below:

$$\text{Return to fixed resource} = \frac{\text{Gross margin per unit of enterprise}}{\text{Fixed resource requirement per unit of cnterprise}}$$

Examples are given in the last column of Table 13.1. Such information allows the planner to compare the returns in different enterprises and to select those that give a high return to scarce resources. At the same time enterprise dominance may be revealed. This arises when there is an enterprise which, while being constrained in the same way as a second enterprise, gives a lower return to the fixed resources, so that it is dominated and will not enter the plan. Provided this is recognised when data are being assembled, it can be eliminated, so reducing the quantity of data that has to be handled during planning.

Recapitulation

Before turning to a demonstration of the principles involved in planning procedures, we may briefly recapitulate the main points of what has gone before.

1. Over a specific period of time the amount of certain resources available can be regarded as fixed.
2. The fixed resources act as both quantitative and qualitative constraints on the enterprises and together with non-material constraints – including personal preferences and attitudes – they determine what enterprises are feasible, the maximum output that can be expected from them, and how they should best be organised.
3. The enterprises make different demands on and give different returns to the fixed resources.
4. The planning objective is to select that combination of enterprises that gives the greatest return – as measured by gross margins – to the fixed resources and other constraints. More specifically, because some resources are in scarcer supply (and are therefore more restrictive) than others, they are allocated to those enterprises where the return to them is highest, so maximising the return to all the resources.
5. Profit is derived by deducting the cost of servicing the fixed resources from the total gross margin.

6. Different plans can be derived by assuming varying sets of fixed resources, so that short-term planning merges into longer-term planning.

7. The data required in planning fall under three broad heads:

(*a*) The amount and quality of fixed resources and other constraints.

(*b*) The outputs of the feasible enterprises together with their requirements of fixed and variable resources.

(*c*) Prices of inputs and outputs.

Principles in planning. A graphic example

Having examined the background to planning, we are now in a position to consider different planning techniques. Before doing so, however, some of the principles involved in planning may be demonstrated by a simple example involving only two enterprises.

Elements of the problem

Although the problem is a very limited one, the data presented in the first part of Table 13.2 are representative of all the necessary elements of short-term, deterministic, farm planning models. The resources available to the farmer are listed in the first column. Land, labour, tractor work and working capital represent material, shared resources, while the potato quota is a specific non-material resource.[1] Together they permit potatoes and wheat to be grown, which have gross margins of £720 and £400 per ha respectively and make differing calls on the fixed resources. (It is assumed that they are organised in an optimal way.) In consequence, as the second part of the table shows, while potatoes give the higher return to land, summer labour and spring tractor work, wheat does so for spring labour and capital. The objective is to discover that area in the two crops which maximises the gross margin, in the light of the fixed resources available.

Planning framework

In Table 13.3 the limits imposed on the production of wheat and potatoes (columns 3 and 5) are derived by dividing the available

[1] The peculiar nature of this resource mix stems from the example being deliberately chosen to demonstrate principles in planning and not to provide a realistic answer to a real-life problem. To add verity, however, it could be assumed that the owner of a very large mainly cereal farm, growing no root crops at present and with resources left over from his current farming operations, is thinking of taking on another 75 ha of land and also of including potatoes as a new enterprise (so that the quota applies to the whole and not just the additional land).

TABLE 13.2. *Data for planning*

1. *Elements of a plan*

			Enterprises	
			Potatoes	Wheat
Unit (hectare):			1	1
Return (gross margin) per unit (£):			720	400
Resources available			Resource requirement	
Land	(hectares)	75	1	1
Spring labour – Mar./Apl.	(hours)	412½	7½	3¾
Summer labour – Aug./Sept.	(hours)	325	2½	5
Spring tractor work	(hours)	450	5	3¾
Working capital[a]	(£)	20,000	400	100
Potato quota	(hectares)	48	1	0

2. *Return (gross margin) per unit of resource*

Resource	Unit	Potatoes (£)	Wheat (£)
Land	1 hectare	720	400
Spring labour – Mar./Apl.	1 hour	96	107
Summer labour – Aug./Sept.	1 hour	288	80
Spring tractor work	1 hour	144	107
Working capital[a]	£1	1.8	4.0
Potato quota	1 hectare	720	—

[a] For seed, fertiliser and spray.

TABLE 13.3. *Planning framework – enterprise limits*

			Potatoes		Wheat	
		(1) Resources available	(2) Resources required per ha	(3) Maximum hectares (1)/(2)	(4) Resources required per ha	(5) Maximum hectares (1)/(4)
Land	(hectares)	75	1	75	1	75
Spring labour	(hours)	412½	7½	55	3¾	110
Summer labour	(hours)	325	2½	130	5	65
Spring tractor work	(hours)	450	5	90	3¾	120
Working capital	(£)	20,000	400	50	100	200
Potato quota	(hectares)	48	1	48	—	—

resources (column 1) by their respective requirements (columns 2 and 4). Not unexpectedly, some resources are more limiting than others, with quota the most restrictive on potatoes (48 ha) and summer labour on wheat (65 ha). This same information is shown graphically in Figure 13.1.

In each of the individual figures, the vertical axis (*OP*) represents ha of potatoes and the horizontal axis (*OW*) ha of wheat. In Figure 13.1*a* land is plotted as the first constraint. Table 13.3 shows that land limits the farmer to 75 ha of potatoes or 75 ha of wheat and these two points, L_p and L_w, on the respective axes are joined by a straight line. This is the framework imposed by land on the production of potatoes and wheat, showing the maximum that can be produced either alone or in combination. For example, at *x* the combination is 55 ha of potatoes and 20 ha of wheat while at *y* it is 10 ha potatoes and 65 ha wheat. It is impossible to produce outside the area OL_pL_w, for doing so implies that the land available is exceeded. While, on the other hand, it is quite feasible to produce within the same area, it is illogical to do so, as it implies leaving land idle when it is the only constraint. Thus *logical* and *feasible* production is confined to the boundary L_pL_w.

In Figure 13.1*b*, the boundary imposed by $412\frac{1}{2}$ hours of spring labour is similarly plotted, running from 55 ha potatoes, SL_p, to 110 ha wheat, SL_w, with the various combinations of the two crops that exactly use up the labour in between. For example, *z* represents 30 ha potatoes and 50 ha wheat ($30 \times 7\frac{1}{2}$ hours $+ 50 \times 3\frac{3}{4} = 412\frac{1}{2}$ hours).

The boundaries for land and spring labour are combined in Figure 13.1*c*. From what has gone before it will be appreciated that logical and feasible production is confined to the two-segmented curve SL_pDL_w; that is the inner boundary resulting from the intersection of the two individual boundary lines. Spring labour is more limiting on potatoes than is land, so the boundary starts at SL_p, where there are 55 ha potatoes with 20 ha land idle. Wheat is then added at the expense of potatoes until, with 35 ha potatoes and 40 ha wheat, point *D* is reached, where both land and labour are fully used.[1] After point *D*, land is more limiting than spring labour, which therefore starts to become spare, until at L_w (75 ha wheat) $131\frac{1}{4}$ hours are idle.

[1] Proof:

	Hectares		Hours per hectare		Total hours
Potatoes	35	×	7.5	=	262.5
Wheat	40	×	3.75	=	150.0
	75				412.5

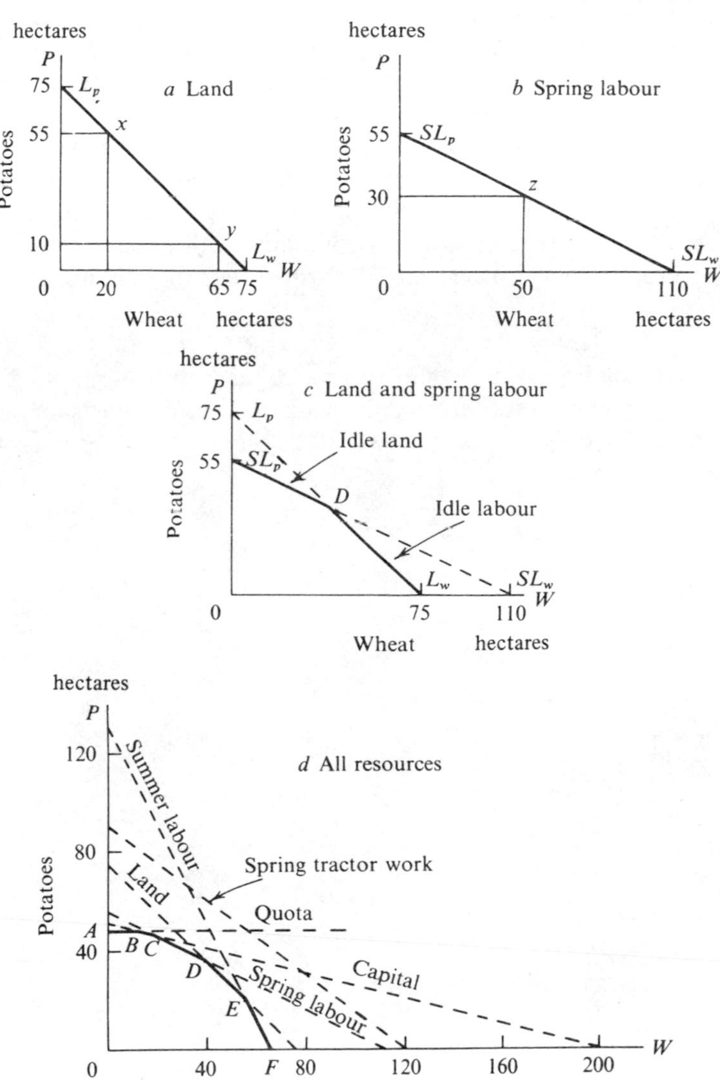

Fig. 13.1. The planning framework

Finally the six constraints in the example are combined in Figure 13.1*d*. With the exception of spring tractor work, which never proves limiting (because it is dominated by the other resources and can therefore be discarded as a constraint), they form the framework *A-B-C-D-E-F* of the planning problem or, to put it more formally, the production possibilities curve for potatoes and wheat. Resources are never all fully used at the same time, the maximum being two at a time at points *B*,*C*,*D* and *E*. Conversely, at least three resources are always left partly unused. This accords closely with practical farm planning, where, because of indivisibilities combined with imbalance between resources, seldom, if ever, are all farm resources fully utilised.

Substitution ratios

The planning framework is shown on a larger scale in Figure 13.2. The separate segments result from different resources running short as the combination of potatoes and wheat changes. When one resource

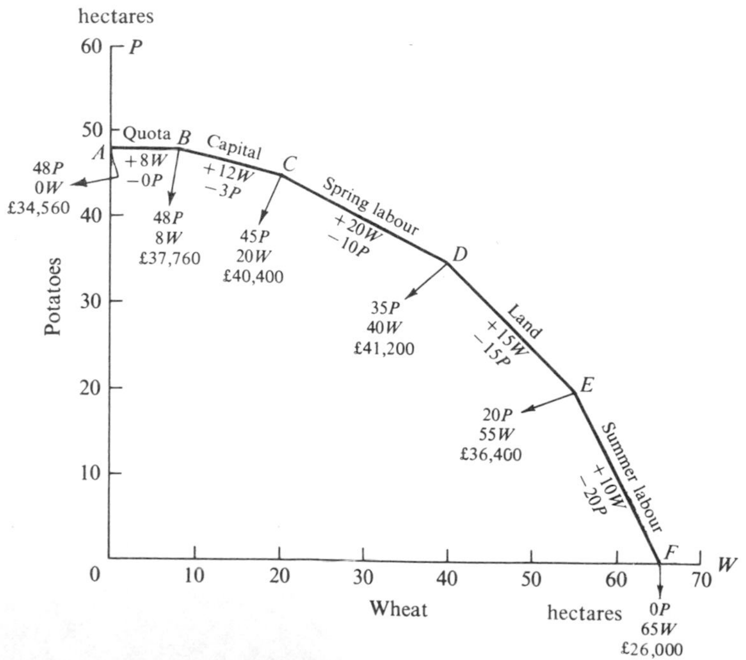

Fig. 13.2. The planning framework, substitution ratios and feasible solutions

TABLE 13.4. *Rates of substitution between potatoes and wheat*

Resources	Resources required per hectare		Substitution ratios. 1 hectare wheat replaces:		Gross margin gained or lost		
	(1) Wheat	(2) Potatoes	(3) [(1)/(2)]		(4) Wheat (£)	(5) Potatoes (£)	(6) Net (£)
Potato quota (hectares)	0	1	—		—	—	—
Working capital (£)	100	400	0.25	acres	+400	−180	+220
Spring labour (hours)	3.75	7.5	0.5	of	+400	−360	+40
Land (hectares)	1	1	1	potatoes	+400	−720	−320
Summer labour (hours)	5	2.5	2		+400	−1,440	−1,040

ceases to be scarce and another becomes so, the slope of the curve changes or, in other words, another segment starts. The significance of these changes of slope is that the rates of substitution between potatoes and wheat are changing. Table 13.4 shows how they are derived. For example, if land is fully utilised (segment *DE*) and potatoes are being grown, adding 1 hectare wheat entails the sacrifice of 1 hectare potatoes, giving a 1:1 substitution ratio. If the same conditions apply to spring labour, adding 1 hectare wheat implies the sacrifice of 0.5 hectares potatoes – a 1:0.5 ratio – as the latter require twice as much spring labour as wheat. Moving clockwise round the planning boundary between *B* and *F* entails an increasing sacrifice of potatoes for each hectare wheat gained. Segment *AB*, resulting from the potato quota, shows indifference between the two crops – a supplementary relationship – for, until *B* is reached, wheat can be added without the sacrifice of any potatoes. (The ratios could equally well be expressed in terms of the amount of wheat lost for each hectare potatoes gained.)

Maximisation procedure

Although a solution can be reached in one step in a simple two-dimensional example (see Appendix 13.2), the purpose here is to simulate the procedures involved in handling more complex situations, where there are more than two enterprises.

The aim is to search round the boundary *A* to *F* (which, as seen previously, represents the path of feasible and logical production) until the maximum gross margin is attained. This is achieved by substituting, up to the limit, the enterprise that gives the higher return to any shared resource which becomes exhausted, for that giving the lower return. (Throughout, reference should be made to Tables 13.2 and 13.4 and to Figures 13.1 and 13.2.)

The starting point is the point of origin *O* in Figure 13.2, where all resources are uncommitted and no gross margin is generated. As there are four shared resources that are all potentially scarce, it is not obvious which of them, in fact, will prove to be most limiting in the optimal solution, so land is selected arbitrarily.

First solution (A). Potatoes give a higher return to land than wheat and are most limited by the quota constraint. The first solution is thus 48 ha of potatoes with gross margin £34,560.

Second solution (B). No shared resource is fully used yet, so wheat can be introduced. The most restrictive resource is capital, the £800 still available permitting 8 ha of wheat (800/100). With 48 ha potatoes and 8 ha wheat, gross margin totals £37,760.

Third solution (C). Capital is the first shared resource to become exhausted, and as wheat gives a higher return to it than potatoes, some of the latter will be replaced. The substitution ratio for capital is that 1 ha wheat replaces 0.25 ha potatoes. Of the resources still spare – land, spring and summer labour – it is spring labour ($22\frac{1}{2}$ hours) that most limits the amount of wheat that can be introduced. As 1 ha of wheat requires 3.75 hours of spring labour but 0.25 ha of potatoes release 1.875 hours (7.5 × 0.25), net requirement per ha is 1.875 hours, limiting wheat to 12 ha (22.5/1.875) at the expense of 3 ha of potatoes. With 45 ha of potatoes (48 – 3) and 20 ha of wheat (8 + 12) gross margin totals £40,400.

Fourth solution (D). Spring labour becomes the second shared resource to be exhausted, to which wheat gives the higher return. The substitution rate for spring labour is that 1 ha wheat replaces 0.5 ha of potatoes. Of the resources still not fully used – land and summer labour – the former (10 ha) is most limiting, permitting another 20 ha of wheat [10/(1 – 0.5)] to substitute for a further 10 ha of potatoes. With 35 ha of potatoes (45 – 10) and 40 ha of wheat (20 + 20) gross margin totals £41,200.

Land becomes the third shared resource to become exhausted, but as wheat gives a lower return per ha than potatoes, the limit of profitable substitutions has been reached and the optimal solution obtained. If, for purposes of illustration, fixed costs are assumed to be £20,000, profit is £21,200.

This elementary example has allowed procedures to be simulated that will be found to be closely reflected in the more formal planning techniques, such as programme planning and linear programming (Chapters 14 and 15). At the same time, a number of the assumptions on which it is based (and which are discussed in Appendix 13.4) are common to many of the more generally applied planning techniques, and may give rise to difficulties when attempting to represent actual farming situations.

Long-term development

Thus far we have been involved only with principles and procedures pertinent to short-term, static planning, that is planning within a framework resulting from a particular pattern of farm resources and constraints – fixed in respect both of quantity and quality – within which specific enterprises may be operated by given techniques. Here the concern is with the development of the farm over time, when the framework itself may shift, thus no longer acting as an inflexible barrier to change beyond its boundaries.

In Figure 13.3, this concept of long-term development is related to theoretical principles (propounded in Chapter 2) on the assumption that farm production is expanding over time (it may, of course, contract). Figure 13.3*a* concerns a multi-product firm in which the iso-cost (production possibilities) curve is pushed further away from the point

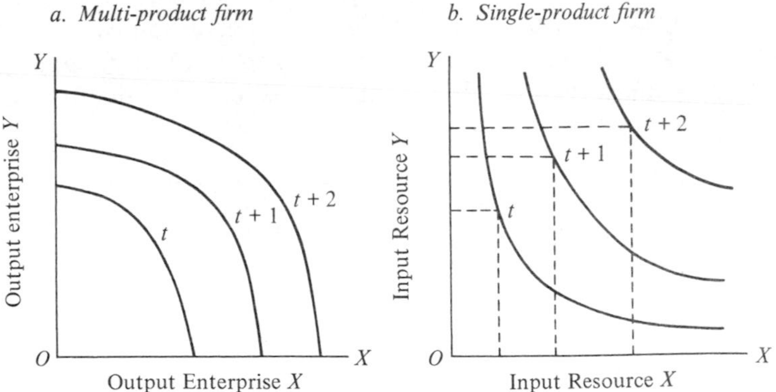

Fig. 13.3. Development over time.

of origin O over successive time periods (t, $t + 1$, $t + 2$). On the other hand, Figure 13.3*b* refers to a single-product business, but in this case it is the iso-product curve that moves outward (the dotted lines represent discrete amounts of the two resources – say labour and capital – available in each time period).

Factors directly linked to changes in the planning framework

As was seen on p. 290, the planning framework results from relating the resources available to the unit requirements for them by individual enterprises, and this gives the clue to the various ways in which it may shift.

Changing the pattern of resources and other constraints. The acquisition or disposal of resources is perhaps the most obvious cause of shifts in the planning framework, whether it concerns material items such as land, labour and capital goods, or non-material ones such as contract and rotational constraints.[1] Frequently there is a close relationship between different constraints, so that a change in one leads to a change in another. For example, the purchase of a bigger and improved potato harvester, while raising machine capacity in terms of the area that can be harvested will, at the same time, lower labour requirements per hectare – so that labour capacity at harvest rises too. In turn this may be sufficient to 'activate' a rotational constraint hitherto non-operative because labour was the more limiting.

Changing the pattern of available enterprises. The second way in which the planning framework may change is by the introduction of a new enterprise not previously considered and, therefore, not contributing to the existing framework (or, conversely, by the elimination of an enterprise which has been so contributing). For example, if oilseed rape were to be introduced in Figure 13.1*d* in place of potatoes the planning framework would be radically changed. In many instances

[1] It must be remembered that a change in the level of a resource is not synonymous with a move to a new planning situation *unless* the planning framework changes in consequence. Thus, for example, if in Figure 13.1*d* (p. 295) an extra tractor is acquired, so adding to the availability of spring tractor work, there is no change because the latter is already in surplus supply; whereas, if extra spring labour is acquired, the framework does change because it is potentially in scarce supply (although not actually so in the optimum plan). Conversely if a tractor is disposed of, the effect on spring tractor work would have to be of sufficient magnitude for it to contribute to the framework, for there to be a change in the planning situation.

bringing in a new enterprise will, in fact, go hand in hand with investment in new resources as, for example, when the introduction of pigs is dependent on the erection of a piggery.

Changing the pattern of available techniques. Finally, the introduction of a previously unconsidered technique may change an enterprise's unit requirement for particular fixed resources and so lead to shifts in the planning framework. For example, work study in a dairy herd may lead to the adoption of better work routines which lower labour requirements per cow, thus raising the number of cows that the work-force can manage. Like introducing a new enterprise, investment in new resources may also be implied, as when the adoption of a new technique is dependent on the purchase of new machinery.

Factors not directly linked to changes in the planning framework

Long-term price movements (as opposed to short-term fluctuations) are obviously of importance in the long-term development of a farm – as was acknowledged in Chapter 1 – yet no mention has been made of them in relation to changes in the planning framework. It is pertinent to consider why this should be so.

Product prices and gross margins. Turning first to product prices, Figure 13.4, which relates different iso-revenue curves to a fixed production possibilities curve (see pp. 36–9), makes it clear that changes in prices involve movement around the latter and not shifts to new curves. When the price of *Y* is twice that of *X* the optimal combination of *X* and *Y* is at *A*, when it equals that of *X* it is at *B*, and when it is half that of *X* it is at *C*. In short, if *Y* is high-priced relative to *X* mostly *Y* is produced, but as its price falls relative to *X* so a clockwise movement is made round the planning boundary with more of *X* produced at the expense of *Y*. To give another example. If, in Figure 13.2, wheat gross margins had been so high relative to those of potatoes that wheat only was being grown (*F*), a lowering of wheat price leading to the introduction of potatoes in no way alters the planning framework.[1]

[1] With a segmented two-dimensional planning curve, there is less sensitivity to changes in individual prices and gross margins than with a continuous curve such as in Figure 13.4. For example, if the ratios used in the latter are instead applied to potatoes and wheat in Figure 13.2, the optimal solution is *D* when $GM_p = 2GM_w$, *D* to *E* when $GM_p = GM_w$, and *E* to *F* when $GM_p = \frac{1}{2}GM_w$.

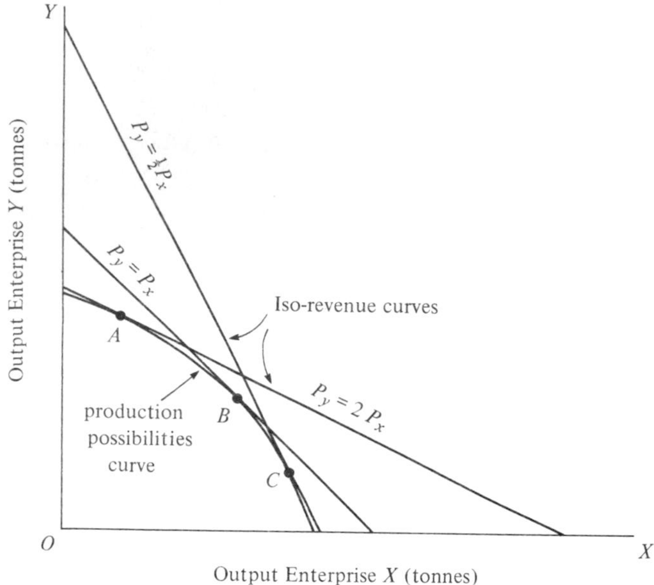

Fig. 13.4. Changing price ratios.

However, as has been seen, in practical planning gross margins rather than prices are used to determine the optimal short-term combination of enterprises, and it follows that the other components of the gross margin apart from price, namely, yield, levels of variable inputs and their prices, also result only in movements along the planning boundary. For example, the application of additional fertiliser to a crop may raise its yield sufficiently to increase its gross margin, and this in turn may lead to its expansion to its current rotational maximum, which is simply a short-term adjustment. Or, a rise in the price of purchased feed, with a consequent lowering of a livestock gross margin, may lead to a reduction of herd or flock size, which again is simply a short-term shift within given resource constraints.

Fixed costs. Next there are changes in the prices (costs) of fixed resources such as rent, wages or machinery charges. Such cost changes in a given complement of resources are, at first sight, quite divorced from either long- or short-term planning since they do not result directly either in shifts in the planning framework or in movements along it. This accords with practice as when, say, an increase in rent reduces farm income but has no effect on the amount of land available to the farmer.

However, although price (and gross margin) changes do not themselves affect the short-term planning framework, and do not therefore *directly* involve long-term planning, they may do so *indirectly* because, if they are considered likely to be long-term in nature, they may lead the farmer to change his existing structure of resources and constraints. For instance, if a farmer is already growing cereals to a rotational maximum – say seventy-five per cent of the arable – and their gross margins improve relative to other crops, he may raise the rotational limit to eighty per cent as a matter of long-term policy if he feels that the change in values is likely to be of a fairly permanent nature, thus shifting his planning boundary. (Such a long-term change must be distinguished from 'cross-cropping', that is, a temporary shift from defined rotational limits to take advantage of a favourable short-term change.) Similarly, an increase in the wages bill relative to machinery charges may lead a farmer to rely more on the latter at the expense of the former, or an increase in rent may persuade a farmer to intensify production in order to maintain his net income.

Objectives. Finally, a farmer's objectives may alter over time, particularly in relation to his family commitments, or a sudden change in his financial situation – because of an inheritance for instance. Such changes in objectives may lead indirectly to changes in the short-term planning framework, just as prices and costs may do. For example, a farmer may farm intensively while he has to support several children, but more extensively when they are all self-sufficient.

Planning and long-term development

Up to now, long-term 'planning' and 'development' have been largely used synonymously. It is however, necessary at this stage to make a distinction between them. The former, when interpreted precisely, implies that the time period directly incorporated in a plan – the planning 'horizon' – is longer than that of the purely short-term, being perhaps ten years or more, rather than a single year at a time. The latter, in contrast, concerns the nature of the farm situation over time and thus embraces, in addition to deliberately planned changes, those that are unplanned (in the sense of being forced on the farmer) such as the loss of land to non-agricultural developments and, further, allows for the intentional maintenance of an unchanged plan. Viewed this way, a short-term plan may remain unchanged for a long period in a farm's development while a long-term plan may, perhaps due to unforeseen circumstances, need modification almost before it has begun to be implemented. Our concern here is with planned long-term development which, as has been seen, implies flexibility in planning frameworks, and we now turn to review briefly the three main approaches to its accomplishment.

Formal long-term planning techniques. The first approach is to utilise formal long-term planning techniques. Compared with those used in short-term planning, new dimensions are added in that they incorporate directly into the model both time-periods longer than that of a single year, and permit the planning framework to change within the time horizon covered by the plan. In addition, where, as is commonly the case, cash flows are discounted to present values, the latter become the objective (or part of it) to be maximised. One such technique is dynamic (multi-period) linear programming (dynamic programming is another – for comments on both techniques see Chapter 17). Typically, this permits capital surpluses to be carried forward from one year to the next and incorporates borrowing opportunities, so that investment in new resources or stock can be made at alternative stages during the life of the plan. Thus the planning framework at the end of the life of the plan may be (although not necessarily) very different from that at the start.

Informal long-term planning techniques. The second approach is the use of informal methods of long-term planning, involving the discounting techniques discussed in Chapter 3 (pp. 61–8) and discussed further below in Chapter 14 (pp. 324–7). The significant difference compared with those in the first category is that, although they also allow for periods longer than a single year and for changes in the planning framework, the latter are *pre-ordained* by the planner and not formulated independently during the actual computations. Typical examples of their use is in investment appraisal of a particular project or in assessing the 'developmental' period involved in, say, the establishment of a dairy herd over a number of years. It has also been suggested that they offer a realistic approach to the assessment of alternative courses of development for the whole farm.[1] The cash flows represent annual net farm incomes (*pre* or *post* tax deductions) while the concept

[1] See: Gunn, H. J. and Hardaker, J. B. (1967) 'Long-term Planning – a Re-examination of Principles and Methods'. *Journal of Agricultural Economics*, **XVIII**, No. 2.

of growth – rather than simply the maximisation of annual cash flows – is allowed for in that the terminal value of assets is included in the computation. Thus, for example, a farmer could compare a plan with a high level of personal consumption and a low level of on-farm investment with a consequent low terminal asset value, with another giving high levels of on-farm investment and terminal value but lower levels of annual personal consumption. In addition, other objectives such as minimum levels of consumption can be incorporated. (See also Appendix 13.5.)

Series of short-term plans. The last approach is by a series of short-term plans which, over a period of time, encompass long-term development (utilising such planning methods as budgeting and programme planning (Chapter 14), linear programming (Chapter 15), and parametric linear programming (Chapter 17)). Although it can be argued that this may result in piecemeal development in that there is often no obvious continuing relationship between one plan and the next, it is in practice the commonest approach to planning long-term development (supplemented by the discounting techniques in special situations). This is so for several reasons – quite apart from there being no evidence that development accomplished in this *ad hoc* manner is necessarily inferior to that achieved by calculating a smaller number of long-term plans.

The first concerns operational feasibility for, as is acknowledged later (Chapter 17, pp. 428–9), formal techniques such as dynamic linear programming and dynamic programming, because of their data requirements, time and cost, tend to fall mainly, if not exclusively, within the province of the researcher, whereas most short-term planning techniques can be readily applied to individual farm situations by farmers and advisers. Secondly, and closely linked with the first point, the longer the period covered by a plan the greater the uncertainty as to events and the quantitative values to be placed upon them, including personal factors such as family size and levels of taxation. At least with a short-term plan there is a fair chance that intelligent estimates can be made for a year or two ahead that turn out not to be too wide of the mark. If circumstances do change, their likely effect on farm organisation can then be assessed by means of new short-term plans. This, in turn, accords with the often opportunistic approach of many farmers to farm development, in that plans are changed in the light of events rather than in anticipation of them (particularly in crop production). For example, the fact that a farm worker suddenly quits the farm may lead to a short-term planning assessment as to whether or not to replace him, whereas if he had not left no such change would have been contemplated. Finally, while long-term planning incorporates long-term constraints and objectives as part of the planning process, this is not to imply that they are absent from short-term planning, where they also contribute to the planning framework. Some examples were given in Chapter 1, such as the long-term objective of survival in farming, which might be expressed in a short-term plan as limitations on the size of risky enterprises or, again, of rotational constraints on crops designed to preserve the long-term condition of the soil.

Whatever the means adopted for planning long-term development, decisions and subsequent actions taken in this sphere are likely to be of far greater consequence than those set in a background of purely short-term planning. This is because investment in 'fixed' resources is usually (but not necessarily) implied, and these resources can be categorised as 'flow' resources, in that they are not all used-up at one point in time, but are available to give a flow of services over many years (see p. 47). For example, the investment misallocated in setting up a new livestock enterprise which is subsequently abandoned because budgeted performance proves to be unattainable, will have more deleterious effects on farm development than a similar, incorrect, short-term decision to expand an enterprise within existing resources. While the latter can probably be put right fairly quickly, the former may well leave a graphic reminder of a farming 'white elephant' in the form of unused and unwanted buildings and equipment, which have absorbed scarce capital, thus diverting it from other uses.

Tax planning

A major feature of long-term planning in practice is tax planning – particularly attempting to minimise the impact of capital taxation on the continuation of the farming business within the family. A description of the details of such taxation is inappropriate in this text, since the precise types and levels of such taxation vary considerably from one country to another and also from time to time within a country – especially from one government to the next. In the UK the main concern at present (1979) is the Capital Transfer Tax (a form of Inheritance Tax), whereby an increasing proportion of the estimated value of the property is paid in taxation on the death of the owner or transfer during lifetime; its potential impact on the larger farm is considerable and could well require the sale of part of the farm in order to pay it.

Ways of trying to reduce the destructive effect of such taxes, as far as the owner is concerned, include transfers of assets to other members of the family before death, dividing the assets equally between the owner and his wife by drawing up an appropriate Will, creation of a tenancy (which reduces the value of the land considerably), letting the farm to a family partnership, using partnerships to transfer profits, giving a high level of remuneration to children employed on the farm (which can be partly loaned back to the business) and life assurance. It will be virtually imperative to engage the services of a highly skilled and experienced accountant to advise on the most appropriate approach, which will differ in almost every individual case according to personal and other circumstances.

Appendix 13.1: Short-term planning data

The categories of data given below are typical of those required in short-term planning. In the longer term additional information is required, such as: the lines of development of most interest to the farmer, his long-term aspirations, his attitudes to the employment of more or less labour, the availability of capital for the acquisition of additional resources and the availability of labour and housing in the vicinity.

A. Resources (Qualitative aspects are important, particularly in relation to enterprise performance)

1. *Productive land*

Area of ploughable land and soil type.
Area of non-ploughable land and type (e.g. permanent pasture, orchard, etc.).
Area suitable/not suitable for specific purposes.

2. *Regular labour* (including members of the family)

Numbers available, whether stockmen or arable workers and whether full-time or part-time.
Amount and type of manual work the farmer is prepared to undertake.

3. *Casual labour* (for tasks on which the farmer is prepared to employ casual)

Task, period covered, numbers available (with details of gangs where applicable), rates of work and remuneration.

4. *Contract work*
Similar details as for casual labour above.

5. *Buildings*
Capacities of those buildings that may limit the size of specific enterprises (e.g. cowsheds, pig fattening houses, corn storage).
Capacities and uses of general purpose buildings.

6. *Machinery*
Major types of machinery and their approximate capacities, given the working conditions on the farm.

7. *Services*
Availability of electricity, piped water, fences, roads etc.

8. *Working capital*
Whether adequate and whether any seasonal difficulties of supply are likely to arise.

B. Enterprises (Those which the farmer now has or is prepared to have)

9. *Crop types and rotation*
For each type of crop (e.g. cereals, legumes, roots etc.), the maximum hectares or proportion of the arable that the farmer is prepared to grow for reasons of fertility, disease risk, preference, quotas, contracts etc. Also the minimum (frequently zero).

10. *Individual cash crops* (including grains and pulses for livestock feeding)

I Details as for (9) above, but for individual crops.
II Output, i.e. anticipated yield and price (incl. subsidies).
III Variable costs. Approximate details of major variable costs (seeds, fertilisers, sprays, casual, contract, transport etc.).
IV Labour peaks (either actual, or potential with a change in cropping). Period concerned and labour available. Crops and tasks

involved, rates of work, including details of teams and equipment. (If given as 'hectares per day' specify length of working day.)

V Links between crops.

11. *Individual livestock* (give outline of system in each case)

I Output, i.e. anticipated yield and price.
Cull or surplus stock sales.

II Variable costs, such as purchased and home-grown concentrates (quantity and price), miscellaneous items (vet bills, medicines etc.), livestock purchases.

III Fodder crops
(*a*) Output of conserved crops and requirement per animal; stocking rates for grazed crops.
(*b*) Other details as for (10) above.
(*c*) Availability of by-products.

IV Labour
If specialised and self-contained, the maximum number of animals that can be handled.
If non-specialised and undertakes other tasks, the hourly requirement per day.

V Building requirements (double-check with (5) above).

Appendix 13.2: Theoretical basis for solution of potato/wheat mix problem

The production theory in Chapter 2 implies that the optimal combination of potatoes and wheat is obtained when:

$$(\Delta P/\Delta W) = (P_w/P_p)$$

where ΔP is the amount of potatoes sacrificed for ΔW, a given increase in wheat output, and P_p and P_w are their respective gross margins.

The relationship $(\Delta P/\Delta W)$ gives the marginal rates of substitution between potatoes and wheat for the different resources as shown by the slopes of the segments in Figure 13.2. If a gross margin ratio line (P_w/P_p, that is, 400/720) is drawn so that it just touches the planning boundary, the point where it does so represents the optimal combination of potatoes and wheat. Such a line runs from 57.2 ha on the potato axis to 103 ha on the wheat axis, touching the planning boundary at point *D* (it may also be designated an iso-gross margin curve, as all points on it result in a gross margin of £41,200).

Appendix 13.3: Marginal value products

In the optimal solution of the potato/wheat mix problem, land and spring labour are both fully used, while other potentially scarce resources have proved to be in adequate supply. It may be of assistance, in terms of the possibility of obtaining more of the two scarce resources, to place a value on their marginal (last) units, namely the last ha of land and the last hour of spring labour. This can be done by calculating the least-cost way of withdrawing them from production (which implies drawing new boundaries in Figure 13.2).

Land. If one ha of land is withdrawn (spring labour is also scarce), it will be taken from wheat, which gives a lower return per ha than potatoes. However, doing so leaves 3.75 hours of spring labour idle, sufficient for 0.5 ha potatoes which, if grown, means another 0.5 ha must be taken from wheat and a further 1.875 hours spring labour is released. Thus, if possible, sufficient wheat should be withdrawn to enable both the land (other than the hectare 'lost') and spring labour to be fully utilised by potatoes. This is so when two ha of wheat are withdrawn:

	Land (hectares)	*Spring labour* (hours)	*Gross margin* (£)
Withdraw 2 hectares wheat	−2	−7.5	−800
Grow 1 extra hectare potatoes	+1	+7.5	+720
Balance	−1	—	−80

The £80 net loss is the value of the marginal hectare, and the new optimal solution, on 74 ha, is 36 ha of potatoes and 38 ha of wheat, giving £41,120 gross margin. In most cases the marginal value product can also be interpreted as the gain consequent upon the acquisition of one extra unit of resource. This is true here, and the most paying way of utilising an extra hectare of land is thus to sacrifice 1 ha of potatoes and grow 2 more ha of wheat, for a gain of £80.[1]

Labour. A similar calculation may be made for spring labour. If one hour is withdrawn (land is also scarce), the following is the adjustment

[1] The marginal value product remains at £80 for a further 5 ha when, with 30 ha of potatoes and 50 ha of wheat, summer labour becomes scarce and the rate of substitution between potatoes and wheat changes.

that leads to the least loss in gross margin:

	Spring labour (hours)	*Land* (hectares)	*Gross margin* (£)
Withdraw 0.26 hectares potatoes	−2	−0.26	−192.0
Grow an extra 0.26 hectares wheat	+1	+0.26	+106.6
Balance	−1	—	−85.4

The marginal value product of 1 hour of spring labour is thus £85.4 and this can also be interpreted as the gain consequent upon the supply of an extra hour. If this represented a real case, the farmer would presumably make strenuous efforts to improve his current use of labour or to acquire additional labour.

Appendix 13.4: Planning assumptions

Quite apart from the adequacy or otherwise of the data used in constructing a farm planning model, there is the question of the validity of the model itself; in other words, its ability to represent realistically the actual farming environment. All the assumptions that follow are inherent in the planning procedure demonstrated in Chapter 13 and, indeed, are common in whole or part to most planning techniques.

Linearity. The relationship between inputs and output in an enterprise is assumed to remain unchanged irrespective of the level of the enterprise in the solution. For example, if 1 hectare land, 5 hours of summer labour and £100 working capital generate £400 gross margin when devoted to wheat, 100 hectares land, 500 hours of summer labour and £10,000 of capital generate £40,000 gross margin.

Constant marginal rates of substitution are thus implied between factors and between products. (See also Chapter 15, pp. 364–6.)

Independence (additivity). Following on from the assumption of linearity, enterprises are assumed to be independent of one another, so that the total resource requirements and the total product of a number of enterprises taken together are simply the sums of their individual inputs and outputs. For example, the yields of wheat, barley and beans, and their requirements of fertilisers and sprays, are assumed to remain the same irrespective of the proportions of the arable land devoted to them. (See also Chapter 15, p. 367.)

Divisibility (continuity). Resources and enterprises are assumed to be divisible into fractional units, so that a solution may, for example, include 45.371 cows requiring 31.238 hectares land. Apart from the relatively minor task of adjusting solutions, more serious problems may arise when indivisible units, such as specialised labour, buildings and machinery, are involved (see Chapters 15 and 17).

Exact data (single-valued expectations). All the coefficients in planning models are assumed to be known with certainty, so that the seasonal variation in outputs and inputs that occurs in practice is not accounted for in any formal manner. The total gross margins from very different plans are thus all assumed to have an equal chance of being achieved, and the plan with the highest gross margin is taken to be the optimum. (It has to be acknowledged, however, that even if planning techniques in general did allow for variability in coefficients, data for individual farms would in most cases not be available.)

Short-term static plans. Solutions are short-term and static, in that they are bounded by a given set of fixed resources and are assumed to be repeatable from year to year. There is thus no allowance for the gradual development of a farm plan over time, such as is necessary if the solution suggests a radical departure from the current organisation.

Finiteness. Finiteness in planning models simply acknowledges that the opportunities available to farmers are not unlimited. It may thus appear a somewhat trite assumption. However, if looked at from another angle, a common weakness in planning models results from inadequate acknowledgement of the opportunities that do, in fact, face the farmer. This occurs, in particular, with the assumption that each enterprise is organised in a single unique manner.

Appendix 13.5: Growth theory

A number of theories relating to the growth of the firm have been developed over the past twenty or so years. Basically there are two alternative approaches: the traditional (or neo-classical) and the behavioural. The latter has been developed more recently than the former. The growth plan is determined through the endogenous and exogenous variables that affect the behaviour of the farm firm in different ways at different points of time.

The traditional theory seeks to find the optimal rate of growth during the planning period, which is in fact often taken to be the indefinite future. A number of alternative analytic models have been developed, those of Baumol, Williamson and Penrose being particularly well known. Prices and the production function are assumed to be known with certainty, and the objective is usually taken to be profit maximisation. Differential calculus and the Lagrangean multiplier have usually provided the operational structure, but as early as 1955 Swanson used multi-period (dynamic) linear programming to this end (see pp. 424–8). The objective when using the latter technique has usually been to maximise net worth over time, normally discounted.

The 'behavioural' theory (the term is taken from biological science) relates to the way in which the firm responds to particular motivation within its environment, with a multiplicity of variable factors acting upon it. In trying to understand and predict the behaviour of the firm to different stimuli, the assumptions of perfect knowledge and profit maximisation are dropped. Stressed rather are the intrafirm relationships and the firm's organisational structure, the multiple goal function, including the 'satisficing' concept, and the continual search for more and better information in order to improve decision-making. Systems analysis is used, and linear programming has often been employed for this purpose. However, the latter technique is inappropriate when uncertainty, integer variables and mutually exclusive activities are incorporated into the model. Simulation is then used, with the aim of arriving at near-optimal solutions at a reasonable cost.

Selected references:

Baumol, W. J. (1962) 'On the Theory of Expansion of the Firm'. *American Economic Review*, **52**, 2.

Eisgruber, L. M. and Lee, G. E. (1971) 'A Systems Approach to Studying the Growth of the Farm Firm', in Dent, J. B. and Anderson, J. R. (eds.), *Systems Analysis in Agricultural Management*. John Wiley & Sons Australasia Pty Ltd.

Irwin, G. D. (1968) 'A Comparative Review of Some Firm Growth Models'. *Agricultural Economics Research*, **20**, 3.

Penrose, E. T. (1959) *The Theory of the Growth of the Firm*. John Wiley, New York.

Renborg, U. (1970) 'Growth of the Agricultural Firm: Problems and Theories'. *Review of Marketing and Agricultural Economics*, **38**, 2.

Swanson, E. R. (1955) 'Integrating Crop and Livestock Activities in Farm Management Activity Analysis'. *Journal of Farm Economics*, **37**, 1249–58.

Williamson, J. (1966) 'Profit, Growth and Sales Maximisation'. *Economica*, **33**, 129.

14: Budgeting and programme planning

BUDGETING

Budgeting is the most widely used method of farm planning. In some ways, however, it is better described as an *aid* to, rather than a *method* of, farm planning. Other techniques described in this book offer means of selecting a farm plan. In budgeting, a farm plan is drawn up using a combination of experience, judgement and intuition; the process of budgeting itself is used only in evaluating the farm plan in financial terms. It could be argued that this is only a method of farm planning comparable with other techniques if more than one plan is drawn up for the farm and budgeting is used to help decide which to choose.

In this chapter budgeting is described mainly in relation to assessing annual profitability, that is, the expected effect on the trading account (see Chapter 19). This is in contrast to capital budgeting, in which the total required to implement a change of plan, or a complete new plan, is estimated; this procedure has already been described, in Chapter 3, pp. 53–6. The two effects can be combined to forecast changes over time in the balance sheet (see Chapter 20).

Budgeting may be defined as the detailed quantitative statement of a farm plan, or a change in farm plan, and the forecast of its financial result. It sets out (*a*) the physical aspects of the plan: what to produce, how much, and the resources needed, and (*b*) the financial aspects of the plan: the expected costs and returns and, therefore, profit. The term 'farm budget' is often used, however, solely, in regard to (*b*).

An important distinction is that made between partial and complete budgeting:

(i) *Partial budgeting* is used when only a partial change in the existing plan is being considered, so that some – possibly most – of the cost and receipt items on the farm will not alter. Thus only the changes in costs and receipts are calculated.

(ii) *Complete budgeting* is used when a plan for a 'new farm' or 'new farmer' is required. It may also be used where a major change in an existing farm is being considered – one which will affect most, perhaps all, of the cost and receipt items on the farm. A 'partial' change can have very large side-effects on the whole farm economy; for example, the effect of doubling the size of a dairy herd on a mixed arable–livestock farm.

Because of the many possible interactions of a major change in plan, it is often easier to prepare a complete rather than a partial budget. However, partial budgeting is in some ways more searching: it explicitly asks all the right questions (see below). Furthermore, it is possible with complete budgeting to alter, without realising it, items which in fact will not alter, at least not as a result of the change in farm plan (see further: ''Normalized' present plan', p. 321 below).

Partial budgeting

Partial budgeting has been described as 'a rough form of marginal analysis', in that it looks at the changes that will occur in costs and receipts as a result of a (marginal) change in the farm plan. The change may be very minor, e.g. buying a sprayer instead of hiring a contractor, or adding five more sows to a pig breeding herd, or very large, e.g. disposing of a dairy herd and substituting sheep and cereals on the area released.

There are three main types of change:

(i) *Product substitution.* Here, one enterprise is substituted for another, e.g. potatoes for sugar beet. Whenever a land-using enterprise is introduced, discarded or changed in size this type of substitution is usually involved.

(ii) *Change of enterprises without substitution.* This may occur when non-land-using enterprises, such as pigs or poultry, are introduced or expanded, discarded or reduced, or where the stocking rate of an existing area of grassland is altered.

(iii) *Factor substitution.* Here, 'factor' is used in the widest sense of the word. Often a change in production techniques is involved. Examples are buying a machine instead of hiring a contractor, changing from hand harvesting to machine harvesting a crop, adding fertiliser to grass and increasing the stocking rate, buying hay instead of making it on the farm. In the first example, medium-term capital is substituted for short-term capital; in the second, machinery (medium-term capital) is substituted for labour (and short-term capital); in the third, short-term capital is substituted for land; in the last, short-term capital is substituted for land, machinery and labour.

These three types of change are not mutually exclusive. Two or even all three may go together. For example, irrigation plus extra fertiliser on grassland (iii) could be combined with increasing the number of livestock on the existing area of grass (ii) or substituting cash crops for part of the grass (i), or some increase in livestock plus some substitution of cash crops for grass.

Four questions are asked in a partial budget, two of which relate to the financial losses arising from the contemplated change (i.e. the debit side) and two of which relate to the consequential financial gains (i.e. the credit side):

A. Debits

What loss of (present) revenue occurs?
What extra (new) costs are incurred?

B. Credits

What extra (new) revenue is obtained?
What (present) costs are no longer incurred?

The discussion in Chapter 2 (pp. 43–5) concerning fixed and variable costs in the more general management sense (as opposed to the narrower gross margin interpretation) is highly relevant to this technique. Only those changes in costs that occur as a result of the contemplated change are considered. At one extreme these may include depreciation and interest on new buildings, e.g. if the introduction or expansion of a dairy herd is being considered; at the other extreme even the fertiliser and seed used on a crop may be excluded, since the costs have already been incurred and will not be affected by the decision, e.g. in deciding whether or not a vegetable crop is worth harvesting when market prices are very low.

Increases or decreases in labour-hours or machinery-hours costed at so much per hour are not included. The labour bill may alter as a result of (*a*) a change in the number of regular workers employed, (*b*) the amount paid to casual workers, (*c*) the amount of overtime worked, or (*d*) the level of any premiums or bonuses paid. If none of these occurs there is no entry for labour in the partial budget. Similarly, machinery depreciation is only affected if the number or size of machines has to be altered as a result of the change. The basic test for each item of cost or receipt is whether or not the entry for that item in the trading account will be changed.

The partial budget may be set out on 'traditional' lines or in gross margin form, both of which are illustrated in the example given in Table 14.1. The gross margin method simplifies those partial budgets concerned with enterprise substitution, because it deals in convenient 'packages'. Although the calculation of the gross margins themselves entails some extra work to begin with, it is very easy afterwards to see the effect of various other possible substitutions. On the other hand, the very facility with which this can be done has its dangers. It is easier to forget changes that may occur in the gross margin when the size of an enterprise alters, or to forget possible changes in 'fixed' costs.

Complete budgeting

Complete budgeting relates to the entire farm plan; thus all the physical data are included and all cost and receipt items have to be calculated. The procedure can be divided into six steps:

(i) *Listing available resources and stating objectives.* The many physical, financial and personal factors that have to be taken into account in determining a farm plan have been discussed in Chapters 1 and 13. It is imperative to understand at the outset the farmer's objectives and to allow for his likes and dislikes in determining the plan. An inventory should then be made of the farm's available resources and constraints. Managerial ability must be judged and allowed for, together with the skill of the available labour force. It is easy to draw up apparently brilliant farm plans on paper, and to forget that someone has to make them work.

(ii) *Estimating crop areas and livestock numbers.* In deciding on the farm plan (or alternative plans) in terms of crop acreages and grazing livestock numbers, the procedure tends to vary depending on whether arable crops or livestock predominate. On the mainly arable farm, crop areas are usually calculated first: a rotation is decided, allowing for any restrictions on areas of individual crops (e.g. potato quota, pea contract). Stock numbers are then determined, according to the area of leys and permanent pasture (if any). On an arable farm, permanent pasture is normally only included if an area is unploughable, e.g. marshland or steep slopes. If there are different soil types the

TABLE 14.1. *Example of partial budget*
Purchase potato harvester (£6,000) and increase potatoes from 20 to 25 hectares, growing 5 hectares less barley.

Debits	(£)	Credits	(£)
Revenue forgone		*Extra revenue*	
Barley output: 5 ha at £300	1,500	Potato output: 5 ha at £1,600	8,000
Damaged potatoes: 1 tonne/ha on 20 ha = 20 tonnes at £38 (£50 per tonne for ware – £12 for chats)	760		
	2,260		8,000
Extra costs		*Costs saved*	
Potato variable costs: 5 ha at £750	3,750	Barley variable costs: 5 ha at £90	450
Harvester: deprecn, interest, repairs	2,220	Reduced casual labour: 20 ha at £100 (150 – 50)	2,000
Extra storage: deprecn. and interest	750	Combine harvester – fuel and repairs: 5 ha at £15	75
Extra fuel, and repairs to tractors, etc.	300		
	7,020		2,525
Total debits	9,280		
Extra profit	1,245		
	10,525	Total credits	10,525
		Gross margin layout	
Gross margin forgone		*Extra gross margin*	
Barley: 5 ha at £210 (300 – 90)	1,050	Potatoes: 5 ha at £850 (1600 – 750)	4,250
Damaged potatoes (as above)	760	Casual labour saved (as above)	2,000
	1,810		6,250
Extra fixed costs		*Fixed costs saved*	
Harvester (as above)	2,220	Combine harvester (as above)	75
Extra storage (as above)	750		
Extra fuel and repairs (as above)	300		
	3,270		75
Total debits	5,080		
Extra profit	1,245		
	6,325	Total credits	6,325

rotations may be different for each. Because fields vary in size, it is necessary to check that the rotation when applied to individual fields adds up to a reasonably level area of each crop each year over a period; this is especially important on a smallish farm with rather large fields. However, more *ad hoc* alterations to cropping are made today than was once the case, changes being made according to soil and weed conditions in individual fields and variations in expected gross margin levels from year to year.

As an example, a farmer with 110 hectares, mainly interested in grain production but not prepared to risk growing continuous cereals, and with no interest in or possibility of growing roots or vegetables, may choose a rotation of 2 wheats, 3 barleys and a 2-year ley. He also has 12 hectares of unploughable pasture. He will thus have 28 hectares of wheat, 42 hectares of barley, 28 hectares of ley and 12 hectares of permanent pasture. He does not want the expense of erecting buildings for cattle (which cannot be outwintered in his conditions) and he therefore chooses sheep for fat lamb production. He is not particularly expert with either sheep or grass, but thinks he can reasonably manage 9 ewes to the hectare all the year round, which is slightly better than average. He will thus have a 360-ewe flock.

On the mainly livestock farm, however, the procedure is different. If the farm is all grass, a balance has to be obtained between the stocking rate, the labour available and the numbers of different types of livestock – ensuring that these comprise units of a sensible economic size. Where the farm is not all grass, the stock numbers are likely to be decided first and arable crops calculated as a residual, that is, the reverse of the arable farm procedure. Suppose the farmer referred to above is instead mainly interested in dairying and wants a one man unit of 80 Friesian cows, rearing just enough heifers for replacement purposes. He thinks he can manage a stocking rate better than the national average, but realises he is not particularly expert in grassland management; he thus bases his calculations on 0.5 forage hectares per livestock unit (defined and explained in Appendix 14.1). The cows and followers total 110 livestock units. He therefore needs approximately 55 hectares of grass, leaving 55 hectares for cereals. With 12 hectares of permanent pasture he can have a rotation of approximately 4-year ley, 2 wheats, 3 barleys. Sometimes distances from the buildings can mean that two or more different rotations are required on different parts of the farm. Thus our example farmer may choose to have longer leys (or possibly put down more permanent pasture) close to the buildings and shorter leys and more cereals further away.

Calculating land requirements for grazing livestock by means of livestock units is a fairly crude method, but widely practised; it is easy and quick, and the more exact and time-consuming calculations may not be felt to be worthwhile in view of the dependence on weather and other variable factors. However, at least an approximate check should be made of the grazing and bulk fodder requirements related to the land area from which it has been calculated that these are to be supplied. The full procedure would be to estimate these requirements by calculating rations on a nutritional basis and then to work out the area needed according to estimated yields. The principles involved in the selection of feedstuffs are discussed in Chapter 9.

(iii) *Estimating physical inputs and outputs.* The next step is to calculate the physical requirements of the variable inputs, e.g. concentrate feed, fertiliser, seed, and the physical production expected, i.e. yields. The question of data sources is discussed at the beginning of Chapter 19 (p. 496), and the sections below headed 'Sensitivity analysis' and 'Criticisms of budgeting' are also relevant.

(iv) *Estimating factor and product prices: calculating costs and returns.* Prices must be estimated next and applied to the physical data already obtained. Thus costs and returns for each item of input and output are calculated, by multiplying together the estimates of quantity and price.

(v) *Estimating 'fixed costs'.* Four important cost items – regular labour, machinery, rent and general overheads – remain to be calculated, together with other payments, such as interest and mortgages. Both the labour and machinery calculations have been fully discussed in previous chapters (Chapters 5, pp. 132–42, and 4, pp. 83–91 respectively). General overhead expenses can be estimated in detail, or an approximate total figure can be obtained from data handbooks. Rent and mortgage payments are 'given'. Tenant's capital requirements can be estimated by means of a capital budget, as shown in Chapter 3, and interest payments calculated by applying the expected rate of interest to the proportion borrowed.

In some circumstances it may be considered desirable to include those items of fixed costs used in calculating management and investment income; that is, a rental value is included for an owner-occupied farm, the value of unpaid labour is charged, and salaried management, interest payments and ownership expenses are excluded (see further Chapter 20, p. 525). It is far more likely, however, that the farmer is interested only in his *actual* situation and the expected profit (or loss) given that situation. In that case all his *actual* expenses, such as ownership costs and interest payments, must be included, but no *notional* charges, such as estimated rents and unpaid labour. If he is also interested in seeing how his plans compare with the results from other farms then these standardisation procedures can be carried out separately afterwards.

(vi) *Totals and layout*. The task then remains of setting out the information, totalling the costs and returns and calculating the expected profit from the (or each) plan. Table 14.2 demonstrates how *not* to set out a budget if it is to be of any value, unless it is accompanied by schedules providing further details of the assumptions. Table 14.3 illustrates a budget layout which includes the important physical and price assumptions without being excessively lengthy.

Additional notes on budgeting

1. *'Normalised' present plan.* When complete budgeting is used to estimate the effect of proposed changes, the budget for the changed plan (or plans) should always be compared with a 'normalised'

TABLE 14.2. *Farm budget* (inadequate layout)

Expenditure	(£)	Returns	(£)
Seed	7,850	Potatoes	22,800
Fertiliser	12,240	Wheat	21,600
Feed	1,300	Barley	20,310
Livestock	6,590	Oats	4,480
Labour	13,200	Sheep	11,010
Power and machinery	11,400	Wool	810
Rent and rates	11,950	Cattle	10,860
Sundries	12,690		
Total	77,220		
Farm profit	14,650		
	91,870	Total	91,870

(N.B. £800-worth of home-produced oats and £900 of barley are fed to livestock; £550 of home-grown barley is used for seed.)

TABLE 14.3. *Farm budget* (full layout)

Gross Margins				
Potatoes (16 ha)				(£)
Output £1425 (28 tonnes at £50, 2 tonnes chats at £12.50)				
Variable costs £750 (seed 275, fert. 135, sprays 60, cas. lab. 150, sundries 130)				
GM: 16 at £675				10,800
Wheat (48 ha)				
Output £450 (5 tonnes at £90)				
Variable costs £100 (seed 25, fert. 45, sprays 30)				
GM: 48 at £350				16,800
Barley (64 ha)				
Output £340 (4.25 tonnes at £80)				
Variable costs £90 (seed 20, fert. 50, sprays 20)				
GM: 64 at £250				16,000
Oats (16 ha)				
Output £330 (4.4 tonnes at £75)				
Variable costs £80 (seed 20, fert. 45, sprays 15)				
GM: 16 ha at £250				4,000
Sheep (300 ewes, fat lamb production)				
Output: lambs 420 at £23 =	9,660			
wool 295 fleece at £2.75 =	810			
cull ewes 65 at £20 =	1,300			
cull rams 2 at £25 =	50			
	11,820			
less ewe replacements, 75 at £40	3,000			
ram replacements, 2 at £100	200			
	3,200			
Output		8,620		
Variable costs (excl. forage) £7.5 per head (concentrates 5, other 2.5)		2,250		
GM (excl. forage)			6,370	
Beef (50 beef cows, single suckling)				
Output: calves (inc. calf sub.), 47 at £180 =	8,460			
cull cows, 8 at £300 =	2,400			
	10,860			
less cow replacements, 9 at £350 =	3,150			
calf purchases, 3 at £80 =	240			
	3,390			
Output		7,470		
Variable costs (excl. forage) £40 per head (concentrates 30, other 10)		2,000		
GM (excl. forage)			5,470	
Total forage GM (excl. forage variable costs)			11,840	
Carried forward...			11,840	47,600

TABLE 14.3. (cont.)

Brought forward		11,840	47,600
Forage variable costs			
16 ha permanent pasture at £40 (fert.)	640		
48 ha leys at £100 (seed 25, fert. 70, sprays 5)	4,800	5,440	
Total forage GM (deducting forage variable costs)			6,400
Total gross margin			54,000
Fixed costs			
Regular labour: 3 men at £3,600 (inc. insurance and overtime)			10,800
Machinery: depreciation 3,950, repairs 3,400, fuel & elec. 2,550, contract work 900, vehicle tax and insurance 600			11,400
Rent and rates			11,950
General overhead expenses: 208 ha at approx. £25			5,200
Total fixed costs			39,350
Farm profit (54,000–39,350):			14,650

budget for the present plan, that is, a profit forecast based on the same yield, price and factor cost assumptions as in the forward budget(s). If this is not done the farmer cannot be sure to what extent the estimated change in profit is simply due to changes in these assumptions – possibly caused largely by recent or expected price changes. Making a comparison with the trading account for the previous year or even several years is not good enough. Partial budgeting avoids this problem, but it could be a complex procedure in the case of widespread alterations in the farm plan.

2. *Two or more, or 'central', budgets*. The farmer may wish to consider two or more alternative plans, in which case a separate budget is of course normally required for each. If the differences between the alternatives are not great, however, it may be sufficient to have a detailed 'central' budget, together with partial budgets showing the effect of marginal differences in plan.

3. *Reasons for budgeting*. Budgeting is not necessarily used simply as a means of trying to derive highly profitable plans. Even if the farmer has only one plan in mind the single budget will give him useful information concerning the net income he can expect to make. He may simply want to know whether the plan he wishes to pursue will give him an adequate income, bearing in mind his personal commitments and desired

standard of living. He may want the budget to help persuade his bank manager to lend him enough to carry out the plan; in this case he may also require a capital (or cash flow) budget (Chapter 3). Or, alternatively, the budget may be used for budgetary control (see Chapter 21, pp. 555–64).

Budgeting in relation to long-term farm development

Long-term farm development, in so far as it is 'planned' at all, is commonly carried out by making a number of short-term plans at different points in time supplemented, if necessary, by discounting procedures (Chapter 13). Budgeting can be used for this purpose, its relative complexity depending largely on the type and intricacy of the particular situation being planned. Before developing this point, the types of budget that may be required are reviewed, distinguishing between those that are concerned with aspects of the trading account (here designated 'trading' budgets) and those dealing with aspects of capital usage and requirements.

Trading budgets

Final trading budget. We have already seen that final trading budgets are designed to show whether some plan, when fully executed, is likely to add to or detract from the annual profitability of farming operations, and thus to help decide whether it will be worthwhile going ahead with its implementation. Such budgets are equally pertinent both to short-term changes within an existing planning framework and to long-term changes when the framework shifts.

Development trading budget. However, although it is often possible to execute purely short-term changes relatively quickly, long-term developments commonly require several years between their initiation and full implementation. For example, suppose a dairy herd is being introduced on a farm that was previously nearly all under cash crops. Leys have to be sown and become established, buildings have to be erected and the right quality animals have to be found and purchased. Perhaps young stock will be bought, to be reared on the farm. Even if down-calving heifers are purchased the yields in the first years will be relatively low. In such cases it may be necessary to prepare a series of development (or 'build up') budgets over time to supplement the final trading budget; (unlike budgets for the final plan, these annual budgets may have to include valuations, at least as far as some types of livestock are concerned). Even if the latter should show the change to be worth making, development budgets may reveal such low or non-existent profits in the intervening years that the project should never be started. Without development budgets farmers may get into serious financial difficulties because of their failure to appreciate how long it may take to get a highly promising farm plan fully established.

Capital budgets

As long-term changes frequently call for extra investment on the farm, capital budgets may be required in addition to trading budgets. They serve to provide answers to such questions as how much capital will be required, when and for how long, and whether a reasonable return is likely to be obtained on the investment. They are linked closely to trading budgets in that the latter usually form the basis for estimating at least a significant part of capital requirements and cash flows.

Simple capital budget. The simple capital budget seeks mainly to answer the first question posed above, namely, the amount of capital that will be needed in a new plan, with a view to determining whether sufficient will be available (from the farmer's own resources or by borrowing).[1] No account is taken of the timing of capital requirements; instead an estimate is made of the total capital needed at a fixed point in time. This may be either when the project is initiated, thus including mainly long- and medium-term items (and coinciding with the calculation of 'initial' capital in discounting exercises) or, more commonly, when the project is fully operational, so that working capital requirements and any offsetting receipts are included also (thus coinciding with the stage covered in a final trading budget).

Cash flow budget. Unlike the simple capital budget, the cash flow budget (see Chapter 3, pp. 53–6) assesses the ebb and flow of capital requirements over time and, in terms of setting up a new plan, may be regarded as the capital counterpart of the development budget. The latter, indeed, is the most likely source of data on which capital estimates are based.

[1] It can also be used in the calculation of 'return on capital' and as a basis for determining relevant interest and depreciation charges for incorporation in trading budgets.

Discounted cash flow budget. This is the most sophisticated form of capital budget for, in addition to the elements contained in the other capital budgets, it allows for the 'time value' of money (see Chapter 3, pp. 61–8).

Use of budgets in diverse planning situations

It now remains to relate these different types of budget to planning long-term changes on the farm (remembering they may be either complete or partial in form). Two factors determine their relevance to particular planning situations. First, whether or not the proposed change can be completed relatively quickly and, secondly, whether or not it involves significant capital investment. Four planning situations thus arise.

Change can be completed quickly and requires no significant investment. This is the simplest situation and all that is usually required is a final trading budget. An example is the raising of a rotational limit on wheat by allowing it to be grown for an extra year at the expense of barley. A partial budget should suffice to assess the difference in their gross margins together with any consequential changes such as on subsequent yields, or on fertiliser and spray needs of other crops.

Change can be completed quickly and requires significant investment. Here a simple capital budget should suffice in addition to a trading budget. An example is the erection of extra grain storage capacity on a farm.

Change cannot be completed quickly and requires no significant investment. In this case, development budgets may be needed in addition to a final trading budget but capital budgets should not be necessary – unless there are substantial cash flow effects. An example is a rotational change which cannot be made all at once, such as the expansion of sugar beet beyond the limit of the present contract to that imposed by the capacity of the existing machinery and labour force.

Change cannot be completed quickly and requires significant investment. This combination gives rise to the need for both development trading budgets and capital cash flow budgets, and is thus the most complex of the various combinations to plan. An example is given by the expansion of a dairy herd in Table 3.11 (p. 65). Although this shows simply the end-product of the various calculations, they would be derived from development and final trading budgets, probably together with cash flow budgets, while a simple capital budget might also be required to derive the initial capital requirement.

Criticisms of budgeting

Several criticisms can be made of budgeting, but most of them apply equally to all planning techniques. Thus it can be argued on theoretical grounds that budgeting assumes linear relationships (see Chapter 13, p. 311 and that it virtually ignores diminishing returns and complementarity relationships between enterprises (see Chapter 2). Given the necessary information, however, allowance can be made for these aspects.

There is also the problem of estimating yields, especially in the case of new farmers or those beginning new enterprises, and estimating prices. Because of an inevitable (though variable) degree of uncertainty, some argue that budgeting is worthless. Again, this criticism applies equally to all planning techniques. Certainly it cannot be denied that uncertainty exists and that even the most skilful and experienced adviser will be unable to forecast results exactly, especially in each individual year. Nevertheless, making calculations based on 'best estimates' is better than having no guidelines at all. Any sensible person accepts that yield and price fluctuations will cause 'errors' in the forecast for individual years. The necessity to consider this point is dealt with in Chapter 16 (under 'Sensitivity analysis'). More crucial would be bad errors in estimating the *average* levels over a period of years, particularly in the *relative* levels for different products – and especially if large amounts of fixed capital have been invested in enterprises in which the level of performance has been overestimated. When in doubt, product prices and yields should always be forecast cautiously, and costs should be put on the high side, but not to a fault. If *excessive* caution is shown in making plans, few would ever start or continue in farming.

Finally, budgeting can be criticised as being an inefficient technique if a profit-maximising plan is being sought. Many budgets may be needed before a high-profit plan is obtained, and still there would be no certainty that substantially more profitable plans did not exist. The more experienced the adviser and the simpler the farm the less truth there is in this. Also, by no means all farmers seek maximum profits. Nevertheless, other techniques can be more effective, providing the advantages they offer are fully exploited. Budgeting is also more subject to personal bias on the part of the adviser than other, more objective, techniques.

Planning using gross margins per hectare

The term 'gross margin planning' (or 'ordered budgeting') is sometimes used when gross margins per hectare are calculated for each land-using enterprise and used to help decide on the farm plan or plans. Essentially the technique of budgeting is employed, using gross margins (defined in Chapter 2, pp. 45–6), which eases the computational task where several plans are being considered. The only difference is that the method is slightly less intuitive than 'traditional' budgeting as used before the gross margin concept became widespread, in that the gross margins per hectare are used as guidelines to the selection of enterprises. However, it is still by no means a formalised technique. Where a farm's past records are being used to supply the necessary data, as is usual (except, of course, where the farmer is new to the farm), a number of difficulties can arise in calculating the gross margins. One of these is referred to in Appendix 14.1; others are discussed in Chapter 20 (pp. 534–5).

When using gross margins per hectare as a guide to future farm plans the figures for the different enterprises are compared, with a view possibly to substituting enterprises with high gross margins for those with low ones. Four important points have to be remembered, however. First, the different enterprises may be utilising very different types of land: there may be only a limited area of the farm suitable for growing potatoes, for example, and the sheep may be partly or entirely grazing unploughable land with few alternative uses. Secondly there are the rotational effects: if, for instance, a farmer expands his cereal area at the expense of his area of leys, his cereal yields will probably fall and his cereal variable costs rise – more fertiliser being required to try to stem the drop in yields and more sprays probably being needed to keep the land clean (see further Chapter 12, pp. 272–4). Given the same complement of labour and machinery, the timeliness of operations will deteriorate. If he follows traditional cropping practice, his area of wheat will be reduced compared with his barley and oats area. Thirdly, different enterprises obviously have different requirements for the various 'fixed' resources – regular labour, machinery and buildings – and working capital. The gross margin per hectare does not cover this aspect, of course; it is only one feature of the enterprise, albeit a very important one. Finally, expansion of an existing enterprise may necessitate a large increase in fixed costs, such as a new building, an extra man or a larger machine.

For all these reasons, a simple comparison of gross margins per hectare has only a very limited use for farm planning, except perhaps as a rough initial guide. Obviously per hectare figures are meaningless for most pig and poultry enterprises, and some intensive beef systems are the same or only marginally different. Farm planning incorporates all the above aspects of the enterprises available for selection.

In gross margin terms the four main ways of raising the profitability of a farm may be summarised as follows:

(i) Increase the total gross margin of the farm by improving the gross margins of the existing enterprises.
(ii) Increase the total gross margin of the farm by changing the 'enterprise-mix', by substituting one or more enterprises for one or more others; the factors that limit this approach have been discussed above.
(iii) Increase the total gross margin by expanding an existing enterprise or introducing a new one, without needing to reduce other enterprises, e.g. by expanding or introducing pigs or poultry or catch crops.
(iv) Reduce the level of fixed costs – mainly labour and machinery expenses.

The first of these should always be investigated thoroughly before any further steps are taken. The last three can be combined in five different ways:

(*a*) Raising total gross margin with approximately the same level of fixed costs. For example, expanding the potato area or the number of cows at the expense, say, of barley or sheep, without any increase in regular labour, machinery depreciation or building costs – except for some slight increase in fuel and repairs, or the cowman's wage.
(*b*) Raising total gross margin, accepting that fixed costs will also rise significantly. Obviously the former must rise by more than the latter if the change is to improve profitability. An example would be the introduction of potatoes or dairy cows on a farm where there had been none before, or a substantial expansion in the size of these enterprises, resulting in extra regular labour, machinery and building costs.
(*c*) Keeping the same farm plan and thus total gross margin, but reducing the level of fixed costs, i.e. the number of regular men

or machinery expenses. As the size of the labour force on a farm declines, reducing it further becomes increasingly difficult, and eventually impossible. In fact the majority of farms have too few men for cuts to be possible without a considerable reduction in the intensity of the system, and of course many have no hired labour at all. On some larger farms a net saving through further substitution of machinery for labour is still possible. On many, however, social reasons prevent short-term reductions in the labour force.

(*d*) Reducing total gross margin by simplifying the system, at the same time reducing the total fixed costs still more. The classic example is introducing continuous or mainly cereal production in place of systems which include root crops and/or livestock. If the simpler, more specialised system makes possible a large reduction in labour and machinery, farm profits may rise despite the reduced output. For various reasons the popularity of this particular example has declined in the UK in recent years, but less extreme examples do sometimes occur, e.g. the deletion of small, poor-performance pig or dairy enterprises, or small areas of moderately yielding root crops or vegetables, may still enable bigger savings in fixed costs than the loss in total gross margin.

(*e*) Increasing total gross margin and yet at the same time achieving savings in fixed costs. This is not easy to do, unless the farm has been very poorly managed in the past.

The choice between these alternatives on any particular farm depends on many aspects of the farm and the farmer: his comparative advantage in different types of crops and livestock, his likes and dislikes, skills and non-skills, his aims and ambitions, the availability of capital and his attitude to investment.

PROGRAMME PLANNING

While budgeting and gross margin planning are informal techniques that allow the financial implications of potential changes in farm organisation to be assessed, programme planning is on several counts more formal. First, it has the definite goal of profit maximisation. Secondly, an explicit procedure is used in an attempt to reach this goal.

Thirdly, labour, machinery and capital requirements can be built directly into the procedure whereas with budgeting, which deals mainly in 'per hectare' terms, they are usually assessed separately, if at all. In consequence, programme planning lies between simpler 'hand' planning techniques, on the one side, and more sophisticated computer techniques, such as linear programming, on the other.

Stages in programme planning

The principles and procedures in programme planning are very similar to those illustrated in the graphic potato/wheat mix example in Chapter 13 (pp. 292–9). It is thus a process of selecting enterprises in order of their return to potentially scarce resources, with substitutions at the margin when resources run short. However, whereas the graphic procedure – designed simply to illustrate principles – permitted only two enterprises to be handled, programme planning is not limited in this way and so allows the planning of real farm situations.

The main stages may first be specified, before being illustrated with a practical example. They are:

1. Simplify by determining which resources are potentially scarce, eliminating those that are not. Similarly, eliminate non-viable enterprises.

2. Calculate the gross margins of the remaining enterprises per unit of the remaining potentially scarce shared resources.

3. Select one of the resources as being potentially the most limiting (land is usually selected, unless another resource appears likely to be critically limiting). Introduce, up to its maximum, that enterprise which gives the highest gross margin per unit of the resource (but excluding, at this stage, enterprises giving infinite returns to the resource).

4. Continue to introduce successively, and up to their respective maxima, those enterprises with the next highest gross margins per unit of the selected resource until either:
   (i) the resource in question (the first resource) is exhausted; or
   (ii) another resource (the second resource) is exhausted, while some of the first resource still remains.

5. *If the first resource is exhausted*, introduce, if possible, an enterprise that does not require any of the first resource (i.e. gives infinite returns to it). If there is a choice of such enterprises, select them in descending order of their returns to another potentially scarce resource. If a second resource is exhausted in the process, proceed to stage 6 below. If not, proceed to stage 8.

6. *If another resource is exhausted*, select to it by substituting the

enterprise that is not yet in the plan (or is not yet in to its maximum) and which gives the highest return to this second resource, for the enterprise already in the plan which gives the lowest.

7. Continue such substitutions with enterprises entering in descending order, and leaving in ascending order, of their returns to the second resource until:

(*a*) another resource is exhausted, in which case select enterprises giving a high return to this resource as in stage 6; or

(*b*) it no longer pays to continue to make substitutions to the second resource. In which case, introduce, if possible, an enterprise that does not require any of the second resource. If there is a choice of such enterprises, select them in descending order of their returns to another potentially scarce resource. If another resource is exhausted in the process, select enterprises giving a high return to it as in stage 6 above. If not, proceed to stage 8.

8. When it appears that there are no more gainful substitutions to be made, double-check the solution both for total gross margin and total use of resources. Subtract fixed costs to obtain net profit.

9. It may be worthwhile checking on the solution, by starting the whole selection procedure again, choosing a different resource as the first limiting resource.

The first two stages are pre-planning ones, in that the actual selection procedure does not begin until stage 3. In addition, as with other planning procedures, before any of these stages can be carried out, the relevant information has to be assembled, adjusted as far as possible so that it applies to an 'average' season and checked to ensure that it cannot be improved upon technically.

An example

This preliminary collection and checking of data is assumed to have been performed for a 120-hectare, 4-man arable farm, and the resulting information is collated in Table 14.4 in the same matrix form as was introduced in Chapter 13 (Table 13.2). There are fourteen constraints – one for land, four for labour, six for rotation, one for fixed capital (accommodation) and two arising from institutional considerations – the majority of which are common to more than one enterprise. They permit eight enterprises – seven crop and one livestock – to be carried on, their gross margins being shown at the top of, and their resource requirements in the body of, the matrix. In one case – sugar beet – alternative methods of organisation are specified. Sugar beet (regular)

TABLE 14.4. *Data for planning – multi-enterprise situation*

	Unit:	Winter wheat 1 ha	Spring barley 1 ha	Spring oats 1 ha	Winter beans 1 ha	Spring beans 1 ha	S.beet (reg.) 1 ha	S.beet (cas.) 1 ha	Maincrop potatoes 1 ha	Weaner prodn. 1 sow
Gross margin (£)	—	310	250	225	240	205	600	590	580	102
Resources and constraints										
Land (hectares)	120	1	1	1	1	1	1	1	1	0
Labour (hours)										
Spring (Mar.–mid April)	1,003	2.5	7.5	7	0	8.75	10	10	25	3
Early summer (May–mid June)	1,320	0	0	0	0	0.75	30	10	3.75	3
Late summer (Aug.–mid Sept.)	1,240	5	5	5	6.25	3	0	0	1.25	3
Autumn (Oct.–mid Nov.)	930	10	0	0	12.5	0	25	25	50	3
Rotation (hectares)										
Max. cereals	90	1	1	1	0	0	0	0	0	0
Max. wheat	48	1	0	0	0	0	0	0	0	0
Max. oats	20	0	0	1	0	0	0	0	0	0
Max. legumes	24	0	0	0	1	1	0	0	0	0
Max. sugar beet	30	0	0	0	0	0	1	1	0	0
Max. potatoes	24	0	0	0	0	0	0	0	1	0
Accommodation (sows)										
Max. sows	20	0	0	0	0	0	0	0	0	1
Institutional (hectares)										
S.beet contract	10	0	0	0	0	0	1	1	0	0
Potato quota	12	0	0	0	0	0	0	0	1	0

assumes that singling is by regular staff, resulting in a high requirement of 30 hours of regular labour per ha in the early-summer period. In contrast, sugar beet (casual) assumes the employment of casual labour for this task, so reducing the regular labour requirement by 20 hours and the gross margin by £10 per hectare.

Simplification (stage 1)

It would be quite feasible to begin planning with the data in Table 14.4. However, in order to reduce the volume of subsequent calculations and to make the fundamental issues as clear as possible, it is desirable to eliminate any data which can be shown to be superfluous, in that their inclusion or exclusion will make no difference to the solution. Such data take two forms. First, there are resources and constraints that cannot prove limiting on enterprises because the latter are more closely constrained in other ways. Secondly, there are enterprises that will never enter the solution because others will always be selected in preference.

Redundant resources and constraints. Simple inspection by eye is sufficient to reveal whether any of those constraints specific to individual enterprises are redundant. In our example, the rotational limits on sugar beet and potatoes can both be eliminated, as their respective contract and quota constraints are more limiting.

Matters have to be taken further with shared resources, particularly labour, because inspection by eye is insufficient to reveal whether or not any are superfluous. Instead, it is necessary to check whether they will run short when the enterprises that make the biggest demands on them are introduced in descending order of their requirements for each resource. If they do not, then they cannot prove limiting and may be excluded from further planning. This is done in Table 14.5 for the four labour periods. Take the spring period as an example. Potatoes have the highest labour requirement at that time (25 hours per ha), so they are introduced up to their maximum of 12 ha of quota. Sugar beet is next (10 hours per ha) entering to its maximum of 10 ha of contract, and in turn is followed by spring beans ($8\frac{3}{4}$ hours per ha) up to the 24 hectares permitted on rotational grounds. Finally, the remaining 74 ha are taken up by barley ($7\frac{1}{2}$ hours per ha) with, in addition, 20 sows (3 hours per head), as they make no direct calls on land. Potential labour consumption may thus rise as high as 1225 hours, so that, with only 1003 hours available, the spring period must be included in the planning process as being potentially limiting.

TABLE 14.5. *Simplification – checking potential scarcity of labour*

Spring

	hectares	hours per ha	total hours
Potatoes	12	× 25	300
Sugar beet	10	× 10	100
Spring beans	24	× $8\frac{3}{4}$	210
Barley	74	× $7\frac{1}{2}$	555
Sows (20)	—	× (3)	60
Total	120		1,225
Labour available			1,003
Labour potentially scarce			

Early Summer

	hectares	hours per ha	total hours
Sugar beet	10	× 30	300
Potatoes	12	× $3\frac{3}{4}$	45
Sows (20)	—	× (3)	60
Spring beans	24	× $\frac{3}{4}$	18
Barley	74	× 0	0
Total	120		423
Labour available			1,320
Labour not scarce			

Late Summer

	hectares	hours per ha	total hours
Winter beans	24	× $6\frac{1}{4}$	150
Cereals	90	× 5	450
Sows (20)	—	× (3)	60
Potatoes	6	× $1\frac{1}{4}$	8
Total	120		668
Labour available			1,240
Labour not scarce			

Autumn

	hectares	hours per ha	total hours
Potatoes	12	× 50	600
Sugar beet	10	× 25	250
Winter beans	24	× $12\frac{1}{2}$	300
Wheat	48	× 10	480
Sows (20)	—	× (3)	60
Barley	26	× 0	0
Total	120		1,690
Labour available			930
Labour potentially very scarce			

The same applies to autumn labour but, in contrast, labour cannot run out in either early or late summer, even if the most labour-consuming enterprises should enter the solution to their limits, and they can thus be excluded. At the same time, these latter two periods demonstrate that it is possible for land to run short while labour is still available, so that land must also be included as being potentially scarce.[1]

Redundant enterprises. The next object is to eliminate any enterprise that can never enter the solution because, while being constrained as much as (or more than) another enterprise, it gives a lower return to all the potentially scarce resources (that is, the resources other than those eliminated in the previous step).

Spring oats, when compared with spring barley, are an example of such a 'dominated' enterprise. Their respective gross margins per unit of the potentially scarce resources are:

	Spring oats (£)	*Spring barley* (£)
Land (1 hectare)	225	250
Spring labour (1 hour)	32 (225/7)	33 (250/7$\frac{1}{2}$)

while neither requires autumn labour. Although there is a specific limit of 20 ha of oats, this is part of the overall cereal limit of 90 hectares, so that barley will always be selected in preference to oats. The latter can therefore be excluded together with their individual limitation (thus cutting out yet another constraint).

In a similar fashion, once the early summer labour period has been eliminated, sugar beet (casual) is constrained in precisely the same way as sugar beet (regular) and as it gives a gross margin £10 per ha lower than the latter, it too can be excluded.

As a consequence of simplification, the original matrix of fifteen rows and ten columns is reduced to one of ten rows and eight columns, without affecting in any way the solution ultimately to be obtained.

[1] This is perhaps hardly surprising. Nonetheless, the aim is to maintain objectivity as far as possible. If labour were extremely scarce, an optimal solution might suggest that some land should be left idle.

Gross margin per unit of shared resource (stage 2)

The next stage involves calculating the gross margins of the different enterprises per unit of the *shared* resources. (There is no need to do so for those constraints specific to single enterprises.) This is done in Table 14.6, in which enterprises are shown in descending order of their gross margins per hectare of land and per hour of spring and autumn labour respectively. Those enterprises making no call on a resource (and, therefore, giving infinite returns to it) are listed last because it usually proves to be better in practice, when selecting enterprises that give infinite returns to a specific resource, to leave them until that resource has been exhausted by the enterprises that make specific demands on it (rather than selecting them first because they give the highest returns to that resource).

Planning procedure (stages 3 to 8)

With the first two stages completed, the actual planning process can be initiated by selecting one of the shared resources as being potentially the most limiting. Table 14.5 shows that although autumn labour is likely to be more limiting than spring labour, there are no *a priori* reasons for choosing it rather than land, which thus becomes the first resource to which enterprises are selected. The subsequent steps in the planning process are shown in Table 14.7, which also demonstrates a suggested layout in which only the shared resources appear explicitly.

Select to land (Table 14.7, steps i to iii). Table 14.6 shows that of the enterprises actually requiring land, sugar beet has the highest gross margin per ha (£600). Dividing the resource availabilities by the respective demands that 1 ha of sugar beet makes on them – so giving the maximum area that each permits – reveals the contract constraint as being the most limiting at 10 ha, and it is at this level that sugar beet is introduced (step i).

Potatoes give the next highest gross margin per ha (£580). Of the shared resources remaining after the introduction of sugar beet, land permits 110 ha (110/1), spring labour 36.1 ha (903/25) and autumn labour 13.6 ha of potatoes (680/50). As these levels are all in excess of the quota limit (12 ha), the latter is most limiting, and it is at this level that potatoes enter (step ii).

Wheat gives the third highest gross margin per ha (£310). The most limiting resource with sugar beet and potatoes already in the plan is autumn labour, which permits only 8 ha (80/10). With wheat in the

TABLE 14.6. *Returns to potentially scarce shared resources*

Land		Spring labour			Autumn labour		
	Gross margin per hectare (£)			Gross margin per hour (£)			Gross margin per hour (£)
Sugar beet	600	Wheat	(310/2.5)	124	Sows	(102/3)	34
Potatoes	580	Sugar beet	(600/10)	60	Wheat	(310/10)	31
Wheat	310	Sows	(102/3)	34	Sugar beet	(600/25)	24
Barley	250	Barley	(250/7.5)	33	Winter beans	(240/12.5)	19
Winter beans	240	Spring beans	(205/8.75)	24	Potatoes	(580/50)	12
Spring beans	205	Potatoes	(580/25)	23			
No limit							
Sows		Winter beans			Barley		
					Spring beans		

TABLE 14.7. *Programme planning example. Stages in planning* (select to land)

Step	Enterprise selection			Land		Spring labour		Autumn labour		Max. Cereals		Max. Legumes		Gross margin change (£)	Cumulative gross margin (£)
		Amount (ha)	Cum. level (ha)	Used (ha)	Unused (ha)	Used (hrs)	Unused (hrs)	Used (hrs)	Unused (hrs)	Used (ha)	Unused (ha)	Used (ha)	Unused (ha)		
Resources available at start:				—	120	—	1,003	—	930	—	90	—	24	—	0
(i)	S. beet	10	10	10	110	100	903	250	680	—	90	—	24	6,000	6,000
(ii)	Potatoes	12	12	12	98	300	603	600	80	—	90	—	24	6,960	12,960
(iii)	Wheat	8	8	8	90	20	583	80	0	8	82	—	24	2,480	15,440
	Potatoes	−1.2	10.8	−1.2	91.2	−30	613	−60	60	—	82	—	24	−696	14,744
(iv)	Sows (nos.)	20	20	—	91.2	60	553	60	0	—	82	—	24	2,040	16,784
	Potatoes	−8	2.8	−8	99.2	−200	753	−400	400	—	82	—	24	−4,640	12,144
(v)	Wheat	40	48	40	59.2	100	653	400	0	40	42	—	24	12,400	24,544
	Potatoes	−2.8	0	−2.8	62	−70	723	−140	140	—	42	—	24	−1,624	22,920
(vi)	W. beans	11.2	11.2	11.2	50.8	—	723	140	0	—	42	11.2	12.8	2,688	25,608
(vii)	Barley	42	42	42	8.8	315	408	—	0	42	0	—	12.8	10,500	36,108
(viii)	S. beans	8.8	8.8	8.8	0	77	331	—	0	—	0	8.8	4	1,804	37,912
	W. beans	−11.2	0	−11.2	11.2	—	331	−140	140	—	0	−11.2	15.2	−2,688	35,224
(ix)	Potatoes	2.8	2.8	2.8	8.4	70	261	140	0	—	0	—	15.2	1,624	36,848
	S. beans	8.4	17.2	8.4	0	74	187	—	0	—	0	8.4	6.8	1,722	38,570
	Wheat	−22	26	−22	22	−55	242	−220	220	−22	22	—	6.8	−6,820	31,750
(x)	Potatoes	4.4	7.2	4.4	17.6	110	132	220	0	—	22	—	6.8	2,552	34,302
	Barley	17.6	59.6	17.6	0	132	0	—	0	17.6	4.4	—	6.8	4,400	38,702
(xi)	S. beans	−4.4	12.8	−4.4	4.4	−39	39	—	0	—	4.4	−4.4	11.2	−902	37,800
	Barley	4.4	64	4.4	0	33	6	—	0	4.4	0	—	11.2	1,100	38,900

Solution and double check to Table 14.7

Enterprise	Land (hectares)	Spring labour (hours)	Autumn labour (hours)	Gross margin (£)
Sugar beet	10.0	100	250	6,000
Potatoes	7.2	180	360	4,176
Spring beans	12.8	112	—	2,624
Wheat	26.0	65	260	8,060
Barley	64.0	480	—	16,000
	120.0			
Sows 20		60	60	2,040
		997	930	38,900
		spare 6		
		1,003	less Fixed costs	30,000
			Net profit	8,900

solution at this level, autumn labour becomes the first shared resource to be exhausted (step iii).

Select to autumn labour (Table 14.7, steps iv to viii). The exhaustion of autumn labour while there are still 90 ha of land available, brings the plan to stage 6 of the planning procedure (as outlined on p. 331), and selection now switches to the resource that is actually scarce. Leaving aside for the time being barley and spring beans which require no autumn labour, Table 14.6 shows that of the enterprises not yet in the plan, sows give the highest gross margin per hour of autumn labour (£34), while of those already in the plan, potatoes give the lowest (£12); thus the former will enter at the expense of the latter. The maximum of 20 sows requires 60 hours of autumn labour and this calls for the sacrifice of 1.2 ha of potatoes (at 50 hours per hectare) (step iv).

Wheat gives the next highest return to autumn labour (£31 per hour) and although there are already 8 ha in the plan, the rotation permits 48 ha. There are still 10.8 ha of potatoes in the plan from which autumn labour can be withdrawn, so the next step is to determine which resource is most limiting on wheat. Land permits 91.2 ha (91.2/1), spring labour 221 ha (553/2.5), autumn labour (via potatoes) 54 ha (10.8 × 50/10) and the remaining wheat rotation 40 hectares. The latter is thus most restrictive, and 40 ha of wheat enter the plan for the sacrifice of 8 ha of potatoes (40 × 10 = 8 × 50) (step v).

Sugar beet offers the third highest return to autumn labour (£24 per hour), but is already in the plan at its maximum. Winter beans are next

(£19 per hour) and of the resources still available, it is the 140 hours of autumn labour still held by the remaining 2.8 ha of potatoes that are most restrictive, limiting beans to 11.2 ha (2.8 × 50/12.5) (step vi).

All the potatoes having been eliminated, of the enterprises now in the plan, it is winter beans that give the lowest gross margin per hour of autumn labour. Thus no more of the latter should be introduced and no more worthwhile substitutions can be made to autumn labour. This leaves spring beans and barley which do not require autumn labour. The latter is selected first as it gives the higher gross margin per ha (£250 compared with £205). Of the remaining resources, cereal rotation is the most limiting on barley, allowing 42 ha (maximum cereals 90 ha less wheat 48 ha) and once it has been introduced (step vii) the land remaining limits spring beans to 8.8 ha (step viii).

Select again to land (Table 14.7, steps ix to xi). Land is now scarce in addition to autumn labour and it is necessary to check that, in pursuing selection to the latter to its ultimate limits, returns to land have not been sacrificed unnecessarily. Of the four enterprises that give the highest returns per ha (Table 14.6), three – sows, sugar beet and wheat – are already in the plan at their respective maxima, and attention thus focusses on the remaining one – potatoes – which has previously been completely eliminated from the plan. If potatoes are to be re-introduced, both autumn labour and land have to be obtained from enterprises already in the plan. Of the latter, winter beans give the lowest returns to autumn labour, 4 ha providing enough labour for 1 ha of potatoes (50/12½). The only crop available to utilise the balance of 3 ha of land is spring beans. The gains and losses of this substitution are:

	(£)
Sacrifice 4 ha winter beans at £240 gm per ha	−960
Gain 1 ha potatoes at £580 gm per ha	+580
Gain 3 ha spring beans at £205 gm per ha	+615
Net gain	235

The substitution is worthwhile, as each 4-hectare 'unit' adds £235 to gross margin, and is limited to 2.8 units when all 11.2 ha of winter beans have been replaced by 2.8 ha of potatoes and 8.4 ha of spring beans (step ix).

If there are to be any more potatoes, land and labour must come from another source. This cannot be sugar beet because it gives a higher return than potatoes to *both* land and autumn labour. Only wheat remains, of which 5 ha must be sacrificed to provide sufficient autumn labour for 1 ha of potatoes (50/10). Barley can take up the 4 ha remaining, since the sacrifice of wheat releases cereal land. Testing the value of this substitution:

	(£)
Sacrifice 5 ha wheat at £310 gm per ha	−1,550
Gain 1 ha potatoes at £580 gm per ha	+580
Gain 4 ha barley at £250 gm per ha	+1,000
Net gain	30

The substitution is just worthwhile. The limiting factor is now the amount of spring labour available. Each 5-ha unit of potatoes and barley requires 55 hours of spring labour $[(1 \times 25) + (4 \times 7\frac{1}{2})]$, while each five ha of wheat releases $12\frac{1}{2}$ hours, giving a net requirement of $42\frac{1}{2}$ hours. With 187 hours of spring labour available at this point, 4.4 units can be substituted ($187/42\frac{1}{2}$), namely, 4.4 ha of potatoes and 17.6 ha of barley, at the expense of 22 ha of wheat (step x).

Spring labour is now scarce in addition to land and autumn labour, but as 4.4 ha of cereal rotation are now spare, 4.4 ha of barley, with a higher gross margin per ha, can replace 4.4 ha of spring beans, and spring labour moves back into slight surplus (step xi).

Check selection to spring labour. With the shared resources all virtually exhausted, it is obvious that this plan must be the optimum or very close to it. Nevertheless, it is worth checking whether there is any advantage to be had by selecting to spring labour (ignoring the slight surplus). Potatoes give the lowest return to spring labour, while wheat (of those enterprises actually utilising it) gives the highest. In obtaining autumn labour, the sacrifice of 1 ha of potatoes permits 5 ha of wheat. This in turn entails the sacrifice of 5 ha of barley to obtain the necessary cereal land. The odd hectare remaining can be put into spring beans. Balancing the gains and losses:

	(£)	(£)
Sacrifice 1 ha potatoes at £580 gm per ha	−580	
Sacrifice 5 ha barley at £250 gm per ha	−1,250	−1,830
Gain 5 ha wheat at £310 gm per ha	+1,550	
Gain 1 ha spring beans at £205 gm per ha	+205	+1,755
Net loss		75

The substitution is not worth making. Nor is the sacrifice of potatoes for winter beans (which give an infinite return to spring labour). It can thus be concluded that the optimal solution has indeed been obtained. It remains to double-check the solution, as in the last part of Table 14.7, and to deduct the fixed costs (assumed here to be £30,000) to arrive at the optimal net profit of £8900.

Commentary

The steps taken in this planning example have been deliberately set out rather pedantically in order to demonstrate the application of 'rules', as far as they can be formulated. Undoubtedly an experienced planner, particularly one who had previously met problems involving similar resource and enterprise patterns to those on the farm under study, could take short cuts. These might result partly from his judgement of what were likely to be profitable enterprise combinations and partly from his anticipation of those substitutions that would probably lead to 'dead-ends'. For instance, in the previous example it is fairly evident that if the 'root' crops are initially introduced to their limits, most of the available autumn labour will be consumed. An alternative would be to set aside sufficient labour to permit at least a proportion of sows and wheat (the enterprises giving a high return to autumn labour) to enter the solution, and then to bring in the root crops with the labour remaining.

In addition (as indicated in stage 9 of the planning procedure, p. 332), unless one resource is critically short, it may be advantageous to plan more than once with the same data, taking a different resource as being initially limiting on each occasion. In relatively easy problems, this may provide confirmation of the optimal solution by another route. In more difficult problems, where the planner may have become tied down in complex substitutions, it may offer an easier path to the solution.

In summary, the broad stages involved in the application of programme planning are as follows:

1. Collection, analysis and adjustment of planning data.
2. Simplification of data preparatory to planning.
3. Application of planning procedure.

Evaluation of programme planning

There is a large degree of formality in programme planning, as exemplified by its dependence on basic planning concepts: fixed and variable costs, gross margin per unit of scarce resource, marginal substitution, and optimal allocation of scarce resources with account taken of opportunity costs. This makes it a valuable means of teaching planning principles. Nevertheless, it depends heavily on a trial-and-error process of seeking an optimal solution, as is well demonstrated by the example in Table 14.7, where potatoes first enter to their maximum, are then entirely eliminated, finally to re-enter and stabilise at a level sixty per cent of their maximum. It is also illustrated by the usually arbitrary nature of the selection of the first limiting resource. In the previous example land was chosen, but in the event the planning process would have been less complex and would have required a smaller number of substitutions if autumn labour had been selected first instead (see Appendix 14.2).

Again, the lack of complete rigour is shown by the fact that several alternative ways have been suggested for determining the starting point of the calculations and the action to be taken when a resource is exhausted (see Appendix 14.3). Furthermore, although substitutions may not be too difficult to foresee when there are only two limiting resources and a few alternatives between which to deploy them, matters are very different with more complex problems. Then substitutions may occur between combinations of several enterprises together (rather than between single ones), in order to balance the demands on, and supplies of, a number of resources that have all become exhausted at one and the same time. Thus the likelihood of an optimal solution being reached depends in part on the skill and experience of the planner and in part on the complexity of the problem. There is also the danger that complex problems may be deliberately over-simplified in an attempt to contain the arithmetic within manageable proportions. This is particularly likely to be the case on those livestock farms where a large range of alternative feedstuffs are available. It should be part of the planning problem to discover the optimal pattern of feeding, but often a fixed pattern is assumed for the sake of simplicity.

It has been suggested that conceptually and in its degree of sophistication, programme planning lies between budgeting and linear programming. This, however, is the root cause of its fallibility as a planning technique and why it is so little used in practice, namely, that it falls between two stools, lacking the advantages of either of the other techniques and with few advantages of its own to offer in compensation. On the one hand, it needs more data than budgeting, but cannot easily deal with problems such as 'lumpy' inputs, interdependence of enterprises and non-linearity (see Chapters 13 and 15). On the other hand, as noted above, it may be incapable of dealing satisfactorily with situations that could be readily solved by linear programming with no arithmetical effort and with the benefit of 'by-product' information also (see Chapter 15, pp. 360–2).

Programme planning does, however, have the advantage, compared with a *single* linear programming computer run, of greater flexibility, in that obviously severe restrictions that come to light during the calculations can be examined and possibly eased during the procedure, and enterprises that are too small can be deliberately avoided. On the same count, the 'logic' behind solutions can be explicitly demonstrated, because of the availability of the steps by which they have been obtained, so that they are likely to be more readily accepted by the farmer. Also, since the technique is capable of providing optimal or near optimal solutions in relatively simple cases, it offers the planner a means of making a preliminary summary review of a complex problem, before he turns to other techniques to obtain a more detailed solution.

Nevertheless, if the problem is one requiring a more complex technique than budgeting, and all the data needed for programme planning are available, most would argue that linear programming is the obvious technique to use, given the availability of a computer organisation to undertake the work, and the willingness on the part of the farmer to pay for it.

Appendix 14.1: Livestock units and forage allocation

Livestock units and forage hectares

The livestock unit concept is employed to enable different types and age-groups of livestock to be put on a common basis. A livestock unit is based on the estimated energy requirements of a Friesian cow with an average yield of milk, and the livestock units for the various categories of livestock relate to their relative energy requirements. These may be expressed in various degrees of detail and can be extended, for example, to cover different breeds. Table 14.8 gives a list of livestock units.

The total number of grazing livestock units on a farm is a matter of simple calculation. The following is an example:

	LU per head		*Total LU*
70 dairy cows	at 1.0		70
10 heifers over 2 years old	at 0.8	8.0	
18 heifers 1 – 2 years old	at 0.6	10.8	
23 heifers under one-year old	at 0.4	9.2	28
280 ewes	at 0.2		56
	Total		154

The forage area of a farm consists mainly of grassland, both permanent and temporary, but may also include kale, fodder turnips, etc. If there were 77 forage hectares available for the livestock in the above example, the stocking density (or rate) would be 0.5 forage ha per LU (i.e. 77 ÷ 154) – or 2 LU per ha. For the purpose of making this calculation, rough grazing is usually converted to the equivalent area of average quality grassland. Also, any forage hectares used exclusively for pigs or poultry, and the hectare equivalent of any home-grown fodder fed to barley beef, are deducted.

In order to calculate the forage area required to support a given number of livestock of varying types (for both grazing and conserved bulk fodder – mainly hay and silage), the total livestock units are first calculated, then divided by the estimated livestock units per forage hectare that the farmer thinks he can achieve given his level of grassland management, the quality of the soil and the amount of fertiliser (especially nitrogenous) that he intends to use. His relative dependence on bulk fodder as compared with concentrate feeds should be taken into account, and the forage hectare-equivalents of straw (supplemented by concentrates) and any purchased bulk fodder (such as hay) are deducted. Problems that arise in calculating comparative measures of stocking density are further discussed in Appendix 20.1.

TABLE 14.8. *Livestock units*

Dairy cows	1.0
Beef cows (excl. calves)	0.7
Other cattle over 2 years old (incl. bulls)	0.8
Semi-intensive beef (6 to 16–20 months old)	0.7
Other cattle 1 to 2 years old	0.6
Other cattle under 1 year old	0.4
Lowland ewes (incl. lambs under 6 months old)	0.2
Rams, tegs, lambs for fattening (over 6 months old)	0.2
Hill ewes	0.1

Notes:

1. The above figures are per head and relate to average numbers of stock over the whole year, based on monthly recording, i.e. the livestock units *relate to requirements over a twelve-month period.* Where stock are kept for only part of a year, therefore, the livestock unit figure should be reduced *pro rata*.

2. Judgement can be used in adjusting individual figures according to variations in breed, system, yield, etc.

Allocation of grassland

Where gross margins per hectare are required for grazing livestock, and more than one type of livestock graze the same area either at the same time or at different times of the year, the problem of area allocation arises. There are two main possibilities. One is to record the quantities of bulk food, such as hay and silage, fed to each type of livestock and allocate the hectares needed to produce them according to yields per hectare, and to allocate grazing by grassland recording. The latter involves recording which fields are occupied by each type of stock each day. However, not only are both the recording and calculations tedious but the results tend to be of dubious value, largely because the quality of the grazing varies so much at different times of the year; further complications arise when different types of stock are grazed together concurrently. The other possibility is to allocate on a livestock-unit basis. To return to the above example, livestock units per forage ha were calculated as being 2. The cows would thus be allocated 35 hectares (70 LU ÷ 2), the heifers 14 hectares (28 ÷ 2), and the sheep 28 hectares (56 ÷ 2). If forage variable costs totalled £5390, i.e. £70 per ha (5390 ÷ 77), £2450 (35 ha × £70) would be allocated to the cows, £980 to the heifers, and £1960 to the sheep.

The livestock unit calculation has its uses as an approximate method of allocation because it is simple and the gross margin per hectare figures so derived give some indication of the contribution different grazing livestock enterprises are making, and low figures compared with standards may help illuminate a weak enterprise. It does however have its drawbacks and the results must always be treated with caution, since they could be misleading. For example, the main dairy grazing area may well receive more fertiliser and have a higher stocking rate than outlying land, yet each may provide both conservation and grazing, leaving only the aftermath for other stock. It may be that the cows are overstocked and the sheep understocked. Further, livestock units themselves are at best fairly crude measures of relative forage requirements. For these reasons, some authorities advise against allocation and treat forage costs as common to all the grazing livestock on the farm. Planning procedures using this basis are described in the next section of this appendix. There is also the important point that a dairy herd obviously makes far greater demands on the 'fixed' resources of the farm than, say, sheep; but this aspect is not related to the method of allocation, which is the point at issue here.

Difficulties also arise over purchased bulk foods, such as hay, brewers' grains and chat potatoes. It is normal practice to deduct these as variable costs in arriving at the overall gross margin per forage hectare. When using figures so derived in farm planning, however, it is important to realise that they could be misleading, because such treatment may contravene the proportionality rule for variable costs (see Chapter 2, p. 45). Thus, if more livestock are kept on a given forage area, with little or no improvement in the productivity of that land, the cost of bought bulk feeds per head for the extra stock will be higher than the average figure in the past. The same point can arise with rented keep. It is also debatable whether these costs should be deducted when calculating measures for efficiency comparisons (see further Appendix 20.1, last paragraph).

It is normally a straightforward matter to allocate bought bulk feed and rented keep, because they are usually intended for specific types of stock. In treating these items as variable costs, however, the point made above must be remembered: the proportionality rule may be contravened. Another point to bear in mind is that this practice may invalidate comparisons made between different types of stock on the same farm. When bulk fodder is purchased or keep is rented, it is because there is insufficient forage available on the farm for the number of livestock being kept. It may be quite arbitrary – a matter of convenience or convention – which type of livestock receives the bought, as opposed to the home-grown, feeds. It could be unfair and misleading, therefore, to penalise one type of stock for the inadequacy of home food supplies and not the others.

Non-allocative procedures

As mentioned above, because of these various allocation problems, some prefer not to allocate the forage area where mixed grazing is practised. Only the overall gross margin per hectare is calculated, that is, the figure obtained from all the grazing livestock enterprises combined, together with any lesser items such as occasional hay sales. There are then two possibilities.

The first is to retain the present ratios of the different types of stock, e.g. (from the earlier example) 4 ewes per dairy cow (together with the minimum number of dairy followers for replacement purposes). Possible ways of increasing the gross margin per forage hectare are then examined, e.g. by extra fertiliser use or more intensive grazing management, and finally it is decided whether to expand or reduce the forage area as compared with the area under cash crops.

The alternative procedure, which is more usual, is *not* to accept the present stocking ratios, which means that the possibility of substituting one grazing enterprise for another, or expanding one and not the others, is examined. For this purpose, gross margins per head of each type of stock are calculated, but ignoring forage variable costs, which are treated as common to all the grazing livestock. By comparing the ratios of these figures of gross margins per head excluding forage, the potential profitability of substitutions can be gauged. For example, if the figures are £300 per dairy cow and £25 per ewe, the ratio would be 12:1, which means that if an extra cow could be kept at the expense of less than 12 ewes it would pay to make the substitution (and *vice versa*), assuming fixed costs remained unaltered. In this way the possibility of raising overall gross margin per forage hectare can be explored. Subsequently, the two steps described in the previous procedure can be taken, i.e. considering other ways of raising the gross margin per forage hectare and the possibility of substituting forage area for cash crops, or *vice versa.*

A snag with the second procedure is the difficulty of calculating gross margins per head, even excluding forage. It is relatively easy for say, dairy cows, beef cows and ewes, where average numbers during the year can usually be estimated fairly readily, but even here difficulties can arise, especially when numbers are changing substantially, and it can be virtually impossible in heifer-rearing and many systems of beef production, because of varying numbers of stock of different ages. Some calculate figures per livestock unit, but these tend to be of little value. In practice, therefore, often only the *total* figures for the enterprises, excluding forage variable costs, can be calculated. Some of the various steps described above have then to be taken virtually concurrently, since they often affect one another. Such factors as the availability of buildings, hedges and fences, distances from buildings, type of soil and topography, availability of capital and labour, and the economic size of the livestock units, have all to be considered.

Appendix 14.2: Alternative path to solution of programme planning example

Table 14.9 demonstrates the order of enterprise selection and substitution in the programme planning example, when autumn labour is

TABLE 14.9. *Stages in programme planning example* (select to autumn labour)

Step	Enterprise selection			Land		Spring labour		Autumn labour		Max. Cereals		Max. Legumes		Gross margin change (£)	Cumulative gross margin (£)
		Amount (ha)	Cum. level (ha)	Used (ha)	Unused (ha)	Used (hrs)	Unused (hrs)	Used (hrs)	Unused (hrs)	Used (ha)	Unused (ha)	Used (ha)	Unused (ha)		
Resources available at start:				—	120	—	1,003	—	930	—	90	—	24	—	0
(i)	Sows (nos)	20	20	—	120	60	943	60	870	—	90	—	24	2,040	2,040
(ii)	Wheat	48	48	−48	72	120	823	480	390	48	42	—	24	14,880	16,920
(iii)	S. beet	10	10	10	62	100	723	250	140	—	42	—	24	6,000	22,920
(iv)	W. beans	11.2	11.2	11.2	50.8	—	723	140	0	—	42	11.2	12.8	2,688	25,608
(v)	Barley	42	42	42	8.8	315	408	—	0	42	0	—	12.8	10,500	36,108
(vi)	S. beans	8.8	8.8	8.8	0	77	331	—	0	—	0	8.8	4	1,804	37,912
(vii)	W. beans	−11.2	0	−11.2	11.2	—	331	−140	140	—	0	−11.2	15.2	−2,688	35,224
	Potatoes	2.8	2.8	2.8	8.4	70	261	140	0	—	0	—	15.2	1,624	36,848
	S. beans	8.4	17.2	8.4	0	74	187	—	0	—	0	8.4	6.8	1,722	38,570
(viii)	Wheat	−22	26	−22	22	−55	242	−220	220	−22	22	—	6.8	−6,820	31,750
	Potatoes	4.4	7.2	4.4	17.6	110	132	220	0	—	22	—	6.8	2,552	34,302
	Barley	17.6	59.6	17.6	0	132	0	—	0	17.6	4.4	—	6.8	4,400	38,702
(ix)	S. beans	−4.4	12.8	−4.4	4.4	−39	39	—	0	—	4.4	−4.4	11.2	−902	37,800
	Barley	4.4	64	4.4	0	33	6	—	0	4.4	0	—	11.2	1,100	38,900

taken initially as the most limiting resource instead of land. The steps may be briefly outlined:

Select to autumn labour (steps i to vi). Sows, wheat and sugar beet are the three enterprises giving the highest gross margins per hour of autumn labour (in that order, see Table 14.6), and sufficient resources are available to enable them all to be introduced to their respective maxima.

Winter beans gives the fourth highest return to autumn labour, but scarcity of the latter limits them to 11.2 ha. (Stage 5 of the procedure as outlined on p. 331 has thus been reached, in which the first resource to which selection is being made is exhausted.)

Barley, to the limit of cereal permission, and spring beans, to the limit of the remaining land (neither require autumn labour), complete the selection to labour.

Select to land (steps vii to ix). Land is now scarce as well as autumn labour, so that selection is made on the basis of returns per ha. The last three steps are identical to those in Table 14.7 and are explained on pp. 341–2.

Appendix 14.3: Alternative methods of starting the programme planning procedure

Various ways of starting the programme planning procedure have been suggested. Here we list them briefly:

(i) Select in order of gross margins per hectare.

(ii) Select in order of gross margins per unit of the resource subjectively expected to be the most limiting.

(iii) Start with the enterprise giving the highest total gross margin when introduced to its limit, and proceed on the basis of the scarcest remaining (or limiting) resource.

(iv) Rank the enterprises in descending order of their gross margins per unit of the various scarce resources. Illustrating this with the data from Table 14.6:

Enterprise	*Land*	*Spring labour*	*Autumn labour*	*Total*
Sows	1	4	3	8
Sugar beet	2	3	5	10
Potatoes	3	7	7	17
Wheat	4	2	4	10
Barley	5	5	1=	11
Winter beans	6	1	6	13
Spring beans	7	6	1=	14

Add together the individual rankings and select on the basis of increasing order of the value of the total ranking, that is, sows, sugar beet, wheat and so on.

(v) Prepare a series of plans by selecting in order of gross margins per unit of each resource in turn, stopping when that or another resource becomes exhausted (that is, without proceeding to substitute at the margin). The plan giving the highest total gross margin is then taken and the marginal substitution procedure carried out on that plan.

15: Linear programming

Linear programming is a technique based on the processes of matrix algebra, which given suitably formulated data, is capable of producing optimal, mathematical solutions in terms either of maximising or of minimising some stated objective. It thus lends itself readily in farm planning to the determination of the combination of enterprises and techniques that maximises the returns to a particular set of fixed resources. Similarly, though less commonly so as a direct farming application, it can be used to discover the least-cost way of producing a stated output, as in the computation of minimum-cost rations.

For all practical purposes, linear programming requires access to a computer, for although computations can be performed by hand they become very time-consuming and there is a considerable risk of cumulative errors arising. Two basic sets of input data are required to solve a problem by computer. One concerns the problem itself – thus falling within the province of the planner – and is contained in a 'matrix' or two-way table. The other – the *program* – consists of instructions about the manipulations to be performed on the matrix. The latter is the responsibility of the specialist and is, in any case, a once-and-for-all task that need not concern the computer user, except insofar as it affects the way in which the planning data must be presented to the computer and the form in which the computer output – the solution to the problem – is obtained.[1]

The use of linear programming and a computer, by removing the burden of computation from the planner, makes it possible for far more data to be handled and for more comprehensive solutions to be obtained. In addition, the latter are optimal in the arithmetical sense. These attributes, however, must not obscure the fact that the computer is simply a sophisticated type of calculating machine. In consequence, the validity of the solution depends not so much on the computer as on

[1] Programs for linear programming routines are normally available in the 'libraries' of computer laboratories.

the accuracy of the data on which the computation is based, and on the skill and understanding with which relationships between resources and enterprises on the farm are translated into matrix form. It follows that the main concern of the planner should be to ensure a realistic specification of the problem, a topic dealt with in depth in Chapter 18. In the meantime, the present chapter aims to give an insight into the processes of linear programming and the assumptions on which it is based, to illustrate the form in which data are presented to the computer and the type of output obtained, and to assess its value as a farm planning technique.

Principles and procedures in linear programming

The process of linear programming may be formally defined as follows:

> Linear programming maximises (or minimises) a linear function of variables that are subject to linear inequalities and must assume non-negative levels.

The component parts of this definition may be considered in greater detail, assuming the aim is to *maximise* farm income.

'Maximise a linear function of variables'. The linear function of variables to be maximised comprises the 'profit' equation or planning objective of the model and is referred to as the 'objective function'. The variables contained in it (except for zeros) are money values arising from the various operations that farmers carry out. Although they are frequently expressed as gross margins, the separate operations embraced by the latter concept – namely, purchase of inputs (variable costs), production and sale of output (yield × price) – may also be treated independently of one another in linear programming. For example, fodder may be produced separately from the livestock that draw on it, or buying and selling may appear as independent operations. Many different values are thus encompassed in the objective function and whether they are gross margins, partial gross margins, sale prices, purchase prices or variable costs, all are designated 'net revenues', while the operations of which they are the financial expression are called 'activities'.

The aim of planning is to seek that combination of activities which maximises the total value of their net revenues in the objective function. Net profit is then derived by deducting the fixed costs.

If the simple, two-dimensional example from Table 13.2 (p. 293) is used in illustration, the linear function to be maximised, namely, the objective function, is:

$$\text{Objective function (£)} = 720p + 400w$$

where p and w are hectares of potatoes and wheat respectively, and 720 and 400 their net revenues (gross margins in this instance). In the optimal solution (p. 298), the values assumed in the objective function are:

$$\text{Objective function} = (£720 \times 35) + (£400 \times 40) = £41{,}200$$

The function is linear because, irrespective of the actual levels of potatoes and wheat (which may range from all potatoes and no wheat to all wheat and no potatoes), their net revenues are assumed to remain unchanged.

'Subject to linear inequalities'. Linear inequalities refer to the operation of the individual constraints, of which there are six in Table 13.2 – land, spring and summer labour, spring tractor work, working capital and potato quota. Taking first the aspect of linearity, the constraints in Figure 13.1 are all represented by straight lines. For example, that for spring labour is expressed by:

$$7.5p + 3.75w = 412.5 \text{ (hours)}$$

and that for summer labour:

$$2.5p + 5w = 325 \text{ (hours)}$$

Linearity implies that irrespective of the levels of potatoes and wheat introduced, their unit requirements of labour (and of other fixed resources) remain unchanged.

Next we turn to the inequalities. To insist that the fixed resources must all be exactly consumed by the activities – as is implied by the equality signs above – is impracticable. If there should happen to be a solution where this were possible, it would probably not be optimal. In consequence, the constraints are expressed as inequalities. For example,

$$\text{Spring labour (hours): } 7.5p + 3.75w \leq 412.5$$
$$\text{Summer labour (hours): } 2.5p + 5w \leq 325$$

The amounts of spring and summer labour taken up by potatoes and wheat must be 'less than or equal to' ($\leq$) the respective amounts available. (Obviously they cannot exceed the availabilities.)[1,2]

In the optimal solution, spring labour is fully consumed:

$$\text{Spring labour (hours): } (7.5 \times 35) + (3.75 \times 40) = 412.5$$
$$412.5 = 412.5$$

whereas there are 37.5 hours of summer labour spare:

$$\text{Summer labour (hours): } (2.5 \times 35) + (5 \times 40) < 325$$
$$287.5 < 325$$

'Activities at non-negative levels'. Although the need for activities to be at non-negative levels may appear a somewhat trite condition to impose, it is nevertheless technically necessary when employing a computer. Without it, a supply of a resource might be increased by bringing in at a negative level an activity that required that resource. Or again, the value in the objective function might be increased by bringing in at negative levels activities like fodder crops, whose variable costs represent negative net revenues.

To recapitulate in less formal terms, linear programming seeks the combination of activities that maximises the value of the objective function, while paying due regard to the constraints imposed on them.

Disposal activities. As inequalities are not readily handled, disposal activities (also variously called 'slack variables' and 'difference factors') are introduced, one into each inequality. Their role is to absorb the excess, if any, of resources available over resources used, so that each inequality can be expressed as an equation. It follows that one unit of a disposal activity represents one unit of an unused resource.

For example, if l_i is the disposal activity for one hour of spring labour

[1] In addition, 'greater than or equal to' ($\geq$) constraints may sometimes be required, and so may equalities (see Chapter 18, p. 440).

[2] In the linear programming matrix it is usual for the two sides of the expression to change places. If b_i is the constraint on the ith row of a matrix and a_{ij} represents the demands made upon it by one unit of the activity in the jth column, instead of:

$$a_{ij} \leq b_i$$

we have in the linear programming matrix:

$$b_i \geq a_{ij}.$$

and l_{ii} for one hour of summer labour, the former inequalities become:

Spring labour (hours): $7.5p + 3.75w + li = 412.5$
Summer labour (hours): $2.5p + 5w + lii = 325$

and the values in the optimal solution are:

Spring labour (hours): $(7.5 \times 35) + (3.75 \times 40) + (1 \times 0) = 412.5$
Summer labour (hours): $(2.5 \times 35) + (5 \times 40) + (1 \times 37.5) = 325$

Whereas spring labour is entirely consumed by potatoes and wheat so that its disposal activity is at zero level, that for summer labour takes up the $37\frac{1}{2}$ hours spare at that time, so keeping both sides of the equation in balance.

Data input – layout of linear programming matrix

In the matrix, relationships between resources and activities on the farm are translated into a form suitable for processing by linear programming. The first part of Table 15.1 shows a common layout. The activities head the matrix and since the first entry is their contribution to the objective function, the latter constitutes the first row (although an alternative format is for it to be the last row). The levels of resources and constraints appear in the first column of figures (known as the *B* column), while the input requirements and output contributions of the activities appear in the body of the matrix.[1,2] As the disposal activities are formed automatically in the computer (from instructions given in the program), the matrix builder does not have to write them in explicitly and they are thus excluded from the table. The matrix can be interpreted either vertically or horizontally. Reading down a column shows the amalgam of resources and constraints required by a particular activity together with any output from it, while reading across a row shows the demand and supply situation in respect of a given resource or constraint.

The second part of Table 15.1 illustrates this matrix layout with some of the data from the programme planning example (Table 14.4).

[1] As will be seen in Chapter 18, in addition to those activities that simply consume resources there may be others which supply or transfer resources or commodities.

[2] The size of the matrix is specified as $m \times n$ where m is the number of rows and n the number of columns. The resources and other constraints make up a column vector of m rows (the *B* column), while the values in the objective function make up a row vector of n columns. The input–ouput matrix by which they are linked thus has as many rows as there are constraints and as many columns as there are activities.

TABLE 15.1. *Layout of linear programming matrix*

1. *Outline layout*

	ACTIVITIES producing, selling, buying, transferring
	OBJECTIVE FUNCTION net revenues made up of gross margins, partial gross margins, variable costs, prices
RESOURCES and CONSTRAINTS Land Labour Capital Personal Institutional Husbandry	INPUT–OUTPUT MATRIX resources or constraints consumed or supplied per unit of each activity

2. *Layout with example data*

		WHEAT	BARLEY	WBEANS	SBEANS	SBEETR	SBEETC	POTS	SOWS
	0	310	250	240	205	600	590	580	102
LAND	120	1	1	1	1	1	1	1	0
LAB SP	1,003	2.5	7.5	0	8.75	10	10	25	3
LAB ES	1,320	0	0	0	0.75	30	10	3.75	3
LAB LS	1,240	5	5	6.25	3	0	0	1.25	3
LAB AU	930	10	0	12.5	0	25	25	50	3
MX CER	90	1	1	0	0	0	0	0	0
MX WHT	48	1	0	0	0	0	0	0	0
MX LEG	24	0	0	1	1	0	0	0	0
MX SBT	10	0	0	0	0	1	1	0	0
MX POT	12	0	0	0	0	0	0	1	0
MX SOW	20	0	0	0	0	0	0	0	1

It is necessary to label the rows and columns so that they can be identified in the solution. The present example is based on a program which permits letters – occupying not more than six spaces – to be used, which makes for easy identification. Other programs may allow only figures to be used for labelling, which may be carried out automatically in the computer. The data are fed into the computer either in rows or columns, usually on punched paper tape or punched cards.

A valuable feature of most programs is that they permit the 'over-writing' of coefficients in the matrix, so that more than one solution can be obtained from the same computer output. The data for the original matrix are fed into the computer together with the data that are to be substituted. Having obtained a solution from the former, the computer substitutes the fresh data and calculates further solutions. Solutions obtained in this way from revised matrices can be used to test the effects of changes in prices, in resource levels, in techniques or any combination of the three. It may often be preferable to break the process down into two stages, so that substitutions are made only after perusal of the solution to the original matrix. When this is so, there is no need to recalculate the original matrix when returning it to the computer with the substitute data.

Computations (Simplex method)[1]

The first stage in the computations consists of adding disposal activities, each representing one unit of a constraint, to the data fed in from the matrix (the 'real' activities). Marginal value products (see Appendix 13.3) – all of which are zero at this stage, because no resources are exhausted – are formed for each disposal activity. Similarly, 'net marginal opportunity costs' (see Appendix 15.1 below) are expressed for each real activity, taking, at this stage, the same values as those in the objective function, but with signs reversed.

This is the 'first feasible solution' which, with all resources idle, forms the starting point for subsequent calculations. These proceed stage by stage on somewhat similar lines to those illustrated in the potato/wheat mix and programme planning examples in Chapters 13 and 14 respectively. Each stage (iteration) represents a new solution that leads to an increase in total net revenue, and results either from the introduction of new activities or from changes in the levels of activities that have been brought in previously. An incoming activity replaces the resource which limits it the most, so that the latter becomes expressed in terms

[1] A worked example is demonstrated in Appendix 15.1.

of that activity.[1] In this way, marginal rates of product substitution are calculated, as are marginal rates of factor substitution for those resources not so replaced (or which replace other resources). Thus coefficients in the input–output matrix, at each iteration, represent the changes in the level of resources, and of those activities already in the solution, that will occur if one unit of an activity is introduced. Marginal value products and net marginal opportunity costs continue to be calculated, the activity that adds the highest value (per unit) to net revenue being selected as the next to be introduced at each stage. Finally, when no more positive gains are to be had, computations are brought to a halt.

Computer output and its interpretation

An example of computer print-out – that is, the solution to a problem – is shown in Table 15.2 for the programme planning example from Table 14.7 (with which it may be compared). Commonly, some or all of the following information is included (the numbering coincides with that in the table):

1. Total farm net revenue.
2. The levels of those activities included in the solution.
3. The quantities that remain of partially used (or unused) resources.
4. The amount of change necessary in the net revenues of excluded activities for them to merit inclusion in the solution – assuming no changes in any other coefficients. For example, the net revenue of sugar beet (casual) would need to increase by £10 per ha (from £590 to £600), when it would be at the same level as sugar beet (regular).
5. The marginal value products of those resources or constraints that are fully utilised in the solution – assuming all other coefficients are unchanged, e.g., an extra hectare of land permits another £189.1 net revenue to be generated, or an extra hour of autumn labour, another £6.9.
6. The amount by which the net revenue of each activity included in the solution can rise or fall (taken on its own and with all other coefficients unchanged) before new solutions with respectively more or less of that activity are necessary, if farm net revenue is to be maximised. For example, if the net revenue of sugar beet (regular) falls by more than £10 per ha, it should be eliminated and replaced by sugar beet

[1] Consequently, there cannot be more activities in the final solution than there are constraints in the matrix.

TABLE 15.2. *Example of computer print-out*[a]

FPC/120/4MEN				
NO.ITNS		8		
RETURN	①	38910.9091		
BASIS		AMOUNT	RANGE	
ACTIVITIES				
WHEAT	②	25.2727	−22.8291	15.0000
BARLEY	②	64.7273	−15.0000	22.8293
SBEANS	②	12.6545	−33.4285	45.8824
SBEETR	②	10.0000	−10.0000	NO LIMIT
POTS	②	7.3455	−75.0000	585.0000
SOWS	②	20.0000	−75.8182	NO LIMIT
			⑥	
RESOURCES				
LAB ES	③	922.9636		
LAB LS	③	682.8545		
MX WHT	③	22.7273		
MX LEG	③	11.3455		
MX POT	③	4.6545		
NOT IN BASIS		AMOUNT	RANGE	
ACTIVITIES				
WBEANS	④	35.4545		
SBEETC	④	10.0000		
RESOURCES				
LAND	⑤	189.0909	−10.4400	9.3600
LAB SP	⑤	1.8182	−187.5000	192.0000
LAB AU	⑤	6.9091	−605.9995	384.0000
MX CER	⑤	47.2727	−11.0118	12.2824
MX SBT	⑤	220.0000	−10.0000	18.9818
MX SOW	⑤	75.8182	−20.0000	67.3333
			⑦	

[a] Obtained from program prepared by G. B. Aneuryn-Evans.

(casual), whose net revenue is assumed to be unchanged. On the other hand, the net revenue of sugar beet (regular) can rise indefinitely (NO LIMIT) without requiring a change in its level, because it is already at its maximum in the plan. Another example is given by potatoes, whose net revenue can fall by £75 per ha (to £505) or rise by £585 (to £1165) without their present selected level of 7.3 ha changing.

7. The number of units of each fully used resource (taken in isolation) that can be added to or subtracted from its availability in the plan, before its marginal value product – as indicated in the solution – would change (because of the exhaustion of a resource that is not limiting in the solution). For example, 10.4 ha of land could be subtracted from, or 9.4 ha added to, the present 120 ha with no change in the marginal value product of land of £189 per hectare.

The first five items are normally available as part of the general linear programming routine (they form part of the final iteration of the computations) and it is only necessary to retrieve them, by instructing the computer to include them in the print-out. By contrast, the last two require additional calculations to be performed, and whether they are available therefore depends on the degree of sophistication of the program.

The interpretation and use of these various categories of data may be briefly considered.

Total farm net revenue (1). This is often the same as total farm gross margin, with profit derived by deducting the fixed costs (mainly the cost of supplying and servicing the resources). However, it is possible for some, even all, of the fixed costs to be included as buying activities in the matrix, so that total net revenue and total gross margin no longer correspond.

The level of activities in the solution (2). Certain adjustments are usually necessary to activity levels in the solution, which should in any case be regarded only as a guide to the future development of the farm. First, as shown in Table 15.2, the computer may print the activity levels to several places of decimals (necessary to avoid cumulative errors building up during the computations), which therefore require rounding up or down (the programme planning solution in Table 14.7 shows the effect of assuming integral quantities). Secondly, and more importantly, some activities may come in at trivial levels or at levels that do not consitute logical units, so that quite large changes in the solution may be required.[1]

Scarce and plentiful resources (3, 5 and 7). Taken together, items 3, 5 and 7 distinguish those resources that are plentiful from those that are scarce

[1] See pp. 366–7 for discussion of how such manifestations of the 'integer' problem may be treated.

and thus limit the further development of the solution. They may suggest that some resources in excess supply could with advantage be discarded or contracted while others, being scarce, should if possible be used in a more technically efficient manner, or perhaps be expanded in the longer term. In the latter case, the higher the level of the marginal value product of a scarce resource (5) in relation to the cost of acquiring more of it, the greater the likelihood of such acquisition being worthwhile. This likelihood is further increased if the range in its marginal value product (7) indicates that a large amount could be added before its marginal value product would start to fall (as it must, because as more and more is added, the stage is eventually reached where it ceases to be scarce and its marginal value product falls to zero). For example, the small 'sideline' unit of 20 sows producing weaners for sale in the solution in Table 15.2, could be completely eliminated or increased by 67 sows without changing the marginal value product of £76 per sow.[1] This suggests that it might be worthwhile for the farmer to expand it into a specialised unit of, say 80 sows, replacing one of the arable workers by a stockman. To discover the full effect of such reorganisation – which would include a reduction in the area of root crops – another solution would have to be obtained, with three arable workers instead of four and with 80 sows permitted.

If all the major resources in a solution are fully utilised and their marginal value products are low, the implication is that a sound balance has been achieved between the different resources with regard to the opportunities available.

Marginal value products can also be used to determine whether the inclusion of some activity not put in the original matrix can be justified. If the net revenue of such an activity is capable of covering the sum of the products of its requirements of scarce resources and their respective marginal value products, its inclusion will add to the total net revenue, although replanning is required to discover what changes are needed in the original solution in order to accommodate it. Suppose in our example that second-early potatoes are being considered. Of the fully used resources, each hectare of second-earlies needs one hectare land and 25 hours of spring labour, there being a sufficiency of labour at other times, as well as 4.6 ha of potato quota to spare. Their

[1] This is less than the net revenue of £102 per sow, because the opportunity cost of a sow's labour requirement is charged, namely, 3 hours of spring labour at £1.82 and 3 hours of autumn labour at £6.91 = £26.

inclusion would be justified, providing their net revenue amounted to at least £234.6 per hectare [(1 × £189.09) + (25 × £1.82)].

Objective function values (4 and 6). Both the increases required in the net revenues of excluded activities for them to justify a place in the solution (4), and the size of the changes in net revenues of included activities that necessitate alterations in their levels if farm net revenue is to be maximised (6), are calculated on the assumption that all other values except the one under consideration remain unchanged. They thus need to be interpreted with caution, for long-term price changes of single commodities in isolation are unlikely to occur very often. With this caveat in mind, they do to a limited extent indicate the relative stability of the solution in the face of changing prices. If large changes in values are required to bring about a change in the solution, stability is suggested, while small changes suggest instability. The latter further indicate that there are other (sub-optimal) solutions where, although activity levels are different, total net revenues will be almost the same as that of the optimal solution. In consequence, if the matrix were re-run with the relevant price changes incorporated in turn, a choice of several solutions would be made available.

A further point is that where large changes in net revenues are needed to induce new plans, there can be greater confidence that, even if their values were uncertain in the first place, the solution will nevertheless be the same as that obtaining if the true values had been known and incorporated (providing the latter are not too widely different from the values actually assumed).

Theoretical considerations

The assumptions underlying much of planning – linearity, divisibility, independence, single-valued expectations and short-term, static situations (Appendix 13.4) are all relevant to linear programming, particularly as they are built into the matrix before planning starts and thus inevitably influence the solution. In consequence, it is necessary to consider ways in which they can be modified when they are not thought to give a fair representation of a particular planning situation.

Linearity. Non-linear rates of transformation or substitution between factors or products, arising from the law of diminishing returns (variable proportions) or from scale effects, can be dealt with by representing discrete points on their functions as activities in the matrix. For example, suppose there is the following relationship between increasing intensity of labour use and the output per ha of a hypothetical product X:

1 HECTARE PRODUCT X	
Total units of labour input	*Total units of output*
1	5
2	8
3	10
4	11

Such a function, demonstrating diminishing returns to labour, can be shown in the matrix as four separate activities, as follows (with output valued at £10 per unit):

Product:	X_1	X_2	X_3	X_4
Net revenue (£)	50	80	100	110
Land (hectares)	1	1	1	1
Labour (units)	1	2	3	4

If the product came into the solution, X_1 would be selected if labour was critically short in relation to land and X_4 if land was critically short relative to labour. X_2 and X_3 represent 'compromise' positions with respect to the use of land and labour.

Exactly the same treatment applies when the concern is more with variable proportions, as exemplified in the example of beef production in Table 9.1 (p. 204), where successive additions of given quantities of silage to the diet replace decreasing amounts of concentrates. Allowing for the two different weight gains of 68 kg and 91 kg, each with four alternative rations, eight beef production activities would be required to represent the situation.

This method of taking discrete points on functions only approximates to the smooth, continuous curves of theory. For instance, in the beef production example, the optimal ration might lie between those specified in the matrix and similarly with the optimal weight gain. However, there are many occasions when such treatment accords closely with conditions on the farm and, in any case, the paucity of suitable response data renders even this simplified approach uncommon.

Representing a function as a number of separate activities fails, however, to provide a workable solution when there are increasing returns (or decreasing costs). This is demonstrated by the dairy herd example (p. 477), where hours per cow fall from 7.50 to 6.25 as herd size doubles from 20 to 40 cows. If, with labour scarce, 20 cows entered the solution, half the 40-cow unit would be selected in preference to the 20-cow unit (because of the divisibility assumption), thus falsely appearing to economise on labour. In consequence, it becomes necessary either to run the matrix more than once, each time forcing in a different herd size, or to use the approximation procedure outlined on p. 478.

Divisibility (continuity). The assumption that resources and activities are divisible into infinitesimally small units often causes no particular problems, other than the need to make minor adjustments in the solution to bring activities to integral levels. In other cases, however, it may lead to illogical solutions. This is because it is impossible to instruct the computer that an activity must either enter the solution at a specific level or else be excluded; for example, that there should be a unit of 60 cows or none at all.[1] Similarly, activities in the matrix that permit resources such as labour, buildings and machinery to be acquired if needed, cannot be made to do so in whole units. Again, it is impossible to constrain the matrix so that, if one particular activity is selected, another is not included. The latter is a problem that often occurs when an enterprise is subdivided into one or more alternative activities, representing different methods of production, as with pork, bacon and heavy hog production or with milk production from high-yielding, concentrate-fed cows as opposed to lower-yielding, bulk-fed cows.

In cases where it is necessary to assume one out of a choice of several specific sizes for an activity, a solution is first obtained in which it is free to find its own level. It may happen that the latter coincides with requirements or is close enough to need only minor adjustments. If not, two more solutions are obtained, in which the activity is forced in at integral levels that bracket the original value. As an illustration, suppose that in the previous dairy herd example – where there must be 60 cows or none – 57 cows were introduced in the first solution. This could probably be rounded to 60 with no particular difficulty. If it were 37 cows, however, the matrix would be run twice more, once excluding cows and once forcing in 60. The difference in the fixed costs of the

[1] It is possible to insist on minimum or specific levels of activity, but this gives rise to inflexibility in those cases where an optimal solution would have excluded the activity.

two plans could then be compared with the difference in their net revenues, in order to decide which plan was best.

Independence (additivity). Many examples arise on farms of enterprises which are not independent of one another. Perhaps the most obvious case is the way in which different crops interlock in rotations or the way different classes of livestock may combine to make better use of grazing. Or interdependence may simply arise because the farmer insists that if one activity is introduced then another must be brought in as well. For example, if bacon production comes into the plan, weaner production must also be included.

One way in which this problem can be handled is to combine the enterprises concerned into a single activity, as exemplified by the compounding of rotations (pp. 451–3). Another method, which, however, establishes only a 'one-way' relationship, is to leave them as separate enterprises, but to link them so that one cannot be introduced unless the other has first entered the solution. For example, wheat may be made dependent on non-cereal crops entering the solution, but the latter are not dependent on wheat.

Single-valued expectations. The linear programming solution is obtained using exact, not probabilistic, data. However, as discussed in Chapter 16 (pp. 384–9) and in Chapter 18 (pp. 487–90), it is possible to take account of uncertainty in an *ad hoc* fashion, which may accord quite closely with the farmer's own reactions to it. Solutions obtained in this way, however, although more likely to be acceptable to the farmer, may not be optimal, because the use of a probabilistic model might have resulted in the same net revenue with less risk, or a greater net revenue with the same risk. It follows that in planning situations where there is a high degree of uncertainty – as on horticultural holdings – it may be desirable to use a model incorporating risk and uncertainty (see Chapter 17), providing that both the necessary data and the facilities to enable it to be applied are available.

Short-term, static solutions. The large element of fixed resources usually incorporated in the linear programming matrix means that relatively short-term situations are being studied. When solutions are not widely different from the current farm organisation, they may represent the farmer's problems adequately. When, however, they differ widely, several years may be required to attain the suggested organisation, as is true of longer-term planning in general. In such circumstances, it may be preferable to use a technique in which a dynamic element is incorporated (see Chapters 13, 14 and 17).

Evaluation of linear programming

Linear programming may be appraised under two heads. The first concerns its inherent characteristics as a planning technique. The second concerns its characteristics as a practical planning tool, in short, its operational feasibility.

Linear programming as a planning technique

One of the main advantages of linear programming, compared with the other methods of planning so far considered, is that complex situations can be studied in a more comprehensive and realistic manner (particularly when 'over-writing' techniques are available, see p. 359), because computations are carried out by the computer and not by the planner. For example, a given problem may be studied in greater depth, as when, in planning a livestock farm, a whole range of potential feedstuffs is included, instead of the simplifying assumption being made of a set pattern of feeding, which may be unavoidable with budgeting and programme planning. Or again, a far greater range of plans may be encompassed by changing the assumptions in respect of resource availability, prices and input–output coefficients, because of the ease with which fresh data can be incorporated and new solutions obtained. In this way, the farmer can gain a general picture of the lines along which his farm might develop, instead of just a single solution based on present resources and practices.

Linear programming also gives a greater degree of objectivity than simpler techniques. Admittedly, personal bias may become incorporated in the planning coefficients – indeed, this may be necessary as far as the attitudes of the farmer are concerned – but once the matrix has been set up, the solution is quite independent of the planner. This frequently results in interesting and unanticipated possibilities coming to light in the solution, which would not even have been contemplated in the normal course of events. Greater objectivity is also likely to be applied in the process of collecting and analysing data for the construction of the matrix, because issues have to be faced which might be glossed over in other methods of planning. For example, the need to specify labour availability and requirements on arable farms, means that this aspect is more likely to be critically reviewed than would otherwise be the case. At the same time, the task of formally assembling planning data can be a salutary exercise for the farmer, because it shows him just how much he does and does not know of the many resource–enterprise relationships on his farm which may be vital to successful business management.

A further advantage of linear programming is that it produces a unique, optimal solution, whereas budgeting is unlikely to do so and programme planning is likely to do so only in simpler cases. However, this is a benefit that can easily be overstated. The first reason for this is that the solution is optimal only in terms of the efficiency with which the matrix has been constructed and the accuracy of the data. Secondly, solutions should not be interpreted too literally, but rather should be used as signposts to potential developments (in practice, it would be exceptional for a first solution to be adopted in its entirety). Thirdly, there are likely to be other solutions that may differ quite fundamentally from the optimal solutions, but which have almost as high a total net revenue and which may be more acceptable to the farmer (perhaps because they involve less change or are considered less risky). There is thus the danger that the optimal solution may blind the planner to other potential avenues of development. Finally, the optimal solution may not be optimal in terms of profit, because it is net revenue that is being maximised. This may result in an activity entering the solution at a level that does not cover its specific fixed costs, such as those of specialised machinery.

As has already been seen (pp. 360–2), the output from linear programming includes additional data, such as marginal value products, quite apart from the 'standard' solution showing activity levels and total net revenue (or gross margin with simpler techniques). Although such extra information has to be interpreted carefully, it may be useful in suggesting the lines along which further development might take place and the fact that it is available can thus be counted as an advantage.

The validity of some of the assumptions of linear programming (which are common, in part at least, to most other techniques) has already been discussed (pp. 364–8), together with the measures that may be needed on occasion to overcome their shortcomings. Although such measures may successfully meet the situation, they nevertheless lead to greater complexity and size of matrix and may require it to be run several times. However, this must not be over-emphasised for, in practice, such adjustments are frequently unnecessary. Admittedly, this may be partly because sufficiently detailed and reliable data are not available for problems to arise, a point that leads us on to consider linear programming in the context of a practical planning tool.

Linear programming and operational feasibility

One of the main arguments raised against linear programming as a practical planning tool is that it calls for a large volume of very precise data which are unlikely to be available on the individual farm. While neither the problem of lack of data nor the ability of the computer to handle large amounts can be questioned, this does not mean that a large volume of data *has* to be handled, nor is there any valid reason why the data should be more accurate than those used in other methods of planning. Not unnaturally, the availability of the computer may encourage the planner to use more data, if only to avoid the simplifications necessary with 'hand' techniques. Also, the first step is usually to assemble the data – a process that may give the impression that linear programming therefore needs more data than other simpler techniques – whereas with the latter, some may be held in abeyance until a later stage. For example, in gross margin planning, labour supply and demand are often ignored during the process of selecting enterprises, the feasibility of labour-use in the solution being checked afterwards. If enterprise requirements exceed the labour available, further planning has to be carried out. Although there is no reason why linear programming should not be used in exactly the same way, it is normal practice to include the labour data at the start, so that it follows that the solution is kept within the bounds of feasibility.

This is not to imply that linear programming is a technique that should be used irrespective of the amount of data to be handled. If only a relatively small amount of data is required to express a problem realistically, techniques such as partial budgeting may be more appropriate.[1]

Since linear programming is a computer technique that requires a specialised knowledge of matrix building, a formal organisation is necessary if it is to be operated as a planning service. The steps involved include the collection, analysis and verification of data, setting them up in matrix form, transforming them into computer input and processing by computer. The subsequent output then has to be interpreted and put in a form suitable for the final step, namely, the communication of solutions to the farmer. One requirement, if these operations are to be performed, is access to a computer laboratory with suitably trained staff, which is not likely to be a problem (in

[1] Although there is a danger that what appears at first sight to be a simple planning problem may turn out to have far-reaching implications for the organisation of the whole farm, and therefore justify comprehensive planning methods.

developed countries, at least). Another requirement is an organisation for the handling of data both before and after processing by the computer, and it is here that the biggest difficulties are likely to arise. Data handling calls for expertise of two types in particular. One is in the province of the 'field adviser' who, in addition to the ability to communicate with farmers, needs to be familiar with farming and its problems, the data that are required to enable problems to be solved, and alternative sources of data when those on the farm require supplementing. The other concerns the matrix builder, who requires the necessary skills to translate farm data into realistic models.[1] These two aspects are not, however, mutually exclusive. The matrix builder is more likely to set up realistic models if he has a fair knowledge of circumstances on the farm. The field adviser is better equipped if he has some knowledge of how the matrix has been set up, particularly if he has to explain to the farmer *why* the computer has selected a certain organisation as optimal. Ideally, therefore, these tasks should be performed by the same individual, although the number of cases that could then be handled is likely to be reduced. This leads to another factor, namely, the extent to which farmers are prepared to accept plans in which they have been little involved, beyond discussing the problem and supplying the data. Cases certainly occur where farmers are reluctant to accept solutions, although they are based on constraints and relationships to which they have previously assented. In part, at least, this may arise because they are insufficiently aware of the implications of the model, a problem likely to be accentuated if matrix construction is an operation remote from the farm.

There is also the question of time and cost, a relatively small part of which is concerned with actual computer processing in linear programming. Any form of comprehensive, whole-farm planning, whether carried out by linear programming, programme planning or by setting up a number of complete budgets, is bound to be time-consuming, although as experience is gained – particularly of the problems on specific types of farm – the time required for the planning process (including matrix construction) can be considerably reduced. However,

[1] The 'MASCOT' system, operated by the Farm Advisory Service of the Agricultural Division of I.C.I., includes a computer program (Matrix Generator) that automatically sets up farm data in the form of a linear programming matrix, thus eliminating the need to construct a separate matrix for each individual farm case. A less sophisticated way of achieving this is to establish standardised matrices representative of specific farm types, into which the relevant data for individual farms are inserted.

in general, comprehensive planning cannot be had 'on the cheap'. Consequently, even if the use of linear programming should prove more costly, its advantages are likely to justify the extra expense.

Representative farms and management objectives

In areas where there is reasonable homogeneity in at least some of the major resources – particularly with respect to natural factors, such as soil type, topography and climate – linear programming can be used to obtain solutions to 'modal' or 'representative' farm situations, in order to guide planning on individual farms.[1] In this way some of the benefits of comprehensive computer planning can be made available to a greater number of farmers in an area than would be the case with the individual programming of farms.

Since farms are likely to display considerable variation around a particular modal situation (when account is taken of both quantitative and qualitative aspects of farm resources), more than one model is required if differences in factors such as farm size, the number of workers and the availability of buildings are to be accommodated. Once a basic model has been constructed, however, use of the 'over-writing' technique (p. 359) permits the rapid calculation of solutions covering a whole range of situations.

This is not to imply that the availability of such solutions makes individual farm planning unnecessary. Instead they provide a basis for the formulation of 'management objectives' that complement, rather than substitute for, individual planning. In short, use is made of the inferences drawn from modal solutions and not the solutions themselves.

More specifically, management objectives can assist in planning with simpler techniques on the individual farm, in that they may:

1. Suggest profitable ways of allocating resources in the short term.
2. Suggest potential paths of development in the longer term (by a comparison of models in which resources and opportunities vary).
3. Distinguish resources likely to prove limiting from those which are not, and which can, therefore, be excluded when planning.
4. Distinguish activities which usually enter solutions from those which do not, and which need not, therefore, be considered in planning.

[1] Given the necessary agencies to undertake the work, such as universities or Government advisory services.

5. Give greater confidence that simplification (carried out on the basis of 3 and 4 above) is less likely to lead to unrealistic or sub-optimal solutions, because it is based on the outcomes of comprehensive models.

6. Widen the vision of farmers and advisers by suggesting lines of development that would not otherwise have been contemplated.

Appendix 15.1: Example of stages in linear programming computations

The linear programming computations in Table 15.3 are based on the potato/wheat mix example in Chapter 13 (pp. 292–9), with which they may be compared. Barley has been added as a third activity, but as it never enters the solution the stages here are the same as those in Chapter 13.

The table shows the outcome of the computations at each stage. It does not show the additional computations on which they are based. Signs are to be interpreted as follows. In the *Z–C* row, positive signs indicate a potential reduction in net revenue, and negatives a potential gain. In the body of the matrix, positive signs indicate either a resource required or reduction in an activity already in the plan. Negatives indicate either a resource saved or expansion of an activity already in the plan.

First feasible solution

This consists of the data from the matrix with the addition of a disposal activity for each constraint and with two extra rows, the *Z* row and the *Z–C* row. For disposal activities, both the latter show the marginal value products of scarce resources, that is the gain or loss of sacrificing (putting into disposal or non-use) one unit of a fully used resource. For real activities, the *Z* row shows marginal opportunity costs and the *Z–C* row net marginal opportunity costs, the latter indicating the net gain or loss of introducing one unit of activity.

Since at this stage all resources are idle (in disposal) the marginal value products are all zeros. Nor are any of the real activities being operated, so the *Z–C* row simply shows their net revenues with negative signs (that is the net revenue to be gained if one unit is introduced).

To move to the second feasible solution, the activity with the greatest negative value in the *Z–C* row is introduced up to its maximum. This is potatoes (−720).

TABLE 15.3. *Stages in linear programming* (Simplex procedure)

	Resources and constraints		B	Land (1 hectare)	Spring labour (1 hr)	Summer labour (1 hr)	Working capital (£1)	Potato quota (1 hectare)	Potatoes (1 hectare)	Wheat (1 hectare)	Barley (1 hectare)
	C (£ net revenue)			0	0	0	0	0	720	400	350
				Disposal activities					Real activities		
	1st feasible solution										
	Land	(hectares)	75	1	0	0	0	0	1	1	1
	Spring labour	(hours)	412.5	0	1	0	0	0	7.5	3.75	7.5
	Summer labour	(hours)	325	0	0	1	0	0	2.5	5	5
	Working capital	(£)	20,000	0	0	0	1	0	400	100	85
	Potato quota	(hectares)	48	0	0	0	0	1	1	0	0
	Z (MVP or marginal opportunity cost)	(£)	0	0	0	0	0	0	0	0	0
	Z–C (MVP or net marginal opp. cost)	(£)	0	0	0	0	0	0	–720	–400	–350
	2nd feasible solution										
	Land	(hectares)	27	1	0	0	0	–1	0	1	1
	Spring labour	(hours)	52.5	0	1	0	0	–7.5	0	3.75	7.5
	Summer labour	(hours)	205	0	0	1	0	–2.5	0	5	5
	Working capital	(£)	800	0	0	0	1	–400	0	100	85
720	Potatoes	(hectares)	48	0	0	0	0	1	1	0	0
	Z	(£)	34,560	0	0	0	0	720	720	0	0
	Z–C	(£)	34,560	0	0	0	0	720	0	–400	–350
	3rd feasible solution										
	Land	(hectares)	19	1	0	0	–0.01	3	0	0	0.15
	Spring labour	(hours)	22.5	0	1	0	–0.375	7.5	0	0	4.312
	Summer labour	(hours)	165	0	0	1	–0.05	17.5	0	0	0.75
400	Wheat	(hectares)	8	0	0	0	0.01	–4	0	1	0.85

720	Potatoes	(hectares)	48	0	0	0	0	1	1	0	0
	Z	(£)	37,760	0	0	0	4	−880	720	400	340
	Z−C	(£)	37,760	0	0	0	4	−880	0	0	−10
	4th feasible solution										
	Land	(hectares)	10	1	−0.4	0	0.005	0	0	0	−1.75
	Potato quota	(hectares)	3	0	0.133	0	−0.005	1	0	0	0.75
	Summer labour	(hours)	112.5	0	−0.1	1	0.038	0	0	0	−10.625
400	Wheat	(hectares)	20	0	0.533	0	−0.01	0	0	1	3.5
720	Potatoes	(hectares)	45	0	−0.133	0	0.005	0	1	0	−0.75
	Z	(£)	40,400	0	117.33	0	−0.4	0	720	400	860
	Z−C	(£)	40,400	0	117.33	0	−0.4	0	0	0	510
	5th feasible solution										
	Working capital	(£)	2,000	200	−80	0	1	0	0	0	−315
	Potato quota	(hectares)	13	1	−0.26	0	0	1	0	0	−1
	Summer labour	(hours)	37.5	−7.5	0.66	1	0	0	0	0	2.5
400	Wheat	(hectares)	40	2	−0.26	0	0	0	0	1	0
720	Potatoes	(hectares)	35	−1	0.26	0	0	0	1	0	1
	Z	(£)	41,200	80	85.33	0	0	0	720	400	720
	Z−C	(£)	41,200	80	85.33	0	0	0	0	0	370

Second feasible solution

Potatoes are introduced up to the limit set by quota (48 ha) and overwrite the quota row. The *B* column shows the resources remaining to be 27 ha land, 52.5 hours spring labour, 205 hours summer labour and £800 capital. Total net revenue is £34,560 (48 ha × £720).

Coefficients in the potato quota disposal column (which is 'inactive' in that all potato quota is used and none is therefore in disposal) show the effect of making one ha of quota idle (i.e. putting it into disposal). One ha of potatoes is sacrificed at a cost (MVP) of £720, and with an addition to the 'pool' of unused resources of 1 ha land, 7.5 hours spring labour, 2.5 hours summer labour and £400 capital.

The highest negative value in the *Z–C* row is that of wheat (–400), which is therefore introduced to its limit in the next stage.

Third feasible solution

The working capital available in the previous stage (£800) limits wheat to 8 ha, and the working capital row becomes overwritten by wheat. In consequence, additions to or subtractions from the capital supply by the various activities are now expressed indirectly in terms of hectares of wheat.

The *B* column shows that with 8 ha of wheat and 48 ha of potatoes, net revenue is £37,760, and there are 19 ha of land, 22.5 hours of spring labour and 165 hours of summer labour to spare. As capital and quota are fully used they both have non-zero values in the *Z–C* row, as does barley, which is the only real activity that has not yet been introduced. The coefficients in these three activities are to be interpreted as follows:

Working capital. If £1 of the fully used capital is put into disposal, it is obtained by sacrificing 0.01 ha wheat (which requires £1 capital), valued at £4 (MVP). There is a consequent gain in unused resources of 0.01 ha land, 0.38 hours spring labour and 0.05 hours summer labour.

Potato quota. If 1 ha of potato quota is put into disposal, 1 ha of potatoes is sacrificed, so releasing sufficient capital (£400) for 4 ha of wheat to be grown, giving a net gain (MVP) of £880 [(4 ha wheat × £400) – (1 ha pots × £720)]. On balance, additional requirements of other resources are as follows:

Land: 3 hectares (4 ha wheat – 1 ha pots)
Spring labour: 7.5 hrs [(4 ha wheat × 3.75 hrs) – (1 ha pots × 7.5 hrs)]
Summer labour: 17.5 hrs [(4 ha wheat × 5 hrs) – (1 ha pots × 2.5 hrs)].

Barley. If 1 ha of barley is introduced, 0.85 ha of wheat are sacrificed to gain the necessary working capital, leading to a net gain ($Z-C$) of £10 [(1 ha barley × £350) – (0.85 ha wheat × £400)]. Additional amounts of other resources are required as follows:

Land: 0.15 hectares (1 ha barley – 0.85 ha wheat)
Spring labour: 4.31 hrs [(1 ha barley × 7.5 hrs) – (0.85 ha wheat × 3.75 hrs)]
Summer labour: 0.75 hrs [(1 ha barley × 5 hrs) – (0.85 ha wheat × 5 hrs)].

The highest negative $Z-C$ value is for potato quota (–880), indicating that some of it should be put to disposal in carrying out the substitution between potatoes and wheat shown above.

Fourth feasible solution

Spring labour limits the increase in wheat to 12 ha (total 20 ha) at the expense of 3 ha potatoes (total 45 ha). Net revenue is £40,400 and there are 10 ha land, 3 ha potato quota (which overwrite spring labour) and 112.5 hours summer labour to spare.

If 1 hour of spring labour is put to disposal, 0.133 ha potatoes are grown at the expense of 0.533 ha wheat, with a loss of £117.33 [(0.133 ha pots × £720) – (0.533 ha wheat × £400)].

Only working capital now displays a negative value in the $Z-C$ row, indicating that in the next stage it will be put into disposal, in the process of obtaining spring labour by sacrificing 0.005 ha potatoes for each 0.01 ha wheat gained.

Fifth feasible solution

Land limits the gain in wheat to 20 ha (40 ha in all) with the sacrifice of 10 ha potatoes (leaving 35 ha). Net revenue is £41,200, and there are small amounts of working capital, quota and summer labour to spare.

As there are now no negative values in the $Z-C$ row, no more gainful substitutions can be made and the optimal solution has been obtained.

Computer print-out

The minimum amount of data printed out in the usual form of output consists of the B column and the $Z-C$ row. If this is re-arranged and set up in the same form as in Table 15.2, it appears as follows:

RETURN	41,200
BASIS	AMOUNT
ACTIVITIES	
WHEAT	40
POTS	35
RESOURCES	
LAB SM	37.5
CAPITAL	2,000
QUOTA	13
NOT IN BASIS	AMOUNT
ACTIVITIES	
BARLEY	370
RESOURCES	
LAND	80
LAB SP	85.33

Appendix 15.2: The hand calculations

The calculations needed to carry out linear programming 'by hand' are illustrated by the example given in Table 15.3, changing from the 2nd matrix (feasible solution, stage or iteration) to the 3rd. We will call the former the 'old' matrix and the latter the 'new' matrix.

At each iteration:

1. Check whether there are any activities with a negative $Z-C$; if there are, the plan with the highest possible total net revenue (TNR) has not yet been obtained.
2. If more than one activity has a negative $Z-C$, the one with the largest negative $Z-C$ is selected (Wheat: 400).
3. Calculate an extra column, R, for the old matrix. In this, the figure in each row is obtained by dividing the figure in the B column by the coefficient in the selected activity column, e.g. Land: $27 \div 1 = 27$; Spring labour: $52.5 \div 3.75 = 14$; Summer labour: $205 \div 5 = 41$; Working capital: $800 \div 100 = 8$; Potatoes $48 \div 0 =$ infinity. These figures represent the maximum amount of wheat that can be grown as determined by each constraint taken on its own.
4. Introduce the selected activity (wheat) into the next plan (iteration) at the maximum level permitted by the most limiting constraint

(working capital: 8 hectares). We shall refer to the 'outgoing column' (wheat in the 2nd iteration), the 'outgoing row' (working capital in the 2nd iteration) and the 'incoming row' (wheat in the 3rd iteration).

5. Recalculate all the coefficients, including the new B column (the level of real activities in the new plan and the resources remaining, i.e. the level of the disposal activities), the new $Z-C$ row and the new TNR.

This procedure is repeated until there are no negative Z–Cs in the matrix last produced.

The actual calculations required when changing from one matrix to the next are as follows:

(i) Divide each figure in the outgoing row (working capital) by the 'outgoing pivot', which is the figure where the outgoing row intersects the outgoing column (wheat): 100. This gives the incoming row (wheat).

(ii) Subtract from each figure in the old matrix the product of the figure in the same column in the incoming row and the figure in the same row in the outgoing column; (e.g. Spring labour for barley = $7.5 - (0.85 \times 3.75) = 4.312$).

(iii) The Z of each column activity in the new matrix is then found, by multiplying each coefficient in the column by the net revenue per unit of the activity to which the row relates, and summing the resulting figures; (e.g. for barley: $[0.85 \text{ (wheat)} \times 400] + [0 \text{ (potatoes)} \times 720] = 340$; the disposal activities can be ignored since their net revenues are zero).

(iv) The new $Z-C$ figures are then calculated; (e.g. barley, $340–350 = -10$). Alternatively, the $Z-C$ figures can be calculated using the formula given in (ii) above; (e.g. for barley: $-350 - (0.85 \times -400) = -10$); the Z figures then do not need to be calculated.

(v) The new TNR is found by multiplying the level of each activity by its net revenue per unit and summing the resulting figures; (e.g. wheat (8 × £400) + potatoes (48 × £720) = £37,760).

Appendix 15.3: The Basic equations

No attempt is made in the following to explain the matrix algebra used in linear programming.

For the sake of simplicity, let us assume that a plan is required with only two possible activities and two constraints. The matrix is as follows:

Activity:			*A*	*B*
Net revenues (£):			300	200
Constraints	Land (ha)	300	2	2
	Capital (£)	4,000	20	30

By using simultaneous equations a plan can be found that fully uses all resources, so that:

Use of land:	$2A + 2B$	$= 300$
Use of capital:	$20A + 30B$	$= 4000$
Objective function:	$300A + 200B$	$=$ TNR

where A = the number of units of A in the plan
and B = " " " " " B " " " .

There are three equations and three unknowns (A, B, TNR). There can therefore be only one (the 'unique') solution.

This is where $A = 50$ and $B = 100$. The TNR = £35,000.

However, if we are prepared to leave some resources unused, it can easily be observed that there is a plan giving a higher TNR. This is 150 units of A, which leaves 1000 units of capital unused but gives a TNR of £45,000.

To achieve this (as explained on pp. 356–7) we introduce disposal activities, which allow non-use of resources, into the equations. We then have:

Use of land:	$2A + 2B + 1L + 0C$	$= 300$
Use of capital:	$20A + 30B + 0L + 1C$	$= 4000$
Objective function:	$300A + 200B + 0L + 0C$	$=$ TNR

Where L = the number of units of land (left unused)
and C = " " " " " capital (" ").

We now have five unknowns and only three equations, which is described mathematically as a problem that is 'under-identified', i.e. there is no unique solution. The number of possible solutions is virtually infinite. Linear programming finds the one giving the highest TNR.

This is achieved using three sets of equations as follows (two have already been described on pp. 354–6):

(i) *The profit equation.* This gives the TNR (Z_0) of any plan. In the above example it was:

$$Z_0 = 300A + 200B + 0L + 0C = \text{TNR}.$$

(ii) *The production possibility equations.* These describe the constraints within which the maximum TNR plan must be obtained. In the above example these were:

$$2A + 2B + 1L + 0C = 300$$
$$20A + 30B + 0L + 1C = 4000$$

(iii) *The criterion equation.* This is the means by which we know whether the TNR of any given plan can be further increased (see Appendix 15.2). It compares Z (the opportunity cost) with C (the net revenue) of an activity. For barley in the 3rd feasible solution of Table 15.3 this is:

$$\begin{aligned} Z-C &= [(0.85 \times 400) + (0 \times 720)] - 350 \\ &= 340 - 350 = -10. \end{aligned}$$

If the $Z-C$ of an activity is negative, TNR can be increased by its selection; the greater the negative sum the greater the increase.

Thus linear programming maximises the profit equation, subject to the production possibility equations (i.e. the constraints), by means of the criterion equation.

16: Uncertainty and farm organisation and planning

A major feature of farm production, to which many references have already been made, is the lack of knowledge of the future levels of inputs, outputs and prices, not simply for some long distant point in time but often for only short periods ahead. Uncertainty is synonymous with imperfect knowledge and is reviewed in this chapter from two main aspects: first, how farmers may react to it in their efforts to run viable and long-surviving businesses and, secondly, how it may be accommodated in practical farm planning.

Imperfect knowledge and the farmer

The farmer is commonly regarded as having to bear a greater burden of uncertainty than managers in most other industries. Some indication of this is given by the high degree of variability in farm incomes from year to year. For example, an East Midlands study revealed that the incomes of individual farmers diverged annually by an average of plus or minus fifty per cent from their ten year mean.[1] As seen in Chapter 1, the main cause of such variation is the natural and biological element, both in farm resources and products, which results in many factors over which the farmer has little control.

However, by itself the high degree of variability in farming is only part of the problem, for if farmers knew in advance what variations were going to occur they would be better equipped to make the necessary allowances for them. The nub of the problem is that they are largely unpredictable, to a degree that depends both on the item under review – for example, future prices as compared with future yields – and on the breadth of experience and knowledge of the individual decision-maker – for instance, a beginner in farming as opposed to one who has run the same farm for many years. In consequence, measures taken to reduce variability also have an impact on the degree of uncertainty. For example, irrigating a crop in dry seasons to maintain

[1] Jones, R. B. (1969) 'Stability in Farm Incomes'. *Journal of Agricultural Economics*, **XX**, No. 1.

yields, while leaving unchanged the uncertainty of when such seasons will occur, reduces yield variability and thus also the level of yield uncertainty.

Attitudes to uncertainty, and profit maximisation

Profit maximisation (within the bounds imposed by relevant long-term constraints) would be a more adequate objective for farmers if they were indifferent to the problems arising from uncertainty. Indeed some farmers – particularly those with strong capital foundations to their businesses and a high average level of income – may show a preference for risk, by devoting a considerable proportion of their resources to projects with highly uncertain outcomes, where the very real possibility of failure is balanced by the chance of a high pay-off. Although farmers in general may occasionally commit a small part of their resources to such highly 'risky' projects, they tend rather to be 'risk-averse' in that they are prepared to sacrifice some of their profits to measures that help counter the potentially deleterious effects of uncertainty on their businesses. Such an attitude is quite understandable for, in addition to being faced with a high degree of uncertainty, there are many factors which reduce their ability to stand up to its consequences, thus exacerbating the problem. One is that they are usually the sole managers (and often owners) of their businesses, having to meet the full financial consequences of their decisions and actions. Another is that their businesses are often quite small, thus making it harder for them to acquire capital (by saving or by borrowing) to tide them over difficult periods. It also means that they are usually 'price-takers' for both the goods and services they purchase and the products they sell. Furthermore, a high proportion of their resources are relatively inflexible – for example, land, family labour and specialised forms of capital – and cannot readily be dispensed with or turned to other uses in tight situations. Finally, the family nature of much of farming makes farmers more aware of their social obligations towards providing the needs of their families, in addition to sustaining their farming operations.

Uncertainty thus leads to aims and behaviour different from those that would apply if farmers were simply profit-maximisers. Although, as already acknowledged, their reactions to uncertainty result largely from their innate and subjective judgement as individuals, survival is likely to rank high on their list of objectives, because if the business does not survive other objectives are rendered null and void. Broadly interpreted, survival implies the farmer's ability to meet his farm and personal commitments – with the emphasis on those that are unavoidable such as rent and income-tax – without depleting his capital resources, since that would lead to lowered earning power and profits in the future. In consequence, farmers may aim for plans that have a good chance of bringing in sufficient income to cover their commitments rather than ones which, while maximising profits, give a greater risk of income falling too low in some seasons. A closely linked aim is to reduce the degree of income variation from year to year, not only because a stable income is more easily equated with a fixed level of commitments, but also because financial planning and organisation are rendered less troublesome. Yet another aim is to strengthen the financial standing of the business so that it is more resilient in the face of difficult seasons or unexpected disasters.

The extent to which farmers deem it necessary to take action to ensure the survival of their businesses, depends (apart from their degree of risk aversion) on the interplay between the level of their capital reserves, on the one hand, and the likelihood of unfavourable events occurring, coupled with their relative severity, on the other. Thus action may be taken against events that appear potentially crippling to the business, even if their occurrence is likely to be remote, while nothing may be done about more frequently occurring events because their consequences appear relatively trivial. We now turn to consider the type of measures that farmers can take to protect their businesses, before considering how allowances can be made for them in farm planning.[1]

Dealing with uncertainty – measures to reduce variability and uncertainty in farm incomes

Selection of enterprises

The relative stability of farm income from year to year hinges largely on the enterprises selected, since they are the major cause of variation. Two points are relevant. First, the degree of variation between seasons (that is, the extent of deviation from mean outcome measured in physical or financial terms – see p. 396) differs from one enterprise to another. For example, on the whole, root crops are more variable than cereals, and pigs more variable than dairy cows. Thus farmers can achieve greater stability in farm income by concentrating on enterprises (alone or in combination) that vary little from year to year (so, conversely, excluding or keeping to a low level those that vary a lot).

[1] Although the emphasis is on measures concerned with enterprise combination, aspects of enterprise organisation are also included.

Secondly, enterprises do not necessarily respond in the same way to seasonal stimuli, either in direction or degree (as Figure 1.1. on p. 11 makes clear), so that farmers may combine them in the hope that if some perform badly in particular seasons, there will be others that perform well – or at least less badly.

Such diversification is at its most obvious when several enterprises are involved with their own distinct forms of output, for example, crops and livestock, or cereals and root crops, but it sometimes occurs as part of the technical process within individual enterprises. This is so in dairy herds where, in addition to milk, there are sales of unwanted calves, surplus heifers and cull cows: a relationship that the farmer may deliberately strengthen by selecting a dual purpose breed which evens out somewhat the respective contributions from milk and meat. A similar situation arises in those enterprises where there are distinct stages in the process which can be carried out on different farms. For example, a pig producer who elects to carry out both rearing and fattening removes the risk of income fluctuations through changes in weaner prices, to which the specialist rearer or fattener is subject. Diversified output also arises when there are 'joint products' such as mutton and wool, beef and hides, or cereal grain and straw. However, their value in stabilising income must not be exaggerated, since one part of the combined output (the first in the examples just quoted) usually constitutes a far greater proportion of total sales than the other. For instance, a high price for wool would do little to offset low lamb prices in a ewe flock.

In addition to its rôle in income stabilisation, diversification may be used as a measure of protection against occasional uncertain events whose occurrence would place heavy strains on the business. For example, a dairy specialist might add a poultry unit to his operations as a hedge against the possibility of his herd having to be destroyed because of an outbreak of foot and mouth disease.

Contract and futures trading

In theory, a forward contract to buy or sell at a 'fixed' price converts price uncertainty into price certainty. In fact, for selling, at least, this may be far from the case. Unavoidable variations in quality mean that prices actually to be received remain uncertain and, together with variations in yields, result in uncertain and variable receipts. Indeed, a forward contract may introduce its own uncertainty. For example, if a farmer contracts ahead to sell potatoes at a price based on 'normal' harvest yields and, in the event, actual yields turn out to be below average, he forgoes the compensatory effect on prices that farmers selling on the open market could reasonably expect. In short, he sells a below average yield at a price below average for that season.

Futures contracts offer a better hedge against such uncertainties because, being negotiable, they can be bought or sold at the prices currently ruling for such transactions. For example, a cereals producer who takes out a futures contract to sell grain can either let the contract mature and deliver the grain to a futures store or, conversely, dispose of the grain locally and cancel ('close out') the contract by buying a contract to receive grain.[1]

Dealing with uncertainty – measures to increase the resilience of the farm business

There are two closely related aspects to building resilience into the farm business in light of future uncertainties. The one – stability – is largely concerned with ways of ensuring that a particular pattern of farming can be maintained intact, while the other – flexibility – involves means of increasing the farmer's freedom to alter his existing system, so that he is not confined in a straitjacket where change is only possible at high cost.

Stability

Measures to stabilise the farm business cover a wide spectrum, ranging from those that are aimed simply at reducing the inherent variability of an existing system – and are mainly technical in nature – to those which, more importantly, seek to ensure that it can be carried on in spite of unfavourable chance events that might otherwise threaten its survival. For example, exceptional storm damage on a cereal farm, a serious outbreak of disease on a livestock holding, or a disastrous fire on either, might leave the farmer unable to meet his financial commitments, with the consequent risk that he could be forced out of business if his creditors should insist on prompt settlement. Various financial steps, which are mainly concerned with maintaining solvency, can be taken to buffer the farm against such eventualities.

Asset structure. As a longer-term measure of protection, the business may be 'geared' so that the farmer owns a major proportion of the capital, as opposed to that which is borrowed; while, against the

[1] See, for instance, Mackel, C. (1975) 'The Futures Market – a Key to Stable Grain Prices?' *Farm Management Review*, **No. 5**, Agricultural Economics Division, North of Scotland College of Agriculture.

sudden short-term emergency, a substantial part of the assets may be kept 'liquid', so that they can be turned into cash at relatively short notice. Both measures are discussed elsewhere in the book (pp. 73–4, 545–7). Here we simply acknowledge that an over-cautious approach to both gearing and liquidity may mean that a high price is paid in opportunities lost for further investment in the expansion or intensification of farm operations.

Borrowing. Rather than taking action in anticipation of unfavourable events, the farmer may wait instead until they have actually occurred and then rely on borrowing to meet any deficiencies. However, there is still a close link with the level of gearing and liquidity for, if the one is high and the other low, there may be difficulty in finding lenders (at least, at 'reasonable' rates of interest). Conversely, the larger a farmer's debt-free collateral, the riskier the plans that he can afford to adopt.

Formal insurance. Yet another measure is to transfer the costs arising from such eventualities as fire, theft and disease to external insurance agencies, in return for the payment of annual premiums. Clearly, such a transfer of responsibility does nothing to reduce the likelihood of the insured event occurring, and this is important, because even when a farmer's assets are adequately insured there may be consequential costs which are not covered. For example, a farmer who receives compensation for a grain store destroyed by fire shortly before harvest is not similarly recompensed if he receives a lower price for his grain because he is forced to sell it 'off the combine'.

In addition to measures for gaining stability on the financial side, there are others which are basically matters of technical organisation.

Informal insurance. There are many practices open to farmers – such as the routine inoculation of seed, vaccination of stock, or spraying of crops – which may be compared with formal insurance, because they are often implemented with no knowledge of whether the event against which they are directed will actually occur (as opposed to taking action after the event, such as when disease has been diagnosed). However, unlike formal insurance, they do lead to a reduction in the likelihood of specific events occurring, or in their severity (otherwise there would be no point in incurring their cost). Somewhat similarly, the insistence of many livestock producers on rearing their own young stock is a form of insurance against introducing disease onto their farms and against the possibility of paying excessively high prices for replacement stock.

Another type of informal insurance arises in respect of the uncertainty facing the arable farmer about the time available and the work requirements for performing tasks such as harvesting crops. By maintaining a labour and machinery complement in excess of that needed in 'normal' seasons he is more certain of being able to complete them. The cost of such measures depends both on the frequency with which abnormal seasons occur and the extent of over-capacity in normal ones. Some part of it, at least, should be offset by retrieving output that would otherwise have been lost, or by saving expenditure on alternative 'emergency' measures, such as the hire of contractors, to complete the task.

Flexibility

Although maintaining a flexible system is usually viewed as a means of reacting to unfavourable events, it has a positive side as well, in that it may allow the farmer to take more ready advantage of favourable changes.

Resource flexibility. The farmer may gain flexibility in his operations by manipulating the qualitative aspects of resources, in two main ways. First, by investing in capital items which, because they are not too highly specialised, can readily be put to more than one use. Examples are machines such as the combine harvester which can cope with a variety of cereals, pulses and other crops, or buildings which can be adapted to house a variety of livestock. Secondly, by relying on shorter-lived, cheaper capital items – such as pole barns rather than more elaborate brick structures – so that, if necessary, projects can be abandoned relatively early in their lives, without leaving money tied up uselessly in investments which technically still have many years to run (this is also a form of 'time-flexibility'). However, as acknowledged in the pig buildings example (pp. 107–8), a price may have to be paid in terms of lowered performance compared with that which could have been obtained from more specialised and longer-lasting investments.

A more drastic alternative is not to invest in those capital items that can be hired instead. Even if the latter should prove more expensive in operating costs, it does away with the risk of a redundant piece of equipment with only a scrap value being left on the farmer's hands.

Product flexibility. Product flexibility implies having more than one form of output on a farm, the balance of which can be altered in the face of changing market forces. Diversification into several distinct enterprises is an obvious example, always providing that their balance is not too rigidly prescribed in advance, as with a 'strict' rotation. Similarly, product flexibility may be gained to some extent from within certain individual enterprises. For example, a milk producer faced with favourable beef prices relative to those for milk might, by less rigorous culling of his herd, cut down the number of heifer calves retained as herd replacements, so increasing the numbers available for fattening (crossing his heifers with a beef bull if necessary).

A more specialised form of product flexibility arises when more than one marketing opportunity occurs for a particular product over a period of time (it is, therefore, another form of 'time-flexibility'). There are many examples. Some varieties of potato can be lifted as 'second-earlies' in summer but, if prices are disappointing at that time, can be left to bulk-up and be sold later as 'maincrop'. In face of a weak pork market, it may be feasible to fatten pigs to heavier weights, selling them instead as baconers or heavy hogs. If cereal prices are low after harvest, grain can be stored in the hope of higher prices as the season advances (given the necessary storage capacity). In the first two examples flexibility stems from the opportunity to continue the production process instead of terminating it, but in the last one the production, but not the marketing process, is complete. In all of them, the producer has greater freedom of action than if he could only sell his produce at one point in time.

The cost of uncertainty

We have seen, in passing, that uncertainty gives rise to various costs. These may be divided into 'involuntary' costs occurring independently of any measures that the farmer may take to counter the effects of uncertainty, and 'voluntary' costs which are the direct consequence of such actions.

Involuntary costs. If the farmer were gifted with perfect knowledge of future events (and was technically capable of making the necessary adjustments) he could modify his farming system so that it always provided near optimal results from year to year. Since, however, this ideal state is precluded, the system operated is likely to be sub-optimal in most years, and a 'cost' thus arises which is the difference in value between the actual plan and the theoretical 'perfect knowledge' plan in any one year. Although such differences are not necessarily valued exclusively in money terms (for example, considerable loss of satisfaction may arise) when related to profit-maximisation, they are the opportunity costs arising from the loss of potential profits. Since they occur independently of whether the farmer takes any deliberate action to counter the effects of uncertainty, they are involuntary (or unavoidable) costs.

Voluntary costs. In contrast, there are costs which only arise because the farmer does take active measures to protect his business from an uncertain future. These also commonly take the form of opportunity costs as, for example, when a farmer over a run of years deliberately grows a less profitable crop because it has a more stable outcome than another.[1] But money costs may be incurred too, such as for insurance, the prophylactic treatment of crops and livestock, or the employment of labour and machinery surplus to requirements in all but difficult seasons (with implied opportunity costs in terms of the alternative uses of the money disbursed on such measures).

Uncertainty and farm planning

There are two closely related aspects in taking account of uncertainty in farm planning: first, making allowances for the effect that uncertainty has on the farmer's attitudes and objectives and, secondly, acknowledging the variability inherent in many of the planning parameters. Both may be achieved, to greater or lesser effect, by formal or informal means. Formal measures involve the use of various types of 'risk-programming' – such as dynamic, quadratic or stochastic linear programming (reviewed in Chapter 17) – which acknowledge variability in at least some of the planning coefficients and allow for objectives other than simple profit-maximisation. Informal measures concern the *ad hoc* embodiment of allowances for uncertainty in the more 'workaday' deterministic techniques such as budgeting, programme planning and linear programming, and the implementation of various checks and tests at different stages of the planning process. These two approaches differ fundamentally in that informal techniques depend, to a far greater extent than formal ones, on the prejudgement of issues involving uncertainty, thus losing flexibility in that solutions are partly determined in advance, and may be far from the optimum in a purely risk-planning sense (see p. 287 for one example).

[1] On occasion there may be opportunity gains as, for example, when a farmer contracts ahead to sell grain at a price which, in the event, turns out to be higher than the market price ruling at the time of delivery. Or again, when a stable crop, grown instead of a normally higher profit but more variable alternative, turns out to be more profitable as well. However, such unanticipated gains apply to single seasons rather than to a run of seasons.

Notwithstanding, there is little likelihood of formal techniques being applied at present on any regular basis to individual farms because of their cost and complexity, together with the paucity of reliable probabilistic data with which to formulate valid expectations of an uncertain future. Conversely, the 'unscientific' treatment of uncertainty in deterministic models at least goes some way towards meeting the problem and may in fact be the best that can be achieved in practice. Furthermore, it may often reflect quite closely the manner in which the farmer actually reacts to uncertainty. Consequently, it is largely our concern in the rest of this chapter.

Incorporating attitudes to uncertainty

We have seen earlier that the risk-averse farmer is prepared to adopt measures which, while reducing the level of potential profits, increase the likelihood of his obtaining them. Taken together, such measures – excepting some, like insurance, which are simply incorporated in fixed costs – involve all the elements of the planning process. Some act as constraints, for example, the imposition of upper limits on the size of risky enterprises. Others concern enterprise inputs, as with the 'inflation' of labour requirements above those applicable to 'normal' seasons, because the farmer wants to ensure that he can cope when conditions are difficult. Yet others affect the enterprise returns, such as the use of cautious gross margins in enterprises with which the farmer is unfamiliar. The manner in which they can be incorporated in a deterministic planning model is reviewed in greater detail in Chapter 18 (pp. 487–90), in the context of adjustments to the linear programming matrix, but they apply equally to budgeting and gross margin planning, where account is taken of them as the calculations proceed.

Taking account of variability and imperfect knowledge

Although it may not be too difficult to allow (in a purely mechanical way) for the farmer's attitudes to uncertainty in deterministic planning, this is far from the case when the concern is to reflect the high degree of variability which in practice exists in inputs and outputs. As was acknowledged in Appendix 13.4 (p. 312), planning coefficients take specific values as though they were known with certainty. In consequence, even if the physical data used in planning were to be based on records that accurately reflected the seasonal variability that might be anticipated, their expression as single coefficients – usually averages – in deterministic models would effectively conceal the underlying variation. Nevertheless, various steps can be taken that go some way towards ameliorating the problem, in that they attempt to assess how critical is the assumption of single-valued expectations, or to assign values to data that are not readily quantified. Depending on their purpose they may be carried out before, during or after planning, or they may be linked directly to operational decisions.

Analysing the probability of events occurring

The formulation of expectations about the frequency with which unfavourable events are likely to occur is central to decisions as to whether measures should be taken to counter them. To take a simplified illustration, suppose a farmer wants to know whether he should spray a crop every year in case serious disease should strike. From past experience he reckons that disease is likely to halve the expected gross margin – from £480 to £240 per hectare – but normal output should be achieved if £60 per hectare is spent on spraying materials (he has the necessary labour and equipment). To summarise the outcomes:

	No spraying		*Spraying*
(£ per ha)	*Normal season*	*Abnormal season*	
Output	600	360	600
Variable costs	120	120	180
	480	240	420

The nub of the problem is whether the average gross margin from a combination of normal and abnormal seasons – which depends on their relative frequency – is more or less than that obtained from spraying. If the farmer thinks that disease will occur once in three seasons, the average gross margin based on this *subjective probability* is:

(£480 + £480 + £240)/3 = £400 per hectare.[1]

As this is less than that obtained by spraying, the latter is worthwhile. If, however, the farmer reckons that disease hits badly in only one season in five, the position is reversed:

(£480 + £480 + £480 + £480 + £240)/5 = £432 per hectare.

[1] The likelihood of events taking place may be formally expressed as probabilities (P), which always sum to 1 when all probabilities are included (just as percentages always sum to 100). Expressing our two examples in this way:

Break-even analysis

However, in practice the farmer may often be in considerable doubt about the likelihood of particular events occurring, or of the level of other important variables which may affect the issue. In such instances some guidance may be had from 'break-even' analysis, where the aim is to find that level of the variable in question which just balances the net return between different courses of action, so that it is a matter of indifference which of them is pursued. An assessment can then be made as to whether the break-even level is likely to be achieved. To continue with our spraying example, and putting it another way, the average gross margin from not spraying will equal that of spraying when the occasional loss of £240 per hectare (£480 − £240) is just balanced by the £60 cost incurred every year for spraying, which is one year in four ((£480 − £240)/60). Confirmation is given by calculating the average cost of not spraying, assuming disease occurs once in four seasons:

$$(£480 + £480 + £480 + £240)/4 = £420 \text{ per hectare,}$$

which is the same as that obtained from spraying. If the farmer considers that the disease will occur more than one year in four he should spray. If the frequency is less he loses by doing so.

Often it is the level of yield or price, or both, that is in doubt. Suppose the farmer is satisfied that abnormal seasons are likely to occur about one year in five, but is less sure as to the extent to which gross margin is likely to be reduced by disease. The break-even gross margin, where it is a matter of indifference whether crops are sprayed, occurs when the five-year average gross margin of unsprayed crops equals that of those sprayed, the level of gross margin in abnormal seasons being the

---

Abnormal season:	*1 year in 3*			*1 year in 5*		
	P	£	£	*P*	£	£
	0.67	× 480 =	320	0.8	× 480 =	384
	0.33	× 240 =	80	0.2	× 240 =	48
	1.00		400	1.0		432

In practice there would usually be a greater range of probable outcomes (often varying continuously), resulting in a more detailed probability distribution. In addition, the probability of a particular event may be conditional on another event occurring. See, for example, Martin Upton (1976) *Agricultural Production Economics and Resource Use*, Oxford University Press, pp. 133–45.

unknown (X) to be solved:

$$(£480 + £480 + £480 + £480 + £X)/5 = £420 \text{ per hectare}$$
$$X = £180 \text{ per hectare.}$$

Only if disease is likely to cut gross margin per hectare by more than £300 (480 − 180) to below £180 is it worthwhile spraying when disease is expected to occur one year in five.

As a final example, let us assume a farmer is trying to decide whether he should invest in equipment for irrigating 16 hectares of maincrop potatoes. The capital cost is estimated to be £8000. Depreciation and interest charges per annum amount to £1200, or £75 per hectare, and with other costs averaging £25, the total cost is £100 per hectare. As he is doubtful about the extra yield he is likely to obtain, he can readily calculate the break-even yield needed just to cover the extra costs. At an average price of £50 per tonne (net of an allowance for harvesting and marketing the extra yield) this is 100/50, i.e. 2 tonnes, which represents a 7 per cent increase on his present average yield of 28 tonnes per hectare.

Sensitivity analysis

Another method of assessing a situation where there is considerable uncertainty about the validity of one or more of the key assumptions is the use of sensitivity analysis, in which the effect of differences in the key variables is shown. This is more likely to be required for yields or prices than for costs. It would be particularly desirable, for example, for someone starting a large dairy herd; the initial calculations could be based, say, on a yield of 4500 litres per cow and a price of 10p per litre, and the effect of a difference either way of, say, 100 litres in yield or 0.25p per litre in price could be given as extra information. It is possible in fact to draw a graph to illustrate the effect on profit or return on capital of a complete range of price and/or yield levels (e.g. Figure 16.1); this has been described as 'parametric budgeting' (cf. 'parametric programming' Chapter 17, pp. 421–4). The same might be done for cereal yields and prices on a mainly cereal-growing farm. A separate estimate of the lowest likely level of profit (or maximum likely loss) in the event of a bad year may be valuable or even essential to a man just beginning farming with little spare capital. Where there are several enterprises, however, there are likely to be some counterbalancing effects; for example, except where climatic extremes occur, it is rare for the yields (and prices) of all crops to be poor in the same year (see further pp. 398–400 below).

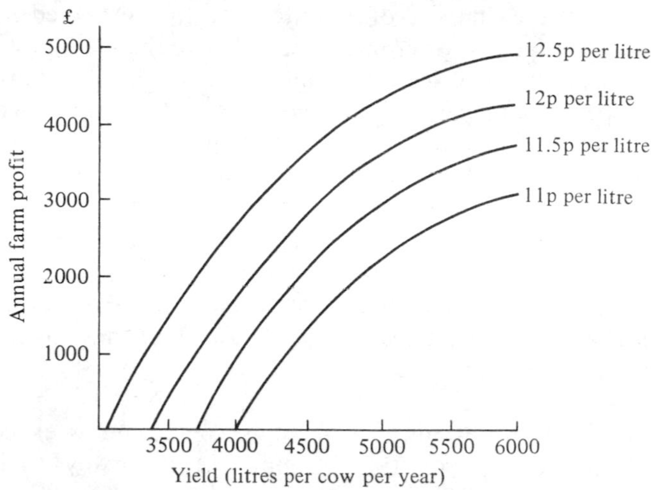

(Example: a specialist dairy farm of 40 hectares, showing variation in farm profitability with variations in milk yield per cow and milk price per litre).

Fig. 16.1. 'Parametric budgeting'

Real costs

When assessing the virtue of specific measures to counter uncertainty, it is often necessary to balance the real costs against the benefits that are likely to accrue. As has been seen elsewhere in the book (pp. 209–11, 224–5, 244–8), real costs are the sum of the variable costs and the net opportunity costs (of diverting scarce fixed resources from other uses) to implement the measure in question. For instance, if in our previous example of spraying (p. 392), the farmer had to divert labour (at $1\frac{1}{2}$ hours per hectare) from other tasks where its marginal value was £8 per hour, the real cost would be £72 per hectare (v.c. £60 + o.c. £12) and not the £60 shown before when labour was assumed to be freely available.

Often, however, there will be no similar and valid basis for calculating the benefits in terms of a reduction in risk. For example, farmers may rear their own young-stock, rather than rely on bought-in animals, on the grounds of disease risk; or make their own hay requirements, rather than purchase them, because of the risk of the latter's quality being inferior; or own machines themselves, rather than share with neighbours or hire a contractor, because of the risk of potential yield losses due to lack of timeliness. But often their assessment of these alternative actions, in terms of the differences to be expected in disease incidence, hay quality, or crop yields, will be of the sketchiest nature, perhaps being based solely on intuition, to which a previous unfortunate experience may have contributed. In such instances, where the benefits from risk-avoidance measures cannot readily be quantified, their real costs should still be calculated, for a sounder assessment can then be made of the value of the particular action in question. If the real costs should prove to be high, the farmer may well decide to change his policy, or to seek a less costly way of implementing it. In addition, where the alternative is to purchase rather than to produce on the farm (as in the examples on pp. 211 and 246), they enable break-even prices to be calculated.

The problem of variation in planning coefficients is exacerbated when, as is often the case, they respond in varying ways to different seasonal conditions. This is illustrated in Figure 1.1 (p. 11) by wheat and potato yields which moved in the same direction in only one year of the six (1966), and even then to a very different degree. It is to this problem that we now turn, first in the context of the reduction of variation both in single and multiple enterprise situations and, secondly, in respect of ways in which some allowance can be made for it in practical planning.

Reduction of variation

Seasonal variation within enterprises

Variations in outcome from year to year can be measured in both absolute and proportionate terms. For example, suppose a survey of a sample of farms shows that the gross margin of an enterprise *A* varies as follows in four main types of season, each of which is regarded as having an equal chance of occurring ($P = 0.25$).

Season type:	*I*	*II*	*III*	*IV*	*Mean*	*Standard deviation (SD)*	*Coefficient of variation (CV)*
GM of *A* (£)	54	38	26	42	40	10	25

A simple way to sum up this seasonal variation is to calculate the *mean deviation*, in which the sum of the deviations of each observation from the mean (ignoring signs) is divided by the number of observations. This gives £8 in our example: $\{(54 - 40) + (38 - 40) + (26 - 40) + (42 - 40)\}/4$.

However, here (and subsequently) we rely on the more sophisticated (and more generally useful) *standard deviation* (σ), in which each deviation is squared before being summed and divided by the number of observations (n) – thus giving the *variance* (σ^2), the square root of which is the standard deviation. This is £10 in our example: $\sqrt{[(14^2 + 2^2 + 14^2 + 2^2)/4]}$.[1] The advantage of the standard deviation is that given normally distributed observations, confidence limits can be attached to ranges of values each side of the mean.[2] For example, ninety per cent of observations are likely to fall within plus or minus 1.657 standard deviations of the mean and ninety-five per cent within plus or minus two standard deviations. In enterprise *A* (with mean gross margin £40 and SD £10), where the observations concern individual seasons, gross margin would thus be expected to fall within the range £23.4 – £56.6 in nine seasons out of ten, and between £20 and £60 in nineteen seasons out of twenty. Proportional variation can in turn be measured by dividing the standard deviation by the mean – giving the coefficient of variation (v) – which can be expressed in percentage terms (v%). In our example this is 25 per cent [(10 × 100)/40].

Now let us compare enterprise *A* with two others, respectively less and more variable, assuming that there can be only one enterprise on the farm.

		A	*B*	*C*
Mean gross margin	(£)	40	40	100
Standard deviation	(£)	10	5	30
Coefficient of variation	(%)	25	12½	30

B is clearly preferable to *A* because variation is halved for the same gross margin. In addition, in nineteen years out of twenty the gross margin should not fall below £30 in *B*, whereas it may fall as low as £20 in *A*. The choice between *B* and *C* is less obvious. While *B* is still preferable if reduction of variation is the only aim, *C* offers not only a far higher mean gross margin, but a higher minimum one as well, since the latter should not fall below £40 in nineteen years out of twenty.

[1] Standard deviation can also be defined as the square root of the squared deviations multiplied by their probabilities, which is $\sqrt{\{(14^2 \times 0.5) + (2^2 \times 0.5)\}}$ in the above example. In small samples it is conventional to apply a correction factor which in the first formulation consists of dividing by one less than the number of observations ($n - 1$).

[2] A 'normal' distribution is one that is unimodal with observations symmetrically distributed either side of the mean – the majority clustering quite closely round it. The equation of the normal curve is expressed in terms of the mean and standard deviation of a distribution. Although it is idealised in form, observations of natural phenomena often conform to it quite well.

It is thus evident that reduction of variation is not necessarily a sound objective in itself but must be related to expected levels of mean and minimum return. Indeed, even if the gross margin of *C* were only £70, so that it might fall as low as £10 (given the same level of probability), the extra income that would be received over a series of years or the chance of a high gross margin season occurring would be attractive to many. Confronted with such a choice the decision-maker has to balance (or 'trade-off') the advantages of higher incomes against the disadvantages of greater variation and lower minimum incomes (a theme to which we return shortly).

Seasonal variation between enterprises

The overall variation in outcome of a combination of enterprises depends on two other factors in addition to the variability of individual enterprises. First, the relationship between the seasonal behaviour of the different enterprises making up the mix and, second, the proportions in which they are combined.

Relationships between enterprises. We saw earlier (p. 385) that diversification, aimed at reducing income variation, depends on the selection of enterprises that react in different ways to varying seasonal stimuli. The latter implies not just whether their reactions are in the same or in opposite directions, but the relative strength of the relationship. It can be measured statistically by the *correlation coefficient* (r) which ranges in value from $+1$ to -1, the two extremes on the scale indicating respectively that two variables move in the same or in opposite directions (the $+$ and $-$ signs) and that they are correlated in the strongest possible manner ('perfect' correlation), in that their annual deviations from the mean bear the same proportional relationship to each other throughout. As we move towards zero from ± 1 so the strength of the association weakens, until at zero there is no discernible relationship.[1]

If two enterprises were perfectly negatively correlated ($r = -1$), variation could be completely eliminated by combining them in such proportions that the variation in one exactly offset that of the other (which is when their proportions are in inverse ratio to their standard deviations). Compare the following two enterprises where $r = -1$.

[1] The first step in arriving at the correlation coefficient is to calculate *covariance* (cov) – a measure of the joint variation between two variables – by multiplying together the deviations from their respective means, summing them and dividing the total by the number of observations (n): $\text{cov}\, xy = \Sigma(x - \bar{x})(y - \bar{y})/n$. The covariance is then divided by the product of the standard deviations of the two variables to obtain the correlation coefficient: $r = \text{cov xy}/\sigma_x \sigma_y$.

Season type:	*I*	*II*	*III*	*IV*	*Mean*	*SD*	*CV%*
GM of *A* (£)	54	38	26	42	40	10	25
GM of *D* (£)	12	44	68	36	40	20	50

The standard deviation of *D* is twice that of *A*, and in any one season *D* varies twice as much from its mean as does *A* but in the opposite direction (e.g. season I, *A* up £14, *D* down £28). In consequence, a mix of two thirds *A* and one third *D* reduces seasonal variation to zero.

Season type:	*I*	*II*	*III*	*IV*	*Mean*	*SD*	*CV%*
GM (£) $\frac{2}{3}$rds *A*	36.0	25.3	17.3	28.0	26.7	6.7	25
$\frac{1}{3}$rd *D*	4.0	14.7	22.7	12.0	13.3	6.7	50
Total	40.0	40.0	40.0	40.0	40.0	0	0

Unfortunately such an idealised situation is hardly likely to prevail. In practice enterprises (particularly crops) are often positively correlated, but even here a combination may reduce variation. To demonstrate this, we break enterprise *A* down into two separate activities, each with the same mean and standard deviation (in order to hold 'other things equal').

Season type:	*I*	*II*	*III*	*IV*	*Mean*	*SD*	*CV%*
GM (£) A'	54	38	26	42	40	10	25
A''	54	42	38	26	40	10	25
$A' + A''$	108	80	64	68			
$\frac{1}{2}A' + \frac{1}{2}A''$	54	40	32	34	40	8.6	21.5

A' and A'' move in the same direction in seasons I and III, and in opposite directions in seasons II and IV, resulting in a correlation coefficient of +0.48. However, the coefficient of variation of 25 per cent if they are produced on their own is reduced to 21.5 per cent if they are combined in equal proportions. Variation continues to diminish as the correlation coefficient moves towards zero and then on into increasing negative values:

Correlation coeff. A'/A''	+1	+0.5	0	−0.5	−1
CV% $\frac{1}{2}A' + \frac{1}{2}A''$	25.0	21.6	17.7	12.5	0

Thus the fact that there may be no negative correlation between enterprises does not imply that variation cannot be reduced by combining them. The extent of its reduction, at any given value of the correlation coefficient, depends on the degree of variability in the individual enterprises.

Variation in individual enterprises. It is only to be expected that as a less variable enterprise is substituted for a more variable one, so the overall variation is reduced even if there is perfect positive correlation. This is shown below, where increasing amounts of activity B (p. 397) are added to A, assuming a correlation coefficient of $r = +1$.

Proportions of A and B:	100*A*	90*A*/10*B*	50*A*/50*B*	10*A*/90*B*	100*B*
CV%	25.00	23.75	18.75	13.75	12.50

Conversely, if D (p. 399), which is twice as variable as A, is substituted for the latter and $r = +1$, the overall variation steadily increases:

Proportions of A and D:	100*A*	90*A*/10*D*	50*A*/50*D*	10*A*/90*D*	100*D*
CV%	25.00	27.5	37.5	47.5	50

Nevertheless, such an increase in variability is not inevitable, for the overall variation depends not just on the degree and direction of correlation but on the proportion of the mix made up by the more variable enterprise. To continue with the same example, if $r = +0.4$, as D is introduced overall variation falls slightly below the 25 per cent level of A on its own, but only providing D does not exceed 11 per cent of the mix.[1]

Recapitulation

To recapitulate on the reduction of variation by combining enterprises, we may first remind ourselves of the factors that influence the overall variability of a mix, namely:

1. The degree of absolute and proportional variation of the individual enterprises comprising the mix.
2. The direction and degree of correlation between them.
3. The proportions in which they are combined.

The first two factors may be to some extent under the indirect control of the farmer in that he may take measures that reduce variation, such as a high standard of husbandry or the use of irrigation. But for any

[1] Overall variation may be reduced, provided an appropriate mix is selected, if the covariance of the two variables is less than either's individual variance. In our example the variance (σ^2) of A is 100 and of D is 400, while their covariance when $r = +0.4$ is 80 ($0.4 \times 10 \times 20$). The latter is less than either of the individual variances. If r rose to 0.5, covariance would be 100, equalling the variance of A. There would then be no reduction in variation by adding D to A. (For proof, see Upton (1976) *op. cit.*, pp. 190–2.)

given standard of farming, it is only the last factor that is under his direct control, and even here his freedom to alter enterprise proportions may be restricted by constraints imposed by rotation, livestock accommodation and so on.

Next we summarise the inferences that arise from our consideration of the effect of enterprise selection on the reduction of variation:

1. Although in order to reduce variation to a low level it is necessary to combine strongly negatively-correlated enterprises of low variability, even quite strongly positively correlated ones may allow variation to be reduced.
2. Diversifying into two or more enterprises is not an automatic way of reducing variation compared with the specialised production of one enterprise.
3. In any case, a low level of variation taken on its own is not necessarily a reliable measure of the financial risks facing the farm business, and thus the reduction of variation is not necessarily a sound objective for the risk-averse manager.

An example

These factors are demonstrated in Table 16.1. Part 1 shows the degree of variation in individual crops, wheat and barley being relatively stable while potatoes are highly variable, with sugar beet in between. Next, the relationships between them are summed up in a correlation matrix. For example, wheat is negatively correlated with barley and potatoes but positively correlated with sugar beet, as are potatoes. The degree of correlation is relatively strong throughout, falling below 0.6 in only one instance.

These data are used in the second part of the table, to assess the variability of seven potential cropping systems (*A* to *G*) by means of the coefficient of variation (col. *c*).[1] Plan *B* is the least variable, because wheat and barley are negatively correlated and are themselves stable crops. In contrast, plan *G* varies the most because barley and potatoes are positively correlated and potatoes are highly variable. Compared with plan *A* – barley alone – diversifying into plans *B*, *C* and *F* reduces overall variability, but in plans *D*, *E* and *G* it is increased.

[1] For the method of calculating the standard deviation of a mix see, for example, Murphy, M. C. (1971) 'Risk Evaluation in Farm Planning – A Statistical Approach'. *Journal of Agricultural Economics*, **XXII**, No. 1.

TABLE 16.1. *Variability in cropping – an example*

1. *Crop variation and correlation* (South Cambs, 1964–6)

Variation	*Gross margin* (£ per ha)	*Standard deviation* (£ per ha)	*Coefficient of variation* (%)
Wheat	81	19	23
Barley	75	15	20
S. Beet	165	50	30
Potatoes	232	135	58

Correlation Matrix

	Wheat	*Barley*	*S. Beet*	*Potatoes*
Wheat	1	−0.60	0.62	−0.70
Barley	−0.60	1	−0.35	0.69
S. Beet	0.62	−0.35	1	0.82
Potatoes	−0.70	0.69	0.82	1

Source: Based on Murphy, M. C. (1968), *The Appraisal of Risk and Uncertainty in East Anglian Farming*. Dept. of Land Economy, Cambridge University.

2. *Crop combinations. Variation of gross margin and ability to meet fixed commitments* (per 40 hectares)

Plan	*Enterprise combination* Barley	Wheat	Potatoes	S. Beet	*Gross margin:* *Mean* (*a*)*	*SD* (*b*)	*CV* (100*b*/*a*) (*c*)	*Min.*[1] (*a*–1.657*b*) (*d*)	*Fixed commitments*[2] (*e*)	*Max. fall below FC*[1] (*f*)	*Probability of falling below fixed commitments* *Per cent* (*a* − *e*/*b*)[3] (*g*)	*1 in* n *years* (100/*g*) (*h*)
	hectares				£	£	%	£	£	£	%	years
A	40	—	—	—	3,000	600	20	2,006	2,700	−694	31	3
B	20	20	—	—	3,125	309	10	2,613	2,700	−87	8	12
C	20	10	—	10	3,962	565	14	3,026	3,100	−74	6	16
D	20	10	10	—	4,638	1,444	31	2,245	3,100	−855	14	7
E	20	10	5	5	4,300	980	23	2,676	3,100	−424	11	9
F	27	—	—	13	4,199	646	15	3,129	3,100	+29	4½	22
G	27	—	13	—	5,098	2,094	41	1,628	3,100	−1,472	17	6

[1] In 9 out of 10 years.

[2] Minimum sum to meet essential commitments including farm requisites and services, and personal expenditure.

[3] Refer to table of probabilities for the normal curve.

SD = Standard deviation. *CV* = Coefficient of variation.

* Rounding differences arise (in converting original data in acres to hectares).

Minimum returns and fixed commitments

However, we have already acknowledged that reduction of variability may, on its own, be an inadequate objective in countering uncertainty, and needs to be related to the level of returns that are likely to accrue. In turn the latter may be balanced against fixed commitments, for the ability to generate sufficient income to cover them with a reasonable degree of certainty may be an important objective, particularly for the business that is short of capital or is in danger of over-trading. This aspect is considered in cols. *d* to *h*, where fixed commitments (col. *e*) are assumed to be £2700 per 40 hectares when there are no root crops and £3100 when there are. Minimum incomes – in nine years out of ten (col. *d*) – are calculated by deducting 1.657 standard deviations from the mean in each plan. Next, fixed commitments are deducted from minimum incomes, the resulting negative values (col. *f*) in all plans except *F* indicating that there is the likelihood – to a greater or lesser degree – that fixed commitments cannot always be met at the given level of probability.[1] Finally, the problem is looked at another way by calculating the probability of failure to meet fixed commitments, first on a percentage basis (col. *g*) and secondly in terms of frequency (col. *h*).[2]

This additional information enables a more critical judgement to be made of the plans in terms of risk aversion – particularly when they are arrayed in order of ascending mean gross margin, as in Figure 16.2. Plans *A*, *B* and *C* are dominated by plan *F* because it gives both a higher mean and minimum gross margin together with less likelihood of failure to meet fixed commitments; thus it would be illogical to select any of the former. Plans *E*, *D* and *G* have increasingly high mean gross margins accompanied, however, by steadily falling levels of minimum gross margins and a greater risk of failure to meet fixed commitments. Whether or not a farmer would prefer any of them to plan *F* depends on his degree of risk aversion and the extent to which he is prepared to trade off one against the other. However, to concentrate solely on the

[1] The extent of the shortfall depends on the degree of variability of the plan and the relative proximity of mean gross margin and fixed commitments. For example, although plan *G* has the highest margin between mean gross margin and fixed commitments its high degree of variability results in the probability of a large fall below the mean. On the other hand, the vulnerability of plan *A* is more the consequence of the mean gross margin being so narrowly above fixed commitments rather than of a high degree of variability (which is half that of *G*).

[2] Based on the formula: $t = (c - \overline{x})/\sigma_x$ where $\overline{x}$ = mean gross margin, c = fixed commitments and σ = standard deviation. The value t is referred to a table of the normal probability integral (single tail) to give the relevant probability.

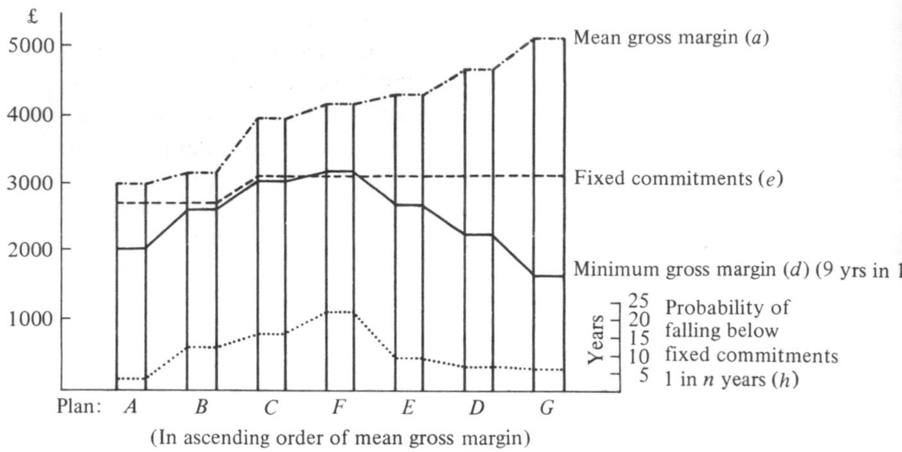

(Suffixes refer to columns in part 2 of Table 16.1)

Fig. 16.2. Crop combinations in South Cambs. (1964–6)

negative tail of the distribution is to take a pessimistic view of outcomes, for all but the most highly risk averse of farmers would be just as interested in maximum likely incomes. Nevertheless, the main point is that the decision-maker is in a better position to make sound judgements as to his future course of action if he has additional information on the variability of a plan as well as its mean outcome.

Variability and practical planning

A procedure

The question arises as to the way in which such additional information may be provided in practical planning (as distinct from the research-oriented techniques reviewed in Chapter 17). The steps involved are outlined below:

1. Determine the physical outputs of enterprises (and the variable inputs if possible) in different seasons from the past (records are essential here).
2. Construct seasonal gross margins by applying prices applicable to future plans to the seasonal physical data from step 1.
3. Average the seasonal gross margins of the different enterprises, giving due weight to the frequency with which different seasons seem likely to occur.

4. Use these averages to obtain a gross-margin maximising solution (as is normal in most deterministic planning).

5. Calculate the total gross margins accruing to this solution in the different seasons and in the average season.

The planner now has an array of total gross margins not only for the average situation but for each of the individual seasons also. Providing the latter are reasonably representative of what may be expected to occur in the future he thus has information both on maximum and minimum incomes and their frequency.

An example

A simplified example is given in Table 16.2, the first part of which shows gross margins for three types of season (anticipated to occur two, five and three years in ten respectively), on the assumption that steps 1 and 2 detailed above have already been taken. The mean gross margins of £196, £162 and £156 per hectare for enterprises *P*, *Q* and *R* are weighted averages calculated from the seasonal gross margins (step 3) [e.g. £196 in $P = (£215 \times 0.2) + (£255 \times 0.5) + (£85 \times 0.3)$]. In part 2 of the table, an optimum solution – 30 ha *P*, 50 ha *Q*, 20 ha *R* – is derived from the average gross margins (step 4). (It can be seen by eye that this solution is optimal in maximising returns to land – the only scarce resource – given the individual enterprise constraints.) In part 3, the amounts of the different enterprises in the optimum solution are multiplied by their mean and seasonal gross margins per hectare to give total mean and seasonal gross margins (step 5) (e.g. enterprise *P*, season *I*: 30 × £215 = £6450, season *II*: 30 × £255 = £7650 and so on).

In this example, total gross margin may fall as low as £11,300 per 100 hectares in three years in ten (season type *III*).[1] If the farmer regards this as too risky, he can modify the plan in order to reduce variability and so raise minimum gross margin. For example, as the gross margin of *P* is at its lowest and that of *R* at its highest in season type *III*, eliminating the former in favour of the latter reduces variability very considerably, and raises minimum gross margin to £14,750 (plan 2 in part 4 of the table), £3450 higher than before. However, as this entails a sacrifice of £1200 in mean gross margin, plan 3 might be preferred, where only half of *P* is transferred to *R*. Minimum gross margin is now £13,025, which is £1725 higher than in the original plan, while the sacrifice in mean gross margin is cut by a half to £600.

[1] The data in part 3 of the table can be used to calculate the standard deviation and coefficient of variation of the mix, namely, ±£4015 and 23.5 per cent respectively.

TABLE 16.2. *The average gross margin plan and seasonal variability*

1. *Seasonal gross margins* (per hectare)

	Season type: I	II	III	*Mean*
Probability:	0.2	0.5	0.3	
	£	£	£	£
Enterprise P	215	255	85	196
Q	280	155	95	162
R	80	160	200	156

2. *Optimum solution based on mean gross margins* (per 100 ha)

Enterprise	*Planning constraints* (ha)		*Solution* (ha)
P	Max. 30	Max. 80 (P + Q)	30
Q	Max. 80		50
R	Max. 50		20

3. *Optimum solution – mean and seasonal gross margins* (per 100 ha)

Enterprise	*ha*	*Season type:* *I* (0.2)	*II* (0.5)	*III* (0.3)	*Mean*
		£	£	£	£
P	30	6,450	7,650	2,550	5,880
Q	50	14,000	7,750	4,750	8,100
R	20	1,600	3,200	4,000	3,120
	100	22,050	18,600	11,300	17,100

4. *Alternative plans – mean and seasonal gross margins* (per 100 ha)

Plan	*Enterprises* (ha) *P*	*Q*	*R*	*Season type:* *I* (0.2)	*II* (0.5)	*III* (0.3)	*Mean*
				£	£	£	£
2	0	50	50	18,000	15,750	14,750	15,900
3	15	50	35	20,025	17,175	13,025	16,500

Appendix 16.1: Decision analysis[1]

During the past decade or so increasing interest has been shown in the subject of decision analysis, or decision theory. This formalised approach to decision-making starts from the premise that any decision is uncertain, i.e. unpredictable as to its precise – or sometimes even approximate – outcome. Accepting this, all current information rele-

[1] The authors wish to thank Dr. Paul Webster (Wye College) for useful comments on this appendix.

vant to a particular decision – or as much as can be obtained in the time available – should be set out and used logically. As new information arises, this is incorporated in those decisions of a continuing nature. The decision-maker then chooses between alternative courses of action in a logical manner, according to his own estimates of the likelihood of different outcomes occurring, and according to his attitude to taking risks. The resulting choice is often referred to as 'the best bet' decision. In this event the outcome may well be different, but at least the possibility should have been known and allowed for when the decision was made.

The decision tree

The first step is to set out logically the choice available in terms of alternative courses of action, the possible variable factors ('events') that will affect the outcome of each alternative choice, the subjectively estimated probability of each of these occurring, and the financial outcomes. A simple example is given in Figure 16.3, which also illustrates the sequential nature of many decisions. A decision tree consists of two types of 'fork'. One is an 'act' fork giving alternatives between which the decision-maker has to choose; the other is an 'event' fork, which relates to alternative possible events (e.g. prices or yields). The

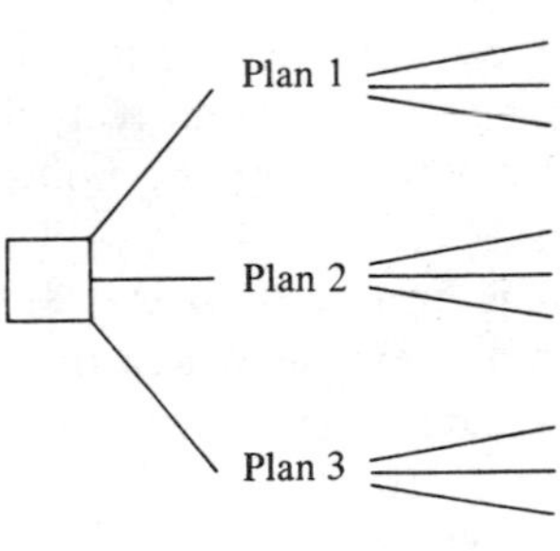

Act	Event and probability	Season type	Outcome £	EMV £	CE £
Plan 1	0.1	I	30,000	14,600	12,000
	0.7	II	16,000		
	0.2	III	2,000		
Plan 2	0.1	I	20,000	13,800	13,600
	0.7	II	14,000		
	0.2	III	10,000		
Plan 3	0.1	I	25,000	14,200	13,200
	0.7	II	15,000		
	0.2	III	6,000		

Note: EMV = expected money value, CE = certainty equivalent (see p. 408)

The CEs assume a risk-averse farmer. Thus although Plan 1 gives the highest EMV it gives the lowest CE, and Plan 2, although it gives the lowest EMV, gives the highest CE and is thus the preferred course of action.

Fig. 16.3. A decision tree

most preferred act fork, i.e. course of action, is found working from right to left.

Subjective probabilities. The concept of subjective probabilities has already been described (pp. 392–3). To summarise, the likelihood of any event actually happening has to be estimated, between the levels 0 and 1, so that the total of the probabilities equals 1.

Almost certainly circumstances will alter as time passes, and the estimate of the likelihood of alternative events occurring in the future will change. Sometimes nothing can be done about it, because the decision has already been made and executed, e.g. a crop that has been sold. But often action can be modified, e.g. the level of concentrate feeding when the quality/quantity of bulk fodder or grazing turns out to be different than anticipated. *Bayes Theorem* indicates how subjective probabilities should be amended in a logical manner in the light of new information: *prior* probabilities are converted to *posterior* probabilities on the basis of the likelihood of occurrence of the new information.

Certainty equivalents. Next the decision-maker's attitude to risk has to be determined. Suppose there is a choice: between receiving £1000 for certain and a 50–50 chance of either £2000 or nothing. The 'risk-averse' type of person would choose the former. The 'risk-preferer' (or 'risk-taker') would prefer the latter. A person on the borderline is said to be 'risk-indifferent'. The majority of farmers appear to be risk-averse, but this varies according to the amount of money at risk (see p. 384). (Compare the decision whether to spray a crop grown on only a small area of the farm against a disease which may result in a relatively slight loss in yield with deciding whether or not to insure the buildings against fire.)

Let us assume the £1000 for certain is preferred. If this sum is gradually reduced it will eventually reach a level at which the risk-averse person is indifferent between the gamble and the for-certain sum; below this amount he will prefer the 50–50 chance. For a highly risk-averse person this could occur at, say, £600. This is known as the 'certainty equivalent' (CE) for this individual for this particular set of possible outcomes. On the other hand the gambler may require, say, £1250 for certain to compensate him for losing the chance of getting £2000.

The long-run (average or expected) outcome of a gamble is said to be its EMV (expected money value), e.g. it is £1000 in the example above.

For the risk-indifferent person, CE = EMV, and the 'risk premium' is defined as the EMV minus the CE.

The individual decision-maker's CE of each course of action in the decision tree can be determined. Whichever alternative gives the highest CE is the best bet choice for that person. However, the need to establish the CEs separately for each decision can be circumvented if a person's 'utility function' is known.

The utility function

This describes an individual's attitude to increasing amounts of money, which clearly relates to his attitude to risk, i.e. the proportional difference between CE and EMV. For instance, the 'risk-averse' curve in Figure 16.4 shows decreasing marginal utility as the sum of money increases. Hence lower cash values are given more weight than higher values when deciding between alternative possible outcomes. An individual's utility function is measured by asking the person a series of questions relating to choices between alternative money outcomes with varying degrees of risk (Dillon (1971), p. 22 *et seq.*).

For a particular individual, the utility of any financial outcome can be read off from that person's utility curve. The utility is found for each

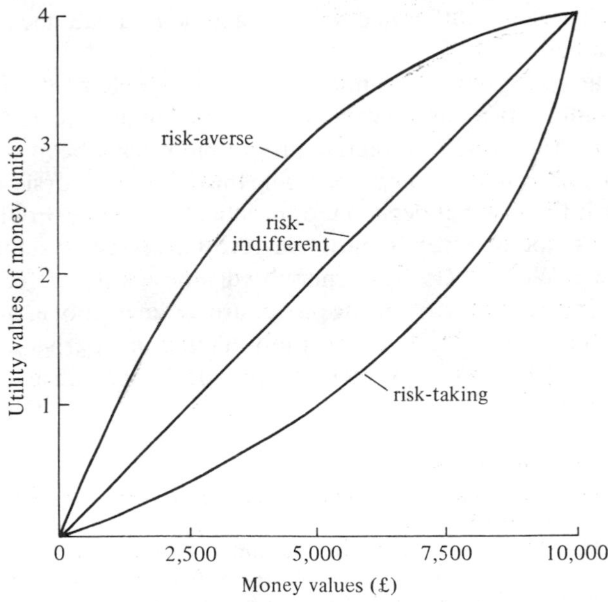

Fig. 16.4. Utility functions

outcome of an action. These utilities are then weighted according to the probability of each possible outcome (as when calculating the EMVs), to give the 'expected utility' (EU) of the course of action. The action giving the highest EU is selected. The CE of each action can now be read off from the same utility curve, but this is not necessary to give the preferred course of action. The above procedure is the essence of '*Bernoulli's Principle*'.

Potential practical usefulness

Proponents of decision analysis argue that theirs is the only practical approach to decision-making, since the outcome of any action is never known for certain, especially in farming, and, furthermore, allowance must be made for the individual's attitudes to risk. Thus establishing the range of possible outcomes and ascribing to them subjective probabilities, and so on, is the only realistic approach to the problem.

While there is no doubt truth in this and the approach is therefore to be encouraged, especially for particularly difficult and important decisions, it has to be acknowledged that few farmers are likely to go to such pains to help them make any decision, let alone all of them, particularly because however 'good' a decision is, in the sense that all aspects of it have been thoroughly researched and analysed in the way described above, it still may prove to be the wrong decision as things turn out. There is a difference between a good or a bad decision and a good or a bad result.

A few attempts have been made to incorporate elements of decision analysis into established farm planning techniques (e.g. Lin *et al.* (1974)). Furthermore, interactive programmes have been written for use on portable, micro-computers using the decision analysis approach to arrive at the best bet decision for practical, everyday problems, e.g. whether or not to spray a particular crop against a specific pest or disease (e.g. Webster (1977)). Undoubtedly these will proliferate in the future, using at least *parts* of the procedure outlined above, such as the decision tree, since improved decision-making in a perpetual climate of uncertainty is a matter of such vital practical importance to successful management.

Selected references

1. Anderson, J. R., Dillon, J. L. and Hardaker, J. B. (1977) *Agricultural Decision Analysis.* Iowa State University Press.
2. Coyle, R. G. (1972) *Decision Analysis.* The Camelot Press Ltd (an introductory text).
3. Dillon, J. L. (1971) 'An Expository Review of Bernoullian Decision Theory in Agriculture: Is Utility Futility? *Review of Marketing and Agricultural Economics,* **39**, No. 1.

4. Halter, A. N. and Dean, G. W. (1971) *Decisions under Uncertainty, with Research Applications*. South-Western Publishing Co.
5. Lin, W., Dean, G. W. and Moore, C. V. (1974) 'An Empirical Test of Utility vs. Profit Maximisation in Agricultural Production'. *American Journal of Agricultural Economics*, **56**, No. 3.
6. Lindley, D. (1973) *Making Decisions*. John Wiley and Sons, Ltd.
7. Makeham, J. P., Halter, A. N. and Dillon, J. L. (1968) *Best Bet Farm Decisions*. Guidebook No. 6, Univ. of New England.
8. Officer, R. R. and Halter, A. N. (1968) 'Utility Analysis in a Practical Setting'. *American Journal of Agricultural Economics*, **50**, No. 1.
9. Raiffa, H. (1968) *Decision Analysis*. Addison-Wesley Publishing Co.
10. Webster, J. P. G. (1976) 'Analysing Risky Decisions'. *Farm Management*, **3**, No. 3. (A short, simply written article, with examples.)
11. Webster, J. P. G. (1977) 'The Analysis of Risky Farm Management Decisions: Advising Farmers about the Use of Pesticides'. *Journal of Agricultural Economics*, **XXVIII**, No. 3.

17: Further programming techniques

Conceptual criticisms of linear programming

The previous chapter ended with an evaluation of linear programming. Some of the criticisms levelled at this technique relate to its practical difficulties compared with budgeting and programme planning, but others relate to its conceptual inadequacy. That is to say, they criticise the linear programming model for inadequately representing the 'real world' situation. It is these criticisms that have led to the development of other computer techniques relating to the planning of a business, which are the subject of this chapter.

These shortcomings of linear programming may be summarised under three headings:

1. *Structural.* This refers to the assumptions of linearity and continuity. The latter means that 'integers', or indivisible units, cannot be dealt with in a fully acceptable manner. This difficulty relates in particular to units of building and machinery cost, and the desirability of avoiding units too small either to cover the associated specific fixed costs adequately or to be worth the managerial effort required. As a result, the maximum total net revenue plan may not be that providing the maximum profit, since the extra fixed costs may exceed the extra net revenue compared with a 'sub-optimal' plan. As has been seen in Chapter 15, difficulties involved with the linearity assumption can largely be overcome, by defining separate activities to describe different points on, or sectors of, a curve depicting diminishing returns. Given the difficulty of obtaining accurate data specific to individual herds and fields, this is often a sufficient representation of reality in practical terms. The problem of indivisibility and decreasing costs is more difficult, but, again as we have seen, there are ways of tackling this, especially by re-running the programme with different assumptions and comparing the results. Nevertheless, a more direct way of solving these problems would save time and probably be more accurate.

2. *Dynamics*. Linear programming provides a solution for a given production period, usually a year. The adjustments required to move from the existing plan to the recommended plan may take several years. There may be alternative ways of making this adjustment. Resources may need to be accumulated over a period of years, from within the farm. The linear programming optimal plan may not suit the longer-term aims of the farmer. All these problems of longer-term planning require a 'dynamic' treatment rather than the 'static' approach of linear programming.

3. *Objectives and uncertainty*. Even if the plan producing maximum total net revenue does provide the highest profit, other objectives of the farmer may be more important, e.g. long-term growth of capital assets, and these may be better obtained from a different plan. When considering this point, it must be re-stressed that linear programming only maximises within the limits imposed and with the data given; thus allowances can be made for personal preferences and, to some extent, for risk. Nevertheless, the linear programming model is 'deterministic', that is, it assumes single values for net revenues, constraints and resource requirements, as though perfect knowledge existed. In fact the real world is an uncertain world, especially when it comes to making plans for some time in the future. This uncertainty affects farmers' decisions – and it affects different farmers differently. An important aspect of a farmer's objectives relates to his attitude to risk and uncertainty.

Other computer programming techniques

The main techniques so far developed to deal with these three criticisms are listed below. The inadequacies of 'ordinary' linear programming which are tackled by each technique are given alongside.

1. Integer Programming.**(*)	Structural.
2. Separable Programming.	Structural.
3. Monte Carlo Method.****	Structural; Objectives.
4. Parametric Programming.*****	Structural and uncertainty – but only to a very limited extent.
5. Dynamic Linear Programming.***	Dynamics; Objectives – to a limited extent.

6. Dynamic Programming.*	Dynamics primarily; Structural and Uncertainty also.
7. Quadratic Programming.**	Objectives and Uncertainty.
8. Stochastic Linear Programming.	Objectives and Uncertainty.
9. Game Theory.**	Objectives and Uncertainty.
10. MOTAD.***	Objectives and Uncertainty.

The number of asterisks following each technique is a measure of its potential usefulness for practical advisory purposes during the 1980s, so far as can be judged at present. Ordinary linear programming would have five asterisks – an important point to bear in mind when considering these other techniques. In deciding on the number given to each technique, the following criteria have been used:

1. Data requirements.
2. The likely general availability of the required computer routines.
3. The level of advisory expertise required to understand and apply the technique.
4. The practical significance of the particular problems tackled by the technique and the extent to which useful guidelines are provided by them and not by linear programming.

A brief outline of the method and object of each of these techniques follows. Those with apparently negligible practical potential in the near future are given little attention.

Integer programming

Being able to use integers (that is, whole numbers with no fractional or decimal parts) in a computer model has considerable advantages. Of at least four distinct approaches to integer (or 'discrete') programming one of the two most frequently described is the 'cutting plane' method devised by Gomory. This consists of an augmented linear programme. After the ordinary linear programming solution is found, additional constraints are automatically generated in such a way as eventually to produce a solution entirely in integer values. The original feasible linear programming area is gradually pared down until the choice is made between the integer values closest to the original linear programming feasible boundary. The other, and perhaps more promising, is the 'branch and bound' method, which solves a sequence of ordinary linear programming problems in which upper and lower bounds are imposed on the values of all integer variables. The optimal solution is sought from a 'tree', the branches and sub-branches of which represent alternative problems generated by the programme.

Practical experience of using integer programming, particularly in farming, is at present very limited, although programmes are now available and being tested on farm situations. It appears to take a considerable amount of computer time and not always to provide the optimum integer solution. Even more useful for farming will be 'mixed' (as compared with 'pure') integer programmes, in which only *some* of the variables have to be integers (instead of all of them).

As alternatives to 'pure' integer programming, various so-called 'cut-and-try' methods using ordinary linear programming can be applied. As these have already been described in Chapter 15 they will only be summarised here. The most obvious method is re-running the programme with different integer levels forced in. For example, it could be run with no cow activity, with 75 cows forced in and then again with 150 forced in. Allowance can be made for decreasing labour requirements per head of livestock as numbers increase. Again, programmes can be run with two alternative potato activities, one assuming hand picking and the other the use of a potato harvester. The differences in fixed costs are compared with the differences in net revenues of the alternative solutions. A problem here is the large number of re-runs needed if there are several integer choices. For all possible combinations of four alternative integer situations to be considered 15 runs would be needed; five would require 31. This is not difficult to do, but interpretation of the many results may take a long time.

The other main alternative is to revise the matrix in the light of the original linear programming solution and re-run. Instead of the automatic generation of new constraints, as in the Gomory method, one or more variables can be forced in at the closest acceptable integer level once the non-integer solution is found; the other variables can then find their new level. This may be done in successive stages. There is no guarantee that the ultimate solution will be optimal, but it may be considered close enough to be acceptable. For individual farm planning the time required would preclude making several attempts in order to compare the results.

Separable programming

Because its practical value in the near future appears to be very limited, little will be said about this technique. Its main object is to allow for increasing returns. It has similar possibilities to integer programming as regards dealing with indivisibilities, but it has been less applied even than integer programming and the likely availability of computer routines seems to be less promising. An advantage is that it probably requires less computer time than integer programming, but it is more difficult to formulate the model. The technique deals with non-linear functions, and it is used to restrict the possible combinations of certain activities that can be selected in the optimal plan.

Monte Carlo method

This technique was rapidly accepted, developed and tested in farm planning after its inception in Sweden in the mid-1960s. The reason is that it has several obvious advantages compared with linear programming and the computer routines required are less difficult to write than those for mathematical programming techniques.

The particular advantage of the technique is that it works in integer values of any required 'step size'. A minimum as well as a maximum size can be included for each enterprise, without needing to force in the enterprise to achieve this, as in linear programming. For example, the choice can be made, all in one run of the programme, between 0, 75, 150 and 225 cows. Fixed costs, e.g. of a machine or building, can be included as well as variable costs, again without having to force in the item if it is not required. The choice can be made between different numbers of regular workers, each costing, say, £3500 a year. Also, it is possible to prescribe that if activity *X* is included one or more other specified activities must be excluded, if these are held to be incompatible.

It is not a maximising technique, however. The solutions are random feasible plans. Usually the top ten or twenty plans (as measured by total net revenue) are printed out. The top plan will fall short of the linear programming solution by an amount depending on the number of 'runs', the complexity of the matrix and the effect of the integer values. Because of the latter, however, the net profits of the top plans (after deducting the fixed costs) could be higher than that of the linear programming solution. In any case the difference is likely to be so small as to be insignificant, considering the uncertainty attached both to the data and to the future.

Another advantage is that the farmer is given a *choice* of plans. He may prefer a sub-optimal plan because it is simpler to operate or less risky. Furthermore, other criteria can be supplied as well as the total net revenue of the plans, e.g. capital requirements and a measure of risk. The farmer can thus balance different objectives in making his choice. The computer can even plot points on a graph with, say, initial (or, 'set-up') capital requirements on one axis and profit on another; furthermore a third criterion, e.g. the approximate return on capital, or the estimated range in annual profit, can be plotted at each point on the graph represented by a plan.

The method of computation uses the simulation technique and is basically simple. A matrix is required, similar to linear programming but with some differences. An example is shown in Table 17.1. Minimum and maximum levels for each activity are included in the activity columns. The maximum number of activities to be included in any plan and the number of plans to be calculated (that is, 'runs') are specified. The matrix consists of two sections, one containing 'primary' activities (at specified integer levels), the other 'derived' activities, including buying and selling activities. The primary activities section is the same as in a linear programming matrix; only these activities are used in the selection procedure. If any activity (e.g. wheat II) requires a supplying activity (e.g. wheat I) the latter has to be chosen before the former. In the centre block of the matrix, the coefficients indicate the supply and use of derived activities by primary activities. The derived activities are linked to their respective primary activities by 'markers' (−1) and do not use any of the 'real' constraints; two levels of prices can be specified for each where appropriate: a selling price and a (higher) buying price. The levels of the derived activities are calculated after each plan has been formed, by balancing the amounts produced and used by the primary activities.

The data are first read into the computer and each activity is given an identifying number. In any one run the first activity is chosen by selection of a random number. Next an integer level for that activity is chosen, again at random, between the upper and lower size limits. The resource requirements of that activity at the chosen level are deducted from the total resources available and the remaining resource levels computed; if resource supplies are insufficient for the chosen level to operate, the size of the activity is reduced to the maximum which available resources allow. The procedure is repeated with a second activity, this time matching it against the resources remaining having included the first activity. The process continues until the specified number of activities has been selected. If at this stage surplus resources remain, each activity is taken in the order of its original selection and expanded until a constraint is reached, except that the upper size limit set for each activity cannot be exceeded. Finally the levels of the derived activities are calculated in relation to the levels of the selected primary activities, to balance the requirements and surpluses of common factors or products, and the total net revenue obtained.

TABLE 17.1. *Monte Carlo method: example of matrix*

	Fixed resources	Primary activities								Derived activities		
		(1) Grass seed 1 acre	(2) Pots. 1 acre	(3) Grow barley 1 acre	(4) Wheat I 1 acre	(5) Wheat II 1 acre	(6) Cows I 1 cow	(7) Cows II 1 cow	(8) Bacon pigs 30 pigs	(9) Barley 1 ton	(10) Straw 1 ton	(11) Grazing ley 1 acre
Net revenues		25	60	−3	42	36	110	120	177	23 21	5 3	8
1. Land (acres)	200	1	1	1	1	1	1.2	1.2				
2. Labour I (hrs)	550	1	10	2	2	2	3	2.5	15			
3. Labour II (hrs)	450		1	2.7	2.7	2.7	3	2.5	15			
4. Cereals (acres)	130			1	1	1						
5. Wht. I Wht. II Tie	0				−1	1						
6. Cows (no.)	70						1	1				
1. Barley (tons)				−1.5			1.25	1.25	5.1	−1		
2. Straw (tons)			1	−1.2	−1	−1	0.75	0.75			−1	
3. Grazing (acres)							1.2	1.2				−1
Cumulative frequency[a]		10	25	37	50	62	71	86	100			
Minimum activity levels		10	15	10	10	10	30	50	1			
Maximum activity levels		50	30	70	50	50	50	70	4			

Number of iterations: 1000
Maximum number of primary activities per plan: 6

[a] The differences between the 'cumulative frequency' row figures for adjacent activities measure their chance of selection, thus giving the weighting referred to on p. 377, e.g. potatoes have a 15% chance of selection (25–10) and barley 12% (37–25).

Source: Donaldson, G. F. and Webster, J. P. G. (1968) *An Operating Procedure for Simulation Farm Planning – Monte Carlo Method.* Wye College, University of London.

This whole plan-building procedure is repeated the specified number of times, say 3000. It is conceivable for all these plans to be stored and printed out. However, apart from the time that would be needed to look at them at all, most are likely to be of very little interest, being entirely randomly selected with no specified objective. Instead the first, say, twenty plans can be stored and each subsequent plan tested against those already stored. If the total net revenue of the new plan exceeds that of the lowest of the plans so far stored the new plan replaces the lowest plan. This continues until the top twenty of the total number are obtained. They are then printed out (Table 17.2 shows the top ten for the data given in Table 17.1) and the selection made by the farmer. As already explained, the levels of other criteria can also be printed out with each plan, and the results may even be graphed. Furthermore, various forms of analysis can be done within the program specification, such as the number of times each activity enters those solutions giving a total net revenue above a certain level.

This technique does appear to have considerable practical potential, although the use made of it in the UK during the 1970s has been disappointing. The amount of computer storage space needed might have been a difficulty not long ago, but recent developments of machines with greatly expanded capacity have overcome this possible limitation. The technique is 'wasteful' of computer time and the computer cost exceeds that of linear programming, unless many re-runs are made with the latter. However, the proportionate increase in total cost is likely to be small when the adviser's time is included. A dilemma arises in deciding on the number of runs required with farms of differing complexity. It may be worthwhile on complicated farms to use linear programming to reduce the number of activities included in the Monte Carlo procedure. It is also possible to economise in computer time by weighting activities subjectively (see footnote to Table 17.1), so as to give those thought most likely to enter the best plans a better chance of being selected – although there are obvious difficulties and potential drawbacks to doing so. Furthermore, 'heuristic' procedures (which broadly means, 'finding out from experience') have been developed to improve the efficiency of the method in terms of computer time per useful plan by a 'narrowing down' process: after a certain number of runs, or even continuously, information about the most profitable plans so far selected can be used to adjust the 'sampling parameters' (such as the upper and lower limits to the size of individual activities) in the direction of the most profitable plans, so that less computer time is wasted in selecting obviously unprofitable plans. A

TABLE 17.2. *Monte Carlo method: output tableau – top ten plans*

Plan no.	(1)	(2)	(3)	(4)	(5)	(6)	(7)	(8)	(9)	(10)
Total net revenue	10,471	10,325	10,318	10,302	10,286	10,272	10,260	10,247	10,247	10,239
Primary activities										
1. Grass seed (acres)	11	28	23	21	28	17	20	10	0	13
2. Potatoes (acres)	20	21	19	18	15	21	15	20	20	20
3. Grow barley (acres)	0	0	17	30	0	24	0	15	37	27
4. Wheat I (acres)	50	45	47	48	47	50	50	47	50	27
5. Wheat II (acres)	32	22	10	0	21	0	22	25	0	27
6. Cows I (no.)	0	0	0	0	0	0	0	0	0	0
7. Cows II (no.)	70	70	70	69	70	70	70	66	70	70
8. Bacon pigs (30)	0	0	0	1	4	0	4	0	0	0
Derived activities, (+ sign = sell, − sign = buy, or use)										
1. Barley (tons)	−87.50	−87.50	−62.00	−46.35	−107.90	−51.50	−107.90	−60.00	−32.00	−47.00
2. Straw (tons)	+9.50	−6.50	+5.90	+14.25	+0.50	+5.30	+4.50	+20.50	+21.90	+13.90
3. Grazing leys (acres)	−84.00	−84.00	−84.00	−82.80	−84.00	−84.00	−84.00	−79.20	−84.00	−84.00

Source: Donaldson, G. F. and Webster, J. P. G. (1968) *An Operating Procedure for Simulation Farm Planning – Monte Carlo Method.* Wye College, University of London.

dilemma remains however – if the 'top twenty' are all very similar and close to the linear programming solution the technique gives little extra choice of plans; if, on the other hand, they are all very different and some way from the linear programming solution, there will be the suspicion that still better plans exist. But the big advantage obtained from using integers remains.

Parametric programming

The matrix for parametric programming is the same as for linear programming. The only difference is that one or more items in the matrix are allowed to vary. The technique is therefore referred to alternatively as *variable resource* or *variable price programming*. In the former, one or more of the constraints are allowed to vary, so that a series of optimum plans is produced over a range of, say, farm areas or capital availability. In the latter, one or more of the prices are allowed to vary, so that, similarly, a series of optimum plans is provided for a range of prices for one or more products. It is possible, as an alternative, to re-run a linear programming matrix with several different discrete levels of availability for one or more resources, or with different price assumptions for one or more products. Parametric programming differs in that the level of the variable is altered continuously over a complete range. The necessary computer routines are fairly easily obtainable.

The resource whose supply level is altered in variable resource programming for planning individual farms is most likely to be capital, but it could be any other constraint. The technique has a greater potential application however in modal farm planning, where linear programming solutions are being used as guidelines for a number of farms whose resource levels, e.g. land area, will obviously differ.

In the modified simplex method of variable resource programming the criterion for introducing activities into the plan is modified to ensure that the variable resource (say, capital) is always invested in the activity which will provide the highest marginal return to that resource. In the computation, an extra row is included to provide the required information. For each level of capital input, therefore, the optimum plan is obtained. When a selected activity reaches its limit, the amount of capital required, the plan and the total net revenue of that plan are calculated. Given this position, the unselected activity now showing the highest marginal revenue to capital is chosen and the process is repeated. This normally continues until no further increase in total net revenue is possible, that is, until the marginal value product of the variable resource becomes zero, indicating that it has become surplus to the availability of other resources. Intermediate plans can be found from plotting the resulting 'key' plans, as shown in Figure 17.1. The lines drawn between any two adjacent key points, where the investment opportunities change, are straight – because of the linearity assumption. The reduction in the slopes of successive lines denotes falling marginal returns to the variable resource as its supply increases. It is possible to produce plans at successive equal additions to the variable resource supply, e.g. at £5000, £10,000, £15,000, etc. of capital.

In two-resource variable programming, the optimum plans are first found for each resource in turn, assuming the other resource to be in unlimited supply. This is done in effect by running two one-resource variable programmes – say for land and capital. In this way an 'area' is defined outside which further land or capital supply, at any given level of the other resource, will not enable any increase in total net revenue to be obtained. Plans are then found for any combination of land and capital within this bounded area. The interpretation of the results is far more complex than for one-resource variable programming. In principle it is possible to vary more than two resources, but the problem of interpreting the results then becomes very large.

Variable price programming is most often used in farm policy research, namely to derive 'normative supply functions', that is, to predict how farmers *should* react to changes in the relative price level of a commodity. It can also be used in farm planning, however – particularly by applying it to modal farm situations.

In one-price variable programming the price of one product is varied over a given range, with all other prices given. It is necessary to have a supply row and a selling activity for the product (say, wheat); that is, it is not enough to have a single combined 'produce and sell' activity. First the optimum plan at the minimum price level in the required range is computed. Subsequently, critical price levels at which the optimum plan changes are calculated, and the plans and total net revenues are derived for these levels. By this means a series of wheat price ranges are obtained, at each of which a given area (or production) of wheat remains optimal. Beyond each critical price level the optimal wheat area increases. This is depicted in Figure 17.2.

Two-price variable programming is feasible but much more complicated. Let us assume that the two commodities of interest are wheat and barley. First the optimal plan is derived, given the minimum prices for both together. Optimal plans are then obtained for the other extremes of the price ratios, using one-price variable programming.

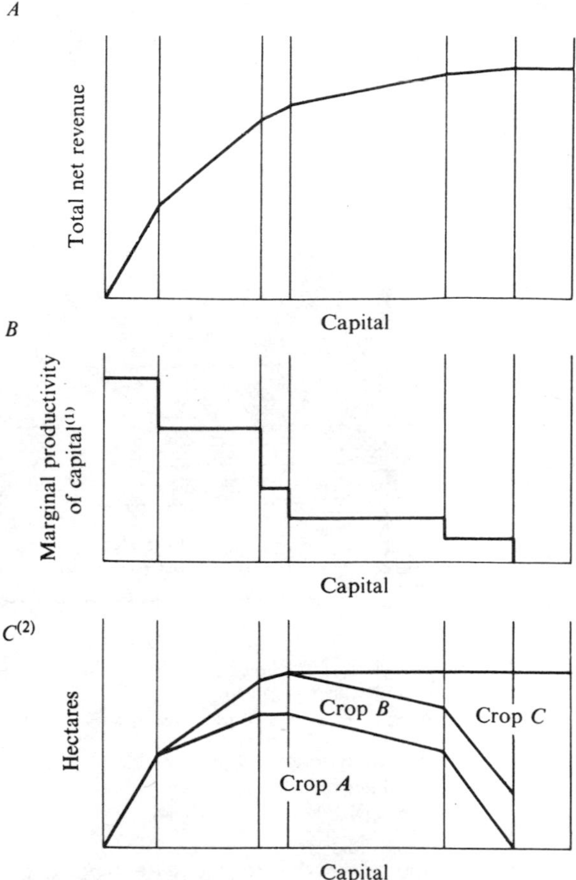

[1] Increase in total net revenue per additional unit of capital

[2] Alternatively, each activity may be plotted on a separate graph

Fig. 17.1. Variable resource programming – illustration of results
A. Total net revenue
B. Marginal productivity of capital
C. Plans

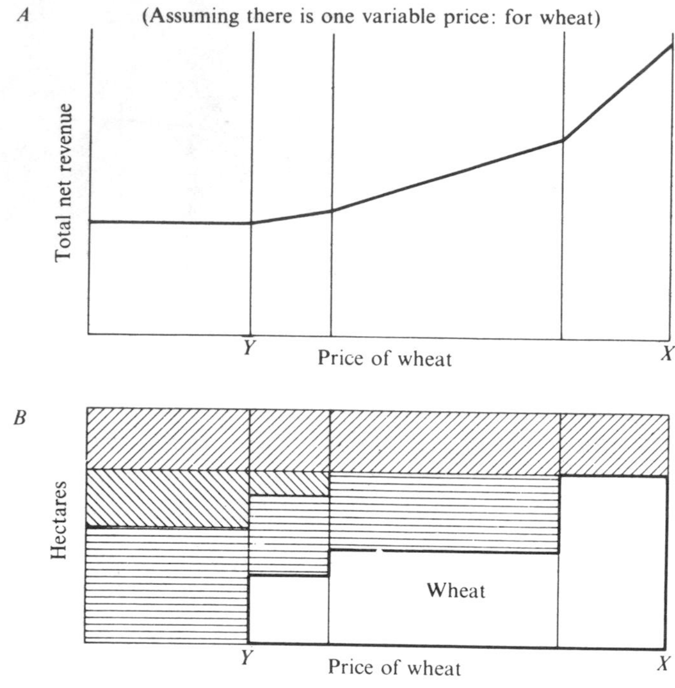

The different types of shading depict three other activities
X = maximum of wheat price range
No wheat enters the plan until price reaches Y

Fig. 17.2. Variable price programming – illustration of results
A. Total net revenue
B. Plans, with hectares of wheat

Thus plans are obtained over the whole wheat-price range at the minimum barley price and at the maximum barley price; similarly plans are derived over the whole barley-price range at both the minimum and the maximum prices for wheat. This defines a bordered area. Optimum plans for any combination of wheat and barley prices within this area can be derived by a succession of one-price variable solutions across the area. These same methods may be used for varying three or more prices, but the interpretation of results soon becomes far too complex to handle.

Dynamic linear programming

The limitations of a single-period, or static, approach such as ordinary linear programming were outlined on p. 413 above. Dynamic linear programming uses the ordinary linear programming model and computations, modified only in that more than one period is included in the model, these periods being interlinked. Hence the alternative names 'multi-period linear programming', 'sequential linear programming' or 'intertemporal linear programming'. The period can be of any chosen length, e.g. three months, one year or five years. In fact it does not have to be of the same duration for the whole model – a farmer may, for example, seek fairly detailed time plans in the near future but be satisfied with broad outline policy guides in the more distant future.

A series of interdependent optimal plans is obtained from the model, that is, the optimum in one year allows for optimal requirements in all other periods also. The sum of all the periods considered is often referred to as the 'planning horizon' (this term has already been used in a more general sense in Chapter 13). The build-up and possible re-investment of resources, especially capital, over time can be planned, transfers occurring from one period to the next. The model is 'dynamic' only in the sense that inputs and outputs are dated, not in the sense that variability of prices and other coefficients are incorporated.

The matrix takes the shape shown in Figure 17.3. Period 2 is linked to period 1 by the contents of block *X*; period 3 is linked to period 2

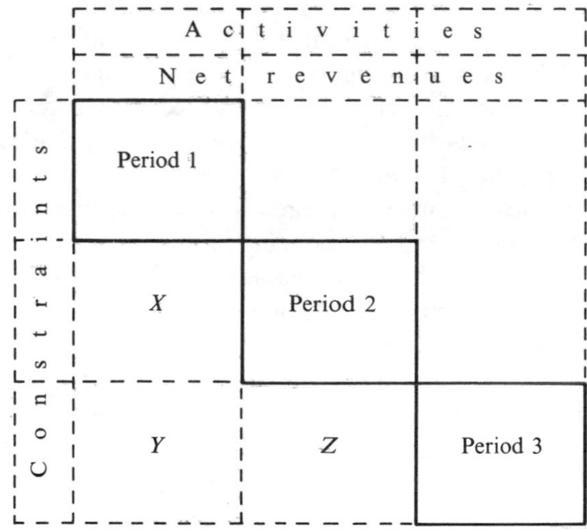

Fig. 17.3. Dynamic linear programming – structure of matrix

by block Z and to period 1 indirectly through blocks X and Z, but possibly also directly through Y. Any number of periods can be included, as long as the computer being used has sufficient capacity to handle the resulting matrix size.

Most dynamic linear programming models are concerned with studying the build-up and optimum use of capital through time. In this case there is a capital (or 'income') row for each period, which allows for withdrawal of funds to meet both variable and fixed costs and living expenses, and capital can be transferred from one period to the next. A simple example is shown in Table 17.3. Thus each activity has a positive coefficient (its total variable costs) in the capital row for period K and a negative coefficient (its output) in period $K + 1$. Fixed costs and living expenses can either be forced in as a capital requirement, as shown in Table 17.3, or deducted cumulatively from the capital constraints for successive periods, as below:

Capital (period 1)	6,000 $\geqq$	no fixed cost
Capital (period 2)	1,750 $\geqq$	activity required
Capital (period 3)	−2,750 $\geqq$	

The supply of capital in each period will depend on the original sum available, the size of the annual deduction for fixed costs and personal expenses, and the annual cash returns of the activities in the selected plan relative to their demands for variable capital. A capital transfer activity in each period can pass on unused capital from one period to the next for possible future use, if this is more profitable than present use. Any variable can be changed over time according to expectations and long-term plans, e.g. prices can be altered, new enterprises can be introduced or old ones dropped, or allowance may be made for an anticipated rise or fall in soil fertility.

Usually the net revenues for each activity are discounted to give present values, the objective thus being to maximise the present value of future incomes over the entire planning horizon. Thus in Table 17.3, for example, a 7 per cent discount rate is assumed and the net revenue for pigs, which is £60 a year, becomes 52.4 in period 2, that is, $60/(1 + 0.7)^2$, or 60×0.873. Perennials such as fruit orchards can be included; their activity columns would contain the returns less variable costs in each capital row of all the planning periods after planting (these would of course be negative sums at first), and the net revenue would be the discounted net returns over the whole planning horizon. Investments in fixed resources, borrowing throughout the planning horizon,

TABLE 17.3. *Dynamic linear programming – example of matrix layout*

	Period 1			Period 2			Period 3		
	Pigs	Beef	Fixed costs	Pigs	Beef	Fixed costs	Pigs	Beef	Fixed costs
Net revenue	56.1	28.0	0	52.4	26.2	0	49.0	24.5	0
Period 1									
Capital (£) 10,000 ≥	120	70	1						
Labour (hrs) 600 ≥	20	8							
Fixed costs/ personal expenses (£) 4,000 =			1						
Period 2									
Capital (£) 0 ≥	−180	−100		120	70	1			
Labour (hrs) 600 ≥				20	8				
Fixed costs/ personal expenses (£) 4,250 =						1			
Period 3									
Capital (£) 0 ≥				−180	−100		120	70	1
Labour (hrs) 600 ≥							20	8	
Fixed costs/ personal expenses (£) 4,500 =									1

and salvage values (that is, disposal, or sale, values of assets at the end of the planning horizon) can also be allowed for. Some studies have made the objective the maximisation of revenue-earning capacity or net worth in the final period. Maximising net worth is of particular interest in that variations in salvage values compared with the original cost of investments allow for the fact that some investments, e.g. buildings and machinery, fall in value, while others may increase, e.g. livestock and land.

Dynamic linear programming thus has considerable potential and interest, and yet it has been little used. There are three main reasons for this. First, it can only optimise future *expectations*, and obviously many factors and circumstances may change unexpectedly over time. Secondly, the matrix can become extremely large, e.g. even a 20-column by 12-row annual matrix over 10 years becomes 200 × 120, and a 60 by 40 over 20 years becomes 1200 × 800. Not long ago few, if any, computers could handle such large matrices, but this is no longer much of a problem in many countries. In any case the size of the matrix can be reduced – and probably would be – by using ordinary linear programming to pick out the key activities and constraints, or the problem may be solved in stages (i.e. a few years, or periods) at a time. Furthermore, only broad guidelines over time should be expected from the model. Thirdly, incorporating the required capital items realistically and allowing for discounting takes thought and therefore time, and the continuity assumptions (i.e. non-integers) limit the reality and add to the difficulties of model-building. Dynamic integer or dynamic mixed integer programming would overcome this last disadvantage.

Dynamic programming

While fascinating intellectually, dynamic programming has little significance for practical farm planning at the present time and so will be dealt with relatively briefly. It is a mathematical technique entirely different from dynamic linear programming, but its main objective is broadly the same: namely, to obtain an optimal policy over a succession of periods, or 'stages' – the decisions made in any one period or stage controlling the 'state' in which the process will be found in the following stage. In fact the decision problems that can be handled by dynamic programming do not have to be dynamic in the temporal sense, provided the decision problem can be dealt with in sequential stages, one at a time. The technique starts by looking at the final stage or period and works back to the initial or current period.

Conceptually dynamic programming is far more impressive than dynamic linear programming. It can handle non-linear and integer problems. It can also incorporate stochastic elements, that is, probability distributions for variables, instead of having to assume single, 'deterministic' levels for each variable. Thus the sensitivity of the optimal policies to variations in the parameters can readily be examined, and results are obtained not just for the particular situation being studied but for an entire range of related situations. Furthermore, the matrix size can be far smaller than for dynamic linear programming for a similar problem. The technique has been applied to such problems as crop rotations, inventories, e.g. fodder reserves, and replacement policy, e.g. livestock culling.

Unfortunately there are two major drawbacks to its practical use for everyday advisory work. The first is that the very flexibility of the technique means that an infinite variety of models can be constructed, and virtually a new computer program has to be written individually for each different problem, whereas linear programming uses a single basic model. Secondly, the data requirements are far more stringent even than for linear programming; whole functions have to be defined. Large firms may be able to justify the cost; individual farms cannot.

Another technique, *recursive programming*, has affinities to dynamic programming in that it deals with a sequence of interrelated decisions over time. It does not however seek to devise optimal rules for decision-making, but only to *explain* changes that occur. It has thus so far been mainly applied to studies of supply response in sectors of the agricultural industry rather than to individual farm planning.

Quadratic programming

Quadratic programming tackles the problem of random variations in enterprise outputs, as caused by annual fluctuations in yields and prices. It provides the maximum profit (or net revenue) plan at any given level of income variation (or risk) or – which in fact comes to the same thing – the plan with the lowest income variation (risk) for any given level of profit. Thus in selecting a farm plan the farmer can take into account not only the *average* profit to be expected but also the *minimum* profit (or maximum loss) that is likely to occur in bad years. The technique does not however cover seasonal variations in inputs, except insofar as these can be handled by linear programming.

The technique uses a modification of the simplex method of linear programming. Measures of stochastic variation in net revenues, caused by yield and price changes, are included in the income function. It is not enough to include the variance[1] of each activity separately. Allowance must also be made for co-variance, that is, relationships between the variance of different pairs of activities; for example, the weather in any one year may benefit several crops together, or possibly benefit one crop but be detrimental to another. In other words, the income variations of all combinations of crops have also to be incorporated. Thus, co-variances for each pair of enterprises must be included as well as the variance for each. This information is included in what is consequently called a 'variance–co-variance matrix'. An example is given in Table 17.4. The technique minimises the variance for a given 'expected' (i.e. average) total net revenue (or, maximises the latter for a given variance). The usual procedure is to obtain first of all the normal linear programming result, and its level of variance; then, for successive lower levels of total net revenue, that plan is obtained which minimises variance at each level.

The total net revenues of successive plans can then be plotted against the variance. With a 'normal' frequency distribution (that is, one that is symmetrically distributed on either side of the mean) there is a 95 per cent chance that a result will be within twice the standard deviation of the mean expected level. For example, with a mean level for net revenue of £10,000 and a standard deviation of £1000, in 19 cases out of 20 the net revenue in any one year will be between £8000 and £12,000, that is, there is only a 1 in 40 chance that it will fall below £8000. Lower levels of minimum income may be calculated with even safer levels, e.g. 1 in 100 or 1 in 200. These minimum levels can be plotted against average expected levels, as shown in Figure 17.4. The farmer is unlikely to select a plan with an expected net revenue below X (where the corresponding minimum net revenue is at its highest), since these plans also have a lower minimum level of net revenue. Beyond that the farmer can choose between a plan with a higher expected net income but with more risk (of a lower minimum net income in any one year) and one with a lower expected net income but less risk (i.e. a higher minimum income). Another advantage of the technique is that the farmer is afforded a

[1] The *variance* measures the amount by which a range of results varies around an average (i.e. mean) figure. It is calculated by summing the squares of deviations (i.e. differences from the mean) and dividing by the number of observations less 1. The square root of the variance is the *standard deviation*.

TABLE 17.4. *Quadratic programming – example of variance–co-variance matrix*

	Wheat	Barley	Sugar beet	Early potatoes	Late potatoes	Broad beans	Dwarf beans	Vining peas
Wheat	**12.8**	7.8	−9.7	0	0	0	5.8	10.8
Barley	7.8	**8.5**	−8.0	−19.0	−13.5	4.7	4.7	0
Sugar beet	−9.7	−8.0	**379**	−126	−89.7	0	31.6	59.0
Early potatoes	0	−19.0	−126	**1,053**	523	51.8	52.6	98.3
Late potatoes	0	−13.5	−89.7	523	**531**	0	0	0
Broad beans	0	4.7	0	51.8	0	**1,018**	104	193
Dwarf beans	5.8	4.7	31.6	52.6	0	104	**1,053**	197
Vining peas	10.8	0	59.0	98.3	0	193	197	**917**

Source: Camm, B. (1962) 'Risk in Vegetable Production on a Fen Farm'. *The Farm Economist*, **X**, no. 2.

Notes:

The bold figures are the variances; the remainder are co-variances.

The figures below the diagonal of variances simply duplicate the figures above the variances.

A positive co-variance implies a positive correlation between the annual outputs of the two crops; a negative co-variance means there is a negative correlation. Zero implies an insignificant correlation coefficient.

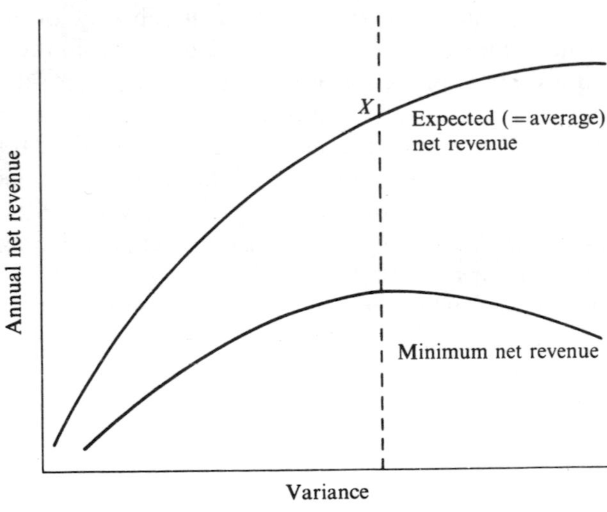

Fig. 17.4. Quadratic programming – expected and minimum net revenue

choice of sub-optimal plans, one of which he may prefer on grounds other than risk.

Clearly, then, this technique has a useful advantage over ordinary linear programming. Furthermore, computer routines should not be too difficult to obtain. The major problem preventing more use in practice is obviously that of data. It is difficult enough to obtain the information required to construct a variance–co-variance matrix from an area, let alone an individual farm. Some have criticised the technique, too, because it still leaves the farmer with a difficult choice, while others have argued that in any case the choice is inadequate – that his objectives may be far too complex for him to be able to choose between plans satisfying the single criterion of minimum risk at any given level of total net revenue. Furthermore, the statistical assumption of normal distributions for the net revenues may not be valid. Finally, the technique suffers from the inadequacies of ordinary linear programming, such as the continuity assumption.

Stochastic linear programming

Stochastic linear programming is another form of risk programming. Its scope is broader than that of quadratic programming, in that it can handle random variations in resource supplies and input coefficients as well as net revenues. Each variable subject to risk variation has its range of possible values specified as a probability distribution. Of the two possible approaches to stochastic linear programming the one usually applied involves solving a number of ordinary linear programmes with values of the variables drawn from the probability distributions. Thus a procedure is required for obtaining sets of random variations from the complete range. If the probabilities are normally distributed this is apparently not too difficult to do. However, the very limited use that has been made of the technique, which has been known about in agricultural economics since the mid-1950s, indicates the practical difficulties involved in its application. Estimating probability distributions for all items in the matrix likely to be subject to random variation (which means a major proportion of them) would obviously be an enormous task. Furthermore the technique is demanding of computer time. Thus it is likely to be useful only for research purposes.

Game theory

Game theory has not been used in practical advisory work, but it merits some attention in this chapter because of the important aspects of decision-making to which it relates and because developments that have been suggested offer at least some possibility for its practical application in the future.

Game theory deals with decision-making, or 'choice of strategies', in the face of the uncertainty of the real world. Because of the time-lag in production, the 'price-taking' nature of the industry, its dependence on weather, pests and diseases, and so on, farmers and farm managers have to make their decisions with a greater degree of uncertainty than managers in most other sectors of industry. These factors are largely uncontrollable and unpredictable.

The theory of games was developed to analyse the situation where a conflict of interests occurs between two or more decision-makers. It studies the results of alternative possible courses of action (or 'strategies') for one person, given that the other person(s) are also looking after their own interests at the same time and acting accordingly. In agriculture the farmer or farm manager is taking the decisions and the 'opponent' is 'Nature', which represents all the aspects of uncertainty mentioned above. Nature is, however, passive; in other words, it cannot change as a result of the action taken.

Thus the farm planning problem is conceived as the farmer 'playing a game' against Nature. He has to decide his course of action, or strategy, given various 'states of nature', namely, different possible price and weather conditions, etc. that may occur in the future planning period. A 'payoff matrix' is drawn up, which represents the whole set of possible returns from different activities in different years (or 'states of nature'). Table 17.5 illustrates such a matrix, the figures being the gross margins per acre for each enterprise in the different years.

TABLE 17.5. *Game theory – example of payoff matrix*

	Gross margins (£ per acre) over 5 years States of nature (years)				
Activity	(1)	(2)	(3)	(4)	(5)
Spring wheat	31.3	28.4	30.2	48.7	31.2
Winter wheat	47.6	38.8	40.6	51.4	48.3
Barley	46.1	33.5	33.9	39.6	40.0
Early potatoes	105.0	61.1	109.8	187.8	98.5
Maincrop potatoes	50.8	22.9	186.1	104.6	120.2
Peas	50.3	105.9	99.5	76.1	90.1
Clover seed	23.2	86.0	41.8	77.7	54.0
Cows	59.0	51.9	57.0	60.4	58.4
Sheep	25.8	35.8	25.8	26.5	29.7

Source: McInerney, J. P. (1969) 'Linear Programming and Game Theory Models – Some Extensions'. *Journal of Agricultural Economics*, **XX**, No. 2.

Given this information, various strategies are possible, depending on the farmer's decision criteria, which in turn depend on his personality and his circumstances. There are four 'classic' criteria, each requiring different strategies.

1. *Wald's criterion (maximin).* Here, the farmer tries to choose 'the best of the worst', that is, he selects that combination of activities which will maximise his minimum income. This gives the farmer maximum security in that his lowest likely income is higher than for any other plan. If he pursues this strategy he can be regarded either as a pessimist or simply as ultra-careful. A farmer may take such a course because he has only a small equity in his business, large family responsibilities, or because he has only recently started farming and wants to 'feel his way' to begin with.

2. *Laplace's criterion.* In this case the farmer simply assumes that each state of nature is equally likely to occur and tries to maximise his expected income on that basis. This is in fact what ordinary linear programming normally does, in that the maximising plan is usually (though not necessarily) calculated using the best estimates of average net revenues for each activity.

3. *Hurwicz's criterion.* For this criterion an 'optimism-index' has to be estimated for the farmer. This is used to weight the probability of the best and worst likely results. The expected 'payoff' is then calculated for each row (or strategy) and the highest selected. For a complete pessimist the answer is the same as would result from using Wald's maximin criterion. Obviously the problem here is to select the correct 'optimism-index'; this can vary for an individual from day to day. Furthermore, the model considers only the extreme values and ignores other relevant data in the complete set.

4. *Savage's Regret criterion.* This model is based on the difference between the *actual* payoff to the farmer following a particular strategy and that which he *could have* obtained had he known in advance the state of nature which in fact prevailed. This measures his dissatisfaction, or 'regret', at the opportunities missed, which the model aims to minimise. The principle is one of optimism in contrast to the pessimism of the Wald criterion, but on its own it is hardly likely to have practical significance.

Of these criteria, it has already been observed that the Laplace is virtually the same as linear programming. Of the others the Wald (maximin) appears to have the highest potential practical value. Like the other criteria it can be used with the normal linear programming computer routine. Some work has indicated that the results may in fact produce a plan with almost as high an average total net revenue as linear programming, but with a much higher minimum level. Particularly low levels that are very unlikely to occur should be excluded from the payoff matrix. Others have suggested a blend of the Wald and the Savage Regret criteria. Another possibility is to apply the criteria to a quite different type of payoff matrix, one produced by calculating the linear programming solution for each state of nature (i.e. year) separately and then applying each solution to all the other years; the payoff matrix then comprises the total net revenues of the different plans in different years.

The main limitation to the technique's practical potential is again the problem of data availability. If the data have virtually to be 'invented', its benefit is obviously arguable. But compared with quadratic programming it does give a definitive answer, instead of leaving the choice to the farmer, it can be used with linear programming computer routines, which are more easily available, and no variance–co-variance matrix has to be calculated. However, both tackle only the uncertainty as regards 'payoff', not those concerning resource availabilities and requirements, for example, for which other techniques or approximations would be needed.

Focus-loss and MOTAD

Since 1967 there have been a number of other attempts to make some form of risk programming more practically possible by reducing both the computational and the data requirements (compared especially with quadratic programming) and yet at the same time satisfying the essence of the farmer's problem.

One approach is based on the suggestion that the farmer is not so much interested in the whole feasible range of outcomes as in the extreme possible outcomes, both favourable (called 'focus-gain') and, far more important, unfavourable ('focus-loss'). A 'safety-first' policy can aim to minimise the probability of attaining a critically low minimum total net revenue (TNR), maximise this minimum TNR, or maximise the expected TNR subject to some specified probability of attaining at least this minimum level. The focus-loss procedure aims at the last: it concentrates on the probability of obtaining some critically low TNR together with providing the 'expected' (i.e. likely average) outcome. The conventional linear programming format can be used, with various additions to the matrix. It is referred to as the FLCP (focus-loss constrained programming) model.

The concept of an inviolate minimum TNR can easily be criticised, on the grounds that it is too simplistic. For example, most farmers would probably be prepared to accept a slightly lower TNR than a presupposed minimum one year in ten if the likely outcomes in the other nine years were well above those for any safer plan. Decision analysis (Appendix 16.1, pp. 406–11) examines these same problem-areas more realistically.

The Maximin criteria used in Game Theory (p. 434 above) has a similar objective – to maximise the worst possible payoff that nature is likely to inflict. Further consideration of this approach has led to the development of a model with features similar to those of quadratic programming but one that is far simpler to use, utilising parametric programming. It uses the same gross margin data to calculate the mean absolute deviation as a substitute for variance. This has been shown in practice to be little, if any, inferior to using the standard deviation. Farm plans are derived which, for each level of expected income, achieve the minimisation of total absolute deviation (hence the name, MOTAD). Since the sum of the positive total absolute deviations must equal the sum of the negative ones, and since also decision-makers are mainly worried about below average outcomes, only the minimisation of negative values need be considered. The results appear to be very similar to those given by quadratic programming.

Appendix 17.1: Further reading: selected references

General

Beale, E. M. L. (1968). *Mathematical Programming in Practice.* Pitman and Sons (Especially Chapter 13 – Quadratic Programming, Chapter 14 – Separable Programming, Chapter 15 – Integer Programming, and Chapter 17 – Stochastic Programming.)

McInerney, J. P. (1971) 'Developments in Planning Techniques with a Practical Potential in the 1970s'. *First International Farm Management Congress.* Farm Management Association.

Nix, J. (1969) Annotated Bibliography on Farm Planning and Programming Techniques. *Farm Management*, **1**, No. 7.

Reisch, E. M. (1970) 'Recent Advances in Farm Planning in W. Europe and North America.' *XIVth International Conference of Agricultural Economists.*

Weinschenck, G. (1968) 'Recent Developments of Quantitative Analysis on the Micro-level'. *International Seminar on Economic Models and Quantitative Methods for Decisions and Planning in Agriculture.*

Integer programming

Beale, E. M. L. (1965) Survey of Integer Programming, Chapter 17 of *Programming for Optimal Decisions.* Penguin Books.

Butterworth, K. (1972) 'Practical Application of Integer Programming to Farm Planning'. *Farm Management*, **2**, No. 3.

LP methods:

Camm, B. M., and Rothlisberger, P. (1965) 'Planning a Swiss Farm: a Study in Discrete Programming'. *The Farm Economist*, **10**, No. 9.

Monte Carlo method

Carlsson, M., Hovmark, B., and Lindgren, I. (1969) 'A Monte Carlo Method for the Study of Farm Planning Problems'. *Review of Marketing and Agricultural Economics*, **37**, No. 2.

Donaldson, G. F. and Webster, J. P. G. (1968) *An Operating Procedure for Simulation Farm Planning – Monte Carlo Method.* Department of Agricultural Economics, Wye College (University of London).

Thompson, S. C. (1967) *An Approach to Monte Carlo Programming*, Study No. 3, Department of Agriculture, University of Reading.

Parametric programming

Heady, E. O. and Chandler, W. (1958) *Linear Programming Methods* (Chapters 7 and 8). Iowa State College Press.

Dynamic linear programming

Loftsgaard, L. D. and Heady, E. O. (1959) 'Application of Dynamic Programming Models for Optimum Farm and Home Plans'. *Journal of Farm Economics*, **41**, 51.

Stewart, J. D. and Thornton, D. S. (1962) *A Study in Phased Development Solved with the Aid of Linear Programming*. Miscellaneous Studies No. 24, Department of Agricultural Economics, University of Reading.

Dynamic programming

Burt, O. R. and Allison, J. R. (1963) 'Farm Management Decisions with Dynamic Programming'. *Journal of Farm Economics*, **45**, No. 1. 121.

Combination of enterprises

Throsby, C. D. (1964) 'Some Dynamic Programming Models for Farm Management Research'. *Journal of Agricultural Economics*, **16**, No. 1.

Quadratic programming

Camm, B. M. (1962) 'Risk in Vegetable Production on a Fen Farm'. *The Farm Economist*, **10**, No. 2.

McFarquar, A. M. M. (1961) 'Rational Decision Making and Risk in Farm Planning'. *Journal of Agricultural Economics*, **14**, No. 4.

Stochastic linear programming

Johnson, S. R., Teterfiller, K. R. and Moore, D. S. (1967) 'Stochastic Linear Programming and Feasibility Problems in Farm Growth Analysis'. *Journal of Farm Economics*, **49**, 908.

Game theory

Agrawal, R. C. and Heady, E. O. (1968) 'Applications of Game Theory Models in Agriculture'. *Journal of Agricultural Economics*, **19**, No. 2.

Hazell, P. B. R. (1970) 'Game Theory – an Extension of its Application to Farm Planning under Uncertainty'. *Journal of Agricultural Economics*, **21**, No. 2.

McInerney, J. P. (1967) 'Maximin Programming – An Approach to Farm Planning under Uncertainty'. *Journal of Agricultural Economics*, **18**, No. 2.

McInerney, J.P. (1969) 'Linear Programming and Game Theory Models – Some Extensions'. *Journal of Agricultural Economics*, **20**, No. 2.

Focus-loss and MOTAD

Boussard, J. M. and Petit, M. (1967) 'Representation of Farmers' Behaviour under Uncertainty with a Focus-loss Constraint'. *Journal of Farm Economics*, **49**, No. 4.

Hazell, P. B. R. (1971) 'A Linear Alternative to Quadratic and Semi-variance Programming for Farm Planning under Uncertainty'. *American Journal of Agricultural Economics*, **53**, No. 1.

Kennedy, J. O. S. and Francisco, E. M. (1974) 'On the Formulation of Risk Constraints for Linear Programming'. *Journal of Agricultural Economics*, **25**, No. 2.

18: Matrix construction

Although matrix construction is considered in this chapter mainly from the viewpoint of linear programming, much of it is fundamental to many of the other techniques discussed in Chapter 17, such as multi-period linear programming, parametric programming, quadratic programming and Monte Carlo simulation. Indeed, some of its basic aspects are also applicable to programme planning.

As was seen in Chapter 15, matrix construction concerns the translation of farm resource – enterprise relationships into a series of mathematical equations that are suitable for processing by computer, and the fundamental problem of the planner is to ensure that such relationships are expressed realistically. In attempting to do this, two points should be kept in mind. First, the purpose of a matrix is not to detail every facet of farm organisation but simply to represent its essential features. Secondly, solutions are not meant to provide management with detailed blueprints of desirable courses of action, but rather to point the way to adjustments that are likely to prove profitable.

This chapter begins by considering the basic relationships between resources and activities and the functions performed by the latter. It then turns, more specifically, to operations with the major resources.

Basic operations

Resource – activity relationships

The most frequent relationship between activities and resources (and other constraints) is that already considered on page 356, where the amount of a resource consumed by the activities must be 'less than or equal to' its supply. To recapitulate, suppose that on an arable farm, legumes – beans and peas – must not exceed 40 hectares:

	Beans (1 hectare)	*Peas* (1 hectare)		*Constraints*
Maximum legumes (hectares)	1	1	≤	40

or, as it is usually written in the matrix, with the resource or constraint first (in the *B* column):

Constraint	*B*		*Beans* (1 hectare)	*Peas* (1 hectare)
Maximum legumes (hectares)	40	≥	1	1

The combined area of peas and beans cannot rise above a maximum of 40 ha, but, on the other hand, it can assume any level below 40 ha (including zero ha).

Two other relationships may also be required. The first is simply the converse of the relationship above (in that the sign is reversed) and is applicable when it is wished to specify some minimum level of an activity. Taking the legume example again:

Constraint	*B*		*Beans* (1 hectare)	*Peas* (1 hectare)
Minimum legumes (hectares)	40	≤	1	1

The combined area of beans and peas must be 'greater than or equal to' 40 hectares. In short, they may occupy an area above the minimum of 40, but cannot fall below it.

Lastly, it may be required that an activity takes on a fixed and predetermined level in the solution, so that the apposite relationship is signified by an equality sign:

Constraint	*B*		*Beans* (1 hectare)	*Peas* (1 hectare)
Legume requirement (hectares)	40	=	1	1

Land in legumes must be exactly equal to 40 hectares, although in this example there is some flexibility, in that it can be satisfied by beans or peas alone or by any combination of the two totalling 40 hectares.

Of these three relationships, it is the first that is automatically catered for in linear programming computations. If either of the other two are required, an instruction to this effect must be specified.[1,2]

[1] As was seen earlier (p. 357), with the 'less than or equal to' constraint, the coefficient in the disposal activity is positive. With the 'greater than or equal to' constraint it is, therefore, negative.

[2] Although disposal activities enable inequalities to be treated as equalities, the matrix builder is not concerned with this mathematical stratagem, but with the *actual relationships that exist between activities and constraints*. For this reason and for clarity of exposition, signs expressing such relationships are shown in the rest of this chapter, although it is not normally necessary to include them as part of matrix input, any more than it is necessary to include disposal activities.

Specification of supply and demand

So far it has been seen that with the usual 'less than or equal to' constraint, activities cannot rise above the particular levels specified by the positive coefficients in the column of resources and other constraints (the *B* column). Looked at in another way, the latter represent either the supply of material resources, such as land and labour, or the 'giving of permission' to undertake various activities, in the case of non-material factors such as institutional or rotational constraints. In contrast, positive coefficients in the body of the matrix represent the demands of the activities for resources or for 'permission' and it follows, therefore, that *negative* coefficients represent supply, as is illustrated by the following example:

Constraint	*B*		*Beef store* (1 beast)	*Yearling heifer* (1 beast)
Maximum pasture (hectares)	20	≥	0.3	0.2

There is a supply of 20 ha of permanent pasture, while the requirements per head of beef stores and yearling heifers are 0.3 ha and 0.2 ha respectively. If the 20 hectares is now transferred to the right-hand side of the expression, so that its sign changes in the process, we have:

Constraint	*B*		*Beef store* (1 beast)	*Yearling heifer* (1 beast)	*Pasture supply* (20 ha)
Maximum pasture (hectares)	0	≥	0.3	0.2	−20

Regardless of which way the permanent pasture constraint is set up, the effect is the same. For example, suppose there are 50 beef stores and 25 yearling heifers in the solution:

Constraint	*B*		*Beef store*		*Yearling heifer*		*Pasture supply*
Activity levels:			(50 beasts)		(25 beasts)		(20 ha)
Maximum pasture (hectares)	20	≥	15	+	5		—
			(0.3 × 50)		(0.2 × 25)		
or Maximum pasture (hectares)	0	≥	15	+	5	−	20
			(0.3 × 50)		(0.2 × 25)		(−20 × 1)

In each case the supply of, and demand for, pasture is in balance and no additional animals can be carried without breaking the supply constraints. Conversely, it is feasible to carry no animals at all.

Reverting to the first formulation, suppose that agisted pasture is also available. This can be shown as an activity with a negative coefficient in the pasture row indicating supply:

Constraint	*B*		*Beef store* (1 beast)	*Yearling heifer* (1 beast)	*Agisted pasture* (1 hectare)
Maximum pasture (hectares)	20	≥	0.3	0.2	−1

As matters stand, however, the agisted pasture is not constrained in any way and is also without cost, so that it can rise to infinity, giving, in turn, permission for an infinite number of animals to be carried. To remedy this a separate constraint is necessary, specifying the maximum agisted pasture available (assumed here to be 8 ha and with the simplifying assumption that it can be rented in any quantity up to that amount). At the same time its cost (£90 per ha) must be entered in the objective function as a negative value (as it subtracts from the value of the function) along with the net revenues of beef stores and heifers (positive values) – assumed to be £35 and £40 per head respectively.[1]

	B		*Beef store* (1 beast)	*Yearling heifer* (1 beast)	*Agisted pasture* (1 hectare)
Objective function (£ net revenue)		=	35	40	−90
Constraints					
Maximum pasture (ha)	20	≥	0.3	0.2	−1
Maximum agisted pasture (ha)	8	≥	0	0	1

A maximum of 28 hectares of pasture are available, 20 ha on the farm and a further 8 ha that can be rented. Suppose that all this pasture is used, carrying 50 beef stores and 65 heifers. Values under the different activities are as follows:

	B		*Beef stores*		*Yearling heifers*		*Agisted pasture*	*Row total*
Activity levels:			(50 beasts)		(65 beasts)		(8 hectares)	
Objective function (£ net revenue)		=	1,750 (35 × 50)	+	2,600 (40 × 65)	−	720 (−90 × 8)	3,630

[1] Some programs require the signs in the objective function to be the opposite of this, negatives meaning addition to and positives subtraction from its value.

Constraints								
Maximum pasture (hectares)	20	≥	15 (0.3 × 50)	+	13 (0.2 × 65)	−	8 (−1 × 8)	20
Maximum agisted pasture (hectares)	8	≥	0	+	0	+	8 (1 × 8)	8

Total net revenue generated is £3630, and total supply and demand of pasture are in balance.

It may also be noted that, as the 20 ha of pasture on the farm is without cost in the matrix (it is included in the fixed costs which are deducted afterwards), it will always be used up first, before any agisted pasture is rented. Additionally, the latter will only be called upon if animals are capable of covering its cost.

Finally, suppose that there is only agisted pasture available. The row showing its supply and the demands made on it appears as follows:

Constraint	*B*		*Beef store* (1 beast)	*Yearling heifer* (1 beast)	*Agisted pasture* (1 hectare)
Agisted pasture (hectares)	0	≥	0.3	0.2	−1

This type of relationship, where there is a zero in the *B* column and with supply arising from an activity (or activities), is common in linear programming (sometimes being designated a 'tie-line'). Fodder crops supplying livestock with bulky food, the passing of rotational permission from one crop to another, or the hiring of casual labour are all examples. Where feed (or other resource) supply activities occur with costs (negative net revenues) in the objective function, it is part of the planning problem to discover the least-cost way of incorporating them in the solution if they are required. In consequence, the linear programming procedure in maximising net revenue will of necessity also minimise feed costs at the level of output chosen, taking into account the opportunity costs of resources used to supply the different types of feed.

Basic operations with activities

In turning to consider the basic functions that activities perform and the manner in which they are transcribed in a linear programming matrix, two points need to be emphasised. First, there are often alternative ways of setting them up and, secondly, this usually affects coefficients in both the input–output matrix and the objective function, because the two are closely linked.

Activities can be divided into four main types, according to their function, namely:

(i) Producing activities,
(ii) Selling activities,
(iii) Purchasing activities,
(iv) Transfer activities.

These functions are not necessarily mutually exclusive, as more than one may be undertaken in the same activity. To enable them to be performed, resources or commodities – material and non-material – are consumed which, as has been seen previously, may be supplied both from the fixed resources of the farm and by activities in the matrix. In addition, the consumption of working capital is implied where costs occur in the objective function, even if working capital constraints are not specifically built into the matrix.

Operations with barley are taken to illustrate the writing of these various functions into a matrix.

Producing activity

	B		*Produce barley* (1 hectare)
Objective Function (OF) (£ net revenue)		=	−80
Barley grain (tonnes)	0	≥	−4
Land (hectares)	*X*	≥	1
Harvest labour (hours)	*Y*	≥	4

One hectare barley yields 4 tonnes of grain (the straw is assumed burnt), consuming farm resources in the process. Variable costs for seed, fertiliser and sprays amount to £80 per hectare and since, like the agisted pasture in the previous example, they subtract from the value of the objective function, that is, they constitute a negative net revenue, also bear a minus sign. Land and labour at harvest are shown as being representative of fixed resource requirements in general (they are not shown subsequently, although their inclusion is implied).

However, production without utilisation would be a pointless exercise. Suppose that bacon pigs can be fattened, requiring 0.2 tonnes of grain and contributing a net revenue of £23 per pig.[1]

	B		*Produce barley* (1 hectare)	*Produce and sell bacon* (1 pig)
OF (£ net revenue)		=	−80	23
Barley grain (tonnes)	0	≥	−4	0.2

Because of the link in the grain row, bacon production cannot be undertaken unless barley is first produced, one hectare sufficing for 20 pigs. In this sense, therefore, the production of barley 'gives permission' for pigs to be kept.

Selling activity. If barley is assumed to be saleable for £85 per tonne, as well as being fed to pigs, this may be shown as a separate selling activity, linking in with the grain row.

	B		*Produce barley* (1 hectare)	*Sell barley* (1 tonne)	*Produce and sell bacon* (1 pig)
OF (£ net revenue)		=	−80	85	23
Barley grain (tonnes)	0	≥	−4	1	0.2

However, if the only outlet for barley is to sell it, separate producing and selling activities are not required, as they can be combined into one activity. The need for the grain row is also obviated. In our example, a net revenue of £260 per ha [(4 × 85) − 80 which is the same as gross margin] replaces the £80 variable costs in the objective function. The pig activity is another example in which producing and selling are combined, a relationship that occurs frequently in matrix building.

Purchasing activity. A greater degree of flexibility is gained in our example if a barley purchasing activity is included, for pigs can then be kept independently of whether or not barley is grown on the farm. The

[1] The net revenue of £23 per pig differs from gross margin per pig in that barley is not directly charged. The total cost per pig of supplying barley in a plan consists of £4 of variable costs [(0.2t/4t) × £80], together with the opportunity costs arising from the use of one twentieth of a hectare of land (assuming it to be fully used) and of any other scarce resources associated with it in the growing of barley.

purchase price of barley (£102 per tonne) becomes a negative entry in the objective function, while the one tonne of grain so acquired appears as supply in the grain row.

	B		*Produce barley* (1 hectare)	*Sell barley* (1 tonne)	*Purchase barley* (1 tonne)	*Produce and sell bacon* (1 pig)
OF (£ net revenue)		=	−80	85	−102	23
Barley grain (tonnes)	0	≥	−4	1	−1	0.2

Transfer activity. A transfer activity is not a real activity in the farming sense, but is a device to pass a resource or commodity from one row to another, so adding flexibility to the linear programming model. It is distinguished by having a zero in the objective function, so that it neither adds to nor detracts from the value of the latter.[1]

To pursue the same example further, assume that barley can be fed to winter-fattened beef stores in addition to pigs. However, while the beef animals can also be fed home-produced oats (a winter variety which yield 4.25 tonnes of grain per hectare, and which have variable costs amounting to £75 per hectare) or purchased sugar beet pulp as substitutes for barley, the pigs cannot. In consequence, the supply of starchy concentrates to beef animals must be shown on a row separate from the barley supply to pigs, otherwise the latter would be able to consume oats and beet pulp.

	B		*Produce and sell bacon* (1 pig)	*Produce and sell beef* (1 beast)	*Produce barley* (1 ha)	*Produce oats* (1 ha)	*Buy pulp* (1 tonne)	*Transfer barley* (1 tonne)
OF (£ net revenue)		=	23	46	−80	−75	−90	0
Barley grain (tonnes)	0	≥	0.2	0	−4	0	0	1
Starchy concs. (tonnes barley equiv.)	0	≥	0	0.4	0	−3.42	−0.91	−1

In these circumstances, the function of the transfer activity is to pass barley from the barley supply row through to the starchy concentrates row, so that barley fed to pigs is kept distinct from barley fed to beef

[1] Occasionally, as will be seen later (p. 471), where there are several transfer activities, very small negative values may be applied in order to achieve a specific preference ordering.

animals.[1] The barley transfer activity receives its requirements from the barley production activity, and for every 1t received passes on 1t to the starchy concentrates row, which includes also the supply from oats and pulp. Since the latter have different feeding values, they are brought to a common denominator by the use of 'barley equivalents' (based on net energy values that, in terms of crude weight, mean that 1t pulp and oats = 0.91t and 0.805t barley respectively).

If, for example, there are 20 beef animals, which receive their starchy concentrate requirements entirely in the form of barley, activity levels in the matrix are as follows:

Level:	*B*	*Produce and sell beef* (20 beasts)	*Produce barley* (2 hectares)	*Transfer barley* (8 tonnes)	*Row total*
OF (£ net revenue)	=	920	−160	0	760
Barley grain (tonnes)	0 ≥	0	−8	8	0
Starchy concs. (tonnes barley equiv.)	0 ≥	8	0	−8	0

[1] It might seem that an easy solution would be to allow the barley activity to supply both rows at once, thus:

	B	*Produce barley* (1 hectare)	*Produce and sell bacon* (1 pig)	*Produce and sell beef* (1 beast)
OF (£ net revenue)	=	−80	23	46
Barley grain I (tonnes)	0 ≥	−4	0.2	0
Barley grain II (tonnes)	0 ≥	−4	0	0.4

Unfortunately this duplicates the barley supply, with the result that the same hectare yields 8t, 4t to pigs and 4t to beef. For a formulation with two grain supply rows to be feasible, there have to be two 'produce barley' activities:

	B	*Produce barley I* (1 hectare)	*Produce barley II* (1 hectare)	*Produce and sell bacon* (1 pig)	*Produce and sell beef* (1 beast)
OF (£ net revenue)	=	−80	−80	23	46
Barley grain I (tonnes)	0 ≥	−4	0	0.2	0
Barley grain II (tonnes)	0 ≥	0	−4	0	0.4

However, if there were other activities that could supply starchy concentrate to both bacon and beef, they would also have to be duplicated, so that the number of columns would be increased, compared with the use of a single transfer activity.

Sometimes a transfer activity may be used to pass on the supply of a resource or commodity in terms different from those in which it has been received. For example, the starchy concentrates row could be expressed directly as megajoules of net energy in the various feedstuffs:

	B		*Produce and sell bacon* (1 pig)	*Produce and sell beef* (1 beast)	*Produce barley* (1 ha)	*Produce oats* (1 ha)	*Buy pulp* (1 tonne)	*Transfer barley* (1 tonne)
Barley grain (t)	0	≥	0.2	0	−4	0	0	1
Starchy concs. ('000 MJ NE)	0	≥	0	3.3	0	−27.8	−7.4	−8.1

In short, for every 1t of barley grain consumed in the transfer activity, 8100 megajoules net energy are passed on to the starchy concentrates row.

Joint products. The barley example may also be used to show some of the manipulations that may be needed in dealing with joint products, in this case, grain and straw.

It has been assumed up to now that there is no use for the straw and that it is all burnt. Turning to the other extreme, suppose all the straw can be utilised. One way of dealing with this is to incorporate it directly with the grain producing activity. If barley straw yields 2t per ha, variable costs (for twine) are £4 per ha and 7 hours of arable labour are required per ha for baling and carting the straw, a combined grain/straw activity may be constructed as below (for comparison the previous 'grain-only' activity is shown also):

	B		*Produce barley grain and straw* (1 hectare)	*Produce barley grain only* (1 hectare)
OF (£ net revenue)		=	−84	−80
Barley grain (tonnes)	0	≥	−4	−4
Barley straw (tonnes)	0	≥	−2	0
Land (hectares)	*X*	≥	1	1
Labour (hours)	*Y*	≥	11	4

In a similar manner, if all the straw could be sold and there was no consumption of grain or straw on the farm, they could be combined in a single 'produce and sell grain and straw' activity.

In some cases, for example, in the production of lambs and wool, such treatment is likely to be adequate. With barley, however, it lacks flexibility, for if labour is scarce at harvest time, it may well be preferable to grow a greater area of barley with the straw burnt, rather than a smaller area with the straw collected. (Indeed, it is common in arable areas for straw to be baled only in quantities sufficient to meet livestock requirements on the farm, while the remainder is burnt.)

In such circumstances, a separate straw handling activity is required. Assuming this supplies the beef activity with its requirement of 1 tonne of litter straw per head:

	B	*Produce barley grain and straw* (1 hectare)	*Bale and cart straw* (1 hectare)	*Produce and sell beef* (1 beast)
OF (£ net revenue)	=	−80	−4	46
Produce & utilise barley grain (tonnes)	0 ≥	−4	0	0.4
Produce barley straw (tonnes)	0 ≥	−2	2	0
Utilise barley straw (tonnes)	0 ≥	0	−2	1
Land (hectares)	X ≥	1	0	0
Labour (hours)	Y ≥	4	7	0

The basic barley activity produces 2t straw per hectare, which at the same time gives permission for straw to be baled and carted. In turn every hectare straw handled – as opposed simply to being available – supplies 2t straw to the straw utilisation row.[1] If there are 20 beef stores requiring 20 tonnes straw and if 50 ha of barley are grown, activity levels are as follows:

Level:	B	*Produce barley grain and straw* (50 hectares)	*Bale and cart straw* (10 hectares)	*Produce and sell beef* (20 beasts)
OF (£ net revenue)	=	−4,000	−40	920
Produce barley straw	0 ≥	−100	20	0
Utilise barley straw	0 ≥	0	−20	20

Ten of the fifty hectares of straw produced are utilised, or 20 tonnes out of 100 tonnes. The remainder is burnt.

The various operations with activities that have so far been considered, are brought together into a single matrix in Table 18.1. They, to-

[1] The similarity to a transfer activity may be noted in the straw handling activity, in that it passes on a commodity from one row to another. Nevertheless, it is not strictly a transfer activity as it is a 'real' activity in the farming sense, with a value in the objective function. As with transfer activities, commodities may be passed on in terms different from those in which they are received. For example, if the straw was being passed on as a coarse fodder for feeding to the beef animals, it might be expressed as energy equivalents.

TABLE 18.1. *Operations with activities*

	B		Produce and sell bacon (1 pig)	Produce and sell beef (1 beast)	Produce barley grain and straw (1 hectare)	Sell barley (1 tonne)	Purchase barley (1 tonne)	Transfer barley (1 tonne)	Produce oats, grain and straw (1 hectare)	Bale and cart straw[a] (1 tonne)	Purchase beet pulp (1 tonne)
Objective function (£ net revenue)		=	23	46	−80	85	−102	0	−75	−2	−90
Constraints											
Barley grain (tonnes)	0	≥	0.2	0	−4	1	−1	1	0	0	0
Starchy concs. (tonnes barley equiv.)	0	≥	0	0.4	0	0	0	−1	−3.42	0	−0.91
Straw supply (tonnes)	0	≥	0	0	−2	0	0	0	−2.5	1	0
Straw (litter) utilisation (tonnes)	0	≥	0.07	1	0	0	0	0	0	−1	0
Land (hectares)	X	≥	0	0	1	0	0	0	1	0	0
Arable labour-cereal harvest (hrs)	Y	≥	0	0	4	0	0	0	4	3.5	0

[a] Straw handling is expressed per tonne rather than per hectare because oat straw is utilised in addition to barley straw.

gether with the resource–activity relationships discussed earlier, are fundamental to linear programming matrices, for the principles upon which they are based apply equally to other resources and activities.

Operations with land

The inclusion of rotational data in linear programming models of arable farms is not meant to impose a rigid straitjacket on cropping systems. Rather, it should allow as much flexibility of cropping as possible, while at the same time acknowledging the effect that growing crops in different proportions and sequences may have on factors such as soil structure and the incidence of weeds and disease, and thus on yields and the amounts of fertilisers and sprays that are required. There are several ways of writing rotational data into a matrix, which meet these conditions with varying degrees of success. To illustrate them, use is made of the example of wheat production in Table 18.2. Where wheat follows wheat (wheat II), yield per hectare is 0.2t lower than where it follows beans (wheat I), in spite of heavier fertiliser dressings. The result is that gross margin is £7 per hectare lower.

Compounding rotations

One way of dealing with rotations is to compound the input–output data for the individual crops into single activities, which are then written into the matrix. For instance, the second part of Table 18.2 shows two rotations in which the proportion of wheat differs:

Rotation *A*: beans – wheat – barley – barley
Rotation *B*: beans – wheat – wheat – barley

The data for the individual crops are summed in the penultimate column to give the net revenue (gross margin in this case) and resource requirements of one unit (4 ha) of rotation, while in the final column this is for convenience brought to a hectare basis – the form in which it would probably be expressed in the matrix.

The advantage of this treatment is that it takes account of the effects of specific rotations on the crops comprising them (that is, it does allow for interdependence), and it provides solutions that are expressed in terms of feasible rotations. There are, however, several factors that in practice make it difficult to apply. First, more than one rotation may be included in a single solution. For example, suppose a solution for a 200-hectare farm indicated 120 ha of rotation *A* and 80 ha of rotation *B*. In such a case it might be possible to organise the farm into two 'blocks', each with its separate rotation. But if 195 ha of rotation *A*

TABLE 18.2. *Rotations with wheat*

1. *Wheat gross margins* (per hectare)

	Wheat after beans (wheat I)		Wheat after wheat (wheat II)	
Yield (tonnes)	5.6		5.4	
	(£)	(£)	(£)	(£)
Value output		142.95		138.13
Variable costs				
Seed	6.30		6.30	
Sprays	2.22		2.22	
Fertilisers	7.04	15.56	9.27	17.79
Gross margin		127.39		120.34

Source: Bullen, E. R. (1966) *J. Min. Agric*: (London), 73, no. 3, 125–130.

2. *Compounding rotations including wheat* (1966 values)

Rotation A (25% wheat)	Winter beans (1 ha)	Winter wheat I (1 ha)	Spring barley (1 ha)	Spring barley (1 ha)	Total (4 ha)	Per hectare
Net revenue (£)	62	127	99	99	387	97
Land (hectares)	1	1	1	1	4	1
Labour: spring (hrs)	0	1.5	6.9	6.9	15.3	3.8
summer (hrs)	6.2	4.9	4.9	4.9	20.9	5.2
autumn (hrs)	11.6	10.4	4.2	4.2	30.4	7.6

Rotation B (50% wheat)	Winter beans (1 ha)	Winter wheat I (1 ha)	Winter wheat II (1 ha)	Spring barley (1 ha)	Total (4 ha)	Per hectare
Net revenue (£)	62	127	120	99	408	102
Land (hectares)	1	1	1	1	4	1
Labour: spring (hrs)	0	1.5	1.5	6.9	9.9	2.5
summer (hrs)	6.2	4.9	4.9	4.9	20.9	5.2
autumn (hrs)	11.6	10.4	10.4	4.2	36.6	9.2

and 5 ha of rotation *B* were suggested, blocking the farm would hardly be a practical proposition, so that the solution would require adjusting. (To compound the two rotations into one would not offer a way out of the problem, because to do so would invalidate the data within them. In short, they would not be additive.) Secondly, unless several rotations are included in the matrix, the cropping of the farm may virtually be dictated in advance, so that planning flexibility is lost.

For example, assume that sugar beet substitutes for the bean shift in rotations A and B and that on a 200-ha farm the maximum contract is 20 ha. Even if the maximum sugar beet were to be grown, the two rotations – together or alone – could not total more than 80 ha (as sugar beet is a quarter of each), so that other rotations would be needed to allow the whole farm to be cropped. Finally, and arising from the last point, where more than a few alternative crops can be grown on the same farm, a considerable number of different rotations may be feasible and therefore need to be written into the matrix. Mitigating against this, however, is the paucity of suitable rotational data relevant to the individual farm.

Constraints on individual crops

Another way of handling rotational data is to place limitations on individual crops or groups of crops. The reasoning behind this treatment is that the input–output data for crops will not change unduly, providing they are grown within certain specified proportions of the arable land. To continue with the example of wheat; when it amounts to 25 per cent of the arable (rotation A) its net revenue is £127 per ha, but when it expands to 50 per cent (rotation B) average net revenue for both shifts taken together falls slightly, to £123.5 per hectare. The latter could, therefore, reasonably be taken to represent wheat net revenue on a farm where wheat is permitted to make up half the arable. Admittedly, it would only be an approximation, as its true level would vary both with the proportion of wheat grown within the prescribed limits, and with the sequence in which it was grown. (However, as seen earlier – Chapter 13, p. 289 – such small changes in net revenue might well be accommodated by a single optimal solution.) Furthermore, if sufficiently comprehensive data are available to enable a distinction to be made between successive shifts of the same crop, each shift can be individually constrained (see p. 454 below).

Constraints on individual crops most commonly concern maxima that must not be exceeded, with the occasional insistence on minimum limits. Where minima are not explicitly defined crops can run at zero level, although there may sometimes be implied minima on them, arising from the maxima imposed on other crops. For example, on a 200-ha cash-cropping farm where the combined maxima for non-cereal crops is 120 hectares, there is an implied minimum of 80 ha cereals.

Constraints on individual crops may be stated as absolute values where the arable area is fixed, but must take the form of proportional values if it can vary. In either case, potential flexibility of cropping depends on the combined maxima of individual crops exceeding the arable area, for if they only equal it the rotation has been determined in advance (assuming all the land is used). For example, if beans, barley and wheat were the only crops available and were constrained to not more than 25, 50 and 25 per cent respectively of the arable area, there is no flexibility, for the constraints have simply defined rotation *A*.

Absolute constraints. As has already been seen, crop maxima may be expressed in absolute terms as being 'less than or equal to' and crop minima as being 'greater than or equal to' specified areas. This is illustrated in the second part of Table 18.3, where the first six constraints define crop maxima and the last two crop minima. Several other points arise from this example matrix.

1. As the combined maxima for all crops total 306 hectares (150 ha cereals + 50 ha potatoes + 66 ha sugar beet + 40 ha beans) compared with an arable area of 200 ha, flexibility of cropping is ensured.
2. Although there is no stated minimum for cereals, the combined maxima of non-cereal crops of 156 ha ensure that at least 44 hectares will be grown.
3. It is sometimes possible to reduce matrix size by compounding constraints. Row 3, 'maximum barley and cereals', is an example. Both may rise to 75 per cent of the arable area and, as barley is a constituent of cereals, they may be combined in one row instead of there being a separate row for each.
4. If response data are sufficiently detailed to enable a distinction to be made between the yields from different shifts of the same crop, the total crop constraint may be replaced by constraints on the individual shifts. We take as an example the first and second wheats after a break crop (with 10 per cent difference in yields) and, as in Table 18.3, with the total area of wheat not exceeding 100 of the 200 hectares of arable available.

			Wheat I (1 hectare)	*Wheat II* (1 hectare)
Net revenue (£)		=	330	300
Arable land (hectares)	200	≥	1	1
Max. wheat I (hectares)	50	≥	1	0
Max. wheat II (hectares)	50	≥	0	1

TABLE 18.3. *Constraints on individual crops*

1. *Crop maxima and minima*

Maximum percentage of arable land: wheat 50, barley 75, cereals 75, potatoes 25, sugar beet 33, beans 20
Minimum percentage of arable land: 'roots' 10, beans 5

2. *Absolute rotational constraints*

	hectares	Wheat (1 ha)	Barley (1 ha)	Potatoes (1 ha)	S. beet (1 ha)	Beans (1 ha)
Arable land	200 ≥	1	1	1	1	1
Max. wheat	100 ≥	1	0	0	0	0
Max. barley and cereals	150 ≥	1	1	0	0	0
Max. potatoes	50 ≥	0	0	1	0	0
Max. sugar beet	66 ≥	0	0	0	1	0
Max. beans	40 ≥	0	0	0	0	1
Min. roots	20 ≤	0	0	1	1	0
Min. beans	10 ≤	0	0	0	0	1

3. *Proportional rotational constraints*

a. Unscaled			Wheat (1 ha)	Barley (1 ha)	Potatoes (1 ha)	S. beet (1 ha)	Beans (1 ha)	P. pasture (1 ha)
Croppable land (hectares)	200	≥	1	1	1	1	1	1
Max. wheat	0	≥	0.50	−0.50	−0.50	−0.50	−0.50	0
Max. barley and cereals	0	≥	0.25	0.25	−0.75	−0.75	−0.75	0
Max. potatoes	0	≥	−0.25	−0.25	0.75	−0.25	−0.25	0
Max. sugar beet	0	≥	−0.33	−0.33	−0.33	0.66	−0.33	0
Max. beans	0	≥	−0.20	−0.20	−0.20	−0.20	0.80	0
Min. roots	0	≥	0.10	0.10	−0.90	−0.90	0.10	0
Min. beans	0	≥	0.05	0.05	0.05	0.05	−0.95	0

b. Scaled			Wheat (1 ha)	Barley (1 ha)	Potatoes (1 ha)	S. beet (1 ha)	Beans (1 ha)	P. pasture (1 ha)
Croppable land (hectares)	200	≥	1	1	1	1	1	1
×2[a] Max. wheat	0	≥	1	−1	−1	−1	−1	0
×4[a] Max. barley and cereals	0	≥	1	1	−3	−3	−3	0
×4[a] Max. potatoes	0	≥	−1	−1	3	−1	−1	0
×3[a] Max. sugar beet	0	≥	−1	−1	−1	2	−1	0
×5[a] Max. beans	0	≥	−1	−1	−1	−1	4	0
×10[a] Min. roots	0	≥	1	1	−9	−9	1	0
×20[a] Min. beans	0	≥	1	1	1	1	−19	0

[a] Scaling factor.

Each wheat activity is limited to half the maximum wheat area. If 50 ha or less of wheat are grown, wheat I will always be selected in preference to wheat II, because of its higher net revenue. In spite of the greater degree of precision obtained, however, this may still only approximate to the true position. For example, suppose a solution on 200 hectares of arable land indicated a three-course rotation of 67 ha of non-cereal crops, followed by 67 ha of wheat, followed by 67 hectares of barley; the 67 ha of wheat after non-cereals would be represented by 50 hectares of wheat I and 17 hectares of wheat II.

Proportional constraints. When the arable area cannot be fixed in advance because it is not known at what level non-rotational crops, such as permanent pasture or orchards, will enter the plan, absolute rotational constraints are not applicable. For example, if potatoes cannot exceed 25 per cent of the arable area on a 200-hectare farm, their limit is 50 hectares in absolute terms. If, however, 80 ha of permanent pasture are included, only 120 ha of arable are available, of which 25 per cent is 30, not 50, ha. (Conversely, if the potato constraint remained at 50 ha, it would represent over 40 per cent of 120 hectares.)

Proportional constraints represent a special case of giving and receiving 'permission'. Maximum constraints may be taken first and illustrated with the example of potatoes (Table 18.3), which cannot exceed 25 per cent of the arable land, the area of which in turn depends on the combined hectares of potatoes, wheat, barley, sugar beet and beans (designated p, w, b, sb and be respectively). This may be stated in the usual matrix form, with the constraint (that is, the arable area available) on the left of the expression and the activity being constrained (potatoes) on the right:

$$0.25(p + w + b + sb + be) \geq p.$$

Potato land must be less than or equal to one-quarter of the combined area of potatoes, wheat, barley, sugar beet and beans (that is, the total arable area). Now transferring the left side of the expression to the right:

$$0 \geq p - 0.25(p + w + b + sb + be)$$

and simplifying: $0 \geq (p - 0.25p) - 0.25w - 0.25b - 0.25sb - 0.25be$

$$0 \geq 0.75p - 0.25w - 0.25b - 0.25sb - 0.25be.$$

The final row is the form in which the constraint is written in the matrix, as shown in part 3*a* of Table 18.3. However, time may be saved in data punching if fractions are scaled to integral quantities by bringing the smallest value to unity, which in this instance involves multiplying throughout by 4:

$$0 \geq 3p - w - b - sb - be.$$

This form is shown in part 3*b* of the table. Three ha of non-potato crops are required to give permission for 1 ha of potatoes to be grown [0 = (1 ha potatoes × 3) + (3 ha non-potato crops × −1)]. If, on 200 hectares of arable, 50 ha of potatoes are grown, 150 ha of non-potato crops are thus required to give permission. It is impossible to have more potatoes, say 51 hectares, because 153 ha of non-potato crops would then be required, so exceeding the arable area by 4 ha (51 + 153 = 204). If there were 80 ha of permanent pasture, so that the arable fell to 120 hectares, potatoes could rise to a maximum of 30 hectares, with 90 hectares of non-potato crops giving permission.

Minimisation is simply the converse of maximisation, as is demonstrated by the same potato constraint, for in stating that potatoes must not exceed 25 per cent of the arable area, it is also implied that non-potato crops must be a minimum of 75 per cent. Crops being constrained to a minimum pass on permission for other crops to be grown. For example, root crops must be a minimum of 20 ha of the 200 hectares of arable land in Table 18.3. Twenty ha of root crops are thus required to allow 180 hectares of non-root crops [0 = (20 ha root crops × −9) + (180 ha non-root crops × 1)]. If less than the minimum root land were to be selected, say 18 hectares, then 20 ha of land would go idle, because permission would be given for only 162 ha of non-root crops (18 × −9). Conversely, root crops can rise above the minimum, in which event some of the permission they create is unused.

Absolute and proportional constraints may also be applied for other than rotational reasons, for example, in the imposition of contracts and quotas. The potato quota may be taken as an example. Suppose that on a 200-ha arable farm there is a potato quota for 35 ha, but the farmer is prepared to grow potatoes up to the rotational limit of 50 hectares, paying £120 per hectare penalty on the excess:

			Quota potatoes (1 hectare)	*Penalty potatoes* (1 hectare)
Net revenue (£)		=	850	730
Arable land (hectares)	200	≥	1	1
Max. potato quota (hectares)	35	≥	1	0
Max. potatoes (hectares)	50	≥	1	1

As quota potatoes have the higher net revenue, they will always enter solutions before penalty potatoes. If the latter are also grown, they take up the 15 ha of rotation remaining after the inclusion of 35 hectares of quota potatoes.

Although the use of absolute and proportional constraints does not require the detailed specification of crop responses under different rotations (and is thus a realistic tool in view of the amount of data likely to be available), a problem arises in that it may be difficult to formulate even approximate rotations from the proportions indicated in a solution. This is because it is not just a question of the amounts of different crops to be grown, but also of the *sequence* in which they should be grown. For example, in Table 18.3, potatoes cannot rise above a maximum of 25 per cent of the arable or sugar beet above 33 per cent. But it is also implied that potatoes should not be grown on the same land more than 1 year in 4 or sugar beet more than 1 year in 3. If, on a 200-hectare farm, 50 ha of potatoes, 66 ha of sugar beet and 84 ha of barley were indicated, it would be extremely hard to make up a practical rotation meeting the necessary conditions, and adjustments to the solution would therefore be necessary.

Links between crops

The giving and receiving of permission between crops can be used in a different way from that used in proportional constraints (where all arable crops participate) to ensure that certain crop sequences are established.

We return to the wheat example (bottom p. 454), where wheat I may only follow non-cereal crops, while wheat II, naturally, can only follow wheat I:

			Wheat I (1 hectare)	*Wheat II* (1 hectare)	*Barley* (1 hectare)	*Non-cereal crops* (1 hectare)
Net revenue (£)		=	330	300	255	*X*
Arable land (hectares)	200	≥	1	1	1	1
Max. wheat I (hectares)	0	≥	1	0	0	−1
Max. wheat II (hectares)	0	≥	−1	1	0	0

Non-cereal crops provide permission, 1 ha for 1 ha, for wheat I, which in turn does the same for wheat II. Wheat II thus cannot exceed the hectares of wheat I, nor wheat I the hectares of non-cereals.

However, suppose it is considered desirable to have a smaller proportion of second wheat; for example, only half of wheat I may be followed by wheat II. This is achieved by allowing every hectare of wheat I to pass only half a hectare of permission to wheat II:

			Wheat I (1 hectare)	*Wheat II* (1 hectare)	*Non-cereal crops* (1 hectare)
Max. wheat I (hectares)	0	≥	1	0	−1
Max. wheat II (hectares)	0	≥	−0.5	1	0

These examples assume that each hectare of non-cereal crop can be followed by a hectare of wheat, but, for husbandry reasons, this may not always be the case. For example, the amount of permission passed on by leys of duration longer than one year depends on the life of the ley which determines the proportion ploughed each year. Again, not all the sugar beet crop may be lifted in time for winter wheat to be sown. In such cases, less than a hectare of permission is passed on for each hectare of the relevant non-cereal crop that is grown.

			Wheat I (1 ha)	*Potatoes* (1 ha)	*1-yr ley* (1 ha)	*2-yr ley* (1 ha)	*3-yr ley* (1 ha)	*Sugar beet* (1 ha)
Max. wheat I (hectares)	0	≥	1	−1	−1	−0.5	−0.33	−0.6

In this example, only half the two-year ley and one-third of the three-year ley area are ploughed each year, and are therefore available to be followed by wheat. Similarly, only 60 per cent of the sugar beet crop is lifted in time for wheat to be sown. On the other hand, potatoes and 1-year ley pass on permission hectare for hectare.

Another complication is that while some crops may be followed by two wheats in succession, others may be followed only by one. Suppose that two wheats in succession may follow only leys of 2 years or longer duration:

			Wheat I (1 ha)	*Wheat II* (1 ha)	*Potatoes* (1 ha)	*1-yr ley* (1 ha)	*2-yr ley* (1 ha)	*3-yr ley* (1 ha)	*Sugar beet* (1 ha)
Max. wheat I (hectares)	0	≥	1	0	−1	−1	−0.5	−0.33	−0.6
Max. wheat II (hectares)	0	≥	0	1	0	0	−0.5	−0.33	0

Wheat I no longer passes on permission to wheat II, which now receives it direct from two-year and three-year leys.

So far it has been assumed that enough data are available for a distinction to be made between wheats I and II. Where this is not the case and there is only a single wheat activity to represent them both, constraints similar to those already considered can still be applied. For example, if non-cereal crops can be followed only by one wheat, there is a straightforward giving and receiving of permission hectare for hectare:

			Wheat (1 hectare)	*Non-cereal crops* (1 hectare)
Max. wheat (hectares)	0	≥	1	−1

If, however, there can be two wheats, each hectare wheat is shown as receiving two hectares of permission:

			Wheat (1 hectare)	*Non-cereal crops* (1 hectare)
Max. wheat (hectares)	0	≥	1	−2

Other proportions can be dealt with similarly. Thus if only half the first wheat can be followed by a second, the relevant coefficient under non-cereal crops is (−) 1.5.

Finally, when two wheats can follow some crops but not others, the permission given by the former is doubled:

			Wheat (1 ha)	*Potatoes* (1 ha)	*1-yr ley* (1 ha)	*2-yr ley* (1 ha)	*3-yr ley* (1 ha)	*Sugar beet* (1 ha)
Max. wheat (hectares)	0	≥	1	−1	−1	−1 (−0.5×2)	−0.66 (−0.33×2)	−0.6

For example, if there were 40 ha of 2-year ley, permission would be given for 40 hectares of wheat – 20 ha of first-year and 20 ha of second-year wheat after ley.

Crop links thus provide a useful means of ensuring that a given sequence of crops is obtained. Naturally they must not be too rigidly applied, or cropping patterns may be determined in advance. Commonly they are used in conjunction with absolute or proportional constraints.

Land of differing types or quality

Frequently there are contrasting types of soil on the same farm. The consequences are threefold. First, certain crops may be specific to one soil type only. Secondly, yields and resource requirements of those crops that can be grown over the whole farm may differ from one soil type to another and, thirdly, their rotational constraints are also likely to be different. When this is the case, the matrix can be divided into sub-matrices according to the number of soil types that need to be differentiated. The outline example in Table 18.4 assumes two soil types – heavy and light – each with its own cropping and rotation. The remainder of the matrix is taken up with those resources and constraints, such as labour, that are common to both.

Land and intermediate commodities – the forage complex

On farms where grazing livestock can be carried, defining relationships between forage supply activities – notably grassland, both grazed and conserved – and livestock activities constitutes an important part of the planning problem. The aim of planning is to discover the least-cost pattern of feed supply with which to meet livestock requirements, particularly in terms of the opportunity costs of forgone alternatives (see Chapter 9, pp. 209–11). It follows that the specification of forage supply in the matrix should be as flexible as possible. Given the large range of potential forage activities which may be supplying several types of livestock, it is clear that the forage complex can build up into a large and intricate part of the matrix.

The relationships between the supply of forage and the requirements of livestock for feed can be handled in several ways:

(*a*) Fixed feeding patterns with combined forage/livestock activities.
(*b*) Fixed feeding patterns with separate forage and livestock activities.
(*c*) Flexible feeding patterns with separate forage and livestock activities.

Fixed feeding patterns with combined forage/livestock activities. This method incorporates the land and labour needed for the provision of a fixed and predetermined pattern of fodder supply, directly in the livestock activities. Net revenue per animal is normally identical with gross margin, since forage variable costs are deducted from output.

For example, the following two dairy-cow activities might be incor-

TABLE 18.4. *Land of differing types*

			Heavy soil					Light soil			
			Wheat (1 ha)	Barley (1 ha)	Beans (1 ha)	Clover ley (1 ha)	Perm. past. (1 ha)	Wheat (1 ha)	Barley (1 ha)	Potatoes (1 ha)	Sugar beet (1 ha)
Net revenue (£)		=	320	240	260	80	−40	300	250	850	530
Heavy soil (hectares)	120	≥	1	1	1	1	1				
Max. wheat (hectares)	0	≥	1	0	−2	−2	0		All zeros		
Max. legumes (hectares)	0	≥	−1	−1	4	4	0				
Light soil (hectares)	80	≥						1	1	1	1
Max. wheat (hectares)	0	≥			All zeros			1	0	−1	−0.6
S. beet contract (hectares)	10	≥						0	0	0	1
October labour (hours)	850	≥	5	2	5	0	0	4	0	12	6
Combine harvester (hectares)	160	≥	1	1	1	0	0	1	1	0	0

porated in a matrix, one assuming that hay provides the cows' bulky fodder requirements in winter and the other that silage fulfils this function:

		Dairy cows fed hay (1 cow)		*Dairy cows fed silage* (1 cow)	
Net revenue (£)	=	220		224	
Land (hectares)	$X \geq$	0.64	grazing 0.36	0.60	grazing 0.36
			hay 0.28		silage 0.24
Arable labour					
May/mid June (hours)	$Y \geq$	1.9		4.2	
Mid June/June (hours)	$Z \geq$	3.7		0.6	

Flexibility in the overall feeding pattern is given by the relative proportions of the two activities in the solution. For example, if 10 cows fed hay and 30 cows fed silage were selected, the inference would be that a ration based mainly on silage should be fed. Conversely, if the solution indicated 38 cows fed hay and 2 cows fed silage, an all-hay ration would be inferred, with marginal adjustments to the solution.[1]

If there is only a limited number of alternative forage activities, this method may suffice. Otherwise it requires a proliferation of livestock activities, each assuming differing feeding patterns, if true flexibility is to be obtained.

Fixed feeding patterns with separate forage and livestock activities. This method is simply an extension of the previous one. Instead of the forage activities being included directly in the livestock activities, they are shown separately, supplying the latter with their fixed patterns of feed requirements.

[1] Strictly activities may not be additive in this fashion. In our example, a cow's response might be different if a ration based partly on hay and partly on silage were to be fed, instead of either all hay or all silage. If this were known to be the case and data were available, additional activities with varying levels of hay and silage input could be incorporated in the matrix. The additivity problem arises here because of the underlying assumption of constant marginal rates of substitution between the two feeds. This is the common assumption in dealing with feed supply from alternative sources in a matrix and, indeed, is a common assumption in practical rationing.

Turning again to the same dairy-cow example:

		3-yr ley grazed (1 ha)	3-yr ley 2 cuts hay (1 ha)	3-yr ley 2 cuts silage (1 ha)	Dairy cows fed hay (1 cow)	Dairy cows fed silage (1 cow)
Net revenue (£)	=	−77	−81	−77	270	270
Land (hectares)	$X \geq$	1	1	1	0	0
Grazing (hectares)	$0 \geq$	−1	0	0	0.36	0.36
Hay (hectares)	$0 \geq$	0	−1	0	0.28	0
Silage (hectares)	$0 \geq$	0	0	−1	0	0.24
Arable labour						
May/mid June (hrs)	$Y \geq$	0.8	5.8	16.5	0	0
Mid June/July (hrs)	$Z \geq$	1.8	11.0	0	0	0

The net revenues of the hay and silage-fed cows rise by £50 and £46 respectively, because fodder variable costs are now incurred via the forage activities, as too are the land and labour requirements for producing forage.

Although this treatment of forage supply may appear merely as an unnecessarily complicated version of the first method, it has the advantage that rotational constraints, such as leys passing on permission for wheat to be grown, are more easily handled.

Flexible feeding patterns with separate forage and livestock activities. This method has some similarity to the previous one, in that there are separate forage activities, but there is greater flexibility in the provision of grazing, and livestock no longer have rigid and predetermined requirements of particular feedstuffs. The latter are now expressed in terms such as energy or hay equivalents, which provide a common denominator for the output from the various forage activities.

Table 18.5 illustrates this treatment with part of a forage complex, which itself is simply part of a larger matrix.

Grazing. Grazing is divided into an early-summer period (April to June) and a late-summer period (July to September), so that some allowance can be made for the seasonal pattern of grass output, which is assumed here to be one-third higher in the first period. In addition, such a division allows grazing after hay and silage cuts to contribute to livestock requirements in the second period.

Where different types of livestock, such as cattle and sheep, graze the same grassland, better utilisation and thus higher stocking rates may be achieved. One way of allowing for this is to have combined livestock activities (in addition to single ones), with better stocking

TABLE 18.5. *The forage complex*

		3-yr ley grazed (1 hectare)	3-yr ley 1 cut hay then grazed (1 hectare)	3-yr ley 2 cuts hay (1 hectare)	3-yr ley 1 cut silage then grazed (1 hectare)	3-yr ley 2 cuts silage (1 hectare)	Marrow-stem kale (unthinned) (1 hectare)	Transfer metab. energy ('000 MJ)	Dairy cow (1 cow)	Beef store summer (1 beast)	Beef store winter (1 beast)
Net revenue (£)	=	−77	−79	−81	−77	−77	−80	0	270	35	46
Land (hectares)	$X \geq$	1	1	1	1	1	1	0	0	0	0
Grazing											
Apr–June (hectares)	$0 \geq$	−1.33	0	0	0	0	0	0	0.36	0.3	0
July–Sep. (hectares)	$0 \geq$	−1	−1	0	−1	0	0	0	0.36	0.3	0
Winter forage[a]											
Oct.–Dec. ('000 MJME)[b]	$0 \geq$	0	0	0	0	0	−69.6	−1	5.7	0	3.6
Jan.–Mar. ('000 MJME)[b]	$0 \geq$	0	−26.0	−40.7	−28.4	−47.5	0	1	5.7	0	3.3
Max. kale in ration (tonnes crude wt)	$0 \geq$	0	0	0	0	0	45	0	−2.2	0	−1.6
Arable labour											
May/mid June (hours)	$Y \geq$	0.7	5.7	5.7	16.3	16.3	3.2	0	0	0	0
Mid June/July (hours)	$Z \geq$	1.7	10.9	10.9	0	0	0.7	0	0	0	0

[a] For maintenance only.
[b] MJME = megajoules metabolisable energy.

rates than the individual activities on their own. If it is known in advance that grazing will be shared, as, for example, between dairy cows and heifer replacements, average grazing rates based on livestock units may be employed (see Appendix 14.1).

In addition, it may be necessary to distinguish between areas that can be grazed by all types of livestock and those that are accessible only to some. For instance, in our example, distant fields on the farm might be available to beef stores but not to dairy cows. Similarly, some areas may be suitable only for conservation because lack of fences or water supplies prohibits grazing.

Winter feeding. The output of forage to provide the livestock with a maintenance ration during the winter period (October to March) is expressed as metabolisable energy (measured in units of a thousand megajoules). Winter is also divided into two three-month periods. This is necessary where one or more foods can contribute to one period but not to the other. In this example, marrow-stem kale provides forage in the first half of winter but not in the second. Following on from this, the outputs of hay and silage are shown in the second period with a transfer activity moving any requirements into the first period. If it were the other way round, kale could be transferred from the first to the second period, implying that it could be fed in late winter.

In addition, whereas it is feasible for livestock to receive either all hay or all silage, a limit is placed on the quantity of kale that can be fed (assumed to be 25 kg and 18 kg daily for dairy cows and 'winter' beef cattle respectively). This is achieved by the animals 'giving permission' for this amount to be fed if required.

This treatment is more flexible than the others, although, like them, it assumes constant rates of substitution between feeds. If we want to specify livestock requirements in greater detail, perhaps by including protein requirements and dry matter limits, it is necessary to have a sub-matrix for each type of livestock, with a repetition of the forage crops in each. If this is not done, it becomes possible for surplus nutrients from one type of animal to be passed on to another. If there are several different types of animal, this more detailed specification naturally leads to a rapid increase in matrix size.

Operations with labour

In writing labour constraints into a matrix, it is necessary to distinguish between labour used on crops and labour used on livestock. Whereas the former is characterised by seasonal peaks and troughs, the latter presents, on the whole, an even work requirement from day to day and is also less influenced by the weather.

Selection of peak labour periods

The availability and requirements of labour for fieldwork are usually entered in a matrix as man-hours or -days for those periods, such as spring drilling, cereal and root harvests, when labour is likely to run short.[1] The selection of the relevant periods to be included in the matrix may be based partly on previous experience on the farm. It must be kept in mind, however, that if radical changes in farm organisation are possible, periods that have caused no trouble in the past may do so in the future, and should therefore be included as well. For example, there may currently be labour to spare at cereal harvest on an arable farm where root crops, with their high labour requirements, are also grown. If, however, the latter are eliminated and the labour force reduced, the cereal harvest may present the main peak in labour requirements.

Length and degree of flexibility in peak periods

In deciding on the length of peak periods, a course has to be steered between over-restriction and excessive flexibility as to when work can be performed. If, say, two-week periods are taken within which labour coefficients for each job are rigidly specified, the choice of farm plan may be unnecessarily limited. On the other hand, if very long periods are taken, the choice may become unrealistically wide. The length to be selected is usually contingent on natural crop cycles, because certain operations need to be carried out within specified periods of time if yields are not to suffer. In consequence, periods do not necessarily coincide with calendar months, nor need they be of the same length at different times of the year.

Difficulties, however, may arise when there are important operations to be carried out on several different crops at the same time of year, whose time-spans do not coincide. Although the time available for some crop operations may correspond in length with the peak labour periods selected in the matrix, with others it may be shorter and with yet others longer. For example, suppose that on a farm where cereals and root crops are grown, October is taken as being representative of the autumn labour peak and that the following operations have to be accommodated at that time:

[1] As was seen in Chapter 5, the hours available for productive work are less than the total hours actually available, because various deductions have to be made to allow for factors such as the effects of weather on the workability of the land.

Operation	*Time span available*
Cultivate and drill wheat	October
Harvest potatoes	1st half October
Harvest sugar-beet	Last week September to end November
Plough for spring sown crops	September to December

While the time available for wheat drilling corresponds with the peak period of October, that for potato harvest is of shorter duration and that for sugar beet harvest and ploughing of longer duration.

Crop operation time and length of peak labour period are the same. The treatment of labour for those crop operations that, like wheat, have the same time span as the peak period is quite straightforward. For example, if four men are available and supply 672 hours in October, and wheat requires 9 hours per ha, the labour constraint on wheat is simply:

			Wheat (1 hectare)
Arable labour–October (hours)	672	≥	9

Crop operation time is shorter than peak labour period. The time span available for harvesting potatoes, in the example, is only half the October peak. If potatoes were treated in the same way as wheat, it would be possible for them to draw on labour from the second half of October. To prevent this happening, they have to be restricted within the overall peak period. One way of handling the situation is to divide October into two periods, allowing potatoes to draw only on the first one, while a transfer activity passes surplus labour through to crops, like wheat, that can draw on the full labour supply.

			Wheat (1 hectare)	*Potatoes* (1 hectare)	*Transfer labour* (1 hour)
Labour 1st half October (hours)[1]	370	≥	0	40	1
Labour 2nd half October (hours)[1]	302	≥	9	0	−1

Potatoes can draw on only 370 hours while, on the other hand, wheat can draw on the full 672 hours.

[1] Because of declining workability of the land as the month advances, 55 per cent of labour is assumed available in the first half and 45 per cent in the second.

Crop operation time is longer than peak labour period. The time span available for the sugar beet harvest in the example is over twice the length of the peak October period. One way of dealing with this is to allocate to the peak period that proportion of the sugar beet harvest that usually falls within it. Suppose that the beet harvest is distributed as follows:

Harvest sugar beet	*September*	*October*	*November*	*Total*
Proportion of harvest (%)	10	45	45	100
Labour (hours per hectare)	3	15	15	33

Fifteen hours are thus allocated to the October period.

Such treatment may suffice where there is little flexibility in the time when an operation must be performed, but this is not generally true of sugar beet. Insisting that 45 per cent of the beet must be harvested in October (and similarly with other months) means that there is no flexibility about when it may be lifted and the hectares appearing in a solution may be severely curtailed, because of competition with potatoes and wheat at that time. Instead, flexibility can be gained by having two sugar beet activities, one assuming that all the harvest (except the ten per cent in September) is carried out in October and the other that it is done in November.

			Sugar beet I *harvest Oct.* (1 hectare)	*Sugar beet* II *harvest Nov.* (1 hectare)
Labour – October (hours)	672	≥	30	0
Labour – November (hours)	400	≥	0	30

There is no need to have additional sugar beet activities with varying proportions of harvest in October and November, because the latter will be indicated by the proportions in which sugar beet I and sugar beet II are selected in the solution.

If it is regarded as unfeasible to lift *all* the beet in any one month, there can instead be activities for early- and late-harvested beet. If two-thirds is the maximum that can be lifted in each month, the division is as follows:

			Sugar beet I *early harvest* (1 hectare)	*Sugar beet* II *late harvest* (1 hectare)
Labour – October (hours)	672	≥	20	10
Labour – November (hours)	400	≥	10	20

Ploughing for spring sown crops, which extends from September to December, could be handled in a similar way to sugar beet, with, say, four activities, 'plough September', 'plough October', 'plough November' and 'plough December', respectively. Another method is to use transfer activities, each drawing on labour for a particular period and passing it on to the operation in question. On the assumption that the aim is to complete the ploughing as early as possible, fractional but increasing penalties may be imposed in the objective function for succeeding periods, so that early ploughing is preferred to that carried out later. This ensures, for example, that December ploughing is not selected when there are still hours to spare in earlier months.

			Barley (1 hectare)	*Plough Sept.* (1 hr)	*Plough Oct.* (1 hr)	*Plough Nov.* (1 hr)	*Plough Dec.* (1 hr)
Net revenue (£)		=	250	0	−0.00001	−0.0001	−0.001
Max. arable labour							
September (hours)	750	≥	1.5	1	0	0	0
October (hours)	672	≥	0	0	1	0	0
November (hours)	400	≥	0	0	0	1	0
December (hours)	370	≥	0	0	0	0	1
Ploughing (hours)	0	≥	3.3	−1	−1	−1	−1

If complete flexibility were regarded as too risky, because too high a proportion of ploughing might be left until late in the season, it could be insisted that, say, half the ploughing (1.6 hours) should be carried out in September and October, with the remaining half performed at any time. In short, partial flexibility could replace complete flexibility.[1]

Extending the time available for crop operations

Labour peaks arise partly because of the planner's insistence that certain crop operations must be carried out within specified periods, usually with the object of avoiding the yield losses that may otherwise be incurred. It may be worthwhile, however, reducing the pressure on labour by extending the time-spans within which operations may be performed, even if there are some yield losses in consequence. For

[1] Strictly, because of husbandry constraints, the sequence of cropping must be known before the degree of flexibility in ploughing can be accurately determined. This is because limits to flexibility may arise both in ploughing *before* a crop – as with winter wheat – and in ploughing *after* a crop – as with sugar beet. This applies equally to the application of 'conventional' inflexible labour constraints.

example, October is commonly regarded as the optimal month for drilling winter wheat. Suppose that there is likely to be a loss in net revenue of £40 per ha if it is drilled in November. This can be accommodated in a matrix, with a consequent gain in flexibility, in the same manner as shown for sugar beet harvest, namely by having two activities, in which the operation is performed respectively in October and November. In the case of wheat, however, net revenue is £40 per ha lower in the latter period because of the potential loss in yield

			Wheat drilled October (1 hectare)	*Wheat drilled November* (1 hectare)
Net revenue (£)		=	330	290
Labour – October (hours)	672	≥	9	0
Labour – November (hours)	400	≥	0	9

Team-work

Certain tasks are undertaken by men working together in teams. In order to illustrate a method of handling this, we may still keep to the previous example (p. 469) but, for simplicity, assume that potatoes may be harvested throughout October and that sugar beet requirements are specified as a fixed proportion (15 hours plus 1.5 hours for one man loading with tractor and foreloader). Furthermore, suppose that both potatoes and sugar beet require a team of three regular workers at harvest. Ignoring the teams for the moment the labour constraint for October could be set up as follows:

			Wheat (1 hectare)	*Potatoes* (1 hectare)	*Sugar beet* (1 hectare)
Arable labour (4 men) – October (hours)	672	≥	9	40	16.5

When treated in this manner it is possible for the combined acreage of potatoes and sugar beet to exceed the labour (504 hours) that *three* men supply. In short, they can draw on the labour of the fourth man who is not part of the team. To avoid the possibility of impracticable solutions arising in this way, a distinction should be made between men working in teams of three and men working singly.[1]

[1] If other constraints, such as quota or contract, were sufficiently limiting to keep the combined area of potatoes and sugar beet below that level where the three man labour supply was exceeded, there would be no need to allow explicitly for teams.

			Wheat (1 hectare)	Potatoes (1 hectare)	Sugar beet (1 hectare)	Labour transfer (1 hour)
Arable labour – October						
3-man team (hours)	504	≥	0	40	15	1
Men working singly (hours)	168	≥	9	0	1.5	−1

Potatoes and sugar beet can now call on only three men for harvesting, while, conversely, all four men are available to perform tasks that do not require team-work. If the crops utilising October labour in a solution were 26 ha wheat, 6 ha potatoes and 12 hectares sugar beet, all October labour would be used, being distributed in the following manner:

Level:			Wheat (26 ha)	Potatoes (6 ha)	Sugar beet (12 ha)	Labour transfer (84 hours)	Row total
Arable labour – October							
3-man team (hours)	504	≥	0	240	180	84	504
Men working singly (hours)	168	≥	234	0	18	−84	168

Another way of formulating this constraint, which eliminates the transfer activity, is to distinguish between three-man teams and the total labour available:

			Wheat (1 hectare)	Potatoes (1 hectare)	Sugar beet (1 hectare)
Arable labour – October					
3-man team (hours)	504	≥	0	40	15
Total labour: 4 men (hours)	672	≥	9	40	16.5

The repetition of the harvest requirements for potatoes and sugar beet in the second row prevents the same labour being used twice. If the cropping were as in the first formulation, there would be 84 hours to spare in the first row with full utilisation in the second row.

It may also be necessary to carry machinery constraints implicitly within the labour constraints. Continuing with the same example, suppose the sugar beet harvest is performed by a two-man and not a three-man team (harvest requirements in October falling from 15 hours to 12 hours per ha). With four men available, two harvest teams would seem possible, but this is precluded because there is only one harvester.

The new situation may be dealt with by having two transfer activities.

			Wheat (1 ha)	*Pota-toes* (1 ha)	*Sugar beet* (1 ha)	*Labour transfer I* (3-man hrs)	*Labour transfer II* (1 hr)
Arable labour – October							
3-man team (hours)	504	≥	0	40	0	3	0
2-man team (hours)	0	≥	0	0	12	−2	1
Men working singly (hours)	168	≥	9	0	1.5	−1	−1

Labour surplus to the three-man team is passed on via labour transfer I, two men to the two-man team and the third to the operations with men working singly. In turn, the latter receive any surplus labour from the two-man team, by way of labour transfer II.

If the cropping were as before, but with 30 ha of wheat instead of 26 (the extra 4 ha utilise the labour released from sugar beet by the replacement of the three-man team with the two-man team), activity levels would be:

Level:			*Wheat* (30 ha)	*Pota-toes* (6 ha)	*Sugar beet* (12 ha)	*Labour transfer I* (88 units of 3 hrs)	*Labour transfer II* (32 hours)	*Row total*
Arable labour – October								
3-man team (hours)	504	≥	0	240	0	264	0	504
2-man team (hours)	0	≥	0	0	144	−176	32	0
Men working singly (hours)	168	≥	270	0	18	−88	−32	168

'Overhead' labour

The labour requirements of activities in a matrix usually refer only to essential operations that must be carried out in specific periods. It is thus assumed that general farm maintenance, such as hedging and ditching, can be performed in less busy periods. Similarly, while labour supply coefficients in peak periods are adjusted for weather effects, together with some allowance for unforeseen contingencies, such as sickness, it is usually assumed that holidays are taken in off-peak periods. If this is not the case, deductions can be made from the available labour in the appropriate periods. It is possible also to have a 'safety net', by including a total annual labour constraint with the total overhead labour requirement deducted.

Overtime, casual labour and contract services

A common way of dealing with overtime is to add it to ordinary time, thus treating it as a fixed cost to be deducted from total net revenue when calculating net profit. A more accurate method is to have activities for purchasing overtime, up to suitably constrained limits, in specific periods. Cereal harvest labour (4 men) is treated in this manner in the following outline example:

		Wheat (1 hectare)	*Barley* (1 hectare)	*Buy overtime* (1 hour)
Net revenue (£)	=	320	250	−1.3
Cereal harvest				
Ordinary hours	872 ≥	5	5	−1
Overtime hours	368 ≥	0	0	1

The amount of overtime assumed available may be the maximum that the men are prepared to work, or preferably, a lower figure that allows some surplus to cover bad seasons. If opportunities for overtime occur at most times of the year, there is the possibility that the annual total could rise above that which the men would normally be prepared to work. To prevent this, an annual overtime constraint may be used, which specifies the maximum that can be worked and which is drawn on by the separate overtime activities in the different peak periods.

Casual labour can be treated in the same way, but only if it can be used on *all* the tasks that have to be performed in a particular period. Where this is not the case, it is necessary to distinguish between tasks on which casual labour can and cannot be used. One way is to have those tasks that casual labour (as well as regular) can perform on a row separate from those that can be carried out only by regular labour, with a transfer activity passing regular labour between them. This method is illustrated by an example from early summer, where casual labour can be used only on sugar beet singling.

		Maincrop potatoes (1 ha)	*Spring beans* (1 ha)	*Sugar beet* (1 ha)	*Hire casual labour* (1 hour)	*Transfer regular labour* (1 hour)
Net revenue (£)	=	850	230	770	−1.5	0
Regular labour (hours)	1,320 ≥	4	0.8	10	0	1
Sugar beet singling (hours)	0 ≥	0	0	20	−1	−1
Max. casual labour (hours)	400 ≥	0	0	0	1	0

If casual labour can be employed only on a single task, a simpler method is to duplicate the activity in question. In our example, one sugar beet activity would use regular labour for singling, and the other, casual labour – the cost being deducted from its net revenue (as in the programme planning example, Table 14.4 p. 333).

The hire of contract services – which include a labour element and concern specific operations such as ploughing and sugar beet harvesting – can be dealt with in the same manner as casual labour.

Labour transfer between crops and livestock

Labour – particularly on small farms – is often non-specialised, undertaking a variety of tasks on both crops and livestock. This gives rise to the problem that, because of weather limitations on fieldwork, the effective working week is shorter for crops than for livestock, which are relatively independent of its influence.

As labour availabilities are usually expressed in terms of hours available for fieldwork, one method of dealing with this is to scale down livestock requirements in the same ratio as that of the length of the crop week and the length of the livestock week. For example, if on a mixed arable farm with four men the effective working week in October is 38 hours for crops and 57 hours for livestock, the former is one-third less than the latter. This is the proportion by which livestock requirements are reduced:

			Wheat (1 hectare)	*Potatoes* (1 hectare)	*Dairy cows* (1 cow)	*Pork production* (1 sow)
October labour (hours) (available for fieldwork)	672	≥	9	40	4.4 (6.6×0.66)	3.8 (5.7×0.66)

Dairy cows and sows requires 6.6 and 5.7 hours per head respectively in October, and these requirements are reduced by one-third to 4.4 and 3.8 hours.

Another method is to have separate fieldwork and total labour (that is the hours available for livestock) constraints for each period. The cropping requirements appear in both rows, but those for livestock appear only in the total labour row:

			Wheat (1 hectare)	*Potatoes* (1 hectare)	*Dairy cows* (1 cow)	*Pork production* (1 sow)
October labour (hours)						
Total (57 × 31/7 × 4)	1,010	≥	9	40	6.6	5.7
Fieldwork (38 × 31/7 × 4)	672	≥	9	40	0	0

In this manner, livestock activities can draw on the full 1010 hours, but crops are constrained by the more limiting 672 hours of fieldwork available.

Yet another method is to employ a transfer activity, which in passing fieldwork hours on to livestock inflates them in the necessary ratio [1.5 times in this case (57/38)]. The illustration below introduces, in addition, another factor, in that it is assumed that only one man out of the four can work on livestock.

		Wheat (1 hectare)	*Potatoes* (1 hectare)	*Dairy cows* (1 cow)	*Pork Prodn.* (1 sow)	*Transfer fieldwork* (1 hour)
October labour (hours)						
Fieldwork	672 ≥	9	40	0	0	1
Livestock max. hours	168 ≥	0	0	0	0	1
Consumption of labour by livestock	0 ≥	0	0	6.6	5.7	−1.5

The total labour force is shown on the fieldwork row, with the transfer activity passing on 1.5 hours to livestock for each fieldwork hour consumed. However, the middle row constrains the amount transferred to a maximum of 168 fieldwork hours, representing one of the four men.

Spreading livestock labour 'overheads'

Another problem likely to arise in cases where labour is transferable between crops and livestock is that average labour requirements per head for the latter vary with the number of animals kept, because of the 'overhead' element in stockwork, such as time spent fetching animals or cleaning equipment. It follows that, on the one hand, the number of animals in the solution needs to be known if the relevant labour coefficients are to be inserted in the matrix, but on the other hand, that the labour coefficients actually used may determine the number of animals selected. Still pursuing the previous example, suppose that the cows are limited to a maximum of forty, because of the size of the cowshed, while if there are to be any cows on the farm the farmer is not prepared to accept a unit of less than twenty. Labour coefficients in October for the minimum and maximum herd sizes and for the mid-point are:

Herd Size (cows)	20	30	40
October hours per herd	150	200	250
October hours per cow	7.50	6.66	6.25

One possible way of handling the situation might appear to be to include the three separate herd sizes. However, if labour were scarce and, say, 20 cows came into the solution, half the 40-cow unit, with labour requirements of only 125 hours (250/2), would be selected, rather than the 20-cow unit requiring 150 hours.

There is no simple and at the same time mathematically elegant way of handling the problem. Instead, one method is to run the matrix several times, each time forcing in (by means of equality signs) units of different sizes, to which the appropriate labour coefficients are applied. The solutions are then compared for profitability with a further one in which no animals are permitted. In our example, there could be four solutions with, respectively, 0, 20, 30 and 40 cows. With 'overwriting' techniques this is a simple method to apply, but the number of solutions required proliferates rapidly if there is more than one type of livestock to be dealt with, with several potential unit sizes for each.

Another similar method is to approximate to the livestock requirements by forcing in a livestock unit which is flexible in size. The example below (still based on the previous assumptions) also shows fieldwork labour linking through by a scaled transfer activity.

			Dairy unit: *20 cows*	*30 cows*	*40 cows*	*Transfer fieldwork* (1 hour)
October labour						
Fieldwork (hours)	672	≥	0	0	0	1
Consumption of labour by dairy cows (hours)	0	≥	150	200	250	−1.5
Force in dairy unit (cows)	1	=	1	1	1	0

Such a formulation ensures either that one of the three units (20, 30 or 40 cows) is selected, or else that fractions of two *adjacent* units, which total to unity and thus give at least an approximation to the true labour coefficient, enter the solution. For example, if 34 cows are included in the solution, the combination that satisfies this number of cows and the requirement that the dairy unit should equal unity is 0.6 of the 30-cow unit and 0.4 of the 40-cow unit:

Cow numbers:	(0.6×30)	+	(0.4×40)	=	34
Dairy unit:	0.6	+	0.4	=	1

Total hours amount to 220 $[(200 \times 0.6) + (250 \times 0.4)]$, an average of 6.47 hours per cow, which falls between the 6.66 and 6.25 hours per cow of the 30- and 40-cow units respectively.

If the minimum herd size of 20 cows is selected it may indicate that no cows are preferable, so a solution in which the herd is eliminated should also be obtained and the profitability of the two plans compared.

Specialist livestock labour

Constraints on the availability of specialist livestock labour – that is, stockmen who work full-time on one type of animal (which may include replacements) – can usually be expressed simply in terms of the maximum number of animals that can be handled. (This method also eliminates the need to specify decreasing labour inputs per animal as unit size increases.) If, while still working only on livestock, stockmen can work on more than one type of animal, it is still possible to express labour constraints in terms of maximum unit size, scaling one type of livestock in terms of the other in a manner similar to that for the transfer of labour between crops and livestock. For example, if a stockman could look after a maximum of either 60 cows on their own or 50 cows with followers, the labour constraint could be expressed in terms of the maximum number of cows alone:

	Dairy cows *(1 cow)*	*Dairy cows and followers* *(1 cow)*
Livestock labour (cow units) 60 ≥	1	1.2

Flexibility in the size of labour force

In longer-term planning or when a new farm is being considered, the aim may be to discover the optimal size of labour force. One way of doing this is to run the matrix several times, assuming different numbers of men and also, perhaps, different machinery complements. Their cost is deducted as a fixed cost from net revenue, so that the highest profit plan may be located, and thus the optimal labour and machinery complement.

Another method is to have an activity that hires regular labour by the man, so supplying a given number of hours to each labour period, as in the following example:

			Wheat (1 hectare)	*Barley* (1 hectare)	*Potatoes* (1 hectare)	*Hire regular labour* (1 man)
Net revenue (£)		=	320	250	850	–3,265
Labour						
March/mid Apl. (hours)	0	≧	2.5	7.5	25	–250
May/mid June (hours)	0	≥	0	0	4	–330
Aug./mid Sept. (hours)	0	≥	5	5	1.2	–310
Oct./mid Nov. (hours)	0	≥	9	0	40	–230

However, the difficulty in the case of non-integer programs is that the optimal solution will almost certainly express the labour force to a fraction of a worker, for example, 4.321. If the fraction is close to a whole number and the farm is a large one, the nearest whole number can reasonably be accepted. Otherwise the matrix needs to be re-run with, in the above example, 4 men and 5 men, and the plans compared for profitability.

Operations with capital

Fixed capital

In writing fixed capital constraints into a matrix, a distinction may be made between capital already committed on the farm and additional capital which may be incorporated as a consequence of planning.

Existing fixed capital. The numbers of livestock or hectares of crops that can be carried on a farm may be limited by the capacities of existing buildings and machinery, and it is usually in this form that the latter appear as constraints in a matrix. The time element is important in this respect. With livestock, this is because in continuous production the time taken to process individual batches partly determines throughput and thus the annual capacity of buildings. With crops, the time available to operate machines is one of the determinants of their capacity.

First, an example may be taken from livestock production. Suppose there is a pig fattening house in which the farmer is prepared to undertake either pork, bacon or heavy hog production. Allowing for their different spatial requirements, 100 porkers or 83 baconers or 66 heavy hogs can be carried at any one time, while the different lengths of time taken to fatten them permit 3.71, 2.48 and 2.17 batches per year respectively. Annual capacity – the product of these two factors – thus amounts to 371 porkers or 206 baconers or 143 heavy hogs. In setting this up in matrix form, porker capacity is taken as the common denominator with baconer and heavy hog requirements appropriately scaled.

		Porkers (1 pig)	*Baconers* (1 pig)	*Heavy hogs* (1 pig)
Fattening house capacity (porker units)	371 ≥	1.0	1.8	2.6

Thus baconers are constrained to a maximum of 206 (371/1.8) and heavy hogs to 143 (371/2.6).

Another example may be taken of machinery capacity in crop production. Suppose a three-metre-cut combine harvester clears 6.4 ha of cereals or 4 ha of spring beans in an eight-hour working day and that twenty 'cutting' days are available for cereals, the last five of which overlap with the harvesting of spring beans. In addition, a further seven days are available for the latter after cereal harvest is finished. Stating this in terms of hours of combining:

		Cereals (1 ha)	*Spring beans* (1 ha)	*Transfer combining* (1 hour)
Cereals – combine capacity (hours)	160 ≥	1.25	0	1
Spring beans – combine capacity during cereal harvest (hours)	40 ≥	0	0	1
Spring beans – combine capacity after cereal harvest (hours)	56 ≥	0	2	– 1

The first row expresses combine capacity for cereals. The transfer activity permits a maximum of 40 hours to be passed to spring beans, which can also draw on another 56 hours not available to cereals.

Additional fixed capital. The opportunity to purchase new capital items, such as machinery, may be incorporated directly in the matrix. The annual cost of servicing the capital item appears in the objective function as a negative net revenue, while permission to include appropriate activities is passed on in the body of the matrix. For example, suppose a farmer, because of increasing difficulty in obtaining casual labour, is thinking of purchasing a one-row potato harvester as an alternative to the use of an elevator digger as at present. Its capacity is reckoned as 12 ha with an annual charge for depreciation, interest, spares and repairs of £1320.

			Potatoes elevator digger (1 hectare)	*Potatoes 1-row harvester* (1 hectare)	*Acquire potato harvester* (1 machine)	*Hire casual labour* (1 hour)
Net revenue (£)		=	850	800	– 1,320	– 1.5
Max. potatoes – machine harvested (hectares)	0	≥	0	1	– 12	0
Regular labour – potato harvest (hours)	*X*	≥	38	53	0	0
Casual labour – potato harvest (hours)	0	≥	80	40	0	– 1

The purchase of the machine permits 12 ha of mechanically harvested potatoes to be grown, thus allowing the casual labour requirement per hectare to be halved.

However, there is a difficulty with this approach. If, say, 6 ha of machine-harvested potatoes are included in the solution, only half a machine's annual costs will be incurred in passing on the necessary 6 ha of permission. Allowing capital items to be acquired directly in the matrix is thus likely to be no more than a rough guide to future policy. A generally more satisfactory approach is to run the matrix twice, once with the capital item incorporated (and with its annual costs included with the other fixed costs) and once without. In our example, one run would thus include the opportunity to grow up to 12 ha of machine-harvested potatoes, with £1320 added to fixed costs, while the other would not.

Working capital

The characteristic ebb and flow of working capital – particularly on arable farms – has already been noted (Chapter 12, p. 270). On the one hand, capital is generated by sales of farm produce and by borrowing. On the other, it is consumed in the process of defraying variable costs, such as purchased feeds, seeds and fertilisers; and fixed costs, such as wages, rent, machinery repairs, overheads, interest and repayments of capital. In addition, private expenditure, including taxation, must be added to fixed costs.

Although it is not difficult to handle working capital in a matrix, problems nevertheless arise in practical applications. One is that of obtaining relevant data, for not only must the levels of cash flows be predicted, but also their timing. Another is that information is needed on seasonal capital requirements, which include private expenditure, in addition to the usual farm fixed costs. Also, it has to be decided when the financial year should be assumed to start and how much working capital will be available at that time. In consequence, if planning seems unlikely to change the existing pattern of farming very much, and if in the past shortage of working capital has not been a problem, it is probably safe to exclude it from the matrix, at least in the first instance.

Incorporating working capital. There are two main ways of incorporating working capital into a matrix. One is to use transfer activities to pass surplus capital from one period to another during the year. The other is to accumulate the ebbs and flows of capital in successive periods.

These two methods may be illustrated, using the data in the first part

TABLE 18.6. *Working capital*

1. *Consumption (+ve) and production (−ve) of working capital*

	Working capital requirements (farm and private) (£)	Winter wheat (1 hectare) (£)	Spring barley (1 hectare) (£)	Maincrop potatoes (1 hectare) (£)	Pork production (12 pigs) (£)
Quarter I (Jan.–Mar.)	11,850	−195	−101	−185	−10
Quarter II (April–Jun.)	11,460	19	11	−343	−10
Quarter III (July–Sept.)	12,940	56	0	120	−10
Quarter IV (Oct.–Dec.)	10,590	−200	−160	−442	−10
Total[a]	46,840	−320	−250	−850	−40

[a] The totals of the individual activities equal their net revenues.

2. *Use of transfer activities*

	B		Wheat (1 hectare)	Barley (1 hectare)	Potatoes (1 hectare)	Pork (12 pigs)	Transfer activities QI–QII (£1)	QII–QIII (£1)	QIII–QIV (£1)	Pay-off activity (£1)
Net revenue (£)		=	320	250	850	40	0	0	0	0.0001
Working capital										
Quarter I (£)	−11,850	≥	−195	−101	−185	−10	1	0	0	0
Quarter II (£)	−11,460	≥	19	11	−343	−10	−1	1	0	0
Quarter III (£)	−12,940	≥	56	0	120	−10	0	−1	1	0
Quarter IV (£)	−10,590	≥	−200	−160	−442	−10	0	0	−1	1

3. *Use of cumulative capital balances*

	B		Wheat (1 hectare)	Barley (1 hectare)	Potatoes (1 hectare)	Pork (12 pigs)
Net revenue (£)		=	320	250	850	40
Working capital						
Quarter I (£)	−11,850	≥	−195	−101	−185	−10
Quarter II (£)	−23,310	≥	−176	−90	−528	−20
Quarter III (£)	−36,250	≥	−120	−90	−408	−30
Quarter IV (£)	−46,840	≥	−320	−250	−850	−40

of Table 18.6. The first column of figures shows the capital required to service the fixed resources – assuming a 150-ha, 3-man farm – and to defray private expenditure in the four quarters of the year (if necessary, the periods can be shorter than this). It is assumed that there is neither capital on hand nor capital owing at the start of the year. If this were not so, the former would be deducted and the latter added to the requirement in the first period. The capital requirements represent constraints on the farming system that have to be satisfied by the activities, and they therefore appear in the *B* column, taking *negative* values. (Conversely, if there are surpluses of working capital in any periods, the signs are positive.) For example, the first quarter appears as follows:

	B		*Wheat* (1 hectare)	*Barley* (1 hectare)	etc.
Working capital – Quarter I (£)	–11,850	≥	–195	–101	

The negative sign in the *B* column indicates that the activities must generate at least £11,850 of working capital in the first quarter.

The remaining columns in the first part of Table 18.6 show the quarterly requirements or supply of working capital in four representative activities. The signs have the usual meaning of those appearing in the body of the matrix. Thus positive signs indicate net capital consumption, arising either from variable costs alone or from variable costs exceeding sales in particular quarters. Negative signs indicate net capital supply arising from sales alone or from sales exceeding variable costs.

The second part of the table demonstrates the use of transfer activities to pass on any capital surplus from one quarter to the next, assuming the 'trading' year starts on 1 January. The 'pay-off' activity is simply a convenient device by means of which any capital surplus to requirements is accumulated at the end of the year. The fractional but positive net revenue in the objective function ensures that the transfer activities pass surplus capital through from period to period, even if it is not required directly to finance operations.

The alternative method of accumulating capital balances from one period to the next is shown in the last part of the table.

As is usual with the unmodified linear programming procedure, solutions refer to purely static situations. For example, although a considerable capital surplus may accrue at the end of the year, there is no provision for long-term development through re-investment. If capital proves limiting in some periods – because supply exactly matches consumption – the planner knows that the introduction of greater flexibility at such times may permit further expansion of the plan. Similarly, the fact that it may prove impossible to obtain a feasible solution from a matrix because, for example, more capital is required at some point of the year than the activities can provide, indicates that assumptions require changing.

Greater flexibility can be introduced in two main ways. One is by varying the assumptions concerning the levels and timings of cash flows and of working capital requirements for meeting fixed costs and private expenditure. For example, cereals and potatoes may be sold at or soon after harvest or else be stored for later sale. Fertilisers and other requisites may be purchased shortly before they are actually required or else purchased earlier at a discount in off-season periods. Bills may be settled promptly or payment delayed. Such modifications can be obtained either by running more than one matrix or by incorporating additional activities – such as 'wheat sold early', 'wheat sold late' into a single matrix.

The other way of increasing flexibility is to introduce 'formal' borrowing (apart from the credit obtained by delaying payments).

Incorporation of borrowing. Borrowing can be allowed for in the matrix by deducting the maximum obtainable credit from the capital required at that time (or adding it to any capital in hand). For instance, if it is assumed that £5000 is borrowed from the start of the year in the example in Table 18.6, the initial capital required – £11,850 – falls to £6850. If transfer activities are being used, the amounts of capital (*B* column) in the periods after the capital injection remain unchanged, as the transfer activities pass on any additional surplus capital. With accumulated capital balances, however, it is necessary to adjust capital in the subsequent periods too, so that it becomes £18,310, £31,250 and £41,840 in our example.

In deriving the net profit of a solution, repayment of the principal must be deducted along with other fixed costs from net revenue. Interest must be deducted too. In its simplest form this is interest on the whole sum borrowed for the full year. However, if interest is paid only on the sum outstanding at any time, its amount can be more accurately assessed by reference to the solution. For example, suppose that with £5000 credit available from the start of the year, the capital shown surplus in each quarter is £6400, £4100, £0 and £5700 respectively.[1] Com-

[1] If cumulative balances are used, the availability of working capital is shown in the solution either as a fully used, or as an idle, resource in the different periods. If transfer activities are used, it is shown by the levels of the transfer activities and the pay-off activity.

paring these figures with the £5000 credit shows the amount actually borrowed in each period to be £900 and £5000 in the second and third quarters respectively, and nothing in the first and last quarters (as capital availability exceeds the credit allowed by £1400 and £700 respectively).

Another approach is to incorporate borrowing activities directly in the matrix. The partial formulation below (showing just the last two quarters) assumes that up to £5000 can be borrowed in each quarter at 16 per cent interest, and that repayment of capital and interest (£104) is made in the subsequent quarter (or in an additional end-of-year capital row in the case of the last quarter).

	B		*Wheat etc.* (1 ha)	*Borrow £100: QIII*	*QIV*	*Transfer £1: QIII–QIV*	*QIV–year end*	*Pay-off activity* (£)
Net revenue (£)		=	320	−4	−4	0	0	0.0001
Capital *QIII* (£)	−12,940	≥	56	−100	0	1	0	0
Capital *QIV* (£)	−10,590	≥	−200	104	−100	−1	1	0
Capital, end of yr (£)	0	≥	0	0	104	0	−1	1
Capital limit *QIII* (£)	5,000	≥	0	100	0	0	0	0
Capital limit *QIV* (£)	5,000	≥	0	0	100	0	0	0

Operations reflecting management attitudes to uncertainty

One characteristic of most planning models is the assumption of perfect knowledge of future events. This is reflected in price, yield and input coefficients, which are 'single-valued', since no allowance is made for seasonal variation in their values. As already acknowledged (p. 391), the relatively limited use of such techniques as quadratic programming and stochastic linear programming which allow for variation in some of the planning parameters, is largely because of the paucity of relevant data with which to evaluate an uncertain future.

Here we consider how, nevertheless, some allowance can be made in the 'standard' linear programming matrix for problems arising because knowledge is mostly far from perfect. As seen in Chapter 16 (pp. 390–2), this requires account to be taken both on the way in which uncertainty moulds the attitudes and objectives of the farmer, and of the year-to-year variability inherent in his operations, particularly in respect of enterprise outcomes. To take them in turn.

Incorporating attitudes to uncertainty

Exclusion of enterprises. The farmer may refuse to consider certain enterprises as potential 'entrants' into a farm plan, because he regards them as 'too risky'. This may result from his having had very little experience of them in the past or, conversely, from previous experience which has been unfavourable, such as with crop failures. In the longer term it may also reflect a form of capital rationing, in that the farmer is not prepared to invest in enterprises which may require considerable capital and which may take some time to reach fruition.

In the matrix, such attitudes are reflected simply by the omission of enterprises, even though they are feasible in terms of the available resources. If desired, the matrix can be run twice, once including and once excluding the enterprises in question. A comparison of the net profits of the two solutions enables the farmer to evaluate better the soundness of his attitudes.

Maximum size of enterprises. Imposing maximum size limits on certain enterprises, because they are regarded as 'risky', is simply an extension of the first point above. Although the farmer is prepared to countenance the enterprise on the farm, he does not want it to absorb more than a small part of the available resources nor to make more than a limited contribution to farm income. In the matrix, such constraints on maximum size take their place with other non-material limitations, such as contracts and quotas.

Inclusion of enterprises. In contrast with a refusal to consider certain enterprises, the farmer may insist that others must appear in the solution. This may be because he regards the outcomes of such enterprises as relatively stable, or it may be simply a question of preference.

In the matrix, such an enterprise may be dealt with by use of the 'greater than or equal to' sign (see p. 440), so that it is compelled to enter at a minimum level. If it does enter the solution at the minimum, it suggests that a lower (including zero) level may be preferable. In this event, it may be worth running the matrix again, without the minimum constraint, so that the enterprise can find its own level, enabling a cost to be put on the specification of a minimum size.

Number of enterprises. The farmer, on the principle of not having 'all his eggs in one basket', may insist on some minimum number of enterprises. In the case of cropping farms, this can be handled in a similar way to rotational constraints, so that no single crop is permitted to take up 100 per cent of the arable area. Or else one crop can 'give permission' for another to be grown. The latter approach is also relevant for livestock farms. For example, a dairy farmer may insist on rearing his own herd replacements. In the matrix, the heifer-rearing activity 'gives permission' for dairy cows to be kept. If herd life is reckoned as four years, the relationship could be expressed as follows:

		Milk production (1 dairy cow)	*Heifer rearing* (1 heifer)
Replacement policy	$0 \geq$	1	−4

Milk production cannot be undertaken unless heifers are reared, one heifer allowing four cows to be kept (as a herd life of four years gives a replacement rate of one-quarter of the cows each year).

Yet another method is to combine certain activities. This approach could be used in the example above, and another example is furnished by the writing of complete rotations into the matrix (see pp. 451–3).

Adoption of 'cautious' standards. 1. *Net revenues.* The adoption of 'cautious' net revenues is also advocated as a means of allowing for uncertainty in planning. If the principle is applied to *all* activities and their net revenues remain in the same ratio to one another (so that the solution stays the same as if they had not been adjusted), all that may be gained is an understatement, rather than a possible overstatement, of total net revenue. However, if cautious net revenues are deliberately applied to specific enterprises, about whose output the farmer is less certain than he is with others, it becomes a valid means of reducing their likelihood of selection or of reducing the level at which they are selected.

2. *Resource levels and requirements.* Deflating resource levels – or inflating resource requirements – is another way of acknowledging uncertainty. The reduction of labour availability at peak periods, to allow for weather effects and other contingencies, is one example. The more strongly the farmer wishes to be able to complete operations within a certain time period from season to season, the more should the availability of labour be reduced. In other words, the unfavourable season rather than the average season is being catered for. Similar action may be taken with machinery, in that the capacity written into the matrix may be below that which could be achieved in a reasonable year. Such

measures may accord quite closely with the farmer's action in being, say, 'over-combined', so that he is ensured of being able to 'snatch' the harvest on the few available cutting days in a wet season.

Allowing for seasonal variability

We saw in Chapter 16 (pp. 404–6) that, given the necessary data on year to year variations in enterprise outcomes, it is possible to obtain solutions which, in addition to maximising weighted average gross margins, also provide information on the likely levels of farm gross margin in particular types of season. As shown in the example below (based on the data in Table 16.2, p. 406), such measurement of variability can readily be accommodated in the linear programming matrix.

Enterprise:		*P*	*Q*	*R*	*Net revenue, season:*		
					I	*II*	*III*
		(1 ha)	(1 ha)	(1 ha)	(£)	(£)	(£)
OF (£ average net revenue)	=	196	162	156	0	0	0
Net revenue, season type: I	0 =	−215	−280	−80	1	0	0
II	0 =	−255	−155	−160	0	1	0
III	0 =	−85	−95	−200	0	0	1
Land (hectares)	100 ≥	1	1	1	0	0	0

Apart from the usual type of farm constraint (represented here by land) there is an extra row and column for each seasonal type. Seasonal net revenues (gross margins) appear – with negative signs – under their respective enterprise heads, while the use of equality relationships ensures that their values in the solution are totalled in the seasonal net revenue columns, thus appearing in the solution as included activities.

A simpler formulation which obviates the need for the extra columns is to replace the equalities by the usual 'less than or equal to' relationship. Showing this for Season I only:

Enterprise:		*P*	*Q*	*R*
		(1 ha)	(1 ha)	(1 ha)
OF (£ average net revenue)	=	196	162	156
Net revenue, season type I	0 ≥	−215	−280	−80

Total seasonal net revenues now appear as unused resources in the solution.

Allowing for minimum net revenue

If the farmer is concerned that a plan should be capable of supplying some minimum level of net revenue in each season, the last formulation can be adjusted by replacing the zeros in the *B* column by the specified minimum revenue with minus sign, thus indicating, as in the case of working capital (p. 485), that at least that amount of net revenue must be generated. To use the same example, but assuming a minimum level of £14,750 net revenue is required:

Enterprise:			*P* (1 ha)	*Q* (1 ha)	*R* (1 ha)
OF (£ average net revenue)		=	196	162	156
Minimum NR, season type: I	−14,750	≥	−215	−280	−80
II	−14,750	≥	−255	−155	−160
III	−14,750	≥	−85	−95	−200

Reference to Table 16.2 shows that since the solution which maximises average net revenue in this example does not satisfy the minimum net revenue constraint in season type *III* (where it falls to £11,300), a sub-optimal solution (in terms of average net revenue) would be selected – assuming a feasible one exists, as is the case here (Plan 2, Table 16.2). If this formulation is used, it is advisable to run another matrix excluding the minimum net revenue constraints so that the price paid in terms of average net revenue forgone (if any) may be ascertained.

PART IV

THE CONTROL OF RESOURCES AND ENTERPRISES

It is one thing to make a plan; it is quite another to put it into operation and make sure that it works. Major changes in plans are made infrequently on most farms – perhaps only two or three times in a working lifetime. But control is a continuous process: checking the progress that is being made, making adjustments necessary because of changing circumstances or to bring a plan that is drifting back onto course.

The word 'control' can be used in a variety of senses, some narrow, some broad. In this book it is treated in three parts, each given a separate chapter. Chapter 19 describes the recording of the information required. Chapter 20 discusses ways of analysing the data recorded. Chapter 21 deals with the actual procedure of applying methods of control to the farm business.

19: Data recording

Introduction – why record?

This chapter is placed before that on analysing the data because the information must obviously be made available before it can be utilised. To serve as an introduction, general reasons for keeping farm records are given below. This is followed by a description of what records should be kept, together with explanations as to why these particular items are necessary. The details of how recording should be done are included as appendices, since they are intended mainly for reference purposes and can be omitted by readers whose interest is more general. In fact, some may prefer to obtain a more specific understanding of the uses to which such data can be put before reading this chapter, so that they can better appreciate the recommendations that are made. In this case they are advised to read Chapters 20 and 21 before the present chapter.

In the descriptions of the recording techniques contained in the appendices, some of the details given may seem petty and superfluous. They are deliberately included, however, because they are often not appreciated, and one of the most important reasons for farmers not keeping records that would be valuable to them is that they do not know precisely what needs to be done. Sometimes recording is started but later abandoned because it proves to be too difficult or not to be giving the information required. Often these faults can be rectified by a clearer appreciation of recording procedures.

Records need to be kept for three main purposes: to check on performance, to guide future decisions and to provide planning data. Some excuse themselves from paying proper attention to this side of management by stressing the 'historical' aspect of recording. They argue that the information relates to what is past, whereas a manager must constantly be looking ahead, not wasting time on post mortems, or in dreaming of what might have been. However, it is only through recording that a check can be made on how performance has compared with past plans, and to a large extent this is a continuous, contemporary process, not at all 'historical': this is largely the subject-matter of Chapter 21. Furthermore, records should reveal the strengths in a business that can be exploited and the weaknesses that must be removed: an aspect covered in Chapter 20. Finally, records provide data for use in making or revising future plans.

Planning involves both selecting the right technique and obtaining the necessary data. It is usually the latter that provides the greater problem for advisers. 'Standard data' are available to some extent, but are rarely sufficiently detailed to be applied with full confidence to individual farms. Variations in, for example, soil type, climate, machinery size and building layouts affect crop yields, labour requirements, and so on. Even if standard data were available in far greater detail than at present, circumstances on the individual farm would frequently fall between different categories, since it would be optimistic to expect data to be provided to cover a continuous range of differences. Furthermore, it would be virtually impossible to cover one vital variable, except very crudely: namely, quality of management. This varies according to such factors as skill, experience, personality and objectives.

As a result, the majority of advisers would argue that the most suitable data to apply are those obtained from the farm itself, from its past records. These should obviously reflect the particular conditions of the individual farm and the quality of its labour and management. Unfortunately the data can never be perfect. Apart from possible errors and inaccuracies in recording, circumstances and people alter. Changes occur in technology and in the prices of both inputs and outputs; the composition of the labour staff may change; the farmer or manager's experience will increase and his objectives and motivation may alter. Nevertheless, data from the farm itself still provides the best available guide to the future, even though such information may need to be 'normalised' (that is, adjusted on the basis of expectations in a 'normal' future year), because of exceptional circumstances in the past or changing conditions, while, in any event, future price expectations must be applied to the physical data recorded.[1]

However, there is no point in recording simply for the sake of it. Records should not be kept unless they can be profitably used.

[1] More formally, there are at least five alternatives for estimating yields, prices and other data for use in budgeting and programming: (i) standard data; (ii) averages of past results; (iii) modes (or most typical levels) derived from past results; (iv) any of the first three, adjusted for estimated differences or changes in management, conditions, technology and prices; (v) average weighted figures, based on (subjectively

Recording incurs costs as well as providing returns, whether the costs consist of fees for professional assistance or the value of the time of the farmer, manager or members of his family, which could either have been used for other work on the farm or for leisure. The law of diminishing returns applies to money or the value of time spent in recording, just as it does to any other variable resource, and there comes a point where the further records, extra detail or additional accuracy are not sufficiently useful to be worth the extra costs incurred to provide them.

Good farm records should satisfy three criteria: they should serve a definite purpose, be easy to complete and be up-to-date, so that any action needed can be taken as early as possible.

What to record

This section describes what physical and financial records are required and the specific reasons for keeping them. Views differ with regard to both what and how to record. The recommendations made below refer to the minimum records that are felt to be necessary for management purposes, and in each case a method of recording is suggested in the appendices which is felt to be as simple as possible, while at the same time being adequate. In most cases alternative methods exist.

(Footnote continued)
assessed) probabilities; this is a more formal version of (iv); the sum of the probabilities for each possible level must equal one; to take the yield of wheat as an example:

Yield range (t/ha)	Probability (total = 1)		Mid-point of range		
5.5–5.7	0.1	×	5.6	=	5.6
5.2–5.4	0.2	×	5.3	=	10.6
4.9–5.1	0.2	×	5.0	=	10.0
4.6–4.8	0.3	×	4.7	=	14.1
4.3–4.5	0.1	×	4.4	=	4.4
4.0–4.2	0.1	×	4.1	=	4.1
			weighted average (='expected') yield		4.88

In the case of a 'normal' distribution (e.g. 5.3:0.1, 5.0:0.2, 4.7:0.4, 4.4:0.2, 4.1:0.1), in which the 'pattern' of expectations is the same both above and below the most likely level (and the intervals between successive levels are equal), the average, the mode and the weighted average of the possible levels are identical.

Financial records

A major reason for keeping financial records is in order to provide information regarding the profitability of the whole farm business over a given period. This enables an analysis to be carried out to reveal the economic strengths and weaknesses of the farming system and to provide data to help in the preparation of revised plans and budgets. The information is normally presented in the form of a trading account (or profit and loss account[1]), and the period is usually one year, i.e. twelve calendar months, although not necessarily from 1 January to 31 December. The trading account needs to be sufficiently detailed to be of use for subsequent diagnosis, although it is unnecessary to include in it all the detail available. An example, for the farm budgeted in Tables 14.2 and 14.3, is shown in Table 19.1. A balance sheet is also required, showing the overall capital position of the farm business; this is discussed in detail in the next chapter.

The following financial records should be kept. The first four are needed to produce the trading account.

A cash analysis book. This provides the main record of receipts and expenses, and is set out in such a way as to enable each item to be recorded under an appropriate heading, e.g. milk and potatoes on the receipts side, fertiliser and machinery repairs on the expenses side.

A petty cash book. Small items of receipt and expenditure paid in cash need to be recorded separately.

A statement of debtors and creditors. At the end of the financial year it is necessary to compile a list of those who owe money (debtors) and those to whom money is owed (creditors), together with the amounts and the items for which the money is owed or owing. These sums relate to sales and purchases made during the financial year and they must therefore be included in the trading account for that year. Similarly, sums owed and owing at the beginning of the year will have been paid during the year and must be excluded, because they in fact relate to

[1] In accountancy a distinction is often made between the trading account and the profit and loss account. The trading account, besides including revenue and valuation changes, incorporates those charges which are considered to be directly attributable to putting goods into saleable condition; this gives a gross profit (or loss) from which the remaining ('overhead') costs incurred in carrying on the business are deducted in the profit and loss account.

TABLE 19.1. *Farm trading account* (at 31 March)

Opening valuation	(£)	*Receipts*	(£)
Cattle	10,082	Cattle	11,425
Sheep	7,854	Sheep	12,291
Wheat	7,697	Wool	747
Barley	596	Wheat	17,313
Hay	846	Barley	18,318
Straw	180	Oats	4,192
Concentrate feed	305	Potatoes	25,126
Seed	719	Produce consumed	105
Fertiliser	1,230	Private use of car, electricity	360
Sprays	105	Cottage rents	552
Fuel	160	Contract receipts	194
Tillages, etc.	2,394	Miscellaneous (wayleaves, etc.)	56
Total opening valuation	32,168	Total receipts	90,679
Expenditure		*Closing valuation*	
Cattle purchases	2,177	Cattle	10,511
Sheep purchases	2,760	Sheep	7,378
Seed	7,212	Wheat	11,052
Fertiliser (net of subsidy)	11,497	Barley	460
Concentrate feed	1,482	Hay	994
Wages and National Insurance	12,150	Straw	180
Machinery and vehicle repairs	3,532	Concentrate feed	390
Fuel, oil, electricity	2,239	Seed	373
Vehicle tax and insurance	477	Fertiliser	749
Contract and hire	774	Sprays	135
Machinery and vehicle depreciation	4,273	Fuel	160
Transport	346	Tillages, etc.	3,063
Sprays	1,497	Total closing valuation	35,445
Water	334		
Veterinary charges and medicine	403		
Farm repairs	4,001		
Rent and rates	11,872		
General insurance	551		
Postage and telephone	209		
Accountancy charges	450		
Bank charges and interest	1,673		
Miscellaneous expenses	4,684		
Total expenses	74,593		
Farm profit	19,363		
	126,124		126,124

Note: Most trading accounts presented by accountants show less detail than is included above, two or more items often being combined, e.g. fertiliser, seed and sprays, or (all) grain.

sales and purchases made in the previous financial year. The opening list of debtors and creditors for the current year will clearly be the same as the closing list for the previous year.

Valuations. Revenue and expenditure do not give the complete picture of the value of production and inputs used during the year, even after adjustments for debtors and creditors. With inputs this is because of differences in the amount and value of materials in store at the end of the financial year compared with the beginning. On the output side it is because of changes in the amount and value of unsold (or unconsumed) livestock and crops on the farm at the beginning and end of the year. If the total value of inputs in store at the end of the year exceeds that at the beginning then the value of inputs used during the year has been less than the expenditure upon them, and *vice versa*. If the total value of crops and livestock is greater at the end than at the beginning then the value of output has been greater than the revenue, and *vice versa*. Allowance for such changes has therefore to be made in the trading account and in the enterprise schedules. Furthermore, the value of assets in store must be included in the balance sheet in calculating the capital position and net worth of the business (Chapter 20, p. 543). As will be discussed in Appendix 19.1 (p. 511), the date of valuation is important.

Enterprise outputs. It is also necessary to record the financial output of each crop or livestock enterprise for the 'harvest year' or production cycle. Enterprise outputs are an essential part of the calculation of gross margins, but they are of such importance that they should be recorded even if gross margins are not. They are major determinants of profitability and variations in them from year to year are largely responsible for annual changes in total farm profit. Much of the required information can come from a fully detailed cash analysis book, but records of *internal transfers* and *produce consumed* are also needed. Both of these refer to production that is used but not sold. 'Internal transfers' relate to the product of one enterprise which is used on the same farm by another enterprise; examples are barley fed to pigs, or calves from the dairy herd used for beef production. These need to be valued and credited to the enterprise producing them and charged against the enterprise receiving them. 'Produce consumed' relates to production that is consumed by the farm household or by the farm employees.

Enterprise variable costs. If gross margins are to be calculated separate records are needed for the allocation of variable costs. Easily the most important of these on many farms are *concentrate feedingstuffs*, the level of which has a considerable bearing on the profitability of most livestock enterprises. This is particularly true of pigs, poultry and intensive beef production; it has least significance for sheep and the summer fattening of beef. Often a rough allocation at the end of the year of fertiliser, seed, sprays and miscellaneous livestock variable costs is good enough for practical purposes, particularly as complete accuracy can be difficult to achieve, even with careful recording, because of the carry-over from one year to another. For arable enterprises and grass, field records (see p. 517) can be used to facilitate this allocation, the amounts being roughly costed according to prices paid during the year, e.g. for different types of fertiliser. Only a rough check need be made with the annual accounts, to ensure that the sums allocated are *approximately* the same as the sums spent, allowing for valuations of materials in store and used on growing crops at the beginning and end of the year. This is sufficient particularly where the main enterprises consist of livestock and/or cereals, since the variable costs (excluding concentrate feedingstuffs) are low compared with output; hence the estimate of gross margins is little affected by slight inaccuracies in the allocation of variable costs, and the difficult task of accurate reconciliation is not worthwhile. The more arable and horticultural crops with high variable costs that are grown the stronger the case for fuller and more accurate allocation and reconciliation.

Labour costs. Elaborate recording and calculations of labour costs per enterprise are not in general recommended, and certainly not for each field. For arable farming and horticulture the results can be highly misleading (see further Chapter 20, pp. 538–9), apart from being time-consuming and costly. If, for any reason, such calculations are wanted, they should be done as simply as possible, e.g. by totalling annual hours per enterprise and multiplying by the average labour cost per hour of all the workers, rather than by recording and costing separately the number of hours of ordinary time and overtime spent by each worker on each crop. There is a better case to be made for costing labour used for livestock enterprises, especially where full-time specialist stockmen are employed; this is partly because the results are more meaningful and partly because the task is relatively simple, requiring no elaborate system of recording and calculations.

As will be discussed below, there is a stronger argument in favour of recording *physical* data on labour use.

Machinery costs. It may be desirable to record separately at least some of the costs associated with different machines on the farm, in particular depreciation, repairs and possibly fuel. On most farms it is not worth the trouble required to record these items as a regular procedure. However, where, for example, machinery repair costs appear to be excessive, a farmer may rightly want to find the reasons.

Physical records

Physical data concerning the farm and its performance are essential to implement the financial information already described. This is so for all three uses of farm records as set out at the beginning of this chapter: to check current performance, for directly controlling the business and its constituent parts; to aid the analysis of past results, in attempting to detect weaknesses and strengths to guide future decisions; and to provide planning data. In so far as prices of both outputs and inputs (particularly the former) are subject to continual change, the physical data is in many ways of greater importance than the financial information. This is particularly true regarding the provision of planning data.

The following are the physical records that should be kept.

A monthly record of livestock numbers. This is required for each livestock category, together with the details for each month of numbers born, bought or transferred in, and numbers that have died, been sold and transferred out. In this way full control is kept over many important aspects of livestock enterprises. Items like mortality and sales are recorded for subsequent cross-checking if necessary, and an accurate record of numbers is ensured for such annual calculations as milk yield per cow and weaners per sow, and for estimating the stocking rate.

Production of breeding livestock, e.g. litres of milk, weaners born and reared, lambs born and reared. This information is needed for measuring important determinants of profitability. Obviously, some of the data can be derived from the monthly recording of numbers just outlined.

Breeding records. In the case of dairy cows and sows, it is of considerable importance to keep a check on the breeding performance of each animal. This is vital to profitability, and is a valuable aid to culling.

Concentrate feedingstuffs. It is necessary to know the quantity of concentrate feed consumed by each category of livestock, as well as its cost.

Crop yields. The yield per hectare of each crop grown is in most cases the main factor affecting the profit contribution of individual crop enterprises.

Field records and rotation record. Records for individual fields should cover crop grown, variety, fertiliser and spray use, date sown and harvested, and approximate yield if possible. The larger the farm and the less well known it is to the farmer or manager and his staff the more useful these records are. Obviously, if the farm is a small one or the farmer has been on it a long time he may feel he knows the individual fields and their idiosyncracies well enough to make recording superfluous.

Sometimes recording the cultivations on each field is advocated. There is little point in this, however, unless it is felt that some useful lessons might ultimately be learnt – for instance, if different cultivation techniques are being tried and the effects on yields are to be compared. Individual field costing is not recommended. Neither is it worthwhile, usually, to record the grazing of individual fields, unless the farmer wishes to compare the effect on output of different grass varieties or fertiliser treatments under his particular conditions, to help him decide future policy on these points. A case may be made for such recording to help allocate the forage area and hence variable costs to different categories of grazing livestock on the farm. These attempts, however, tend to be complicated by such factors as the quality of the grazing at different times of the year, and estimating the performance of the animals on different fields is extremely difficult, except in rather general terms.

Labour records. In contrast to allocating labour *costs* to individual enterprises – especially in the case of crops – a strong case can be made for recording the number and timing of labour *hours* spent on each enterprise where seasonal labour requirements vary, as they do with all crops. Such information may be used partly to check on efficiency, by comparing the labour used for various jobs with standards, but, more important, it is extremely valuable when planning enterprise changes, particularly on arable farms and horticultural units. This is not meant to imply that comprehensive labour use records should be kept on every farm. Where the farming system has relatively few enterprises (counting all spring-sown cereals as one enterprise and all autumn-sown cereals as another) there is often little to be learnt from labour recording, except possibly where the farm is large and several men are employed. On slightly more complicated farms notes can be made of gang-sizes and rates of work achieved on the critical jobs at particularly busy times of the year. Only on a farm or holding with a fairly complex cropping programme is more comprehensive recording worthwhile, and then not necessarily over the whole year; if there are slack periods not much will be gained by recording how the labour is used at such times, particularly as there may be an element of 'filling time' on some tasks.

The remainder of this chapter consists of three appendices giving details of *how* the records advocated above can be kept. Appendix 19.1 covers financial records, Appendix 19.2 physical records, and Appendix 19.3 makes recommendations concerning office procedure.

Appendix 19.1: How to record – financial records

The scope of this book is such that it cannot hope to contain a complete manual on accountancy. Only the main methods of financial recording for management purposes and the important points that should be kept in mind are considered below. No attempt will be made to cover every aspect relevant solely to tax assessment, which is the province of the accountant. Further details that apply to office procedure in general are added in Appendix 19.3.

Cash analysis book

There are two alternative layouts: either receipts are entered on the left-hand side and expenses on the right-hand side, or receipts are entered in one part of the book and expenses in another. The latter provides more space and is thus to be preferred on most farms. The general layout is shown in Figure 19.1. Each item is entered twice, once under a single column for all entries on the left (headed 'amount') and again, on the same line, under the appropriate 'analysis' column to the right. Headings for expenses are similar for most farms, but for receipts they

Receipts

Date	Detail	Cheque no.	Amount	Contra	Cattle	Sheep	etc.
			£	£	£	£	£

Expenses

Date	Detail	Cheque no.	Amount	Contra	Feed	Seed	etc.
			£	£	£	£	£

Fig. 19.1. Layout of cash analysis book

obviously vary widely according to the type of farming. Suggestions for headings are given below.[1]

Expenses

Contra
Petty cash (PC if included with private drawings)
Livestock purchases
Feed
Seed, plants (P) and bulbs (Bu)
Fertilisers and lime (F), sprays (S)
Wages and national insurance: (R) = regular labour
(C) = casual labour
Machinery, tractor and vehicle repairs
Fuel and oil (FO), electricity (E) and coal (C), glasshouse fuel (GF)
Contract and hire (C), transport (T)
General insurance (G), vehicle tax and insurance (VTI)
Rent, rates (Ra), water (W)
Property repairs (to buildings, fences, etc.)
Sundries (including vet. and med. (V), Office expenses and professional charges (O))
Baler twine (BT) and sack hire (SH)
Capital (machinery, buildings, etc.)
Private drawings
Bank charges and interest (B), mortgage (M), other ownership expenses (OE)
Marketing expenses (other than transport), including packing materials (PM); bought-in produce (BP)
Spare column

Obviously any inappropriate items can be omitted, e.g. livestock purchases and feed on a farm with no livestock; this may allow other items grouped to be split into more than one column.

[1] As advocated in *Keeping Financial Records* (1968). Short Term Leaflet No. 48, Ministry of Agriculture, Fisheries and Food.

Receipts

Contra
Milk
Eggs and poultry
Cattle,
Sheep,
Pigs,
Cereals,
(Wheat, barley and oats should have separate columns if they are main crops and there are enough spare columns; otherwise use W for wheat, B for barley, O for oats to distinguish between them) .
Potatoes
Other crops – in separate columns as far as possible
Contract work
Miscellaneous,
Capital sales and capital grants (CG)

The number of headings chosen has to be given careful forethought. On the one hand, to avoid subsequent further analysis (or breakdown) of individual columns as far as possible, there should be separate headings for each main item. Obviously, however, the total number of columns available will set a limit, unless the analysis is to continue over more than a pair of facing pages, which is best avoided. But, in any case, to have separate columns for items, even important ones, that only have one or a few entries during the year is wasteful of space and unnecessary. The answer in such cases is to amalgamate two or three of these items and use coding to help the subsequent analysis at the end of the period. These could be in the form of single letters or numbers on the right of the column (or in a separate narrow column if the book is so laid out); examples are given in the list above. The key to the coding should be given at the front of the book.

Usually the items are entered when payments are actually made or receipts obtained. If it is wished to record purchases and sales when made, prior to payment, (which may be preferable for control purposes – see Chapter 21) they should be ticked off when paid. Cheque numbers and as many details as possible should be entered for subsequent checking and reference, e.g. quantities of grain or numbers of animals sold and the price, so that the cash analysis book is fully used as a means of recording transactions, not simply sums of money. Complications such as contra payments, payments on account, and 'composite' payments for several widely differing items should be avoided as far as possible.

The simplest way to deal with unavoidable contra payments is to include a contra column after the amount column in both the payments and receipts sections. A 'contra' sum is then included in both. For example, if sales of barley worth £400 were set off against a bill for fertiliser (£350) and seed (£200) of £550 the relevant columns would be as follows:

EXPENSES				RECEIPTS		
Amount (£)	*Contra* (£)	*Fertiliser* (£)	*Seed* (£)	*Amount* (£)	*Contra* (£)	*Barley* (£)
150	400	350	200	—	400	400

The sums in the 'amount' plus 'contra' columns must equal the sum of the figures in the analysis columns, only the actual net sum paid or received being entered in the 'amount' columns. Payments received which are made net of certain deducted expenses, e.g. for marketing, can be dealt with in the same way if it is felt worthwhile to record separately the gross receipts and the expenses deducted; the latter would be the sum included in both 'contra' columns, the net sum paid being entered in the 'amount' column on the receipts sheet.

Where payments on account are unavoidable, because some payments must be made but financial circumstances make it impossible to settle the whole account, it is far preferable to select certain items from the total account and pay those, rather than pay a round sum. Subsequent checking is then made much easier.

It is usually best to record expenses net of discounts. If there are several different cost items in the bill, which therefore need allocating to more than one column, an approximate allocation of the total discount should be made. An alternative is to record the gross amounts in the analysis columns and have a separate column for discounts: the net sum is recorded in the 'amount' column, so that the figures in the 'amount' column plus the 'discount' column equal the sum of the analysis columns.

When each sheet is completed, the columns should be added and the totals inserted at the foot. The total of each of the two 'amount' columns – plus the 'contra' and 'discount' columns if included – should equal the sum of the analysis columns. After checking, and correcting if necessary, the totals should be carried forward to the top of the next sheet, so that the totals are cumulative from the beginning of the financial year.

Periodically (at least quarterly) the entries in the cash analysis book should be checked against the bank statement. The opening bank balance plus total receipts less total expenses should equal the opening bank balance for the following reconciliation period. The latter sum, plus the total value of any cheques sent to suppliers that have not yet been paid in to the bank by the payee, should equal the final balance as shown in the bank statement.

Petty cash

Recording is simplified considerably if payments are made by cheque rather than cash, and if all cash receipts are banked. They will then be straightforward entries in the cash analysis book. It is obviously impossible, however, to avoid cash transactions entirely, particularly for minor day-to-day expenses. A useful method of reducing the recording problem to a minimum is to employ the 'float' system. A round sum is drawn from the bank by cheque to cover several weeks' likely minor expenses. This is recorded as 'petty cash' in the detail column of the expenses sheet in the cash analysis book and also entered in an analysis column headed 'petty cash'. This sum is recorded under receipts in a petty cash book. Payments should be recorded in a diary or pocketbook as soon as possible after they occur and entered under expenses in the petty cash book as follows:

Date	*Detail*	(£)
4 Feb.	Meal at market	1.45
4 Feb.	Publications	2.20
6 Feb.	Petrol	4.10

It is often most convenient for the expenses to be paid out of private cash and the appropriate sums, as recorded in the petty cash book, taken from the petty cash box afterwards. When all but, say, about £10 of the petty cash has been spent, a further sum for petty cash should be drawn by cheque, sufficient to bring the sum back to the original amount, e.g. if the original sum were £50 and £10.20 were left, £39.80 should be drawn. At the end of the year the petty cash book expenses are analysed and 'posted' to the appropriate columns of the cash analysis book. The petty cash column total can then be ignored when the amount and analysis columns are reconciled.

Receipts of cash in small sums are best kept separate and recorded either in another petty cash book (for 'receipts') or in a separate part of the same book. When the sum is large enough to be worth paying into the bank the amount should be recorded in the receipts petty cash book and also included in the receipts sheet of the cash analysis book, with 'cash' in the 'detail' column and the sum allocated to the appropriate analysis columns. If such receipts are used for payment of petty cash expenses both recording and subsequent analysis are needlessly complicated. The sum would need to be recorded as an outgoing in the petty cash receipts book or section and as a receipt in petty cash expenses. If this is practised frequently, it may be easier to have a single book with left-hand pages for expenses and right-hand pages for receipts.

If recording complications are to be minimised, money for private expenses should be kept separate from the petty cash receipts and expenses. Wage payments should also be kept separate, though when sums are drawn for wages that are not exactly the sum needed (the details of which will be kept in the wages book), any deficit can be made up from petty cash and surpluses paid in to petty cash. These amounts will have to be recorded in the expenses petty cash book(s) under expenses and receipts respectively. Sometimes a cheque is drawn for cash to cover jointly wages, private expenses and petty cash. 'Cash' would then be entered in the 'detail' column of the cash analysis book and the total allocated between the three appropriate analysis columns. Some prefer to record all cash drawings in one column ('cash drawn') and record its allocation separately.

Debtors and creditors

The names of debtors and, separately, the names of creditors, together with the appropriate amounts owed or owing, can be simply listed on two halves, or sides, of a sheet of paper. When the debts are paid after the end of the year the items can be marked as a debtor (D) or creditor (C) in the 'detail' column when entered in the cash analysis book and ticked off on the list of debtors and creditors.

The debtors and creditors can be analysed under the appropriate headings on separate sheets in the receipts and expenses sections respectively of the cash analysis book, and each column totalled. The cumulative, annual column totals of receipts and expenses during the year are then adjusted as follows, to give the sums to enter in the trading account:

Receipts + debtors at end of year – debtors at beginning of year.
Expenses + creditors at end of year – creditors at beginning of year.

Valuations

For the most part valuation is a process of estimation, because the current value of most assets cannot be known with certainty unless they are actually sold. Alternative bases are available, according to the use for which the valuations are required. Once the basis has been decided it should be the same for both opening and closing valuations. The closing valuation is made for the last day of the financial year and forms the opening valuation for the following year. If values are updated, as for breeding livestock in particular, then both the opening and closing valuations should be calculated using the same (revised) per unit figures in estimating the annual profit for the year for management purposes. Valuation recommendations, based on the need for meaningful figures for management guidance, are given below:

Saleable crops in store: at estimated market value less costs, such as marketing expenses, still to be incurred; the value can be either at the time of valuation or at the expected date of sale; the latter tends to be the more straightforward for subsequent analysis, provided an allowance is made for possible loss of saleable produce while in store.

Growing crops: at variable costs (as defined in gross margin calculations) to the date of valuation; for management purposes it is usually best to ignore 'cultivations' and manurial residues – they mean more recording and calculations and are as likely to mislead analysis and decision-making as to aid them.

Saleable crops ready for harvesting but still in the ground: preferably these should be valued like saleable crops in store, less estimated harvesting costs, but they can alternatively be treated as growing crops.

Fodder stocks (home-grown): for the calculation of gross margins from livestock these are best calculated at variable costs. Alternatively they can be valued at estimated market value – based on hay-equivalent value according to quality. Minor, fortuitous changes in stocks of fodder, because of varying weather conditions, the severity or length of the winter or minor changes in livestock numbers, are in many ways better ignored. This cannot be done, however, where a build up or run down of fodder stocks is the result of deliberate policy. Fodder crops still in the ground, e.g. kale, should be treated as growing crops.

Stocks of purchased materials (including fodder): at cost net of discounts (where known) and subsidies (where applicable).

Livestock: at current market value less cost of marketing; fluctuations in market value expected to be temporary should be ignored.

Machinery and equipment: at original cost (net of any investment grants), less accumulated depreciation to date of valuation.[1]

On a farm where arable production is important, the financial year for management purposes should preferably begin and end at the time when there are likely to be least crops in store; this obviously reduces the amount of estimation needed and allows accurate calculation of crop outputs at the same time as the annual account is completed. On a farm growing cereals and potatoes, however, these crops may not be sold until April, May or even June, by which time the following year's spring corn and root crops will have been sown. If the complication of having to record materials used on growing crops is to be minimised, the year needs to end at the end of March or early April, although this may still be too late to avoid the problem on a light land farm.[2] On farms with a dairy herd or a grazing beef cattle enterprise a spring year end is again to be preferred, since it allows the complete grass cycle to be covered within the same financial year, including both the summer grazing and the feeding of the conserved grass. For sheep a late autumn year end is usually preferable.

Enterprise Outputs

If all the produce is sold it is possible for all the information required to calculate enterprise outputs to be obtained from the cash analysis book, particularly if each enterprise can be spared a separate column in the receipts section. This is not usually possible, however, and even if it were it would be desirable to transfer the data (or at least to summarise them) onto separate sheets at the end of the year, rather than to leave them scattered over many pages.

Thus separate records should be kept for each enterprise. An ordinary ledger book will suffice, with one or more separate pages for each enterprise, according to the likely number of entries. However, since it is often difficult to forecast, until after a few years' experience, how many pages will be needed for each enterprise, there is much to be said for having loose-leaf sheets, kept in an appropriate type of file. This has the additional advantage of allowing successive years' records

[1] But see Appendix 19.4 (Inflation Accounting).

[2] The desirability, for management purposes, of valuing when crops and livestock on hand are low clashes with that for purposes of tax equalisation between seasons, which requires sufficient stocks on hand to enable values to be suitably adjusted. Many arable farmers compromise by having a December valuation; by then they know whether it has been a good or bad year and there are still sufficient stocks on hand to adjust the values accordingly.

of each enterprise to be kept together subsequently. Sufficient columns are needed for the following information: date, quantity, price (although this is often not worth including for each entry if it has to be calculated) and value. A wider column should be left for notes, which can include the name of the buyer if required. The first column can be used to insert numbers for checking back to the cash analysis book entries, but if the date entered is the same this should be sufficient to allow any subsequent checking. If an enterprise has more than one distinctive type of output it is preferable to keep a separate sheet for each; for example, dairy cows require three: for milk, culls and calves. Where many small sales take place, e.g. eggs at the farm gate, it is better to record them separately, possibly in a small notebook, and insert only periodic (say weekly) totals in the main sheets.

These enterprise records must include not only sales, but also the amount and value of internal transfers and produce consumed on the farm by the household and employees. Some may prefer to have separate sheets to record each of these; the case for this is strongest where there are many entries during the year; where this is so use may again be made of preliminary rough entries in notebooks with the subsequent transfer of periodic totals to the main sheets.

At the end of the financial year, further entries will be needed in order to calculate enterprise outputs, namely, debtors and opening and closing valuations. Where there is a closing valuation, subsequent entries will have to be made as the produce in store is sold or used on the farm, to check the harvest year output (see Chapter 20, p. 534).

Each livestock enterprise should have a separate sheet to record purchases of livestock and/or internal transfers from another livestock enterprise. Every internal transfer has to be recorded twice: as a credit (sale) to one enterprise and a debit (purchase) to the other. The value entered should be the nearest estimate to market value at the time of transfer.

Concentrate feedingstuffs

Recording this item is a relatively simple task if each type of concentrate feed is purchased for a specific type of livestock and fed only to that class of livestock (e.g. dairy nuts, calf weaner pencils). The expenses sheets in the cash analysis book can be used. If there are enough columns available, a separate feed column can be included for each category of livestock, with quantities being written in the detail column. Otherwise feed can be recorded in a single column with initials of the type of stock (e.g. DF for dairy followers) added either alongside the sum in the (feed) column or in the detail column. In this case the details have to be transferred at the end of the year, or more frequently if required, onto separate records (further cash analysis sheets could be used) in order to add the sums of money and physical quantities for each type of livestock separately. As with any cost item, adjustments need to be made for creditors, deducting the amounts owed at the beginning of the year and adding the amount owed at the end. It is also necessary to add the quantity and value of stocks at the beginning of the recording period and deduct those at the end, unless the amounts are small and much the same at each end of the period. Where monthly amounts are wanted, it will almost certainly be insufficient to use only the cash analysis book. A separate record is required of all quantities coming onto the farm at the time of delivery and the way in which they are allocated, and a periodic reconciliation of the two is needed, as described subsequently.

Even where monthly amounts are not required, a more complex system of recording is needed where some or all types of feedingstuffs purchased are used by more than one type of stock. Home-mixing is often involved, frequently using home-produced grain. Recording is in this case greatly simplified if all deliveries and issues are made to and from a central store. As delivered, the different types of feed are recorded in separate columns. Again the cash analysis book layout can be used. The date and supplier are listed. For each type of feed there needs to be a narrow column for quantities and a wider column for cost. Every time food is issued from the central store a note has to be made of four items: the date, type of food, quantity and category of stock. Barn record cards can be used, either made of stiffish material or attached to a board, with four columns. The cards must always be kept in the same place, with a pencil or biro attached. On completion, or at the end of the recording period, the card(s) must be sent to the farm office and replaced by a new card. Alternatively, pads of feed record slips can be used, giving this same information; one slip is used for each issue and filed on a spike or in a box, from where they are periodically collected for analysis. A small notebook is another alternative. Where mixes are used it is best to record only the name or number of the mix and the quantity. A separate list needs to be kept, either in the barn or the office, of the composition of each mix.

Each week, fortnight or month the details from the barn record cards or slips are entered onto feed record sheets, one for each type of livestock. An example of the layout is shown in Figure 19.2. The total amount of each mix fed to each type of livestock should be calculated

Dairy cows

Date	Barley		Oats		Flaked Maize		Bran & Mids		etc.	
	tonne	£	tonne	£	tonne	£	tonne	£	tonne	£

Fig. 19.2. Feed record sheet

and separated into the individual ingredients before recording on the feed record sheets, each item being subsequently valued. Where only annual amounts are wanted, quantities only of farm grain need be recorded, an approximate average value being placed on them at the end of the year; the figure for the average value of grain may then be slightly less accurate but this is balanced by the large reduction in the number of calculations required.

Periodically a reconciliation should be made between quantities delivered to the store and the amounts issued. A monthly check may be too time-consuming while an annual check may make it difficult to discover the reasons for discrepancies, which could be large before being revealed; quarterly is thus a suitable compromise. Deliveries during the period plus opening stocks less closing stocks should equal issues during the period. The reconciliation can be simplified by omitting farm grain. It is difficult, indeed often impossible, to check the latter, because amounts held in bulk are usually known only very approximately, especially if stored in heaps on the floor. The only real answer here is to weigh accurately the quantities used and record them. This is essential if the gross margins, not only of the livestock but also of the cereal enterprises, are to be properly calculated. A double check can be provided by weighing off, say, two tonnes at a time from the grain store and recording these as deliveries to the central food store, subsequently reconciling them with issues in the same way as for purchased concentrates.

To obtain monthly amounts fed to enterprises for control purposes the amounts issued to each type of stock must be adjusted for changes in stocks. The total fed equals the amounts issued plus closing stocks less opening stocks. These adjustments may be unnecessary if the amounts in stock are trivial compared with the total used during the period.

Fertiliser and seed

Any records of fertiliser and seed costs should be kept simple, for reasons already given (p. 501). Seed is obviously bought specifically for a particular enterprise; it is often possible, therefore, to record sufficient detail in the cash analysis book – either in the detail column or partly in the detail column and partly in the seed column (possibly by using a system of coding); these data can be transferred to separate enterprise records subsequently as required. Alternatively, fuller details can be recorded on one or more pages in a ledger.

Fertiliser is likely to be less straightforward. Quantities and costs of purchases may again be obtained from the expenses sheets of the cash analysis book. However, if payment of bills is delayed and the complication of allowing for creditors is to be avoided, pages in a ledger can be used for recording deliveries, which can be ticked off as paid for and entered in the cash analysis book. Allocation can be recorded on a barn card or in a notebook kept in the fertiliser store, as recommended for concentrate feedingstuffs. Alternatively, one of the farm staff (e.g. the arable foreman on a large farm) can record dates, quantities used and the crops in a pocketbook kept on his person. Periodically the details are transferred to a fertiliser-use record kept in a ledger. The relevant pages can be divided into columns, one for each crop. Alternatively, the fertiliser-use pages (or page – depending on the number of crops and the size of the farm) can be divided into sections, one for each crop. Quantities can be recorded initially, costs being inserted subsequently. At the end of the year a rough reconciliation should be attempted, allowing of course for opening and closing stocks.

As has already been suggested, however, a rougher calculation, consisting of an end-of-year allocation assisted by the field records suggested below, will often be sufficient.

Other variable costs

On farms where contractors or casual labour are employed for work on specific enterprises, separate pages should be kept in a ledger for the recording of the amounts paid and the enterprises concerned. Separate pages can also be kept to record veterinary and medicine and other miscellaneous variable livestock expenses, together with their allocation, if this cannot be done simply and adequately in the cash analysis book.

Machinery costs

Records of machinery expenses largely relate to the calculation of depreciation and the resulting estimate of valuation; this is discussed fully in Chapter 4. Otherwise they are likely to consist mainly of repairs to particular machines or types of machine (e.g. tractors), although some farmers may, at least from time to time, wish to check on fuel costs. It may not be possible to record sufficient information in the 'detail' and 'machinery repairs' columns of the cash analysis book for this purpose and, even if it is, subsequent analysis will be needed. The best course is to have a separate page in the cash analysis book for such analysis. The total repair bills are included in the 'amount' column and the analysis columns are allotted to different machines or types of machine. If a farmer only wants to record the costs of a few items of machinery, however, separate pages in a ledger will suffice, one, for example, for combine repairs, and others, say, for tractor expenses and farm vehicles. Items should be recorded here at the same time as the payments are entered in the cash analysis book. Tax and insurance can also be added if required.

Appendix 19.2: How to record – physical records

Some physical records have already been covered above, because they have been incorporated with financial records. These include quantities of concentrate feedingstuffs and crop yields. Livestock production has also been partly covered, in that it has been recommended that physical quantities, such as milk produced and calves sold and retained, should be recorded together with their value. Items such as egg production, the number of weaners reared (and either sold or transferred to the fattening enterprise) and lambs sold or retained should also be covered by such means. Sometimes, however, these records may be insufficient. Thus, with pig breeding and lamb production, numbers born and mortality should be recorded. These, together with other items, such as the dates of farrowing of each sow, should be entered in a notebook kept by the pigman or shepherd, for subsequent recording on enterprise pages in a ledger.

Monthly record of livestock numbers

Much of the above information can be obtained from a monthly reconciliation of livestock numbers. It is not enough to record end-of-month numbers only; the derivation of each figure is needed as a check. This type of record must show, for each type of livestock, some or all of the following items, as appropriate: (*a*) opening numbers, numbers born, numbers bought, numbers transferred in, and (*b*) deaths, numbers sold, numbers transferred out, closing numbers. The total of the items in (*a*) should equal the total of the items in (*b*). Two alternatives are possible – either to have a monthly sheet covering all types of livestock, or one sheet, covering the twelve calendar months, for each type of stock. The latter is to be preferred, the layout being shown in Figure 19.3.

Calves under 6 months old

	Oct.	Nov.	Dec.	Jan.	etc.
Start of month	30	31	30	28	27
Births	5	4	1	2	
Purchases	3	4	4	3	
Transfers in	4	4	3	3	
Total	42	43	38	36	
Deaths	1	—	2	—	
Sales	3	2	3	2	
Transfers out	7	11	5	7	
End of month	31	30	28	27	
Total (= Check)	42	43	38	36	

Fig. 19.3. Monthly reconciliation of livestock numbers

Breeding checks

Various types of chart are available which allow for both recording and control simultaneously. Because they are usually regarded as a means of control their description is left until Chapter 21 (p. 570). Some of the data from these charts, such as calving or farrowing dates, can be transferred to books or cards for more permanent records.

Field records

Field records can be kept in an ordinary bound ledger, or in a loose-leaf file, or on cards. There is one page, or card, per field per year. The virtue of loose-leaf files or cards is that successive years for each field can be put together to make a continuous record. Also, data for any single crop can easily be assembled as required. If only a few items are recorded, one sheet or card may be used for more than one year, thus saving on space requirements over a period of years. These records will form a type of diary for each field, for subsequent reference. The items to be recorded include crop grown, variety, fertilisers and sprays used, date sown and harvested. Yields should be recorded as accurately as possible, without going to excessive trouble trying to keep lots separate. Often these can be only roughly estimated, as is usually the case with cereals, but an approximate figure is undoubtedly better than nothing. Notes should be added, recording observations about the field, e.g. concerning drainage, fertility or soil peculiarities. Many of these items may first be written in a notebook carried by a member of the farm staff – the head tractor driver, arable foreman or the farm manager – and subsequently transferred to the field records.

Rotation record

This should be kept on a single sheet of paper, unless the number of fields is so large as to make it impossible. The names and/or numbers of the fields (and their areas if required) are listed down the left-hand side and the remaining space is divided into, say, ten columns, representing successive years. The crop grown on each field in each year is entered in the appropriate space. This is illustrated in Figure 19.4. Over a period of years an overall impression is given of the rotations on the farm. This is aided visually by colouring in each rectangle, e.g. grass green, barley yellow, potatoes red. If the farm is divided into approximate rotational 'blocks' of fields it is obviously desirable to group these together on the page and, similarly, to keep all fields of permanent pasture, rough grazing or orchard together.

Name of Field	OS No.	Ha	1970	1971	1972	1973	etc.
Snape	307	15.3	Potatoes	Wheat	Barley	Barley	
Little Chequers	286	6.7	Barley	Barley	Oats	Potatoes	
Great Chequers	293	13.2	Ley	Wheat	Wheat	Barley	
Upper Westwell	312	12.9	Ley	Ley	Ley	Wheat	
Lower Westwell	297	15.4	Ley	Ley	Wheat	Wheat	
Dale Hill	301	14.4	P. pasture	P. pasture	P. pasture	P. pasture	
etc.							

Fig. 19.4. Rotation record

Farm map

A large-scale wall map should be kept in the farm office. With the aid of a chinagraph pencil on a transparent sheet, the current history of the field (e.g. cropping, varieties, manuring) can be recorded and is always instantly visually available. At convenient intervals this information can be transferred to the field records suggested above. Alternatively, the information can be copied onto smaller scale maps, one for each year, kept as permanent annual field records.

Labour data

On farms with elaborate cropping systems and where many jobs are performed at peak times (and on many horticultural units labour may be fully deployed on essential productive work for most or even all of the year) the tasks may be recorded on time-sheets, but these are laborious to analyse where a large staff is employed and are often inaccurate. Time-sheets are more useful as a means of recording ordinary time and overtime worked for calculating wages, and as a means of transferring useful information from the field to the office, than for recording the labour hours spent on different jobs.

On farms with a limited number of major tasks at peak times, the information required about these can be recorded in a way that requires far less subsequent analysis than time-sheets. The method involves recording certain details of each task, either in a pocketbook kept by the head tractor driver, arable foreman or manager, or on specially prepared small cards. One page or card is needed for each job, unless it covers a long period, in which case two or more pages or cards, each covering one or two weeks, will be required per job. The task, such as maincrop potato harvesting, is written at the top. Normally there will be one entry per day. Columns are needed for the date, the gang size (i.e. numbers of workers employed), hours worked and hectares completed. Sometimes the latter can best be bracketed over more than one day, e.g. for the completion of a whole field. Other items which might be useful subsequently can also be entered, either at the top, in an extra column, or as footnotes, e.g. the type of machine employed, the number of tractors and trailers in use. Notes can also be added, for later reference, relating to weather and soil conditions, especially if these are exceptional. The pages from the pocketbook or the cards, which can be kept within a stiff-covered pocketbook during the period of recording, should be filed, in chronological order, either by crop or by operations.

Appendix 19.3: Office procedure[1]

All the recording procedures which have been described in Appendices 19.1 and 19.2 are considerably simplified if there is order rather than

[1] In preparing this Appendix, particular reference has been made to *Office Organisation for Farm and Horticultural Businesses* (1967), Short Term Leaflet No. 47. Ministry of Agriculture, Fisheries and Food.

chaos in the farm office. On a farm large enough to have an office separate from the house, it is important that it should be readily identifiable by those visiting the farm and that it should have a letter-box in case no one is about, for the posting of delivery notes, etc. In the office all papers should be sorted and grouped in a systematic manner so that they may be found easily and quickly.

Correspondence

There should be three trays (see paragraph 2, p. 521) for incoming correspondence. All unopened letters (or letters opened by a secretary but not yet seen by the farmer), unchecked delivery notes and miscellaneous papers should be placed in the 'in' tray (no. 1). Once read and considered those letters and other material of no further use may be thrown away, those requiring further action should be put in the 'pending' tray (no. 2), while others may go directly into the 'filing' tray (no. 3) or be filed away immediately. The contents of the 'pending' tray, as they are dealt with, are similarly either placed in the filing tray or filed straight away. An alternative is to put those papers requiring action on a specific day – such as agenda for meetings – into a loose-leaf diary.

Copies of outward letters should always be kept. If these are hand-written, it is possible to obtain letter books with pages numbered in pairs, so that a carbon copy is left in the book.

Purchases

Three more trays are needed for the systematic treatment of purchases. Every delivery should be accompanied by a delivery note, which must go promptly to the farm office if not presented there by the person delivering the goods. Having first checked that the goods delivered are as described in the notes, the latter are put in a tray (no. 4), where they remain until invoices are received. Once the invoices are to hand, they are checked against the relevant delivery note or notes, which are then attached to the invoices and placed in another tray (no. 5) to await the receipt of the statement. When a statement is received it is in turn checked against the relevant invoices, attached to them and placed in tray no. 6 for payment. Once paid, by cheque, the cheque stub should preferably be numbered, the same number being put on the statement; this is to facilitate later checking, if needed, especially by the accountant at the end of the year. The invoices and statements should be retained, not sent with the cheque. Instead a compliments slip should be enclosed, giving the invoice number(s), or the name and address of the farmer can be stamped on the back of the cheque, where the invoice number(s) can be written also. Once paid, the details should be entered in the expenses sheets of the cash analysis book. Subsequently, receipts should be attached to the statements and invoices. These papers should be stored securely and chronologically in a box file with a retaining clip. The cheque books stubs should be similarly stored in a suitable box.

Sales

It is suggested that the farmer should keep a book of delivery notes, with carbon copies. These are kept in tray no. 7, where sales notes also are kept, having been attached to the relevant delivery note. Any similar documents relating to promises to pay, e.g. relating to forthcoming subsidy payments, are kept in the same tray until payment is made. When cheques, payments advice and credit notes are received they are checked against and attached to the sales notes or other appropriate documents from tray no. 7 and placed in tray no. 8. Brief details of each sale should be included on the paying-in slip stub, together, preferably, with a number which is also put on the sales or credit note. Once again this will aid any later checking that may be needed and will be of considerable assistance to the accountant. Details are entered on the receipts sheets of the cash analysis book. The papers should then be stored, as for invoices etc., in a separate box file, with the paying in slips in a suitable sized box – perhaps together with the cheque book stubs.

Eight trays may seem an inordinate number. Naturally they need not cover too much desk or table space, since trays with two or more tiers are available: there could therefore be a three-tier tray for correspondence, another for purchases, and a two-tier tray for sales. Of course it is possible to amalgamate the contents of all three trays for purchases into one, and both sales trays into one, and indeed this might be quite satisfactory on a farm with a relatively small amount of business. On the larger farm, however, more trays will mean greater order and save time in searching for papers. Instead of trays, some may prefer to use other types of container, such as box files, or even simply a series of bull clips hanging from hooks on the wall.

Filing

Outward letters should be filed in chronological order; letter books used for handwritten letters only need the first and last dates written on the cover before storage. Inward letters and papers are more numerous and only those likely to be of any further possible use should be kept. Unless they are very numerous those retained can be filed together, the best method probably being to keep them in alphabetical order of the name of the writer, firm or organisation. Where there is more than one letter from a single source, the papers within that group should be filed in chronological order. Separate files need only be kept if there is a substantial amount of paper connected with a particular firm, organisation or subject e.g. relating to the erection of a new building, or a costings scheme.

Diaries

Two alternatives to the usual type of desk diary can be very useful. One is a wall diary, with a space for each day covering a three, six or twelve-month period. In busy offices a loose-leaf diary has much to commend it, with a page for each day. The advantage of this is that as well as reminders, letters and papers can be inserted in the appropriate days in the future, thus avoiding having to search for them later. Another point is that the diary can be continuous: it can cover more or less than twelve months and pages can be added and withdrawn at one- or two-month intervals.

Mail-in recording

In preparing this chapter, it has been envisaged that the records are being kept by the farmer himself, perhaps with the aid of his wife or a part- or full-time secretary. 'Mail-in' record-keeping services have been developed in some countries (including to a limited extent in the U.K.), although not without considerable development problems, particularly when computerised.

For an international review of progress and experience with EDP (electronic data processing) in farming to date, including major schemes such as Canada's impressive CANFARM, the reader is referred to Rowe, A. H. (1971) 'Computerised Systems of Accounting and Control of Farm Business Management', First International Farm Management Congress, Farm Management Association. (See also 'Combined planning and control', pp. 474–6.)

Appendix 19.4: Inflation accounting

High rates of inflation have raised the problem of how to deal with its effects on annual accounts. It is a complex subject. If inflation is ignored, the accounts can give a misleading picture of the true level of profits and of the financial standing of the business. Regarding the former, profits are exaggerated when the depreciation of an asset is based on its 'historic cost' (i.e. the original purchase price) rather than the replacement cost (i.e. the current cost of buying the same asset) and when appreciation in the value of stocks and work-in-progress during the year is included. As a result, if the profit calculated on historic costs were withdrawn from the business, either its physical assets would be run down or borrowing would be increased (usually, in practice, meaning increasing overdrafts). With regard to the balance sheet, historic cost undervalues many of the assets, which leads to misleading calculations being made of such important financial measures as net worth and return on capital.

Several alternative accounting systems have been proposed, including Current Purchasing Power, Replacement Cost and Current Cost Accounting. Each has its particular strengths and weaknesses and consequently no one method has become universally accepted. The second method is the simplest, but the last (CCA) was preferred and hence recommended by a UK group appointed to consider the alternatives in 1974–5 (the Sandilands Committee).

In CCA, assets are included in the accounts not at historic cost but at their 'value to the business' at the balance sheet date. Stocks are valued in the trading account on the same basis, at the date of sale of the resulting output. The 'value to the business' is defined as being the loss to the business if it were to be deprived of the asset. Usually this is its current replacement cost, and depreciation is based on this figure. With regard to stocks and work-in-progress the 'value to the business' is the lower of current replacement cost and 'net realisable value' (i.e. sale value less disposal costs). The difference between 'value to the business' and historic cost is called a 'holding gain'; this is included as a 'revaluation reserve' in the balance sheet. The surplus for the year after the above adjustments is called the 'operating gain'.

No further detail or example will be given here,[1] but the essential features should be clear: because an asset is valued in the balance sheet at replacement cost and depreciation is based on this amount, and because of the revaluation of stocks and work-in-progress as described, 'false' profits through inadequate depreciation allowances and increases in stocks due to inflation are eliminated.

[1] For a more detailed, but still fairly brief, description, together with a farm business example, see Hill, G. P. (1977–8) 'Current Cost Accounting'. *Farm Management*, **3**, No. 7.

20: Data analysis

Chapter 19 has described what records should be kept and how to keep them. The present chapter discusses the use that may be made of this information to guide future decisions. It begins by describing how information from the trading account can be used to provide broad 'whole farm' measures of economic performance and subsequently considers those which help show the success or otherwise of the individual enterprises. It ends by looking at the balance sheet – the capital and liquidity aspects of the business.

Account analysis

Although any system which involves the detailed examination of a set of accounts could be described as 'account analysis', the term is usually applied to an investigation of the trading account from the point of view of the farm business as a whole, with relatively little attention being paid to the individual enterprises. Although aspects of this approach were known before 1950, it was from about this time that the system became widely developed and popularised in the United Kingdom. It represented a directly opposite approach to that of cost accounting, or complete enterprise costing, which treats every individual enterprise on the farm as though it can be regarded as a self-contained business. This latter system is further discussed below. Account analysis emphasises the integrated nature of the farm business and its essence lies in calculating various 'efficiency factors' or 'indices' to compare with standards (average or 'premium' figures) obtained from other, similar farms.[1]

Because the system is based essentially on comparisons with other farms, the accounts are first adjusted to put all farms on a similar

[1] In England and Wales these standards are derived mainly from the Farm Management Survey, the results of which are usually published annually by the agricultural economics departments of ten universities. The three Scottish Colleges of Agriculture provide a similar service.

financial basis.[1] For the purposes of comparison, all farms are treated as though they are tenanted, pay for all their manual labour and have no charges for interest or management. The following adjustments are therefore made: a rent is added for owner-occupied property, the basis being the average rent being paid for farms of similar quality and size in the area; any manual labour supplied by the farmer or his family is charged at the average rates that would have to be paid to employees; any mortgage payments and other expenses of owner occupation, and any payments for management and interest, are deducted from the farm expenses. The costs, so adjusted, represent the total inputs of the farm. When these are deducted from the total gross output of the farm the resulting figure is called the 'management and investment income'. This represents the return to management and investment in tenant's capital. It cannot be regarded as a 'profit' figure as such; charges for management and interest on all tenant's capital, whether borrowed or not, would have to be deducted before arriving at the 'pure' profit to the entrepreneur as defined in economic theory. The management and investment income per ha, compared with other farms of similar type and size, is the starting point of the subsequent analysis to trace reasons for differences. If the figure is a poor one then output is too low, costs are too high, or both are at fault. Each in turn is studied in detail, output aspects being sub-divided into those relating to the intensity of the system being pursued and those measuring the yield levels being obtained.

Per hectare figures for the various items of cost and gross output are calculated, after adjusting the totals for valuation changes. If the valuations have not been made on the basis of the recommendations made in Appendix 19.1 (p. 510) they should be modified accordingly.

The cost figure for each item, e.g. fertiliser, equals expenditure plus opening valuation, less closing valuation and any subsidies. The value of private use should be deducted from expenditure, for example, for the farm car, or electricity and coal. Machinery costs must include depreciation, less any profit made on the sale of machinery or plus any loss on disposal; this profit or loss on sale is the difference between the written-down value and the sale price.

The gross output figure for each product equals revenue (which includes subsidies), plus closing valuation, less opening valuation and

[1] Should comparisons be confined to previous years' results on the same farm or a budget forecast, as referred to later, these adjustments are unnecessary (see further, p. 535).

less purchases of livestock, livestock products and any other produce brought for resale. The value of produce consumed in the farm-house or supplied to employees without payment should be added; that part of the value supplied to the farm workers should also be added to the cost of labour on the other side of the account.

Table 20.1 shows the figures calculated from the trading account data given in Table 19.1 (p. 499), together with the adjustments that have been outlined. Obviously per hectare figure comparisons with

TABLE 20.1. *Account analysis – initial presentation of data*

Inputs	Total (£)	Per ha (£)	Gross outputs	Total (£)
Fertilisers	11,978	67.6	Cattle	9,677
Power and machinery[a]	10,935	52.6	Sheep	9,802
Labour[b]	13,850	66.6	Wheat	20,668
Rent and rates[c]	11,320	54.4	Barley	18,182
Sundries	12,445	59.8	Oats	4,192
Sub-total	60,528	291.0	Potatoes	25,126
Bought feed	1,397[d]		Forage and tillage valn. changes	(+)817
Bought seed	7,558[d]		Other receipts	355
Total inputs	69,483			
Management and investment income	19,336	93.0		
	88,819		Total gross output	88,819

(derived from the trading account data in Table 19.1)

[a] Machinery and vehicle repairs + fuel, oil, electricity + vehicle tax and insurance + contract and hire + machinery and vehicle depreciation; less private use of car and electricity.

[b] Includes £1,700 for farmer's own manual labour (half-time).

[c] £552 for cottage receipts deducted.

[d] Since the bought feed and seed figures depend not only on the farming system (as for the other inputs), but also on the relative dependence of the farm on home-produced as compared with purchased feed and seed, per hectare figures have no relevance and are therefore not given.

For calculation of other inputs and gross outputs, see text.

Check: management and investment income (£19,336) = farm profit (Table 19.1) (£19,363) plus bank charges and interest (£1,673) less value of farmer's manual labour (£1,700).

Gross output per hectare: £427.

Net output per hectare (Gross output less bought feed and seed): £384.

Management and investment income = gross output less total inputs *or* net output less sub-total inputs.

other farms have only a limited value. Apart from the more general points made on the next page, much clearly depends on the particular size, system and circumstances of the farm in question. As regards the farming system, the specific combination of enterprises and the general level of intensity obviously have a major effect on the per hectare cost figures. On the gross output side, per hectare figures for individual items are virtually meaningless for efficiency comparisons. Their only value is in helping to give an overall picture of the farming system, but percentages of total gross output are preferable for this purpose. Even in this respect the figures may have little value, because they do not include internal transfers – which also affect the costs. Thus, if most or all of the barley is kept on the farm for feed and seed, not only will the gross output figure be very low compared with the true output of barley, but the feed and seed costs will also be misleadingly low. Preferably, therefore, the internal transfer figures should be included, on both sides, although most of the limitations of per hectare comparisons still remain.

For whole-farm figures this internal transfer effect is eliminated by using net output instead of gross output, since net output is gross output less bought feed and bought seed. Farms are thus put on a similar basis, whether they buy in all of their feed and seed or are largely or entirely self-sufficient. Since one farm may have a higher gross output than another simply because it sells all its produce and buys in all its requirements, net output should always be used in preference to gross output for efficiency comparisons.

For reasons which will be discussed below, the use of the account analysis system has declined since the early 1960s. Consequently this chapter makes no attempt to give a comprehensive survey of the efficiency ratios that have been used in this system in the past.[1] Measures of stocking rate are still widely used, however; these have already been described in Appendix 14.1 and are further discussed in Appendix 20.1. Labour and machinery measures are also still of interest, partly because of the importance of these two cost items and partly because they have not been superseded by later developments; they are therefore discussed in some detail below, under gross margin analysis.

Criticisms of account analysis

Two main criticisms have led to a decline in the use of this system: one is the limited value of inter-farm comparisons, the other the inadequate

[1] Readers are referred to the following books for fuller descriptions of the technique: 1. Norman, L. and Coote, R. B. (1971). *The Farm Business* (Chapter 1). Longman. 2. Blagburn, C. H. (1961). *Farm Planning and Management* (Chapter 2). Longmans.

amount of information that is provided for taking specific action to improve the situation.

As regards inter-farm comparisons, farms have to be put into groups and there is no ideal way of doing this. The type of farming is the basis most commonly employed, the usual criterion being either the proportion of total standard output (= regional or national average yield × average price) or standard man-days (see Chapter 5, p. 133) provided by the main types of enterprise, e.g. dairy, arable, etc. The farms within a group, however, may then be in quite different areas, and on very different soils – which could be especially important in the case of arable farming. Another point is that farms within the group may not be typical. Representative standards could only be assured by basing them on a large number of randomly selected farms. But it is almost impossible to get a high response rate to a random survey when details of the whole-farm accounts are required. If the total sample of farms is only a few hundred, because this is all resources will allow, there is, at the extremes, a choice between having a reasonably large number of farms within each group but only a few, rather ill-defined groups, or a large number of well-defined groups with only a small number of farms in each. In the former case the individual farm being studied may differ widely in size and type from others in the group; in the latter the group is particularly susceptible to any peculiarities in the farms in the sample.

The value of comparative standards is even more limited for farms of above average efficiency. 'Premium' figures, such as the averages of the fifty per cent of farms with the highest management and investment income per hectare or return on tenant's capital, are necessarily based on even smaller samples than the overall averages. Because of the possibility of chance or accountancy errors relating to a single year's results, premium figures should be based only on data from the consistently best farms over a period of at least three consecutive years. The reasons for these better results, however, may differ widely.

A strong theoretical criticism is that most of the measures are ratios depicting average relationships, such as net output per £100 labour, whereas, as we have seen in Chapter 2, it is what happens at the margin that is important to decision making. Thus a farmer may take action that improves his net output per £100 labour and yet still be worse off, or *vice versa* (see Chapter 5, p. 127).

Above all, however, the fact that every farm is different limits the application of inter-farm comparisons. The resources available differ in both quantity and quality on every farm and any combination is inevitably unique. This point becomes still more relevant when differences in managerial potential and objectives are considered.

The other major criticism of account analysis is that even if it enables weaknesses to be detected in the farming system it fails to provide enough information to enable them to be rectified. Following the analysis, it is necessary to obtain details of enterprise outputs and variable costs if budgeting or other methods of farm planning are to be pursued; thus there is much to be said in favour of a system of analysis that incorporates the provision of such information. This criticism can be summed up by saying that the whole-farm approach is too general, and that more attention must be paid to the individual enterprises.

Because of these limitations other approaches have gained ground. The first main criticism has resulted in increasing emphasis being placed on comparisons of a farm's results with its own achievements in previous years, or with a previously prepared budget. These are discussed in detail in the next chapter. The farm is compared, as it were, only with or within itself. The second main criticism (together to some extent with the first) has resulted in the increased popularity of gross margin analysis. This is linked to the idea of obtaining enough information about a farm to be able to re-plan it, as required, in the light of its own resources and the farmer's ability, and hence to establish realistic targets to meet the farmer's objectives. The emphasis is thus placed on what the farmer ought reasonably to be able to accomplish, given his situation, rather than on comparisons with the results of other farmers, with possibly quite different resources and objectives.

It should, however, be emphasised that the account analysis system was developed essentially to give guidance to farmers with very few records and therefore little detailed information about their farm and its enterprises. It could be applied with only a detailed trading account together with crop areas and livestock numbers. Subsequent improvements have required more data from the farm.[1] Furthermore, it was never intended as more than a general initial check and guide. It can still provide reassurance or warning for a farmer who has little idea how his profitability compares with that of others, provided he is satisfied that the farmers supplying the standards are reasonably similar. It can indicate possible reasons for low profits which can subsequently be investigated in greater detail. No experienced adviser,

[1] This applies to both gross margin analysis and the M.A.1. – M.A.2. system now widely used in the UK. The latter falls somewhere between 'traditional' account analysis and gross margin analysis in its consideration of individual enterprises, and thus in its enterprise data requirements.

however, would draw too many conclusions from a single efficiency measure, without taking into account both the farm circumstances and other related efficiency factors. Furthermore, although all farms are different, there are many with strong similarities, for example, small, all-grass dairy farms. It is the arable farms and horticultural holdings where account analysis tends to be of least use, and where frequent enterprise changes, requiring planning data, are most likely. It is so difficult to make inter-holding comparisons in horticulture, and so little comparative data are available for different types of holding, that any account analysis tends to be of the very general type found in industry. Since per hectare of the holding figures are virtually useless where, for example, there is a variable percentage of the holding under different types of glass, the sort of calculations made are return on capital and output or profit per £100 expenses: that is, broad, non-diagnostic measures of the overall efficiency of the business.

Gross margin analysis

Gross margin analysis has become widespread in the UK since about 1960, when it was first popularised amongst farm management advisers. Gross margins have been defined in Chapter 2 (pp. 45–6). The same farm figures as illustrated in Tables 19.1 and 20.1 are shown in gross margin form in Table 20.2. The analysis comprises two parts: the gross margins themselves and the fixed costs.

Comparison of gross margins

The gross margins per hectare or per head of livestock are compared with standards obtained from other farms, preferably of similar type. Thus, wherever possible, and unless only very broad comparisons are required, arable crop gross margins should be compared only with those from farms of similar soil type, and dairy herd figures should be compared only with figures for the same breed and possibly the same system. With this reservation in mind, the comparison gives a useful idea of the production and economic efficiency of an enterprise. However, annual variations must be allowed for and preferably average figures over several seasons should be obtained, both for the individual farm and for the compilation of standards.

For all three major types of enterprise – cash crops, non-grazing livestock and grazing livestock – a major reason for differences in gross margin levels, given similar conditions, is the level of yield obtained, whether this be tonnes of potatoes per ha, egg yield per bird, or milk yield per cow. Considering only discrepancies between individual farm

TABLE 20.2. *Gross margin account*

Fixed costs	Total (£)	Gross margins	(£)	Total (£)	Per ha (£)
Regular labour	10,050	*Cattle*: Output	9,677		
Power and machinery	10,935	Variable costs (excl. forage)	2,063[b]		
Rent and rates	11,320	GM (FVCs[c] not deducted)		7,614	
General overhead exps.	7,989	*Sheep*: Output	9,842[d]		
Total fixed costs[a] (194 per ha)	40,294	Variable costs (excl. forage)	2,193[b]		
		GM (FVCs not deducted)		7,649	
				15,263	
		Forage variable costs		3,594	
		GM from forage area		11,669	182
		Wheat: Output	20,668		
		Variable costs	3,842		
		GM		16,826	350
		Barley: Output	19,512[e]		
		Variable costs	6,058[f]		
		GM		13,454	210
		Oats: Output	4,922[g]		
		Variable costs	1,339		
		GM		3,583	224
		Potatoes: Output	25,191[d]		
		Variable costs	10,460		
		GM		14,731	921
Farm profit[a] (101 per ha)	21,036	Other receipts and valuation changes		1,067[h]	
	61,330			61,330	295

[a] Bank charges and interest have been excluded from fixed costs, but no allowance for unpaid manual labour has been included.

[b] Cattle and sheep variable costs include the value of home-grown concentrate feed (£1,550).

[c] FVCs = forage variable costs.

[d] Sheep and potatoes: produce consumed is allocated between these two enterprises.

[e] Barley output includes £820 for home-grown feed and £510 for home-grown seed.

[f] Barley variable costs include the market value of home-grown seed.

(Footnotes to Table 20.2, cont.)

[g] Oats output includes £730 for home-grown feed.

[h] Forage valuation changes could be incorporated in overall forage output (sometimes forage variable costs are adjusted but this is not recommended). Tillage valuation changes can usually be eliminated from gross margin (and indeed other management) accounts (see text); any fertiliser and seed in the ground (on unharvested crops) at the time of the valuation should be allocated to the appropriate year's crop.

It is possible to put the data in the above account in brief summary form (with no detail of the derivation of the gross margin figures), together with separate schedules for the individual enterprises, e.g.:

			(£)
Potatoes: Output			25,191
	Variable costs:		
	Fertiliser	2,241	
	Seed	3,692	
	Sprays	747	
	Casual labour	2,100	
	Other	1,680	
			10,460
			14,731

The full variable cost allocation in the above account is as follows:

	Fert.	Seed (inc. HG)	Sprays	Cas. Lab.	Concs. (inc. HG)	Vet. and Med.	Misc.	Total
Cattle					1,494	176	393	2,063
Sheep					1,453	227	513	2,193
Wheat	2,352	1,336	154					3,842
Barley	3,449	2,175	434					6,058
Oats	787	471	81					1,339
Potatoes	2,241	3,692	747	2,100			1,680	10,460
Grass	3,149	394	51					3,594
Total	11,978	8,068	1,467	2,100	2,947	403	2,586	29,549

(HG = Home-grown)

Note: This table is primarily intended to illustrate the layout of a gross margin account, and for this purpose the outputs and variable costs have been taken from the figures for the financial year. In practice – as explained in the text (p. 000) – adjustments are needed on most farms to give the true 'harvest year' gross margins for crops.

performance and standards, price is usually of less importance, because it tends to affect all producers similarly in the same season. The level of concentrate feed is another vital determinant for most types of livestock, especially non-grazing stock such as pigs, poultry and barley beef. Per hectare figures for grazing livestock are also strongly influenced by the stocking rate. These are the *main* factors, but there are many others, which will be looked at in more detail in a later section of this chapter (headed 'enterprise checks'). Again it must be emphasised that it is the levels of output and, for most types of livestock, concentrate feed costs that are the major determinants of the gross margin levels. This is why these factors were stressed in Chapter 19, on recording. It is also the reason why, in so far as the gross margin calculations use estimates of output that also incorporate valuations, these valuations must be as realistic as possible and must be subsequently checked for accuracy wherever feasible – as with crops in store that are subsequently sold. This point is returned to below.

It is important not to compare the gross margin figures alone, but also to look at the composition of the variable costs. This is obviously required if the possible reasons for any discrepancies are to be fully explored, but it is also necessary because the items of variable cost incurred can vary from farm to farm. For example, a farmer who engages a contractor to combine harvest his cereals will have the charge, say £40 per ha, deducted from the gross margin. Most people, however, do their own combining with their own equipment, in which case the expenses are included in the fixed costs and therefore are not deducted in deriving the gross margin. Thus the standard will probably include no such figure in the variable costs. To take another example, for potato harvesting a farmer may use casual labour (a variable cost) or regular labour (a fixed cost), a contractor's machine (a variable cost) or his own (a fixed cost). Thus it is necessary to see the details of the variable cost items included in deriving the standards.

Allied to this point, where there are substantially different treatments given to the same enterprise on a farm, separate gross margins need to be calculated for each treatment if useful comparisons are to be made, since to strike an average gives meaningless results. Obviously winter wheat and spring wheat, maincrop and second early potatoes, should be regarded as separate enterprises. So should big varietal differences, e.g. Record and King Edward potatoes grown on the same farm. Separate gross margins should also be calculated if there are major differences in the method of production of the same enterprise, for example, if one dairy herd is fed in winter on self-feed silage, whilst another relies on bought hay and brewers' grains, or straw with concentrate supplement. Another example would be if part of the potato area were hand picked by casual labour and part were mechanically harvested. In the latter case, however, it would be necessary only to record separately the harvesting variable costs (since an average of the two would have no meaning); there would be no point in dividing the growing costs, such as seed and fertiliser, nor the output–unless a check were being sought on possible effects on yield of the method of harvesting. Minor differences in treatment should normally be ignored, unless deliberately made for purposes of comparison.

Making comparisons between the gross margins of the different enterprises on a mixed farm might possibly be considered to be part of the analysis of the farming system. This practice is better considered, however, as a possible prelude to planning and is subject to several important reservations (see Chapter 14, pp. 328–9).

Some problems in calculating gross margins

For livestock enterprises the gross margin is normally calculated from the output and variable costs during the financial year, both having been adjusted for valuation changes. The date of the financial year-end makes little difference to non-grazing enterprises. Preferences exist for grazing enterprises, as discussed in Chapter 19 (p. 511), but it is rarely worthwhile to go to the trouble of carrying forward forage variable costs, especially when some new leys are being established on the farm more or less every year. For arable crops, too, the easiest way to calculate gross margins is to take the output and variable costs for each enterprise during the year and divide by the hectares harvested that year. This can be highly inaccurate, however, and the results can sometimes even be nonsensical. The gross margins should relate to the production period, from initial field preparation until final sale; this is often called the 'harvest year' and it can spread over two or even three financial years. Thus, if fertiliser and seed are applied for a crop during the financial year preceding that in which harvesting occurs, their cost must be carried forward. If part or all of the crop is in store at the end of the financial year in which harvesting takes place, a 'provisional' gross margin can be calculated using a realistic valuation (see p. 510), but when the crop is ultimately sold or used on the farm the provisional figure should be corrected. There is nearly always some difference between the valuation and ultimate value, because of inaccuracies in estimating both quantities and price. Strictly speaking any such discrepancy should appear separately in the financial account of the year when the produce is used or sold, as a profit or loss on the opening valuation; that is, it should not be attributed to the crops being harvested in the current financial year.

Another common problem is the allocation of forage hectares, and the variable costs thereof, where more than one type of livestock graze the same area, either at the same time or at different times of the year. The possible approaches to this difficulty have been fully discussed in Appendix 14.1, where an associated problem – that of the allocation of bought bulk feed and rented keep – is also considered. The last paragraph of Appendix 20.1 discusses the question whether the overall gross margin per hectare from the forage area in any year should be calculated from the hectares of forage crops grown during that year or from an adjusted figure.

Analysis of fixed costs

The gross margin approach has contributed little new in the analysis of fixed costs compared with the account analysis system, except for the crude and not very useful rule-of-thumb that total fixed costs should not exceed two-thirds of the total gross margin. Labour and machinery costs can be related to the total gross margin of the farm but little is gained by this compared with relating them to net output. This is not to say, however, that the gross margin system ignores the fixed costs; on the contrary, it is still a most important part of the analysis.

Per hectare cost figures can be used, for regular labour and machinery for example, as in the initial stages of account analysis, but their obvious inadequacy has already been discussed. In describing the account analysis system a number of adjustments to the accounts for the purpose of calculating management and investment income were outlined. These included adjustments to the fixed costs, such as charging for unpaid manual labour, estimating a rent on owner-occupied land, and excluding ownership expenses. The only purpose in making these adjustments, however, is to put all farms on a similar basis, to enable a fairer comparison of their economic efficiency to be made. But if no such comparison is intended and the only concern is to see whether the farm is covering its own particular fixed expenses adequately, whatever their composition may be, there is no point in making the adjustments.

Apart from per hectare figures, the overall efficiency of labour and machinery use, which should always be considered together, can be measured by relating a total farm output measure to the input costs and comparing with standards. Examples are net output per £100 labour, per £100 machinery and per £100 labour and machinery. Total farm gross margin can be used instead of net output, but standards are less easily obtained and the results are of similar value. Casual labour is included in labour cost in the case of net output per £100 labour but not for gross margin per £100 labour; the value of unpaid labour is also included in the former case and usually, but not always, in the latter. The general form of the calculation is:

$$\frac{\text{net output (or gross margin)} \times 100}{\text{labour (and/or machinery) cost}}.$$

These measures[1], like others described in this section, can be criticised on all the grounds mentioned on pp. 528–9 above, including the fact that they describe *average* relationships only (see further Chapter 5, p. 127). A further criticism of these measures is that net output and total gross margin are affected by factors that have little or nothing to do with the efficiency with which the labour force or machinery is managed. Factors such as natural soil fertility, or the amount of fertiliser used, have a large effect on the net output or total gross margin. (These and similar aspects are futher discussed in Chapter 5, pp. 127–32). Consequently, other measures have been devised which avoid this financial effect, by relating to purely physical measures of labour and machinery requirement.

The labour measures use the standard man-day (SMD) concept described and illustrated in Chapter 5 (page 133, Table 5.2). The number of SMDs theoretically required is compared with the number available. The measure is:

$$\frac{\text{SMDs required} \times 100}{\text{SMDs available}}.$$

The higher the figure, the better is the apparent labour efficiency, the general norm being 100. The term 'labour efficiency index' has been applied both to this and to the variant described immediately below.

Sometimes the measure is extended to cover the level of wages paid, since labour expenses may be high not because an excessive amount of labour is employed but because a high wage-level is paid, which is not balanced by more efficient labour use. A theoretical labour bill is

[1] It is also possible to calculate expected levels of labour, machinery and other fixed costs according to total farm gross margin or net output by means of regression equations. See Universities of Bristol and Exeter, *Farm Management Handbook, 1971*, p. 41.

calculated, by multiplying the total number of SMDs required by the average labour cost per SMD, and related to the actual labour cost (plus the value of unpaid labour), as follows:

$$\frac{\text{SMDs required} \times \text{average labour cost per SMD} \times 100}{\text{labour cost of the farm}}.$$

Again, 100 is the norm, and the higher the figure the better the labour efficiency.

Yet another measure, which avoids the difficulties involved both in assessing the total SMDs available and of obtaining an up-to-date average labour cost per SMD, is labour cost per 100 SMDs. The formula for this is:

$$\frac{\text{labour cost of the farm} \times 100}{\text{SMD required}}.$$

Comparisons are made with averages obtained from other farms.

In the case of machinery, the costs per tractor unit can be calculated, as described in Chapter 4 (pp. 82–3, Table 4.1), and compared with standards (Table 4.7, p. 122).

All these measures are only diagnostic; they cannot in themselves supply a remedy. Further, more detailed investigation, taking full account of the particular circumstances of the farm, is needed before any remedial action can be taken. In the case of labour this can be done with the aid of gang work-day charts (see Chapter 5, p. 140) for the field work and part-time stockmen, together with a study of the number of full-time stockmen in relation to the number of stock carried, taking the layout of the buildings into account where appropriate. The gang-work day chart is also relevant as regards machinery use, in combination with a detailed study of the amount and age of machinery on the farm and possibly the depreciation, repair and fuel costs of some or all of the major machinery items.

Cost accounting

In cost accounting, or complete enterprise costing, not only are the outputs and variable costs allocated to individual enterprises, as for gross margins, but the fixed costs are also allocated. That is to say, all labour and machinery costs, rent and general overhead expenses are fully allocated. As a result, a net profit or loss is calculated for each enterprise, and the sum of these equals the total profit or loss for the whole farm. On the face of it such a procedure would appear to have much to commend it, since different enterprises obviously make widely differing demands on the labour and machinery force on the farm: compare, for example, sheep and potatoes. The system was at one time recommended by several influential farm economists/accountants but a very small proportion of farmers followed their advice and few farm economists, if any, still recommend the system. This is for several reasons, which are largely related to points of principle made in Chapter 2.

First, many farm costs are 'joint costs', that is, they are shared between two or more or possibly all the enterprises on the farm. It is therefore possible to allocate them only arbitrarily. For example, farm overhead expenses can be distributed among the enterprises according to the number of hours of direct labour attributable to each. Such expenses include general repairs and indirect labour costs, that is, labour that cannot be allocated directly to an enterprise, either because bad weather prevents field staff from working outside or because the work is not directly allocable, such as hedging and ditching and repairing machinery. However, any method of distribution is only an artificial device for allocating costs which are essentially unallocable.

Secondly, the system ignores the concept of supplementary relationships. Thus labour used is costed according to the current hourly rate, and a share of building costs or rent (in the case of a catch crop) is charged, even if the resources would still be there if the enterprises were eliminated; the resources might simply be left unused, but their costs would still be incurred. Hence an enterprise making use of such spare resources may appear to be making a loss, but if it were dropped total farm profit would fall, because its output would be forgone and yet many of the costs would continue as before. A further point is that a large amount of labour is sometimes employed on a particular task simply because there is little else to do at that time of year.

Neither can complementary relationships be handled, but this is equally true of gross margin costing. Attempts have been made to overcome this deficiency by crediting and debiting 'cultural residues' to different enterprises, according to whether they are considered to be of benefit or detrimental to subsequent crops. But because the amounts can only be arbitrary little is gained by this practice.

Thirdly, the principle of opportunity cost is completely ignored. The point made above concerning supplementary relationships reflects one aspect of this. Labour is charged at the same hourly rate, whether it is being used at a time when there is no other productive work to do or at a time when many critical jobs are waiting to be done in an exceptionally busy period.

Fourthly, and again this is linked with previous points, all inputs are recorded as though they are variable in the gross margin sense, that is, as though their total cost will vary in proportion to the size of the enterprise. As we have seen, this is clearly not so. Some are fixed whatever the type or size of enterprise selected, while others consist of indivisible, or integer, units of cost, e.g. regular labour, buildings, machinery. The integer costs will be at a given total level over a certain range and outside this range will rise, or fall, in 'steps' (see further Chapter 2, p. 47).

For these reasons, the value of cost accounting is very limited, because the net profits and losses obtained per enterprise have little significance as guides to re-planning on the individual farm (see also the example in Chapter 12, pp. 260–2). Yet there are still further, very important disadvantages: it is troublesome, time-consuming and therefore costly. This is true both of the amount of recording needed and the subsequent analysis and calculations required. Time-sheets, tractor sheets, fuel records, and so on, have to be kept in detail and analysed. Yet the results are of less value to individual farm planning than gross margins.

This does not mean that the full costing of individual enterprises should be entirely condemned, for it does have some uses. For example, such costings, on a representative sample of farms at periodic intervals, give useful indications of general trends in the profitability of an enterprise; they can also supply useful physical data for planning and show the technological changes occurring over time. Again, for price-fixing purposes for individual enterprises there is little alternative. However, none of these points relates to the complete costing of all enterprises on the individual farm. The previous chapter contained some discussion on the question of recording seasonal labour requirements, at least at peak times, and certain machinery cost items, either to provide planning data or to make comparisons with figures from other farms. These can be considered as useful extensions to gross margin costing without going nearly as far as complete cost accounting, but even they are by no means necessary on every farm, every year.

Enterprise checks

As has already been explained earlier in this chapter, a single figure for the gross margin alone is insufficient for a full and effective examination of the performance of an enterprise. For this, both the output and details of the variable costs are required. For those farmers wishing to study at least their main enterprises in greater depth, however, further details are needed concerning the derivation of both the output and the costs. This is by no means the same thing as cost accounting.

Detailed enterprise checks have more significance for livestock enterprises than for crops. With crops, unless it is felt worthwhile to carry out some periodic checks on labour use and specific machinery expenses (e.g. a combine or potato harvester), only a breakdown of the output into yield and price is required in addition to the details of the variable costs.

With livestock, on the other hand, many more useful details can be obtained and many more efficiency measures can be calculated. The investigation process often begins by calculating the 'margin over concentrates' per head; this is usually the enterprise output less concentrate costs, although for dairy cows output in this connection is usually taken as meaning simply the value of milk produced. With enterprises such as pigs, poultry and barley beef, where concentrate costs form such a high proportion of total costs, the measure 'food costs per £100 output' is a simple one to derive (given reasonably accurate feed allocation where there is more than one livestock enterprise on the farm) and it is at the same time a useful indication of the profitability of the enterprise. Another advantage of this measure is that it avoids the necessity for calculating the average number of head of livestock, which is often difficult. The general form of the calculation is:

$$\frac{\text{enterprise (e.g. pig) food costs} \times 100}{\text{enterprise (e.g. pig) output}}$$

However, such measures have their limitations, not only because there are other important costs besides concentrate food, e.g. labour and buildings, but also because they are non-diagnostic; that is, they provide only a yardstick of profitability and do not explain why the figure is high or low; thus no action is possible to improve the position until a further more detailed study has been made.

It would be space-consuming and tedious to repeat here the form this diagnosis can take for each of the livestock enterprises. The method is similar in every case and there are many schemes available from commercial firms and other organisations in the UK which farmers can join. The procedure will thus be outlined for one enterprise only, dairy cows. The main measures required for other enterprises are, however, listed in Appendix 20.2. Up-to-date average figures for comparison are available from various sources.[1]

[1] e.g. Nix. J. *Farm Management Pocketbook*. Wye College, University of London.

The main revenue and cost items required for checking the profitability of a dairy enterprise are as follows (per cow):

1. Value of milk production (sales + used on farm)
2. Value of culls } herd depreciation } net
3. Value of replacements } } replacement
4. Value of calves (sold and retained) } cost
5. Cost of concentrate food
6. Cost of other purchased foods and keep rented
7. Other variable costs (excluding forage)
8. Forage variable costs
9. Labour costs
10. Annual building costs

There are obviously other costs, such as the rental value of the land, but many of these are either relatively minor or there is little or nothing that can be done to change them. Others, such as conservation costs, may be important, but they require much more recording; on most farms this is not worth the effort involved, but on some, certainly, periodic calculations could prove to be of value, particularly where there is a wish to compare alternative systems.

Detailed investigations would normally begin by calculating one or more of the following:

Margin over concentrates per cow (= 1 − 5)
Output less concentrates per cow (= (1 + 2 + 4) − (3 + 5))
Gross margin per cow (= Output less concentrates − (6 + 7 + 8)).

In order to derive per hectare figures, or course, these would have to be divided by forage hectares per cow.

Further investigation of the value of milk production would initially involve calculating the two items from which the figure is derived: milk yield per cow and price per litre. Each of these can then be further investigated, the former by calculating the lactation yield and average calving interval (or, less usefully, the average percentage of dry cows), the latter by measuring seasonality (percentage of winter milk) and average grade and other bonuses. Net replacement costs can be examined by calculating value per cull sold, mortality rate, value per head of replacements, average herd life, value per calf, calves born live per 100 cows and calf mortality. Concentrate costs can be divided into quantity (tonnes) per cow and price per tonne; concentrates (kg) per litre and concentrate costs (p) per litre can be calculated. Labour costs can be separated into labour hours per cow and cost per hour.

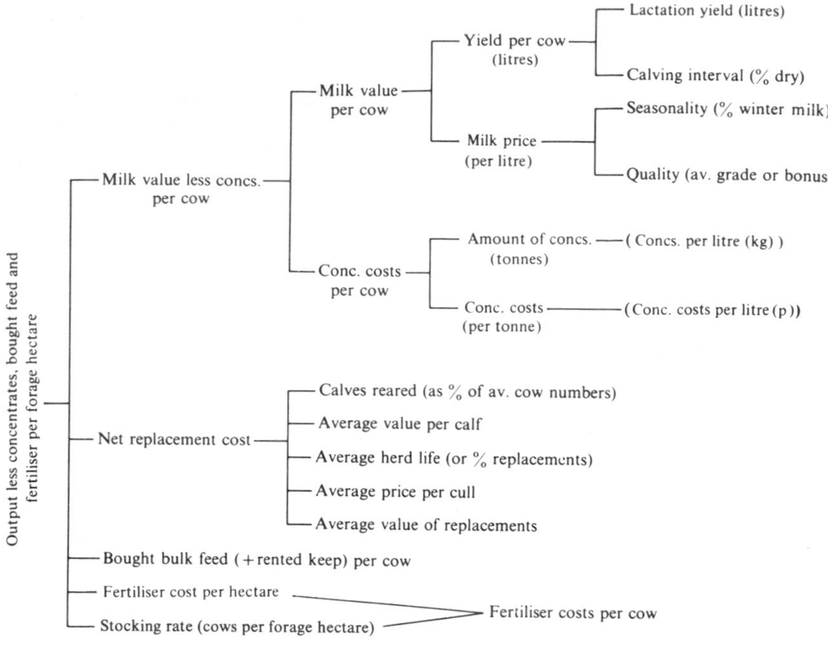

Fig. 20.1. Outline analysis of profitability of milk production

In this way, a full diagnosis of the enterprise can be made and weaknesses noted for future or immediate action. The procedure is illustrated in Figure 20.1. Further aspects of this analysis will be described in the next chapter.

The balance sheet

The balance sheet presents the capital position of the farm business at a point in time – normally the end of the financial year. This is in contrast to the trading account, which shows the profitability of the business enterprise over a given period, normally one year. The latter will clearly affect the former, especially over a period of years, but much will also depend on the extent to which funds are withdrawn from the business for private spending and further capital investment, as well as for tax payments.

Two major problems in trying to interpret balance sheets are, first, that the layouts presented differ widely and are often difficult to comprehend and, secondly, the assets are often very much undervalued, which makes the compilation of analytical ratios meaningless.

In summary form the layout of the balance sheet can be illustrated as follows:

	(£)		(£)
Liabilities	30,000	Assets	50,000
Net capital	20,000		
	50,000		

On the right-hand side are the assets of the business, that is, what the business is worth. On the left are the liabilities, that is, what the business owes. The net capital (otherwise known as the capital balance, net worth, or equity) is the balancing item; thus assets (£50,000) − liabilities (£30,000) = net capital (£20,000). This is the sum that would remain to the owner if the business were sold and all the liabilities paid; to put it colloquially, it is his stake in the business. In a sense the net capital can be regarded as a liability, in that it can be said to represent the claim of the proprietor against the business (that is, what the business 'owes' him), as opposed to the claims of others, or the 'outside' claims. Unlike the other liabilities, however, the proprietor's claim is a residual, not a given sum. If there were a net capital deficit instead of a surplus this would have to be included on the assets side to balance, and it would mean that the business was insolvent. The details on the assets side of the balance sheet show how the capital is being used in the business, and those on the liabilities side the sources of that capital.

The assets in the balance sheet are subdivided into different types of capital, according to the time period involved. However, the actual terms used may differ and it is sometimes difficult to decide how to classify borderline items. The basic distinction is between fixed and current assets, although the former can be further sub-divided into long-term and medium-term assets. The items included in each of these have already been described in Chapter 3 (pp. 50–1) and so will not be listed in full detail here. Current assets are those likely to be liquidated at least within the financial year (or the production period if this is longer). They include growing crops, crops in store, unfinished fatstock, debtors and cash in hand and at the bank. Although these assets are often described as being readily convertible into cash this is not always the case; their degree of liquidity varies, as is discussed further below. Assets are normally listed in order of their liquidity. It must always be remembered that the current value of most of the items can only be estimated.

Liabilities, also, are usually divided into three types, again according to the time element. These are (apart from the owner's equity): long-term, medium-term and current. The former are long-term loans such as mortgages. Current liabilities can be called in at any time and require virtually immediate payment. In between there are liabilities which require settlement in more than one year but less than about five. Sometimes long-term and medium-term liabilities are referred to jointly as deferred liabilities, in contrast to the current liabilities.

A typical balance sheet, containing items in each category mentioned above, is given in Table 20.3. It relates to the same farm whose trading account was given in Table 19.1.

Many calculations can be made and ratios derived from the balance sheet which attempt to show the strengths and weaknesses in the capital position of the business. Only a selection of these will be presented, since they can otherwise become confusing rather than helpful. Apart from the *profitability* of a business, as illustrated by the trading account – preferably over at least 2 or 3 years – there are 2 other

TABLE 20.3. *The balance sheet*

Liabilities	(£)	Assets		(£)
Loan from A. Smith	15,000	Grain store[a]		5,230
Bank overdraft	8,247	Improvements to property[a]		1,860
Creditors	1,077	Vehicles		3,067
	24,324	Machinery and equipment		14,711
		Closing valuation:		
		Sheep	7,378	
		Cattle	10,511	
		Growing crops, cults., materials in store	4,870	
		Crops in store	12,686	35,445
		Debtors		2,432
		Cash in bank		
Net capital	38,496	Cash in hand		75
	62,820			62,820

[a]The farm is tenanted, but the farmer has paid for certain fixtures and improvements with the agreement of the landlord. On an owner-occupied farm, the value of the land, house, cottages and buildings is usually placed at the top of the list of assets.

features that are vital to its basic strength and ability to survive: its *stability* and *liquidity*. Another important attribute is *flexibility*. Finally, *growth* is a further aspect of creditworthiness that a potential lender to the business likes to see.

Stability is particularly reflected in the owner's share in the business, that is, his net capital, or equity. A simple way to measure this is to calculate the 'per cent equity', that is, the owner's net capital as a percentage of the total value of the assets. In Table 20.3 this is

$$\frac{38{,}496}{62{,}820} \times 100 = 61 \text{ per cent.}$$

Usually, however, it is calculated as the 'net capital ratio', which consists of total assets divided by total liabilities excluding the owner's equity. From Table 20.3 again we have:

$$\frac{62{,}820}{24{,}324} = 2.58.$$

The higher the per cent equity or the net capital ratio the safer is the business and the less vulnerable to an unexpected drop in the value of its assets, or occasional trading losses. This point has already been illustrated in Chapter 3, when discussing the principle of increasing risk (pp. 73–4). The lower the per cent equity, or the nearer the net capital ratio is to 1, the less inclined will a potential lender be to put money into the business, other things being equal. The more risky the type of business, the higher the net capital ratio needs to be. The higher the 'gearing', that is, the ratio loan capital: own capital (equity), the greater the chance of getting a very high return on one's own capital, but also the greater the chance of going bankrupt. High gearing should therefore only be considered where consistently good profits seem certain to be made. On the other hand, low gearing may mean that profitable investment opportunities are being forgone. Another aspect of this is the 'ratio of times covered' that is, the profits of the business divided by the annual fixed interest charges; the lower this is, the more vulnerable is the business.

The aspect of stability just described relates to the long-term solvency of the business. However, it also has to survive in the shorter run, weathering the temporary stresses and strains that may occur. An important measure in this regard is the 'current ratio', which is calculated as:

$$\frac{\text{current assets}}{\text{current liabilities}}$$

In Table 20.3, this is

$$\frac{20{,}063^{1}}{9{,}324^{2}} = 2.15.$$

The higher the figure, the safer is the firm in the short run, because the more likely it is to survive unexpected demands from creditors or the bank manager by being able to obtain the necessary funds quickly.

A current ratio of 2:1 (or 2, as calculated above) is usually considered to be reasonably safe, but much depends on the type of business and the time of year. Often in farming the ratio is well below 2:1, because a bank overdraft tends to be regarded as at least a medium-term liability rather than the current liability which, strictly speaking, it is. The more liquid the current assets, the lower the ratio can safely be. Thus, still more crucial to the *immediate* solvency, as opposed to the *ultimate* solvency as measured by the net capital ratio, is the 'liquidity ratio'. This is measured as:

$$\frac{\text{liquid assets}}{\text{current liabilities}}$$

Some current assets are either immediately available or can be made so in a very short time, e.g. cash in hand or at the bank, whether in current or deposit account, and crops in store. These are the liquid assets. Others may either be difficult to convert into cash in the short term – for instance, growing crops and possibly some debtors – or can probably be sold only at a loss or at least to the detriment of the profitability of the business, e.g. trading livestock. If liquid assets were insufficient to cover current liabilities, the business could be in serious financial difficulty if the short-term creditors started pressing for payment, even though the ultimate solvency of the business might be perfectly sound. Thus a business in this position might need to obtain further long-term loans so as to be able either to reduce the current liabilities or to increase the liquid assets. The total value of the fixed assets should always be exceeded by the long-term liabilities plus the owner's equity. Otherwise part of the fixed assets are being financed from short-term lending, which is a dangerous position that could lead to a forced sale of some of the fixed assets.

[1] Growing crops, etc. + crops in store + debtors + cash in hand.

[2] Bank overdraft + creditors.

The term 'overtrading' is used to describe the situation where there is a shortage of cash or, more accurately, where liquid assets fall seriously short of current liabilities. This can occur through too rapid expansion with inadequate cash reserves. The time lag in production means that expenses are being incurred without a corresponding increase in sales. Creditors and bank borrowing (where permitted) may increase rapidly. If the bank and/or some of the major creditors become doubtful about their chances of getting their money back they may demand payment, or they may be forced to do so because of a credit squeeze; the business could then be in severe difficulties.

The flexibility aspect of the business can be judged partly in the light of the financial ratios between current liabilities and current assets described above, but also according to the balance of the different types of asset. Thus if too high a proportion of the assets are fixed there may be insufficient working capital to exploit them profitably. In this case either loans should be obtained on the security of part of the fixed assets so as to be able to increase the current and medium-term assets, or, if this is either impossible or for some reason considered to be undesirable, the possibility of selling part of the fixed assets should be considered. This is largely the reasoning behind the sale and lease-back of land.

To conclude this section with some general points: first, the reference made earlier to the valuation of assets must be repeated: the ratios described have little or no meaning unless the assets are realistically valued, even though such valuations can at best only be estimated. Another point is that the ratios have to be looked at in relation to each other, so as to give an overall picture of the financial structure of the business. Further, it must be remembered that the balance sheet relates to a point in time; on a farm, a month or two earlier or later the position may look markedly different. Finally, probably even more important than the *level* of ratios discussed are the *trends* in those levels – a matter discussed in the next section.

The flow of funds and the capital account

It is extremely important to know whether the equity and liquidity positions are improving or worsening, particularly in the latter case, where the trends may act as an early warning that action must be taken to avoid serious difficulties. The changes in the composition of the total assets and liabilities and the level of net capital need to be studied. Normally the previous year's figures are given alongside the current figures in the balance sheet, which makes possible a quick grasp of the recent situation.

Of particular interest to farmers is the change that has occurred during the year in their cash balance or level of bank overdraft. Obviously this will depend on the amount of cash that has gone into the business compared with that which has been withdrawn. The relevant details can be set out in a statement showing the 'flow' or 'source and disposition' of funds.

The starting point is the trading account profit (or loss) for the year. There are many reasons, however, why this may bear little relation to the change in the farmer's cash situation during the year. The following will affect the position, either because they are non-cash items or because they are not included in the trading account:

Non-cash items:

1. Changes in valuations of livestock, crops in store, growing crops and materials in store.
2. Changes in debtors and creditors.
3. 'Notional' allowances, such as produce consumed in the farmhouse, private use of car and house fuel; or any 'imputed' costs, e.g. for board and lodging for workers, or payments to the family not actually made.
4. Depreciation.
5. Profit or loss on sale of machinery or equipment.

Items not in trading account:

1. Capital payments, receipts and grants, e.g. for machinery and buildings.
2. Additional loans and loan repayments.
3. Private drawings (these may include withdrawal of cash to invest outside the farm business).
4. Tax payments.
5. Extra cash introduced into the business apart from loans.

These items, together with the profit or loss from the trading account, are incorporated in a statement, the layout of which is shown in Table 20.4. It is not easy at first to understand why some of the individual non-cash items are included as a 'source' or 'disposal' of funds. Those described as sources are items which, by their inclusion in the trading account, either (*a*) have decreased the profit in a way not reflected in the net cash position – either because no cash has been paid out for the cost items concerned (depreciation, loss on sale of machinery, 'imputed' costs), or because a reduction in output has occurred through a decrease in valuation, or (*b*) have not affected the trading profit but

TABLE 20.4. *Flow of funds statement*

Source of funds	Disposal of funds
Trading account profit	Trading account loss
Decrease in valuation	Increase in valuation
Decrease in debtors	Increase in debtors
Increase in creditors	Decrease in creditors
'Imputed' costs	'Notional' receipts (or cost deductions)
Depreciation	
Loss on sales of machinery, etc.	Profit on sales of machinery, etc.
Capital receipts and grants	Capital payments
Additional loans	Loan repayments
Cash introduced	Private drawings
Private receipts	Tax payments
Balance (deficit)	Balance (surplus)

Note: If the total 'sources' exceeds the total 'disposals' the balance will appear on the disposal side (that is, a surplus will have been produced) and *vice versa*.

have increased the cash available (decrease in debtors, increase in creditors). Similarly, under disposal come items which either (*a*) have increased the profit in a way not reflected in the net cash position–either because no cash has been received for the output items concerned ('notional' receipts, such as produce consumed, profit on sale of machinery) or because a higher output has occurred through an increase in valuation, or (*b*) have not affected the trading profit but have decreased the cash available (increase in debtors, decrease in creditors).

The various items affect the composition of the balance sheet in different ways. The following directly alter the net capital figure: the trading profit or loss, private drawings and tax payments, 'notional' receipts, 'imputed' costs and extra capital brought into (or taken out of) the business. Others appear directly as changes in liabilities and assets: changes in valuation, and debtors and creditors. The remainder also affect the composition of the liabilities and assets: additional loans and loan repayments, depreciation. Depreciation appears as a reduction in the value of the machinery, equipment and building assets. It is balanced on the liabilities side by a corresponding reduction in the net capital (through its deduction as a cost in the trading account). Profit or loss on sale of machinery can be regarded, respectively, as a reduction in or addition to depreciation.

It follows that the trading account and balance sheet can be reconciled. The profit, and its derivation, must tie up with the way the capital

TABLE 20.3. *The balance sheet including a capital account*

Liabilities: Start of year (£)	Liabilities		Liabilities: End of year (£)	Assets: Start of year (£)	Assets		Assets: End of year (£)
20,000	Loan from A. Smith:			5,880	Grain store:	5,880	
	Start of year:	20,000			less depreciation[a]	650[b]	5,230
	less repaid during year:	5,000	15,000	2,060	Improvements to		
6,503	Bank overdraft		8,247		property:	2,060	
1,954	Creditors		1,077		less depreciation[a]	200[b]	1,860
Capital account:				3,987	Vehicles:	3,987	
	Opening net capital	29,949			less depreciation[a]	920	3,067
	Add:						
	Capital introduced			11,224	Machinery and equipment:		
	(to repay loan)	5,000			Opening valuation	11,224	
	Net profit for year	19,363			plus purchases[c]	7,650	
		54,312				18,874	
	Deduct:				less sales[c]	810	
	Drawings (private & tax)	15,351			depreciation[a]	3,353	
	Produce consumed	105				4,163	14,711
	Private use of car and				Valuation:		
	electricity	360		7,854	Sheep		7,378
		15,816		10,082	Cattle		10,511
					Growing crops, cults.,		
29,949	*Closing net capital*		38,496	4,913	materials in store		4,870
				9,319	Crops in store		12,686
				(32,168)	(Total valuation)		(35,445)
				3,027	Debtors		2,432
				60	Cash in hand		75
58,406			62,820	58,406			62,820

[a] Depreciation for the year.
[b] Depreciation on tenant's fixtures has been included under rent and rates in the trading account in Table 19.1.
[c] Purchases and sales during the year.

position of the business has altered during the year. The procedure involved is known as 'proving the account' and the statement that sets this out is known as the 'capital account'. Often this is incorporated in the liabilities side of the balance sheet. This is in fact done in Table 20.5, which illustrates many of the points discussed above.

For the account to be proved the net capital at the end of the year must equal the net capital at the beginning of the year + trading account profit (or less trading account loss) + 'imputed' costs + cash introduced into the business, including any private receipts – private drawings, tax payments, and 'notional' receipts.

As already mentioned, depreciation of assets is balanced by an appropriate deduction from the trading profit. Loan repayments or additional loans are balanced by changes in the total and the ratios of the various assets. An increase in net capital may be reflected in a reduction in bank overdraft, by the repayment of a loan from another source, by an increase in assets, or by a combination of all three.

Appendix 20.1: Assessing stocking rate and gross margin per forage hectare.

The calculation of livestock units per forage hectare has been described in Appendix 14.1. Using this calculation, a farmer may appear to have a very high stocking rate, but this may not be a true reflection of his ability to grow and manage grass, since he may be heavily dependent on purchased fodder or rented keep. A figure for 'adjusted forage hectares' can be calculated to allow for this point and other apparent discrepancies. The adjustments are to add the hectare equivalents of:

- keep rented,
- purchased fodder,
- decreased valuation of stocks of home-grown fodder (although changes resulting from yield and use variations caused by weather conditions may be ignored),
- catch crops and grazing from cash crops of hay or seed.

To deduct the hectare equivalents of:

- keep let,
- 'occasional' fodder and seed sales (hay and seed are treated as cash crops where their sale is regular policy),

increased valuation of stocks of home-grown fodder (but see note above).

Some authorities prefer to omit some or even all of these adjustments and simply take them into account in interpreting the figure for forage hectares per livestock unit.

The overall gross margin per hectare of forage can be related to either forage hectares or adjusted forage hectares. In the former case, any costs for bought fodder or rented keep, together with changes in fodder valuations and occasional hay or seed sales, are incorporated in the calculation of the gross margin. In the latter case they are not. The gross margin per adjusted forage hectare is a more meaningful figure if the intention is to compare the efficiency of grassland management with that on other farms. However, the gross margin per forage hectare is the relevant figure if the intention is to study the contribution of the forage area to covering the fixed costs and providing a profit on the farm concerned.

Appendix 20.2: Livestock efficiency measures

The following are further measures used in diagnosing the economic efficiency of major livestock enterprises other than dairy cows (which are discussed on pp. 541–2). They are needed to examine the reasons for variations shown by broader measures of comparison such as margin over concentrates, gross margin, or gross margin less direct labour costs and deadstock depreciation.

Single suckling beef

Calving percentage (number of calves born per 100 cows served)
Calf mortality
Calving interval
Mortality of beef cows
Average herd life
Average weight of calves sold (or transferred to fattening enterprise)
Average age of calves when sold (or transferred to fattening enterprise)
Average value of calves when sold (or transferred to fattening enterprise)

Fattening beef

Liveweight gain per day
Value per head of calves or stores brought in
Mortality
Price per kg of fat cattle sold
Grading: percentages of each category
Concentrates per head

Price of concentrates per kg.
Killing out percentages
Conversion ratio, i.e. kg concentrates per kg liveweight gain (barley beef)

Sheep

Lambing percentage (lambs reared per 100 ewes put to ram)
Lambs born alive per 100 ewes (put to ram)
Lamb mortality
Ewe mortality (%)
Barren ewes (%)
Average flock life
Average price of culls
Average price of replacements
Average value per lamb
% lambs sold fat, % stores and % retained for breeding
Average price per lamb sold fat
Average value per lamb not sold fat

Pig Rearing

Pigs reared to 8 weeks per sow per year, comprising:
- Average number of litters per sow per year (or farrowing index)
- Pigs born alive per litter
- Mortality of piglets

Average price of cull sows (and gilts)
Sow (and gilt) mortality
Average weight of piglets at 8 weeks
Average price per piglet sold (or valuation when transferred for fattening)
Average weight of piglets when sold (or transferred)
Value of food per sow, comprising:
- Weight of food per sow
- Price of food per cwt

Pig fattening

Average cost and weight per weaner or store brought in
Average value of fat pig sold (preferably separately for each category if more than one, i.e. porkers, cutters, baconers, heavy hogs), comprising:
- Weight of pigs sold
- Average price per kg

Mortality
Cost of food per kg liveweight gain, comprising:
- Conversion ratio: kg of food per kg liveweight gain
- Price of food per tonne

Grading: % in each category (where appropriate)

Laying poultry

Egg production per bird[a] in a specified period (e.g. 48 or 52 weeks)
Average price per egg
Grading (in different size groups and % seconds)
Mortality[a]

Cost of food per bird[a] comprising:
    Quantity of food per bird[a]
    Price of food per tonne
    Price per point-of-lay bird
    Price per cull bird.

[a] Based on number of birds initially housed.

Table poultry

Weight per bird
Price per bird
Mortality
Weeks housed
Batches per house per year
Grading
Cost of food per bird, comprising:
    Quantity of food per bird
    Price of food per tonne

In all cases other measures, such as labour cost per head, labour hours per head, and deadstock (i.e. buildings and machinery) depreciation per head, may be computed where this is felt to be appropriate, as it normally will be in the case of enterprises employing full-time staff and where specialist buildings have been erected. However, little action can be taken with regard to the latter once the building has been erected, and sometimes there may be little that can be done to alter labour costs.

21: Methods of control

Until the 1960s, controlling the business was a neglected aspect of farm management. Yet many would argue that it is the most important part. It rather depends on how broadly the term 'control' is interpreted. At one extreme it might be thought of in terms of a single procedure – the annual checking of actual results against a budget forecast; on the other hand it might justifiably be held to cover every aspect of administering the farm business. In the latter case the term would encompass not only the subject-matter of the last two chapters – recording and analysis – but very much more, including all day-to-day decision-making.

It is obviously not sufficient simply to make plans and put them into operation. It is also essential to check periodically to see how the plans are progressing and whether the objectives are being achieved. Any unfavourable deviations from the charted course must be corrected as soon as possible, insofar as it is within the power of management to do so. It may be necessary to adjust the plans themselves, if changing circumstances make this appear to be desirable. The present chapter describes techniques available for this purpose.

Annual budgetary appraisal

The broadest type of performance check is to compare the actual annual financial results achieved with a budget forecast. The process of budgeting has been described in Chapter 14. The simplest form of budgetary appraisal is illustrated in Table 21.1. This consists merely of putting budgeted and actual results alongside one another and calculating the difference. Simple and crude as this may be, it is better than nothing. Where the profit is above or below the expected level, the comparison gives a rough idea why. Even if the profit is close to the budgeted figure it may be because favourable differences have approximately cancelled out unfavourable differences. It is extremely important to know this, because favourable features should be examined to see whether they can be further exploited in the future, and unfavourable features must be studied to see whether they can henceforth be avoided.

TABLE 21.1. *Variations from budget*

	Budget (£)	Actual (£)		Extra profit variation (£) (Output above budget)	Lower profit variation (£) (Output below budget)
Outputs					
Milk	37,800	35,828		—	1,972
Wheat	26,325	29,345		3,020	—
etc.	...	...		...	...
Total	133,815	135,048		5,079	3,846
			Net	1,233	—
				(Input below budget)	(Input above budget)
Inputs					
Fertiliser	6,300	5,850		450	—
Machinery	12,900	13,905		—	1,005
etc.	...	...		...	...
Total	110,955	117,879		3,513	10,437
			Net	—	6,924
Profit	22,860	17,169		—	5,691

However, the above procedure only *describes* differences, it does not *explain* them. If profitability is low, it shows which particular sectors of the farm output and cost structure are responsible, but it fails to clarify which aspects of management are at fault and therefore need to be rectified. It may be, however, that the budget was over-optimistic in some respects and needs modification in future to make it more realistic. This is especially likely in the case of a farm budgeted for the first time, where few records have been kept in the past, or where a major change in policy has occurred, including enterprises introduced for the first time, or, in particular, where the farmer is new to the farm.

Explanation of differences requires a further breakdown of each item. The following are the factors that can cause variations:

Outputs: the size of enterpises in the *plan* (i.e. number of hectares, number of livestock);
yield (per hectare or per head);
price per unit of output.

Inputs: the size of enterprises in the *plan* (as above);
quantity of input per hectare or per head;
cost per unit of input.

For some items of output and input this three-stage breakdown is possible, but for others it clearly is not. It is straightforward for arable crops where the results are calculated on a 'harvest year' basis. Otherwise it is necessary to check separately the validity of the opening valuation, as regards both quantity and price. The analysis is also clear-cut for milk, egg, weaner pig and fat lamb production. In all cases, however, valuation differences in breeding stock have to be checked. This is likely to be still more important with fattening livestock, where 'yields' and 'price per unit' may often be difficult to calculate. In the case of inputs, while it may be relatively straightforward to analyse differences in seed, fertiliser and concentrate feed costs under the three headings given above, this is not possible for such expenses as labour, machinery and general overheads; in fact only quantities and cost per unit are relevant – in some cases not even these. Usually, unanalysed differences in sub-items of these costs will suffice, e.g. the division of machinery expenses into depreciation, repairs, fuel, contract hire charges and other expenses. Judgement must be used in deciding what level of detail it is worthwhile pursuing. It depends on how important the item is, how big the deviation is and how easy it is to get the required information. It is obviously a waste of time to spend hours tracing small changes in a minor item of output or cost; often the reason may be known and there is little point in proving it exactly, especially as it does in any case only relate to what is past. However, if, for example, machinery repairs prove to be substantially in excess of the budget estimate, perhaps for two or three years running, it could be worthwhile making a detailed study of that item, looking for possible economies in the future.

An analysis should be attempted for all the enterprise outputs, except those of minor significance. As already outlined, the reasons for variations can be separated into differences in plan, in yield and in price. Tables 21.2 (*a*) and (*b*) show the required calculations in the case of milk and wheat production respectively. Tables 21.2 (*c*) and (*d*) analyse variations in dairy cattle output, excluding milk production, and a fattening beef enterprise respectively; in such cases it will often be too complicated to attempt an accurate division between plan, yield and price differences and a roughly estimated division will have to suffice if it is felt desirable to complete the comprehensive table referred to below – but the value of such a procedure will then obviously be limited and its worthwhileness debatable. Where the product of an enterprise is retained on the farm, the value at which it has been internally transferred is used in place of the sale price. Table 21.2 (*e*) shows an analysis of poultry feed cost variations.

These calculations can be done on separate sheets of paper or they can be incorporated in a comprehensive layout, as shown in Table 21.3. The value of the latter alternative is that all the results are summarised on one sheet of paper, but supplementary sheets may still be needed if certain items, e.g. labour costs, are felt to be worth further analysis. It is not necessary to try to allocate all the variations between the three reasons for differences given in Table 21.3; as has been pointed out above, this will often be impossible except by using largely arbitrary estimates. The comparison between budget and actual can also be made in terms of gross margins and fixed costs, in which case supplementary sheets are certainly needed to analyse the differences in the former.

This procedure of annual budgetary appraisal can be criticised on several grounds. The discrepancies may be caused by either faults in budgeting or circumstances outside the control of management, and no correcting action may be possible. The first point – the questionable accuracy of budgeting – has already been discussed briefly; over time, the accuracy should steadily improve but, in any case, it is better to have a broad guide based on the best possible estimates than to drift along aimlessly. Certainly it is true, also, that in farming many variations are largely, sometimes entirely, outside the farmer's control, for example, weather effects on yields and price fluctuations caused by market conditions. Despite the validity of these points, the knowledge that builds up over time about the effect on profitability of changes in various factors can prove extremely valuable for future planning, for example, when deciding whether it is worthwhile installing irrigation or storage for a particular crop, or whether some enterprises are too variable in results to be acceptable. There is built up a deeper understanding of the cost and return structure of the business – of the key items that are important to profitability and those that are of little account. Furthermore, even if the reasons for a discrepancy are clear and no action can be taken to correct the situation, it is highly desirable to have a quantitative measure of the financial effects; attention is drawn to what is happening and future plans may well have to be amended.

Two other criticisms, namely, that some cost items are 'given', making the question of control irrelevant, and that the annual check is too late, that is, too infrequent, are discussed in the next section.

Whole farm budgetary control

By the time the end-of-year budgetary appraisal can be carried out it is certainly too late to correct some of the damage that might have been done by taking wrong decisions during that financial year. How much

TABLE 21.2. *Analysing the variance – actual versus budget*
(*a*) *Milk production*

Cause of difference	Plan (cows)	Yield (litres)	Price (per litre)	£
Budget	80	4,500	10.5p	37,800
Actual	76	4,365	10.8p	35,828
Difference	−4	−135	+0.3p	−1,972
Share of difference	−£1,886[a]	−£1,166[b]	+£1,080[c]	−1,972

[a] Plan: −4 cows × 4,365 litres × 10.8p (use *actual* yield and *actual* price).
[b] Yield: −135 litres gal × 80 cows × 10.8p (use *forecast* plan and *actual* price).
[c] Price: +0.3p × 80 cows × 4,500 litres (use *forecast* plan and *forecast* yield).

(*b*) *Wheat production*

Cause of difference	Plan (ha)	Yield (tonnes)	Price (per tonne)	£
Budget	65	4.5	£90.00	26,325
Actual	71	4.9	£84.35	29,345
Difference	+6	+0.4	−£ 5.65	+3,020
Share of difference	+£2,480[a]	+£2,193[b]	−£1,653[c]	+3,020

[a] Plan: 6 ha × 4.9 tonnes × £84.35.
[b] Yield: 0.4 tonnes × 65 ha × £84.35.
[c] Price: £5.65 × 65 ha × 4.5 tonnes

(*c*) *Dairy cattle output (excluding milk production)*

	Budget (£)	Actual (£)	Extra profit variation (£)	Lower profit variation (£)
Closing valuation	24,600 (82 cows at £300)	22,200 (74 cows at £300)	—	2,400
Sale of culls (inc. deaths)	4,160 (16 at £260)	4,940 (20 at £247)	780	—
Sale of calves	2,280 (38 at £60)	2,664 (36 at £74)	384	
Value of calves retained	1,710 (38 at £45)	1,575 (35 at £45)		135
Total	32,750	31,379	1,164	2,535 (−1,371)

Less				
Opening valuation	23,400 (78 cows at £300)	23,400 (78 cows at £300)	—	—
Heifers transferred in	5,100 (15 at £340)	4,420 (13 at £340)	680	—
Heifer/cow purchases	1,800 (5 at £360)	1,179 (3 at £393)	621	—
Total	30,300	28,999	1,301	—(+1,301)
Output	+2,450	+2,380	2,465	2,535 (−70)

(*d*) *Beef output*

	Budget (£)	Actual £)	Extra profit variation (£)	Lower profit variation (£)
Closing valuation	7,200 (30 at £240)	7,905 (31 at £255)	705	—
Sales	9,900 (30 at £330)	8,424 (27 at £312)	—	1,476
Total	17,100	16,329	705	1,476 (−771)
Less				
Opening valuation	6,300 (30 at £210)	6,300 (30 at £210)	—	—
Purchases	2,700 (30 at £90)	3,108 (28 at £111)	—	408
Total	9,000	9,408	—	408 (−408)
Output	8,100	6,921	705	1,884 (−1,179)

(*e*) *Poultry feed costs (egg production)*

Cause of difference	Plan (no. of birds)	Feed per bird	Cost of feed per tonne	(£)
Budget	5,000	40 kg	£110	22,000
Actual	5,500	43 kg	£121	28,616
Difference	+500	+ 3 kg	£ 11	+6,616
Share of difference	+£2,601[a]	+£1,815[b]	+£2,200[c]	+6,616

[a]Plan: + 500 × 43 kg × £121 (use *actual* use per head × *actual* cost per tonne).
[b]Use per head: + 3 kg × 5,000 × £121 (use *forecast* plan × *actual* cost per tonne).
[c]Cost: + £11 × 5,000 × 40 kg (use *forecast* plan × *forecast* use per head).

TABLE 21.3. *Budgetary appraisal – comprehensive layout*

	Budget		Actual		Difference		Analysis of difference[a]		
	Details	(£)	Details	(£)	+Profit	−Profit	Plan[b]	Yield[c]	Price[d]
Milk	80 cows × 4,500 l × 10.5p	37,800	76 cows × 4,365 l × 10.8p	35,828	—	1,972	−1,866	−1,166	+1,080
Cattle		10,550		9,301	—	1,249			
Wheat	60 ha × 4.5 t × £90	26,325	71 ha × 4.9 t × £84.35	29,345	3,020	—	+2,480	+2,193	−1,653
etc.		59,140		60,574	2,059	625			
					5,079	3,846			
Total outputs		133,815		135,048	1,233	—	—	—	—
							Plan[b]	Amount[e]	Cost[f]
Seed		4,680		4,943	—	263			
Fertiliser		9,450		8,916	534	—			
Feed: Poultry	5,000 × 40 kg × £110	22,000	5500 × 43 kg × £121	28,616	—	6,616	+2,601	+1,815	+2,200
Cows (etc.)		14,700		14,256	444	—			
Labour	6 men × 3,150	18,900	6 men × £3,282	19,692	—	792	—	—	+792
etc.		41,225		41,456	—	231			
					978	7,902			
Total inputs	—	110,955	—	117,879	—	6,924	—	—	—
Profit	—	22,860	—		—	5,691	—	—	—

[a] For any item where it is impossible to allocate as shown (see text) one or two columns only may be used, or two or all three columns can be grouped, or the analysis may be omitted altogether. For this reason no totals are entered.
[b] Difference caused by discrepancy in number of ha of crops or number of head of livestock.
[c] Difference caused by discrepancy in yield per ha or per head.
[d] Difference caused by discrepancy in price per unit of output.
[e] Difference caused by discrepancy in amount used per ha or per head.
[f] Difference caused by discrepancy in cost per unit of input.

too late it is depends to some extent on how quickly the annual accounts are completed, but even if they are available almost immediately after the end of the financial year, it will still be too late in indicating some perhaps crucial decisions that ought to have been taken. Despite its lateness, however, the procedure is still of value, partly – as has already been argued – because of the financial picture of the business and its most important elements that is built up, but also because *some* useful action, as regards future cropping and stocking for example, can still be taken in the future as a result of the analysis.

For the financial appraisal to be fully worthy of the name 'control', however, it should be carried out more frequently, that is, either monthly or at least quarterly. It will then be possible to check discrepancies earlier and to take action accordingly, as required. Apart from management action as regards farm policy, frequent financial checking may be necessitated by extreme shortage of capital, which may require adjustment in dates of buying materials, selling produce or paying bills. This situation could call for monthly checks for financial control, whatever the type of farm. In fact in businesses operating very close to overdraft limits, or in a dangerous liquidity position, calculations may be needed even more frequently than monthly. The technique required in these situations is described in Chapter 3, pp. 53–6. A cash flow statement has to be drawn up. As explained in Chapter 3, this is different from a budgeted trading account, in that such non-cash items as valuations and depreciation are omitted.

For control purposes three, preferably six, columns are required: for the budgeted and actual monthly figures, the cumulative budgeted and actual figures to date, and the differences. A dilemma often arises as to whether figures should be inserted when deliveries occur (to or from the farm) or when payments are made. The best plan is to budget for payment to be made soon after delivery, to include the items soon after the delivery dates and to tick off when payment is made. If funds permit, bills should be paid promptly, to minimise recording problems. If cost items are not entered until paid and long delays occur, the control procedure will give a false picture of the situation that is building up. Table 21.4 illustrates the layout of the information needed.

On the other hand, on many types of farm not in such a precarious financial position, there may be very little to be gained by frequent checks. With arable crops, not much action can be based on financial recording to help 'control' the production of the crop; most of the production variable costs have been determined and already incurred once the crop has been sown, and any further

TABLE 21.4. *Monthly and cumulative cash flow cost checks*

Month(s)	October			November		October – November			December		October – December			etc.
Item	Budget (£)	Actual (£)	Diffce. (£)	Budget (£)	Actual (£)	Budget (£)	Actual (£)	Diffce. (£)	Budget (£)	Actual (£)	Budget (£)	Actual (£)	Diffce (£)	
Regular labour	620	594	−26	600	612	1,220	1,206	−14	580	623	1,800	1,829	+29	
Casual labour	40	74	+34	—	30	40	104	+64	—	—	40	104	+64	
Machinery repairs etc.	200	163	−37	200	98	400	261	−139	200	426	600	687	+87	

Notes:

(1) 30 Sept. year-end.

(2) If felt to be desirable, a monthly difference column can be added.

action to be taken before harvesting is purely technical, based primarily on physical appraisal. On *any* type of farm, many costs are outside the farmer's immediate control because there is little or nothing that he can do about them, at least within the financial year; examples are rent, mortgage expenses, and interest payments.

On mainly arable farms, therefore, it can be concluded that there is little to be gained from monthly or even quarterly recording, unless the cash flow situation is fairly critical, that is, unless *financial* control in the sense of controlling monthly sales and expenditure is very important, in contrast to *operational* control, which relates to the need to adjust the actual farming policy. However, on any large-scale farm, arable or otherwise, it is often difficult to realise that certain items of expenditure are running at a high level and should if possible be regulated, e.g. machinery repairs or miscellaneous expenditure, and a quarterly check, at least on selected cost items, has therefore much to commend it.

As a useful compromise between end-of-year appraisal only and quarterly checks, on any type of farm, an estimate can be made in October (relating to a 1 April–31 March budget) of how near the year's actual outcome looks like comparing with the budget. This estimate will embrace what has happened during the first half of the financial year and what seems likely to happen over the remainder of the period. Estimated discrepancies may provide useful indicators of action needed before the end of the year or the following spring. Estimating the year's profit in advance can also help in deciding when to replace machinery in order to achieve the biggest tax advantage.

Budgetary control in livestock production

In contrast to arable crops, there are some livestock enterprises for which budgetary control in the full sense is well suited. These include milk production, pigs, poultry and barley beef. For these, variable inputs (primarily concentrate feedingstuffs) are very important cost items, the level and composition of which can be frequently altered and directly affect production, which varies continually throughout the year. Thus full managerial control, in the sense of being able to take frequent decisions that affect both inputs and outputs, is both possible and desirable. Although an experienced specialist stockman with a small enterprise may be capable of realising almost immediately when results are falling off and be able quickly to identify the cause and put it right, this becomes more and more difficult as livestock units become larger. Monthly recording of the vital elements of profitability that are

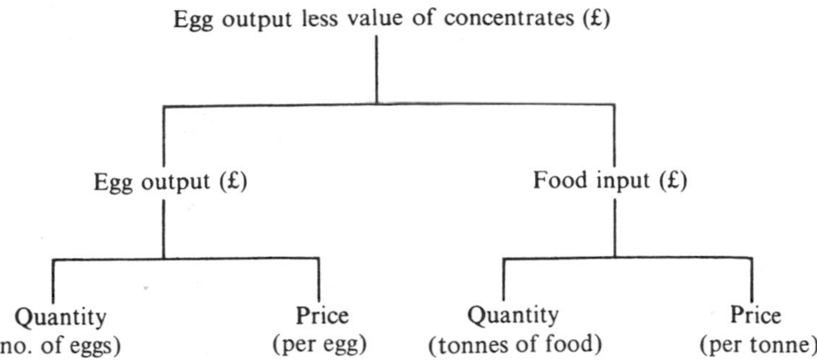

Fig. 21.1. Items for monthly recording: egg production

within the control of management supplies the necessary information to allow policy adjustments to be made, especially as regards feeding, before it is too late.

There is no point in monthly recording of items that are either obvious or outside the power of management to control. In a dairy enterprise, for example, these would include building depreciation and labour costs and even grazing and conservation expenditure, important though these are to profitability. The items capable of continuous control are concentrate feed and output; therefore, these are the only ones that justify frequent recording. The relevant profit factors are shown in Figure 21.1 for egg production; the same chart layout could be used for other livestock enterprises. Enterprises such as pigs or barley beef, where sales are less continuous than is the case with milk and eggs, are more difficult. This is because output can only be accurately determined by careful weighing and valuation of the stock at the end of each month. This is not only labour-consuming but the valuation is clearly subject to error.[1] However, the larger the herd and the more continuous its production (in contrast to 'batch' production) the less necessary monthly valuations become. Furthermore, as we shall see, incorporation of a forecast largely – if not entirely – overcomes this problem. Less frequent calculations, such as quarterly or six-monthly, help avoid the need for within-year valuations, or at least such frequent valuations, but control is then weakened. Some prefer to operate a three or six-month moving average, without valuations, possibly using efficiency measures instead of comparisons with the budget. This avoids many problems but is less effective as a means of control.

[1] Nevertheless, monthly valuations, carried out as accurately as possible, cannot be avoided for some purposes.

If this frequent recording is to be used for control purposes, the results must obviously be compared with some sort of 'norm' to see whether or not progress is satisfactory. There should be both monthly and cumulative figures (see Table 21.5). Some managers may be satisfied with simply charting the cumulative figures against one or more previous years, or simply towards an end-of-year target for annual margin over concentrates. This has some merit, but it does not constitute 'control'. There is no reason to suppose that previous years' results are suitable targets for the current year – unless they proved highly profitable – and striving towards an annual figure would almost certainly mean that failure to reach it would be observed too late for suitable action to be taken.

Some procedures compare the farm's monthly results with averages for a group of farms for the same month, or arbitrarily split an annual target into monthly amounts – often in equal steps, i.e. £390 a year margin of milk value less concentrate costs equals £33 a month. But, again, neither comes properly under the category of 'control'. For this, a forecast must be made for the individual farm concerned, taking its own circumstances and potential performance level into account. The forecast must incorporate the expected seasonality of production, which can of course vary widely from farm to farm. Opinions vary as to what extent the forecast should be based on past performance (possibly adjusted for some improvement expected from deliberate policy changes) and to what extent it should be based on a 'target' in the sense of expecting a level of performance on a par with the achievements of the best producers. The former is more realistic and, because it is obviously easier to achieve, there is more chance of the stockman and manager receiving the boost to morale provided by exceeding the forecast; on the other hand, there is little to be proud of in reaching an easy target, and if actual results should still fall short of a modest forecast there will be far more disappointment than if there is failure to reach a target set deliberately high. Some like and need to aim for a high target, others are more suited to trying to beat a forecast based on a slight improvement in past results. It all depends on the psychology of the worker(s) involved, together with the ambitions of the farmer-manager.

The above discussion relates to establishing the 'level' of forecast, in the sense of margin over concentrates per head. This is a composite of output level and quantity of concentrates. The latter, in the case of ruminant livestock, needs to be related to the quantity and quality of bulk feeds, as well as the output level that is sought. The seasonality

TABLE 21.5. *Monthly and cumulative checks for livestock – milk production*

Month(s)	October			November		October–November			December		October–December			etc.
	Target	Actual	Diffee.	Target	Actual	Target	Actual	Diffee.	Target	Actual	Target	Actual	Diffee.	
1. *Whole herd*														
No. of cows	76	75	−1	78	76	77	75.5	−1.5	80	79	78	76.3	−1.7	
No. of dry cows	25	22	−3	15	14	20	18.0	−2.0	5	5	15	13.7	−1.3	
Milk produced (litres)	24,225	23,780	−445	31,500	30,350	55,725	54,130	−1,595	37,500	35,600	93,225	89,730	−3,495	
Concs. fed (tonnes)	8.65	9.77	+1.12	12.70	12.47	21.35	22.24	+0.89	15.10	13.99	36.45	36.23	−0.22	
Milk value (£)	2,422	2,412	−10	3,150	3,095	5,572	5,507	−65	3,750	3,630	9,322	9,137	−185	
Conc. costs (£)	1,038	1,173	+135	1,524	1,545	2,562	2,718	+156	1,812	1,746	4,374	4,464	+90	
Margin over Concs. (£)	1,384	1,239	−145	1,626	1,550	3,010	2,789	−221	1,938	1,884	4,948	4,673	−275	
2. *Per cow*														
Milk yield (litres)	319	317	−2	404	399	724	717	−7	469	451	1.195	1,176	−19	
Concs. fed (kg)	11.4	13.0	+1.6	16.3	16.4	27.7	29.5	+1.8	18.9	17.7	46.7	47.5	+0.8	
Milk value (£)	31.9	32.2	+0.3	40.4	40.7	72.4	72.9	+0.5	46.9	45.9	119.5	119.7	+0.2	
Conc. costs (£)	13.7	15.7	+2.0	19.5	20.3	33.3	36.0	+2.7	22.7	22.1	56.1	58.5	+2.4	
Margin over concs. (£)	18.2	16.5	−1.7	20.9	20.4	39.1	36.9	−2.2	24.2	23.8	63.4	61.2	−2.2	
3. *Other measures*														
Milk price per litre (p)	10.0	10.1	+0.1	10.0	10.2	10.0	10.2	+0.2	10.0	10.2	10.0	10.2	+0.2	
Conc. costs per tonne (£)	120	120	+ —	120	124	120	122	+2	120	125	120	123	+3	
Concs. fed per litre (kg)	0.36	0.41	+0.05	0.40	0.41	0.38	0.41	+0.03	0.40	0.39	0.39	0.40	+0.01	
Conc. costs per litre (p)	4.3	4.9	+0.6	4.8	5.1	4.6	5.0	+0.4	4.8	4.9	4.7	5.0	+0.3	
Per cent dry cows	32.9	29.3	−3.6	19.2	19.4	26.0	23.8	−2.2	6.2	6.3	19.2	18.0	−1.2	

Notes:

(1) 30 Sept. year end.

(2) If felt to be desirable, a monthly difference column could be added.

TABLE 21.6. *Milk production – lactation curves according to month of calving* (100 = average yield for herd)

Month of Calving	Jan.	Feb.[a]	Mar.	Apr.	May	June	July	Aug.	Sept.	Oct.	Nov.	Dec.	Jan.	Feb.[a]	Mar.	Apr.	May	June	July	Aug.	Sept.	Oct.
January	14.4	13.6	14.2	13.1	12.2	10.1	8.8	7.0	4.6	2.8	0.2											
February		12.6	15.1	14.4	13.8	11.7	10.7	9.1	7.0	5.1	3.1	0.4										
March			14.7	16.2	15.5	13.0	12.0	10.3	8.0	6.3	4.2	2.7	0.1									
April				15.1	16.7	14.1	13.1	11.6	9.4	7.9	6.1	4.6	3.2	0.2								
May					16.1	15.9	14.8	13.0	10.7	9.1	7.2	5.9	4.3	2.7	0.3							
June						15.0	16.7	15.0	12.4	10.7	8.8	7.6	6.3	4.4	3.7	0.4						
July							15.3	15.8	13.4	11.7	9.5	8.6	7.5	5.8	5.6	4.3	0.5					
August								14.9	14.5	12.8	10.5	9.4	9.2	6.5	6.6	5.8	4.4	0.4				
September									14.2	14.5	12.2	10.9	9.7	8.0	8.3	7.8	6.6	4.3	0.5			
October										14.4	13.9	12.9	11.3	9.2	9.6	9.1	8.1	5.6	3.6	0.3		
November											13.6	14.7	13.2	10.7	11.1	10.5	9.8	7.6	5.9	3.6	0.3	
December												14.4	14.8	12.2	12.5	11.7	10.9	8.8	7.3	5.2	2.9	0.3

[a]Add $3\frac{1}{2}\%$ in leap year.

Derived by G. Allanson, Wye College, from data supplied by Production Division, Milk Marketing Board.

Figures for each month of calving weighted by the resulting lactation yield and the percentage of cows in the national herd calving in each month.

pattern has to be based on expected dates of calving or farrowing, or dates of rearing or buying pullets for egg production or stock for fattening. These expectations, e.g. for milk and egg production, are then linked to the production curves of the animals.

To illustrate from milk production, Table 21.6 shows the monthly milk yield per 100 litres of annual yield per cow to be expected from each cow calving at different months of the year. Thus if, for simplicity, we assumed that, in a mainly autumn-calving herd of 80 cows on 1 October, 10 had calved the previous Dccember, 10 in August and 20 in September, and 20 dry cows were expected to calve during October and 20 in November, the expected milk production in October, for a 4,500 litre average herd, would be:

		litres
December calvers:	10 × 45 × 0.3 =	135
August calvers:	10 × 45 × 12.8 =	5,760
September calvers:	20 × 45 × 14.5 =	13,050
October calvers:	20 × 45 × 7.2[a] =	6,480
November calvers:	20 × 45 × — =	—
	Total	25,425

[a] *7.2 (= ½ of 14.4) assumes the new calvings are spread evenly through the month.*

This number of litres would be multiplied by the expected milk price for the month to give the expected financial output. There are various levels of refinement. For example, separate tables are available for heifers. Separate calculations can be made for each individual cow, using its own expected production based on past performance. Obviously such elaborations add to the amount of work required, although not very much if the calculations are computerised. A compromise method is to place a cow in one of, say, three or four expected output categories. In some schemes the targets are adjusted to allow for the *actual* number of calvings in each month, once known. Others prefer to keep their original targets in view and take into account variations between expected and actual calvings when analysing differences compared with forecast. The latter course is easier and has much to commend it; otherwise there is a risk of adjusting the forecast downwards to allow for what could be not unfavourable external circumstances but managerial deficiencies, thus reducing the pressure to take the necessary steps towards improvement.

Physical controls

Certain physical controls are extremely important, especially in livestock production. Physical quantities, such as levels of production and amounts of food, will normally be recorded, checked and adjusted together with the financial data, as described in the last section.

Charts containing breeding details are very important to the profitability of some livestock enterprises. This is not true of animals such as sheep, where all the stock are served at one time of the year and give birth at another. But it is for stock such as dairy cows and sows, where it is important to keep the breeding cycle as short as the continued good health and productivity of the animals will allow, with no long periods when production is either nil or very low. Each successive heat missed costs cumulatively more. For each dairy cow, for example, a check should be kept on the dates of the following: calving, coming on heat, serving or AI, pregnancy confirmation, and expected subsequent calving. In this way, any cow that is giving trouble can be spotted early: if it is proving difficult to get in calf it has to be carefully watched and the decision made whether it is worth persevering with or whether it should be culled; obviously much will depend on its lactation yield potential. There are a number of cow- and sow-breeding charts available. Many are rectangular with one row per cow; the columns can represent either calendar weeks or the number of weeks after calving (regardless of the actual date). The latter makes it simple to mark off critical periods after calving with vertical lines, but it is less easy to keep track of the dates. Some farmers use pegboards. Circular charts are also available and becoming increasingly popular. All work on the same principle and aim at quick identification of trouble areas, so as to allow for action to be taken to put the matter right as quickly as possible.

Another visual aid that can be used for day-to-day control, this time in the important area – especially to arable farmers – of fieldwork operations, is the gang-work day chart (see Chapter 5, p. 140). In any season, comparison of *expected* operational progress as outlined on this chart and *actual* progress to date gives a clear indication of how far behind or ahead of schedule the year's operations are. Using this chart makes it easier to plan priorities and predict the need for more overtime work or hiring contractors in a difficult season than if all the information is carried in the head. Clearly, the larger and the more complex the farm the truer this is.

In order to be able to check progress on critical jobs quickly a further visual aid may be used: a work progress chart. A separate chart is needed for each major job, e.g. potato harvesting, autumn/winter ploughing, winter wheat drilling. The information required is the date when it is hoped to start the job, the date it is hoped to finish it, and the hectares to be covered. The period involved depends – as in the gang-

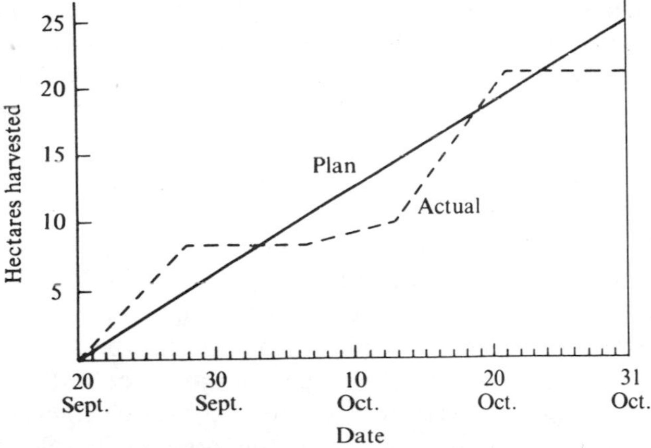

Potato harvesting (25 hectares) is planned to begin on September 20th and to be completed by 31st October (estimated 25 available working days, allowing for bad weather and soil conditions = 1 hectare per working day). The plan line is drawn straight, but normally progress would be expected to be faster at first (steeper slope) and gradually decline (reducing slope) with worsening conditions as winter approaches.

In the example, good progress is made from Sept. 20th. to Sept. 28th. (high per cent of workable days and fast rate of work in good conditions), bad weather stops work from Sept. 29th. to Oct. 7th., there is slow recovery from Oct. 8th. to the 13th., the weather is good and progress rapid from Oct. 14th. to 21st., after which bad conditions again prevent harvesting, leaving 3 hectares unlifted on Oct. 31st.

Fig. 21.2. Work progress chart – potato harvesting.

work day chart – on the expected crop, weather and soil conditions, and on the way in which the job fits into the overall farm plan – for example, potato harvesting dates often depend partly on whether or not sugar beet is also grown. Figure 21.2 illustrates the chart for potato harvesting. Matching 'actual' against 'plan' shows immediately not only whether the job is behind or ahead of schedule, but also by how much.

Management by objectives

Budgetary control forms a major part of the approach to running a business known as 'management by objectives' (MBO). This concept was first publicised in UK farming circles towards the end of the 1960s. In detail it contains nothing new; its exponents claim it to be a complete system of management, with an emphasis on control mechanisms, aimed at avoiding entire dependence on short-term, *ad hoc* decision making based primarily on intuition. It has been defined as 'the active process of determining and guiding the course of a business towards its objectives'. The following is a brief outline of the MBO procedure.

The first step is to analyse the environment in which the firm will have to operate in the future. This comprises both external and internal factors. The manager can have little or no control over many of the external factors, for example the state of the economy, Government legislation, demand prospects, imports, technical developments and competition from other firms and products. The internal factors include the resources and skills available, and the firm's present financial position and level of performance. The analysis endeavours to detect both threats to the business and opportunities that lie ahead. Future plans must include ways of dealing with the former and exploiting the latter.

The second step is to draw up strategic, long-term plans, which outline the way in which the business is to develop during a specified future time period. In farming this is normally between five and ten years, according to such factors as the main types of enterprise, the likelihood of technological and major price changes, and the amount of capital sunk in fixed equipment, including buildings. The strategy comprises three parts, which take on progressively more detail and form the main elements of the MBO system.

The first part is to define the *purpose* of the business – a subject already touched upon in the first pages of this book. This is a general statement of what the farmer wants from his farm business. It may be maximisation of profits with a given level of investment; it may be to meet certain family commitments and achieve a given standard of living; it may be to aim at a specified rate of growth – either because this is felt necessary to ensure future survival, or solely for its own sake, or to be able to set up a son in a farm of his own; it may be simply for enjoyment, provided there is sufficient income to live comfortably. Whatever it is, the farmer-manager should be clear about his purpose in being in the business of farming.

The second part is more specific: it is to state unequivocally what results are to be achieved and by what dates – in order to satisfy the purpose of the business. These are the specific *objectives*. For example, the aim may be a profit of £75 per hectare in three years' time, or a return on tenant's capital of 20 per cent after two more years.

There is no point, however, in stating wildly over-optimistic targets that there is no possible chance of reaching. They have to be capable of achievement, and the third part of the strategy states in detail what has to be done in order to realise the objectives. *Goals* are established, which give the levels of performance to be achieved; for example, a margin over concentrates per cow of £400. At the same time there has to be a detailed assessment of what is required in order to attain each of the specified goals: the financial and physical resources needed, the feeding and breeding policies to be followed. Further, the data to be recorded have to be decided, together with the frequency of recording and the control mechanism to be employed. 'Key tasks' are identified, which are of particular importance to the success of the plans.

After the strategy has been agreed in the detail indicated, the third step is to make tactical plans for immediate action to be taken which will affect performance during the coming year and help achieve the goals specified in the strategic plans. Critical problems that could jeopardise future profits have to be solved. Any major weaknesses revealed in the initial analysis of the environment have to be tackled.

Control procedures are an essential part of MBO. These indicate where and when changes in tactical plans are needed, which could be very frequently. It is also advisable to review the strategic plan periodically in the light of changing circumstances: perhaps every three or six months for relatively minor changes, and every two years for more fundamental, long-term changes.

One of the particularly important features of MBO has yet to be mentioned. This is the complete involvement of personnel at every level in drawing up the detailed goals. Not only top management but unit or subordinate managers should understand the purpose and objectives of the business, and agree the goals and the control procedures to be employed within their own sections, in order to fit into the overall strategy for the firm. In a large farming business, unit managers will also involve workers in the unit – especially skilled men, such as cowmen. In this way, everyone knows what is expected of him and is committed to the achievement of the plan and the performance levels set; these have not been *imposed* from above – the men have themselves helped design and approve them. The phrase 'participative management' is sometimes used to describe this approach. At the other extreme is the completely authoritarian control exerted by 'the man at the top' (see further Chapter 5, pp. 152–3). If top management simply 'goes through the motions' of consultation and participation, and subordinates feel that they are being pressurised or squeezed by targets that are set for them, the system will fail. Discontent and cynicism and inadequate performance will result, and performance will probably be worse than in an authoritarian system.

Combining planning and control

This book has studied farm planning and control largely as though they are two separate subjects. It has been hinted more than once, however, that both can be interpreted in either a narrow or a broad sense. If planning is held to include not only long-term, strategic decision-making, in the sense of major changes in the farm economy or enterprise-mix, but also short-term tactical adjustments in order to adapt to changing circumstances; and if control is taken to mean not only annual checks on performance but the continual recording and analysis of data results and day-to-day adjustment according to changing events – then the two obviously overlap. In essence, then, it can certainly be argued that both are aspects of the same problem and that it is essential, therefore, for them to be fully integrated. This in fact takes us back to the first chapter of this book, where this same point was made (p. 16) and illustrated, in Figure 1.2.

Such an approach would combine both planning and control procedures. Since circumstances are continually changing, plans need constant revision. Ideally data should be supplied at frequent intervals for control purposes, and linked with planning techniques that modify policies in accordance with the information provided. Up-to-date information should be fed in continually, indicating how circumstances are altering (e.g. relative prices) and how the level of technical performance is comparing with expectations. In the light of this, targets should be altered and plans changed, in order better to satisfy the objectives of the business. Clearly, changes requiring only minor alterations, say in the enterprises being pursued and the capital required, can be made far more frequently than large-scale changes. Within a given enterprise (and this applies mainly to livestock), an optimising technique could be operated, using the most recent data provided in a given control period to enable targets to be revised for the coming period. Some would draw a distinction here between 'decisions', which relate to the following control period, and 'plans', which refer to many periods ahead. Both can be changed, but only to a limited extent – except in the case of any plans made over a very long period (e.g. more than ten years ahead).

System-simulation models

The systems approach and the use of simulation methods to examine the working of a 'system' were briefly described[1] in Appendix 4.2 (pp.

[1] For a full description, see further Dalton, G. E. (ed.) (1975) *Study of Agricultural Systems*, Applied Science Publishers Ltd, especially Chapter 3: Dent, J. B., 'The Application of Systems Theory in Agriculture'.

116–8), before referring to their use in the choice of machinery. They have also been referred to in Appendix 13.5 (p. 312) with regard to growth of the firm theory. Finally, the use of simulation in farm planning (Monte Carlo method) has been described in Chapter 17 (pp. 416–21).

There has been a considerable development in the application of these approaches to livestock enterprises during the 1970s,[1] which are exemplified by computer models of dairy[2] and pig herds[3] that incorporate all the relevant physical and financial variables and enable the effect of changes in any of them to be evaluated. For example, the effect on pig throughput, financial output and profitability of variations in the farrowing index, number of weaners born per litter, mortality, liveweight gain per day and so on can be rapidly found, thus facilitating the virtually continual updating of forecasts according to current level of performance.

There are two alternative ways of developing such models so that they can be used by many producers.[4] The first is the representative farm approach, used to examine the broad implications of major changes in farm policy. The other, referred to as the 'skeleton' model, includes the basic parameters of a production system and reflects the sequence and timing of management decisions. Results applicable to the individual farm are obtained when its own data are fed in. Although more expensive to develop than a model designed specifically for one farm, the cost to the individual user is far less. Validation can be a problem but this is substantially less for skeleton models than for most other simulation models.

Data for the individual farm are stored in a computer file to which the manager has access and which can be amended at any time. Once the process is learnt, the latter should be able to use the model without outside assistance. Present performance can be continually checked against forecast, or target, and any changes in policy felt to be necessary can be evaluated before being implemented. Similarly the effect of any changes in external parameters can be quickly estimated. An

[1] Early examples are described in Dent, J. B., and Anderson, J. R. (1971) *Systems Analysis in Agricultural Management* (Chapter 13), John Wiley & Sons Australasia Pty. Ltd. See also Charlton, P. J. (1972) 'Financing Farm Business Growth', *Farm Management*, **2**, No. 2 (relating to a pig unit).

[2] Street, P. R. (1973) *Nottingham University Dairy Enterprise Simulator*. Dept of Agriculture and Horticulture, Univ. of Nottingham.

[3,4] Blackie, M. J. and Dent, J. B. (1974) 'The Concept and Application of Skeleton Models in Farm Business Analysis and Planning'. *Journal of Agricultural Economics*, **XXV**, No. 2.

information system – the recording, storage and quick retrieval of data – is an integral part of this approach. Centralised computer facilities are required, with an efficient system of data transmission to and from individual farms.

Such models attempt to meet the criticism farmers often make that their main worry lies not in making long-term plans, but in making the important day-to-day decisions. They need to know, on a virtually continual basis, 'what is', 'what is wrong' and 'what to do about it'. But however sophisticated and mathematically precise such models become, it is impossible to think of human judgement being wholly superseded, especially where circumstances change so much and so rapidly as in farming. The systems approach outlined would aim simply to *serve* management – by feeding it with continually updated information, suitably analysed, together with suggestions for optimal decisions in order to help it arrive at better decisions. It could not *replace* it.

This chapter has therefore completed the overall picture outlined in the opening chapter of the book, and the last two sections have emphasised the integrated nature of the many and varied problems that have to be resolved in the process of farm planning and control. The farmer has to decide his objectives; his available resources must be allocated, both in the organisation of his enterprises and in the combination of those enterprises, so as to meet the objectives in a profitable way; furthermore, control must be continually exercised in order to check whether the objectives are being met and, if they are not, to enable corrective action to be taken as soon as possible. If the terms 'planning' and 'control' are broadly interpreted, therefore, both are taking place simultaneously and continually, and it is the task of the farmer-manager to ensure that the necessary decisions are taken and the required action implemented quickly and effectively.

Selected further reading

(Where more than one reference is made to a book or article, only the name(s) of the author(s) and the year are given on the second and subsequent occasions).

Chapter 1

Bradford, L. A. and Johnson, G. L. (1953) *Farm Management Analysis*. John Wiley and Sons. Chapters 1–3.

Castle, E. N., Becker, M. H. and Smith, F. J. (1972) *Farm Business Management* (second edition). Macmillan. Chapter 1.

Heady, E. O. (1952) *Economics of Agricultural Production and Resource Use*. Prentice-Hall. Chapter 1, (pp. 3–13).

Heady, E. O. and Jensen, H. R. (1954) *Farm Management Economics*. Prentice-Hall. Chapter 1.

Chapter 2

Bishop, C. E. and Toussaint, W. D. (1958) *Introduction to Agricultural Economic Analysis*. John Wiley and Sons. Chapters 2–11.

Bradford, L. A. and Johnson, G. L. (1953). Chapters 8–12.

Britton, D. K. and Hill, B. (1975) *Size & Efficiency in Farming*. Saxon House.

Castle, E. N., Becker, M. H. and Smith, F. J. (1972). Chapter 2.

Dillon, J. L. (1968) *The Analysis of Response in Crop and Livestock Production*. Pergamon Press.

Heady, E. O. (1952). Parts 1 and 2.

Heady, E. O. and Dillon, J. L. (1961) *Agricultural Production Functions*. Iowa State College Press.

Heady, E. O. and Jensen, H. R. (1954). Chapter 4.

Rae, A. E. (1977) *Crop Management Economics*. Crosby Lockwood Staples. Chapters 1–4.

Upton, M. (1973). *Farm Management in Africa*. Oxford University Press. Chapters 1–4.

(1976) *Agricultural Production Economics and Resource-use*. Oxford University Press.

Chapter 3

Castle, E. N., Becker, M. H. and Smith, F. J. (1972). Chapter 8.

Chisholm, A. H. and Dillon, J. L. (1967) *Discounting and Other Interest Rate Procedures in Farm Management*. Professional Farm Management Guidebook No. 2, University of New England.

Clery, P. (1975) *Farming Finance*. Farming Press Limited.

Edwards, A. E. and Rogers, A. (eds.) (1974) *Agricultural Resources*. Faber and Faber Ltd. Chapter 7 (by Hill, B.).

Kerr, H. W. T. (1966) *Methods of Appraising New Capital Investments in Agriculture*. Farmers Report 161, University of Nottingham.

Merrett, A. J. and Sykes, A. (1963) *The Finance and Analysis of Capital Projects*. Longmans, Green & Co.

(1966) *Capital Budgeting and Company Finance*. Longmans, Green & Co.

Norman L. and Coote, R. B. (1971) *The Farm Business*. Longman Group Ltd. Chapter 5.

Chapter 4

Bradford, L. A. and Johnson, G. L. (1953). Chapter 19.

Castle, E. N., Becker, M. H. and Smith, F. J. (1972). Chapters 9, 13, 14.

Centre for Agricultural Strategy (1976). *Land for Agriculture*. College of Estate Management, Reading.

Clery, P. (1975). Chapters 4 and 6.

Culpin, C. (1968) *Profitable Farm Mechanisation*. Crosby Lockwood & Son.

Dancey, R. (1970) 'The Economics of Buying More Land'. *Farm Management*, **1**, No. 8.

Dent, J. B. and Anderson, J. R. (1971) *Systems Analysis in Agricultural Management*. John Wiley & Sons Australasia Pty. Ltd; Chapter 14 (by van Kempen, J. H.).

Donaldson, G. F. (1970) *Farm Machinery Capacity*. Royal Commission on Farm Machinery. Queen's Printer for Canada, Ottawa.

Edwards, A. E. and Rogers, A. (eds.) (1974). Chapter 5 (by Edwards, A. E.)

Finney, J. B. (1978) 'Choosing Farm Machinery'. *Farm Management*, **3**, No. 8.

Heady, E. O. and Jensen, H. R. (1954). Chapters 12 and 14.

James, P. J. (1973/4) 'Obtaining Machinery – A Review of the Financing Alternatives'. *Farm Management*, **2**, No. 7.

Ministry of Agriculture, Fisheries and Food (1969) *Labour and Machinery*. Aids to Management No. 6, HMSO.

Sturrock, F. G., Cathie, J. and Payne, T. A. (1977) *Economies of Scale in Farm Mechanisation*. Agricultural Economics Unit, Department of Land Economy, University of Cambridge.

Chapter 5

Armstrong, J. (1975) 'The Role of Authority in Enlightened Man Management'. *Farm Management*, **2**, No. 12.

(1970) 'Towards a More Effective Farm Staff'. *Farm Management*, **1**, No. 9.

Bradford, L. A. and Johnson, G. L. (1953). Chapter 19.

Heady, E. O. and Jensen, H. R. (1954). Chapter 13.

Ministry of Agriculture, Fisheries and Food (1969).

Norman, R. G. (1971) 'The Scope for Industrial Labour Management Techniques in Agriculture'. *Farm Management*, **2**, No. 1.

Chapters 6 to 11

Barnard, C. S., Halley, R. J. and Scott, A. H. (1970) *Milk Production*. Iliffe Books. Chapters 2–4, 6.

Heady, E. O. and Jensen, H. R. (1954) Chapters 8–10.

Norman, L. and Coote, R. B. (1971) Chapters 6 and 7.

Organisation for Economic Co-operation and Development, Documentation in Agriculture and Food: (1966) *Poultry Production*. No. 81.

(1968) *Beef Production*. No. 82

(1969) *Cow Milk Production*. No. 83

Ridgeon, R. F. and Sturrock, F. G. (1969) *Economics of Pig Production*. Ag. Econ. Report No. 65, Department of Land Economy, Cambridge University.

Chapter 12

Bradford, L. A. and Johnson, G. L. (1953). Chapter 13.

Castle, E. N., Becker M. H. and Smith, F. J. (1972). Chapter 11.

Folley, R. R. W. (1973) *Intensive Crop Economics*. Heinemann Educational Books.

Heady, E. O. and Jensen, H. R. (1954). Chapters 6 and 7.
Rae, A. E. (1977).

Chapter 13

Gunn, H. J. and Hardaker, J. B. (1967) 'Long-Term Planning – A Re-examination of Principles and Methods'. *Journal of Agricultural Economics*, **XVIII**, No. 2.

Chapter 14

Castle, E. N., Becker, M. H. and Smith, F. J. Chapter 5.
Clarke, G. B. and Simpson, I. G. (1959) 'A Theoretical Approach to Profit Maximisation Problems in Farm Management'. *Journal of Agricultural Economics*, **XIII**, No. 3.
Kerr, H. W. T. and Thomas, H. A. (1967) *An Exercise in Planning*. Farmers' Report No. 166, Department of Agricultural Economics, University of Nottingham.
McFarquhar, A. M. M. (1962) 'Research in Farm Planning Methods in Northern Europe'. *Journal of Agricultural Economics*, **XV**, No. 1. (pp. 81–8).
Organisation for Economic Co-operation and Development, Documentation in Food and Agriculture (1962) *Programme Planning*. No. 45.
Rae, A. E. (1977) Chapter 5, (pp. 106–24).
Richards, P. A. and McConnell, D. J. (1967) *Budgeting, Gross Margins and Programme Planning*. Professional Farm Management Guidebook No. 3, University of New England.
Sturrock, F. G. (1971) *Farm Accounting and Management*. Pitman, Chapters 14–18.
Wallace, D. B. and Burr, H. (1963) *Planning on the Farm*. Report No. 60, Agricultural Economics Unit, Department of Land Economy, University of Cambridge.

Chapter 15

Barnard, C. S. (1963) 'Farm Models, Management Objectives and the Bounded Planning Environment'. *Journal of Agricultural Economics*, **XV**, No. 4.
Beneke, R. R. and Winterboer, R. (1973) *Linear Programming Applications to Agriculture*. Iowa State College Press. Chapters 1, 2 (pp. 10–29).
Boles, J. N. (1955) 'Linear Programming and Farm Management Analysis'. *Journal of Farm Economics*, **XXXVII**, No. 1.
Candler, W. and Musgrave, W. F. (1960) 'A Practical Approach to the Profit Maximisation Problems in Farm Management'. *Journal of Agricultural Economics*, **XIV**, No. 2.
Dent, J. B. and Casey, H. (1967) *Linear Programming and Animal Nutrition*. Crosby Lockwood. Chapters 3 and 4.
Hardaker, J. B. (1971) *Farm Planning by Computer*. Ministry of Agriculture, Fisheries and Food, Technical Bulletin No. 19. HMSO. Chapters 1, 4, 8, 10.
Heady, E. O. (1954) 'Simplified Presentation and Logical Aspects of Linear Programming Technique'. *Journal of Farm Economics*, **XXXVI**, No. 5.
Heady, E. O. and Candler, W. (1958) *Linear Programming Methods*. Iowa State College Press. Chapters 1–3.
McFarquhar, A. M. M. (1961) 'The Practical Use of Linear Programming in Farm Planning'. *Farm Economist*, **IX**, No. 10.
Puterbaugh, H. L., Kehrberg, E. W. and Dunbar, J. O. (1957) 'Analysing the Solution Tableau of a Simplex Linear Programming Problem in Farm Organisation'. *Journal of Farm Economics*, **XXXIX**, No. 2.

Smith, V. E. and Barnard, C. S. (1960) 'Cost Allocation and the Detection of Unprofitable Ventures'. *Journal of Farm Economics*, **XLII**, No. 3.

Throsby, C. D. (1970) *Elementary Linear Programming*, Random House.

Chapter 16

Castle, E. N., Becker, M. H. and Smith, F. J. (1972). Chapters 7, 10 (pp. 211–14).

Heady, E. O. (1952). Chapters 15–17.

Heady, E. O. and Jensen, H. R. (1954). Chapter 17.

Jones, R. B. (1969) 'Stability in Farm Incomes'. *Journal of Agricultural Economics*, **XX**, No. 1.

Mackel, C. (1975) 'The Futures Market – a Key to Stable Grain Prices?'. *Farm Management Review*, No. 5, Agricultural Economics Division, North of Scotland College of Agriculture.

Murphy, M. C. (1971) 'Risk Evaluation in Farm Planning – A Statistical Approach'. *Journal of Agricultural Economics*, **XXII**, No. 1.

Rae, A. E. (1977). Chapters 12, 13 (pp. 414–8).

Upton, M. (1976).

Chapter 17

See Appendix 17.1.

Chapter 18

Beneke, R. R. and Winterboer, R. (1973). Chapters 2 (pp. 29–35), 3–13.

Casey, H. (1968) *Linear Programming and Farm Planning*. Department of Agricultural Economics, University of Reading.

Hardaker, J. B. (1971). Chapters 5–7, 9.

Heady, E. O. and Candler, W. (1958). Chapter 6.

Rae, A. E. (1977). Chapter 8.

Stewart, J. D. (1961) 'Farm Operating Capital as a Constraint – A Problem in the Application of Linear Programming'. *Farm Economist*, **IX**, No. 10.

Chapter 19

Brown, D. (1973) 'Farm Office Organisation'. *Farm Management*, **2**, No. 5.

Camamile, G. H. and Theophilus, T. W. D. (1964) *Records for Profitable Farming*. Hutchinson. Chapters 6–9.

Castle, E. N., Becker, M. H. and Smith, F. J. (1972). Chapter 3.

Davies, G. D. D. and Dunsford, W. J. (1967) *The Farm Balance Sheet: Its Construction and Interpretation*. Report No. 167, Department of Agricultural Economics, University of Exeter.

Hosken, M. (1976) *The Farm Office*. Farming Press Ltd.

Kerr, H. W. T. (1968) *Farm Management Accounting*. Farmers' Report No. 168, Department of Agricultural Economics, University of Nottingham.

Ministry of Agriculture, Fisheries and Food (1967) *Office Organisation for Farm & Horticultural Businesses*. Short-Term Leaflet No. 47, HMSO.

(1968) *Keeping Financial Records*. Short-Term Leaflet No. 48, HMSO.

(1967) *Feed Recording*. Short-Term Leaflet No. 49, HMSO.

Nix, J. (1978) *Farm Management Pocketbook*. Farm Business Unit, Wye College, University of London.

Chapter 20

Camamile, G. H. and Theophilus, T. W. D. (1964). Chapter 2.

Candler, W. and Musgrave, W. F. (1960).

Castle, E. N., Becker, M. H. and Smith, F. J. (1972). Chapter 4.

Davies, G. D. D. and Dunsford, W. J. (1967).

Giles, A. K. (1962) *Gross Margins and the Future of Account Analysis*. Miscellaneous Studies No. 23, Department of Agricultural Economics and Management, University of Reading.

Lloyd, D. H. (1970) *The Development of Farm Business Analysis and Planning in Great Britain*. Study No. 6, Department of Agriculture, University of Reading.

Norman, L. and Coote, R. B. (1971). Chapter 1.

Rcid, I. G. (1969) 'Balance Sheet Interpretation'. *Farm Management*, **1**, No. 6.

Chapter 21

Boyer, R. S. (1969) 'Management by Objectives'. *Farm Management*, **1**, No. 5.

Camamile, G. H. and Theophilus, T. W. D. (1964). Chapter 4.

Giles, A. K. (1964) *Budgetary Control as an Aid to Farm Management*. Miscellaneous Studies No. 33, Department of Agricultural Economics and Management, University of Reading.

Rowe, A. H. (1971). 'Computerised Systems of Accounting and Control of Farm Business Management'. *First International Farm Management Congress*, Warwick.

(Simulation: see references in text, p. 574–5n).

Index